GLEIM®

2016 EDITION

INSTRUMENT PILOT

FAA KNOWLEDGE TEST

for the FAA Computer-Based Pilot Knowledge Test

Instrument Rating - Airplane
Flight Instructor - Instrument - Airplane
Instrument Ground Instructor

Instrument Rating - Foreign Pilot
Flight Instructor - Instrument - Added Rating

by

Irvin N. Gleim, Ph.D., CFII

and

Garrett W. Gleim, CFII

Gleim Publications, Inc.
P.O. Box 12848 · University Station
Gainesville, Florida 32604

(352) 375-0772
(800) 87-GLEIM or (800) 874-5346
Fax: (352) 375-6940

Internet: www.gleim.com
Email: admin@gleim.com

For updates to the first printing of the 2016 edition of
Instrument Pilot FAA Knowledge Test

Go To: www.gleim.com/updates

Or: Email update@gleim.com with **IPKT 2016-1** in the subject line. You will receive our current update as a reply.

Updates are available until the next edition is published.

ISSN 1553-6882
ISBN 978-1-58194-649-9

YOU CAN HELP

This 2016 edition is designed specifically for private pilots who aspire to obtain the instrument rating. Please send any corrections and suggestions for subsequent editions to us via the feedback links within the online components, by emailing aviation@gleim.com, or by calling the number above.

A companion volume, *Instrument Pilot Flight Maneuvers and Practical Test Prep*, focuses on the FAA practical test, just as this book focuses on the FAA knowledge test. Save time, money, and frustration--order online at www.gleim.com today! Please bring these books to the attention of flight instructors, fixed-base operators, and others with a potential interest in acquiring their certificates and ratings. Wide distribution of these books and increased interest in flying depend on your assistance and good word. Thank you.

Environmental Statement -- This book is printed on recyclable, environmentally friendly groundwood paper, sourced from certified sustainable forests and produced either TCF (totally chlorine-free) or ECF (elementally chlorine-free).

Our answers have been carefully researched and reviewed. Inevitably, there will be differences with competitors' books and even the FAA. If necessary, we will develop an UPDATE for *Instrument Pilot FAA Knowledge Test*. Visit our website or email update@gleim.com as described above for the latest updates and information on all of our products. Updates for this 2016 edition will be available until the next edition is published. To continue providing our customers with first-rate service, we request that technical questions about our materials be sent to us via the feedback links within the online components. We will give each question thorough consideration and a prompt response. Questions concerning orders, prices, shipments, or payments will be handled via telephone by our competent and courteous customer service staff.

ABOUT THE AUTHORS

Irvin N. Gleim earned his private pilot certificate in 1965 from the Institute of Aviation at the University of Illinois, where he subsequently received his Ph.D. He is a commercial pilot and flight instructor (instrument) with multi-engine and seaplane ratings and is a member of the Aircraft Owners and Pilots Association, American Bonanza Society, Civil Air Patrol, Experimental Aircraft Association, National Association of Flight Instructors, and Seaplane Pilots Association. He is the author of flight maneuvers and practical test prep books for the sport, private, instrument, commercial, and flight instructor certificates/ratings and the author of study guides for the sport, private/recreational, instrument, commercial, flight/ground instructor, fundamentals of instructing, airline transport pilot, and flight engineer FAA knowledge tests. Three additional pilot training books are *Pilot Handbook*, *Aviation Weather and Weather Services*, and *FAR/AIM*.

Dr. Gleim has also written articles for professional accounting and business law journals and is the author of widely used review manuals for the CIA (Certified Internal Auditor) exam, the CMA (Certified Management Accountant) exam, the CPA (Certified Public Accountant) exam, and the EA (IRS Enrolled Agent) exam. He is Professor Emeritus, Fisher School of Accounting, University of Florida, and is a CFM, CIA, CMA, and CPA.

Garrett W. Gleim earned his private pilot certificate in 1997 in a Piper Super Cub. He is a commercial pilot (single- and multi-engine), ground instructor (advanced and instrument), and flight instructor (instrument and multi-engine), and he is a member of the Aircraft Owners and Pilots Association and the National Association of Flight Instructors. He is the author of study guides for the sport, private/recreational, instrument, commercial, flight/ground instructor, fundamentals of instructing, and airline transport pilot FAA knowledge tests. He received a Bachelor of Science in Economics from The Wharton School, University of Pennsylvania. Mr. Gleim is also a CPA (not in public practice).

REVIEWERS AND CONTRIBUTORS

Jim Chaney, Gold Seal CFI, CFII, MEI, AGI, and IGI, is the Gleim 141 Chief Flight Instructor and one of our aviation editors. Mr. Chaney has 16 years of experience as a Flight Instructor, Stage Check Instructor, Assistant Chief Flight Instructor, Chief Flight Instructor, and Director of Flight Operations. He has taught Aviation English at various universities in China. Mr. Chaney researched changes, wrote and edited additions, and incorporated revisions into the text.

Drew S. Glastetter, CFII, MEI, ASES, ATP - SA227, CA212, B737, is one of our aviation editors. Mr. Glastetter researched questions, wrote and edited answer explanations, and incorporated revisions into the text.

The CFIs who have worked with us throughout the years to develop and improve our pilot training materials.

The many FAA employees who helped, in person or by telephone, primarily in Gainesville, Orlando, Oklahoma City, and Washington, DC.

The many pilots who have provided comments and suggestions about *Instrument Pilot FAA Knowledge Test* during the past several decades.

A PERSONAL THANKS

This manual would not have been possible without the extraordinary effort and dedication of Jacob Brunny, Julie Cutlip, Kelsey Olson, Jake Pettifor, Teresa Soard, Justin Stephenson, Joanne Strong, and Elmer Tucker, who typed the entire manuscript and all revisions and drafted and laid out the diagrams and illustrations in this book.

The authors also appreciate the production and editorial assistance of Jessica Felkins, Kristen Hennen, Jeanette Kerstein, Katie Larson, Josh Lehr, Diana León, Cary Marcous, Shane Rapp, Drew Sheppard, Kayley Thomas, and Martha Willis.

Finally, we appreciate the encouragement, support, and tolerance of our families throughout this project.

TABLE OF CONTENTS

NOTE: The FAA no longer releases the complete database of test questions to the public. Instead, sample questions are released on the Airmen Testing page of the FAA website on a quarterly basis. These questions are similar to the actual test questions, but they are not exact matches.

Gleim utilizes customer feedback and FAA publications to create additional sample questions that closely represent the topical coverage of each FAA knowledge test. In order to do well on the knowledge test, you must study the Gleim outlines in this book, answer all the questions under exam conditions (i.e., without looking at the answers first), and develop an understanding of the topics addressed. You should not simply memorize questions and answers. This will not prepare you for your FAA knowledge test, and it will not help you develop the knowledge you need to safely operate an aircraft.

Always refer to the Gleim update service (www.gleim.com/updates) to ensure you have the latest information that is available. If you see topics covered on your FAA knowledge test that are not contained in this book, please contact us at aviation@gleim.com to report your experience and help us fine-tune our test preparation materials.

Thank you!

PREFACE

The primary purpose of this book is to provide you with the easiest, fastest, and least expensive means of passing the instrument rating–airplane knowledge test. The publicly released FAA knowledge test bank does **not** have questions grouped together by topic. We have organized them for you. We have

1. Reproduced all previously released knowledge test questions published by the FAA. We have also included many additional similar test questions, which we believe may appear in some form on your knowledge test.
2. Reordered the questions into 94 logical topics.
3. Organized these topics into 11 study units.
4. Explained the answer immediately to the right of each question.
5. Provided an easy-to-study outline of exactly what you need to know (and no more) at the beginning of each study unit.

Accordingly, you can thoroughly prepare for the FAA pilot knowledge test by

1. Studying the brief outlines at the beginning of each study unit.
2. Answering the question on the left side of each page while covering up the answer explanations on the right side of each page.
3. Reading the answer explanation for each question that you answer incorrectly or have difficulty answering.
4. Facilitating this Gleim process with our **FAA Test Prep Online**. Our software allows you to emulate the FAA test (CATS or PSI). By practicing answering questions on a computer, you will become at ease with the computer testing process and have the confidence to PASS. See pages 17 and 18.
5. Using our **Online Ground School**, which provides you with our outlines, practice problems, and sample tests. This course is easily accessible through the Internet. Also, we give you a money-back guarantee with our **Online Ground School**. If you are unsuccessful, you get your money back!

The secondary purpose of this book is to introduce *Instrument Pilot Flight Maneuvers and Practical Test Prep* and *Pilot Handbook*.

Instrument Pilot Flight Maneuvers and Practical Test Prep is designed to help prepare pilots for their flight training and the FAA instrument rating practical test. Each task, objective, concept, and requirement is explained, analyzed, illustrated, and interpreted so pilots will be totally conversant with all aspects of the instrument pilot practical test.

Pilot Handbook is a textbook of aeronautical knowledge presented in easy-to-use outline format, with many charts, diagrams, figures, etc., included. While this book contains only the material needed to pass the FAA knowledge test, *Pilot Handbook* contains the textbook knowledge required to be a safe and proficient pilot.

Many books create additional work for the user. In contrast, this book and its companion, *Instrument Pilot Flight Maneuvers and Practical Test Prep*, facilitate your effort. They are easy to use. The outline/illustration format, type styles, and spacing are designed to improve readability. Concepts are often presented as phrases rather than as complete sentences – similar to notes that you would take in a class lecture.

Also, recognize that this study manual is concerned with **airplane** flight training, not balloon, glider, or helicopter training. We are confident this book, **FAA Test Prep Online**, and/or **Online Ground School** will facilitate speedy completion of your knowledge test. We also wish you the very best as you complete your instrument rating, in subsequent flying, and in obtaining additional ratings and certificates.

Enjoy Flying Safely!

Irvin N. Gleim
Garrett W. Gleim

July 2015

INTRODUCTION: THE FAA PILOT KNOWLEDGE TEST

The beginning of this introduction explains how to obtain an instrument rating, and it explains the content and procedures of the Federal Aviation Administration (FAA) knowledge test, including how to take the test at a computer testing center. The remainder of this introduction discusses and illustrates the Gleim **Online Ground School** and **FAA Test Prep Online**. Achieving an instrument rating is fun. Begin today!

Instrument Pilot FAA Knowledge Test is one of four books contained in the Gleim **Instrument Pilot Kit**. The other three books are

1. *Instrument Pilot Flight Maneuvers and Practical Test Prep*
2. *Instrument Pilot Syllabus*
3. *Aviation Weather and Weather Services*

Instrument Pilot Flight Maneuvers and Practical Test Prep presents each flight maneuver you will perform in outline/illustration format so you will know what to expect and what to do before each flight lesson. This book will thoroughly prepare you to complete your FAA practical (flight) test confidently and successfully.

Instrument Pilot Syllabus is a step-by-step syllabus of ground and flight training lesson plans for your instrument rating training.

The Gleim *Aviation Weather and Weather Services* combines all of the information from the FAA's *Aviation Weather* (AC 00-6), *Aviation Weather Services* (AC 00-45), and numerous FAA publications into one easy-to-understand book. It will help you study all aspects of aviation weather and provide you with a single reference book.

While the following books are not included in the Instrument Pilot Kit, you may want to purchase them if you do not already have them:

Pilot Handbook is a complete pilot reference book that combines over 100 FAA books and documents, including *AIM*, FARs, ACs, and much more. Aerodynamics, airplane systems, airspace, and navigation are among the topics explained in *Pilot Handbook*. This book, more than any other, will help make you a better and more proficient pilot.

FAR/AIM is an essential part of every pilot's library. The Gleim *FAR/AIM* is an easy-to-read reference book containing all of the Federal Aviation Regulations (FARs) applicable to general aviation flying, plus the full text of the FAA's *Aeronautical Information Manual (AIM)*.

WHAT IS AN INSTRUMENT RATING?

An instrument rating is added to your private or commercial pilot certificate. A new certificate will be issued to you by the FAA upon satisfactory completion of your training program, an FAA knowledge test, and a practical test. A sample private pilot certificate with an instrument rating is reproduced below.

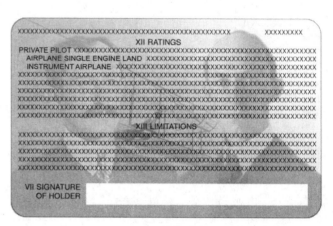

REQUIREMENTS TO OBTAIN AN INSTRUMENT RATING

1. Hold at least a private pilot certificate.

2. Be able to read, write, and understand English (certificates with operating limitations may be available for medically related deficiencies).

3. Hold a current FAA medical certificate.

   a. You must undergo a routine medical examination, which may be administered only by FAA-designated doctors called aviation medical examiners (AME).

   b. Even if you have a physical handicap, medical certificates can be issued in many cases. Operating limitations may be imposed depending upon the nature of the disability.

   c. Your certificated flight instructor-instrument (CFII) or fixed-base operator (FBO) will be able to recommend an AME.

      1) CFII is a flight instructor who has an instrument rating on his or her flight instructor certificate and is authorized to provide instruction for the instrument rating.

      2) An FBO is an airport business that gives flight lessons, sells aviation fuel, repairs airplanes, etc.

      3) Also, the FAA publishes a directory that lists all authorized AMEs by name and address. Copies of this directory are kept at all FAA offices, ATC facilities, and Flight Service Stations (FSSs). Alternatively, go to the Gleim website at www.gleim.com/aviation/amesearch.php.

4. Receive and log ground training from an authorized instructor or complete a home-study course (such as studying this book, *Instrument Pilot Flight Maneuvers and Practical Test Prep*, and *Aviation Weather and Weather Services* or using the Gleim **Online Ground School**) to learn

   a. *Federal Aviation Regulations . . . that apply to flight operations under IFR*

   b. *Appropriate information that applies to flight operations under IFR in the Aeronautical Information Manual*

   c. *Air traffic control system and procedures for instrument flight operations*

      d.   *IFR navigation and approaches by use of navigation systems*

      e.   *Use of IFR en route and instrument approach procedure charts*

      f.   *Procurement and use of aviation weather reports and forecasts and the elements of forecasting weather trends based on that information and personal observation of weather conditions*

      g.   *Safe and efficient operation of aircraft under instrument flight rules and conditions*

      h.   *Recognition of critical weather situations and windshear avoidance*

      i.   *Aeronautical decision making and judgment*

      j.   *Crew resource management, including crew communication and coordination*

5. Pass a knowledge test with a score of 70% or better. All FAA tests are administered at FAA-designated computer testing centers. The instrument rating test consists of 60 multiple-choice questions selected from the airplane-related questions in the FAA's instrument rating test bank. The FAA's published airplane-related questions, along with our own similar questions, are reproduced in this book with complete explanations.

6. Accumulate flight experience (FAR 61.65).

      a.   50 hr. of cross-country flight time as pilot in command, of which at least 10 hr. must be in airplanes

            1)   The 50 hr. includes solo cross-country time as a student pilot, which is logged as pilot-in-command time.

            2)   Each cross-country must have a landing at an airport that was a straight-line distance of more than 50 NM from the original departure point.

      b.   A total of 40 hr. of actual or simulated instrument time in the areas of operations listed in item 7. below, including

            1)   15 hr. of instrument flight training from a CFII

            2)   3 hr. of instrument training from a CFII in preparation for the practical test within 2 calendar months preceding the practical test

            3)   Cross-country flight procedures that include at least one cross-country flight in an airplane that is performed under IFR and consists of

                 a)   A distance of at least 250 NM along airways or ATC-directed routing

                 b)   An instrument approach at each airport

                 c)   Three different kinds of approaches with the use of navigation systems

      c.   If the instrument training was provided by an authorized instructor, a maximum of 20 hr. permitted in an approved flight simulator or flight training device

7. Demonstrate flight proficiency (FAR 61.65). You must receive and log training, and obtain a logbook sign-off (endorsement) by your CFII on the following areas of operations:

      a.   *Preflight preparation*

      b.   *Preflight procedures*

      c.   *Air traffic control clearances and procedures*

      d.   *Flight by reference to instruments*

      e.   *Navigation systems*

      f.   *Instrument approach procedures*

      g.   *Emergency operations*

      h.   *Postflight procedures*

8. Alternatively, enroll in an FAA-certificated pilot school or training center that has an approved instrument rating course (airplane).

      a.   These are known as Part 141 schools or Part 142 training centers because they are authorized by Part 141 or Part 142 of the FARs.

            1)   All other regulations concerning the certification of pilots are found in Part 61 of the FARs.

9. Successfully complete a practical test that will be given as a final exam by an FAA inspector or designated pilot examiner. The practical test will be conducted as specified in the FAA's Instrument Rating Practical Test Standards (FAA-S-8081-4).

    a. FAA inspectors are FAA employees and do not charge for their services.

    b. FAA-designated pilot examiners are proficient, experienced flight instructors and pilots who are authorized by the FAA to conduct flight tests. They do charge a fee.

 The FAA's Instrument Pilot Practical Test Standards are outlined and reprinted in the Gleim *Instrument Pilot Flight Maneuvers and Practical Test Prep* book.

FAA PILOT KNOWLEDGE TEST AND TESTING SUPPLEMENT

1. This book is designed to help you prepare for and pass the following FAA knowledge tests:

    a. Instrument Rating - Airplane (IRA), which consists of 60 questions and has a time limit of 2 hr. 30 min.

    b. Flight Instructor - Instrument - Airplane (FII), which consists of 50 questions and has a time limit of 2 hr. 30 min.

    c. Instrument Ground Instructor (IGI), which consists of 50 questions and has a time limit of 2 hr. 30 min.

        1) This test may include some helicopter-related questions. Just read the question carefully and, if you do not know the answer, take a guess. You need only 35 right out of 50 to pass the test.

    d. Instrument Rating - Foreign Pilot (IFP), which consists of 50 questions and has a time limit of 2 hr. 30 min.

        1) This test emphasizes FARs and weather more than the instrument rating (IRA) knowledge test.

    e. Flight Instructor - Instrument - Airplane - Added Rating (AIF), which consists of 20 questions and has a time limit of 1 hr.

        1) This test is for a CFII (helicopter) who wants to add an airplane rating to his or her CFII certificate.

2. The FAA legends and figures are contained in a book titled *Computer Testing Supplement for Instrument Rating*, which you will be given to use at the time of your test.

    a. For the purpose of test preparation, the appropriate legends and figures are reproduced in this book.

Important Note about the FAA Figure Addendum

In 2014, the FAA released an Addendum A for the *Computer Testing Supplement for Instrument Rating*. This addendum contains over 100 additional figures, including approach plates, approach procedures, departure procedures, A/FD excerpts, etc. The FAA has released some questions referencing certain figures from this addendum. Gleim has included those FAA-released questions and the relevant figures in our instrument rating materials. However, we have not included any of the addendum figures that do not have FAA-released questions. If you answer all of the questions in the Gleim test bank for instrument rating, you will be comfortable using the figures in the addendum to answer similar questions on the knowledge test.

For example, in our test bank, we have the following question:

(Refer to Figure 152 below.) At what point would a pilot execute the missed approach for the Baro Nav and LNAV approaches at LBF?

A. 3,100 feet DA for Baro NAV, or 1.5 NM from the RWY 30 waypoint for LNAV.

B. 3,280 feet DA for Baro NAV, or the BEMXI waypoint for the LNAV.

C. 3,100 feet DA for Baro NAV, or RWY 30 waypoint for the LNAV.

Answer (C) is correct. *(IPH Chap 4)*
DISCUSSION: Fig. 152 shows the DA for the Baro NAV approach is 3,100 feet, and the LNAV approach terminates at the RWY 30 waypoint. It would be appropriate to execute a missed approach from those points.
Answer (A) is incorrect. Although 3,100 feet is the DA for the Baro NAV approach, 1.5 NM from the RWY 30 waypoint is incorrect. The approach plate indicates the waypoint is 1.5 NM from the threshold, not that it is 1.5 NM from the missed approach point. Answer (B) is incorrect. The LNAV MDA, not the Baro NAV DA, is 3,280 feet.

Figure 152. – RNAV (GPS) RWY 30, North Plate Regional Airport Lee Bird Field (LBF).

If you can answer the question on the previous page for Figure 152, you can answer a similar question for the new Figure 253 below.

(Refer to Figure 253 below.) At what point would a pilot execute the missed approach for the Baro Nav and LNAV approaches at OSH?

A. 1,118 feet DA for Baro NAV, or 1.1 NM from the RWY 18 waypoint for LNAV.

B. 1,200 feet DA for Baro NAV, or the DAGTE waypoint for the LNAV.

C. 1,118 feet DA for Baro NAV, or RWY 18 waypoint for the LNAV.

Answer (C) is correct. *(IPH Chap 4)*
DISCUSSION: Fig. 253 shows the DA for the Baro NAV approach is 1,118 feet, and the LNAV approach terminates at the RWY 18 waypoint. It would be appropriate to execute a missed approach from those points.
Answer (A) is incorrect. Although 1,200 feet is the DA for the Baro NAV approach, 1.1 NM from the RWY 18 waypoint is incorrect. The approach plate indicates the waypoint is 1.1 NM from the threshold, not that it is 1.1 NM from the missed approach point. Answer (B) is incorrect. The LNAV MDA, not the Baro NAV DA, is 1,200 feet. DAGTE is the final approach fix.

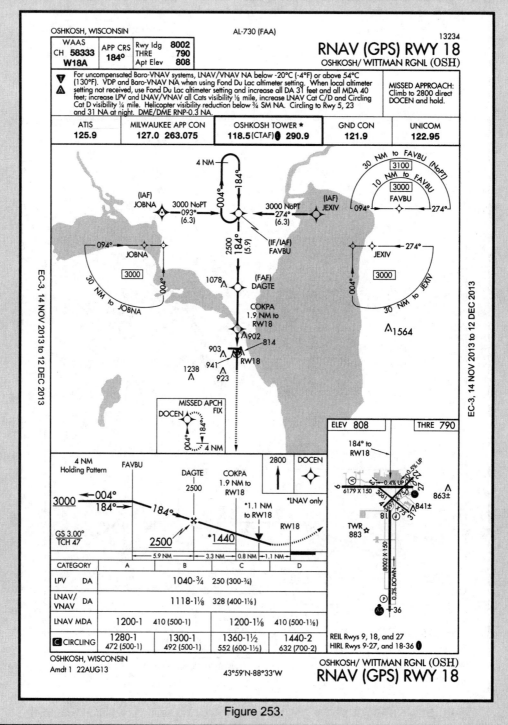

Figure 253.

3. In an effort to develop better questions, the FAA frequently **pretests** questions on knowledge tests by adding up to five "pretest" questions. The pretest questions will not be graded.

    a. You will NOT know which questions are real and which are pretest, so you must attempt to answer all questions correctly.

    b. When you notice a question NOT covered by Gleim, it might be a pretest question.

        1) We want to know about each pretest question you see.

        2) Please email (aviation@gleim.com) or call (800-874-5346) with your recollection of any possible pretest questions so we may improve our efforts to prepare future instrument pilots.

FAA'S KNOWLEDGE TESTS: CHEATING OR UNAUTHORIZED CONDUCT POLICY

The following is taken verbatim from an FAA knowledge test. It is reproduced here to remind all test takers about the FAA's policy against cheating and unauthorized conduct, a policy that Gleim consistently supports and upholds. Test takers must click "Yes" to proceed from this page into the actual knowledge test.

14 CFR part 61, section 61.37 Knowledge tests: Cheating or other unauthorized conduct

(a) An applicant for a knowledge test may not:
(1) Copy or intentionally remove any knowledge test;
(2) Give to another applicant or receive from another applicant any part or copy of a knowledge test;
(3) Give assistance on, or receive assistance on, a knowledge test during the period that test is being given;
(4) Take any part of a knowledge test on behalf of another person;
(5) Be represented by, or represent, another person for a knowledge test;
(6) Use any material or aid during the period that the test is being given, unless specifically authorized to do so by the Administrator; and
(7) Intentionally cause, assist, or participate in any act prohibited by this paragraph.

(b) An applicant who the Administrator finds has committed an act prohibited by paragraph (a) of this section is prohibited, for 1 year after the date of committing that act, from:
(1) Applying for any certificate, rating, or authorization issued under this chapter; and
(2) Applying for and taking any test under this chapter.

(c) Any certificate or rating held by an applicant may be suspended or revoked if the Administrator finds that person has committed an act prohibited by paragraph (a) of this section.

FAA PILOT KNOWLEDGE TEST QUESTION BANK

In an effort to keep applicants from simply memorizing test questions, the FAA does not currently disclose all the questions you might see on your FAA knowledge test. We encourage you to take the time to fully learn and understand the concepts explained in the knowledge transfer outlines contained in this book. **Using this book or other Gleim test preparation material to merely memorize the questions and answers is unwise and unproductive, and it will not ensure your success on your FAA knowledge test.** Memorization also greatly reduces the amount of information you will actually learn during your study.

The questions and answers provided in this book include all previously released FAA questions in addition to questions developed from current FAA reference materials that closely approximate the types of questions you should see on your knowledge test. We are confident that by studying our knowledge transfer outlines, answering our questions under exam conditions, and not relying on rote memorization, you will be able to successfully pass your FAA knowledge test and begin learning to become a safer and more competent pilot.

FAA QUESTIONS WITH TYPOGRAPHICAL ERRORS

Occasionally, FAA test questions contain typographical errors such that there is no correct answer. The FAA test development process involves many steps and people and, as you would expect, glitches occur in the system that are beyond the control of any one person. We indicate "best" rather than correct answers for some questions. Use these best answers for the indicated questions.

Note that the FAA corrects (rewrites) defective questions as they are discovered; these changes are explained in our updates (see page ii). However, problems due to faulty or out-of-date figures printed in the FAA Computer Testing Supplements are expensive to correct. Thus, it is important to carefully study questions that are noted to have a best answer in this book. Even though the best answer may not be completely correct, you should select it when taking your test.

REORGANIZATION OF FAA QUESTIONS

1. In the public FAA knowledge test question bank releases, the questions are **not** grouped together by topic; i.e., they appear to be presented randomly.

    a. We have reorganized and renumbered the questions into study units and subunits.

2. Pages 521 through 530 contain a list of all the questions in FAA learning statement code order, with cross-references to the study units and question numbers in this book.

    a. For example, question 1-17 is assigned the code PLT012, which means it is found in Study Unit 1 as question 17 in this book and is covered under the FAA learning statement, "Calculate aircraft performance - time/speed/distance/course/fuel/wind."

    b. Questions relating to helicopters, gliders, balloons, etc., are excluded.

HOW TO PREPARE FOR THE FAA PILOT KNOWLEDGE TEST

1. Begin by carefully reading the rest of this introduction. You need to have a complete understanding of the examination process prior to initiating your study. This knowledge will make your studying more efficient.

2. After you have spent an hour analyzing this introduction, set up a study schedule, including a target date for taking your knowledge test.

    a. Do not let the study process drag on and become discouraging; i.e., the quicker, the better.

    b. Consider enrolling in an organized ground school course, like the Gleim **Online Ground School**, or one held at your local FBO, community college, etc.

    c. Determine where and when you are going to take your knowledge test.

3. Work through Study Units 1 through 11.

    a. All previously released questions in the FAA's instrument rating knowledge test question bank that are applicable to airplanes have been grouped into the following 11 categories, which are the titles of Study Units 1 through 11:

Study Unit 1	-- Airplane Instruments
Study Unit 2	-- Attitude Instrument Flying and Aerodynamics
Study Unit 3	-- Navigation Systems
Study Unit 4	-- Federal Aviation Regulations
Study Unit 5	-- Airports, Air Traffic Control, and Airspace
Study Unit 6	-- Holding and Instrument Approaches
Study Unit 7	-- Aeromedical Factors
Study Unit 8	-- Aviation Weather
Study Unit 9	-- Aviation Weather Services
Study Unit 10	-- IFR En Route
Study Unit 11	-- IFR Flights

    b. Within each of the study units listed, questions relating to the same subtopic (e.g., thunderstorms, airplane stability, sectional charts, etc.) are grouped together to facilitate your study program. Each subtopic is called a subunit.

    c.   To the right of each question, we present

        1)   The correct answer

        2)   The appropriate source document for the answer explanation [These publications can be obtained from the FAA (www.faa.gov) and aviation bookstores.]

A/FD	*Airport/Facility Directory*	FAA-P-8740-50	On Landings, Part III
AAH	*Advanced Avionics Handbook*	FAR/14 CFR	Federal Aviation Regulations
AC	*Advisory Circular*	FI Comp	Flight Computer
ACL	*Aeronautical Chart Legend*	IFH	*Instrument Flying Handbook*
AFH	*Airplane Flying Handbook*	IPH	*Instrument Procedures Handbook*
AFNA	*Aerodynamics for Naval Aviators*	MHP	*Medical Handbook for Pilots*
AIM	*Aeronautical Information Manual*	NTSB	National Transportation Safety Board Regulations
AvW	*Aviation Weather*	P/C Glossary	Pilot/Controller Glossary (AIM)
AWS	*Aviation Weather Services*	PHAK	*Pilot's Handbook of Aeronautical Knowledge*

           a)   The codes may refer to an entire document, such as an advisory circular, or to a particular chapter or subsection of a larger document.

               i)   See page 531 for a complete list of abbreviations and acronyms used in this book.

        3)   A comprehensive answer explanation, including

           a)   A discussion of the correct answer or concept

           b)   An explanation of why the other two answer choices are incorrect

4.   Each study unit begins with a list of its subunit titles. The number after each title is the number of questions that cover the information in that subunit. The two numbers following the number of questions are the page numbers on which the outline and the questions for that particular subunit begin, respectively.

5.   Begin by studying the outlines slowly and carefully. The outlines in this part of the book are very brief and have only one purpose: to help you pass the FAA knowledge test.

    a.   **CAUTION:** The **sole purpose** of this book is to expedite your passing the FAA knowledge test for the instrument rating. Accordingly, all extraneous material (i.e., topics or regulations not directly tested on the FAA knowledge test) is omitted, even though much more knowledge is necessary to fly safely. This additional material is presented in four related Gleim books: *Instrument Pilot Flight Maneuvers and Practical Test Prep*, *FAR/AIM*, *Aviation Weather and Weather Services*, and *Pilot Handbook*.

6.   Next, answer the questions under exam conditions. Cover the answer explanations on the right side of each page with a piece of paper while you answer the questions.

> Remember, it is very important to the learning (and understanding) process that you honestly commit yourself to an answer. If you are wrong, your memory will be reinforced by having discovered your error. Therefore, it is crucial to cover up the answer and make an honest attempt to answer the question before reading the answer.

    a.   Study the answer explanation for each question that you answer incorrectly, do not understand, or have difficulty with.

    b.   Use our **Online Ground School** or **FAA Test Prep Online** to ensure that you do not refer to answers before committing to one AND to simulate actual computer testing center exam conditions.

7.   Note that this test book contains questions grouped by topic. Thus, some questions may appear repetitive, while others may be duplicates or near-duplicates. Accordingly, do not work question after question (i.e., waste time and effort) if you are already conversant with a topic and the type of questions asked.

8. As you move through study units, you may need further explanation or clarification of certain topics. You may wish to obtain and use the following Gleim books described on page 1:

    a. ***Instrument Pilot Flight Maneuvers and Practical Test Prep***
    b. ***Pilot Handbook***
    c. ***FAR/AIM***
    d. ***Aviation Weather and Weather Services***

9. Keep track of your work. As you complete a subunit, grade yourself with an A, B, C, or ? (use a ? if you need help on the subject) next to the subunit title at the front of the respective study unit.

    a. The A, B, C, or ? is your self-evaluation of your comprehension of the material in that subunit and your ability to answer the questions.

        A   means a good understanding.
        B   means a fair understanding.
        C   means a shaky understanding.
        ?   means to ask your CFI or others about the material and/or questions, and read the pertinent sections in ***Instrument Pilot Flight Maneuvers and Practical Test Prep*** and/or ***Pilot Handbook***.

    b. This procedure will provide you with the ability to quickly see (by looking at the first page of each study unit) how much studying you have done (and how much remains) and how well you have done.

    c. This procedure will also facilitate review. You can spend more time on the subunits that were more difficult for you.

    d. **FAA Test Prep Online** provides you with your historical performance data.

Follow the suggestions given throughout this introduction and you will have no trouble passing the FAA knowledge test the first time you take it.

With this overview of exam requirements, you are ready to begin the easy-to-study outlines and rearranged questions with answers to build your knowledge and confidence and PASS THE FAA's INSTRUMENT RATING KNOWLEDGE TEST.

The feedback we receive from users indicates that our materials reduce anxiety, improve FAA test scores, and build knowledge. Studying for each test becomes a useful step toward advanced certificates and ratings.

MULTIPLE-CHOICE QUESTION-ANSWERING TECHNIQUE

Because the instrument pilot knowledge test has a set number of questions (60) and a set time limit (2.5 hours), you can plan your test-taking session to ensure that you leave yourself enough time to answer each question with relative certainty. The following steps will help you move through the knowledge test efficiently and produce better test results.

1. **Budget your time.** We make this point with emphasis. Just as you would fill up your gas tank prior to reaching empty, so too should you finish your exam before time expires.

    a. If you utilize the entire time limit for the test, you will have about 2.5 minutes per question.

    b. If you are adequately prepared for the test, you should finish it well within the time limit.

        1) Use any extra time you have to review questions that you are not sure about, cross-country planning questions with multiple steps and calculations, and similar questions in your exam that may help you answer other questions.

    c. Time yourself when completing study sessions in this book and/or review your time investment reports from the Gleim **FAA Test Prep Online** to track your progress and adherence to the time limit and your own personal time allocation budget.

2. **Answer the questions in consecutive order.**

    a. Do **not** agonize over any one item. Stay within your time budget.

        1) We suggest that you skip cross-country planning questions and other similarly involved computational questions on your first pass through the exam. Come back to them after you have been through the entire test once.

    b. Mark any questions you are unsure of and return to them later as time allows.

        1) Once you initiate test grading, you will no longer be able to review/change any answers.

    c. Never leave a multiple-choice question unanswered. Make your best educated guess in the time allowed. Remember, your score is based on the number of correct responses. You will not be penalized for guessing incorrectly.

3. **For each multiple-choice question,**

    a. **Try to ignore the answer choices.** Do not allow the answer choices to affect your reading of the question.

        1) If three answer choices are presented, two of them are incorrect. These choices are called **distractors** for good reason. Often, distractors are written to appear correct at first glance until further analysis.

        2) In computational items, the distractors are carefully calculated such that they are the result of making common mistakes. Be careful, and double-check your computations if time permits.

    b. **Read the question carefully** to determine the precise requirement.

        1) Focusing on what is required enables you to ignore extraneous information, to focus on the relevant facts, and to proceed directly to determining the correct answer.

            a) Be especially careful to note when the requirement is an **exception**; e.g., "Which of the following is **not** a type of hypoxia?"

    c. **Determine the correct answer** before looking at the answer choices.

    d. **Read the answer choices carefully.**

        1) Even if the first answer appears to be the correct choice, do **not** skip the remaining answer choices. Questions often require the "best" answer of the choices provided. Thus, each choice requires your consideration.

        2) Treat each answer choice as a true/false question as you analyze it.

    e. **Click on the best answer.**

        1) You have a 33% chance of answering the question correctly by blindly guessing; improve your odds with educated guessing.

        2) For many multiple-choice questions, at least one answer choice can be eliminated with minimal effort, thereby increasing your educated guess to a 50-50 proposition.

4. After you have been through all the questions in the test, consult the question status list to determine which questions are unanswered and which are marked for review.

    a. Go back to the marked questions and finalize your answer choices.

    b. Verify that all questions have been answered.

EDUCATED GUESSING

 The FAA knowledge test sometimes includes questions that are poorly worded or confusing. Expect the unexpected and move forward. Do not let confusing questions affect your concentration or take up too much time; make your best guess and move on.

1. If you don't know the answer, make an educated guess as follows:

   a. Rule out answers that you think are incorrect.

   b. Speculate on what the FAA is looking for and/or the rationale behind the question.

   c. Select the best answer or guess between equally appealing answers. Your first guess is usually the most intuitive. If you cannot make an educated guess, re-read the stem and each answer choice and pick the most intuitive answer. It's just a guess!

2. Avoid lingering on any question for too long. Remember your time budget and the overall test time limit.

SIMULATED FAA PRACTICE TEST

Appendix A, "Instrument Rating Practice Test," beginning on page 507, allows you to practice taking the FAA knowledge test without the answers next to the questions. This test has 60 questions randomly selected from the questions in our instrument rating knowledge test bank. Topical coverage in the practice test is similar to that of the FAA knowledge test.

It is very important that you answer all 60 questions in one sitting. You should not consult the answers, especially when being referred to figures (charts, tables, etc.) throughout this book where the questions are answered and explained. Analyze your performance based on the answer key that follows the practice test.

It is even better to practice with Test Sessions in the Gleim **FAA Test Prep Online**. These simulate actual computer testing conditions, including the screen layouts, instructions, etc., for CATS and PSI.

For more information on the Gleim **FAA Test Prep Online**, see pages 17 and 18.

PART 141 SCHOOLS WITH FAA PILOT KNOWLEDGE TEST EXAMINING AUTHORITY

The FAA permits some FAR Part 141 schools to develop, administer, and grade their own knowledge tests as long as they use questions from the FAA test bank, similar to the questions in this book. The FAA does not provide the correct answers to the Part 141 schools, and the FAA only reviews the Part 141 school test question selection sheets. Thus, some of the answers used by Part 141 test examiners may not agree with the FAA or with those in this book. The latter is not a problem but may explain why you may miss a question on a Part 141 pilot knowledge test using an answer presented in this book.

AUTHORIZATION TO TAKE THE FAA PILOT KNOWLEDGE TEST

Before taking the instrument pilot knowledge test, you must receive an endorsement from an authorized instructor who conducted the ground training or reviewed your home-study in the areas listed in item 4. on page 2, certifying that you are prepared to pass the knowledge test.

For your convenience, a standard authorization form for the instrument rating-airplane knowledge test is reproduced on page 541, which can be easily completed, signed by a flight or ground instructor, torn out, and taken to the test site.

Note that if you use the Gleim **FAA Test Prep Online** or **Online Ground School**, the program will generate an authorization signed in facsimile by Dr. Gleim that is accepted at all CATS and PSI locations.

NOTE: An instructor endorsement is not required for any instructor knowledge test or the instrument rating-foreign pilot knowledge test.

WHEN TO TAKE THE FAA PILOT KNOWLEDGE TEST

1. You must be at least 15 years of age to take the instrument rating knowledge test.

2. You must prepare for the test under the supervision of your CFII by successfully completing a ground instruction course or by using this book as your self-developed home study course.

   a. See "Authorization to Take the FAA Pilot Knowledge Test" above.

3. Take the FAA knowledge test within 30 days of beginning your study.

   a. Get the knowledge test behind you.

4. Your practical test must follow within 24 months.

   a. Otherwise, you will have to retake your knowledge test.

WHAT TO TAKE TO THE FAA PILOT KNOWLEDGE TEST

1. An approved flight computer (ideally the one that you use to solve the test questions in this book, i.e., one you are familiar with and have used before)

2. A pocket calculator you are familiar with and have used before (no instructional material for the calculator is allowed)

3. Authorization to take the knowledge test (see above and page 541)

4. Proper identification that contains your

   a. Photograph
   b. Signature
   c. Date of birth
   d. Actual residential address, if different from your mailing address

NOTE: Paper and pencils are supplied at the examination site.

COMPUTER TESTING CENTERS

The FAA has contracted with two computer testing services to administer FAA knowledge tests. Both of these computer testing services have testing centers throughout the country. To register for the knowledge test, call one of the computer testing services listed below. More information can be found at www.gleim.com/testing_centers.

CATS   (800) 947-4228   PSI   (800) 211-2754

COMPUTER TESTING PROCEDURES

When you arrive at the testing center, you will be required to provide positive proof of identification and documentary evidence of your age. The identification must include your photograph, signature, and actual residential address if different from the mailing address. This information may be presented in more than one form of identification. Next, you will sign in on the testing center's daily log. Your signature on the logsheet certifies that, if this is a retest, you meet the applicable requirements (see "Failure on the FAA Pilot Knowledge Test" on page 15) and that you have not passed this test in the past 2 years.

Next, you will be taken into the testing room and seated at a computer terminal. A person from the testing center will assist you in logging onto the system, and you will be asked to confirm your personal data (e.g., name, Social Security number, etc.). Then you will be given an online introduction to the computer testing system, and you will take a sample test. If you have used our **FAA Test Prep Online**, you will be conversant with the computer testing methodology and environment and will breeze through the sample test. When you have completed your test, an Airman Computer Test Report will be printed out, validated (usually with an embossed seal), and given to you by a person from the testing center. Before you leave, you will be required to sign out on the testing center's daily log.

Each testing service has certain idiosyncrasies in its paperwork, scheduling, and telephone procedures as well as in its software. It is for this reason that our **FAA Test Prep Online** emulates both of the FAA-approved computer testing companies.

YOUR FAA PILOT KNOWLEDGE TEST REPORT

1.   You will receive your FAA Pilot Knowledge Test Report upon completion of the test. An example test report is reproduced on the next page.

     a.   Note that you will receive only one grade as illustrated.

     b.   The expiration date is the date by which you must take your FAA practical test.

     c.   The report lists the FAA learning statement codes of the questions you missed so you can review the topics you missed prior to your practical test.

2.   Use the FAA Listing of Learning Statement Codes on pages 515 through 520 to determine which topics you had difficulty with.

     a.   Look them over and review them with your CFI so (s)he can certify that (s)he reviewed the deficient areas and found you competent in them when you take your practical test. Have your CFI sign off your deficiencies on the FAA Pilot Knowledge Test Report.

3.   Keep your FAA Pilot Knowledge Test Report in a safe place because you must submit it to the FAA inspector/examiner when you take your practical test.

```
┌─────────────────────────────────────────────────────────────────────────┐
│                    Federal Aviation Administration                        │
│                     Airman Computer Test Report                           │
│                                                                           │
│   EXAM TITLE:  Instrument Rating Airplane                                 │
│                                                                           │
│   NAME:  Jones David  John                                                │
│                                                                           │
│   ID NUMBER:  123456789          TAKE:  1                                 │
│                                                                           │
│   DATE: 07/14/14                 SCORE:  82            GRADE:  Pass        │
│   ....................................................................... │
│                                                                           │
│   Knowledge area codes in which questions were answered incorrectly.  See │
│   appropriate knowledge test guide.  A code may represent more than one   │
│   incorrect response.                                                     │
│                                                                           │
│   PLT004  PLT051  PLT125  PLT322                                          │
│                                                                           │
│   EXPIRATION DATE:  07/31/16                                              │
│                                                                           │
│                       DO NOT LOSE THIS REPORT                             │
│   ....................................................................... │
│                                                                           │
│   Authorized instructor's statement (if applicable).                      │
│                                                                           │
│   I have given Mr./Ms. _____ additional instuction in each│
│   subject area shown to be deficient and consider the applicant competent │
│   to pass the test                                                        │
│                                                                           │
│   Last _____ Initail _____ Cert. No. _____ Type ____│
│   (Print Clearly)                                                         │
│                                                                           │
│   Signature_____                                │
│                                                                           │
│                                                      CTD's Embossed Seal   │
└─────────────────────────────────────────────────────────────────────────┘
```

FAILURE ON THE FAA PILOT KNOWLEDGE TEST

1. If you fail (score less than 70%) the knowledge test (which is virtually impossible if you follow the Gleim system), you may retake it after your instructor endorses the bottom of your FAA Pilot Knowledge Test Report certifying that you have received the necessary ground training to retake the test.

2. Upon retaking the test, you will find that the procedure is the same except that you must also submit your FAA Pilot Knowledge Test Report indicating the previous failure to the computer testing center.

3. Note that the pass rate on the instrument rating knowledge test is over 85%; i.e., fewer than 1 out of 5 fail the test initially. Reasons for failure include

   a. Failure to study the material tested and mere memorization of correct answers. (Relevant study material is contained in the outlines at the beginning of Study Units 1 through 11 of this book.)

   b. Failure to practice working through the questions under test conditions. (All of the previously released FAA questions appear in Study Units 1 through 11 of this book.)

   c. Poor examination technique, such as misreading questions and not understanding the requirements.

This Gleim Knowledge Test book will prepare you to pass the FAA knowledge test on your first attempt! In addition, the Gleim *Instrument Pilot Flight Maneuvers and Practical Test Prep* book will save you time and frustration as you prepare for the FAA practical test.

Just as this book organizes and explains the knowledge needed to pass your FAA knowledge test, *Instrument Pilot Flight Maneuvers and Practical Test Prep* will assist you in developing the competence and confidence to pass your FAA practical test.

Also, flight maneuvers are quickly perfected when you understand exactly what to expect before you get into an airplane to practice the flight maneuvers. You must be ahead of (not behind) your CFI and your airplane. Our flight maneuvers books explain and illustrate all flight maneuvers so the maneuvers and their execution are intuitively appealing to you. Visit www.gleim.com/aviation or call (800) 874-5346 and order today!

GLEIM ONLINE GROUND SCHOOL

1. Gleim **Online Ground School (OGS)** course content is based on the Gleim Knowledge Test books, **FAA Test Prep Online**, FAA publications, and Gleim reference books. The delivery system is modeled on the Gleim FAA-approved online **Flight Instructor Refresher Course**.

    a. Online Ground School courses are available for

        1) Private Pilot
        2) Sport Pilot
        3) CFI/CGI
        4) FOI
        5) Instrument Pilot
        6) Commercial Pilot
        7) ATP
        8) Flight Engineer
        9) Canadian Certificate Conversion

    b. OGS courses are airplane-only and have lessons that correspond to the study units in the Gleim FAA Knowledge Test books.

    c. Each course contains study outlines that automatically reference current FAA publications, the appropriate knowledge test questions, FAA figures, and Gleim answer explanations.

    d. OGS is always up to date.

    e. Users achieve very high knowledge test scores and a near-100% pass rate.

    f. **Gleim Online Ground School is the most flexible course available!** Access your OGS personal classroom from any computer with Internet access 24 hours a day, 7 days a week. Your virtual classroom is never closed!

    g. **Save time and study only the material you need to know!** Gleim **Online Ground School** Certificate Selection will provide you with a customized study plan. You save time because unnecessary questions will be automatically eliminated.

    h. **We are truly interactive. We help you focus on any weaker areas.** Answer explanations for wrong choices help you learn from your mistakes.

Register for Gleim Online Ground School today:
www.gleim.com/OGS

or

Demo Study Unit 1 for FREE at
www.gleim.com/aviation/Demos

GLEIM FAA TEST PREP ONLINE

Computer testing is consistent with aviation's use of computers (e.g., DUATS, flight simulators, computerized cockpits, etc.). All FAA knowledge tests are administered by computer.

Computer testing is natural after computer study and computer-assisted instruction is a very efficient and effective method of study. The Gleim **FAA Test Prep Online** is designed to prepare you for computer testing because our software can simulate both CATS and PSI. We make you comfortable with computer testing!

FAA Test Prep Online contains all of the questions in this book, context-sensitive outline material, and on-screen charts and figures. It allows you to choose either Study Mode or Test Mode.

In Study Mode, the software provides you with an explanation of each answer you choose (correct or incorrect). You design each Study Session:

Topic(s) and/or FAA learning statement codes you wish to cover
Number of questions
Order of questions -- FAA, Gleim, or random
Order of answers to each question -- Gleim or random

Questions marked and/or missed from last session -- test, study, or both
Questions marked and/or missed from all sessions -- test, study, or both
Questions never seen, answered, or answered correctly

In Test Mode, you decide the format: CATS or PSI. When you finish your test, you can and should study the questions missed and access answer explanations. The software emulates the operation of FAA-approved computer testing companies. Thus, you have a complete understanding of how to take an FAA knowledge test and know exactly what to expect before you go to a computer testing center.

The Gleim **FAA Test Prep Online** is an all-in-one program designed to help anyone with a computer, Internet access, and an interest in flying pass the FAA knowledge tests.

Study Sessions and Test Sessions

Study Sessions give you immediate feedback on why your answer selection for a particular question is correct or incorrect and allow you to access the context-sensitive outline material that helps to explain concepts related to the question. Choose from several different question sources: all questions available for that library; questions from a certain topic (Gleim study units and subunits); questions that you missed or marked in the last sessions you created; questions that you have never seen, answered, or answered correctly; questions from certain FAA learning statement codes; etc. You can mix up the questions by selecting to randomize the question and/or answer order so that you do not memorize answer letters.

You may then grade your study sessions and track your study progress using the performance analysis charts and graphs. The Performance Analysis information helps you to focus on areas where you need the most improvement, saving you time in the overall study process. You may then want to go back and study questions that you missed in a previous session, or you may want to create a Study Session of questions that you marked in the previous session. All of these options are made easy with **FAA Test Prep Online**'s Study Sessions.

After studying the outlines and questions in a Study Session, you can further test your skills with a Test Session. These sessions allow you to answer questions under actual testing conditions using one of the simulations of the major testing services. In a Test Session, you will not know which questions you have answered correctly until the session is graded.

Recommended Study Program

1. Start with Study Unit 1 and proceed through study units in chronological order. Follow the three-step process below.

    a. First, carefully study the Gleim Outline.
    b. Second, create a Study Session of all questions in the study unit. Answer and study all questions in the Study Session.
    c. Third, create a Test Session of all questions in the study unit. Answer all questions in the Test Session.

2. After each Study Session and Test Session, create a new Study Session from questions answered incorrectly. This is of critical importance to allow you to learn from your mistakes.

Practice Test

Take an exam in the actual testing environment of either of the major testing centers: CATS or PSI. **FAA Test Prep Online** simulates the testing formats of these testing centers, making it easy for you to study questions under actual exam conditions. After studying with **FAA Test Prep Online**, you will know exactly what to expect when you go in to take your pilot knowledge test.

On-Screen Charts and Figures

One of the most convenient features of **FAA Test Prep Online** is the easily accessible on-screen charts and figures. Many of the questions refer to drawings, maps, charts, and other pictures that provide information to help answer the question. In **FAA Test Prep Online**, you can pull up any of these figures with the click of a button. You can increase or decrease the size of the images, and you may also use our drawing feature to calculate the true course between two given points (required only on the private pilot knowledge test).

Instructor Sign-Off Sheets

FAA Test Prep Online is capable of generating an instructor sign-off for FAA knowledge tests that require one. This sign-off has been approved by the FAA and can be presented at the computer testing center as authorization to take your test--you do NOT need an additional endorsement from your instructor.

In order to obtain the instructor sign-off sheet for your test, you must first answer all relevant questions in **FAA Test Prep Online** correctly. Then, select "Sign-Off Sheets" under the "Additional Features" area on the Main page. If you have answered all of the required questions, the instructor sign-off sheet will appear for you to print. If you have not yet answered all required questions, a list of the unanswered questions, along with their location, will appear.

Order FAA Test Prep Online today
(800) 874-5346 or gleim.com

or

Demo Study Unit 1 for FREE at
www.gleim.com/aviation/Demos

Free Updates and Technical Support

Gleim offers FREE technical support to all users of the current versions. Call (800) 874-5346, send an email to support@gleim.com, or fill out the technical support request form online (www.gleim.com/support/form.php). Additionally, Gleim **FAA Test Prep Online** is always up to date. The program is automatically updated when any changes are made, so you can be confident that Gleim will prepare you for your knowledge test. For more information on our email update service for books, turn to page ii.

STUDY UNIT ONE
AIRPLANE INSTRUMENTS

(8 pages of outline)

This study unit contains outlines of major concepts tested, sample test questions and answers regarding airplane instruments, and an explanation of each answer. The table of contents above lists each subunit within this study unit, the number of questions pertaining to that particular subunit, and the pages on which the outlines and questions begin, respectively.

Recall that the **sole purpose** of this book is to expedite your passing of the FAA pilot knowledge test for the instrument rating. Accordingly, all extraneous material (i.e., topics or regulations not directly tested on the FAA pilot knowledge test) is omitted, even though much more knowledge is necessary to fly safely. This additional material is presented in *Pilot Handbook*, *Aviation Weather and Weather Services*, *FAR/AIM*, and *Instrument Pilot Flight Maneuvers and Practical Test Prep*, available from Gleim Publications, Inc. Order online at www.gleim.com.

1.1 COMPASS ERRORS

1. During taxi, you should check your compass to see that it is swinging freely and indicating known headings.

2. The difference between direction indicated by a magnetic compass not installed in an airplane and one installed in an airplane is called **compass deviation**.

   a. Magnetic fields produced by metals and electrical accessories in an airplane disturb the compass needle.

3. Magnetic compasses can be considered accurate only during straight-and-level flight at constant airspeed.

   a. When turning and accelerating/decelerating, the fluid level and compass card do not remain level, and magnetic force pulls "down" as well as toward the pole.

   b. These are known as the magnetic dip characteristics.

4. In the Northern Hemisphere, **acceleration/deceleration error** occurs when an airplane is on an easterly or westerly heading.

   a. A magnetic compass will indicate a turn toward the north during acceleration on an easterly or westerly heading.

   b. A magnetic compass will indicate a turn toward the south during deceleration on an easterly or westerly heading.

   c. Acceleration/deceleration error does not occur on a northerly or southerly heading.

5. In the Northern Hemisphere, **compass turning error** occurs when turning from a northerly or southerly heading.

   a. A magnetic compass will lag (and at the start of a turn indicate a turn in the opposite direction) when turning from a northerly heading.

      1) If turning to the east (right), the compass will initially indicate a turn to the west and then lag behind the actual heading until your airplane is headed east (at which point there is no error).

      2) If turning to the west (left), the compass will initially indicate a turn to the east and then lag behind the actual heading until your airplane is headed west (at which point there is no error).

   b. A magnetic compass will lead or precede the turn when turning from a southerly heading.

   c. Turning errors do not occur when turning from or through an easterly or westerly heading; i.e., turning errors are minimized at 90° and 270° headings.

6. These magnetic dip errors diminish as acceleration/deceleration or turns are completed.

1.2 PITOT-STATIC SYSTEM

1. When both the airspeed indicator pitot tube and the drain hole are blocked, the airspeed indicator acts as an altimeter.

   a. At a given altitude, airspeed changes would not change the indicated airspeed.

   b. During climbs, the indicated airspeed will increase.

   c. During descents, the indicated airspeed will decrease.

   d. These changes occur as a result of the differential between the pressure of the air locked in the pitot tube and the static air vent pressure.

2. If an alternate static source is vented inside an unpressurized airplane, the static pressure is usually lower than outside pressure due to the Venturi effect of the outside air flowing over the cockpit.

   a. The airspeed indicator will indicate a faster-than-actual airspeed.

   b. The vertical speed indicator (VSI) will momentarily show a climb.

   c. The altimeter will read higher-than-actual altitude.

3. If the pitot tube becomes clogged with ice during flight, only the airspeed indicator will be affected.

   a. The altimeter and vertical speed indicator depend upon the static air vents.

   b. If the static ports are iced over, the vertical speed indicator will not reflect climbs and descents because the change in air pressure cannot be detected by the VSI.

4. If the vertical speed indicator is not calibrated correctly (e.g., continually indicates a descent or climb), it can still be used for IFR flight by adjusting for the error when interpreting the indications.

   a. The VSI is not a required instrument for IFR flight. (Nonetheless, the FAA requires you to report the inability to climb/descend at least 500 fpm, and the FAA Instrument Rating PTS requires constant rate climbs/descents.)

5. The Mach meter or Mach indicator shows the ratio of aircraft true airspeed to the speed of sound at flight altitude by means of the pressure differential between static and impact sources, with correction for temperature and altitude.

6. If the outside air temperature increases during a flight at constant power and a constant indicated altitude, true airspeed (TAS) and true altitude will increase.

1.3 ALTIMETER

1. The altimeter indicates the true altitude at the field elevation if the local altimeter setting is used in an accurate altimeter.

   a. Thus, the altimeter indicates altitude in relation to the pressure level set in the barometric window.

2. Altimeters have three "hands" (like a clock's hour, minute, and second hands).

3. The three hands on the altimeter are generally arranged as follows:

   a. 10,000-ft. interval (thin needle with a flared triangular tip)
   b. 1,000-ft. interval (short, fat needle)
   c. 100-ft. interval (long, medium-thickness needle)

4. Altimeters are numbered 0 through 9.

5. To read an altimeter,

   a. First, determine whether the thin needle with the flared triangular tip rests between 0 and 1 (1-10,000 ft.), 1 and 2 (10,000-20,000 ft.), or 2 and 3 (20,000-30,000 ft.).

   b. Second, determine whether the shortest needle is between 0 and 1 (0-1,000 ft.), 1 and 2 (1,000-2,000), etc.

   c. Third, determine at which number the medium needle is pointing, e.g., 1 for 100 ft., 2 for 200 ft., etc.

6. Atmospheric pressure decreases about 1 in. Hg for every 1,000 ft. of altitude gained.

7. The altimeter setting dial allows adjustment for nonstandard pressure.

   a. A window in the face of the altimeter shows a barometric scale that can be rotated.

   b. Rotating the altimeter setting dial changes the scale and the altimeter hands simultaneously in the same direction by 1,000 ft. per 1 in. Hg.

   c. For example, changing from 29.92 in. to 30.92 in. increases indicated altitude by 1,000 ft., or from 30.15 in. to 30.25 in. increases indicated altitude by 100 ft.

8. Prior to takeoff, the altimeter should be set to the current local altimeter setting.

   a. With the current altimeter setting, the indicated altitude of the airplane on the ground should be within 75 ft. of the actual elevation of the airport for acceptable accuracy.

   b. If the current local altimeter setting is not available, use the departure airport elevation.

   c. The local altimeter setting should be used by all pilots in a particular area, primarily to provide for better vertical separation of aircraft.

   d. During an IFR flight in Class E airspace below 18,000 ft. MSL, ATC will periodically provide the current altimeter setting.

9. The standard temperature and pressure at sea level are 15°C and 29.92 in. Hg.

   a. Pressure altitude is the indicated altitude when the altimeter setting is adjusted to 29.92 in. Hg, i.e., the height above the standard datum plane.

   b. Pressure altitude is used in computations of density altitude, true altitude, and true airspeed.

   c. Pressure altitude will equal true altitude when standard atmospheric conditions exist.

   d. Pressure altitude and density altitude are the same at standard temperature.

10. The altimeter must be set to pressure altitude when flying at or above 18,000 ft. MSL.

    a. This setting guarantees vertical separation of airplanes above 18,000 ft. MSL.

11. Since altimeter readings are adjusted for changes in barometric pressure but not for temperature changes, an airplane will be at lower-than-indicated altitude when flying in colder-than-standard air.

    a. On warm days, you will be at a higher altitude (i.e., true altitude) than your altimeter indicates.

12. When pressure lowers en route, your altimeter will register higher-than-actual altitude until you adjust the altimeter for the new altimeter setting.

1.4 GYROSCOPES

1. Listen to your electric gyroscopes for unusual noises after the battery is turned on but before the engine is started.

2. One of the characteristics of a gyro is that it is resistant to deflection of the spinning wheel, which is based on two of Newton's laws of motion.

    a. A body at rest will continue at rest, and a body in motion will continue in motion in a straight line, until acted upon by an outside force.

    b. Deflection of a moving body is proportional to the deflective force applied and inversely proportional to the body's mass and speed.

1.5 HEADING INDICATOR

1. The heading indicator (HI) should be set to the correct magnetic heading 5 min. after the engine is started.

    a. Prior to takeoff, check the heading indicator to determine that it continues to maintain the correct heading after taxi turns.

2. The remote indicating compass (RIC) combines the functions of the magnetic compass and the heading indicator. One component of the RIC is the slaving control and compensator unit, as shown in Figure 143 below.

Figure 143. - Slaved Gyro Illustration.

a. This unit contains a slaving meter needle that indicates the difference between the displayed heading and the actual magnetic heading.

    1) A right deflection (+) indicates a clockwise (right) error in the heading indicator compass card (i.e., the correct magnetic heading is to the right of the indicated heading).

        a) Depressing the right (counterclockwise) heading drive button will move the heading indicator compass card to the left, thus increasing (+) the indicated heading toward the correct value (i.e., from 180° to 190°).

    2) A left deflection (–) indicates a counterclockwise (left) error in the heading indicator compass card (i.e., the correct magnetic heading is to the left of the indicated heading).

        a) Depressing the left (clockwise) heading drive button will move the heading indicator compass card to the right, thus decreasing (–) the indicated heading toward the correct value (i.e., from 190° to 180°).

b. To make corrections to the RIC, the system must be placed in the free gyro mode.

    1) After corrections are made, the system is returned to the slaved mode, which is the normal mode of operation.

1.6 ATTITUDE INDICATOR

1. Prior to IFR flight, you should check the horizon bar, which should be erect and stable within 5 min. of engine warm-up.

    a. The horizon bar should not tilt more than 5° when making taxi turns.

    b. Remember that you can adjust the position of the miniature airplane, but it is the horizon bar that moves to indicate attitude in flight.

        1) The horizon bar remains parallel to the horizon as the airplane's attitude changes.

        2) When using the attitude indicator for pitch attitude corrections, control pressures should be extremely light.

            a) Movements of the horizon bar above or below the miniature aircraft should not exceed one-half bar width.

            b) Additional inputs should not result in more than a one-half bar width correction.

2. **Precession errors** (both pitch and bank) on attitude indicators are greatest when rolling out of a 180° steep turn in either direction.

    a. As the airplane returns to straight-and-level coordinated flight, the miniature aircraft will show a slight climb and a turn in the direction opposite to the turn just made.

        1) If you indicate straight-and-level, you will be descending and turning in the direction of the turn just made.

    b. These precession errors during turns (including coordinated turns) are caused by centrifugal force acting on the pendulous vanes (erection mechanism in the attitude indicator). It results in the precession of the gyro toward the inside of the turn.

3. Attitude indicators also reflect an error during skidding turns, which precesses the gyro toward the inside of the turn.

    a. As the airplane returns to straight-and-level coordinated flight, the miniature aircraft shows a turn in the direction opposite to the skid. Pitch indication is not affected.

4. Deceleration precession makes some attitude indicators incorrectly indicate a descent.

    a. Conversely, acceleration through precession may result in attitude indicators incorrectly indicating a climb.

5.   Remote indicating compasses (RIC) were developed to compensate for the errors and limitations of the older type of heading indicators.

    a.   The two panel-mounted components of a typical system are the pictorial navigation indicator and the slaving control and compensator unit.

    b.   The slaving control and compensator unit has a push-button that provides a means of selecting either the "slaved gyro" or "free gyro" mode.

    c.   This unit also has a slaving meter and two manual heading-drive buttons.

    d.   The slaving meter indicates the difference between the displayed heading and the magnetic heading.

        1)   A right deflection indicates a clockwise error of the compass card; a left deflection indicates a counterclockwise error.

        2)   When the aircraft is in a turn and the card rotates, the slaving meter shows a full deflection to one side or the other.

        3)   When the system is in "free gyro" mode, the compass card may be adjusted by depressing the appropriate heading-drive button.

    e.   A magnetic slaving transmitter is a separate unit mounted remotely, usually in a wingtip to eliminate the possibility of magnetic interference.

        1)   It contains the flux valve, which is the direction-sensing device of the system.

            a)   A concentration of lines of magnetic force, after being amplified, becomes a signal relayed to the heading indicator unit, which is also remotely mounted.

            b)   This signal operates a torque motor in the heading indicator unit that processes the gyro unit until it is aligned with the transmitter signal.

        2)   The magnetic slaving transmitter is connected electrically to the HSI.

1.7 TURN-AND-SLIP INDICATOR

1.   Prior to engine start, the turn-and-slip indicator should indicate the needle centered, the tube full of fluid, and the ball approximately centered.

2.   During taxi turns, the needle should deflect in the direction of the turn, and the ball should move freely opposite the turn due to centrifugal force.

1.8 TURN COORDINATOR (TC)

1.   The miniature aircraft in the turn coordinator indicates rate of roll and rate of turn.

    a.   When the bank is changing, the rate of roll along the longitudinal axis is indicated.

    b.   When the bank is constant, the rate of turn along the vertical axis is indicated.

    c.   Thus, the angle of bank is only indirectly indicated.

2.   On taxi turns, the miniature aircraft indicates a turn in the direction of the taxiing turn, and the ball moves to the outside of the turn due to centrifugal force.

3.   The miniature airplane will show a turn in a wings-level yaw or during a turn while taxiing.

    a.   The TC indicates direction of roll along the longitudinal axis or yaw along the vertical axis and rate of turn.

    b.   The TC does not give a direct indication of the banked attitude of the airplane.

    c.   The TC does not display bank angle and rate of turn indirectly simultaneously.

        1)   During a turn, the TC first shows the rate of bank indirectly and, once stabilized, the rate of turn.

4. For any given airspeed, a specific angle of bank is necessary to maintain a coordinated turn at a given rate. The faster the airspeed, the greater the angle of bank required to obtain a desired rate of turn.

   a. Standard-rate turn

      1) When the turn needle points to one of the small side marks, it indicates that the airplane is turning at a rate of 3° per second.

5. The inclinometer of the TC consists of a sealed, curved glass tube containing kerosene and a ball which is free to move inside the tube. The fluid provides a dampening action which ensures smooth and easy movement of the ball.

   a. A rate of 3° per second is considered a standard-rate turn, and completing 360° of turn requires 2 minute.

   b. The tube is curved so that the ball tends to seek the lowest point, which is the center of the tube during coordinated flight. Two reference markers aid in determining when the ball is in the center.

      1) During a coordinated turn, turning forces are balanced, causing the ball to remain centered in the tube.

      2) If turning forces are unbalanced, i.e., if improper rudder is used, the ball moves away from the center of the tube in the direction of the excessive force.

      3) In a skid, the rate of turn is too great for the angle of bank, and excessive centrifugal force moves the ball to the outside of the turn.

         a) To achieve coordinated flight from a skid, you should increase the bank angle, reduce the rate of turn by reducing the rudder force to center the ball, or use a combination of both.

      4) In a slip, the rate of turn is too slow for the angle of bank, and the lack of centrifugal force moves the ball to the inside of the turn.

         a) To achieve coordinated flight from a slip, you should decrease the bank angle, increase the rate of turn by applying rudder pressure to center the ball, or use a combination of both.

      5) Remember: In slips, you have used too little rudder (or opposite rudder). In skids, you have used too much rudder.

      6) Apply rudder pressure on the side that the ball is exposed; i.e., step on the ball.

      7) The ball then is a visual aid to determine coordinated use of the aileron and rudder control. During a turn, it indicates the quality of the turn, i.e., whether the airplane has the correct rate of turn for the angle of bank.

1.9 GLASS COCKPITS

1. "Glass cockpits," as they are commonly called, integrate many flight instruments with aircraft performance data on one or more screens to give flight status in a convenient, easy-to-read format.

   a. Glass cockpits and advanced avionics were designed to increase safety by enhancing situational awareness, presenting data in an easy-to-understand format, and performing many necessary tasks automatically.

2. A **primary flight display (PFD)** combines many flight instruments into a single presentation.

   a. These could include the altimeter, attitude indicator, vertical speed indicator, turn coordinator, HSI, and airspeed indicator.

   b. Other flight status information that may be displayed on a PFD could include distance and bearing to the next waypoint, ground track, outside air temperature, navigation instruments, and communication frequencies.

    c.   Instrument sensor systems used to display information on a PFD are more sensitive and reliable than traditional gyroscopic instruments.

    d.   A **multi-function display (MFD)** is often used as a backup PFD and is usually used to monitor engine and powerplant performance, fuel status, traffic, route selection, moving maps, approach charts, weather, and terrain avoidance.

3.   As with flying conventional instruments, care is needed to maintain a correct instrument scan to correctly interpret instrument indications and avoid fixation.

4.   All human activity involving technical devices entails some element of risk. Knowledge, experience, and flight requirements tilt the odds in favor of safe and successful flights. The advanced avionics aircraft offers many new capabilities and simplifies the basic flying tasks, but only if the pilot is properly trained and all the equipment is working properly.

5.   While they have many benefits, much more initial and recurrent training is needed to acquire and retain the knowledge and skills necessary to accomplish a flight safely by means of glass cockpits.

    a.   Pilots flying with advanced avionics or glass cockpits must continually learn their system's functions, capabilities, and limitations.

    b.   With failure a possibility of any given system or display, a pilot must be able to perform manually any task being accomplished automatically.

    c.   All aircraft equipped with electric flight instruments must also contain a minimal set of backup conventional instruments, usually consisting of an attitude indicator, airspeed indicator, and altimeter.

    d.   Safety can be hampered or compromised if a pilot is not aware of what data is being presented or if it is used as a substitute for required preflight planning.

6.   Most of the aviation community believes automation has made flying safer, but there is a fear that pilots fail to see that automation is a double-edged sword.

    a.   Pilots need to understand the advantages of automation while being aware of its limitations. Experience has shown that automated systems can make some errors more evident while sometimes hiding other errors or making them less obvious.

    b.   Humans are characteristically poor monitors of automated systems. When passively monitoring an automated system for faults, abnormalities, or other infrequent events, humans perform poorly. The more reliable the system is, the worse the human performance becomes.

    c.   It is a paradox of automation that technologically advanced avionics can both increase and decrease pilot awareness.

7.   Pilots should not become complacent or be lulled into a false sense of security simply because they have advanced avionics. Judgment and aeronautical decision-making serve as the bridge between technology and safety. Any flight you make involves almost infinite combinations of pilot skill, experience, condition, and proficiency; aircraft equipment and performance; environmental conditions; and external influences. Both individually and in combination, these factors can compress the safety buffer provided by your baseline personal minimums.

QUESTIONS AND ANSWER EXPLANATIONS: All of the instrument rating knowledge test questions chosen by the FAA for release as well as additional questions selected by Gleim relating to the material in the previous outlines are reproduced on the following pages. These questions have been organized into the same subunits as the outlines. To the immediate right of each question are the correct answer and answer explanation. You should cover these answers and answer explanations while responding to the questions. Refer to the general discussion in the Introduction on how to take the FAA knowledge test.

Remember that the questions from the FAA knowledge test bank have been reordered by topic and organized into a meaningful sequence. Also, the first line of the answer explanation gives the citation of the authoritative source for the answer.

QUESTIONS

1.1 Compass Errors

1. On the taxi check, the magnetic compass should

    A. swing opposite to the direction of turn when turning from north.
    B. exhibit the same number of degrees of dip as the latitude.
    C. swing freely and indicate known headings.

Answer (C) is correct. *(IFH Chap 5)*
 DISCUSSION: When taxiing, the magnetic compass should be checked to make sure that the compass card is swinging freely and indicating known headings.
 Answer (A) is incorrect. The compass exhibits turning errors only when the airplane is airborne and in a bank. Answer (B) is incorrect. Compass turning errors occur in flight as a result of magnetic dip.

2. What should be the indication on the magnetic compass as you roll into a standard-rate turn to the left from an east heading in the Northern Hemisphere?

    A. The compass will initially indicate a turn to the right.
    B. The compass will remain on east for a short time, then gradually catch up to the magnetic heading of the aircraft.
    C. The compass will indicate the approximate correct magnetic heading if the roll into the turn is smooth.

Answer (C) is correct. *(IFH Chap 5)*
 DISCUSSION: If you roll into a smooth, coordinated, standard-rate turn to the left or right from an east or west heading, the compass will indicate the approximate correct magnetic heading. There are no turning errors on turns from east or west headings.
 Answer (A) is incorrect. The compass will initially indicate a turn in the opposite direction of a bank only when the airplane is turning from a north heading. Answer (B) is incorrect. When the airplane is turning from an east heading, the compass will immediately indicate a turn if the roll into the turn is smooth.

3. What should be the indication on the magnetic compass as you roll into a standard rate turn to the right from an easterly heading in the Northern Hemisphere?

    A. The compass will initially indicate a turn to the left.
    B. The compass will remain on east for a short time, then gradually catch up to the magnetic heading of the aircraft.
    C. The compass will indicate the approximate correct magnetic heading if the roll into the turn is smooth.

Answer (C) is correct. *(IFH Chap 5)*
 DISCUSSION: If you roll into a smooth, coordinated, standard-rate turn to the left or right from an east or west heading, the compass will normally indicate the approximate correct magnetic heading. Acceleration, not turning, errors are found in east or west headings in the Northern Hemisphere.
 Answer (A) is incorrect. The compass will initially indicate a turn in the opposite direction of a bank only when turning from a north heading. Answer (B) is incorrect. When turning from an east heading, the compass will immediately indicate a turn if the roll into the turn is smooth.

4. What should be the indication on the magnetic compass as you roll into a standard rate turn to the right from a westerly heading in the Northern Hemisphere?

    A. The compass will initially show a turn in the opposite direction, then turn to a northerly indication but lagging behind the actual heading of the aircraft.
    B. The compass will remain on a westerly heading for a short time, then gradually catch up to the actual heading of the aircraft.
    C. The compass will indicate the approximate correct magnetic heading if the roll into the turn is smooth.

Answer (C) is correct. *(IFH Chap 5)*
 DISCUSSION: If you roll into a smooth, coordinated, standard-rate turn to the left or right from an east or west heading, the compass will indicate the approximate correct magnetic heading. There are no turning errors on turns from east or west headings.
 Answer (A) is incorrect. The compass will initially indicate a turn in the opposite direction of a bank only when turning from a north heading. Answer (B) is incorrect. When turning from a westerly heading, the compass will immediately indicate a turn if the roll into the turn is smooth.

5. What should be the indication on the magnetic compass as you roll into a standard rate turn to the right from a south heading in the Northern Hemisphere?

  A. The compass will indicate a turn to the right, but at a faster rate than is actually occurring.

  B. The compass will initially indicate a turn to the left.

  C. The compass will remain on south for a short time, then gradually catch up to the magnetic heading of the aircraft.

Answer (A) is correct. *(IFH Chap 5)*
  DISCUSSION: In turns from a southerly heading in the Northern Hemisphere, the compass leads the turn. That is, it indicates a turn in the proper direction but at a faster rate than is actually occurring.
  Answer (B) is incorrect. The compass will initially indicate a turn in the opposite direction if the turn is made from a north, not south, heading. Answer (C) is incorrect. It describes a shallower-than-standard turn from a north, not south, heading.

6. On what headings will the magnetic compass read most accurately during a level 360° turn, with a bank of approximately 15°?

  A. 135° through 225°.

  B. 90° and 270°.

  C. 180° and 0°.

Answer (B) is correct. *(IFH Chap 5)*
  DISCUSSION: In a turn through north or south, the compass indication will usually be incorrect. But in a turn through east or west, the compass indication is usually accurate. Therefore, the compass should be indicating properly when passing through 90° and 270°. This holds true for only medium to shallow bank turns, e.g., 15-30°.
  Answer (A) is incorrect. The compass leads the heading in a turn through south. Answer (C) is incorrect. Compass turning errors are greatest at north and south headings.

7. What causes the northerly turning error in a magnetic compass?

  A. Coriolis force at the mid-latitudes.

  B. Centrifugal force acting on the compass card.

  C. The magnetic dip characteristic.

Answer (C) is correct. *(IFH Chap 5)*
  DISCUSSION: Magnetic dip causes a compass needle to point both down toward the earth and to the magnetic pole. This characteristic causes turning errors.
  Answer (A) is incorrect. The Coriolis force of the spinning Earth affects winds rather than compass indications. Answer (B) is incorrect. Centrifugal force is not related to compass turning errors.

8. What should be the indication on the magnetic compass when you roll into a standard rate turn to the left from a south heading in the Northern Hemisphere?

  A. The compass will indicate a turn to the left, but at a faster rate than is actually occurring.

  B. The compass will initially indicate a turn to the right.

  C. The compass will remain on south for a short time, then gradually catch up to the magnetic heading of the aircraft.

Answer (A) is correct. *(IFH Chap 5)*
  DISCUSSION: In turns from a southerly heading in the Northern Hemisphere, the compass leads the turn. That is, it indicates a turn in the proper direction but at a rate faster than the actual rate.
  Answer (B) is incorrect. The compass will initially indicate a turn in the opposite direction if the turn is made from a north, not south, heading. Answer (C) is incorrect. It describes a shallower-than-standard turn from a north, not south, heading.

9. What should be the indication on the magnetic compass as you roll into a standard rate turn to the right from a northerly heading in the Northern Hemisphere?

  A. The compass will indicate a turn to the right, but at a faster rate than is actually occurring.

  B. The compass will initially indicate a turn to the left.

  C. The compass will remain on north for a short time, then gradually catch up to the magnetic heading of the aircraft.

Answer (B) is correct. *(IFH Chap 5)*
  DISCUSSION: In turns from a northerly heading in the Northern Hemisphere, the compass will initially indicate a turn to the opposite direction. Then the compass heading will lag behind the actual heading until the airplane approaches an east or west heading.
  Answer (A) is incorrect. It describes a turn to the right from a southerly heading. Answer (C) is incorrect. It describes a shallower-than-standard turn from north.

10. What should be the indication on the magnetic compass as you roll into a standard rate turn to the left from a west heading in the Northern Hemisphere?

   A. The compass will initially indicate a turn to the right.

   B. The compass will remain on west for a short time, then gradually catch up to the magnetic heading of the aircraft.

   C. The compass will indicate the approximate correct magnetic heading if the roll into the turn is smooth.

Answer (C) is correct. *(IFH Chap 5)*
   DISCUSSION: If you roll into a smooth, coordinated, standard-rate turn to the left or right from an east or west heading, the compass will indicate the approximate correct magnetic heading. Turning errors appear on turns from north or south headings, not east or west.
   Answer (A) is incorrect. The compass will initially indicate a turn in the opposite direction of a bank only in a turn from a north heading. Answer (B) is incorrect. In a turn from an east heading, the compass will immediately indicate a turn if the roll into the turn is smooth.

11. What should be the indication on the magnetic compass as you roll into a standard rate turn to the left from a north heading in the Northern Hemisphere?

   A. The compass will indicate a turn to the left, but at a faster rate than is actually occurring.

   B. The compass will initially indicate a turn to the right.

   C. The compass will remain on north for a short time, then gradually catch up to the magnetic heading of the aircraft.

Answer (B) is correct. *(IFH Chap 5)*
   DISCUSSION: In turns from a northerly heading in the Northern Hemisphere, the compass will initially indicate a turn to the opposite direction, and the compass heading will lag behind actual until the airplane approaches an east or west heading.
   Answer (A) is incorrect. It describes a turn to the left from a southerly heading. Answer (C) is incorrect. It describes a shallower-than-standard turn from north.

1.2 Pitot-Static System

12. If both the ram air input and the drain hole of the pitot system are blocked, what reaction should you observe on the airspeed indicator when power is applied and a climb is initiated out of severe icing conditions?

   A. The indicated airspeed would show a continuous deceleration while climbing.

   B. The airspeed would drop to, and remain at, zero.

   C. No change until an actual climb rate is established, then indicated airspeed will increase.

Answer (C) is correct. *(AC 91-43)*
   DISCUSSION: When the airspeed indicator pitot tube and drain hole are blocked, the airspeed indicator will react as an altimeter. There will be a constant pressure within the pitot tube, and as the pressure from the static source decreases during a climb, the indicated airspeed on the airspeed indicator will increase.
   Answer (A) is incorrect. As there is an increase in altitude, the airspeed indicator will show an increase in airspeed as the air pressure within the pitot tube is relatively greater than that of the static air. Answer (B) is incorrect. This reaction would occur if the ram air input, but not the drain hole, were blocked.

13. If, while in level flight, it becomes necessary to use an alternate source of static pressure vented inside the airplane, which of the following variations in instrument indications should the pilot expect?

   A. The altimeter will read lower than normal, airspeed lower than normal, and the VSI will momentarily show a descent.

   B. The altimeter will read higher than normal, airspeed greater than normal, and the VSI will momentarily show a climb.

   C. The altimeter will read lower than normal, airspeed greater than normal, and the VSI will momentarily show a climb and then a descent.

Answer (B) is correct. *(IFH Chap 5)*
   DISCUSSION: Most aircraft equipped with a pitot-static system are provided with an alternate source of static pressure for emergency use. This source is usually vented inside the cabin. The pressure within an unpressurized cockpit is slightly lower than the pressure outside the airplane because of the Venturi effect of the air moving past the outside of the cockpit. When the alternate static source is used, the altimeter will read higher than actual, and the vertical speed indicator will momentarily show a climb.
   Answer (A) is incorrect. The altimeter and airspeed indicators will read higher, not lower, than normal, and the vertical speed indicator will momentarily show a climb, not a descent. Answer (C) is incorrect. The altimeter will read higher, not lower, than normal, and the vertical speed indicator will show level flight, not a descent, after the momentary climb.

14. During flight, if the pitot tube becomes clogged with ice, which of the following instruments would be affected?

A. The airspeed indicator only.

B. The airspeed indicator and the altimeter.

C. The airspeed indicator, altimeter, and Vertical Speed Indicator.

Answer (A) is correct. *(IFH Chap 5)*
DISCUSSION: The pitot-static system is a source of pressure for the altimeter, vertical speed indicator, and airspeed indicator. The pitot tube is connected directly to the airspeed indicator, and the static vents are connected directly to all three. The pressure of air coming into the pitot tube (impact air pressure) is compared with the air pressure at the static system vents to determine airspeed.
Answer (B) is incorrect. The pitot tube is connected only to the airspeed indicator, not the altimeter. Answer (C) is incorrect. The pitot tube is connected only to the airspeed indicator, not the altimeter or vertical speed indicator.

15. If both the ram air input and drain hole of the pitot system become blocked, the indicated airspeed will

A. increase during a climb.

B. decrease during a climb.

C. remain constant regardless of altitude change.

Answer (A) is correct. *(PHAK Chap 7)*
DISCUSSION: If both the pitot tube input and the drain hole on the pitot system are blocked, the airspeed indication will increase during a climb. This is due to the decrease in static pressure, allowing the instrument's diaphram to expand showing an indication of greater airspeed.
Answer (B) is incorrect. If both the pitot tube input and the drain hole on the pitot system are blocked, the airspeed indication will increase during a climb and decrease during a descent. Answer (C) is incorrect. If the pitot system and static port become blocked, the indicated airspeed will remain constant.

16. If the pitot tube ram air pressure hole and drain hole become obstructed, the airspeed indicator will operate

A. like an altimeter as the aircraft climbs and descends.

B. like a very sluggish airspeed indicator lagging all the changes by minutes.

C. normally due to the static port pressure changes.

Answer (A) is correct. *(IFH Chap 5)*
DISCUSSION: When the pitot tube and drain hole are blocked, the airspeed indicator will react as an altimeter. There will be a constant pressure within the pitot tube and, as the pressure from the static source decreases during a climb, the indicated airspeed on the altimeter will increase.
Answer (B) is incorrect. The operation of the airspeed indicator has no association with time. Answer (C) is incorrect. When the pitot tube and drain hole are blocked, the airspeed indicator will react as an altimeter. There will be a constant pressure within the pitot tube and, as the pressure from the static source decreases during a climb, the indicated airspeed on the altimeter will increase.

17. If the outside air temperature increases during a flight at constant power and at a constant indicated altitude, the true airspeed will

A. decrease and true altitude will increase.

B. increase and true altitude will decrease.

C. increase and true altitude will increase.

Answer (C) is correct. *(IFH Chap 5)*
DISCUSSION: As temperature increases, pressure levels rise farther above sea level and true altitude increases given a constant indicated altitude. As altitude increases with constant power, true airspeed increases.
Answer (A) is incorrect. TAS increases, not decreases. Answer (B) is incorrect. True altitude increases, not decreases.

18. If, while in level flight, it becomes necessary to use an alternate source of static pressure vented inside the airplane, which of the following should the pilot expect?

A. The vertical speed to show a climb.

B. The vertical speed to momentarily show a descent.

C. The altimeter to read higher than normal.

Answer (C) is correct. *(IFH Chap 5)*
DISCUSSION: Most aircraft equipped with a pitot-static system are provided with an alternate source of static pressure for emergency use. This source is usually vented inside the cabin. The pressure within an unpressurized cockpit is slightly lower than the pressure outside the airplane because of the Venturi effect of the air moving past the outside of the cockpit. When the alternate static source is used, the altimeter and airspeed indicator will read higher than actual, and the vertical speed indicator will momentarily show a climb.
Answer (A) is incorrect. The VSI will show only a momentary, not a steady-state, climb. Answer (B) is incorrect. The VSI indication will be a momentary climb, not a descent.

19. If, while in level flight, it becomes necessary to use an alternate source of static pressure vented inside the airplane, which of the following should the pilot expect?

A. The vertical speed to momentarily show a climb.

B. The gyroscopic instruments to become inoperative.

C. The altimeter and airspeed indicator to become inoperative.

Answer (A) is correct. *(IFH Chap 5)*
   DISCUSSION: Most aircraft equipped with a pitot-static system are provided with an alternate source of static pressure for emergency use. This source is usually vented inside the cabin. The pressure within an unpressurized cockpit is slightly lower than the pressure outside the airplane because of the Venturi effect of the air moving past the outside of the cockpit. When the alternate static source is used, the altimeter and airspeed indicator will read higher than actual, and the vertical speed indicator will momentarily show a climb.
   Answer (B) is incorrect. The gyroscopic instruments are not affected by changes in the pitot-static system. Answer (C) is incorrect. The altimeter and airspeed indicator will read higher than actual, not become inoperative.

20. What would be the indication on the VSI during entry into a 500 FPM actual descent from level flight if the static ports were iced over?

A. The indication would be in reverse of the actual rate of descent (500 FPM climb).

B. The initial indication would be a climb, then descent at a rate in excess of 500 FPM.

C. The VSI pointer would remain at zero regardless of the actual rate of descent.

Answer (C) is correct. *(IFH Chap 5)*
   DISCUSSION: The vertical speed indicator operates from the static pressure source and indicates change in pressure. Thus, if the static pressure ports became iced over, there would be no change in the static pressure, and there would be no indication of descent or climb.
   Answer (A) is incorrect. With no change in pressure, the indication would be level flight, not a climb. Answer (B) is incorrect. With no change in pressure, the indication would be level flight, not a climb or descent.

21. You check the flight instruments while taxiing and find the vertical speed indicator (VSI) indicates a descent of 100 feet per minute. In this case, you

A. may not proceed under IFR until the instrument is corrected by an authorized instrument repairman.

B. may take off under IFR and use 100 feet descent as the zero indication.

C. may take off and proceed under IFR but only in VFR weather conditions.

Answer (B) is correct. *(IFH Chap 5)*
   DISCUSSION: The needle of the vertical speed indicator (VSI) should indicate zero when the aircraft is on the ground or is maintaining a constant pressure level in flight. If it does not indicate zero, you must allow for the error when interpreting the indications in flight. Since the VSI is not a required instrument, you may fly when it is out of adjustment.
   Answer (A) is incorrect. The VSI can be used by making allowances in flight. Answer (C) is incorrect. The VSI is not a required instrument for IFR operations. You may proceed under IFR even if the VSI is out of adjustment, but you should allow for the adjustment of the error while in flight.

22. What information does a Mach meter present?

A. The ratio of aircraft true airspeed to the speed of sound.

B. The ratio of aircraft indicated airspeed to the speed of sound.

C. The ratio of aircraft equivalent airspeed, corrected for installation error, to the speed of sound.

Answer (A) is correct. *(IFH Chap 5)*
   DISCUSSION: The Mach meter indicates the ratio of aircraft true airspeed to the speed of sound at flight altitude. It uses the pressure differential between the impact and static air sources and corrects automatically for temperature and altitude.
   Answer (B) is incorrect. The Mach meter uses true airspeed, not indicated airspeed. Answer (C) is incorrect. Equivalent airspeed is the calibrated airspeed of an aircraft corrected for compressibility flow at a particular altitude. The Mach meter uses true airspeed.

1.3 Altimeter

23. Pressure altitude is the altitude read on your altimeter when the instrument is adjusted to indicate height above

A. sea level.

B. the standard datum plane.

C. ground level.

Answer (B) is correct. *(IFH Chap 5)*
   DISCUSSION: Pressure altitude is the altitude read on your altimeter when the instrument is adjusted to indicate height above the standard datum plane, i.e., an altimeter setting of 29.92 in. The standard datum plane is a theoretical level where the weight of the atmosphere is 29.92 in. of Hg.
   Answer (A) is incorrect. Indicated altitude, not pressure altitude, is the altitude read on your altimeter (when set to the correct altimeter setting) to indicate the approximate height above mean sea level. Answer (C) is incorrect. The height above ground (absolute altitude) may be indicated directly on a radar altimeter, not by adjusting a pressure altimeter to 29.92 in.

24. How should you preflight check the altimeter prior to an IFR flight?

A. Set the altimeter to 29.92" Hg. With current temperature and the altimeter indication, determine the true altitude to compare with the field elevation.

B. Set the altimeter first with 29.92" Hg and then the current altimeter setting. The change in altitude should correspond to the change in setting.

C. Set the altimeter to the current altimeter setting. The indication should be within 75 feet of the actual elevation for acceptable accuracy.

Answer (C) is correct. *(IFH Chap 5)*
   DISCUSSION: Set the altimeter to the local altimeter setting before taking off, and verify that the indication is within 75 ft. of the actual elevation. If the difference is greater than 75 ft., you should consult an instrument repair shop.
   Answer (A) is incorrect. Setting the altimeter to 29.92 and adjusting for temperature gives density altitude, not true altitude. Answer (B) is incorrect. Only indicated altitude, not change in altitude, is checked.

25. How should you preflight check the altimeter prior to an IFR flight?

A. Set the altimeter to the current temperature. With current temperature and the altimeter indication, determine the calibrated altitude to compare with the field elevation.

B. Set the altimeter first with 29.92" Hg and then the current altimeter setting. The change in altitude should correspond to the change in setting.

C. Set the altimeter to the current altimeter setting. The indication should be within 75 feet of the actual elevation for acceptable accuracy.

Answer (C) is correct. *(IFH Chap 5)*
   DISCUSSION: Set the altimeter to the local altimeter setting before taking off, and verify that the indication is within 75 ft. of the actual elevation. If the difference is greater than 75 ft., you should consult an instrument repair shop.
   Answer (A) is incorrect. An altimeter can be adjusted for nonstandard pressure, not temperature. Answer (B) is incorrect. Only indicated altitude, not change in altitude, is checked.

26. The local altimeter setting should be used by all pilots in a particular area, primarily to provide for

A. the cancellation of altimeter error due to nonstandard temperatures aloft.

B. better vertical separation of aircraft.

C. more accurate terrain clearance in mountainous areas.

Answer (B) is correct. *(IFH Chap 5)*
   DISCUSSION: Because the altimeter in each airplane is equally affected by temperature and pressure variation errors, use of the local altimeter setting in a given area provides for better vertical separation of aircraft.
   Answer (A) is incorrect. The altimeter setting does not compensate for nonstandard temperatures aloft. Rather, all altimeters in the area will reflect the same uncompensated amount. Answer (C) is incorrect. Temperatures aloft must also be considered to ensure terrain clearance.

27. If you are departing from an airport where you cannot obtain an altimeter setting, you should set your altimeter

A. on 29.92 inches Hg.

B. on the current airport barometric pressure, if known.

C. to the airport elevation.

Answer (C) is correct. *(IFH Chap 5)*
   DISCUSSION: If you cannot obtain an altimeter setting at an airport, adjust your altimeter so it reads the current airport elevation.
   Answer (A) is incorrect. Setting the altimeter to 29.92 would provide only pressure altitude. Answer (B) is incorrect. The altimeter setting is the current barometric pressure adjusted to sea level.

28. Which altitude is indicated when the altimeter is set to 29.92" Hg?

A. Density.

B. Pressure.

C. Standard.

Answer (B) is correct. *(PHAK Chap 7)*
   DISCUSSION: Pressure altitude is indicated when the altimeter is set to 29.92.
   Answer (A) is incorrect. Density altitude is pressure altitude corrected for nonstandard temperature. Answer (C) is incorrect. Standard altitude is a nonsense concept in this context.

29. (Refer to Figure 83 below.) Which altimeter depicts 12,000 feet?

 A. 2.

 B. 3.

 C. 4.

Answer (C) is correct. *(IFH Chap 5)*
   DISCUSSION: When indicating 12,000 ft., an altimeter has the long hand (100-ft. intervals) on 0, the short hand (1,000-ft. intervals) on 2, and the thin hand with flared tip (10,000-ft. intervals) just over 1, as shown in altimeter 4.
   Answer (A) is incorrect. In altimeter 2, the thin hand is above 2 and the short hand is on 1, indicating 21,000 ft. Answer (B) is incorrect. In altimeter 3, the short hand is on 1, the long hand is on 2, and the thin hand is above 1, indicating about 11,200 ft.

Figure 83. – Altimeter/12,000 Feet.

30. Altimeter setting is the value to which the scale of the pressure altimeter is set so the altimeter indicates

 A. pressure altitude at sea level.

 B. true altitude at field elevation.

 C. pressure altitude at field elevation.

Answer (B) is correct. *(PHAK Chap 7)*
   DISCUSSION: The altimeter setting is the value that permits the altimeter to indicate the true altitude at field elevation. Within the vicinity of a particular airport, the altimeter setting provides an accurate means of separating traffic vertically and also provides obstruction clearance. Note that the use of the word "true" here is not completely accurate because the altimeter setting does not correct for nonstandard temperature.
   Answer (A) is incorrect. The altimeter setting causes the altimeter to indicate true altitude, not pressure altitude, at field elevation, not sea level. Answer (C) is incorrect. The altimeter setting causes the altimeter to indicate true altitude, not pressure altitude.

31. While you are flying at FL 250, you hear ATC give an altimeter setting of 28.92" Hg in your area. At what pressure altitude are you flying?

 A. 24,000 feet.

 B. 25,000 feet.

 C. 26,000 feet.

Answer (B) is correct. *(IFH Chap 5)*
   DISCUSSION: The pressure altitude is 25,000 ft. in your area because at FL 250 your altimeter should be set at 29.92. A flight level (FL) by definition means a pressure altitude.
   Answer (A) is incorrect. FL 250 by definition means a pressure altitude of 25,000 ft., not 24,000 ft. Answer (C) is incorrect. FL 250 by definition means a pressure altitude of 25,000 ft., not 26,000 ft.

32. (Refer to Figure 84 below.) Which altimeter depicts 8,000 feet?

    A. 1.

    B. 2.

    C. 3.

Answer (B) is correct. *(IFH Chap 5)*
    DISCUSSION: When indicating 8,000 ft., an altimeter has the short hand (1,000-ft. intervals) on 8, the long hand (100-ft. intervals) on zero, and the thin hand with flared tip (10,000-ft. intervals) just before 1, as shown in altimeter 2.
    Answer (A) is incorrect. In altimeter 1, both the thin hand and the short hand are on 8, which would indicate something in the vicinity of 88,000 ft. Answer (C) is incorrect. While the short hand is pointing to 8 and the long hand is pointing to 0 (i.e., 8,000), the long thin needle with the flared tip (10,000-ft. indicator) is on 0, not on the fourth tick mark from the 0 toward the 1. Altimeter 3 is either broken or indicating 108,000 ft.

Figure 84. – Altimeter/8,000 Feet.

33. The pressure altitude at a given location is indicated on the altimeter after the altimeter is set to

    A. the field elevation.

    B. 29.92" Hg.

    C. the current altimeter setting.

Answer (B) is correct. *(PHAK Chap 7)*
    DISCUSSION: Pressure altitude, by definition, is indicated altitude when the altimeter setting is 29.92. This is true regardless of area or true altitude.
    Answer (A) is incorrect. You set the altimeter to a barometric pressure, not an elevation. Answer (C) is incorrect. The altitude indicated on the altimeter after it is set to the current altimeter setting is the indicated altitude, not pressure altitude.

34. How can you determine the pressure altitude on an airport without a tower or FSS?

    A. Set the altimeter to 29.92" Hg and read the altitude indicated.

    B. Set the altimeter to the current altimeter setting of a station within 100 miles and correct this indicated altitude with local temperature.

    C. Use your computer and correct the field elevation for temperature.

Answer (A) is correct. *(PHAK Chap 7)*
    DISCUSSION: The pressure altitude is determined by setting your altimeter to 29.92 and reading the altitude indicated. No matter what altitude or location, the altimeter reads pressure altitude when the barometric window is set to 29.92" Hg.
    Answer (B) is incorrect. It describes true altitude. Answer (C) is incorrect. Correcting field elevation for temperature is a nonsense concept.

35. How can you obtain the pressure altitude on flights below 18,000 feet?

A. Set your altimeter to 29.92" Hg and read the pressure altitude on the instrument face.

B. Set your altimeter to the field elevation and read the pressure altitude from the Kollsman window.

C. Contact an ATC facility FSS and request the current pressure altitude for the area.

Answer (A) is correct. *(PHAK Chap 7)*
DISCUSSION: Pressure altitude can be determined anywhere by setting the altimeter to 29.92.
Answer (B) is incorrect. It is much easier to just change the altimeter to 29.92. Answer (C) is incorrect. Pressure altitude is determined by setting your altimeter to 29.92, not by contacting an FSS.

36. At an altitude of 6,500 feet MSL, the current altimeter setting is 30.42" Hg. The pressure altitude would be approximately

A. 7,500 feet.

B. 6,000 feet.

C. 6,500 feet.

Answer (B) is correct. *(IFH Chap 5)*
DISCUSSION: Rotating the altimeter's setting knob to a higher (or lower) barometric setting moves the hands to higher (or lower) indicated altitude at the rate of 1" Hg to 1,000 ft. of altitude. Given the current altimeter setting of 30.42 and the indicated altitude of 6,500 ft., resetting the window to 29.92 would lower indicated altitude by 500 ft. (30.42 – 29.92 = 0.5" Hg = 500 ft.). The new indicated altitude would be 6,000 ft. MSL, which would be pressure altitude.
Answer (A) is incorrect. A pressure change of 0.5" Hg results in an altitude change of 500 ft., not 1,000 ft. Answer (C) is incorrect. Pressure altitude is equal to actual altitude only when the current altimeter setting is 29.92.

37. How does a pilot normally obtain the current altimeter setting during an IFR flight in Class E airspace below 18,000 feet?

A. The pilot should contact ARTCC at least every 100 NM and request the altimeter setting.

B. FSS's along the route broadcast the weather information at 15 minutes past the hour.

C. ATC periodically advises the pilot of the proper altimeter setting.

Answer (C) is correct. *(IFH Chap 5)*
DISCUSSION: During IFR flight in Class E airspace below 18,000 ft. MSL, ATC periodically provides altimeter settings. Thus, you will continually hear the altimeter settings given to other pilots as you monitor ATC.
Answer (A) is incorrect. ATC provides the altimeter setting without being asked. Answer (B) is incorrect. FSSs do not broadcast the altimeter setting at 15 min. past the hour.

38. What is the procedure for setting the altimeter when assigned an IFR altitude of 18,000 feet or higher on a direct flight off airways?

A. Set the altimeter to 29.92" Hg before takeoff.

B. Set the altimeter to the current altimeter setting until reaching the assigned altitude, then set to 29.92" Hg.

C. Set the altimeter to the current reported setting for climb-out and 29.92" Hg upon reaching 18,000 feet.

Answer (C) is correct. *(FAR 91.121)*
DISCUSSION: When you are at an altitude of 18,000 ft. MSL (FL 180) or higher, the altimeter should be set to 29.92, which is pressure altitude. It does not matter whether you are on an airway.
Answer (A) is incorrect. Indicated altitude (using local altimeter settings) should be used up to FL 180. Answer (B) is incorrect. You should set the altimeter to 29.92 upon reaching FL 180, not upon reaching your assigned altitude.

39. En route at FL 290, your altimeter is set correctly, but you fail to reset it to the local altimeter setting of 30.26 in. Hg during descent. If the field elevation is 134 feet and your altimeter is functioning properly, what will it indicate after landing?

A. 100 feet MSL.

B. 474 feet MSL.

C. 206 feet below MSL.

Answer (C) is correct. *(IFH Chap 5)*
DISCUSSION: One inch of pressure equals approximately 1,000 ft. of altitude. If an altimeter should be set to 30.26 but is set to 29.92, it is set .34 in. Hg too low and thus will indicate 340 ft. (1,000 ft. × .34) less than actual altitude. Thus, if the airplane lands at an airport with a field elevation of 134 ft., the altimeter will indicate 206 ft. below sea level (134 ft. airport elevation – 340 ft. altimeter setting error).
Answer (A) is incorrect. The amount of 100 ft. is obtained by subtracting 34 ft. rather than subtracting 340 ft. Answer (B) is incorrect. The amount of 474 ft. is obtained by adding 340 ft. rather than subtracting 340 ft.

40. Which of the following defines the type of altitude used when maintaining FL 210?

    A. Indicated.

    B. Pressure.

    C. Calibrated.

Answer (B) is correct. *(IFH Chap 5)*
    DISCUSSION: Above 18,000 ft. MSL (FL 180), pressure altitude is used to separate traffic. Pressure altitude is the altitude indicated on an altimeter when it is set to 29.92.
    Answer (A) is incorrect. Indicated altitude is the altitude shown on the altimeter after it is set to the current altimeter setting. Pressure altitude, not indicated altitude, is used at or above 18,000 ft. MSL. Answer (C) is incorrect. All altimeters are calibrated.

41. En route at FL 290, the altimeter is set correctly, but not reset to the local altimeter setting of 30.57" Hg during descent. If the field elevation is 650 feet and the altimeter is functioning properly, what is the approximate indication upon landing?

    A. 715 feet.

    B. 1,300 feet.

    C. Sea level.

Answer (C) is correct. *(IFH Chap 5)*
    DISCUSSION: One inch of pressure equals approximately 1,000 ft. of altitude. If an altimeter should be set to 30.57 but is set to 29.92, it is set .65" Hg too low and thus will indicate 650 ft. (1,000 ft. × .65) less than actual altitude. Thus, if the airplane lands at an airport with a field elevation of 650 ft., the altimeter will indicate sea level, i.e., 650 ft. elevation minus the 650 ft. altimeter setting error.
    Answer (A) is incorrect. This figure is obtained by adding 65 ft. rather than subtracting 650 ft. Answer (B) is incorrect. This figure is obtained by adding 650 ft. rather than subtracting 650 ft.

42. Under which condition will pressure altitude be equal to true altitude?

    A. When the atmospheric pressure is 29.92" Hg.

    B. When standard atmospheric conditions exist.

    C. When indicated altitude is equal to the pressure altitude.

Answer (B) is correct. *(IFH Chap 5)*
    DISCUSSION: Pressure altitude will equal true altitude when standard atmospheric conditions exist at the current altitude, i.e, 29.92" Hg and 15°C at sea level.
    Answer (A) is incorrect. To get true altitude from an altimeter, both temperature and pressure must be standard. Answer (C) is incorrect. Nonstandard temperatures will make indicated altitude deviate from true altitude.

43. Under what condition is pressure altitude and density altitude the same value?

    A. At standard temperature.

    B. When the altimeter setting is 29.92" Hg.

    C. When indicated, and pressure altitudes are the same value on the altimeter.

Answer (A) is correct. *(IFH Chap 5)*
    DISCUSSION: Density altitude, by definition, is pressure altitude adjusted for nonstandard temperature. Accordingly, pressure altitude will equal density altitude at standard temperature.
    Answer (B) is incorrect. Pressure altitude has not been adjusted for nonstandard temperature. Answer (C) is incorrect. Neither indicated nor pressure altitude is adjusted for nonstandard temperature.

44. Under what condition will true altitude be lower than indicated altitude with an altimeter setting of 29.92" Hg?

    A. In warmer than standard air temperature.

    B. In colder than standard air temperature.

    C. When density altitude is higher than indicated altitude.

Answer (B) is correct. *(IFH Chap 5)*
    DISCUSSION: When temperature lowers en route, you are lower than your altimeter indicates. Similarly, when you are in colder-than-standard air temperatures, true altitude is lower than pressure altitude.
    Answer (A) is incorrect. When you are in warmer-than-standard air, the true altitude is above pressure altitude. Answer (C) is incorrect. Assuming an altimeter setting of 29.92, if density altitude is higher than indicated altitude, the air is thinner and thus warmer. When you are in warmer-than-standard air, the true altitude is above indicated altitude.

45. Which condition would cause the altimeter to indicate a lower altitude than actually flown (true altitude)?

    A. Air temperature lower than standard.

    B. Atmospheric pressure lower than standard.

    C. Air temperature warmer than standard.

Answer (C) is correct. *(IFH Chap 5)*
    DISCUSSION: When temperatures are warmer than standard, the pressure levels are raised. That is, the altimeter will indicate an altitude lower than that at which the aircraft is actually flying.
    Answer (A) is incorrect. In colder-than-standard air, pressure levels drop. Thus, the altimeter reads higher, not lower, than true altitude. Answer (B) is incorrect. Using the correct altimeter setting adjusts for nonstandard pressure.

46. When an altimeter is changed from 30.11" Hg to 29.96" Hg, in which direction will the indicated altitude change and by what value?

   A.   Altimeter will indicate 15 feet lower.

   B.   Altimeter will indicate 150 feet lower.

   C.   Altimeter will indicate 150 feet higher.

Answer (B) is correct. *(IFH Chap 5)*
   DISCUSSION: Altimeter settings vary approximately 1" Hg for each 1,000 ft. of altitude. When the altimeter setting is changed from 30.11 to 29.96, it is lower by .15" Hg. Thus, the altimeter will indicate 150 ft. lower (1,000 ft. × .15). Remember that the indicated altitude and altimeter setting vary directly; i.e., when the altimeter setting is adjusted up, indicated altitude increases and vice versa.
   Answer (A) is incorrect. A measure of .15" Hg is equal to 150 ft., not 15 ft. Answer (C) is incorrect. When the altimeter setting is lowered, indicated altitude decreases, not increases.

1.4 Gyroscopes

47. Which practical test should be made on the electric gyro instruments prior to starting an engine?

   A.   Check that the electrical connections are secure on the back of the instruments.

   B.   Check that the attitude of the miniature aircraft is wings level before turning on electrical power.

   C.   Turn on the electrical power and listen for any unusual or irregular mechanical noise.

Answer (C) is correct. *(IFH Chap 5)*
   DISCUSSION: Electric gyro instruments can be checked for irregular noises by listening to them after the battery is turned on but before the engine is started. You should notice any bearing clatters, clicks, or other unusual noises. Additionally, you can look at the instruments to see if they are in their expected positions. There are additional tests to pursue after the engine is started.
   Answer (A) is incorrect. Pilots should not be handling or touching electrical connections behind the instrument panel. Answer (B) is incorrect. Due to the construction of the turn coordinator, the miniature aircraft will be wings level before turning on the electrical power. Thus, this indication would not be a practical test for the electric gyro.

48. One characteristic that a properly functioning gyro depends upon for operation is the

   A.   ability to resist precession 90° to any applied force.

   B.   resistance to deflection of the spinning wheel or disc.

   C.   deflecting force developed from the angular velocity of the spinning wheel.

Answer (B) is correct. *(IFH Chap 5)*
   DISCUSSION: Newton's second law of motion states that the deflection of a moving body is proportional to the deflective force applied and is inversely proportional to its mass and speed. For a gyro, the resistance to deflection is proportional to the deflective force. This property is used by the attitude indicator.
   Answer (A) is incorrect. Precession is the name for the reaction to deflection. The gyro uses precession rather than resisting it. Answer (C) is incorrect. The deflective force is applied to, not developed by, the gyro.

1.5 Heading Indicator

49. What pre-takeoff check should be made of a vacuum-driven heading indicator in preparation for an IFR flight?

   A.   After 5 minutes, set the indicator to the magnetic heading of the aircraft and check for proper alignment after taxi turns.

   B.   After 5 minutes, check that the heading indicator card aligns itself with the magnetic heading of the aircraft.

   C.   Determine that the heading indicator does not precess more than 2° in 5 minutes of ground operation.

Answer (A) is correct. *(IFH Chap 5)*
   DISCUSSION: Vacuum-driven gyros take several minutes to get up to speed. After about 5 min., set the heading indicator to the correct magnetic heading. After taxiing to the runup area, verify that the heading indicator still indicates the correct magnetic heading.
   Answer (B) is incorrect. Non-slaved heading indicators must be manually set to the correct magnetic heading. Answer (C) is incorrect. A precession error of no more than 3° in 15 min., not 2° in 5 min., is acceptable for normal operations.

Figure 143. – Slaved Gyro Illustration.

50. (Refer to Figure 143 above.) The heading on a remote indicating compass is 120° and the magnetic compass indicates 110°. What action is required to correctly align the heading indicator with the magnetic compass?

    A. Select the free gyro mode and depress the counter-clockwise heading drive button.

    B. Select the slaved gyro mode and depress the clockwise heading drive button.

    C. Select the free gyro mode and depress the clockwise heading drive button.

Answer (C) is correct. *(IFH Chap 5)*
    DISCUSSION: Some remote indicating compasses (RIC) have a separate slaving control and compensator unit with a deviation meter. The instrument shows any difference between the displayed heading and the magnetic heading. It also provides the controls shown in Fig. 143 to correct any errors. To correct from 120° indicated on the RIC to the magnetic heading of 110°, select the free gyro mode and depress the clockwise heading drive button until 110° heading on RIC is indicated and the deviation meter is centered.
    Answer (A) is incorrect. Using the counter-clockwise drive button would increase the indicated headings, e.g., from 120° to 130° indicated. Answer (B) is incorrect. The RIC must be in the free gyro mode to use the heading drive button.

51. (Refer to Figure 143 above.) When the system is in the free gyro mode, depressing the clockwise manual heading drive button will rotate the remote indicating compass card to the

    A. right to eliminate left compass card error.

    B. right to eliminate right compass card error.

    C. left to eliminate left compass card error.

Answer (A) is correct. *(IFH Chap 5)*
    DISCUSSION: A left compass card error means that the card has rotated too far to the left; i.e., it reads too high a heading. The clockwise adjustment rotates the indicating compass card to the right to eliminate left compass card error. For example, this would change a 120° heading to 110°.
    Answer (B) is incorrect. You adjust to the right for left, not right, error. Answer (C) is incorrect. The clockwise manual heading drive button rotates the compass card to the right, not left.

52. (Refer to Figure 143 above.) The heading on a remote indicating compass is 5° to the left of that desired. What action is required to move the desired heading under the heading reference?

    A. Select the free gyro mode and depress the clockwise heading drive button.

    B. Select the slaved gyro mode and depress the clockwise heading drive button.

    C. Select the free gyro mode and depress the counter-clockwise heading drive button.

Answer (C) is correct. *(IFH Chap 5)*
    DISCUSSION: If the heading on the compass is left of that desired, the compass has rotated too far to the right, which is a right compass error. Thus, the slaving control must be placed in the free mode, and the counterclockwise drive button must be depressed.
    Answer (A) is incorrect. The clockwise heading drive button would correct a left, not a right, card error. Answer (B) is incorrect. The RIC must be in the free gyro mode to use the heading drive button, and the counterclockwise heading drive button should be depressed.

1.6 Attitude Indicator

53. What pre-takeoff check should be made of the attitude indicator in preparation for an IFR flight?

    A. The horizon bar does not vibrate during warmup.

    B. The miniature airplane should erect and become stable within 5 minutes.

    C. The horizon bar should erect and become stable within 5 minutes.

Answer (C) is correct. *(IFH Chap 5)*
    DISCUSSION: The pre-takeoff check for attitude indicators is that, within the 5-min. warmup, the horizon bar should erect to the horizontal position and remain at the correct position. It should remain stable during straight taxiing and taxi turns.
    Answer (A) is incorrect. The horizon bar usually vibrates during warmup as the gyro gets up to speed. Answer (B) is incorrect. The miniature airplane can be adjusted manually but otherwise remains stationary. It is the horizon bar that moves within the instrument face.

54. Which condition during taxi is an indication that an attitude indicator is unreliable?

    A. The horizon bar tilts more than 5° while making taxi turns.

    B. The horizon bar vibrates during warmup.

    C. The horizon bar does not align itself with the miniature airplane after warmup.

Answer (A) is correct. *(IFH Chap 5)*
    DISCUSSION: The horizon bar in an attitude indicator should not tilt more than 5° during a taxi turn. If it does, it is unreliable and should not be used for IFR flight.
    Answer (B) is incorrect. The horizon bar will vibrate as the gyros get up to speed during warmup. Answer (C) is incorrect. The horizon bar aligns itself with the center of the dial, indicating level flight. Then the miniature airplane must be adjusted to align with the horizon bar from the pilot's perspective.

55. During coordinated turns, which force moves the pendulous vanes of a vacuum-driven attitude indicator resulting in precession of the gyro toward the inside of the turn?

    A. Acceleration.

    B. Deceleration.

    C. Centrifugal.

Answer (C) is correct. *(IFH Chap 5)*
    DISCUSSION: The attitude indicator normally erects itself by discharging air equally through four exhaust ports, each of which is partially covered by a pendulous vane. During coordinated (and skidding) turns, centrifugal force moves the vanes from their vertical position, precessing the gyro toward the inside of the turn.
    Answer (A) is incorrect. Acceleration is a force that induces climb/descent errors in the attitude indicator. Answer (B) is incorrect. Deceleration is a force that induces climb/descent errors in the attitude indicator.

56. If a 180° steep turn is made to the right and the aircraft is rolled out to straight-and-level flight by visual references, the attitude indicator

    A. should immediately show straight-and-level flight.

    B. may show a slight climb and turn.

    C. show a slight skid and climb to the right.

Answer (B) is correct. *(IFH Chap 5)*
    DISCUSSION: In 180° coordinated steep turns, when the airplane is rolled out to straight-and-level flight, the attitude indicator will indicate a turn to the opposite direction along with a slight climb.
    Answer (A) is incorrect. When the airplane is rolled out of a coordinated 180° steep turn to straight-and-level flight, the attitude indicator will indicate a turn to the opposite direction with a slight climb; it will not immediately show straight-and-level flight. Answer (C) is incorrect. Evidence of a skid error cannot be read from the attitude indicator, and the turn error would be to the left, not to the right.

57. During normal coordinated turns, what error due to precession should you observe when rolling out to straight-and-level flight from a 180° steep turn to the right?

    A. A straight-and-level coordinated flight indication.

    B. The miniature aircraft would show a slight turn indication to the left.

    C. The miniature aircraft would show a slight descent and wings-level attitude.

Answer (B) is correct. *(IFH Chap 5)*
    DISCUSSION: In 180° coordinated steep turns, when the airplane is rolled out to straight-and-level flight, the attitude indicator will indicate a turn to the opposite direction along with a slight climb. Thus, the indicated turn would be to the left if the steep turn were made to the right.
    Answer (A) is incorrect. The attitude indicator will show a slight climb to the left, not straight-and-level flight, and it does not indicate coordinated flight. Answer (C) is incorrect. It will indicate a slight climb, not a descent, and it will indicate a turning error.

58. During normal operation of a vacuum-driven attitude indicator, what attitude indication should you see when rolling out from a 180° skidding turn to straight-and-level coordinated flight?

  A. A straight-and-level coordinated flight indication.

  B. A nose-high indication relative to level flight.

  C. The miniature aircraft shows a turn in the direction opposite the skid.

Answer (C) is correct. *(IFH Chap 5)*
  DISCUSSION: Similarly to coordinated turns, the attitude indicator will show a bank in the opposite direction when the aircraft is rolled out of a skidding turn. However, there will be no nose-up indication.
  Answer (A) is incorrect. The attitude indicator will show a slight turn in the opposite direction, not straight-and-level flight, and it does not indicate coordinated flight. Answer (B) is incorrect. A nose-high indication will result only when the aircraft is rolling out of a coordinated turn.

59. Errors in both pitch and bank indication on an attitude indicator are usually at a maximum as the aircraft rolls out of a

  A. 180° turn.

  B. 270° turn.

  C. 360° turn.

Answer (A) is correct. *(IFH Chap 5)*
  DISCUSSION: Errors for both pitch and bank indication on an attitude indicator are greatest when rolling out of a 180° turn. This precession error, normally between 3° and 5°, is self-correcting by the part of the heading indicator called the erecting mechanism.
  Answer (B) is incorrect. Pitch and bank errors are usually the greatest after 180°, not 270°, of turn. Answer (C) is incorrect. Pitch and bank errors are usually the greatest after 180°, not 360°, of turn.

60. When an aircraft is decelerated, some attitude indicators will precess and incorrectly indicate a

  A. left turn.

  B. climb.

  C. descent.

Answer (C) is correct. *(IFH Chap 5)*
  DISCUSSION: Deceleration affects some attitude indicators through precession to incorrectly indicate a descent.
  Answer (A) is incorrect. Acceleration and deceleration result in erroneous pitch readings, not turning errors. Answer (B) is incorrect. Acceleration, not deceleration, may result in precession-related errors indicating a climb.

61. During normal flight with a vacuum driven attitude indicator, control pressures normally should not move the horizon bar more than

  A. One bar width, with not more than an additional one bar width for normal flight deviations.

  B. One-half bar width, with not more than an additional one bar width for normal flight deviations.

  C. One-half bar width, with not more than an additional one-half bar width for normal flight deviations.

Answer (C) is correct. *(IFH Chap 4)*
  DISCUSSION: When using the attitude indicator for pitch attitude corrections, control pressures should be extremely light. Movements of the horizon bar above or below the miniature aircraft should not exceed one-half bar width. Additional inputs should not result in more than a one-half bar width correction.
  Answer (A) is incorrect. The FAA recommends no more than a one-half bar width (not one bar width) indication when making pitch changes using the attitude indicator. Answer (B) is incorrect. The FAA recommends no more than a one-half bar width (not one bar width) indication when making pitch changes, either initially or as a follow up to the initial input.

62. When an aircraft is accelerated, some attitude indicators will precess and incorrectly indicate a

  A. climb.

  B. descent.

  C. right turn.

Answer (A) is correct. *(IFH Chap 5)*
  DISCUSSION: Acceleration affects some attitude indicators through precession to incorrectly indicate a climb.
  Answer (B) is incorrect. Deceleration, not acceleration, may result in precession-related errors indicating a descent. Answer (C) is incorrect. Acceleration and deceleration result in erroneous pitch readings, not turning errors.

1.7   Turn-and-Slip Indicator

63. Prior to starting an engine, you should check the turn-and-slip indicator to determine if the

   A.   needle indication properly corresponds to the angle of the wings or rotors with the horizon.

   B.   needle is approximately centered and the tube is full of fluid.

   C.   ball will move freely from one end of the tube to the other when the aircraft is rocked.

Answer (B) is correct. *(IFH Chap 5)*
   DISCUSSION: Prior to starting an engine, you should determine that the needle of the turn-and-slip indicator is approximately centered and that the tube is full of fluid with the ball also approximately centered if the airplane is on a level surface.
   Answer (A) is incorrect. The needle corresponds to rate and direction of turn, not wing or rotor angle. Answer (C) is incorrect. Rocking the aircraft is not necessary. Freedom of movement of the ball is checked during taxi.

64. What indications should you observe on the turn-and-slip indicator during taxi?

   A.   The ball moves freely opposite the turn, and the needle deflects in the direction of the turn.

   B.   The needle deflects in the direction of the turn, but the ball remains centered.

   C.   The ball deflects opposite the turn, but the needle remains centered.

Answer (A) is correct. *(IFH Chap 5)*
   DISCUSSION: During taxi, the turn-and-slip indicator ball should move freely opposite the direction of any turn since centrifugal force forces the ball to the outside. Also, the rate of turn indicator should indicate a turn in the proper direction.
   Answer (B) is incorrect. The ball will deflect opposite to the direction of the turn. Answer (C) is incorrect. The needle deflects in the direction of the turn.

1.8   Turn Coordinator (TC)

65. What indication should be observed on a turn coordinator during a right turn while taxiing?

   A.   The miniature aircraft will show a turn to the left and the ball remains centered.

   B.   The miniature aircraft will show a turn to the right and the ball moves to the left.

   C.   Both the miniature aircraft and the ball will remain centered.

Answer (B) is correct. *(IFH Chap 5)*
   DISCUSSION: On a taxiing turn to the right, the turn coordinator shows a turn to the right, and the ball moves to the left. The centrifugal force of the turn, which is not offset by bank when taxiing, forces the ball opposite to the turn.
   Answer (A) is incorrect. The ball moves to the outside of the turn due to centrifugal force. Answer (C) is incorrect. The miniature aircraft reacts to yaw and shows a turn to the right, and the ball reacts to centrifugal force by moving left.

66. What indications are displayed by the miniature aircraft of a turn coordinator?

   A.   Rate of roll and rate of turn.

   B.   Direct indication of bank angle and pitch attitude.

   C.   Indirect indication of bank angle and pitch attitude.

Answer (A) is correct. *(IFH Chap 5)*
   DISCUSSION: The turn coordinator indicates rate of roll and rate of turn. When the bank is constant, the rate of turn is indicated. When the bank is changing, the rate of roll is also indicated.
   Answer (B) is incorrect. The turn coordinator only indirectly indicates bank angle and has no relationship to pitch attitude. Answer (C) is incorrect. The turn coordinator has no relationship to pitch attitude.

67. What does the miniature aircraft of the turn coordinator directly display?

   A.   Rate of roll and rate of turn.

   B.   Angle of bank and rate of turn.

   C.   Angle of bank.

Answer (A) is correct. *(IFH Chap 5)*
   DISCUSSION: The turn coordinator indicates rate of roll and rate of turn. When the bank is constant, the rate of turn is indicated. When the bank is changing, the rate of roll is also indicated.
   Answer (B) is incorrect. The angle of bank is not directly indicated by the turn coordinator. Answer (C) is incorrect. The angle of bank is not directly indicated by the turn coordinator.

68. What indication is presented by the miniature aircraft of the turn coordinator?

    A. Indirect indication of the bank attitude.

    B. Direct indication of the bank attitude and the quality of the turn.

    C. Quality of the turn.

Answer (A) is correct. *(IFH Chap 5)*
    DISCUSSION: The miniature aircraft of the turn coordinator indicates the rate of roll when bank is changing. When the rotation around the longitudinal axis is zero, the instrument indicates the rate of turn. Thus, it provides only an indirect indication of the angle of bank.
    Answer (B) is incorrect. The turn coordinator does NOT provide a direct indication of bank. Answer (C) is incorrect. The ball in the turn coordinator, not the miniature aircraft, provides information on the quality of the turn.

69. The displacement of a turn coordinator during a coordinated turn will

    A. indicate the angle of bank.

    B. remain constant for a given bank regardless of airspeed.

    C. increase as angle of bank increases.

Answer (C) is correct. *(IFH Chap 5)*
    DISCUSSION: The displacement of a turn coordinator increases as angle of bank (in coordinated flight) increases because the turn coordinator shows rate of turn, which increases as angle of bank increases.
    Answer (A) is incorrect. The angle of bank is only indirectly indicated. Answer (B) is incorrect. When the rate of roll is zero, the turn coordinator provides information concerning the rate of turn, which in turn changes as airspeed changes given a constant bank.

70. What indication should be observed on a turn coordinator during a left turn while taxiing?

    A. The miniature aircraft will show a turn to the left and the ball remains centered.

    B. The miniature aircraft will show a turn to the left and the ball moves to the right.

    C. Both the miniature aircraft and the ball will remain centered.

Answer (B) is correct. *(IFH Chap 5)*
    DISCUSSION: On a taxiing turn to the left, the turn coordinator shows a turn to the left, and the ball moves to the right. The centrifugal force of the turn, which is not offset by bank when taxiing, forces the ball opposite to the turn.
    Answer (A) is incorrect. The ball moves to the outside of the turn due to centrifugal force. Answer (C) is incorrect. The miniature aircraft reacts to yaw and shows a turn to the left, and the ball reacts to centrifugal force by moving right.

71. What does the miniature aircraft of the turn coordinator display?

    A. The indicator first shows the rate of banking and, once stabilized, the rate of turn.

    B. Indirectly bank angle and then directly rate of turn.

    C. Indirectly bank angle and rate of turn.

Answer (A) is the best answer. *(IFH Chap 3)*
    DISCUSSION: The turn coordinator's gimbals frame is angled upward approximately 30 degrees from the longitudinal axis of the aircraft to sense both yaw (along the vertical axis) and roll (along the longitudinal axis). During a turn, the miniature aircraft of the turn coordinator first shows the rate of bank directly and then, once stabilized, the rate of turn.
    Answer (B) is incorrect. The turn coordinator initially shows the rate of bank and then, once stabilized, indicates the rate of turn. Although this answer has validity, it is not the best answer to the question given that the *Instrument Flying Handbook* contains a direct quote of the first sentence in this explanation. Answer (C) is incorrect. The turn coordinator initially shows the rate of bank and then, once stabilized, indicates the rate of turn. The turn coordinator shows rate of turn directly once the turn is stabilized, not indirectly.

72. In a left turn, correct control coordination is indicated by

    A. The ball of the turn coordinator in the center.

    B. The ball of the turn coordinator to the left of center.

    C. The ball of the turn coordinator to the right of center.

Answer (A) is correct. *(IFH Chap 2)*
    DISCUSSION: When turning in either direction, a correctly coordinated turn will be indicated when the ball is centered in the inclinometer portion of the turn coordinator.
    Answer (B) is incorrect. A left-of-center ball in a left turn indicates a slipping turn, which is caused by insufficient rudder input through the turn. To return to coordinated flight, decrease the angle of bank and apply left rudder pressure until the ball is centered. Answer (C) is incorrect. A right-of-center ball in a left turn indicates a skidding turn, which is the result of excessive rudder in the turn. To return to coordinated flight, increase bank angle and right rudder until the ball is centered.

1.9 Glass Cockpits

73. Which is true of glass cockpits?

A. They enhance situational awareness.

B. They require less frequent training.

C. They give less reliable information to the pilot than traditional instruments.

Answer (A) is correct. *(AAH Chap 3)*

DISCUSSION: Glass cockpits integrate flight instruments, increase safety by enhancing situational awareness, present data in an easy-to-understand format, and perform many necessary tasks automatically.

Answer (B) is incorrect. More initial and recurrent training is needed to acquire and retain the knowledge and skills necessary to accomplish a flight safely by means of glass cockpits. Answer (C) is incorrect. Instrument sensor systems, and thus glass cockpits themselves, are more sensitive and reliable than traditional gyroscopic instruments.

74. Which display combines instruments such as an altimeter, attitude indicator, and vertical speed indicator onto one given screen?

A. Multi-function display.

B. Primary flight display.

C. Glass cockpit display.

Answer (B) is correct. *(AAH Chap 3)*

DISCUSSION: A primary flight display (PFD) combines many flight instruments into a single presentation, including the altimeter, attitude indicator, vertical speed indicator, turn coordinator, HSI, and airspeed indicator.

Answer (A) is incorrect. A multi-function display is primarily used for monitoring engine performance, fuel status, traffic avoidance, weather, or route selection. Answer (C) is incorrect. The term "glass cockpit" is used to describe an entire set of instruments other than conventional instruments.

75. Primary flight displays

A. primarily present terrain avoidance.

B. provide traffic information.

C. include instruments like the attitude indicator.

Answer (C) is correct. *(AAH Chap 3)*

DISCUSSION: A primary flight display (PFD) combines many flight instruments into a single presentation, including the altimeter, attitude indicator, vertical speed indicator, turn coordinator, HSI, engine and powerplant information, and fuel status.

Answer (A) is incorrect. Multi-function displays provide terrain avoidance information. Answer (B) is incorrect. Multi-function displays provide traffic avoidance information.

76. In a Technologically Advanced Aircraft, the pilot sees the flight instruments on what?

A. PFD.

B. AHRS.

C. MFD.

Answer (A) is correct. *(AAH Chap 3)*

DISCUSSION: The PFD, or primary flight display, is home to the basic flight instruments in a technologically advanced aircraft.

Answer (B) is incorrect. The AHRS, or attitude heading and reference system, is one input source of flight information that feeds the primary flight display. It is not a viewing system. Answer (C) is incorrect. The MFD, or multi-function display, is home to engine instrumentation, navigation information, and other supplementary information.

77. The lighter workloads associated with glass (digital) flight instrumentation

A. are instrumental in decreasing training requirements.

B. have proven to increase basic flight skills.

C. may lead to complacency by the flightcrew.

Answer (C) is correct. *(RMH Chap 7)*

DISCUSSION: The enhanced situational awareness and automation capabilities offered by a glass flight deck vastly expand its safety and utility, especially for personal transportation use. At the same time, there is some risk that lighter workloads could lead to complacency. Humans are characteristically poor monitors of automated systems. When passively monitoring an automated system for faults, abnormalities, or other infrequent events, humans perform poorly. The more reliable the system is, the worse the human performance becomes. It is a paradox of automation that technically advanced avionics can both increase and decrease pilot awareness.

Answer (A) is incorrect. Risk management is one of the three flight management skills needed to master the advanced avionics (glass) aircraft. The enhanced situational awareness and automation capabilities by a glass cockpit vastly expand its safety and utility. The advanced avionics simplify basic flying tasks and could lead to complacency of those skills. Answer (B) is incorrect. It is helpful to note that all human activity involving technical devices entails some element of risk. Knowledge, experience, and flight requirements tilt the odds in favor of safe and successful flights. The advanced avionics aircraft offers many new capabilities and simplifies the basic flying tasks, but only if the pilot is properly trained and all the equipment is working properly.

78. When a pilot believes advanced avionics enable operations closer to personal or environmental limits,

    A.   greater utilization of the aircraft is achieved.

    B.   risk is increased.

    C.   risk is decreased.

Answer (B) is correct. *(RMH Chap 8)*
    DISCUSSION: Pilots should not be lulled into a false sense of security simply because they have advanced avionics. Judgment and aeronautical decision making serve as the bridge between technology and safety. Any flight you make involves almost infinite combinations of pilot skill, experience, condition, and proficiency; aircraft equipment and performance; environmental conditions; and external influences. Both individually and in combination, these factors can compress the safety buffer provided by your baseline personal minimums. Consequently, you need a practical way to adjust your baseline personal minimums to accommodate specific conditions.
    Answer (A) is incorrect. While one may be able to use an aircraft in more challenging environments, the risks involved with such flights also increase. Therefore, the best answer choice is that risk is increased when a pilot believes advanced avionics enable operations closer to personal or environmental limits. Answer (C) is incorrect. Risk is increased, not decreased, when a pilot believes advanced avionics enable operations closer to personal or environmental limits.

79. The advancement of avionics in light general aviation airplanes has enhanced situational awareness for properly trained pilots. However, there is concern that this technology could lead to

    A.   complacency.

    B.   fatigue.

    C.   resignation.

Answer (A) is correct. *(ASF-Air Safety Foundation)*
    DISCUSSION: Pilots should not become complacent or be lulled into a false sense of security simply because they have advanced avionics. It takes initial and recurrent training to maintain proficiency using this equipment, but pilots should still maintain their skills and knowledge. Judgment and aeronautical decision making serve as the bridge between technology and safety.
    Answer (B) is incorrect. The reason for technologically advanced aircraft is to give the pilot more situational awareness. If the pilot knows his or her aircraft equipment and systems, fatigue should not be a factor while flying. Answer (C) is incorrect. For pilots that have the proper training and knowledge of the equipment and systems of their technologically advanced aircraft, the hazardous attitude of resignation would not be an issue. If a pilot has difficulty using the autopilot or other systems, all that needs to be done is to fall back on the basics of flying by hand, pilotage, and dead reckoning.

80. Automation in aircraft has proven

    A.   to present new hazards in its limitations.

    B.   that automation is basically flawless.

    C.   effective in preventing accidents.

Answer (A) is correct. *(RMH Chap 7)*
    DISCUSSION: Most of the aviation community believes automation has made flying safer, but there is a fear that pilots fail to see that automation is a double-edged sword. Pilots need to understand the advantages of automation while being aware of its limitations. Experience has shown that automated systems can make some errors more evident while sometimes hiding other errors or making them less obvious. When passively monitoring an automated system for faults, abnormalities, or other infrequent events, humans perform poorly. The more reliable the system is, the worse the human performance becomes. It is a paradox of automation that technically advanced avionics can both increase and decrease pilot awareness.
    Answer (B) is incorrect. Automation is not necessarily flawless. Proper use of checklists and systematic training should be used to control common error-prone tasks and notice errors from automation before they become a threat to safety of flight. Answer (C) is incorrect. While automation has prevented accidents, it can also cause accidents from complacency. Therefore, it is not the best answer choice. When passively monitoring an automated system for faults, abnormalities, or other infrequent events, humans perform poorly. The more reliable the system is, the worse the human performance becomes. It is a paradox of automation that technically advanced avionics can both increase and decrease pilot awareness.

END OF STUDY UNIT

STUDY UNIT TWO
ATTITUDE INSTRUMENT FLYING AND AERODYNAMICS

(5 pages of outline)

This study unit contains outlines of major concepts tested, sample test questions and answers regarding attitude instrument flying and aerodynamics, and an explanation of each answer. The table of contents above lists each subunit within this study unit, the number of questions pertaining to that particular subunit, and the pages on which the outlines and questions begin, respectively.

Recall that the **sole purpose** of this book is to expedite your passing of the FAA pilot knowledge test for the instrument rating. Accordingly, all extraneous material (i.e., topics or regulations not directly tested on the FAA pilot knowledge test) is omitted, even though much more knowledge is necessary to fly safely. This additional material is presented in *Pilot Handbook*, *Aviation Weather and Weather Services*, *FAR/AIM*, and *Instrument Pilot Flight Maneuvers and Practical Test Prep*, available from Gleim Publications, Inc. Order online at www.gleim.com.

2.1 TURNS

1. An airplane requires a sideward force to make it turn.

   a. When the airplane is banked, lift (which acts perpendicular to the wingspan) acts not only upward but horizontally as well.

   b. The vertical component acts upward to oppose weight.

   c. The horizontal component acts sideward to turn the airplane, opposing centrifugal force.

   d. The rate of turn (at a given airspeed) depends on the magnitude of the horizontal lift component, which is determined by bank angle.

2. A turn is said to be coordinated when the horizontal lift component equals centrifugal force (the ball is centered).

   a. Centrifugal force is greater than horizontal lift in skidding turns (the ball is on the outside of the turn).

   b. Centrifugal force is less than horizontal lift in slipping turns (the ball is on the inside of the turn).

3. To coordinate a turn, you should center the ball on the turn-and-slip indicator or the turn coordinator.

   a. Center the ball by applying rudder pressure on the side where the ball is (e.g., if the ball is on the left, use left rudder).

4. A standard-rate turn is indicated when the needle is on the "doghouse" (i.e., standard rate) mark on the turn-and-slip indicator.

5. The angle of attack must be increased in turns to maintain altitude because additional lift is required to maintain a constant amount of vertical lift.

   a. Thus, load factor always increases in turns (assuming level flight).

6. If airspeed is increased in a turn, the angle of bank must be increased and/or the angle of attack decreased to maintain level flight.

   a. Conversely, if airspeed is decreased in a turn, the angle of bank must be decreased and/or the angle of attack must be increased to maintain level flight.

2.2 TURN RATES

1. The standard-rate turn is 360° in 2 min., i.e., 3°/sec.

   a. A half-standard-rate turn is 360° in 4 min., i.e., 1.5°/sec.
   b. EXAMPLE: A 150° heading change using a standard-rate turn would take 50 sec. (150° ÷ 3°/sec. = 50 sec.)

2. A turn-and-slip indicator may be calibrated as 2-minute or 4-minute.

   a. On a 2-minute turn-and-slip indicator, a single width deflection of the needle indicates a turning rate of 3° per second, or a standard rate turn (i.e., 360° in 2 minutes).
   b. On a 4-minute turn-and-slip indicator, a single width deflection of the needle indicates a turning rate of 1.5° per second, or a half rate turn (i.e., 360° in 4 minutes). If the needle is on the doghouse, it is indicating a standard rate turn.

3. At a constant bank, an increase in airspeed decreases the rate of turn and increases the radius of the turn.

   a. The rate of turn can be increased and the radius of turn decreased by decreasing airspeed and/or increasing the bank.

2.3 CLIMBS AND DESCENTS

1. Conditions that determine the pitch attitude required to maintain level flight are

   a. Airspeed
   b. Air density
   c. Wing design
   d. Angle of attack

2. When leveling off from a climb or descent to a specific altitude, you must start the level-off before reaching the desired altitude.

   a. Throughout the transition to level flight, the aircraft will continue to climb or descend at a decreasing rate.
   b. An effective practice is to lead the altitude by 10% of the indicated vertical speed.

      1) Since the last 1,000 ft. of a climb or descent should be made at 500 fpm, you will generally use a lead of 50 ft.

   c. To level off from a descent at a higher airspeed than descent speed, begin adding power 100 to 150 ft. above the desired altitude, assuming a descent rate of 500 fpm.

3.   The pitch instruments are the attitude indicator, the altimeter, the vertical speed indicator, and the airspeed indicator.

   a.   The attitude indicator should be used to make a pitch correction when you have deviated from your altitude; then the altimeter and vertical speed indicator are used to monitor the result.

   b.   Altitude corrections of less than 100 ft. should be corrected by using a half-bar-width (i.e., less than a full-bar-width) correction on the attitude indicator.

4.   To enter a constant-airspeed descent from level cruise and maintain cruise airspeed, simultaneously reduce power and adjust the pitch using the attitude indicator as a reference to maintain cruise airspeed.

5.   To enter a constant-airspeed climb from level cruise, increase the pitch such that the artificial horizon indicates an approximate nose-high attitude appropriate for the desired climb speed.

   a.   Then apply the desired climb power setting.

2.4   FUNDAMENTAL INSTRUMENT SKILLS

1.   The three fundamental skills for attitude instrument flying are (in order)

   a.   **Instrument cross-check** -- the continuous and logical observation of instruments for attitude and performance information

   b.   **Instrument interpretation** -- the understanding of each instrument's construction, operating principle, and relationship to the performance of the airplane

   c.   **Airplane control** -- includes the following elements:

      1)   Pitch control
      2)   Bank control
      3)   Power control

2.5   APPROPRIATE INSTRUMENTS FOR IFR

1.   Flight instruments are divided into the following three categories:

   a.   Pitch instruments

      1)   Attitude indicator (AI)
      2)   Altimeter (ALT)
      3)   Airspeed indicator (ASI)
      4)   Vertical speed indicator (VSI)

   b.   Bank instruments

      1)   Attitude indicator (AI)
      2)   Heading indicator (HI)
      3)   Turn coordinator (TC) or turn-and-slip indicator (T&SI)
      4)   Magnetic compass

   c.   Power instruments

      1)   Manifold pressure gauge (MP)
      2)   Tachometer (RPM)
      3)   Airspeed indicator (ASI)

2. For any maneuver or condition of flight, the pitch, bank, and power control requirements are most clearly indicated by certain key instruments. Those instruments that provide the most pertinent and essential information will be referred to as primary instruments. Supporting instruments back up and supplement the information shown on the primary instruments.

	PITCH	BANK	POWER
a. Straight and level			
Primary	ALT	HI	ASI
Supporting	AI, VSI	AI, TC	MP and/or RPM
b. Airspeed changes in straight and level			
Primary	ALT	HI	MP and/or RPM initially
Supporting	AI, VSI	AI, TC	ASI as desired airspeed is approached
c. Establishing a level standard-rate turn			
Primary	ALT	AI	ASI
Supporting	AI, VSI	TC	MP and/or RPM
d. Stabilized standard-rate turn			
Primary	ALT	TC	ASI
Supporting	AI, VSI	AI	MP and/or RPM
e. Change of airspeed in level turn			
Primary	ALT	TC	MP and/or RPM initially
Supporting	AI, VSI	AI	ASI as desired airspeed is approached
f. Transitioning from straight and level to constant airspeed climb			
Primary	AI	HI	MP and/or RPM
Supporting	ASI, VSI	AI, TC	ASI
g. Straight constant airspeed climb			
Primary	ASI	HI	MP and/or RPM
Supporting	AI, VSI	AI, TC	ASI
h. As power is increased to enter a straight, constant-rate climb			
Primary	AI	HI	MP and/or RPM
Supporting	ASI, VSI	AI, TC	--
i. Straight, constant-rate, stabilized climb			
Primary	VSI	HI	ASI
Supporting	AI	AI, TC	MP and/or RPM

3. For straight-and-level flight, the magnetic compass replaces the HI as the primary bank instrument if the HI is inoperative.

4. The ball of the turn coordinator or turn-and-slip instrument indicates the quality of the turn.

2.6 UNUSUAL ATTITUDES

1. For recovery from nose-low unusual attitudes (negative VSI, increasing airspeed, decreasing altitude, airplane below horizon on attitude indicator),

    a. Reduce power to prevent excess airspeed and loss of altitude
    b. Level the wings with coordinated rudder and aileron
    c. Gently raise the nose to level flight attitude

2. For recovery from nose-high unusual attitudes (positive VSI, decreasing airspeed, increasing altitude, airplane above horizon on attitude indicator),

    a. Add power
    b. Lower the nose
    c. Level the wings
    d. Return to the original altitude and heading

3. When recovering without the aid of the attitude indicator, level flight attitude is reached when the altimeter and the airspeed indicator stop prior to reversing their direction of movement and the vertical speed indicator reverses trend.

4. If the attitude indicator has exceeded its limits in an unusual attitude, nose-low or nose-high attitude can be determined by the airspeed indicator and the altimeter.

    a. The vertical speed indicator is also useful but is not as reliable in turbulent air.

2.7 INOPERATIVE INSTRUMENTS

1. To determine an inoperative instrument, analyze each instrument to determine what it is indicating, and determine which instrument is in conflict with the others.

2. Also, consider grouping the instruments by the systems that power them.

    a. The heading indicator and the attitude indicator are vacuum-driven.
    b. The turn coordinator is usually electric.
    c. The airspeed indicator, altimeter, and VSI rely on the static source.

        1) The airspeed indicator also relies on the pitot tube.

            a) Remember that if the pitot tube's ram air and drain hole are clogged, the airspeed indicator acts as an altimeter; i.e., lower altitudes result in lower airspeeds and vice versa.

            b) Also remember that if only the ram air hole is clogged, the pressure in the line will vent out the drain hole, causing the airspeed indication to drop to zero.

2.8 TURBULENCE AND WIND SHEAR

1. In severe turbulence, set power for the design maneuvering speed (V_A), and maintain a level flight attitude.

    a. Attempting to turn or maintain altitude or airspeed may impose excessive load on the wings.

2. Flight at or below V_A means the airplane will stall before excessive loads can be imposed on the wings.

3. When climbing or descending through an inversion or wind-shear zone, you should be alert for any sudden change in airspeed.

QUESTIONS AND ANSWER EXPLANATIONS: All of the instrument rating knowledge test questions chosen by the FAA for release as well as additional questions selected by Gleim relating to the material in the previous outlines are reproduced on the following pages. These questions have been organized into the same subunits as the outlines. To the immediate right of each question are the correct answer and answer explanation. You should cover these answers and answer explanations while responding to the questions. Refer to the general discussion in the Introduction on how to take the FAA knowledge test.

Remember that the questions from the FAA knowledge test bank have been reordered by topic and organized into a meaningful sequence. Also, the first line of the answer explanation gives the citation of the authoritative source for the answer.

QUESTIONS

2.1 Turns

1. What force causes an airplane to turn?

A. Rudder pressure or force around the vertical axis.

B. Vertical lift component.

C. Horizontal lift component.

Answer (C) is correct. *(IFH Chap 4)*
DISCUSSION: An airplane, like any object, requires a sideward force to make it turn. This force is supplied by banking the airplane so that lift is separated into two components at right angles to each other. The lift acting upward and opposing weight is the vertical lift component, and the lift acting horizontally and opposing centrifugal force is the horizontal lift component. The horizontal lift component is the sideward force that causes an airplane to turn.
Answer (A) is incorrect. The rudder pressure coordinates flight only when the airplane is banked. Answer (B) is incorrect. The vertical component of lift counteracts weight and thus affects altitude.

2. The rate of turn at any airspeed is dependent upon

A. the horizontal lift component.

B. the vertical lift component.

C. centrifugal force.

Answer (A) is correct. *(IFH Chap 4)*
DISCUSSION: At a given airspeed, the rate at which an airplane turns depends upon the amount of the horizontal component of lift.
Answer (B) is incorrect. The vertical component of lift determines altitude and change in altitude. Answer (C) is incorrect. Centrifugal force acts against the horizontal lift component, thus acting against turning the airplane.

3. What is the relationship between centrifugal force and the horizontal lift component in a coordinated turn?

A. Horizontal lift exceeds centrifugal force.

B. Horizontal lift and centrifugal force are equal.

C. Centrifugal force exceeds horizontal lift.

Answer (B) is correct. *(IFH Chap 4)*
DISCUSSION: When a turn is coordinated, horizontal lift equals centrifugal force. This is indicated when the ball on the turn coordinator or turn-and-slip indicator is centered.
Answer (A) is incorrect. When horizontal lift exceeds centrifugal force, there is a slipping turn. Answer (C) is incorrect. When centrifugal force exceeds horizontal lift, there is a skidding turn.

4. (Refer to Figure 144 on page 51.) What changes in control displacement should be made so that "2" would result in a coordinated standard-rate turn?

A. Increase left rudder and increase rate of turn.

B. Increase left rudder and decrease rate of turn.

C. Decrease left rudder and decrease angle of bank.

Answer (A) is correct. *(IFH Chap 5)*
DISCUSSION: Illustration 2 in Fig. 144 is a 4-minute turn-and-slip indicator, indicating a slip in which the rate of turn is too slow for the angle of bank, and the lack of centrifugal force causes the ball to move to the inside of the turn. To return to a coordinated standard-rate turn, you should increase left rudder (i.e., step on the ball) and increase the rate of turn. For a 4-minute turn-and-slip indicator, a standard-rate turn is indicated when the needle is on the "doghouse" (i.e., standard rate) mark. It is presently showing a single width needle deflection, which indicates a half-standard-rate turn.
Answer (B) is incorrect. The rate of turn must be increased, not decreased, to establish a standard-rate turn. Answer (C) is incorrect. Left rudder pressure must be increased, not decreased, in a slip to the left.

5. (Refer to Figure 144 below.) Which illustration indicates a coordinated turn?

   A. 3.

   B. 1.

   C. 2.

Answer (A) is correct. *(IFH Chap 5)*
   DISCUSSION: A coordinated turn is one in which the ball is centered as indicated in illustration 3. The horizontal component of lift equals centrifugal force.
   Answer (B) is incorrect. Illustration 1 shows a skidding turn, in which centrifugal force exceeds the horizontal component of lift. Answer (C) is incorrect. Illustration 2 shows a slipping turn, in which centrifugal force is less than the horizontal component of lift.

6. (Refer to Figure 144 below.) What changes in control displacement should be made so that "1" would result in a coordinated standard rate turn?

   A. Increase right rudder and decrease rate of turn.

   B. Increase right rudder and increase rate of turn.

   C. Decrease right rudder and increase angle of bank.

Answer (B) is correct. *(IFH Chap 5)*
   DISCUSSION: Illustration 1 in Fig. 144 is a 4-minute turn-and-slip indicator, indicating a skid in which the rate of yaw is too great for the angle of bank, and excessive centrifugal force causes the ball to move to the outside of the turn. To return to coordinated flight, you should increase right rudder (i.e., step on the ball) to center the ball. On the 4-minute turn-and-slip indicator, a standard-rate turn is indicated when the needle is on the doghouse mark. Presently, it is showing a single needle width deflection, which indicates a half-standard-rate turn. Thus, the rate of turn must be increased to result in a standard-rate turn.
   Answer (A) is incorrect. The rate of turn must be increased, not decreased. Answer (C) is incorrect. Right rudder must be increased, not decreased.

7. (Refer to Figure 144 below.) Which illustration indicates a skidding turn?

   A. 2.

   B. 1.

   C. 3.

Answer (B) is correct. *(IFH Chap 5)*
   DISCUSSION: A skidding turn occurs when centrifugal force is greater than horizontal lift. As shown by illustration 1, the ball is outside the turn.
   Answer (A) is incorrect. Illustration 2 shows a slipping turn. Answer (C) is incorrect. Illustration 3 shows a coordinated turn.

8. (Refer to Figure 144 below.) Which illustration indicates a slipping turn?

   A. 1.

   B. 3.

   C. 2.

Answer (C) is correct. *(IFH Chap 5)*
   DISCUSSION: A slipping turn is one in which the centrifugal force is less than horizontal lift. As shown by illustration 2, the ball is inside the turn.
   Answer (A) is incorrect. Illustration 1 shows a skidding turn. Answer (B) is incorrect. Illustration 3 shows a coordinated turn.

Figure 144. – Turn-and-Slip Indicator.

9. The primary reason the angle of attack must be increased, to maintain a constant altitude during a coordinated turn, is because the

   A. thrust is acting in a different direction, causing a reduction in airspeed and loss of lift.

   B. vertical component of lift has decreased as the result of the bank.

   C. use of ailerons has increased the drag.

Answer (B) is correct. *(IFH Chap 4)*
   DISCUSSION: In comparison to level flight, a bank results in the division of lift between vertical and horizontal components. To provide a vertical component of lift sufficient to maintain altitude in a level turn, an increase in the angle of attack is required.
   Answer (A) is incorrect. Thrust is always a forward-acting force. The reduction in airspeed (assuming constant power) is due to an increase in angle of attack to compensate for the loss of vertical lift in a turn, i.e., to maintain altitude. Answer (C) is incorrect. In a coordinated turn the ailerons are streamlined and no aileron drag exists. When entering or recovering from turns, you can counteract the adverse yaw caused by aileron drag by use of the rudder.

10. During a skidding turn to the right, what is the relationship between the component of lift, centrifugal force, and load factor?

   A. Centrifugal force is less than horizontal lift and the load factor is increased.

   B. Centrifugal force is greater than horizontal lift and the load factor is increased.

   C. Centrifugal force and horizontal lift are equal and the load factor is decreased.

Answer (B) is correct. *(IFH Chap 4)*
   DISCUSSION: In skidding turns, centrifugal force is greater than horizontal lift. The load factor increases in level turns.
   Answer (A) is incorrect. A slipping, not skidding, turn occurs when centrifugal force is less than horizontal lift. Answer (C) is incorrect. Centrifugal force and horizontal lift are equal in a coordinated, not skidding, turn and, in a level turn, the load factor is increased, not decreased.

11. When airspeed is increased in a turn, what must be done to maintain a constant altitude?

   A. Decrease the angle of bank.

   B. Increase the angle of bank and/or decrease the angle of attack.

   C. Decrease the angle of attack.

Answer (B) is correct. *(IFH Chap 4)*
   DISCUSSION: To compensate for added lift, which would result if airspeed were increased during a turn, the angle of attack must be decreased and the angle of bank increased if a constant altitude is to be maintained.
   Answer (A) is incorrect. The angle of bank must be increased, not decreased. Answer (C) is incorrect. As an alternative, the angle of bank can be increased.

12. When airspeed is decreased in a turn, what must be done to maintain level flight?

   A. Decrease the angle of bank and/or increase the angle of attack.

   B. Increase the angle of bank and/or decrease the angle of attack.

   C. Increase the angle of attack.

Answer (A) is correct. *(IFH Chap)*
   DISCUSSION: To compensate for the decreased lift resulting from decreased airspeed during a turn, the angle of bank must be decreased and/or the angle of attack increased.
   Answer (B) is incorrect. The increased vertical lift required must be obtained by a decrease, not an increase, in angle of bank and/or an increase, not a decrease, in angle of attack. Answer (C) is incorrect. The angle of bank can be decreased as well as the angle of attack increased.

13. When airspeed is decreased in a turn, what must be done to maintain level flight?

   A. Increase the pitch attitude and/or increase the angle of bank.

   B. Increase the angle of bank and/or decrease the pitch attitude.

   C. Decrease the angle of bank and/or increase the pitch attitude.

Answer (C) is correct. *(IFH Chap)*
   DISCUSSION: To compensate for the decreased lift resulting from decreased airspeed during a turn, the angle of bank must be decreased and/or the angle of attack increased by increasing the pitch attitude.
   Answer (A) is incorrect. The increased vertical lift required must be obtained by an increase in the pitch attitude and/or a decrease, not an increase, in the angle of bank. Answer (B) is incorrect. The increased vertical lift required must be obtained by a decrease, not an increase, in the angle of bank and/or an increase, not a decrease, in the pitch attitude.

14. The primary reason the pitch attitude must be increased, to maintain a constant altitude during a coordinated turn, is because the

    A. thrust is acting in a different direction, causing a reduction in airspeed and loss of lift.

    B. vertical component of lift has decreased as the result of the bank.

    C. use of pedals has increased the drag.

Answer (B) is correct. *(AFH Chap 3)*
    DISCUSSION: In a constant altitude turn, as the turn is entered, some of the vertical component of lift is transferred to the horizontal component of lift, decreasing the vertical component, requiring the pitch attitude to be increased.
    Answer (A) is incorrect. Relative to the wings, thrust is acting in the same direction. Answer (C) is incorrect. The effects of drag from the rudder are far outweighed by the redistribution of lift.

2.2 Turn Rates

15. If a standard-rate turn is maintained, how much time would be required to turn to the left from a heading of 090° to a heading of 300°?

    A. 30 seconds.

    B. 40 seconds.

    C. 50 seconds.

Answer (C) is correct. *(IFH Chap 5)*
    DISCUSSION: A standard-rate turn means an airplane is turning at a rate of 3°/sec. A left turn from 090° to 300° is a total of 150° (90° to north and another 60° to 300°). Thus, at standard-rate, it would take 50 sec. (150° ÷ 3°/sec.).
    Answer (A) is incorrect. At a standard rate of turn, an airplane would turn left 90° to a heading of 360°, not 300°, in 30 sec. Answer (B) is incorrect. At a standard rate of turn, an airplane would turn left 120° to a heading of 330°, not 300°, in 40 sec.

16. If a half-standard-rate turn is maintained, how long would it take to turn 135°?

    A. 1 minute.

    B. 1 minute 20 seconds.

    C. 1 minute 30 seconds.

Answer (C) is correct. *(IFH Chap 5)*
    DISCUSSION: A standard-rate turn means an airplane is turning at a rate of 3°/sec. Thus, a half-standard-rate turn is at the rate of 1.5°/sec. To turn 135° at half-standard rate would take 90 sec. (135° ÷ 1.5°/sec.) or 1 min. 30 sec.
    Answer (A) is incorrect. An airplane would turn 90°, not 135°, in 1 min. at half-standard rate. Answer (B) is incorrect. An airplane would turn 120°, not 135°, in 1 min. 20 sec. at half-standard rate.

17. If a half-standard-rate turn is maintained, how long would it take to turn 360°?

    A. 1 minute.

    B. 2 minutes.

    C. 4 minutes.

Answer (C) is correct. *(IFH Chap 5)*
    DISCUSSION: A standard-rate turn (3°/sec) takes 2 min. for 360°. A half-standard-rate turn (1.5°/sec.) would thus take 4 min. for 360°.
    Answer (A) is incorrect. A half-standard-rate turn would take 1 min. to turn 90°, not 360°. Answer (B) is incorrect. A standard-rate, not half-standard-rate, turn completes 360° in 2 min.

18. If a standard-rate turn is maintained, how long would it take to turn 180°?

    A. 1 minute.

    B. 2 minutes.

    C. 3 minutes.

Answer (A) is correct. *(IFH Chap 5)*
    DISCUSSION: A standard-rate turn means an airplane is turning at a rate of 3°/sec. To turn 180° at a standard rate would take 60 sec. (180° ÷ 3°/sec.), or 1 min.
    Answer (B) is incorrect. An airplane would turn 180° in 2 min. at a half-standard-rate, not standard-rate, turn. Answer (C) is incorrect. An airplane would turn 540° in 3 min. at a standard rate (3°/sec.)

19. If a half-standard-rate turn is maintained, how much time would be required to turn clockwise from a heading of 090° to a heading of 180°?

    A. 30 seconds.

    B. 1 minute.

    C. 1 minute 30 seconds.

Answer (B) is correct. *(IFH Chap 4)*
    DISCUSSION: A half-standard-rate turn means an airplane is turning at a rate of 1.5°/sec. A turn clockwise from 090° to 180° is a total of 90°. Thus, at a half-standard rate, it would take 60 sec. (90° ÷ 1.5°/sec.).
    Answer (A) is incorrect. It would take 30 sec. to turn 90° at a standard, not half-standard, rate of turn. Answer (C) is incorrect. An airplane would turn 135°, not 90°, in 1 min. 30 sec. at a half-standard rate of turn.

20. During a constant-bank level turn, what effect would an increase in airspeed have on the rate and radius of turn?

    A. Rate of turn would increase, and radius of turn would increase.

    B. Rate of turn would decrease, and radius of turn would decrease.

    C. Rate of turn would decrease, and radius of turn would increase.

Answer (C) is correct. *(IFH Chap 4)*
    DISCUSSION: The radius of turn at a constant-bank level turn varies directly with the airspeed, while the rate of turn at a constant-bank level turn also varies with airspeed. If airspeed is increased during a constant-bank level turn, the radius of turn will increase, and rate of turn will decrease.
    Answer (A) is incorrect. The rate of turn decreases, not increases. Answer (B) is incorrect. The radius of the turn increases, not decreases.

21. Rate of turn can be increased and radius of turn decreased by

    A. decreasing airspeed and shallowing the bank.

    B. decreasing airspeed and increasing the bank.

    C. increasing airspeed and increasing the bank.

Answer (B) is correct. *(IFH Chap 4)*
    DISCUSSION: To increase the rate and decrease the radius of turn, you should decrease airspeed and increase the bank angle.
    Answer (A) is incorrect. Decreasing (shallowing) the bank decreases, not increases, the rate of turn. Answer (C) is incorrect. The airspeed should be decreased, not increased, to increase the rate of turn.

22. If a standard-rate turn is maintained, how much time would be required to turn to the right from a heading of 090° to a heading of 270°?

    A. 1 minute.

    B. 2 minutes.

    C. 3 minutes.

Answer (A) is correct. *(IFH Chap 5)*
    DISCUSSION: A standard-rate turn means an airplane is turning at the rate of 3°/sec. A turn to the right (or left) from 090° to 270° is a total of 180°. Thus, at standard rate, it would take 60 sec. (180° ÷ 3°/sec.), or 1 min.
    Answer (B) is incorrect. It would take 2 min. to turn 180° at a half-standard, not standard, rate of turn. Answer (C) is incorrect. It would take 3 min. to turn 270°, not 180°, at a half-standard, not standard, rate of turn.

2.3 Climbs and Descents

23. Conditions that determine pitch attitude required to maintain level flight are

    A. flightpath, wind velocity, and angle of attack.

    B. airspeed, air density, wing design, and angle of attack.

    C. relative wind, pressure altitude, and vertical lift component.

Answer (B) is correct. *(IFH Chap 4)*
    DISCUSSION: Conditions that determine the pitch attitude required to maintain level flight are airspeed, air density, wing design, and angle of attack. At a constant angle of attack, any change in airspeed will vary the lift. Lift varies directly with changes in air density. An airplane's wing has lift characteristics that are suited to its intended uses. Lift increases with any increase in the angle of attack (up to the critical angle).
    Answer (A) is incorrect. Flight path is the direction of travel of the airplane, which in this case is level flight. Wind velocity is not considered in maintaining level flight. Angle of attack is the resultant pitch attitude to maintain level flight. Answer (C) is incorrect. Relative wind is the direction of airflow produced by an airplane in flight, and the vertical lift component is an aerodynamic force that acts perpendicular to the relative wind. The density, not pressure, altitude is one condition that determines the pitch attitude required to maintain level flight.

24. Approximately what percent of the indicated vertical speed should be used to determine the number of feet to lead the level-off from a climb to a specific altitude?

    A. 10 percent.

    B. 20 percent.

    C. 25 percent.

Answer (A) is correct. *(IFH Chap 6)*
    DISCUSSION: To level off from a climb and maintain a specific altitude, you should start the level-off before reaching the desired altitude. If your airplane is climbing at 500 fpm, it will continue to climb at a decreasing rate throughout the transition to level flight. An effective practice is to lead the altitude by 10% of the indicated vertical speed (i.e., at 500 fpm, use a 50-ft. lead).
    Answer (B) is incorrect. You should begin to level off from a climb at approximately 10%, not 20%, of the indicated vertical speed. Answer (C) is incorrect. You should begin to level off from a climb at approximately 10%, not 25%, of the indicated vertical speed.

25. To level off from a descent to a specific altitude, the pilot should lead the level-off by approximately

A. 10 percent of the vertical speed.

B. 30 percent of the vertical speed.

C. 50 percent of the vertical speed.

Answer (A) is correct. *(IFH Chap 6)*

DISCUSSION: To level off from a descent to a specific altitude, you should start the level-off before reaching the desired altitude. If your airplane is descending at 500 fpm, it will continue to descend at a decreasing rate throughout the transition to level flight. An effective practice is to lead the desired altitude by 10% of the indicated vertical speed (i.e., at 500 fpm, use a 50-ft. lead).

Answer (B) is incorrect. You should begin to level off from a descent at approximately 10%, not 30%, of the indicated vertical speed. Answer (C) is incorrect. You should begin to level off from a descent at approximately 10%, not 50%, of the indicated vertical speed.

26. As a rule of thumb, altitude corrections of less than 100 feet should be corrected by using

A. two bar widths on the attitude indicator.

B. less than a full bar width on the attitude indicator.

C. less than a half bar width on the attitude indicator.

Answer (B) is correct. *(IFH Chap 6)*

DISCUSSION: As a general rule, altitude corrections of less than 100 ft. should be corrected by using a half-bar-width (i.e., less than a full-bar-width) correction on the attitude indicator.

Answer (A) is incorrect. Altitude corrections of less than 100 ft. should be corrected by using a half-bar-, not a two-bar-, width correction on the attitude indicator. Answer (C) is incorrect. Altitude corrections of less than 100 ft. should be corrected by using a half-bar-width correction on the attitude indicator, not less than a half-bar-width.

27. Which instruments should be used to make a pitch correction when you have deviated from your assigned altitude?

A. Altimeter and VSI.

B. Manifold pressure gauge and VSI.

C. Attitude indicator, altimeter, and VSI.

Answer (C) is correct. *(IFH Chap 6)*

DISCUSSION: The pitch instruments are the attitude indicator, the altimeter, the vertical speed indicator, and the airspeed indicator. The attitude indicator gives you a direct indication of changes in pitch attitude when correcting for altitude variations. The rate and direction of the altimeter and vertical speed indicator confirm the correct pitch adjustment was made, and the altimeter is used to determine when you have reached your assigned altitude.

Answer (A) is incorrect. The question implies that you have all instruments available. Without an attitude indicator, you would use the altimeter and vertical speed indicator to make pitch corrections. Answer (B) is incorrect. The manifold pressure gauge is a power, not pitch, instrument.

28. As a rule of thumb, altitude corrections of less than 100 feet should be corrected by using a

A. full bar width on the attitude indicator.

B. half bar width on the attitude indicator.

C. two bar width on the attitude indicator.

Answer (B) is correct. *(IFH Chap 6)*

DISCUSSION: As a general rule, altitude corrections of less than 100 ft. should be corrected by using a half-bar-width correction on the attitude indicator.

Answer (A) is incorrect. As a general rule, altitude corrections in excess of, not less than, 100 ft. should be corrected by an initial full-bar-width correction on the attitude indicator. Answer (C) is incorrect. Altitude corrections of less than 100 ft. should be corrected by using a half-bar-, not a two-bar-, width correction on the attitude indicator.

29. To enter a constant-airspeed descent from level-cruising flight, and maintain cruising airspeed, the pilot should

A. first adjust the pitch attitude to a descent using the attitude indicator as a reference, then adjust the power to maintain the cruising airspeed.

B. first reduce power, then adjust the pitch using the attitude indicator as a reference to establish a specific rate on the VSI.

C. simultaneously reduce power and adjust the pitch using the attitude indicator as a reference to maintain the cruising airspeed.

Answer (C) is correct. *(IFH Chap 6)*

DISCUSSION: To enter a constant-airspeed descent from level cruising flight and maintain cruising airspeed, you should simultaneously reduce the power smoothly to the desired setting and reduce the pitch attitude slightly by using the attitude indicator as a reference to maintain the cruising airspeed.

Answer (A) is incorrect. Airspeed will increase if you adjust the pitch attitude first. Answer (B) is incorrect. Airspeed will decrease if you first reduce power. You use the airspeed, not vertical speed, indicator to maintain a constant airspeed.

30. To level off at an airspeed higher than the descent speed, the addition of power should be made, assuming a 500 FPM rate of descent, at approximately

    A. 50 to 100 feet above the desired altitude.

    B. 100 to 150 feet above the desired altitude.

    C. 150 to 200 feet above the desired altitude.

Answer (B) is correct. *(IFH Chap 6)*
    DISCUSSION: To level off from a descent at an airspeed higher than the descent speed, it is necessary to start the level-off before reaching the desired altitude. At 500 fpm, an effective practice is to lead the desired altitude by approximately 100 to 150 ft. above the desired altitude. At this point, add power to the appropriate level flight cruise setting.
    Answer (A) is incorrect. Leading the desired altitude by 50 to 100 ft. would require the pilot to level off at descent airspeed, not a higher airspeed. Answer (C) is incorrect. When descending at 500 fpm, 150 to 200 ft. above the desired altitude is not a lead point.

31. To level off from a descent maintaining the descending airspeed, the pilot should lead the desired altitude by approximately

    A. 20 feet.

    B. 50 feet.

    C. 60 feet.

Answer (B) is correct. *(IFH Chap 6)*
    DISCUSSION: To level off from a descent at descent airspeed, lead the desired altitude by approximately 50 ft., simultaneously adjusting the pitch attitude to level flight and adding power to a setting that will hold airspeed constant. Trim off the control pressures and continue with the normal straight-and-level flight cross-check.
    Answer (A) is incorrect. You should lead the desired altitude by approximately 50 ft., not 20 ft., when leveling off from a descent at descent airspeed. Answer (C) is incorrect. You should lead the desired altitude by approximately 50 ft., not 60 ft., when leveling off from a descent at descent airspeed.

32. While cruising at 160 knots, you wish to establish a climb at 130 knots. When entering the climb (full panel), it is proper to make the initial pitch change by increasing back elevator pressure until the

    A. attitude indicator, airspeed, and vertical speed indicate a climb.

    B. vertical speed indication reaches the predetermined rate of climb.

    C. attitude indicator shows the approximate pitch attitude appropriate for the 130-knot climb.

Answer (C) is correct. *(IFH Chap 6)*
    DISCUSSION: To enter a constant-airspeed climb from cruising air-speed, raise the miniature aircraft in the attitude indicator to the approximate nose-high indication appropriate to the predetermined climb speed. The attitude will vary according to the type of airplane you are flying. Apply light elevator back pressure to initiate and maintain the climb attitude. The amount of back pressure will increase as the airplane decelerates.
    Answer (A) is incorrect. For the predetermined climb speed, the adjustment should be to the climb attitude, not just a climb indication on the instruments. Answer (B) is incorrect. The airspeed is predetermined, i.e., constant climb speed, not constant climb rate.

33. While cruising at 190 knots, you wish to establish a climb at 160 knots. When entering the climb (full panel), it would be proper to make the initial pitch change by increasing back elevator pressure until the

    A. attitude indicator shows the approximate pitch attitude appropriate for the 160-knot climb.

    B. attitude indicator, airspeed, and vertical speed indicate a climb.

    C. airspeed indication reaches 160 knots.

Answer (A) is correct. *(IFH Chap 6)*
    DISCUSSION: To enter a constant-airspeed climb from cruising air speed, raise the miniature aircraft in the attitude indicator to the approximate nose-high indication appropriate to the predetermined climb speed. The attitude will vary according to the type of airplane you are flying. Apply light elevator back pressure to initiate and maintain the climb attitude. The required back pressure will increase as the airplane decelerates.
    Answer (B) is incorrect. For the predetermined climb speed, you make the adjustment to the climb attitude, not just a climb indication on the instruments. Answer (C) is incorrect. You make an initial pitch adjustment, not an increasing adjustment; i.e., airspeed will decrease gradually.

2.4 Fundamental Instrument Skills

34. What is the third fundamental skill in attitude instrument flying?

    A. Instrument cross-check.

    B. Power control.

    C. Aircraft control.

Answer (C) is correct. *(IFH Chap 6)*
    DISCUSSION: The third fundamental skill in instrument flying is aircraft control. It consists of pitch, bank, and power control.
    Answer (A) is incorrect. Instrument cross-check is the first, not third, fundamental skill in attitude instrument flying. Cross-checking is the continuous and logical observation of instruments for attitude and performance information. Answer (B) is incorrect. Power control is only one component of aircraft control.

35. What is the first fundamental skill in attitude instrument flying?

A. Aircraft control.

B. Instrument cross-check.

C. Instrument interpretation.

Answer (B) is correct. *(IFH Chap 6)*
   DISCUSSION: The first fundamental skill in attitude instrument flying is instrument cross-check. Cross-checking is the continuous and logical observation of instruments for attitude and performance information.
   Answer (A) is incorrect. The third, not first, fundamental skill in attitude instrument flying is aircraft control. Aircraft control is composed of three components: pitch, bank, and power control. Answer (C) is incorrect. The second, not first, fundamental skill in attitude instrument flying is instrument interpretation. For each maneuver, you must know the performance to expect and the combination of instruments that you must interpret in order to control airplane attitude during the maneuver.

36. What are the three fundamental skills involved in attitude instrument flying?

A. Instrument interpretation, trim application, and aircraft control.

B. Cross-check, instrument interpretation, and aircraft control.

C. Cross-check, emphasis, and aircraft control.

Answer (B) is correct. *(IFH Chap 6)*
   DISCUSSION: The three fundamental skills involved in all instrument flight maneuvers are instrument cross-check, instrument interpretation, and aircraft control. Cross-checking is the continuous and logical observation of the instruments for attitude and performance information. Instrument interpretation requires you to understand each instrument's construction, operating principle, and relationship to the performance of your airplane. Aircraft control requires you to substitute instruments for outside references.
   Answer (A) is incorrect. Trim application is only one aspect of aircraft control. Answer (C) is incorrect. Emphasis (along with fixation and omission) are common errors in instrument cross-checking.

37. What is the correct sequence in which to use the three skills used in instrument flying?

A. Aircraft control, cross-check, and instrument interpretation.

B. Instrument interpretation, cross-check, and aircraft control.

C. Cross-check, instrument interpretation, and aircraft control.

Answer (C) is correct. *(IFH Chap 6)*
   DISCUSSION: The correct sequence in which to use the three fundamental skills of instrument flying is cross-check, instrument interpretation, and aircraft control. Although you learn these skills separately and in deliberate sequence, a measure of your proficiency in precision flying will be your ability to integrate these skills into unified, smooth, positive control responses to maintain any desired flight path.
   Answer (A) is incorrect. Aircraft control is the third, not first, skill used in instrument flying. Answer (B) is incorrect. Instrument interpretation is the second, not first, skill and cross-check is the first, not second, skill used in instrument flying.

2.5 Appropriate Instruments for IFR

38. As power is reduced to change airspeed from high to low cruise in level flight, which instruments are primary for pitch, bank, and power, respectively?

A. Attitude indicator, heading indicator, and manifold pressure gauge or tachometer.

B. Altimeter, attitude indicator, and airspeed indicator.

C. Altimeter, heading indicator, and manifold pressure gauge or tachometer.

Answer (C) is correct. *(IFH Chap 6)*
   DISCUSSION: In straight-and-level flight, when reducing airspeed from high to low cruise, the primary instrument for pitch is the altimeter; the primary instrument for bank is the heading indicator; and the primary instrument for power is the manifold pressure gauge or tachometer.
   Answer (A) is incorrect. The primary pitch instrument is the altimeter, not attitude indicator. Answer (B) is incorrect. The primary bank instrument is the heading indicator, not attitude indicator; and the primary power instrument is the manifold pressure gauge or tachometer, not airspeed indicator.

39. What instruments are considered supporting bank instruments during a straight, stabilized climb at a constant rate?

A. Attitude indicator and turn coordinator.

B. Heading indicator and attitude indicator.

C. Heading indicator and turn coordinator.

Answer (A) is correct. *(IFH Chap 6)*
   DISCUSSION: During a straight, stabilized climb at a constant rate, the heading indicator is the primary instrument for bank. The supporting bank instruments are the turn coordinator and the attitude indicator.
   Answer (B) is incorrect. The heading indicator is the primary, not supporting, bank instrument in a straight climb. Answer (C) is incorrect. The heading indicator is the primary, not supporting, bank instrument in a straight climb.

40. Which instruments are considered primary and supporting for bank, respectively, when establishing a level standard-rate turn?

    A. Turn coordinator and attitude indicator.

    B. Attitude indicator and turn coordinator.

    C. Turn coordinator and heading indicator.

Answer (B) is correct. *(IFH Chap 6)*
    DISCUSSION: When you are establishing a level standard-rate turn, the attitude indicator is the primary bank instrument and is used to establish the approximate angle of bank. The turn coordinator is the supporting bank instrument as you check for the standard-rate turn indication.
    Answer (A) is incorrect. The turn coordinator is the primary bank instrument, and the attitude indicator is the supporting bank instrument only after the standard-rate turn is established, not while entering the turn. Answer (C) is incorrect. The turn coordinator is the supporting, not primary, bank instrument, and the heading indicator is neither the primary nor the supporting bank instrument when establishing a standard-rate turn.

41. Which instrument provides the most pertinent information (primary) for bank control in straight-and-level flight?

    A. Turn-and-slip indicator.

    B. Attitude indicator.

    C. Heading indicator.

Answer (C) is correct. *(IFH Chap 6)*
    DISCUSSION: The primary instrument for bank control in straight-and-level flight is the heading indicator.
    Answer (A) is incorrect. The turn-and-slip indicator is a supporting, not primary, bank instrument in straight-and-level flight. Answer (B) is incorrect. The attitude indicator is a supporting, not primary, bank and pitch instrument in straight-and-level flight.

42. Which instruments, in addition to the attitude indicator, are pitch instruments?

    A. Altimeter and airspeed only.

    B. Altimeter and VSI only.

    C. Altimeter, airspeed indicator, and vertical speed indicator.

Answer (C) is correct. *(IFH Chap 6)*
    DISCUSSION: The pitch control instruments are the attitude indicator, altimeter, vertical speed indicator, and airspeed indicator.
    Answer (A) is incorrect. It omits the vertical speed indicator and the airspeed indicator. Answer (B) is incorrect. It omits the airspeed indicator.

43. Which instrument provides the most pertinent information (primary) for pitch control in straight-and-level flight?

    A. Attitude indicator.

    B. Airspeed indicator.

    C. Altimeter.

Answer (C) is correct. *(IFH Chap 6)*
    DISCUSSION: The primary pitch instrument for straight-and-level flight is the altimeter.
    Answer (A) is incorrect. The attitude indicator is a supporting, not primary, pitch instrument in straight-and-level flight. Answer (B) is incorrect. The airspeed indicator is the primary power, not pitch, control instrument in straight-and-level flight.

44. For maintaining level flight at constant thrust, which instrument would be the least appropriate for determining the need for a pitch change?

    A. Altimeter.

    B. VSI.

    C. Attitude indicator.

Answer (C) is correct. *(IFH Chap 6)*
    DISCUSSION: To maintain level flight at constant thrust, the attitude indicator is the least appropriate for determining the need for pitch change. Until you have established and identified the level flight attitude for that airspeed, you have no way of knowing whether level flight as indicated on the attitude indicator is resulting in level flight as shown on the altimeter, vertical speed indicator, and airspeed indicator.
    Answer (A) is incorrect. Since level flight means a constant altitude, the altimeter is the primary pitch instrument in level flight. Answer (B) is incorrect. The vertical speed indicator (as a trend instrument) shows immediately the initial vertical movement of the airplane, which, disregarding turbulence, can be a reflection of pitch change at a constant thrust.

45. The gyroscopic heading indicator is inoperative. What is the primary bank instrument in unaccelerated straight-and-level flight?

A. Magnetic compass.

B. Attitude indicator.

C. Miniature aircraft of turn coordinator.

Answer (A) is correct. *(IFH Chap 6)*
   DISCUSSION: With the gyroscopic heading indicator inoperative, the primary bank instrument in unaccelerated straight-and-level flight is the magnetic compass. Since any banking results in a turn and change in heading, the magnetic compass is the only other instrument that indicates direction.
   Answer (B) is incorrect. Although the attitude indicator shows any change in bank, it does not provide information (i.e., heading) needed to maintain straight flight. Answer (C) is incorrect. The miniature aircraft of the turn coordinator is the primary bank instrument in established standard-rate turns, not in straight flight.

46. What instruments are primary for pitch, bank, and power, respectively, when transitioning into a constant airspeed climb from straight-and-level flight?

A. Attitude indicator, heading indicator, and manifold pressure gauge or tachometer.

B. Attitude indicator for both pitch and bank; airspeed indicator for power.

C. Vertical speed, attitude indicator, and manifold pressure or tachometer.

Answer (A) is correct. *(IFH Chap 6)*
   DISCUSSION: When you are entering a constant airspeed climb, the attitude indicator is the primary pitch instrument, the heading indicator is the primary bank instrument, and the tachometer or manifold pressure gauge is the primary power instrument.
   Answer (B) is incorrect. The heading indicator, not attitude indicator, is primary for bank, and the manifold pressure gauge, not airspeed indicator, is primary for power. Answer (C) is incorrect. The attitude indicator, not vertical speed indicator, is the primary instrument for pitch, and the heading indicator, not attitude indicator, is primary for bank.

47. What is the primary bank instrument once a standard-rate turn is established?

A. Attitude indicator.

B. Turn coordinator.

C. Heading indicator.

Answer (B) is correct. *(IFH Chap 6)*
   DISCUSSION: After a standard-rate turn is established, the turn coordinator is the primary bank instrument.
   Answer (A) is incorrect. The attitude indicator is the primary bank instrument in establishing a standard-rate turn but not for maintaining the turn once established. Answer (C) is incorrect. The heading indicator is the primary bank instrument for straight flight.

48. During standard-rate turns, which instrument is considered "primary" for bank?

A. Heading indicator.

B. Turn and slip indicator or turn coordinator.

C. Attitude indicator.

Answer (B) is correct. *(IFH Chap 6)*
   DISCUSSION: After a standard-rate turn is established, the turn coordinator or turn-and-slip indicator is the primary bank instrument.
   Answer (A) is incorrect. The heading indicator is the primary bank instrument for straight flight. Answer (C) is incorrect. The attitude indicator is the primary bank instrument in establishing a standard-rate turn but not for maintaining the turn once established.

49. What is the primary pitch instrument when establishing a constant altitude standard-rate turn?

A. Altimeter.

B. VSI.

C. Airspeed indicator.

Answer (A) is correct. *(IFH Chap 6)*
   DISCUSSION: The primary pitch instrument in level flight, either straight or turns, is the altimeter.
   Answer (B) is incorrect. The vertical speed indicator is a supporting, not primary, pitch instrument for establishing a level standard-rate turn. Answer (C) is incorrect. The airspeed indicator is the primary power, not pitch, instrument when establishing a constant altitude standard-rate turn.

50. What is the initial primary bank instrument when establishing a level standard-rate turn?

A. Turn coordinator.

B. Heading indicator.

C. Attitude indicator.

Answer (C) is correct. *(IFH Chap 6)*
   DISCUSSION: The initial primary bank instrument when establishing a level standard-rate turn is the attitude indicator.
   Answer (A) is incorrect. Only after the turn is established does the turn coordinator become the primary bank instrument. Answer (B) is incorrect. The heading indicator is the primary bank instrument for straight flight.

51. What is the primary bank instrument while transitioning from straight-and-level flight to a standard-rate turn to the left?

    A. Attitude indicator.

    B. Heading indicator.

    C. Turn coordinator (miniature aircraft).

Answer (A) is correct. *(IFH Chap 6)*
    DISCUSSION: The initial primary bank instrument when establishing a level standard-rate of turn is the attitude indicator.
    Answer (B) is incorrect. The heading indicator is the primary bank instrument for straight flight. Answer (C) is incorrect. Only after the turn is established does the turn coordinator become the primary bank instrument.

52. What instrument(s) is(are) supporting bank instrument(s) when entering a constant airspeed climb from straight-and-level flight?

    A. Heading indicator.

    B. Attitude indicator and turn coordinator.

    C. Turn coordinator and heading indicator.

Answer (B) is correct. *(IFH Chap 6)*
    DISCUSSION: When entering a constant-airspeed climb from straight-and-level flight, the primary bank instrument is the heading indicator. Supporting bank instruments are the turn coordinator and the attitude indicator.
    Answer (A) is incorrect. The heading indicator is the primary, not supporting, bank instrument for straight flight. Answer (C) is incorrect. The heading indicator is the primary, not supporting, bank instrument for straight flight.

53. What is the primary pitch instrument during a stabilized climbing left turn at cruise climb airspeed?

    A. Attitude indicator.

    B. VSI.

    C. Airspeed indicator.

Answer (C) is correct. *(IFH Chap)*
    DISCUSSION: In a climbing left turn at a constant airspeed, the airspeed indicator is the primary instrument for pitch once the climb is established.
    Answer (A) is incorrect. The attitude indicator is a supporting, not primary, pitch instrument in a stabilized climb. Answer (B) is incorrect. The vertical speed indicator is a supporting, not primary, pitch instrument in a stabilized climb.

54. Which instruments are considered to be supporting instruments for pitch during change of airspeed in a level turn?

    A. Airspeed indicator and VSI.

    B. Altimeter and attitude indicator.

    C. Attitude indicator and VSI.

Answer (C) is correct. *(IFH Chap 6)*
    DISCUSSION: The supporting instruments for pitch during a change of airspeed in a level turn are the attitude indicator and the vertical speed indicator. The primary instrument is the altimeter.
    Answer (A) is incorrect. The airspeed indicator is a supporting power, not pitch, instrument during a change of airspeed in a level turn. It becomes the primary power instrument as the desired airspeed is reached. Answer (B) is incorrect. The altimeter is the primary, not supporting, pitch instrument in level flight.

55. Which instrument is considered primary for power as the airspeed reaches the desired value during change of airspeed in a level turn?

    A. Airspeed indicator.

    B. Attitude indicator.

    C. Altimeter.

Answer (A) is correct. *(IFH Chap 6)*
    DISCUSSION: The airspeed indicator is the primary power instrument as the airspeed reaches the desired value during a change of airspeed in a level turn.
    Answer (B) is incorrect. The attitude indicator is a supporting pitch and bank instrument. Answer (C) is incorrect. The altimeter is the primary pitch instrument.

56. As power is increased to enter a 500 feet per minute rate of climb in straight flight, which instruments are primary for pitch, bank, and power respectively?

    A. Attitude indicator, heading indicator, and manifold pressure gauge or tachometer.

    B. VSI, attitude indicator, and airspeed indicator.

    C. Airspeed indicator, attitude indicator, and manifold pressure gauge or tachometer.

Answer (A) is correct. *(IFH Chap 6)*
    DISCUSSION: As the power is increased to enter a constant-rate climb in straight flight, the primary pitch instrument is the attitude indicator until the vertical speed indicator stabilizes at the desired rate of climb (then the vertical speed indicator becomes primary). The primary bank instrument is the heading indicator. The primary power instrument is the manifold pressure gauge or tachometer.
    Answer (B) is incorrect. The vertical speed indicator is the primary pitch instrument once the constant-rate climb is established. Also, the manifold pressure gauge, not the airspeed indicator, is primary for power. Answer (C) is incorrect. The heading indicator, not the attitude indicator, is primary for bank in straight flight.

57. Which instrument indicates the quality of a turn?

A. Attitude indicator.

B. Heading indicator or magnetic compass.

C. Ball of the turn coordinator.

Answer (C) is correct. *(IFH Chap 6)*
    DISCUSSION: The quality (coordination) of a turn relates to whether the horizontal component of lift balances the centrifugal force. It is indicated by the ball of the turn coordinator or the ball in a turn-and-slip indicator. The airplane is neither slipping nor skidding when the ball is centered, indicating the desired quality of a turn.
    Answer (A) is incorrect. The attitude indicator provides both pitch and bank information. Answer (B) is incorrect. The heading indicator and/or magnetic compass show current direction and changes in direction, not quality of a turn.

2.6 Unusual Attitudes

58. While recovering from an unusual flight attitude without the aid of the attitude indicator, approximate level pitch attitude is reached when the

A. airspeed and altimeter stop their movement and the VSI reverses its trend.

B. airspeed arrives at cruising speed, the altimeter reverses its trend, and the vertical speed stops its movement.

C. altimeter and vertical speed reverse their trend and the airspeed stops its movement.

Answer (A) is correct. *(IFH Chap 6)*
    DISCUSSION: As the rate of movement of the altimeter and airspeed indicator needles decreases, the attitude is approaching level flight. When the needles stop and reverse direction, the aircraft is passing through level flight.
    Answer (B) is incorrect. The vertical speed indicator will be lagging, i.e., showing a decrease in vertical movement when vertical movement has stopped. Answer (C) is incorrect. The rate is only slowing and has not stabilized when the altimeter reverses its trend; i.e., it must stop to indicate level flight.

59. If an airplane is in an unusual flight attitude and the attitude indicator has exceeded its limits, which instruments should be relied on to determine pitch attitude before starting recovery?

A. Turn indicator and VSI.

B. Airspeed and altimeter.

C. VSI and airspeed to detect approaching VSI or VMO.

Answer (B) is correct. *(IFH Chap 6)*
    DISCUSSION: If the attitude indicator is inoperative, a nose-low or nose-high attitude can be determined by the airspeed and altimeter. In a nose-high attitude, airspeed is decreasing and altimeter is increasing, and vice versa for nose-low attitudes.
    Answer (A) is incorrect. The turn indicator indicates nothing about pitch attitude. Answer (C) is incorrect. The altimeter, not the VSI, is the primary pitch instrument. Note the FAA answer selection has VSI and VMO, which should be V_{S1} and V_{MO}, respectively.

60. Which is the correct sequence for recovery from a spiraling, nose-low, increasing airspeed, unusual flight attitude?

A. Increase pitch attitude, reduce power, and level wings.

B. Reduce power, correct the bank attitude, and raise the nose to a level attitude.

C. Correct the bank attitude, raise the nose to a level attitude, and reduce power.

Answer (B) is correct. *(IFH Chap 6)*
    DISCUSSION: For nose-low unusual attitudes, one should reduce the power, level the wings, and then increase the pitch to raise the nose to a level attitude.
    Answer (A) is incorrect. The power should be decreased first, then the wings leveled. Answer (C) is incorrect. The power should be reduced before the nose is raised to minimize the load factor.

61. During recoveries from unusual attitudes, level flight is attained the instant

A. the horizon bar on the attitude indicator is exactly overlapped with the miniature airplane.

B. a zero rate of climb is indicated on the VSI.

C. the altimeter and airspeed needles stop prior to reversing their direction of movement.

Answer (C) is correct. *(IFH Chap 6)*
    DISCUSSION: In unusual attitudes, you can determine the attainment of level flight (not vertical movement) when the altimeter and airspeed needles stop prior to reversing their direction of movement.
    Answer (A) is incorrect. The attitude indicator has a tendency to precess during an unusual attitude and may not be reliable. Answer (B) is incorrect. There is a lag or delay in the vertical speed indicator. It cannot be relied on for determining the instant level flight is attained.

62. (Refer to Figure 145 below.) What is the correct sequence for recovery from the unusual attitude indicated?

A. Reduce power, increase back elevator pressure, and level the wings.

B. Reduce power, level the wings, bring pitch attitude to level flight.

C. Level the wings, raise the nose of the aircraft to level flight attitude, and obtain desired airspeed.

Answer (B) is correct. *(IFH Chap 6)*
   DISCUSSION: In Fig. 145, a nose-low attitude is indicated by a negative vertical speed indicator, high airspeed (i.e., near V$_{NE}$), and the airplane below the horizon on the attitude indicator. For nose-low unusual attitudes, the correct sequence for recovery is to reduce power to prevent excessive airspeed and loss of altitude; level the wings with coordinated aileron and rudder pressure to straight flight by referring to the turn coordinator; and raise the nose to level flight attitude by smooth back elevator pressure.
   Answer (A) is incorrect. The wings should be level before you increase back pressure to decrease the load factor during leveling off. Answer (C) is incorrect. The power should be reduced first.

Figure 145. – Instrument Sequence (Unusual Attitude).

63. (Refer to Figure 147 below.) Which is the correct sequence for recovery from the unusual attitude indicated?

A. Level wings, add power, lower nose, descend to original attitude, and heading.

B. Add power, lower nose, level wings, return to original attitude and heading.

C. Stop turn by raising right wing and add power at the same time, lower the nose, and return to original attitude and heading.

Answer (B) is correct. *(IFH Chap 6)*
DISCUSSION: In Fig. 147, a nose-high attitude is indicated by the increasing altitude, the rate-of-climb indication on the vertical speed indicator, and the decreasing airspeed. The correct sequence for recovery is to add power, apply forward elevator pressure to lower the nose and prevent a stall, level the wings with coordinated aileron and rudder pressure to straight flight, and return to original altitude and heading.
    Answer (A) is incorrect. You should both add power and lower the nose before you level the wings. Answer (C) is incorrect. You should both add power and lower the nose before you level the wings.

Figure 147. – Instrument Sequence (Unusual Attitude).

2.7 Inoperative Instruments

64. (Refer to Figure 146 below.) Identify the system that has failed and determine a corrective action to return the airplane to straight-and-level flight.

   A. Static/pitot system is blocked; lower the nose and level the wings to level-flight attitude by use of attitude indicator.

   B. Vacuum system has failed; reduce power, roll left to level wings, and pitchup to reduce airspeed.

   C. Electrical system has failed; reduce power, roll left to level wings, and raise the nose to reduce airspeed.

Answer (A) is correct. *(IFH Chap 5)*
   DISCUSSION: In Fig. 146, the airplane is in a right turn as indicated by the attitude indicator, the heading indicator, and the turn coordinator; thus, the vacuum and electrical instruments are consistent with each other. Since the attitude indicator indicates a climb, which is consistent with the altimeter and the VSI, the airspeed should not be increasing. Thus, the pitot tube ram air and drain holes are blocked, causing the airspeed indicator to react like an altimeter. To return the airplane to straight-and-level flight, you should lower the nose and level the wings to level-flight attitude by use of the attitude indicator.
   Answer (B) is incorrect. The attitude indicator and heading indicator are consistent with the turn coordinator. Answer (C) is incorrect. The turn coordinator, which is normally electric, is consistent with the attitude indicator, which is normally a vacuum system instrument.

Figure 146. – Instrument Sequence (System Failed).

65. (Refer to Figure 148 below.) What is the flight attitude? One system which transmits information to the instruments has malfunctioned.

A. Climbing turn to left.

B. Climbing turn to right.

C. Level turn to left.

Answer (B) is correct. *(IFH Chap 5)*
DISCUSSION: Fig. 148 illustrates a climbing turn to the right. Note that the attitude indicator shows a climbing turn to the right, the heading indicator shows a turn to the right, and both the altimeter and vertical speed indicator indicate a climb. The turn coordinator shows no turn and is malfunctioning.
Answer (A) is incorrect. The turn is to the right, not the left. Answer (C) is incorrect. The attitude indicator, altimeter, and vertical speed indicator all indicate a climb, and the turn is to the right, not left.

Figure 148. – Instrument Interpretation (System Malfunction).

66. (Refer to Figure 149 below.) What is the flight attitude? One system which transmits information to the instruments has malfunctioned.

    A. Level turn to the right.

    B. Level turn to the left.

    C. Straight-and-level flight.

Answer (C) is correct. *(IFH Chap 5)*

    DISCUSSION: In Fig. 149, the vertical speed indicator, altimeter, and turn coordinator all indicate straight-and-level flight. The heading indicator indicates a turn to the south from west, which is a turn to the left. The attitude indicator indicates a turn to the right; i.e., the attitude indicator and heading indicator are in conflict. Thus, the vacuum system must be malfunctioning, and the airplane must be in straight-and-level flight.

    Answer (A) is incorrect. The vacuum system (i.e., the attitude and heading indicators) is inoperative, and the airplane is in straight flight, not a right turn. Answer (B) is incorrect. The vacuum system (i.e., the attitude and heading indicators) is inoperative, and the airplane is in straight flight, not a left turn.

Figure 149. – Instrument Interpretation (System Malfunction).

67. (Refer to Figure 150 below.) What is the flight attitude? One instrument has malfunctioned.

A. Climbing turn to the right.

B. Climbing turn to the left.

C. Descending turn to the right.

Answer (A) is correct. *(IFH Chap 5)*

DISCUSSION: In Fig. 150, the airplane is in a climb as evidenced by the vertical speed indicator, altimeter, and airspeed indicator. The heading indicator indicates a turn from west to north, which is a turn to the right. The turn coordinator also indicates a turn to the right. Thus, the airplane is in a climbing turn to the right. The attitude indicator is the instrument that is malfunctioning since it indicates a level turn to the left.

Answer (B) is incorrect. The attitude indicator is inoperative; thus, the airplane is turning to the right, not left. Answer (C) is incorrect. The airspeed indicator, altimeter, and vertical speed indicator all show that the airplane is climbing, not descending.

Figure 150. – Instrument Interpretation (Instrument Malfunction).

68. (Refer to Figure 151 below.) What is the flight attitude? One instrument has malfunctioned.

    A. Climbing turn to the right.

    B. Level turn to the right.

    C. Level turn to the left.

Answer (B) is correct. *(IFH Chap 5)*
    DISCUSSION: The vertical speed indicator, altimeter, and attitude indicator indicate level flight. The turn coordinator, attitude indicator, and heading indicator indicate a turn to the right. Accordingly, there is a level turn to the right, and the airspeed should not be near the stall speed. Thus, the ram air inlet and the drain hole of the pitot tube are clogged. The airspeed indicator will react the same way as an altimeter, if the static port is open, by showing a decrease in airspeed as altitude decreases and an increase in speed as altitude increases.
    Answer (A) is incorrect. Flight is level, not climbing, according to the vertical speed indicator, altimeter, and attitude indicator. Answer (C) is incorrect. The turn is to the right, not left.

Figure 151. – Instrument Interpretation (Instrument Malfunction).

2.8 Turbulence and Wind Shear

69. If you fly into severe turbulence, which flight condition should you attempt to maintain?

A. Constant airspeed (V_A).

B. Level flight attitude.

C. Constant altitude and constant airspeed.

Answer (B) is correct. *(AvW Chap 11)*
   DISCUSSION: In severe turbulence, you should attempt to maintain a level flight attitude. You will not be able to maintain a constant altitude and/or airspeed, but you should fly at or below design maneuvering speed (V_A) and attempt to maintain a level flight attitude.
   Answer (A) is incorrect. You want to maintain an airspeed at or below V_A, but in severe turbulence, there will be large variations in airspeed, and you will not be able to keep it constant. Answer (C) is incorrect. In severe turbulence, you will not be able to maintain a constant altitude and/or constant airspeed.

70. If severe turbulence is encountered during your IFR flight, the airplane should be slowed to the design maneuvering speed because the

A. maneuverability of the airplane will be increased.

B. amount of excess load that can be imposed on the wing will be decreased.

C. airplane will stall at a lower angle of attack, giving an increased margin of safety.

Answer (B) is correct. *(AvW Chap 11)*
   DISCUSSION: Flight at or below the design maneuvering speed (V_A) means that the airplane will stall before excess loads can be imposed on the wings.
   Answer (A) is incorrect. You should slow the airspeed to reduce excessive loads, not because the airplane will be more maneuverable at a slow airspeed. Answer (C) is incorrect. An airplane will always stall when the critical angle of attack is exceeded.

71. When a climb or descent through an inversion or wind-shear zone is being performed, the pilot should be alert for which of the following change in airplane performance?

A. A fast rate of climb and a slow rate of descent.

B. A sudden change in airspeed.

C. A sudden surge of thrust.

Answer (B) is correct. *(AvW Chap 9)*
   DISCUSSION: When climbing through an inversion or wind-shear zone, the danger is a sudden change in airspeed. If the airplane were to move abruptly from a headwind to a tailwind, the airspeed would slow dramatically, and a stall or rapid descent could be induced.
   Answer (A) is incorrect. A fast rate of climb and a slow rate of descent are usually not a safety problem, as the reverse could be. Answer (C) is incorrect. The amount of thrust does not change as a result of wind shears.

END OF STUDY UNIT

STUDY UNIT THREE
NAVIGATION SYSTEMS

(9 pages of outline)

This study unit contains outlines of major concepts tested, sample test questions and answers regarding navigation systems, and an explanation of each answer. The table of contents above lists each subunit within this study unit, the number of questions pertaining to that particular subunit, and the pages on which the outlines and questions begin, respectively.

Recall that the **sole purpose** of this book is to expedite your passing of the FAA pilot knowledge test for the instrument rating. Accordingly, all extraneous material (i.e., topics or regulations not directly tested on the FAA pilot knowledge test) is omitted, even though much more knowledge is necessary to fly safely. This additional material is presented in *Pilot Handbook*, *Aviation Weather and Weather Services*, *FAR/AIM*, and *Instrument Pilot Flight Maneuvers and Practical Test Prep*, available from Gleim Publications, Inc. Order online at www.gleim.com.

3.1 DISTANCE MEASURING EQUIPMENT (DME) AND LORAN

1. DME displays slant range distance in nautical miles.

2. Ignore slant range error if the airplane is 1 NM or more from the ground facility for each 1,000 ft. AGL.

   a. The greatest slant range error comes at high altitudes very close to the VORTAC.

   b. EXAMPLE: If you are 6,000 ft. AGL directly above a VORTAC, your DME will read 1.0 NM.

3. A pilot can check the Airplane Flight Manual Supplement to determine if a LORAN C-equipped aircraft is approved for IFR operations.

3.2 RADIO MAGNETIC INDICATOR (RMI)

1. The **radio magnetic indicator (RMI)** consists of a rotating compass card and one or more navigation indicators, which point to stations.

2. The knobs at the bottom of the RMI allow you to select ADF or VOR stations.

3. The magnetic heading of the airplane is always directly under the index at the top of the instrument.

4. The bearing pointer displays magnetic bearings to selected navigation stations.

    a. The tail of the indicator tells you which radial you are on or the magnetic bearing FROM the station.

5. DME arcs with the RMI. The RMI needle should point to the right wingtip on right-hand arcs and the left wingtip on left-hand arcs. This assumes a no-wind situation.

    a. Crosswind from the inside of the arc (e.g., left crosswind on a left-hand arc) requires you to turn toward the NAVAID to compensate for the crosswind, putting the RMI needle in front of the wingtip reference.

    b. Crosswind from the outside of the arc requires you to turn to the outside of the arc, putting the RMI needle behind the wingtip reference.

3.3 VOR RECEIVER CHECK

1. The *Airport/Facility Directory* provides a listing of available VOR receiver ground checkpoints and VOTs (VOR receiver test facilities).

2. Over airborne checkpoints designated by the FAA, the maximum permissible bearing error for the VOR receiver is plus or minus 6° of the designated radial.

    a. An alternative to a certified airborne checkpoint is a prominent ground reference point that is more than 20 NM from a VOR station that is along an established VOR airway.

        1) Once over this point with the CDI needle centered, the OBS should indicate plus or minus 6° of the published radial.

3. The maximum difference between two indicators of a dual VOR system is 4° between the two indicated bearings to the VOR.

    a. The CDI needles should be centered and the indicated bearings checked rather than setting to identical radials and looking at the CDI needles.

4. VOTs are available at a specified frequency at certain airports. The facility permits you to check the accuracy of your VOR receiver while you are on the ground.

    a. The VOT transmits only the 360° radial in all directions.

    b. Tune the VOR receiver to the specified frequency, and turn the OBS (omnibearing selector) to select an omnibearing course of either 0° or 180°.

        1) The CDI needle should be centered; if not, then center the needle.

        2) If 0°, the TO/FROM indicator should indicate FROM.

        3) If 180°, the TO/FROM indicator should indicate TO.

        4) The maximum error is plus or minus 4°.

    c. When using an RMI, the head of the needle will indicate 180°.

5. When making a VOR receiver check with your airplane located on the designated ground checkpoint, the designated radial should be set on the OBS.

    a. The CDI must center within plus or minus 4° of that radial with a FROM indication.

3.4 VERY HIGH FREQUENCY OMNIDIRECTIONAL RANGE (VOR) STATION

1. When VORs are undergoing maintenance, the coded and/or voice identification is not broadcast from the VOR.

2. DME/TACAN coded identification is transmitted one time for each three or four times the VOR identification is transmitted.

    a. If the VOR is out of service, the DME identification will be transmitted about once every 30 seconds at 1350 Hz.

3. A full-scale (from the center position to either side of the dial) deflection of a VOR CDI indicates a 10° deviation from the course centerline.

    a. About 10° to 12° of change of the OBS setting should deflect the CDI from the center to the last dot.

4. An (H) Class VORTAC facility has a range of 40 NM from 1,000 ft. AGL to 14,500 ft. AGL, and a range of 100 NM from 14,500 ft. AGL to 18,000 ft.

    a. To use (H) Class VORTAC facilities to define a direct route of flight at 17,000 ft. MSL, the facilities should be no farther apart than 200 NM.

    b. Generally, for IFR operation off of established airways below 18,000 ft., VOR navigational aids should be no more than 80 NM apart.

5. VOR station passage is indicated by a complete reversal of the TO/FROM indicator.

    a. If after station passage the CDI shows a 1/2-scale deflection and remains constant for a period of time, you are flying away from the selected radial.

6. Airplane displacement from a course is approximately 200 ft. per dot per NM on VORs.

    a. At 30 NM out, one dot is 1 NM displacement; two dots, 2 NM.

    b. At 60 NM out, one dot is 2 NM displacement; two dots, 4 NM.

7. Time/distance to station formula. When tracking inbound, make a 90° turn and measure time and degrees of bearing change.

    a. $$Min.\ to\ station = \frac{60 \times Min.\ between\ bearings}{Degrees\ of\ bearing\ change}$$

    b. $$Distance\ to\ station = \frac{TAS \times Min.\ between\ bearings}{Degrees\ of\ bearing\ change}$$

        1) You may also use your flight computer to calculate the distance.

3.5 HORIZONTAL SITUATION INDICATOR (HSI)

1.   The **horizontal situation indicator (HSI)** is a combination of the heading indicator and the VOR/ILS indicator, as illustrated and explained below.

   a.   The azimuth card -- rotates so that the heading is shown under the index at the top of the instrument

   1)   The azimuth card may be part of a remote indicating compass (RIC), or

   2)   The azimuth card must be checked against the magnetic compass and reset with a heading set knob.

   b.   The course indicating arrow -- the VOR (OBS) indicator

   c.   The TO/FROM indicator for the VOR

   d.   Glide slope deviation pointer -- indicates above or below the glide slope, which is the longer center line

   e.   Glide slope warning flag -- comes out when reliable signals are not received by the glide slope receiver

   f.   Heading set knob -- used to coordinate the heading indicator (directional gyro, etc.) with the actual compass

   1)   If the azimuth card is part of an RIC, this knob is normally a heading bug (pointer) set knob that moves a bug around the periphery of the azimuth card.

   g.   Lubber line -- shows the current heading

   h.   Course deviation bar -- indicates the direction you would have to turn to intercept the desired radial if you were on the approximate heading of the OBS selection

   i.   The airplane symbol -- a fixed symbol that shows the airplane relative to the selected course as though you were above the airplane looking down

   j.   The tail of the course indicating arrow -- shows the reciprocal of the OBS heading

   k.   The course setting knob -- used to adjust the OBS

2.   Airplane displacement from a course is approximately 200 ft. per dot per NM on VORs.

   a.   At 30 NM out, one dot is 1 NM displacement; two dots, 2 NM.

   b.   At 60 NM out, one dot is 2 NM displacement; two dots, 4 NM.

3.   A full-scale deflection of a VOR CDI indicates a 10° deviation from the course centerline.

   a.   About 10° to 12° of change of the OBS setting should deflect the CDI from the center to the last dot.

   b.   With the CDI centered, rotate the OBS 180° to change the ambiguity (TO/FROM) indication.

4.   Solve all VOR problems by imagining yourself in an airplane heading in the general direction of the omnibearing setting.

   a.   If you are heading opposite your omnibearing course, the CDI needle will point away from the imaginary course line through the VOR determined by your omnibearing selector.

   b.   Remember that the VOR shows only your location (not your heading) with respect to the VOR.

5.   A few of the questions on the FAA instrument rating knowledge test require you to identify the position of your airplane relative to a VOR given an HSI presentation.

   a.   First, remember that the CDI needle does not point to the VOR. It indicates the position of the airplane relative to VOR radials.

      1)   Irrespective of your direction of flight, the CDI needle always points toward the imaginary course line through the VOR determined by your omnibearing selector.

   b.   The TO/FROM indicator operates independently of the direction (heading) of your airplane. It indicates which side of the VOR your airplane is on, based on the radial set on your omnibearing selector.

      1)   Irrespective of your direction of flight, the TO/FROM indicator shows you whether you are before, on, or past a line 90° (perpendicular) to the course line determined by your omnibearing setting.

6.   The following diagram explains the TO/FROM indicator and the CDI needle.

   a.   Remember that you must rotate the diagram so the omnibearing direction is pointed in the general direction in which your omnibearing selector is set.

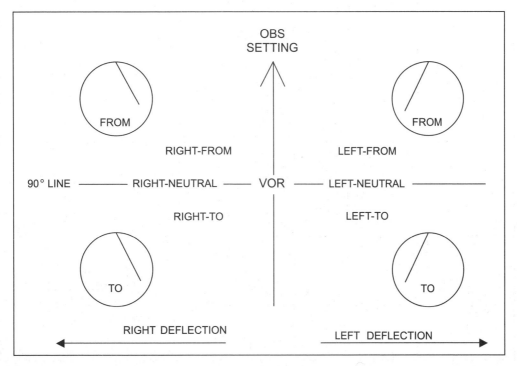

3.6 HSI/LOCALIZER

1. When a VOR is tuned to a localizer frequency (108.10 to 111.95), the OBS (course selection) setting has no impact on the indications of the VOR.

2. When an HSI is tuned to a localizer frequency (108.10 to 111.95), the setting of the front course heading with the head of the needle will eliminate reverse sensing on back courses.

    a. Inbound on a back course, the tail of the needle will be at the top of the instrument, and you will have positive sensing.

    b. If the HSI needle is set to the front course heading, you will have normal sensing on the HSI whether you are flying a front course or a back course approach.

    c. If the HSI needle is set to the back course heading, you will have reverse sensing on the HSI whether you are flying a front course or a back course approach.

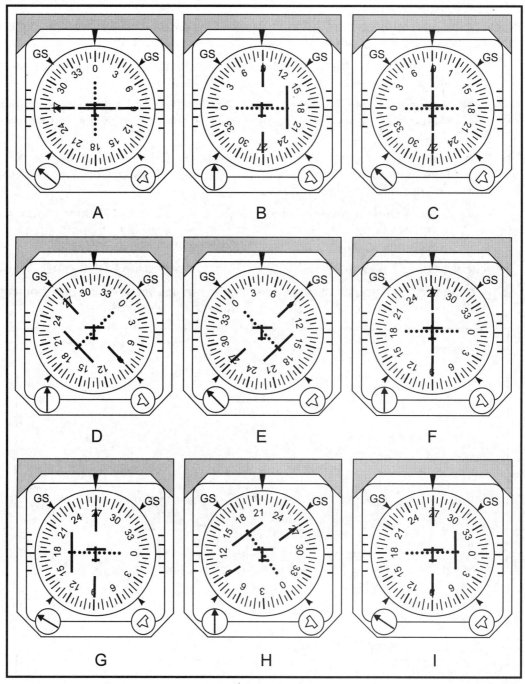

Figure 97. – HSI Presentation.

3.   The localizer information is reported on the face of the HSI instrument just as VOR signals are.

    a.   That is, it is based upon position rather than heading.

4.   Similar to VORs, if you are going in the direction specified for an approach to a runway, a left deflection means you are to the right of course if you are facing in the approximate direction of the localizer.

NOTE: You will use Figure 97, "HSI Presentation" (on the previous page), to answer questions in this section. Be aware that presentations B, C, D, E, and I have backcourse settings of 90°, which means there is reverse sensing irrespective of the airplane's heading.

3.7 GLOBAL POSITIONING SYSTEM (GPS)

1.   You should refer to the flight manual supplement to determine if an installed GPS is Technical Standard Order (TSO) TSO-C129 or TSO-C196 approved for IFR en route and IFR approaches.

    a.   Handheld GPS systems and GPS systems certified for VFR operation may be used during IFR operations only as an aid to situational awareness.

    b.   VFR waypoints are not recognized by the IFR systems and will be rejected for IFR routing.

2.   During IFR en route and terminal operations using an approved TSO-C129 or TSO-C196 GPS system for navigation, the aircraft must be equipped with an approved and operational alternate navigation system that is appropriate to the route.

    a.   Any ground-based navigational facilities required for use with the alternate navigation system (e.g., VORs, NDBs, etc.) must be available and operational along the entire route of flight.

    b.   It is not necessary to actively monitor an alternate means of navigation unless the GPS is not equipped with Receiver Autonomous Integrity Monitoring (RAIM), or RAIM becomes unavailable or predicts an outage.

3.   To effectively navigate by means of GPS, pilots should

    a.   Determine the GPS unit is approved for their planned flight

    b.   Determine the status of the databases

        1)   The current status of navigational databases, weather databases, NOTAMs, and signal availability should be ensured prior to takeoff.

        2)   When in flight, compare the GPS database to the En Route Low Altitude chart. If they are the same, the GPS database is current. Comparing the two can verify the current status of the GPS database.

    c.   Understand how to make and cancel all appropriate entries

        1)   Stressful situations, heavy workloads, and turbulence make data entry errors real problems, and pilots should know how to recover basic aircraft controls quickly.

    d.   Program and review the planned route

        1)   Because each GPS layout can vary widely in type and function (knobs, switches, etc.), programming the units should be verified for accuracy.

        2)   Name changes or spelling mistakes contribute to errors in flying appropriate routes.

    e.   Ensure the track flown is approved by ATC

    f.   Overriding an automatically selected sensitivity during an approach will cancel the approach mode annunciation.

4. One of the primary benefits of satellite-based area navigation (e.g., GPS or RNAV) is that it permits aircraft to fly optimum routes and altitudes.

5. Due to the use of, and reliance on, GPS systems for navigation, it is easy for pilots to lose proficiency in performing manual calculations on courses, times, distances, headings, etc.

    a. Emergency situations (i.e., electrical failures) make it important to maintain proficiency in these calculations.

6. Bear in mind that although handheld GPS units are an excellent aid to situational awareness, they are not an approved navigation source for any IFR operation, regardless of whether you are in visual or instrument meteorological conditions.

7. VFR waypoints have been created for VFR traffic only. These waypoints, identified with five letters and beginning with "VP," are for VFR pilots only. While VFR waypoints are specific to GPS users, they cannot be used in IFR flight plans.

    a. VFR waypoints are not recognized by the IFR systems and will be rejected for IFR routing.

8. There are limitations on and benefits to the operation of GPS units. These must be considered prior to flight.

    a. Aircraft using GPS TSO-C129 or TSO-C196 navigation equipment under IFR must be equipped with an approved and operational alternate means of navigation appropriate to the flight.

    b. GPS is not authorized as a substitute means of navigation guidance when conducting a conventional approach at an alternate airport.

        1) If the approach procedure requires distance measuring equipment (DME), the aircraft must be equipped with the appropriate DME avionics in order to use the approach as an alternate.

    c. GPS database updates are done on a 28-day cycle, which is the same schedule for updating the En Route Low Altitude charts. Compare the two to verify currency.

    d. WAAS improves the accuracy of GPS. If WAAS becomes unavailable, you can safely follow the lateral and vertical (LNAV/VNAV) guidance information displayed on your GPS unit to fly to the LNAV MDA.

    e. Baro-VNAV is an RNAV system function that uses barometric altitude information from the aircraft's altimeter to compute and present a vertical guidance path to the pilot.

3.8 AUTOPILOTS

1. Autopilot systems are automatic flight control systems that keep an aircraft on a set course or in level flight during the en route or approach phase of flight.

    a. Autopilots contain servos, electromechanical devices that translate electrical commands into motion, moving the control surfaces.

2. Autopilot systems can be engaged so that an aircraft will fly a given

    a. Heading (set by turning the heading selection knob, tracking a VOR radial, or following the GPS track),

    b. Altitude (using the altitude hold function),

    c. Climb or descent (at a vertical speed chosen by the pilot), or

    d. Approach.

        1) The approach mode can be used to execute both precision or nonprecision approaches that rely on ground-based navigation facilities or GPS steering.

3. Benefits of using an autopilot system in flight include

   a. A reduction of the physical and mental demands of the pilot

      1) EXAMPLE: During stressful situations, such as flying in a busy terminal area or executing a missed approach in adverse weather conditions, the autopilot puts the pilot in a managerial role of monitoring an aircraft, thus reducing workload.

   b. Improved situational awareness

      1) After engaging the autopilot, it is important to verify that the aircraft is tracking the intended flight profile.

4. Because most autopilots are not capable of changing power settings, pilots must manage the throttle to control all airspeed when the autopilot is engaged.

   a. Care should be taken so aircraft speed limitations are not exceeded in a descent.

   b. Pitch attitude and throttle settings should be monitored in climbs so that the aircraft does not enter a stall.

5. Disadvantages of using an autopilot include

   a. Forgetting to maintain manual flying skills. Because all equipment will fail at some time, a pilot needs to remain proficient in the skills required for manual flying.

   b. Turbulence. Some autopilot systems will disengage or default to certain settings during moderate or severe turbulence.

   c. Malfunction. A pilot should immediately disengage an autopilot system if an unexpected or uncommanded behavior presents itself.

6. A good practice to clarify whether the autopilot is controlling the aircraft is to audibly announce that the autopilot is engaged, similar to the positive exchange of flight controls when flying with two pilots.

QUESTIONS AND ANSWER EXPLANATIONS: All of the instrument rating knowledge test questions chosen by the FAA for release as well as additional questions selected by Gleim relating to the material in the previous outlines are reproduced on the following pages. These questions have been organized into the same subunits as the outlines. To the immediate right of each question are the correct answer and answer explanation. You should cover these answers and answer explanations while responding to the questions. Refer to the general discussion in the Introduction on how to take the FAA knowledge test.

Remember that the questions from the FAA knowledge test bank have been reordered by topic and organized into a meaningful sequence. Also, the first line of the answer explanation gives the citation of the authoritative source for the answer.

QUESTIONS

3.1 Distance Measuring Equipment (DME) and LORAN

1. Which distance is displayed by the DME indicator?

A. Slant range distance in NM.

B. Slant range distance in SM.

C. Line-of-sight direct distance from aircraft to VORTAC in SM.

Answer (A) is correct. *(IFH Chap 9)*
   DISCUSSION: DME (distance measuring equipment) displays line-of-sight direct distance, i.e., slant range, from the aircraft to the VORTAC in nautical miles.
   Answer (B) is incorrect. The measurement is in nautical miles, not statute miles. Answer (C) is incorrect. The measurement is in nautical miles, not statute miles.

2. Which DME indication should you receive when you are directly over a VORTAC site at approximately 6,000 feet AGL?

A. 0

B. 1

C. 1.3

Answer (B) is correct. *(IFH Chap 9)*
   DISCUSSION: Because the DME indicates slant range distance, it will indicate your altitude if you are directly above the VORTAC. One nautical mile equals approximately 6,000 ft., so the DME would read 1 NM.
   Answer (A) is incorrect. The DME would only indicate zero if you were at ground level next to the VORTAC. Answer (C) is incorrect. It would mean that your altitude was about 8,000 ft. AGL (6,000 × 1.3).

3. The greatest DME indication error between actual ground distance and displayed ground distance occurs at

    A. high altitudes far from the VORTAC.

    B. high altitudes close to the VORTAC.

    C. low altitudes far from the VORTAC.

Answer (B) is correct. *(IFH Chap 9)*
    DISCUSSION: Because the DME reads slant range distance, its greatest error occurs at high altitudes very close to the VORTAC. For example, if one were at 12,000 ft. directly over the VOR, the DME would show a distance from the VOR of approximately 2 NM.
    Answer (A) is incorrect. As you get farther away from the station, the slant range error of the DME becomes minimal. Answer (C) is incorrect. The DME has the greatest error at high, not low, altitudes close to, not far from, the VORTAC.

4. As a rule of thumb, to minimize DME slant range error, how far from the facility should you be to consider the reading as accurate?

    A. Two miles or more for each 1,000 feet of altitude above the facility.

    B. One or more miles for each 1,000 feet of altitude above the facility.

    C. No specific distance is specified since the reception is line-of-sight.

Answer (B) is correct. *(IFH Chap 9)*
    DISCUSSION: You should consider the DME slant range error negligible if the airplane is 1 NM or more from the ground facility for each 1,000 ft. of altitude above the elevation of the facility.
    Answer (A) is incorrect. The accuracy is 1 NM, not 2 NM, for each 1,000 ft. AGL. Answer (C) is incorrect. A specific distance is required because the reception is line-of-sight.

5. By which means may a pilot determine if a Loran C equipped aircraft is approved for IFR operations?

    A. Not necessary; Loran C is not approved for IFR.

    B. Check aircraft logbook.

    C. Check the Airplane Flight Manual Supplement.

Answer (C) is correct. *(AIM Para 1-1-15)*
    DISCUSSION: Pilots must be aware of the authorized operational approval level (e.g., VFR or IFR) of a LORAN receiver installed in their aircraft. Approval information is contained in the Aircraft Flight Manual Supplement, on FAA Form 337, in aircraft maintenance records, or possibly on a placard installed near or on the control panel.
    Answer (A) is incorrect. Some LORAN C receivers are approved for IFR operations by the FAA. Answer (B) is incorrect. The operational approval level may be found in the aircraft maintenance records, not necessarily the aircraft logbook.

3.2 Radio Magnetic Indicator (RMI)

6. (Refer to Figure 100 on page 81.) What is the magnetic bearing TO the station as indicated by illustration 4?

    A. 285°.

    B. 055°.

    C. 235°.

Answer (B) is correct. *(IFH Chap 9)*
    DISCUSSION: The magnetic heading of the airplane is always directly under the index at the top of the instrument. The bearing pointer displays the magnetic bearing TO the selected station. In RMI 4, the needle is pointing to 055°, which is the magnetic bearing TO the station.
    Answer (A) is incorrect. This is the magnetic heading, not magnetic bearing. Answer (C) is incorrect. This is the magnetic bearing FROM, not TO, the station.

7. (Refer to Figure 100 on page 81.) Which RMI illustration indicates the aircraft to be flying outbound on the magnetic bearing of 235° FROM the station? (Wind 050° at 20 knots.)

    A. 2

    B. 3

    C. 4

Answer (B) is correct. *(IFH Chap 9)*
    DISCUSSION: A radio magnetic indicator (RMI) consists of a compass card that rotates as the airplane turns. The magnetic heading of the airplane is always directly under the index at the top of the instrument. The bearing pointer displays magnetic bearings TO the selected station. The tail of the indicator tells you which radial you are on or the magnetic bearing FROM the station. Thus, a magnetic bearing of 235° FROM the station is indicated when the tail of the needle is on 235°, as in RMI 3. The airplane's heading is also 235°, which indicates that it is tracking outbound on the 235° MB FROM. The 20-kt. wind from 50° is almost a direct tailwind, which would not require a significant wind correction.
    Answer (A) is incorrect. RMI 2 indicates outbound on the 235° MB TO, not FROM, the station. Answer (C) is incorrect. RMI 4 indicates a large wind correction to the right, e.g., to compensate for a strong crosswind, which does not exist in this question.

8. (Refer to Figure 100 below.) Which RMI illustration indicates the aircraft is southwest of the station and moving closer TO the station?

- A. 1
- B. 2
- C. 3

Answer (A) is correct. *(IFH Chap 9)*
   DISCUSSION: If the airplane is to the southwest of the station and moving toward it, both the heading and the needle should be indicating northeast, which is shown in RMI 1. It indicates a magnetic bearing TO the station of 055°. The magnetic heading is also 055°, which means the airplane is flying to the station.
   Answer (B) is incorrect. RMI 2 shows a heading of 055° and the VOR behind the airplane; i.e., the airplane is northeast, not southwest, of the station and moving away FROM the station. Answer (C) is incorrect. RMI 3 shows a heading of 235° and the VOR behind the airplane, i.e., the airplane moving further FROM, not TO, the station.

9. (Refer to Figure 100 below.) Which RMI illustration indicates the aircraft is located on the 055° radial of the station and heading away from the station?

- A. 1
- B. 2
- C. 3

Answer (B) is correct. *(IFH Chap 9)*
   DISCUSSION: A radial, or bearing FROM, is indicated by the tail of the needle. Thus, the 055° radial is indicated when the tail of the needle is on 055°, as in RMI 2. The heading is also 055°, which means you are flying toward the northeast away from the station and are on the 055° radial.
   Answer (A) is incorrect. RMI 1 indicates flying toward the station on the 235° radial. Answer (C) is incorrect. RMI 3 indicates flying away from the station on the 235° radial.

Figure 100. – RMI Illustrations.

10. (Refer to Figure 104 on page 83.) If the radio magnetic indicator is tuned to a VOR, which illustration indicates the aircraft is on the 010° radial?

    A. 1

    B. 2

    C. 3

Answer (C) is correct. *(IFH Chap 9)*
    DISCUSSION: A radio magnetic indicator (RMI) consists of a rotating compass card and one or more indicators, which point to stations. The tail of the indicator tells you what radial you are on. RMI 3 shows the tail of the indicator on 010°, which means that you are on the 010° radial.
    Answer (A) is incorrect. RMI 1 indicates the 115° radial, not the 010° radial. Answer (B) is incorrect. RMI 2 indicates the 315° radial, not the 010° radial.

11. (Refer to Figure 104 on page 83.) If the radio magnetic indicator is tuned to a VOR, which illustration indicates the aircraft is on the 115° radial?

    A. 1

    B. 2

    C. 3

Answer (A) is correct. *(IFH Chap 9)*
    DISCUSSION: The tail of the RMI indicator tells you what radial you are on. RMI 1 shows the tail of the indicator on 115°, which means that you are on the 115° radial.
    Answer (B) is incorrect. RMI 2 indicates the 315° radial, not the 115° radial. Answer (C) is incorrect. RMI 3 indicates the 010° radial, not the 115° radial.

12. (Refer to Figure 104 on page 83.) If the radio magnetic indicator is tuned to a VOR, which illustration indicates the aircraft is on the 335° radial?

    A. 2

    B. 3

    C. 4

Answer (C) is correct. *(IFH Chap 9)*
    DISCUSSION: The tail of the RMI indicator tells you what radial you are on. RMI 4 shows the tail of the indicator on 335°, which means that you are on the 335° radial.
    Answer (A) is incorrect. RMI 2 indicates the 315° radial, not the 335° radial. Answer (B) is incorrect. RMI 3 indicates the 010° radial, not the 335° radial.

13. (Refer to Figure 104 on page 83.) If the radio magnetic indicator is tuned to a VOR, which illustration indicates the aircraft is on the 315° radial?

    A. 2

    B. 3

    C. 4

Answer (A) is correct. *(IFH Chap 9)*
    DISCUSSION: The tail of the RMI indicator tells you what radial you are on. RMI 2 shows the tail of the indicator on 315°, which means that you are on the 315° radial.
    Answer (B) is incorrect. RMI 3 indicates the 010° radial, not the 315° radial. Answer (C) is incorrect. RMI 4 indicates the 335° radial, not the 315° radial.

Figure 104. – Radio Magnetic Indicator.

14. (Refer to Figure 107 below.) Where should the bearing pointer be located relative to the wing-tip reference to maintain the 16 DME range in a right-hand arc with a right crosswind component?

    A. Behind the right wing-tip reference for VOR-2.

    B. Ahead of the right wing-tip reference for VOR-2.

    C. Behind the right wing-tip reference for VOR-1.

Answer (B) is correct. *(IFH Chap 9)*
    DISCUSSION: Normally, when flying a DME arc with an RMI, the RMI needle will point directly to the VORTAC, and in a no-wind situation it will be on either a 90° or 3 o'clock (for right-hand arc) or 270° or 9 o'clock (for left-hand arc) indication. Since you are flying a right-hand arc, you should be using VOR 2, which points to the right. The right crosswind component will be blowing you away from the VORTAC. You should crab to the right so the VOR 2 bearing pointer is in front of the right wing-tip reference. This indicates you are correcting back into the wind and toward the VORTAC.
    Answer (A) is incorrect. The bearing pointer would be behind the wing-tip reference if you were crabbed away from the VORTAC such as in a left-hand crosswind and a right-hand arc. Answer (C) is incorrect. VOR 1 is pointing toward the left, which would indicate a left-hand, not right-hand, DME arc.

Figure 107. – RMI-DME-ARC
Illustration Wind Component.

15. (Refer to Figure 108 below.) Where should the bearing pointer be located relative to the wing-tip reference to maintain the 16 DME range in a left-hand arc with a left crosswind component?

    A. Ahead of the left wing-tip reference for the VOR-2.

    B. Ahead of the right wing-tip reference for the VOR-1.

    C. Behind the left wing-tip reference for the VOR-2.

Answer (A) is correct. *(IFH Chap 9)*
    DISCUSSION: Since you are flying a left-hand arc, you should be using VOR 2, which points to the left. The left crosswind component will be blowing you away from the VORTAC. You should crab to the left so the VOR 2 bearing pointer is in front of the left wing-tip reference. This indicates you are correcting back into the wind and toward the VORTAC.
    Answer (B) is incorrect. You should use VOR 2 as you are making a left-hand, not right-hand, turn. Answer (C) is incorrect. The needle would be behind the wing-tip if you were crabbed away from, not toward, the VORTAC.

Figure 108. – RMI-DME-ARC
Illustration Wind Component.

3.3 VOR Receiver Check

16. To find the VOR receiver ground checkpoint(s) for an accuracy check, which publication should you consult?

    A. Airman's Information Manual.

    B. En Route Low Altitude Chart.

    C. Airport/Facility Directory.

Answer (C) is correct. *(AIM Para 1-1-4)*
    DISCUSSION: The *Airport/Facility Directory* provides a listing of available VOR receiver ground checkpoints.
    Answer (A) is incorrect. Airman's Information Manual is not a publication. The *Aeronautical Information Manual* is used by pilots and contains general flight information, not data concerning specific airports. Answer (B) is incorrect. En Route Low Altitude Charts do not indicate VOR receiver ground checkpoints.

17. When flying directly over a published airborne VOR checkpoint, what is the maximum error allowed for IFR flight?

    A. Plus or minus 6° of the designated radial.

    B. Plus 6° or minus 4° of the designated radial.

    C. Plus or minus 4° of the designated radial.

Answer (A) is correct. *(AIM Para 1-1-4)*
    DISCUSSION: Airborne checkpoints consist of certified radials that should be received over specific landmarks while airborne in the immediate vicinity of an airport. The maximum tolerance when the CDI is centered is ±6°.
    Answer (B) is incorrect. The tolerance for an airborne checkpoint is ±6°, not +6° or −4°. Answer (C) is incorrect. The tolerance for an airborne checkpoint is ±6°, not ±4°, which is the tolerance for a ground checkpoint or a VOT.

18. When the CDI needle is centered during an airborne VOR check, the omni-bearing selector and the TO/FROM indicator should read

    A. within 4° of the selected radial.

    B. within 6° of the selected radial.

    C. 0° TO, only if you are due south of the VOR.

Answer (B) is correct. *(AIM Para 1-1-4)*
    DISCUSSION: Airborne VOR checkpoints consist of certified radials that should be received over specific landmarks. If no checkpoint is available, a prominent ground point should be selected more than 20 NM from a VOR station that is along an established VOR airway. Once over this point with the CDI centered, the OBS should indicate within 6° of the published radial.
    Answer (A) is incorrect. The maximum error for a ground, not airborne, VOR check is ±4°. Answer (C) is incorrect. You should use a certified airborne checkpoint or select a ground reference that is under an established VOR airway, not a randomly selected radial.

19. When making an airborne VOR check, what is the maximum allowable tolerance between the two indicators of a dual VOR system (units independent of each other except the antenna)?

    A. 4° between the two indicated radials of a VOR.

    B. Plus or minus 4° when set to identical radials of a VOR.

    C. 6° between the two indicated radials of a VOR.

Answer (A) is correct. *(AIM Para 1-1-4)*
    DISCUSSION: If a dual system VOR (units independent of each other except for the antenna) is installed in the airplane, one system may be checked against the other in place of other VOR check procedures. The test consists of tuning both systems to the same VOR and centering the CDI needles, then noting the bearing variation between the two VOR units. It should be less than 4°.
    Answer (B) is incorrect. The CDIs are to be centered, not set to the same radials. Answer (C) is incorrect. It is a maximum tolerance of 4°, not 6°.

20. While airborne, what is the maximum permissible variation between the two indicated bearings when checking one VOR system against the other?

    A. Plus or minus 4° when set to identical radials of a VOR.

    B. 4° between the two indicated bearings to a VOR.

    C. Plus or minus 6° when set to identical radials of a VOR.

Answer (B) is correct. *(AIM Para 1-1-4)*
    DISCUSSION: If a dual system VOR (units independent of each other except for the antenna) is installed in the airplane, one system may be checked against the other in place of other check procedures. The test consists of tuning both systems to the same VOR with the CDI centered and noting the bearing variation between the two VOR units. It should be less than 4°.
    Answer (A) is incorrect. The CDIs must be centered, not set to identical radials. Answer (C) is incorrect. It is a maximum permissible variation of 4°, not 6°, between the indicated bearings.

21. When using VOT to make a VOR receiver check, the CDI should be centered and the OBS should indicate that the aircraft is on the

    A. 090 radial.

    B. 180 radial.

    C. 360 radial.

Answer (C) is correct. *(AIM Para 1-1-4)*
    DISCUSSION: A VOT transmits only the 360° radial. Thus, with the CDI centered, the OBS should indicate 0° with a FROM indication and 180° with a TO indication.
    Answer (A) is incorrect. The VOT transmits only the 360°, not 090°, radial in all directions. Answer (B) is incorrect. The VOT transmits only the 360°, not 180°, radial in all directions.

22. How should the pilot make a VOR receiver check when the aircraft is located on the designated checkpoint on the airport surface?

    A. With the aircraft headed directly toward the VOR and the OBS set to 000°, the CDI should center within plus or minus 4° of that radial with a TO indication.

    B. Set the OBS on the designated radial. The CDI must center within plus or minus 4° of that radial with a FROM indication.

    C. Set the OBS on 180° plus or minus 4°; the CDI should center with a FROM indication.

Answer (B) is correct. *(AIM Para 1-1-4)*
    DISCUSSION: A VOR receiver check is a checkpoint on the airport surface near a VOR. When the aircraft is on the checkpoint, the designated radial should be set on the OBS. The CDI must then center within 4° of the radial. Also, there will be a FROM indication.
    Answer (A) is incorrect. VOR indications are given the same no matter which heading the aircraft is on. The VOR indication is based upon position, not heading. Answer (C) is incorrect. The specified radial, not 180°, should be set on the OBS.

23. (Refer to Figure 81 below.) When checking a dual VOR system by use of a VOT, which illustration indicates the VOR's are satisfactory?

    A. 1

    B. 2

    C. 4

Answer (A) is correct. *(AIM Para 1-1-4)*
    DISCUSSION: A VOT transmits a 360° radial in all directions. Thus, when using an RMI, the tail of each indicator should point to 360°, ±4°.
    Answer (B) is incorrect. Illustration 2 shows the head, not the tail, of one indicator pointing to 360°. Answer (C) is incorrect. Illustration 4 shows the heads, not the tails, of both indicators pointing to 360°.

Figure 81. – Dual VOR System, VOT Check.

24. Where can the VOT frequency for a particular airport be found?

A. On the IAP Chart and in the *Airport/Facility Directory*.

B. Only in the *Airport/Facility Directory*.

C. In the *Airport/Facility Directory* and on the A/G Voice Communication Panel of the En Route Low Altitude Chart.

Answer (B) is correct. *(AIM Para 1-1-4)*
DISCUSSION: The VOT frequency for a particular airport can be found only in the *Airport/Facility Directory*.
Answer (A) is incorrect. VOT frequencies are not listed on approach charts. Answer (C) is incorrect. There is no longer an A/G Voice Communication Panel included on the En Route Low Altitude Chart.

25. (Refer to Figure 82 below.) Which is an acceptable range of accuracy when performing an operational check of dual VOR's using one system against the other?

A. 1

B. 2

C. 4

Answer (C) is correct. *(AIM Para 1-1-4)*
DISCUSSION: When performing an operational check of dual VORs using one system against the other, the difference between the two indicated bearings must be 4° or less. On an RMI, which has two VOR indicators, the VORs should point in the same direction, as in illustration 4 of Fig. 82.
Answer (A) is incorrect. In illustration 1, the needles have a 180° difference. Answer (B) is incorrect. In illustration 2, there is a 10° difference.

Figure 82. – Dual VOR System, Accuracy Check.

26. Which indications are acceptable tolerances when checking both VOR receivers by use of the VOT?

   A. 360° TO and 003° TO, respectively.

   B. 001° FROM and 005° FROM, respectively.

   C. 176° TO and 003° FROM, respectively.

Answer (C) is correct. *(AIM Para 1-1-4)*
   DISCUSSION: A VOT transmits a 360° radial in all directions. Thus, with the course deviation indicator (CDI) centered, the omnibearing selector (OBS) should read 0° with the TO-FROM indicator showing FROM, or the OBS should read 180° with the TO-FROM indicator showing TO, with a maximum error of 4°.
   Answer (A) is incorrect. At 000°, FROM, not TO, should be indicated. Answer (B) is incorrect. The receiver reading 005° FROM exceeds the 4° maximum error limit.

3.4 Very High Frequency Omnidirectional Range (VOR) Station

27. What indication should a pilot receive when a VOR station is undergoing maintenance and may be considered unreliable?

   A. No coded identification, but possible navigation indications.

   B. Coded identification, but no navigation indications.

   C. A voice recording on the VOR frequency announcing that the VOR is out of service for maintenance.

Answer (A) is correct. *(AIM Para 1-1-3)*
   DISCUSSION: The only positive method of identifying a VOR is by Morse Code identification and/or by the recorded voice identification, which is always indicated by use of the word "VOR" following the VOR name. During periods of maintenance, the facility identification is removed, although navigational signals may still be transmitted.
   Answer (B) is incorrect. The coded identification is removed when the station is undergoing maintenance. Answer (C) is incorrect. An out-of-service VOR is not announced by a voice recording.

28. A particular VOR station is undergoing routine maintenance. This is evidenced by

   A. removal of the navigational feature.

   B. broadcasting a maintenance alert signal on the voice channel.

   C. removal of the identification feature.

Answer (C) is correct. *(AIM Para 1-1-3)*
   DISCUSSION: The only positive method of identifying a VOR is by Morse Code identification or by the recorded voice identification, which is always indicated by use of the word "VOR" following the VOR name. During periods of maintenance, the coded and/or voice facility identification is removed, although navigational signals may still be transmitted.
   Answer (A) is incorrect. The navigational signals may continue even though they are not accurate. Answer (B) is incorrect. An out-of-service VOR is not announced by a voice recording.

29. When a VOR/DME is collocated under frequency pairings and the VOR portion is inoperative, the DME identifier will repeat at an interval of

   A. 20 second intervals at 1020 Hz.

   B. 30 second intervals at 1350 Hz.

   C. 60 second intervals at 1350 Hz.

Answer (B) is correct. *(AIM Para 1-1-7)*
   DISCUSSION: The DME/TACAN coded identification is transmitted at 1350 Hz once for each three or four times the VOR or localizer coded identification is transmitted. When either the VOR or the DME is operative, but not both, it is important to recognize which identifier is retained for the operative facility. A single-coded identification repeated at intervals of approximately 30 sec. indicates that the DME is operative and the VOR is not.
   Answer (A) is incorrect. The DME identifier repeats at 30-sec., not 20-sec., intervals at 1350 Hz, not 1020 Hz. Answer (C) is incorrect. The DME identifier repeats at 30-sec., not 60-sec., intervals.

30. What is the meaning of a single coded identification received only once approximately every 30 seconds from a VORTAC?

   A. The VOR and DME components are operative.

   B. VOR and DME components are both operative, but voice identification is out of service.

   C. The DME component is operative and the VOR component is inoperative.

Answer (C) is correct. *(AIM Para 1-1-7)*
   DISCUSSION: The DME/TACAN coded identification is transmitted at 1350 Hz once for each three or four times the VOR or localizer coded identification is transmitted. When either the VOR or the DME is operative, but not both, it is important to recognize which identifier is retained for the operative facility. A single-coded identification repeated at intervals of approximately 30 sec. indicates that the DME is operative and the VOR is not.
   Answer (A) is incorrect. A constant series of identity codes indicates that both the VOR and DME are operative. Answer (B) is incorrect. Voice identification operates independently of the identity codes.

31. For operations off established airways at 17,000 feet MSL in the contiguous U.S., (H) Class VORTAC facilities used to define a direct route of flight should be no farther apart than

    A. 75 NM.

    B. 100 NM.

    C. 200 NM.

Answer (C) is correct. *(AIM Para 1-1-8)*
    DISCUSSION: (H) Class VORTAC facilities have a range of 100 NM from 14,500 ft. AGL up to 18,000 ft. Thus, (H) Class VORTAC facilities should be no farther apart than 200 NM.
    Answer (A) is incorrect. This is the range of an (HH) Class NDB facility, not an (H) Class VORTAC. Answer (B) is incorrect. This is the range of an (H) Class VORTAC at 17,000 ft. MSL; thus the distance between two (H) Class VORTAC facilities can be 200 NM.

32. You are planning an IFR flight off established airways below 18,000 feet MSL. If you use VOR navigation to define the route, the maximum distance between navaids should be

    A. 80 NM.

    B. 40 NM.

    C. 70 NM.

Answer (A) is correct. *(AIM Para 1-1-8)*
    DISCUSSION: (H) Class VOR facilities have a range of 40 NM from 1,000 ft. AGL up to 14,500 ft. AGL and a range of 100 NM from 14,500 ft. AGL up to 18,000 ft. Thus, in general, VOR navigational aids used to describe a route of flight off of established airways below 18,000 ft. (more specifically, below 14,500 ft. AGL) should be no more than 80 NM apart.
    Answer (B) is incorrect. This is the range of an (H) Class VOR from 1,000 ft. AGL to 14,500 ft. AGL. VORs used to describe a route of flight off of established airways below 14,500 ft. AGL should be no more than 80 NM apart. Answer (C) is incorrect. VORs should be no more than 80 NM, not 70 NM, apart to define a route of flight off of established airways below 14,500 ft. AGL.

33. What angular deviation from a VOR course centerline is represented by a full-scale deflection of the CDI?

    A. 4°.

    B. 5°.

    C. 10°.

Answer (C) is correct. *(IFH Chap 9)*
    DISCUSSION: On VORs, full needle deflection from the center position to either side of the dial indicates that the aircraft is 10° or more off course, assuming normal needle sensitivity.
    Answer (A) is incorrect. A deviation of 4° is indicated by a 2-dot deflection on a 5-dot VOR scale. Answer (B) is incorrect. A deviation of 5° is indicated by a 2-dot deflection on a 4-dot VOR scale.

34. Full scale deflection of a CDI occurs when the course deviation bar or needle

    A. deflects from left side of the scale to right side of the scale.

    B. deflects from the center of the scale to either far side of the scale.

    C. deflects from half scale left to half scale right.

Answer (B) is correct. *(IFH Chap 9)*
    DISCUSSION: Full-scale deflection of a CDI occurs when the needle deflects from the center of the scale to either far side of the scale. This indicates that the aircraft is 10° or more off course, assuming normal needle sensitivity.
    Answer (A) is incorrect. It indicates moving from a left full deflection to a right full deflection, i.e., 10° left of course to 10° right of course. Answer (C) is incorrect. It indicates moving from a left half deflection to a right half deflection, i.e., 5° left of course to 5° right of course.

35. When using VOR for navigation, which of the following should be considered as station passage?

    A. The first movement of the CDI as the airplane enters the zone of confusion.

    B. The moment the TO-FROM indicator becomes blank.

    C. The first positive, complete reversal of the TO-FROM indicator.

Answer (C) is correct. *(IFH Chap 9)*
    DISCUSSION: When approaching a VOR, the TO-FROM indicator and the CDI flicker as the airplane flies into the zone of confusion (no signal area). Station passage is shown by complete reversal of the TO-FROM indicator.
    Answer (A) is incorrect. It indicates flight into the zone of confusion over the VOR, not station passage. Answer (B) is incorrect. It is an indication that you are in the zone of confusion over the VOR, not an indication of station passage.

36. Which of the following should be considered as station passage when using VOR?

    A. The first flickering of the TO-FROM indicator and CDI as the station is approached.

    B. The first full-scale deflection of the CDI.

    C. The first complete reversal of the TO-FROM indicator.

Answer (C) is correct. *(IFH Chap 9)*
    DISCUSSION: When approaching a VOR, the TO-FROM indicator and the CDI flicker as the airplane flies into the zone of confusion (no signal area). Station passage is shown by complete reversal of the TO-FROM indicator.
    Answer (A) is incorrect. It indicates flight into the zone of confusion over the VOR, not station passage. Answer (B) is incorrect. It is an indication that you are in the zone of confusion over the VOR, not an indication of station passage.

37. When checking the sensitivity of a VOR receiver, the number of degrees in course change as the OBS is rotated to move the CDI from center to the last dot on either side should be between

    A. 5° and 6°.

    B. 8° and 10°.

    C. 10° and 12°.

Answer (C) is correct. *(IFH Chap 9)*
    DISCUSSION: In addition to VOR receiver checks, course sensitivity may be checked by noting the number of degrees of change in the course selected as you rotate the OBS to move the CDI from center to the last dot on either side. This range should be between 10° and 12°.
    Answer (A) is incorrect. Course change of 5° to 6° should result in a 1/2-scale, not full-scale, needle deflection. Answer (B) is incorrect. Course change of 8° to 10° should result in a 3/4-scale, not full-scale, needle deflection.

38. A VOR receiver with normal five-dot course sensitivity shows a three-dot deflection at 30 NM from the station. The aircraft would be displaced approximately how far from the course centerline?

    A. 2 NM.

    B. 3 NM.

    C. 5 NM.

Answer (B) is correct. *(IFH Chap 9)*
    DISCUSSION: Airplane displacement from a course is approximately 200 ft. per dot per nautical mile for VORs. For example, at 30 NM from the station, a 1-dot deflection indicates approximately 1 NM displacement of the airplane from the course centerline. A full course deflection is 5 dots. With a 3-dot deflection, one would be about 3 NM from the course centerline.
    Answer (A) is incorrect. Two dots, not 3 dots, indicate 2 NM off course. Answer (C) is incorrect. Five dots, not 3 dots, indicate 5 NM off course.

39. An aircraft which is located 30 miles from a VOR station and shows a 1/2 scale deflection on the CDI would be how far from the selected course centerline?

    A. 1 1/2 miles.

    B. 2 1/2 miles.

    C. 3 1/2 miles.

Answer (B) is correct. *(IFH Chap 9)*
    DISCUSSION: Airplane displacement from a course is approximately 200 ft. per nautical mile for VORs. For example, at 30 NM from the station, a 1-dot deflection indicates approximately 1 NM displacement of the airplane from the course centerline. A full course deflection is 5 dots. Since a 1/2-scale deflection on the CDI would be 2 1/2 dots, the airplane would be about 2 1/2 mi. from the course centerline.
    Answer (A) is incorrect. This would be indicated by a 1 1/2-dot deflection. Answer (C) is incorrect. This would be indicated by a 3 1/2-dot deflection.

40. What angular deviation from a VOR course centerline is represented by a 1/2 scale deflection of the CDI?

    A. 2°.

    B. 4°.

    C. 5°.

Answer (C) is correct. *(IFH Chap 9)*
    DISCUSSION: A full course deflection is 5 dots, which is approximately 10°. Since rotation of the OBS to move the CDI from the center to the last dot is approximately 10°, a 1/2-scale deflection would be approximately 5°.
    Answer (A) is incorrect. A full-scale deflection is 10°, not 4°. Answer (B) is incorrect. A full-scale deflection is 10°, not 8°.

41. After passing a VORTAC, the CDI shows 1/2 scale deflection to the right. What is indicated if the deflection remains constant for a period of time?

    A. The airplane is getting closer to the radial.

    B. The OBS is erroneously set on the reciprocal heading.

    C. The airplane is flying away from the radial.

Answer (C) is correct. *(IFH Chap 9)*
    DISCUSSION: If the CDI shows a 1/2-scale deflection to the right, the airplane is flying 5° to the left of course. If it is constant, it means the airplane is flying away from the radial because the 5° off course increases in actual distance as one gets farther away from the VORTAC.
    Answer (A) is incorrect. A steady deflection would indicate the airplane is getting closer to the radial if it were flying TO, not FROM, the station. Answer (B) is incorrect. If you use the reciprocal heading, you get reverse indications from the CDI.

Figure 106. – Aircraft Location Relative to VOR.

42. (Refer to Figure 106 above.) The course selector of each aircraft is set on 360°. Which aircraft would have a FROM indication on the TO/FROM indicator and the CDI pointing left of center?

    A. 1

    B. 2

    C. 3

Answer (B) is correct. *(IFH Chap 9)*
    DISCUSSION: If airplane 2 were heading 360°, the course would be to the left, and the airplane would fly away FROM the VOR. See discussion of VOR orientation presented at the end of the HSI outline.
    Answer (A) is incorrect. If airplane 1 were heading 360°, the course would be to the right, not left. Answer (C) is incorrect. As airplane 3 is heading 360°, it is flying closer TO, not further FROM, the station, and the CDI would be pointing right, not left, of center.

43. (Refer to Figure 106 above.) The course selector of each aircraft is set on 360°. Which aircraft would have a FROM indication on the TO/FROM indicator and the CDI pointing right of center?

    A. 1

    B. 2

    C. 3

Answer (A) is correct. *(IFH Chap 9)*
    DISCUSSION: If airplane 1 set the OBS on 360°, the pilot would see a FROM indication and the CDI needle would displace to the right of center.
    Answer (B) is incorrect. If airplane 2 set the OBS on 360°, the pilot would see a FROM indication and the CDI needle would displace to the left of center. Answer (C) is incorrect. If airplane 3 set the OBS on 360°, the pilot would see a TO indication and the CDI needle would displace to the right of center.

44. Determine the approximate time and distance to a station if a 5° wingtip bearing change occurs in 1.5 minutes with a true airspeed of 95 knots.

    A. 16 minutes and 14.3 NM.

    B. 18 minutes and 28.5 NM.

    C. 18 minutes and 33.0 NM.

Answer (B) is correct. *(IFH Chap 9)*
    DISCUSSION: Use the following formula to compute the time to station:

$$\text{Time to station} = \frac{60 \times \text{Min. between bearings}}{\text{Degrees of bearing change}}$$

$$= (60 \times 1.5) \div 5 = 18\text{min.}$$

Thus, it is 18 min. to the station, which is less than 1/3 of an hour. One-third of 95 is less than 33, and thus must be 28.5 rather than 33.0. On the computer side of your flight computer, put 95 kt. on the outer scale over 60 on the inner scale. Find 18 min. on the inner scale; 28.5 NM is on the outer scale.
    Answer (A) is incorrect. The time is 18 min., not 16 min. Answer (C) is incorrect. Eighteen minutes is less than 1/3 hr., and 1/3 of 95 kt. is less than 33 NM.

3.5   Horizontal Situation Indicator (HSI)

45. (Refer to Figure 95 on page 93.) What is the lateral displacement of the aircraft in NM from the radial selected on the No. 1 NAV?

    A. 5.0 NM.

    B. 7.5 NM.

    C. 10.0 NM.

Answer (A) is correct. *(IFH Chap 9)*
    DISCUSSION: On VORs, the displacement from course is approximately 200 ft. per dot per nautical mile. At 30 NM from the station, one-dot deflection indicates approximately 1 NM displacement of the airplane from the course centerline. At 60 NM, it would be 2 NM for every dot of displacement. Since here, displacement is 2 1/2 dots, the airplane would be 5 NM from the centerline.
    Answer (B) is incorrect. This would be indicated by a 3/4 deflection. Answer (C) is incorrect. This would be indicated by a full deflection.

46. (Refer to Figure 95 on page 93.) On which radial is the aircraft as indicated by the No. 1 NAV?

    A. R-175.

    B. R-165.

    C. R-345.

Answer (C) is correct. *(IFH Chap 9)*
    DISCUSSION: The course selector in Fig. 95 is set on 350° with a FROM reading, indicating that, if the course deviation bar were centered, the airplane would be on R-350. Since a total deflection is approximately 10° to 12°, one-half deflection is 5° to 6°. Here, deflection is less than one-half, so it is about 5°. The course deviation bar indicates that this airplane is to the west of R-350, which would be R-345.
    Answer (A) is incorrect. R-175 would require a TO indicator and a left deflection. Answer (B) is incorrect. R-165 would require a TO indicator.

47. (Refer to Figure 95 on page 93.) Which OBS selection on the No. 1 NAV would center the CDI and change the ambiguity indication to a TO?

    A. 175°.

    B. 165°.

    C. 345°.

Answer (B) is correct. *(IFH Chap 9)*
    DISCUSSION: The course selector in Fig. 95 is set on 350°, resulting in a FROM reading and a 1/2-scale needle deflection. Thus, the airplane is 5° or 6° west of R-350, i.e., R-345. Setting the OBS to the reciprocal course of 165° would center the CDI with a TO indication.
    Answer (A) is incorrect. The airplane is currently on R-345, not R-355. Answer (C) is incorrect. The airplane is currently on R-345 with a FROM, not TO, indication.

48. (Refer to Figure 95 on page 93.) What is the lateral displacement in degrees from the desired radial on the No. 2 NAV?

    A. 1°.

    B. 2°.

    C. 4°.

Answer (C) is correct. *(IFH Chap 9)*
    DISCUSSION: Since, on a standard 5-dot VOR indicator, a full deflection of 5 dots is about 10°, 2 dots means a 4° deflection.
    Answer (A) is incorrect. Each dot is 2°, not 1/2°. Answer (B) is incorrect. Each dot is 2°, not 1°.

49. (Refer to Figure 95 on page 93.) Which OBS selection on the No. 2 NAV would center the CDI?

    A. 174°.

    B. 166°.

    C. 335°.

Answer (A) is correct. *(IFH Chap 9)*
    DISCUSSION: The course selector in Fig. 95 is set to 170° (it is not an HSI; it is a VOR), and the TO-FROM indicator indicates FROM, which means the airplane would be on R-170 if the course deviation bar were centered. Since the bar indicates a left 2-dot deflection, the airplane is 4° to the west of the radial, or on R-174.
    Answer (B) is incorrect. A right, not left, deflection would indicate R-166. Answer (C) is incorrect. On R-335 with an OBS setting of 170°, there would be a TO, not FROM, indication.

50. (Refer to Figure 95 below.) Which OBS selection on the No. 2 NAV would center the CDI and change the ambiguity indication to a TO?

A. 166°.

B. 346°.

C. 354°.

Answer (C) is correct. *(IFH Chap 9)*

DISCUSSION: The course selector in Fig. 95 is set to 170° (it is not an HSI; it is a VOR), and the TO-FROM indicator indicates FROM, which means the airplane would be on R-170 if the course deviation bar were centered. Since the bar indicates a 2-dot left deflection, the airplane is 4° to the west of the radial, or on R-174. To obtain a TO indication, one would have to change the OBS selection by 180° from 174° to 354°.

Answer (A) is incorrect. The airplane is on R-174, not R-346. Answer (B) is incorrect. The airplane is on R-174, not R-166.

Figure 95. – No. 1 and No. 2 NAV Presentation.

51. (Refer to Figure 98 on page 95 and Figure 99 on page 95.) To which aircraft position does HSI presentation "A" correspond?

    A. 1

    B. 8

    C. 11

Answer (A) is correct. *(IFH Chap 9)*
    DISCUSSION: On Figs. 98 and 99, HSI "A" has a VOR course selection of 090°, with a TO indication, meaning the airplane is to the left of the 360/180 radials. It has a right deflection, which means it is north of the 270/90 radials. The airplane heading is 205°, which means airplane 1 is described.
    Answer (B) is incorrect. Airplane 8 is to the right of the 360/180 radials, which would require a FROM, not TO, indication. Answer (C) is incorrect. Airplane 11 is to the right of the 360/180 radials and is south of the 270/090 radials, which would require a FROM, not TO, indication and a left, not right, bar deflection.

52. (Refer to Figure 98 on page 95 and Figure 99 on page 95.) To which aircraft position does HSI presentation "B" correspond?

    A. 9

    B. 13

    C. 19

Answer (C) is correct. *(IFH Chap 9)*
    DISCUSSION: On Figs. 98 and 99, HSI "B" has a VOR course selection of 270° with a FROM indication, meaning that the airplane is to the left of the 360/180 radials. Since it has a right deflection, the airplane is south of R-270. Given a heading of 135°, airplane 19 is described.
    Answer (A) is incorrect. Airplane 9 would require a TO, not FROM, indication and a left, not right, bar deflection. Answer (B) is incorrect. Airplane 13 is to the right of the 360/180 radials, which would require a TO, not FROM, indication.

53. (Refer to Figure 98 on page 95 and Figure 99 on page 95.) To which aircraft position does HSI presentation "C" correspond?

    A. 6

    B. 7

    C. 12

Answer (C) is correct. *(IFH Chap 9)*
    DISCUSSION: On Figs. 98 and 99, HSI "C" has a VOR course selection of 360° with a TO indication, meaning the airplane is south of the 270/090 radials. Since the course deflection bar is to the left, the airplane is to the east of the 180° radial. Given a 310° heading, airplane 12 is described.
    Answer (A) is incorrect. Airplane 6 is north of the 270/090 radials, which would require a FROM, not TO, indication and has a north, not 310°, heading. Answer (B) is incorrect. Airplane 7 is north of the 270/090 radials, which would require a FROM, not TO, indication.

54. (Refer to Figure 98 on page 95 and Figure 99 on page 95.) To which aircraft position does HSI presentation "D" correspond?

    A. 4

    B. 15

    C. 17

Answer (C) is correct. *(IFH Chap 9)*
    DISCUSSION: On Figs. 98 and 99, HSI "D" has a VOR course selection (OBS) of 180°. Its FROM indication means the airplane is south of R-270/90. Since the course deflection bar is to the left, the airplane is west of R-180. Given the heading of 180°, the position describes airplane 17.
    Answer (A) is incorrect. Airplane 4 is north of the 270/090 radials, which would have a TO, not FROM, indication. Answer (B) is incorrect. Airplane 15 would have a centered deflection bar and a north, not 180°, heading.

55. (Refer to Figure 98 on page 95 and Figure 99 on page 95.) To which aircraft position does HSI presentation "E" correspond?

    A. 5

    B. 6

    C. 15

Answer (B) is correct. *(IFH Chap 9)*
    DISCUSSION: On Figs. 98 and 99, HSI "E" has a VOR course selection of 360°. Its FROM indication means the airplane is north of R-270/90. Given the course deflection bar to the left, the airplane is to the east of the 360° radial. Given the 360° heading, the position describes airplane 6.
    Answer (A) is incorrect. Airplane 5 would require a centered deflection bar, and has a south, not 360°, heading. Answer (C) is incorrect. Airplane 15 is south of the 270/090 radials, which would require a centered deflection bar and a TO, not FROM, indication.

56. (Refer to Figure 98 on page 95 and Figure 99 on page 95.) To which aircraft position does HSI presentation "F" correspond?

    A. 10

    B. 14

    C. 16

Answer (C) is correct. *(IFH Chap 9)*
    DISCUSSION: On Figs. 98 and 99, HSI "F" has a VOR course selection of 180° with a FROM indication, meaning that the airplane is south of the 270/90 radials. Since the course deflection bar is centered, the airplane is on R-180. Given a heading of 045° (at the top of the HSI), airplane 16 is described.
    Answer (A) is incorrect. Airplane 10 is east of the 360/180 radials and north of the 270/090 radials, which would require a bar deflection, not a centered bar, and a TO, not FROM, indication. Answer (B) is incorrect. Airplane 14 is east of the 360/180 radials, which would require a bar deflection, not a centered bar.

Figure 98. – Aircraft Position.

Figure 99. – HSI Presentation.

57. (Refer to Figure 109 below.) In which general direction from the VORTAC is the aircraft located?

A. Northeast.

B. Southeast.

C. Southwest.

Answer (A) is correct. *(IFH Chap 9)*
DISCUSSION: The course indicating arrow (OBS) is set to 180°, and the TO-FROM indicator indicates TO (triangle pointing TO arrowhead), which means the airplane is north of the VORTAC. Since the course deviation bar indicates that the airplane needs to be flown to the right, the airplane is to the east of the 360° radial of the VORTAC. Thus, the airplane is northeast of the VORTAC.
    Answer (B) is incorrect. If the airplane were southeast of the VORTAC, there would be a FROM, not TO, indication.
Answer (C) is incorrect. If the airplane were southwest of the VORTAC, there would be a FROM, not TO, indication and a left, not right, bar deflection.

Figure 109. – CDI Direction from
VORTAC.

58. (Refer to Figure 110 below.) In which general direction from the VORTAC is the aircraft located?

A. Southwest.

B. Northwest.

C. Northeast.

Answer (C) is correct. *(IFH Chap 9)*
DISCUSSION: The course indicator arrow (OBS) is set to 60°, and the TO-FROM indicates FROM (opposite the head of the arrow), which means the airplane is northeast of the VORTAC. Since the course deviation bar indicates a deflection of 3 dots to the right, the airplane is to the north of the 60° radial by 6°, which is in the northeast.
    Answer (A) is incorrect. Southwest would require a TO, not FROM, indication. Answer (B) is incorrect. Northwest would require a full right, not a 1/2-scale, deflection.

Figure 110. – CDI Direction from
VORTAC.

59. (Refer to Figure 111 below.) In which general direction from the VORTAC is the aircraft located?

A. Northeast.

B. Southeast.

C. Northwest.

Answer (C) is correct. *(IFH Chap 9)*
DISCUSSION: The course indicator arrow (OBS) is set to 360°, and the TO-FROM indicator is FROM, which means the airplane is north of the VORTAC. Since the course deviation bar is to the right, the airplane is to the west of the 360° radial of the VORTAC. Accordingly, the airplane is to the northwest of the VORTAC.

Answer (A) is incorrect. A left, not right, deflection would indicate the airplane is in the northeast. Answer (B) is incorrect. An indication of TO, not FROM, would indicate the airplane is south of the VORTAC.

Figure 111. – CDI Direction from VORTAC.

3.6 HSI/Localizer

Note: HSI presentations B, C, D, E, and I have backcourse settings of 090°, which means there is reverse sensing irrespective of the airplane's heading.

60. (Refer to Figure 96 below, and Figure 97 on page 99.) To which aircraft position(s) does HSI presentation "A" correspond?

    A. 9 and 6.

    B. 9 only.

    C. 6 only.

Answer (A) is correct. *(IFH Chap 9)*
    DISCUSSION: On Figs. 96 and 97, HSI "A" has a heading of 360° with no localizer deviation, which means the airplane is on the localizer. Airplanes 6 and 9 are on the localizer with a 360° heading.
    Answer (B) is incorrect. The indication will be the same on either localizer. Answer (C) is incorrect. The indication will be the same on either localizer.

61. (Refer to Figure 96 below, and Figure 97 on page 99.) To which aircraft position(s) does HSI presentation "B" correspond?

    A. 11.

    B. 5 and 13.

    C. 7 and 11.

Answer (B) is correct. *(IFH Chap 9)*
    DISCUSSION: On Figs. 96 and 97, HSI "B" has a heading of 090°. It has localizer course setting of 090° with a right deflection, meaning the airplane is south of the localizer. Both airplanes 5 and 13 are described. Note the backcourse setting. If the front course 270° (instead of 90°) had been set, normal (rather than reverse) sensing would be indicated.
    Answer (A) is incorrect. Airplane 11 has a 270°, not 090°, heading. Answer (C) is incorrect. Airplanes 7 and 11 have 270°, not 090°, headings.

62. (Refer to Figure 96 below, and Figure 97 on page 99.) To which aircraft position does HSI presentation "C" correspond?

    A. 9

    B. 4

    C. 12

Answer (C) is correct. *(IFH Chap 9)*
    DISCUSSION: On Figs. 96 and 97, HSI "C" has a heading of 090° with a centered course deviation bar; thus, the airplane is on the localizer with a 090° heading, which describes airplane 12. The backcourse setting (090) has no effect because the deviation bar is centered.
    Answer (A) is incorrect. Airplane 9 has a 360°, not 090°, heading. Answer (B) is incorrect. Airplane 4 has a 270°, not 090°, heading.

63. (Refer to Figure 96 below, and Figure 97 on page 99.) To which aircraft position does HSI presentation "D" correspond?

    A. 1

    B. 10

    C. 2

Answer (C) is correct. *(IFH Chap 9)*
    DISCUSSION: On Figs. 96 and 97, HSI "D" has a heading of 315°. Airplane 2 is the only one with a northwest heading.
    Answer (A) is incorrect. Airplane 1 has a heading of 215°, not 315°. Answer (B) is incorrect. Airplane 10 has a heading of 135°, not 315°.

Figure 96. – Aircraft Position and Direction of Flight.

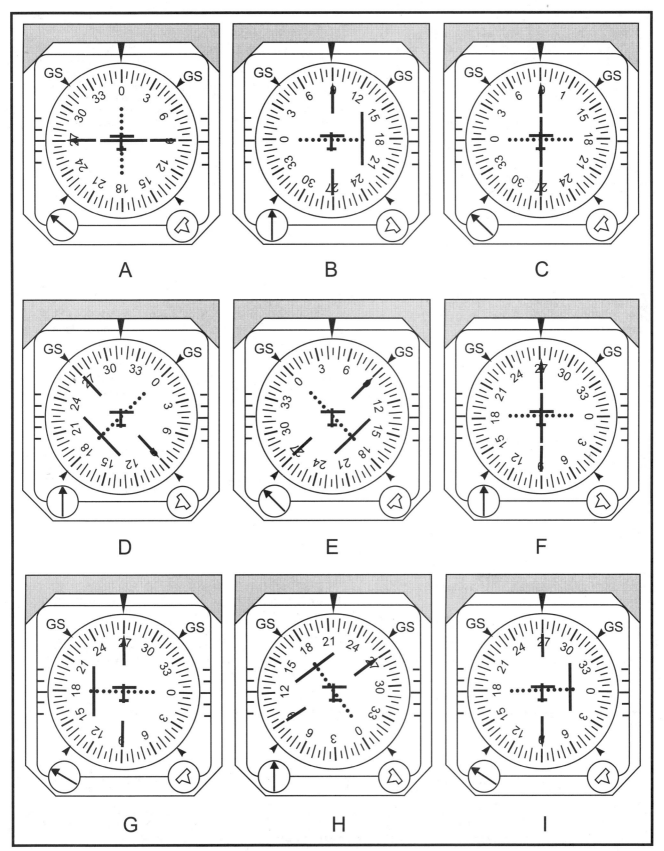

Figure 97. – HSI Presentation.

64. (Refer to Figure 96 below, and Figure 97 on page 101.) To which aircraft position(s) does HSI presentation "E" correspond?

    A. 8 only.

    B. 3 only.

    C. 8 and 3.

Answer (C) is correct. *(IFH Chap 9)*
   DISCUSSION: On Figs. 96 and 97, HSI "E" has a heading of 045°. It has a right deflection with a backcourse HSI setting of 090°. This results in reverse sensing, meaning the airplane is south of the localizer. Thus, airplanes 3 and 8 are described.
   Answer (A) is incorrect. Airplane 3 is also south of the localizer with a 045° heading. Answer (B) is incorrect. Airplane 8 also has a 045° heading and is south of the localizer.

65. (Refer to Figure 96 below, and Figure 97 on page 101.) To which aircraft position does HSI presentation "F" correspond?

    A. 4

    B. 11

    C. 5

Answer (A) is correct. *(IFH Chap 9)*
   DISCUSSION: On Figs. 96 and 97, HSI "F" has a setting of 270° with a centered bar and a 270° heading, which corresponds to airplane 4.
   Answer (B) is incorrect. Airplane 11 would have a left, not centered, course deviation bar. Answer (C) is incorrect. Airplane 5 has a heading of 090°, not 270°.

66. (Refer to Figure 96 below, and Figure 97 on page 101.) To which aircraft position(s) does HSI presentation "G" correspond?

    A. 7 only.

    B. 7 and 11.

    C. 5 and 13.

Answer (B) is correct. *(IFH Chap 9)*
   DISCUSSION: On Figs. 96 and 97, HSI "G" has a localizer setting at 270° with a left deviation, meaning the airplane is north of the localizer. With a 270° heading, it corresponds to airplanes 7 and 11.
   Answer (A) is incorrect. Airplane 11 is also north of the localizer with a 270° heading. Answer (C) is incorrect. Airplanes 5 and 13 have a heading of 090°, not 270°, and are also south, not north, of the localizer.

67. (Refer to Figure 96 below, and Figure 97 on page 101.) To which aircraft position does HSI presentation "H" correspond?

    A. 8

    B. 1

    C. 2

Answer (B) is correct. *(IFH Chap 9)*
   DISCUSSION: On Figs. 96 and 97, HSI "H" has a heading of 215°. Airplane 1 is the only one with a southwest heading.
   Answer (A) is incorrect. Airplane 8 has a heading of 045°, not 215°. Answer (C) is incorrect. Airplane 2 has a heading of 315°, not 215°.

68. (Refer to Figure 96 below, and Figure 97 on page 101.) To which aircraft position does HSI presentation "I" correspond?

    A. 4

    B. 12

    C. 11

Answer (C) is correct. *(IFH Chap 9)*
   DISCUSSION: On Figs. 96 and 97, HSI "I" has a left deviation with a backcourse HSI setting of 090° resulting in reverse sensing. Thus, the airplane is north of the localizer. Airplane 11 has a 270° heading and is north of the localizer.
   Answer (A) is incorrect. Airplane 4 would have a centered CDI, not a right deviation. Answer (B) is incorrect. Airplane 12 would have a centered CDI, not a right deviation, and has a heading of 090°, not 270°.

Figure 96. – Aircraft Position and Direction of Flight.

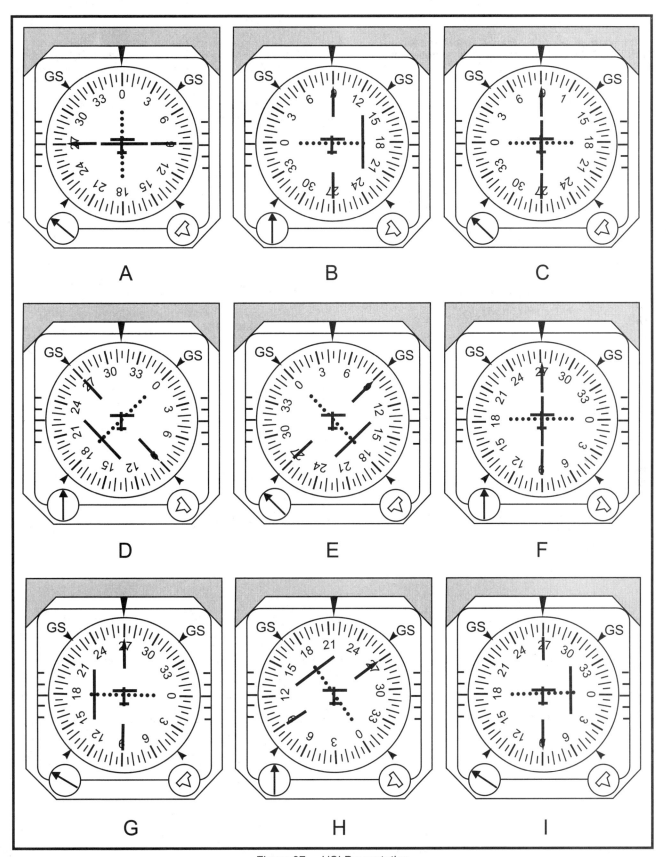

Figure 97. – HSI Presentation.

3.7 Global Positioning System (GPS)

69. How can a pilot determine if a Global Positioning System (GPS) installed in an aircraft is approved for IFR en route and IFR approaches?

    A. Flight manual supplement.

    B. GPS operator's manual.

    C. Aircraft owner's handbook.

Answer (A) is correct. *(AC 20-138A)*
    DISCUSSION: A supplement to the aircraft's POH (flight manual) is required for newly installed equipment. A supplement should state that the GPS is approved for IFR operations (en route and approaches).
    Answer (B) is incorrect. The GPS operator's manual will describe how to operate the GPS unit but will not provide approval for its use in a particular aircraft. Answer (C) is incorrect. The aircraft owner's handbook (i.e., information manual or POH) may not have any information on a GPS unit unless the unit was installed as a standard feature.

70. Hand-held GPS systems, and GPS systems certified for VFR operation, may be used during IFR operations as

    A. the principal reference to determine en route waypoints.

    B. an aid to situational awareness.

    C. the primary source of navigation.

Answer (B) is correct. *(AIM Para 1-1-19)*
    DISCUSSION: In order to use a GPS as the primary means of navigation under IFR or to perform instrument approaches, both the GPS receiver and the aircraft installation must be FAA-approved. Additionally, the receiver must have a current database of waypoints and instrument approach procedures. Hand-held GPS systems and VFR-only GPS systems are not FAA-approved for IFR operations, and may only be used during IFR operations as an aid to situational awareness.
    Answer (A) is incorrect. Hand-held and VFR-only GPS systems are not approved for IFR operations; they may only be used as an aid to situational awareness. Passage of en route reporting points and fixes (i.e., waypoints) must be verified by some other means (e.g., VOR, radar, etc.). Answer (C) is incorrect. Hand-held and VFR-only GPS systems are not approved as the primary source of navigation under IFR; they may only be used as an aid to situational awareness.

71. When may VFR waypoints be used in IFR flight plans?

    A. When GPS is used as the primary source of navigation.

    B. When the waypoints consist of 5 letter identifiers.

    C. VFR waypoints may not be used on IFR flight plans.

Answer (C) is correct. *(PHAK Chap 13)*
    DISCUSSION: VFR waypoints are designed to ease radio congestion in populated areas for VFR traffic only. VFR waypoints are charted on terminal area and sectional aeronautical charts.
    Answer (A) is incorrect. VFR waypoints may not be used in IFR flight plans for instrument navigation. Answer (B) is incorrect. VFR waypoints may not be used in IFR flight plans for instrument navigation.

72. During IFR en route and terminal operations using an approved TSO-C129 or TSO-C196 GPS system for navigation, ground based navigational facilities

    A. are only required during the approach portion of the flight.

    B. must be operational along the entire route.

    C. must be operational only if RAIM predicts an outage.

Answer (B) is correct. *(AIM Para 1-1-19)*
    DISCUSSION: In order to conduct IFR en route and terminal operations using an approved TSO-C129 or TSO-C196 GPS system, the avionics necessary to receive all of the ground-based facilities that are appropriate for the route to the destination airport and to any alternate airport must be installed and operational, and the ground-based facilities necessary for these routes must be operational.
    Answer (A) is incorrect. Ground-based navigational facilities appropriate to the route must be available and operational along the entire route of flight, not just the approach portion. Answer (C) is incorrect. Ground-based navigational facilities appropriate to the route must be available and operational regardless of Receiver Autonomous Integrity Monitoring (RAIM) status. However, unless RAIM predicts an outage, active monitoring of these facilities is not necessary.

73. During IFR en route operations using an approved TSO-C129 or TSO-C196 GPS system for navigation,

    A. no other navigation system is required.

    B. active monitoring of an alternate navigation system is always required.

    C. the aircraft must have an approved TSO-C129 or TSO-C196 and operational alternate navigation system appropriate for the route.

Answer (C) is correct. *(AIM Para 1-1-19)*
    DISCUSSION: Aircraft using GPS under IFR must be equipped with an approved TSO-C129 or TSO-C196 and operational alternate means of navigation appropriate for the route. Active monitoring of alternative navigation equipment is not required if the GPS receiver uses Receiver Autonomous Integrity Monitoring (RAIM). However, active monitoring of an alternate means of navigation is required when the RAIM capability of the GPS equipment is lost or if RAIM predicts an outage.
    Answer (A) is incorrect. Aircraft using an approved GPS system for IFR operations must be equipped with an approved TSO-C129 or TSO-C196 and operational alternate means of navigation appropriate to the flight. Answer (B) is incorrect. Active monitoring of an alternate navigation system is only required when GPS RAIM capability is lost or when an outage is predicted, not at all times.

74. What are the primary benefits of satellite based area navigation (RNAV)?

    A. Provides optimal routing and altitudes.

    B. Radio tuning and controller communication is minimized.

    C. Standard Terminal Arrival Routes and Departure Procedures are not required.

Answer (A) is correct. *(AIM Para 1-1-19)*
    DISCUSSION: The primary benefits of satellite based area navigation (RNAV) are that it permits aircraft to fly optimum routes and altitudes, thereby increasing the efficiency of the entire National Airspace System.
    Answer (B) is incorrect. The primary benefits of satellite based area navigation (RNAV) are the ability to permit aircraft to fly optimum routes and altitudes, not the fact that radio tuning and controller communication is minimized. Answer (C) is incorrect. The primary benefits of satellite based area navigation (RNAV) are the ability to permit aircraft to fly optimum routes and altitudes, not that standard Terminal Arrival Routes and Departure Procedures are not required.

75. A handheld GPS is

    A. not authorized for IFR use.

    B. authorized for IFR use under VMC.

    C. authorized for IFR use under IMC until the runway is in sight.

Answer (A) is correct. *(AIM Para 1-1-19)*
    DISCUSSION: A handheld GPS may be used as an aid to situational awareness in any flight condition, but it is not authorized for any IFR operations.
    Answer (B) is incorrect. While a handheld GPS may be used as an aid to situational awareness in any flight condition, it is not authorized for any IFR operations, regardless of whether you are in instrument or visual conditions. Answer (C) is incorrect. While a handheld GPS may be used as an aid to situational awareness in any flight condition, it is not authorized for any IFR operations, regardless of whether you are in instrument or visual conditions.

76. Effective navigation by means of GPS includes

    A. determining the current status of all databases.

    B. ensuring that ATC approves your planned route.

    C. relying solely on the GPS for course information.

Answer (A) is correct. *(AAH Chap 3)*
    DISCUSSION: A pilot must determine the status of all appropriate databases. If a database is not current, the pilot must use an alternate means of navigation as the primary form.
    Answer (B) is incorrect. Pilots may be, and frequently are, given changes to their requested planned route by ATC. A pilot must ensure that the route flown is approved by ATC whether it was his or her requested plan or not. Answer (C) is incorrect. All systems have the possibility of failing at some point, and it would not be effective to rely solely on a GPS unit for navigation. It is wise to have another means (paper chars, approach plates, etc.) from which to navigate.

77. Why should pilots understand how to cancel entries made on a GPS?

    A. Because GPS units frequently provide wrong or false information.

    B. Because heavy workloads and turbulence can increase data entry errors.

    C. Because published route names commonly change.

Answer (B) is correct. *(AAH Chap 3)*
    DISCUSSION: Stressful situations, heavy workloads, and turbulence make data entry errors real problems, and pilots should know how to recover basic aircraft controls quickly.
    Answer (A) is incorrect. GPS units provide a high degree of accuracy and are unreliable very infrequently. Answer (C) is incorrect. It is not common for names of published routes to change.

78. Reliance on GPS units

A. can cause pilots to lose proficiency in performing manual calculations of time, distance, and heading.

B. will increase a pilot's skill in navigating by visual reference.

C. does not decrease pilot workload.

Answer (A) is correct. *(AAH Chap 3)*

DISCUSSION: Due to the reliance on GPS units for navigation, it is easy for pilots to lose proficiency in performing manual calculations on courses, times, distances, headings, etc.

Answer (B) is incorrect. Reliance on GPS units for navigation does not increase skill in navigating by outside references, such as pilotage. Answer (C) is incorrect. Navigation by GPS does decrease pilot workload.

79. Before a pilot utilizes a GPS route or procedure, what would be an acceptable method of verifying the GPS database is current?

A. Check to see if all waypoints on the GPS route match points on procedure charts.

B. Call FSS/Flight Watch and verify that the GPS database is current.

C. Query the ATC facility issuing your IFR clearance as to database currency.

Answer (A) is the best answer. *(AAH Chap 3)*

DISCUSSION: The way to determine database currency is by checking the database effective dates, presented when the GPS unit is powered on. Most units require the pilot to acknowledge this information before completing the start up cycle. Given the choices presented in this question, checking the GPS procedure against the approach chart is the best alternative to ensuring database currency.

Answer (B) is incorrect. FSS/Flight Watch have no way to determine if your GPS database information is accurate and/or current. Answer (C) is incorrect. ATC has no way to determine if your GPS database information is accurate and/or current.

80. When your aircraft is equipped with a TSO-C129 or TSO-C196 GPS, an airport may not be qualified for alternate use if

A. the only standard approach procedure is GPS at the destination and alternate.

B. the airport has only AWOS-3 weather reporting and no LAAS equipment operational.

C. the airport is next to a restricted or prohibited area.

Answer (A) is correct. *(AIM Para 1-2-3)*

DISCUSSION: Any required alternate airport must have an available instrument approach procedure that does not require the use of GPS.

Answer (B) is incorrect. The AIM states, "any required alternate airport must have an available instrument approach procedure that does not require the use of GPS." Answer (C) is incorrect. It is irrelevant what type of airspace the airport is in or near, any required alternate airport must have an available instrument approach procedure that does not require the use of GPS.

81. When planning an IFR flight using GPS, the pilot should know that VFR waypoints

A. are not recognized by the IFR system and will be rejected for IFR routing.

B. can be used to aid in defining the route in the FAA flight plan if the waypoint name has a 5-letter identifier.

C. can be used to define direct routing under IFR if they are retrieved from a current database and identified by a four-point star.

Answer (A) is correct. *(AIM Para 1-1-18)*

DISCUSSION: VFR waypoints cannot be used for instrument flight planning.

Answer (B) is incorrect. All GPS waypoints have 5-letter identifiers. VFR waypoints consist of five letters beginning with the letters "VP" and cannot be used in IFR flight planning. Answer (C) is incorrect. Although VFR waypoints also are the same four-point star as the IFR waypoint, they cannot be used for IFR flight planning.

82. Prior to using GPS waypoints for RNAV, what can you do to check the current status of the GPS database?

A. Contact the local FSS and have them verify the current status of the database.

B. Contact the ATC/ARTCC that issued the En Route Low Altitude chart to verify the current status of the GPS waypoints.

C. Compare the GPS database to the En Route Low Altitude chart. If they are the same, the GPS database is current.

Answer (C) is correct. *(AIM Para 1-1-18)*

DISCUSSION: GPS database updates are done on a 28-day cycle, which is the same as the schedule for updating En Route Low Altitude charts. You can compare the two to verify currency.

Answer (A) is incorrect. It is not necessary to contact FSS to request verification of your GPS database currency. The FSS will not be able to assist you with determining database currency. They do not issue GPS databases. Answer (B) is incorrect. It is not necessary to contact ATC/ARTCC to request verification of your GPS database currency. ATC/ARTCC will not be able to assist you with determining currency. ATC/ARTCC do not issue GPS databases.

83. While conducting a GPS approach, if you disengage the auto sensitivity, what will occur?

    A. The approach mode annunciation will disengage.

    B. The altitude mode will disengage.

    C. The altitude and heading modes will disengage.

Answer (A) is correct. *(AIM Para 1-1-18)*
    DISCUSSION: Overriding an automatically selected sensitivity during an approach will cancel the approach mode annunciation.
    Answer (B) is incorrect. Altitude mode is an autopilot function, not a GPS function. Answer (C) is incorrect. Altitude and heading modes are autopilot functions, not GPS functions.

84. How does Baro-VNAV provide vertical guidance during an RVAV approach?

    A. GPS equipped airplanes use an existing ILS glide slope signal for vertical guidance for Baro-VNAV approaches.

    B. Baro-VNAV uses defined vertical angles or altitudes as fixes throughout the procedure using the local altimeter setting.

    C. Baro-VNAV uses a series of stepdown fixes.

Answer (B) is correct. *(IPH Chap 5)*
    DISCUSSION: Baro-VNAV is an RNAV system function that uses barometric altitude information from the aircraft's altimeter to compute and present a vertical guidance path to the pilot.
    Answer (A) is incorrect. The Baro-VNAV uses barometric altitude information from the aircraft's altimeter to compute and present a vertical guidance path to the pilot. Answer (C) is incorrect. The Baro-VNAV is a constant descent at approximately a 3.00° glide path. There are no stepdown fixes.

85. GPS systems certified for IFR operations cannot be used as a substitute for DME receivers

    A. to determine aircraft position or a DME fix at altitudes above 24,000 feet.

    B. to fly a DME arc.

    C. in selecting an alternate that requires use of DME.

Answer (C) is correct. *(IPH Chap 1)*
    DISCUSSION: GPS is not authorized as a substitute means of navigation guidance when conducting a conventional approach at an alternate airport if the approach procedure requires DME. The aircraft must be equipped with an appropriate DME in order to use the approach as an alternate.
    Answer (A) is incorrect. There is no rule barring a pilot from using GPS to determine aircraft position above 24,000 feet. Answer (B) is incorrect. There is no prohibition against using GPS to fly a DME arc.

86. When using a TSO-C129 or TSO-C196 GPS for navigation and instrument approaches, any required alternate airport must have

    A. a GPS approach with GBAS that is anticipated to be operational or available at the ETA.

    B. a GPS approach if no WAAS outage is expected.

    C. an approved operational instrument approach procedure other than GPS.

Answer (C) is correct. *(AIM Para 1-1-18)*
    DISCUSSION: Airports with only a global positioning system (GPS) approach procedure cannot be used as an alternate by TSO-129/129A users. Because GPS is not authorized as a substitute means of navigation guidance when conducting a conventional approach at an alternate airport, if the approach procedure requires distance measuring equipment (DME), the aircraft must be equipped with the appropriate DME avionics in order to use the approach as an alternate.
    Answer (A) is incorrect. GBAS is pertinent to a TSO-C161a/162a certified GPS unit, not the TSO-C129 or TSO-C196 specified by this question. Answer (B) is incorrect. WAAS certified GPS units comply with TSO-C145/146, not the TSO-C129 or TSO-C196 units specified by the question.

87. Your aircraft is equipped with a WAAS enabled GPS unit. While performing a GPS approach, you note an "LNAV/VNAV available" indication on the moving map display and horizontal situation indicator. You know that

    A. you can use the LPV minimums line on the IAP chart with this indication.

    B. the indication reflects an artificially created advisory glidepath that you can use to descend to the LNAV MDA.

    C. you can descend to GBAS approach minimums indicated on the IAP.

Answer (B) is correct. *(AIM Para 1-1-20)*
    DISCUSSION: Even if WAAS becomes unavailable, you can safely follow the lateral and vertical (LNAV/VNAV) guidance information displayed on your GPS unit and fly to the LNAV MDA.
    Answer (A) is incorrect. Flying to LPV minimums requires an LPV annunciation on the GPS unit. Answer (C) is incorrect. Equipment requirements for a GBAS in the aircraft is a GBAS receiver. Current avionics conform either to GBAS or WAAS standards. No manufacturer has chosen to build a single avionics package integrating both GBAS and WAAS standards. This aircraft is equipped with a WAAS enabled GPS unit.

88. Aircraft operating under IFR with TSO-C129 or TSO-C196 GPS for en route navigation must also have installed

    A. VOR/DME with RNAV capabilities.

    B. a backup GPS receiver.

    C. the avionics necessary to receive appropriate NAVAIDs along the route.

Answer (C) is correct. *(AIM Para 1-1-18)*
    DISCUSSION: Aircraft using GPS TSO-C129 or TSO-C196 navigation equipment under IFR must be equipped with an approved and operational alternate means of navigation appropriate to the flight.
    Answer (A) is incorrect. There is no specific requirement for VOR/DME with RNAV capabilities to be installed in the aircraft. Answer (B) is incorrect. There is no requirement for the aircraft to have a backup GPS installed.

3.8 Autopilots

89. Which of the following is a benefit of flying with an autopilot?

    A. Pilots will not need to worry about controlling airspeed or throttle settings.

    B. Airspace restrictions will automatically be avoided.

    C. Pilot workload is reduced.

Answer (C) is correct. *(AAH Chap 4)*
    DISCUSSION: Autopilots reduce the physical and mental demands of the pilot.
    Answer (A) is incorrect. Pilots must still manage the throttle to control airspeed when the autopilot is engaged because most autopilots are not capable of changing power settings on their own. Answer (B) is incorrect. It is a pilot's responsibility to avoid all airspace that is restricted or otherwise unavailable for use at a given time.

90. In an autopilot-controlled system, what device actually moves the control surfaces?

    A. Gyroscope.

    B. Servo.

    C. Vacuum pump.

Answer (B) is correct. *(AAH Chap 4)*
    DISCUSSION: Servos are electromechanical devices that translate electrical commands into motion, thus moving the control surfaces.
    Answer (A) is incorrect. Servos, not gyroscopes, translate electrical commands into motion, thus moving the control surfaces. Answer (C) is incorrect. Servos, not vacuum pumps, translate electrical commands into motion, thus moving the control surfaces.

91. To ensure situational awareness while using an autopilot system

    A. pilots must verify that the aircraft is tracking the intended flight profile.

    B. it is important to ensure that all navigational databases are current.

    C. current navigational charts are required.

Answer (A) is correct. *(AAH Chap 4)*
    DISCUSSION: After engaging the autopilot, it is important to verify that the aircraft is tracking the intended flight profile.
    Answer (B) is incorrect. Autopilot systems are not dependent on having current navigational databases. Pilots can use them to maintain a given heading or altitude. Answer (C) is incorrect. While a good practice, having physical paper charts in the aircraft is not a requirement.

END OF STUDY UNIT

STUDY UNIT FOUR
FEDERAL AVIATION REGULATIONS

(6 pages of outline)

This study unit contains outlines of major concepts tested, sample test questions and answers regarding Federal Aviation Regulations (FARs), and an explanation of each answer. The table of contents above lists each subunit within this study unit, the number of questions pertaining to that particular subunit, and the pages on which the outlines and questions begin, respectively.

Recall that the **sole purpose** of this book is to expedite your passing of the FAA pilot knowledge test for the instrument rating. Accordingly, all extraneous material (i.e., topics or regulations not directly tested on the FAA pilot knowledge test) is omitted, even though much more knowledge is necessary to fly safely. This additional material is presented in *Pilot Handbook, Aviation Weather and Weather Services, FAR/AIM,* and *Instrument Pilot Flight Maneuvers and Practical Test Prep,* available from Gleim Publications, Inc. Order online at www.gleim.com.

NOTE: The FAA refers to the Federal Aviation Regulations as "14 CFR" rather than "FARs." The Office of Management and Budget uses FAR as an acronym for Federal Acquisition Regulations. CFR stands for Code of Federal Regulations, and the Federal Aviation Regulations are in Title 14. For example, FAR Part 1 and FAR 61.109 are now referred to as 14 CFR Part 1 and 14 CFR Sec. 61.109, respectively. Due to CFIs' and pilots' widespread use of the acronym FAR, we use FAR and 14 CFR interchangeably to familiarize you with both.

4.1 FAR PART 1

1.1 General Definitions

1. Airports are areas of land or water that are used or intended to be used for the landing and takeoff of aircraft, including any buildings and facilities.
2. A Glide Path Qualification Surface (GQS) is an imaginary surface extending from the runway threshold along the runway centerline to the Decision Altitude (DA) point.

4.2 FAR PART 61

61.3 Requirements for Certificates, Ratings, and Authorizations

1. The pilot in command must hold an instrument rating when operating under IFR or in weather conditions less than the minimums prescribed for VFR flight.
2. An IFR clearance is required when operating in Class A airspace.

61.51 Pilot Logbooks

1. Instrument flight time may be logged when flight is solely by reference to instruments under actual or simulated flight conditions.
    a. The location and type of each instrument approach completed and the name of the safety pilot must be included in the logbook for each simulated instrument flight.
    b. During VMC, a view-limiting device must be used.
2. An instrument flight instructor (CFII) may log instrument time when acting as an instrument flight instructor in actual instrument weather conditions.

61.57 Recent Flight Experience: Pilot in Command

1. In order to act as pilot in command under IFR, one must have logged instrument time (actual or simulated) within the preceding 6 calendar months in either the same category of aircraft (airplane) to be used or in an airplane flight simulator or flight training device and must have performed the following procedures:
    a. At least six instrument approaches
    b. Holding procedures
    c. Intercepting and tracking courses through the use of navigation systems
2. An instrument pilot who does not meet the experience requirements during the prescribed time or 6 calendar months thereafter must then pass an instrument proficiency check.
    a. This check may be conducted by an FAA inspector, an FAA-designated examiner, or a certificated instrument flight instructor.

61.133 Commercial Pilot Privileges and Limitations

1. Commercial pilots without an instrument rating cannot carry passengers for hire on cross-country flights during the day beyond a radius of 50 NM.
    a. Carrying passengers at night is also prohibited without an instrument rating.

4.3   FAR PART 91

91.3 Responsibility and Authority of the Pilot in Command

1. The pilot in command of an aircraft is directly responsible for, and is the final authority as to, determining the airworthiness and operation of that aircraft prior to each flight.

91.21 Portable Electronic Devices

1. The use of certain portable electronic devices is prohibited on aircraft that are being operated under IFR.

91.103 Preflight Action

1. Before beginning any IFR flight, the pilot must obtain and become familiar with information about weather reports and forecasts, fuel requirements, alternatives available if the planned flight cannot be completed, any known traffic delays, runway lengths at airports of intended use, and takeoff and landing distance information.

91.109 Flight Instruction; Simulated Instrument Flight and Certain Flight Tests

1. To operate an airplane in simulated instrument flight, you must have at least a private pilot who is appropriately rated in your aircraft occupying the other control seat as a safety pilot.

91.123 Compliance with ATC Clearances and Instructions

1. If you deviate from an ATC clearance in an emergency, you must notify ATC as soon as possible.

2. If you are given priority by ATC in an emergency, ATC may request that you submit a detailed report within 48 hr. to the manager of that ATC facility.

   a. The report may be required even though no rule has been violated.

3. During an IFR flight in IMC, if a distress condition is encountered, the pilot should immediately declare an emergency and obtain an amended clearance.

   a. Distress is a condition of being threatened by serious and/or imminent danger and of requiring immediate assistance.

91.129 Operations in Class D Airspace

1. If an aircraft's transponder fails during flight within Class D airspace, no deviation is required because a transponder is not required in Class D airspace.

91.131 Operations in Class B Airspace

1. Operations in Class B airspace require two-way radio communications with ATC and a Mode C transponder.

   a. If operating IFR, you must have a VOR receiver.

2. If it is necessary to conduct training operations within Class B airspace, procedures established by ATC for these flights within the Class B airspace will be followed.

91.135 Operations in Class A Airspace

1. An IFR flight plan is required when flying in IFR conditions in controlled airspace and at all times in Class A airspace.

   a. Class A airspace includes the airspace from 18,000 ft. MSL up to and including FL 600.

91.155 Basic VFR Weather Minimums

Cloud Clearance and Visibility Required for VFR

Airspace	Flight Visibility	Distance from Clouds
Class A	Not Applicable	Not applicable
Class B	3 SM	Clear of Clouds
Class C	3 SM	500 ft. below 1,000 ft. above 2,000 ft. horiz.
Class D	3 SM	500 ft. below 1,000 ft. above 2,000 ft. horiz.
Class E		
Less than 10,000 ft. MSL	3 SM	500 ft. below 1,000 ft. above 2,000 ft. horiz.
At or above 10,000 ft. MSL	5 SM	1,000 ft. below 1,000 ft. above 1 SM horiz.

Airspace	Flight Visibility	Distance from Clouds
Class G:		
1,200 ft. or less above the surface (regardless of MSL altitude)		
Day	1 SM	Clear of clouds
Night, except as provided in 1. below	3 SM	500 ft. below 1,000 ft. above 2,000 ft. horiz.
More than 1,200 ft. above the surface but less than 10,000 ft. MSL		
Day	1 SM	500 ft. below 1,000 ft. above 2,000 ft. horiz.
Night	3 SM	500 ft. below 1,000 ft. above 2,000 ft. horiz.
More than 1,200 ft. above the surface and at or above 10,000 ft. MSL	5 SM	1,000 ft. below 1,000 ft. above 1 SM horiz.

1. An airplane may be operated clear of clouds in Class G airspace at night below 1,200 ft. AGL when the visibility is less than 3 SM but more than 1 SM in an airport traffic pattern and within 1/2 NM of the runway.

2. When flying under a "VFR-on-top" clearance on IFR flights, you must fly at VFR altitudes and comply with VFR visibility and distance-from-clouds criteria.

91.157 Special VFR Weather Minimums

1. With some exceptions, special VFR clearances can be requested in Class B, Class C, Class D, or Class E airspace areas.

   a. The flight requirements are to remain clear of clouds and have visibility of at least 1 SM.

2. Flight under special VFR clearance at night is permitted only if the pilot is instrument rated and the airplane is IFR equipped.

91.167 Fuel Requirements for Flight in IFR Conditions

1. When flying IFR, you must carry sufficient fuel to fly to the first airport of intended landing, fly to the alternate airport (if required), and then fly for 45 min. at normal cruising speed.

2. An alternate airport is not required if the destination airport has

   a. At least one approved instrument approach procedure (IAP), and
   b. From 1 hr. before to 1 hr. after the ETA, a forecast of at least

      1) 2,000 ft. ceiling
      2) 3 SM visibility

91.169 IFR Flight Plan: Information Required

1. Intended airports of landing on an IFR flight must have a forecast ceiling of at least 2,000 ft. and visibility of at least 3 SM for 1 hr. before and 1 hr. after the ETA. Otherwise, an alternate must be listed on your IFR flight plan.

2. When a pilot elects to proceed to the selected alternate airport, the landing minimums used should be the minimums specified for the approach procedure selected.

   a. To list an airport with a nonprecision approach as an alternate, the forecast weather must be for at least an 800-ft. ceiling and 2 SM visibility at your ETA.

   b. To list an airport with a precision approach as an alternate, the forecast weather must indicate at least a 600-ft. ceiling and 2 SM visibility at your ETA.

3. If no instrument approaches are prescribed, the minimums for listing an airport as an alternate on an IFR flight are forecast weather allowing descent from the MEA, approach, and landing under basic VFR.

91.171 VOR Equipment Check for IFR Operations

1. When making VOR operation checks, the date, place, bearing error, and pilot signature should be placed in the aircraft log or other record.

2. Operational checks of VORs must be made every 30 days.

3. The maximum allowable tolerance when performing an operational check of a dual VOR system is a 4° variation between the two indicated bearings.

   a. When performing an operational check using a ground-based VOT, the maximum tolerance is ±4°.

   b. When performing an operational check using an airborne checkpoint, the maximum tolerance is ±6°.

4. In addition to the VOR check that must be made at least every 30 days, the altimeter system and the transponder must have been inspected within 24 calendar months.

91.173 ATC Clearance and Flight Plan Required

1. No person may operate an aircraft in controlled airspace under IFR unless that person has

   a. Filed an IFR flight plan and
   b. Received an appropriate ATC clearance.

91.177 Minimum Altitudes for IFR Operations

1. Except when necessary for takeoff or landing, the minimum altitude for IFR flight (if none is prescribed in FAR Parts 95 or 97) is one of the following:

   a. 2,000 ft. above the highest obstacle within a horizontal distance of 4 NM over designated mountainous terrain

   b. 1,000 ft. above the highest obstacle within a horizontal distance of 4 NM over nonmountainous terrain

91.205 Powered Civil Aircraft with Standard Category U.S. Airworthiness Certificates: Instrument and Equipment Requirements

1. For IFR flight, navigation equipment must be appropriate to the ground facilities to be used.

2. Above 24,000 ft. MSL, DME is required if VOR navigational equipment is required.

3. A gyroscopic directional indicator, a gyroscopic attitude indicator, and a gyroscopic rate-of-turn indicator are required for IFR flight.

4. Aircraft being operated under IFR are required to have a slip-skid indicator, a clock with a sweep second pointer or digital presentation, and a pressure-sensitive altimeter.

91.211 Supplemental Oxygen

1. At cabin pressure altitudes above 15,000 ft. MSL, each passenger of the aircraft must be provided with supplemental oxygen.

2. At cabin pressure altitudes above 14,000 ft. MSL, the required minimum flight crew must be provided and use supplemental oxygen during the entire flight time at those altitudes.

3. Pilots can fly at cabin pressure altitudes above 12,500 ft. MSL up to and including 14,000 ft. MSL for up to 30 min. without supplemental oxygen.

    a. If a flight is conducted at these altitudes for more than 30 min., oxygen must be provided to and used by the required minimum flight crew for the time in excess of 30 min.

91.215 ATC Transponder and Altitude Reporting Equipment and Use

1. All aircraft must have and use an altitude encoding transponder (Mode C) when operating

    a. Within Class B airspace
    b. Within 30 NM of the primary Class B airport
    c. Within and above Class C airspace
    d. Above 10,000 ft. MSL except at and below 2,500 ft. AGL
    e. In Class A airspace

2. Request for deviations must be made to the controlling ATC facility.

    a. If the transponder fails during flight, ATC may authorize the aircraft to continue to the airport of ultimate destination.

        1) An aircraft with an operating transponder but without Mode C can request a deviation at any time.

    b. For operation of an aircraft that is not equipped with a transponder, the request for a deviation must be made at least 1 hr. before the proposed operation.

91.411 Altimeter System and Altitude Reporting Equipment Tests and Inspections

1. Each static pressure system and altimeter instrument must be tested and inspected by the end of the 24th calendar month following the current inspection.

4.4 NTSB PART 830

1. NTSB Part 830, "Notification and Reporting of Aircraft Accidents or Incidents and Overdue Aircraft, and Preservation of Aircraft Wreckage, Mail, Cargo, and Records," covers the procedures required for aircraft accident- and incident-reporting responsibilities for pilots.

QUESTIONS AND ANSWER EXPLANATIONS: All of the instrument rating knowledge test questions chosen by the FAA for release as well as additional questions selected by Gleim relating to the material in the previous outlines are reproduced on the following pages. These questions have been organized into the same subunits as the outlines. To the immediate right of each question are the correct answer and answer explanation. You should cover these answers and answer explanations while responding to the questions. Refer to the general discussion in the Introduction on how to take the FAA knowledge test.

Remember that the questions from the FAA knowledge test bank have been reordered by topic and organized into a meaningful sequence. Also, the first line of the answer explanation gives the citation of the authoritative source for the answer.

QUESTIONS

4.1 FAR Part 1

1.1 General Definitions

1. Which of the following terms describes an airport?

A. An area of land or water that is used or intended to be used for the landing and takeoff of aircraft, and includes its buildings and facilities, if any.

B. An area of land that is used for the takeoff and landing of aircraft, but does not include buildings since not all airports have buildings.

C. All runway, taxiway, and ramp areas created for use by aircraft.

Answer (A) is correct. *(14 CFR 1.1)*
    DISCUSSION: Part 1.1 of the Federal Aviation Regulations defines an airport as "an area of land or water that is used or intended to be used for the landing and takeoff of aircraft, and includes its buildings and facilities, if any."
    Answer (B) is incorrect. Part 1.1 of the FARs includes areas of water and any buildings and facilities in the definition of an airport. Answer (C) is incorrect. Part 1.1 of the FARs includes areas of land and water and any buildings and facilities in the definition of an airport.

2. The Glide Path Qualification Surface (GQS) limits the height of obstructions between

A. The final approach fix and the missed approach point.

B. Decision altitude and the runway threshold.

C. Any initial approach fix(es) and the final approach fix.

Answer (B) is correct. *(AC 150-5300-13A)*
    DISCUSSION: The GQS is an imaginary surface extending from the runway threshold along the runway centerline to the Decision Altitude (DA) point.
    Answer (A) is incorrect. The GQS extends to the Decision Altitude (DA) point. Answer (C) is incorrect. The GQS extends to the Decision Altitude (DA) point.

3. The term "airport" means an area of land or water that is

A. Scheduled for use as an airport.

B. Used or intended to be used for the landing and takeoff of aircraft and includes taxiways and other ground movement areas.

C. Used or intended to be used for the landing and takeoff of aircraft and includes its buildings and facilities, if any.

Answer (C) is correct. *(14 CFR 1.1)*
    DISCUSSION: The FAA defines an airport as an area of land or water that is used or intended to be used for the landing and takeoff of aircraft, including buildings or facilities.
    Answer (A) is incorrect. The FAA definition of an airport includes buildings and facilities. This answer option does not include the buildings and facilities stipulated by the FAA definition. Answer (B) is incorrect. This answer option does not include buildings or facilities, which are included in the FAA definition. The FAA definition does not include taxiways and ground movement areas.

4.2 FAR PART 61

61.3 Requirements for Certificates, Ratings, and Authorizations

4. Do regulations permit you to act as pilot in command of an airplane in IMC if you hold a private pilot certificate with ASEL, rotorcraft category, with helicopter class rating and instrument helicopter rating?

A. Yes, if you comply with the recent IFR experience requirements for a helicopter.

B. No. You must hold either an unrestricted airline transport pilot-airplane certificate or an airplane instrument rating.

C. No. However, you may do so if you hold an airline transport pilot-airplane certificate limited to VFR.

Answer (B) is correct. *(14 CFR 61.3)*
    DISCUSSION: Instrument privileges are class-specific. To operate as pilot in command in an airplane in IMC, the pilot would need to have an instrument rating in the airplane class. An unrestricted airline transport pilot-airplane certificate would also meet this requirement.
    Answer (A) is incorrect. Instrument operating privileges are class-specific. Answer (C) is incorrect. The airline transport pilot-airplane certificate would need to be unrestricted for this operation to meet the regulatory requirement.

5. Under which condition must the pilot in command of a civil aircraft have at least an instrument rating?

A. When operating in Class E airspace.

B. For a flight in VFR conditions while on an IFR flight plan.

C. For any flight above an altitude of 1,200 feet AGL, when the visibility is less than 3 miles.

Answer (B) is correct. *(14 CFR 61.3)*
    DISCUSSION: No person may act as pilot in command of a civil aircraft under IFR or in weather conditions less than the minimums prescribed for VFR flight unless (s)he holds an instrument rating.
    Answer (A) is incorrect. An instrument rating is required at all times when operating in Class A, not Class E, airspace. Answer (C) is incorrect. VFR is permitted in uncontrolled airspace during the day with visibilities of as little as 1 SM above 1,200 ft. AGL but below 10,000 ft. MSL.

6. The pilot in command of a civil aircraft must have an instrument rating only when operating

A. under IFR in positive control airspace.

B. under IFR, in weather conditions less than the minimum for VFR flight or in Class A airspace.

C. in weather conditions less than the minimum prescribed for VFR flight.

Answer (B) is correct. *(14 CFR 61.3 and 91.135)*
    DISCUSSION: No person may act as pilot in command of a civil aircraft under IFR, in weather conditions less than the minimums prescribed for VFR flight, or in Class A airspace unless (s)he holds an instrument rating.
    Answer (A) is incorrect. You must have an instrument rating when operating under IFR, in weather conditions less than the minimum for VFR flight, or in Class A airspace, not only under IFR in positive control airspace. Positive control airspace means that ATC will provide separation to all aircraft within that airspace. Answer (C) is incorrect. It omits flying in VFR conditions with an IFR clearance.

61.51 Pilot Logbooks

7. What portion of dual instruction time may a certificated instrument flight instructor log as instrument flight time?

A. All time during which the instructor acts as instrument instructor, regardless of weather conditions.

B. All time during which the instructor acts as instrument instructor in actual instrument weather conditions.

C. Only the time during which the instructor flies the aircraft by reference to instruments.

Answer (B) is correct. *(14 CFR 61.51)*
    DISCUSSION: An instrument flight instructor may log as instrument time that time during which (s)he acts as instrument flight instructor in actual instrument weather conditions.
    Answer (A) is incorrect. The flight conditions must be IMC for the instructor to log flight instruction as instrument time. Answer (C) is incorrect. Instructing in (as well as flying in) actual IFR weather conditions can be logged as instrument time by the instructor.

8. To meet instrument experience requirements of CFR Part 61, section 61.57(c), a pilot enters the condition of flight in the pilot logbook as simulated instrument conditions, what other qualifying information must also be entered?

A. Location and type of each instrument approach completed and name of safety pilot.

B. Number and type of instrument approaches completed and route of flight.

C. Name and pilot certificate number of safety pilot and type of approaches completed.

Answer (A) is correct. *(14 CFR 61.51)*
    DISCUSSION: A pilot may log as instrument flight time only that time during which (s)he operates the aircraft solely by reference to instruments, under actual or simulated instrument flight conditions. Each entry must include the location and type of each instrument approach completed and the name of the safety pilot for each simulated instrument flight.
    Answer (B) is incorrect. The location and type of instrument approaches must be entered along with the safety pilot's name, not the route of flight. Answer (C) is incorrect. The location is required, but the safety pilot's certificate number is not.

9. Which flight time may be logged as instrument time when on an instrument flight plan?

A. All of the time the aircraft was not controlled by ground references.

B. Only the time you controlled the aircraft solely by reference to flight instruments.

C. Only the time you were flying in IFR weather conditions.

Answer (B) is correct. *(14 CFR 61.51)*
    DISCUSSION: A pilot may log as instrument flight time only that time during which (s)he operates the aircraft solely by reference to instruments, under actual or simulated instrument flight conditions.
    Answer (A) is incorrect. VFR flight can be conducted above a cloud layer without visual ground references, i.e., VFR-on-top. Answer (C) is incorrect. Time under the hood (i.e., simulated IFR) as well as actual IFR conditions counts as instrument time.

10. What are the requirements to log an ILS approach in VMC conditions for instrument currency?

A. The flight must remain on an IFR flight plan throughout the approach and landing.

B. The ILS approach can be credited only if you use a view-limiting device and log the name of the safety (pilot).

C. The ILS approach can be credited regardless of actual weather if you are issued an IFR clearance.

Answer (B) is correct. *(14 CFR 61.51, 61.57, 91.109)*
DISCUSSION: To be credited for an ILS approach in VMC, the instrument rated pilot must use a view-limiting device and log the name of the safety pilot. If the instrument rated pilot is doing this for training, a view-limiting device is still required along with an authorized instructor instead of only a safety pilot. The instructor would then endorse the pilot's logbook for the training.
NOTE: The FAA's original question answer selection (B) ends after the word "safety." We added the word "pilot" to complete the sentence.
Answer (A) is incorrect. An IFR flight plan is not required in VMC conditions. However, it is required in IMC conditions. Answer (C) is incorrect. An IFR clearance is not required in VMC conditions. The approach can be credited in IMC conditions with a clearance and without a view-limiting device to remain instrument current.

61.57 Recent Flight Experience: Pilot in Command

11. How long does a pilot meet the recency of experience requirements for IFR flight after successfully completing an instrument proficiency check if no further IFR flights are made?

A. 90 days.

B. 6 calendar months.

C. 12 calendar months.

Answer (B) is correct. *(14 CFR 61.57)*
DISCUSSION: No pilot may act as pilot in command when operating under IFR or in weather conditions less than the minimums prescribed for VFR unless (s)he has, within the past 6 months, logged instrument time under actual or simulated IFR conditions in the category of aircraft involved or in an appropriate flight simulator or flight training device and has performed at least six instrument approaches, holding procedures, and intercepting and tracking courses through the use of navigation systems. An alternative way to remain current is to pass an instrument proficiency check in the category of aircraft involved.
Answer (A) is incorrect. Ninety days refers to takeoff and landing currency to carry passengers. Answer (C) is incorrect. Twelve months is the time whereafter another instrument proficiency check is required.

12. No pilot may act as pilot-in-command of an aircraft, under IFR or in weather conditions less than the minimums prescribed for VFR unless that pilot has, within the preceding 6 calendar months, completed at least

A. six instrument approaches, holding procedures, intercepting and tracking courses using navigational systems, or passed an instrument proficiency check.

B. six instrument flights under actual IFR conditions.

C. three instrument approaches and logged 3 hours.

Answer (A) is correct. *(14 CFR 61.57)*
DISCUSSION: No person may act as pilot in command under IFR or in weather conditions less than the minimums prescribed for VFR unless, within the preceding 6 calendar months, that person has performed and logged under actual or simulated instrument conditions, either in flight in the appropriate category of aircraft for the instrument privileges sought or in a flight simulator or flight training device that is representative of the aircraft category for the instrument privileges sought, at least six instrument approaches, holding procedures, and intercepting and tracking courses through the use of navigation systems. Alternatively, the pilot may pass an instrument proficiency check in the category of aircraft involved.
Answer (B) is incorrect. A pilot must complete, under actual or simulated instrument conditions, at least six instrument approaches, holding procedures, and intercepting and tracking courses through the use of navigation systems, not six instrument flights under actual IFR conditions. Answer (C) is incorrect. A pilot must complete at least six, not three, instrument approaches, holding procedures, and intercepting and tracking courses through the use of navigation systems. There is no required minimum number of hours to be logged.

13. After your recent IFR experience lapses, how much time do you have before you must pass an instrument proficiency check to act as pilot in command under IFR?

A. 6 months.

B. 90 days.

C. 12 months.

Answer (A) is correct. *(14 CFR 61.57)*
DISCUSSION: A pilot who does not meet the recent instrument experience requirements during the prescribed time or 6 months thereafter may not serve as pilot in command under IFR or in weather conditions less than the minimums prescribed for VFR until (s)he passes an instrument proficiency check.
Answer (B) is incorrect. Ninety days refers to the takeoff and landing currency requirements to carry passengers. Answer (C) is incorrect. Twelve months is the time from when you gain IFR currency to when you are required to pass another instrument proficiency check (assuming you have not maintained currency since you gained proficiency).

14. To meet the minimum required instrument flight experience to act as pilot in command of an aircraft under IFR, you must have logged within the 6 calendar months preceding the month of the flight, in the same category of aircraft:

    A. holding procedures, intercepting and tracking courses through the use of navigation systems, and six instrument approaches.

    B. six instrument approaches, three of which must be in the same category and class of aircraft to be flown, and 6 hours of instrument time in any aircraft.

    C. 6 hours of instrument time in any aircraft, and six instrument approaches.

Answer (A) is correct. *(14 CFR 61.57)*
    DISCUSSION: No person may act as pilot in command under IFR or in weather conditions less than VFR minimums unless, within the preceding 6 calendar months, (s)he has performed and logged, under actual or simulated instrument conditions, at least six instrument approaches, holding procedures, and intercepting and tracking courses through the use of navigation systems, in the category of aircraft to be flown.
    Answer (B) is incorrect. All six, not three, approaches must be in the same category and aircraft. Additionally, you must have accomplished holding procedures and intercepting and tracking courses through the use of navigation systems, not accumulated 6 hr. of instrument time. Answer (C) is incorrect. You must have also accomplished holding procedures and intercepting and tracking courses through the use of navigation systems in the same category and class of aircraft, not accumulated 6 hr. of instrument time in any aircraft.

15. To meet the minimum instrument experience requirements, within the last 6 calendar months you need

    A. six instrument approaches, holding procedures, and intercepting and tracking courses in the appropriate category of aircraft.

    B. six hours in the same category aircraft.

    C. six hours in the same category aircraft, and at least 3 of the 6 hours in actual IFR conditions.

Answer (A) is correct. *(14 CFR 61.57)*
    DISCUSSION: No person may act as pilot in command under IFR or in weather conditions less than VFR minimums unless, within the preceding 6 calendar months, (s)he has performed and logged, under actual or simulated instrument conditions, at least six instrument approaches, holding procedures, and intercepting and tracking courses through the use of navigation systems, in the category of aircraft to be flown.
    Answer (B) is incorrect. To be current for IFR, you must have performed six instrument approaches, holding procedures, and intercepting and tracking courses in the same category of aircraft, not accumulated 6 hr. in the same category of aircraft. Answer (C) is incorrect. To be current for IFR, you must have performed six instrument approaches, holding procedures, and intercepting and tracking courses in the same category of aircraft, not accumulated 6 hr. in the same category aircraft with at least 3 hr. in actual IFR conditions.

16. A pilot may satisfy the recent flight experience requirement necessary to act as pilot in command in IMC in powered aircraft by logging within the 6 calendar months preceding the month of the flight

    A. six instrument approaches, holding procedures, and intercepting and tracking courses using navigational systems.

    B. six instrument approaches and 3 hours under actual or 6 hours in simulated IFR conditions; three of the approaches must be in the category of aircraft involved.

    C. 6 hours of instrument time under actual or simulated IFR conditions, including at least six instrument approaches. Three of the 6 hours must be in flight in any category aircraft.

Answer (A) is the best answer. *(14 CFR 61.57)*
    DISCUSSION: Items required by FAR 61.57 to remain current include six instrument approaches, holding procedures, and intercepting and tracking courses using navigation systems.
    Answer (B) is incorrect. The answer does not include holding procedures or intercepting and tracking courses using navigational systems. Answer (C) is incorrect. The answer does not include holding procedures or intercepting and tracking courses using navigational systems.

17. What minimum conditions are necessary for the instrument approaches required for IFR currency?

    A. The approaches may be made in an aircraft, flight simulator, or flight training device.

    B. At least three approaches must be made in the same category of aircraft to be flown.

    C. At least three approaches must be made in the same category and class of aircraft to be flown.

Answer (A) is correct. *(14 CFR 61.57)*
    DISCUSSION: For IFR currency, the six instrument approaches must be made either in the same category of aircraft to be flown or in a flight simulator or training device representative of the aircraft category to be flown, or in any combination of these.
    Answer (B) is incorrect. All six approaches may be done in an approved flight simulator or training device, not necessarily in an airplane. Answer (C) is incorrect. All six approaches may be done in an approved flight simulator or training device, not necessarily in an airplane.

18. What recent instrument flight experience requirements must be met before you may act as pilot in command of an airplane under IFR?

  A. A minimum of six instrument approaches in an airplane, or an approved simulator (airplane) or ground trainer, within the preceding 6 calendar months.

  B. A minimum of six instrument approaches, at least three of which must be in an aircraft within the preceding 6 calendar months.

  C. A minimum of six instrument approaches in an aircraft, at least three of which must be in the same category within the preceding 6 calendar months.

Answer (A) is correct. *(14 CFR 61.57)*
  DISCUSSION: No person may act as pilot in command under IFR or in weather conditions less than VFR minimums unless, within the preceding 6 calendar months, (s)he has performed and logged, under actual or simulated instrument conditions, at least six instrument approaches, holding procedures, and intercepting and tracking courses through the use of navigation systems, in the category of aircraft to be flown, in an approved simulator or flight training device, or in any combination of these.
  Answer (B) is incorrect. All six approaches may be done in an approved flight simulator or flight training device; none are required to be done in an aircraft. Answer (C) is incorrect. All six approaches may be done in an approved flight simulator or flight training device; none are required to be done in an aircraft. In addition, all six approaches, not just three, must be done in the same category of aircraft or a simulator or flight training device representative of that aircraft category.

19. An instrument rated pilot who has not logged any instrument time in 1 year or more cannot serve as pilot in command under IFR, unless the pilot

  A. completes the required 6 hours and six approaches, followed by an instrument proficiency check given by an FAA-designated examiner.

  B. passes an instrument proficiency check in the category of aircraft involved, given by an approved FAA examiner, instrument instructor, or FAA inspector.

  C. passes an instrument proficiency check in the category of aircraft involved, followed by 6 hours and six instrument approaches, 3 of those hours in the category of aircraft involved.

Answer (B) is correct. *(14 CFR 61.57)*
  DISCUSSION: A pilot who does not meet the recent instrument experience requirements during the prescribed time or 6 months thereafter may not serve as pilot in command under IFR or in weather conditions less than the minimums prescribed for VFR until (s)he passes an instrument proficiency check in the category of aircraft involved, given by an FAA inspector, a member of an armed force of the U.S. authorized to conduct flight tests, an FAA-approved check pilot, or a certificated instrument flight instructor. The proficiency check may be completed in an appropriate flight simulator or flight training device.
  Answer (A) is incorrect. An instrument proficiency check by itself provides currency. Additional time and approaches are not required. Answer (C) is incorrect. An instrument proficiency check by itself provides currency. Additional time and approaches are not required.

20. A pilot's recent IFR experience expires on July 1 of this year. What is the latest date the pilot can meet the IFR experience requirement without having to take an instrument proficiency check?

  A. December 31, this year.

  B. June 30, next year.

  C. July 31, this year.

Answer (A) is correct. *(14 CFR 61.57)*
  DISCUSSION: A pilot who does not meet the recent instrument experience requirements during the prescribed time or 6 months thereafter may not serve as pilot in command under IFR or in weather conditions less than the minimums prescribed for VFR until (s)he passes an instrument proficiency check. If the 6 months' recency experience period expires on July 1, the 6 months thereafter would expire on December 31 this year.
  Answer (B) is incorrect. This date represents 12 months instead of 6 months. Answer (C) is incorrect. This date represents 1 month instead of 6 months.

21. How may a pilot satisfy the recent flight experience requirement necessary to act as pilot in command in IMC in powered aircraft? Within the previous 6 calendar months, logged

  A. six instrument approaches, holding procedures, and intercepting and tracking courses using navigational systems.

  B. six instrument approaches and 3 hours under actual or simulated IFR conditions within the last 6 months; three of the approaches must be in the category of aircraft involved.

  C. 6 hours of instrument time under actual or simulated IFR conditions within the last 3 months, including at least six instrument approaches of any kind. Three of the 6 hours must be in flight in any category aircraft.

Answer (A) is correct. *(14 CFR 61.57)*
  DISCUSSION: No pilot may act as pilot in command of a powered aircraft under IFR or in weather conditions less than VFR minimums unless, within the preceding 6 calendar months, (s)he has performed and logged, under actual or simulated instrument conditions, at least six instrument approaches, holding procedures, and intercepting and tracking courses through the use of navigation systems, in the category of aircraft to be flown or in an airplane flight simulator or training device.
  Answer (B) is incorrect. There is no instrument flight time requirement. In addition to the six instrument approaches, you must also log holding procedures and intercepting and tracking courses using navigational systems. Answer (C) is incorrect. There is no instrument flight time requirement. You must log six instrument approaches, holding procedures, and intercepting and tracking courses using navigational systems within the past 6 months, not 3 months.

22. Which additional IFR experience is required for you to meet the recent flight experience requirements to act as pilot in command of an airplane under IFR?

Your present instrument experience within the preceding 6 calendar months is

1. three hours with holding, intercepting and tracking courses in an approved airplane flight simulator.
2. two instrument approaches in an airplane.

    A. Three hours of simulated or actual instrument flight time in a helicopter and two instrument approaches in an airplane or helicopter.

    B. Four instrument approaches in an airplane, or an approved airplane flight simulator or training device.

    C. Three instrument approaches in an airplane.

Answer (B) is correct. *(14 CFR 61.57)*
    DISCUSSION: No person may act as pilot in command under IFR or in weather conditions less than the minimums prescribed for VFR, unless within the preceding 6 calendar months that person has performed and logged under actual or simulated instrument conditions, either in flight in the appropriate category of aircraft for the instrument privileges being sought or in a flight simulator or flight training device that is representative of the aircraft category for the instrument privileges sought; at least six instrument approaches, holding procedures, and intercepting and tracking courses through the use of navigation systems. Having logged only two instrument approaches, the pilot must log four more.
    Answer (A) is incorrect. No minimum time is required; four, not two, more approaches are required; and all approaches must be in an airplane or flight simulator or flight training device representative of an airplane, not a helicopter. Answer (C) is incorrect. Four, not three, more approaches are required to have the required minimum of six.

23. A pilot plans an IFR flight on July 10 of this year. In order to meet IFR currency requirements the pilot must have

    A. performed his or her currency tasks between January 10 and July 10.

    B. performed his or her currency tasks between February 10 and July 10 with none of it before February 10.

    C. completed an IPC within the last year.

Answer (A) is correct. *(14 CFR 61.57)*
    DISCUSSION: For IFR currency, a pilot must meet the recent experience requirements within a 6-calendar-month period to continue to fly as PIC in instrument conditions. After that time, a pilot may meet the requirements within the next 6-calendar-month period but may not act as PIC in instrument conditions until the experience requirements are met. Following that time, the pilot would be required to complete an instrument proficiency check to regain PIC privileges in instrument conditions.
    Answer (B) is incorrect. A pilot has 6 calendar months, not 5, to maintain instrument currency and retain PIC privileges in instrument conditions. Answer (C) is incorrect. An IPC need only be completed if more than 12 calendar months have passed since the pilot was last qualified under the instrument recent experience requirements.

24. Which additional instrument experience, within the preceding 6 calendar months, is required to meet the requirements to act as pilot in command of an airplane under IFR if you already have 3 hours in an instrument simulator (including holding, intercepting, and tracking courses) and two instrument approaches in an airplane?

    A. Another two instrument approaches in an airplane.

    B. Another four instrument approaches in the same category and class.

    C. Another 3 hours of actual or simulated instrument flight time in the same category and class.

Answer (B) is correct. *(14 CFR 61.57)*
    DISCUSSION: Regulations require a total of six instrument approaches in the category and class of aircraft for which instrument currency is sought.
    Answer (A) is incorrect. Regulations require a total of six, not four, instrument approaches to maintain instrument currency. Answer (C) is incorrect. While the additional 3 hours of simulator time would meet that particular requirement, you would still be four instrument approaches short of that requirement.

25. A pilot has an IFR flight plan for July 10 of this year. What is the earliest date the pilot can meet the IFR experience requirements without having to take an IFR proficiency check?

    A. January 10 of this year.

    B. February 10 of this year.

    C. August of last year.

Answer (A) is correct. *(14 CFR 61.57)*
    DISCUSSION: A pilot flying IFR must have performed and logged specific tasks and iterations within the 6 calendar months preceding the month of the flight. January is the sixth month preceding the flight when the pilot met the experience requirements for IFR flight. If (s)he does not complete the requisite tasks before the end of July, a proficiency check would be required in order to exercise the privileges of an instrument-rated pilot.
    Answer (B) is incorrect. February is the fifth month preceding the month of the scheduled flight. The pilot meets the experience requirements to exercise the privileges of an instrument-rated pilot, but February is not the earliest date offered. Answer (C) is incorrect. August of last year is well beyond the 6-month limitation on the experience required to operate as a pilot in IFR conditions.

61.133 Commercial Pilot Privileges and Limitations

26. To carry passengers for hire in an airplane on cross-country flights of more than 50 NM from the departure airport, the pilot in command is required to hold at least

    A. a Category II pilot authorization.

    B. a First-Class Medical certificate.

    C. a Commercial Pilot Certificate with an instrument rating.

Answer (C) is correct. *(14 CFR 61.133)*

    DISCUSSION: To carry passengers for hire, the pilot in command is required to hold at least a commercial pilot certificate. Additionally, to carry those passengers for hire on cross-country flights of more than 50 NM (or at night), (s)he must also hold an instrument rating on the commercial certificate.

    Answer (A) is incorrect. Category II refers to an authorization for reduced ILS approach minimums. Answer (B) is incorrect. A first-class medical certificate is required for operations requiring an airline transport pilot certificate.

27. Which limitation is imposed on the holder of a Commercial Pilot Certificate if that person does not hold an instrument rating?

    A. That person is limited to private pilot privileges at night.

    B. The carrying of passengers or property for hire on cross-country flights at night is limited to a radius of 50 NM.

    C. The carrying of passengers for hire on cross-country flights is limited to 50 NM and the carrying of passengers for hire at night is prohibited.

Answer (C) is correct. *(14 CFR 61.133)*

    DISCUSSION: The applicant for a commercial pilot certificate must hold an instrument rating (airplane), or the commercial pilot certificate must be endorsed with a limitation prohibiting the carriage of passengers for hire in airplanes on cross-country flights of more than 50 NM or at night.

    Answer (A) is incorrect. That person may exercise commercial pilot privileges at night, but with limitations. Answer (B) is incorrect. No passengers may be carried at night without an instrument rating.

28. What limitation is imposed on a newly certificated commercial airplane pilot if that person does not hold an instrument pilot rating?

    A. The carrying of passengers or property for hire on cross-country flights at night is limited to a radius of 50 nautical miles (NM).

    B. The carrying of passengers for hire on cross-country flights is limited to 50 NM for night flights, but not limited for day flights.

    C. The carrying of passengers for hire on cross-country flights is limited to 50 NM and the carrying of passengers for hire at night is prohibited.

Answer (C) is correct. *(14 CFR 61.133)*

    DISCUSSION: The applicant for a commercial pilot certificate must hold an instrument rating (airplane), or the commercial pilot certificate must be endorsed with a limitation prohibiting the carriage of passengers for hire in airplanes on cross-country flights of more than 50 NM or at night.

    Answer (A) is incorrect. The carriage of property (freight) is not limited at night. Answer (B) is incorrect. No passengers may be carried at night, and the flight is limited to 50 NM, not unlimited, for day flights without an instrument rating.

29. A certificated commercial pilot who carries passengers for hire at night or in excess of 50 NM is required to have at least

    A. a type rating.

    B. a first-class medical certificate.

    C. an instrument rating in the same category of aircraft.

Answer (C) is correct. *(14 CFR 61.133)*

    DISCUSSION: A certificated commercial pilot who carries passengers for hire at night or in excess of 50 NM is required to have an instrument rating.

    Answer (A) is incorrect. Even if the airplane requires a type rating, the commercial pilot must have at least an instrument rating to carry passengers for hire at night or in excess of 50 NM. Answer (B) is incorrect. Only a second-class medical certificate is required of commercial pilots. First-class medical certificates are required of airline transport pilots.

30. You intend to carry passengers for hire on a night VFR flight in a single-engine airplane within a 25-mile radius of the departure airport. You are required to possess at least which rating(s)?

A. A Commercial Pilot Certificate with a single-engine land rating.

B. A Commercial Pilot Certificate with a single-engine and instrument (airplane) rating.

C. A Private Pilot Certificate with a single-engine land and instrument airplane rating.

Answer (B) is correct. *(14 CFR 61.133)*
DISCUSSION: A commercial pilot certificate with a single-engine airplane rating is required for a pilot to carry passengers for hire and to operate that class of aircraft. Also, an applicant for a commercial pilot certificate must hold an instrument rating (airplane), or the commercial pilot certificate will be endorsed with a limitation prohibiting carrying passengers for hire on cross-country flights of more than 50 NM or at night.
Answer (A) is incorrect. To carry passengers for hire at night, one must have an instrument rating as well as a commercial pilot certificate. Answer (C) is incorrect. A commercial, not private, pilot certificate is required to carry passengers for hire.

4.3 FAR PART 91

91.3 Responsibility and Authority of the Pilot in Command

31. Who is responsible for determining that the altimeter system has been checked and found to meet 14 CFR Part 91 requirements for a particular instrument flight?

A. Owner.

B. Operator.

C. Pilot-in-command.

Answer (C) is correct. *(14 CFR 91.3)*
DISCUSSION: The pilot in command of an aircraft is directly responsible for, and is the final authority as to, the airworthiness and operation of that aircraft.
Answer (A) is incorrect. The owner is primarily responsible for maintaining the aircraft, but the pilot in command is responsible for determining that the aircraft is airworthy. Answer (B) is incorrect. The operator is primarily responsible for maintaining the aircraft, but the pilot in command is responsible for determining that the aircraft is airworthy.

91.21 Portable Electronic Devices

32. The use of certain portable electronic devices is prohibited on aircraft that are being operated under

A. IFR.

B. VFR.

C. DVFR.

Answer (A) is correct. *(14 CFR 91.21)*
DISCUSSION: The use of portable electronic devices in carrier aircraft and other aircraft operated under IFR is prohibited. This prohibition does not apply to portable voice recorders, hearing aids, heart pacemakers, electric shavers, and other devices that do not interfere with the aircraft's navigation and communication systems.
Answer (B) is incorrect. Portable electronic devices are not prohibited in aircraft operated under VFR. Answer (C) is incorrect. Portable electronic devices are not prohibited in aircraft operated under DVFR (defense VFR).

91.103 Preflight Action

33. Before beginning any flight under IFR, the pilot in command must become familiar with all available information concerning that flight. In addition, the pilot must

A. list an alternate airport on the flight plan and become familiar with the instrument approaches to that airport.

B. list an alternate airport on the flight plan and confirm adequate takeoff and landing performance at the destination airport.

C. be familiar with the runway lengths at airports of intended use, and the alternatives available if the flight cannot be completed.

Answer (C) is correct. *(14 CFR 91.103)*
DISCUSSION: Each pilot in command shall, before beginning a flight, familiarize him/herself with all available information concerning that flight. For a flight under IFR or a flight not in the vicinity of an airport, this information should include weather reports and forecasts, fuel requirements, alternatives available if the planned flight cannot be completed, and any known traffic delays of which (s)he has been advised by ATC. For any flight, the preflight information should include runway lengths at airports of intended use and takeoff and landing distance data.
Answer (A) is incorrect. Listing an alternate airport is not required for all IFR flights, i.e., when the destination is forecast to have ceilings above 2,000 ft. and visibility of at least 3 SM. Answer (B) is incorrect. Listing an alternate airport is not required for all IFR flights, i.e., when the destination is forecast to have ceilings above 2,000 ft. and visibility of at least 3 SM.

34. Before beginning any flight under IFR, the pilot in command must become familiar with all available information concerning that flight including:

A. all instrument approaches at the destination airport.

B. an alternate airport and adequate takeoff and landing performance at the destination airport.

C. the runway lengths at airports of intended use, and the aircraft's takeoff and landing data.

Answer (C) is correct. *(14 CFR 91.103)*
DISCUSSION: Each pilot in command shall, before beginning a flight, familiarize him/herself with all available information concerning that flight. For a flight under IFR or a flight not in the vicinity of an airport, this information should include weather reports and forecasts, fuel requirements, alternatives available if the planned flight cannot be completed, and any known traffic delays of which (s)he has been advised by ATC. For any flight, the preflight information should include runway lengths at airports of intended use and takeoff and landing distance information.
Answer (A) is incorrect. While knowing what approaches are available is a good operating procedure, it is not a required preflight action. Answer (B) is incorrect. A pilot must be familiar with the airplane's takeoff and landing performance at all airports of intended use, not just the destination airport.

91.109 Flight Instruction; Simulated Instrument Flight and Certain Flight Tests

35. What are the minimum qualifications for a person who occupies the other control seat as safety pilot during simulated instrument flight?

A. Private pilot certificate with appropriate category and class ratings for the aircraft.

B. Private pilot with instrument rating.

C. Private pilot with appropriate category, class, and instrument ratings.

Answer (A) is correct. *(14 CFR 91.109)*
DISCUSSION: No person may operate a civil aircraft in simulated instrument flight unless the other control seat is occupied by a safety pilot who possesses at least a private pilot certificate with category and class ratings appropriate to the aircraft being flown.
Answer (B) is incorrect. The safety pilot's certificate must carry an appropriate category and class (but not instrument) rating; e.g., a private pilot (helicopter) may not act as safety pilot in an airplane. Answer (C) is incorrect. The safety pilot does not need to be instrument rated.

91.123 Compliance with ATC Clearances and Instructions

36. When may ATC request a detailed report of an emergency even though a rule has not been violated?

A. When priority has been given.

B. Any time an emergency occurs.

C. When the emergency occurs in controlled airspace.

Answer (A) is correct. *(14 CFR 91.123)*
DISCUSSION: Each pilot in command who is given priority by ATC in an emergency (even though no FAR has been violated) shall, if requested by ATC, submit a detailed report of that emergency within 48 hr. to the manager of that ATC facility.
Answer (B) is incorrect. A written report may be requested when priority is given in an emergency, not any time an emergency occurs. Answer (C) is incorrect. A written report may be requested when priority is given in an emergency, regardless of where the emergency occurs.

37. While on an IFR flight, a pilot has an emergency which causes a deviation from an ATC clearance. What action must be taken?

A. Notify ATC of the deviation as soon as possible.

B. Squawk 7700 for the duration of the emergency.

C. Submit a detailed report to the chief of the ATC facility within 48 hours.

Answer (A) is correct. *(14 CFR 91.123)*
DISCUSSION: Each pilot in command who, in an emergency, deviates from an ATC clearance or instruction shall notify ATC of that deviation as soon as possible.
Answer (B) is incorrect. In an emergency, you must report a deviation from an ATC clearance as soon as possible, not just squawk 7700 during the emergency. Answer (C) is incorrect. A report in 48 hr. is required only if you are given priority during the emergency and ATC requests such a report.

38. During an IFR flight in IMC, a distress condition is encountered, (fire, mechanical, or structural failure). The pilot should

A. not hesitate to declare an emergency and obtain an amended clearance.

B. wait until the situation is immediately perilous before declaring an emergency.

C. contact ATC and advise that an urgency condition exists and request priority consideration.

Answer (A) is correct. *(14 CFR 91.123, P/C Glossary)*
DISCUSSION: Distress is a condition of being threatened by serious and/or imminent danger and of requiring immediate assistance. Thus, during an IFR flight in IMC, if a distress condition is encountered, you should immediately declare an emergency and obtain an amended clearance.
Answer (B) is incorrect. A distress condition is perilous, and you should not hesitate to declare an emergency. Answer (C) is incorrect. You should contact ATC and declare that an emergency, not urgency, condition exists and obtain an amended clearance, not a request for consideration.

39. While on an IFR flight, a pilot has an emergency that causes a deviation from an ATC clearance. What action must be taken?

A. Deviate as necessary and squawk 7700 for the duration of the emergency.

B. Do not deviate until an amended ATC clearance is received and separation from other aircraft is assured.

C. Notify ATC of the deviation as soon as possible and obtain an amended ATC clearance.

Answer (C) is correct. *(14 CFR 91.123)*
DISCUSSION: A pilot may deviate from an ATC clearance if required to do so by an emergency, but the pilot must notify ATC of the deviation as soon as possible and, if on an IFR flight, obtain an amended clearance.
Answer (A) is incorrect. It is not necessary to squawk 7700 as a matter of course when encountering an emergency. However, if the pilot deviates from his or her clearance as a result of an emergency, (s)he is required to notify ATC of the deviation as soon as possible and, if on an IFR flight, obtain an amended clearance. Answer (B) is incorrect. In an emergency, a pilot is permitted to deviate from a clearance as necessary. However, the pilot must notify ATC of the deviation as soon as possible and, if on an IFR flight, obtain a new clearance.

91.129 Operations in Class D Airspace

40. Your transponder is inoperative. What are the requirements for flying in Class D airspace?

A. The entry into Class D is prohibited.

B. Continue the flight as planned.

C. Pilot must immediately request priority handling to proceed to destination.

Answer (B) is correct. *(14 CFR 91.129)*
DISCUSSION: If an aircraft's transponder fails during flight within Class D airspace, no deviation is required because a transponder is not required in Class D airspace.
Answer (A) is incorrect. Since a transponder is not required in Class D airspace, the pilot does not need to depart the Class D airspace. Answer (C) is incorrect. Since a transponder is not required in Class D airspace, a pilot does not need priority handling to proceed to his/her destination.

91.131 Operations in Class B Airspace

41. In addition to a VOR receiver and two-way communications capability, which additional equipment is required for IFR operation in Class B airspace?

A. DME and an operable coded transponder having Mode C capability.

B. Standby communications receiver, DME, and coded transponder.

C. An operable coded transponder having Mode C capability.

Answer (C) is correct. *(14 CFR 91.131)*
DISCUSSION: Unless otherwise authorized by ATC, no person may operate an aircraft within Class B airspace unless that aircraft is equipped with

1. An operable two-way radio,
2. An operable 4096-code transponder having Mode C capability, and
3. For IFR operations, an operable VOR or TACAN receiver.

Answer (A) is incorrect. DME is not required. Answer (B) is incorrect. A standby radio receiver and DME are not required, and the transponder must have Mode C capability.

42. Which of the following is required equipment for operating an aircraft within Class B airspace?

A. A 4096 code transponder with automatic pressure altitude reporting equipment.

B. A VOR receiver with DME.

C. A 4096 code transponder.

Answer (A) is correct. *(14 CFR 91.131)*
DISCUSSION: Unless otherwise authorized by ATC, no person may operate an aircraft within Class B airspace unless that aircraft is equipped with

1. An operable two-way radio,
2. An operable 4096-code transponder having Mode C capability, and
3. For IFR operations, an operable VOR or TACAN receiver.

Answer (B) is incorrect. DME is not required, and a VOR receiver is only required when operating IFR. Answer (C) is incorrect. The 4096-code transponder must also have Mode C capability.

91.135 Operations in Class A Airspace

43. When is an IFR clearance required during VFR weather conditions?

A. When operating in the Class E airspace.

B. When operating in a Class A airspace.

C. When operating in airspace above 14,500 feet.

Answer (B) is correct. *(14 CFR 91.135, 91.173)*
DISCUSSION: No person may operate an aircraft within Class A airspace unless the aircraft is operated under an IFR clearance, regardless of the weather conditions. Class A airspace includes the airspace from 18,000 ft. MSL up to and including FL 600.
Answer (A) is incorrect. An IFR clearance is not required in VMC in Class E airspace. Answer (C) is incorrect. An IFR clearance is not required in VMC in Class E airspace from 14,500 ft. MSL up to but not including 18,000 ft. MSL.

44. When is an IFR flight plan required?

A. When less than VFR conditions exist in either Class E or Class G airspace and in Class A airspace.

B. In all Class E airspace when conditions are below VFR, in Class A airspace, and in defense zone airspace.

C. In Class E airspace when IMC exists or in Class A airspace.

Answer (C) is correct. *(14 CFR 91.135, 91.173)*
DISCUSSION: No person may operate an aircraft in Class E airspace in IMC unless (s)he has filed an IFR flight plan and received an appropriate ATC clearance. Furthermore, under FAR 91.135, no one may operate in Class A airspace unless the aircraft is operated under IFR at a specific flight level assigned by ATC. This implies having filed an IFR flight plan for Class A airspace also.
Answer (A) is incorrect. While an instrument rating is required, an IFR flight plan is not required in Class G airspace. Answer (B) is incorrect. VFR flights are permitted when VFR weather conditions exist in air defense identification zones (ADIZ).

45. Operation in which airspace requires filing an IFR flight plan?

A. Any airspace when the visibility is less than 1 mile.

B. Class E airspace with IMC and Class A airspace.

C. Positive control area, Continental Control Area, and all other airspace, if the visibility is less than 1 mile.

Answer (B) is correct. *(14 CFR 91.135, 91.173)*
DISCUSSION: No person may operate an aircraft in Class E airspace in IMC unless (s)he has filed an IFR flight plan and received an appropriate ATC clearance. Furthermore, under FAR 91.135, no one may operate in Class A airspace unless the aircraft is operated under IFR at a specific flight level assigned by ATC. This implies having filed an IFR flight plan for Class A airspace also.
Answer (A) is incorrect. An IFR flight plan is not required in Class G airspace. Answer (C) is incorrect. An IFR flight plan is not required in uncontrolled Class G airspace.

46. When are you required to have an instrument rating for flight in VMC?

A. Flight through an MOA.

B. Flight into an ADIZ.

C. Flight into Class A airspace.

Answer (C) is correct. *(14 CFR 91.135)*
DISCUSSION: No person may operate an aircraft within Class A airspace at any time unless (s)he is rated for instrument flight and is on an instrument flight plan.
Answer (A) is incorrect. An instrument rating is not required for flight through an MOA in VMC. Answer (B) is incorrect. An instrument rating is not required for flight into an ADIZ (air defense identification zone) in VMC.

91.155 Basic VFR Weather Minimums

47. What is the required flight visibility and distance from clouds if you are operating in Class E airspace at 9,500 feet MSL with a VFR-on-Top clearance during daylight hours?

A. 3 SM, 1,000 feet above, 500 feet below, and 2,000 feet horizontal.

B. 5 SM, 500 feet above, 1,000 feet below, and 2,000 feet horizontal.

C. 3 SM, 500 feet above, 1,000 feet below, and 2,000 feet horizontal.

Answer (A) is correct. *(14 CFR 91.155)*
DISCUSSION: In Class E airspace below 10,000 ft. MSL, the basic VFR weather minimums are flight visibility of 3 SM and a distance from clouds of 500 ft. below, 1,000 ft. above, and 2,000 ft. horizontal.
Answer (B) is incorrect. The visibility requirement is 3, not 5, SM, and the distances from clouds above and below are reversed. It should be 1,000 ft. above and 500 ft. below. Answer (C) is incorrect. The distances from clouds above and below are reversed. It should be 1,000 ft. above and 500 ft. below.

48. What is the minimum flight visibility and distance from clouds for flight at 10,500 feet with a VFR-on-Top clearance during daylight hours? (Class E airspace.)

A. 3 SM, 1,000 feet above, 500 feet below, and 2,000 feet horizontal.

B. 5 SM, 1,000 feet above, 1,000 feet below, and 1 mile horizontal.

C. 5 SM, 1,000 feet above, 500 feet below, and 1 mile horizontal.

Answer (B) is correct. *(14 CFR 91.155)*
DISCUSSION: In Class E airspace at or above 10,000 ft. MSL, the basic VFR weather minimums are flight visibility of 5 SM and a distance from clouds of 1,000 ft. above or below and 1 SM horizontal.
Answer (A) is incorrect. The minimum flight visibility and distance from clouds in Class E airspace below, not at or above, 10,000 ft. MSL are 3 SM, 1,000 ft. above, 500 ft. below, and 2,000 ft. horizontal. Answer (C) is incorrect. The vertical separation from clouds is 1,000 ft. both above and below.

49. (Refer to Figure 92 below.) What is the minimum in-flight visibility and distance from clouds required for an airplane operating less than 1,200 feet AGL during daylight hours in area 6?

A. 3 miles; (I) 1,000 feet; (K) 2,000 feet; (L) 500 feet.

B. 1 mile; (I) clear of clouds; (K) clear of clouds; (L) clear of clouds.

C. 1 mile; (I) 500 feet; (K) 1,000 feet; (L) 500 feet.

Answer (B) is correct. *(14 CFR 91.155)*
DISCUSSION: In Class G airspace at or below 1,200 ft. AGL (area 6 in Fig. 92), the basic VFR weather minimums during daylight hours are in-flight visibility of 1 SM and clear of clouds. Answer (A) is incorrect. The minimum visibility and distance from clouds in VFR flight in area 6 at night, not in daylight, are 3 SM visibility, 1,000 ft. above, 500 ft. below, and 2,000 ft. horizontal. Answer (C) is incorrect. No such combination of requirements exists in any airspace.

50. (Refer to Figure 92 below.) What is the minimum in-flight visibility and distance from clouds required in VFR conditions above clouds at 13,500 feet MSL (above 1,200 feet AGL) in Class G airspace during daylight hours for area 2?

A. 5 miles; (A) 1,000 feet; (C) 2,000 feet; (D) 500 feet.

B. 3 miles; (A) 1,000 feet; (C) 1 mile; (D) 1,000 feet.

C. 5 miles; (A) 1,000 feet; (C) 1 mile; (D) 1,000 feet.

Answer (C) is correct. *(14 CFR 91.155)*
DISCUSSION: In Class G airspace at more than 1,200 ft. AGL and at or above 10,000 ft. MSL (area 2 in Fig. 92), the basic VFR weather minimums are in-flight visibility of 5 SM and a distance from clouds of 1,000 ft. above or below and 1 SM horizontal.
Answer (A) is incorrect. Distances of 1,000 ft. above, 2,000 ft. horizontal, and 500 ft. below are the minimum cloud distances for VFR in Class G airspace above 1,200 ft. AGL and below, not at or above, 10,000 ft. MSL. Answer (B) is incorrect. The visibility minimum is 5 SM, not 3 SM.

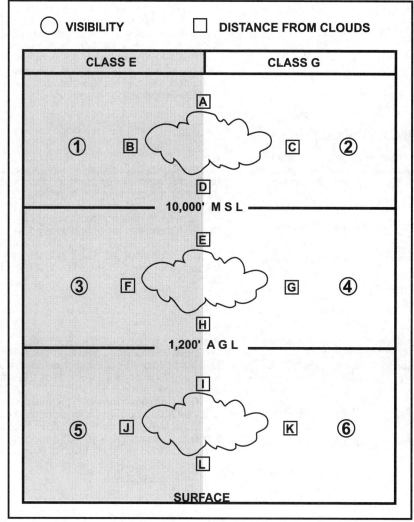

Figure 92. – Minimum In-Flight Visibility and Distance from Clouds.

51. (Refer to Figure 92 on page 124.) What is the minimum in-flight visibility and distance from clouds required for a VFR-on-Top flight at 9,500 feet MSL (above 1,200 feet AGL) during daylight hours for area 3?

A. 2,000 feet; (E) 1,000 feet; (F) 2,000 feet; (H) 500 feet.

B. 5 miles; (E) 1,000 feet; (F) 2,000 feet; (H) 500 feet.

C. 3 miles; (E) 1,000 feet; (F) 2,000 feet; (H) 500 feet.

Answer (C) is correct. *(14 CFR 91.155)*
    DISCUSSION: In Class E airspace at less than 10,000 ft. MSL (area 3 in Fig. 92), the basic VFR weather minimums are in-flight visibility of 3 SM and a distance from clouds of 500 ft. below, 1,000 ft. above, and 2,000 ft. horizontal.
    Answer (A) is incorrect. The visibility required is 3 SM, not 2,000 ft. Answer (B) is incorrect. The visibility required is 3 SM, not 5 SM.

52. (Refer to Figure 92 on page 124.) A flight is to be conducted in VFR-on-Top conditions at 12,500 feet MSL (above 1,200 feet AGL). What is the in-flight visibility and distance from clouds required for operation in Class E airspace during daylight hours for area 1?

A. 5 miles; (A) 1,000 feet; (B) 2,000 feet; (D) 500 feet.

B. 5 miles; (A) 1,000 feet; (B) 1 mile; (D) 1,000 feet.

C. 3 miles; (A) 1,000 feet; (B) 2,000 feet; (D) 1,000 feet.

Answer (B) is correct. *(14 CFR 91.155)*
    DISCUSSION: In Class E airspace at or above 10,000 ft. MSL (area 1 in Fig. 92), the basic VFR weather minimums are in-flight visibility of 5 SM and a distance from clouds of 1,000 ft. above or below and 1 SM horizontal.
    Answer (A) is incorrect. The distance-from-clouds requirements listed are for below, not at or above, 10,000 ft. MSL. Answer (C) is incorrect. The visibility requirement is 5 SM, not 3 SM, and the horizontal separation requirement from clouds is 1 SM, not 2,000 ft.

53. (Refer to Figure 92 on page 124.) What in-flight visibility and distance from clouds is required for a flight at 8,500 feet MSL (above 1,200 feet AGL) in Class G airspace in VFR conditions during daylight hours in area 4?

A. 1 mile; (E) 1,000 feet; (G) 2,000 feet; (H) 500 feet.

B. 3 miles; (E) 1,000 feet; (G) 2,000 feet; (H) 500 feet.

C. 5 miles; (E) 1,000 feet; (G) 1 mile; (H) 1,000 feet.

Answer (A) is correct. *(14 CFR 91.155)*
    DISCUSSION: In Class G airspace at more than 1,200 ft. AGL but less than 10,000 ft. MSL (area 4 in Fig. 92), the basic VFR weather minimums during daylight hours are in-flight visibility of 1 SM and a distance from clouds of 500 ft. below, 1,000 ft. above, and 2,000 ft. horizontal.
    Answer (B) is incorrect. The in-flight visibility of 3 SM is required for a night, not day, flight. Answer (C) is incorrect. In-flight visibility of 5 SM and a distance from clouds of 1,000 ft. above or below and 1 SM horizontal are the VFR weather minimums in Class G airspace above 1,200 ft. AGL and at or above, not below, 10,000 ft. MSL.

91.157 Special VFR Weather Minimums

54. (Refer to Figure 92 on page 124.) What is the minimum in-flight visibility and distance from clouds required for an airplane operating less than 1,200 feet AGL under special VFR during daylight hours in area 5?

A. 1 mile; (I) 2,000 feet; (J) 2,000 feet; (L) 500 feet.

B. 3 miles; (I) clear of clouds; (J) clear of clouds; (L) 500 feet.

C. 1 mile; (I) clear of clouds; (J) clear of clouds; (L) clear of clouds.

Answer (C) is correct. *(14 CFR 91.157)*
    DISCUSSION: In Class E airspace when an airplane is operating under special VFR, the distance-from-clouds requirement is clear of clouds. No one may take off or land an airplane under special VFR unless ground visibility is at least 1 SM. If ground visibility is not reported, the in-flight visibility during takeoff or landing must be at least 1 SM.
    Answer (A) is incorrect. Special VFR permits operation just clear of clouds. Answer (B) is incorrect. Special VFR permits operation just clear of clouds and with a minimum visibility of 1 SM, not 3 SM.

91.167 Fuel Requirements for Flight in IFR Conditions

55. What are the minimum fuel requirements in IFR conditions, if the first airport of intended landing is forecast to have a 1,500-foot ceiling and 3 miles visibility at flight-planned ETA? Fuel to fly to the first airport of intended landing,

A. and fly thereafter for 45 minutes at normal cruising speed.

B. fly to the alternate, and fly thereafter for 45 minutes at normal cruising speed.

C. fly to the alternate, and fly thereafter for 30 minutes at normal cruising speed.

Answer (B) is correct. *(14 CFR 91.167)*
DISCUSSION: In general, no person may operate a civil aircraft in IFR conditions unless it carries enough fuel (considering weather reports, forecasts, and conditions) to complete the flight to the first airport of intended landing, fly from that airport to the alternate airport, and fly after that for 45 min. at normal cruising speed.
Answer (A) is incorrect. An alternate airport is required because the destination airport, from 1 hr. before to 1 hr. after ETA, has a forecast ceiling of less than 2,000 ft. AGL. Answer (C) is incorrect. The fuel requirement after the alternate is 45 min., not 30 min.

56. During your preflight planning for an IFR flight, you determine that the first airport of intended landing has no instrument approach prescribed in 14 CFR part 97. The weather forecast for one hour before through one hour after your estimated time of arrival is 3,000 ft. scattered with 5 miles visibility. To meet the fuel requirements for this flight, you must be able to fly to the first airport of intended landing,

A. and then fly for 45 minutes at normal cruising speed.

B. then to the alternate airport, and then for 45 minutes at normal cruising speed.

C. then to the alternate airport, and then for 30 minutes at normal cruising speed.

Answer (B) is correct. *(14 CFR 91.167)*
DISCUSSION: You may not operate an aircraft (other than a helicopter) under IFR unless it carries sufficient fuel to fly to the first airport of intended landing, fly from that airport to the alternate airport, and fly thereafter for 45 minutes at normal cruising speed. An alternate airport is not required if the forecast weather conditions from one hour before to one hour after your estimated time of arrival call for a 2,000-ft. ceiling and 3 SM visibility, and your destination airport has at least one approved instrument approach procedure (IAP). Because your destination airport (first airport of intended landing) has no IAP, you must file an alternate airport and meet the applicable fuel requirements.
Answer (A) is incorrect. You are required to file an alternate airport and meet the applicable fuel requirements because your destination airport has no IAP. Answer (C) is incorrect. You would be required to carry fuel sufficient for only 30 minutes at normal cruising speed after flying to the alternate airport if you were flying a helicopter, not an airplane. Airplanes must be able to fly for 45 minutes at normal cruising speed.

91.169 IFR Flight Plan: Information Required

57. For aircraft other than helicopters, is an alternate airport required for an IFR flight to ATL (Atlanta Hartsfield) if the proposed ETA is 1930Z?

TAF KATL 121720Z 121818 20012KT 5SM HZ BKN030
 FM2000 3SM TSRA OVC025CB
 FM2200 33015G20KT P6SM BKN015 OVC040
BECMG 0608 02008KT BKN040 BECMG 1012 00000KT
 P6SM CLR=

A. Yes, because the ceiling could fall below 2,000 feet within 2 hours before to 2 hours after the ETA.

B. No, because the ceiling and visibility are forecast to remain at or above 1,000 feet and 3 miles, respectively.

C. No, because the ceiling and visibility are forecast to be at or above 2,000 feet and 3 miles within 1 hour before to 1 hour after the ETA.

Answer (C) is correct. *(14 CFR 91.169)*
DISCUSSION: Since the ETA is 1930Z, you must check the forecast from 1830Z to 2030Z. In the TAF given, you will use the first forecast period (which is valid from 1800 to 2000Z) and the second forecast period (which is valid from 2000 to 2200Z). The lowest visibility and ceiling are forecast from 2000 to 2200Z. The visibility is 3 SM, and the ceiling is 2,500 ft. Thus, no alternate airport is required because the ceiling and visibility are forecast to be at or above 2,000 ft. and 3 SM within 1 hr. before to 1 hr. after the ETA.
Answer (A) is incorrect. The time frame of concern is 1 hr., not 2 hr., before and after the ETA. Answer (B) is incorrect. The ceiling must remain at least 2,000 ft., not 1,000 ft., for an alternate not to be required.

58. Determine the alternate minimums for an airport with a precision approach procedure.

A. 400-foot ceiling and 2 miles visibility.

B. 600-foot ceiling and 2 miles visibility.

C. 800-foot ceiling and 2 miles visibility.

Answer (B) is correct. *(14 CFR 91.169)*
DISCUSSION: Unless otherwise authorized, no person may include an alternate airport that has a precision (ILS) approach in an IFR flight plan unless current weather forecasts indicate that at the ETA at the alternate airport the ceiling is at least 600 ft. and visibility is 2 SM.
Answer (A) is incorrect. A ceiling of 400 ft. is not a standard minimum ceiling used as an alternative airport minimum. Answer (C) is incorrect. The alternate airport minimums for nonprecision approaches are 800 ft. and 2 SM.

59. When a pilot elects to proceed to the selected alternate airport, which minimums apply for landing at the alternate?

A. 600-1 if the airport has an ILS.

B. Ceiling 200 feet above the published minimum; visibility 2 miles.

C. The landing minimums for the approach to be used.

Answer (C) is correct. *(14 CFR 91.169)*
DISCUSSION: When one goes to an alternate airport to land, the landing minimums for the particular approach, not the minimums for listing the airport as an alternate, are the minimums to be used for the approach.
Answer (A) is incorrect. To be listed on the flight plan as an alternate airport, the weather conditions at the estimated time of arrival at the alternate must be a 600-ft. ceiling and 2 SM, not 1 SM, visibility. Answer (B) is incorrect. The published approach minimums, not some adjustment thereof, should be used.

60. If a pilot elects to proceed to the selected alternate, the landing minimums used at that airport should be the

A. minimums specified for the approach procedure selected.

B. alternate minimums shown on the approach chart.

C. minimums shown for that airport in a separate listing of "IFR Alternate Minimums."

Answer (A) is correct. *(14 CFR 91.169)*
DISCUSSION: When one goes to an alternate airport to land, the landing minimums for the particular approach, not the minimums for listing the airport as an alternate, are the approach minimums to be used for the approach.
Answer (B) is incorrect. Alternate minimums shown on the approach chart refer to the weather conditions required to list that airport as an alternate on your IFR flight plan, not to land there. Answer (C) is incorrect. Alternate minimums shown on the approach chart refer to the weather conditions required to list that airport as an alternate on your IFR flight plan, not to land there.

61. What minimum weather conditions must be forecast for your ETA at an alternate airport, that has only a VOR approach with standard alternate minimums, for the airport to be listed as an alternate on the IFR flight plan?

A. 800-foot ceiling and 1 statute mile visibility.

B. 800-foot ceiling and 2 statute miles visibility.

C. 1,000-foot ceiling and visibility to allow descent from minimum en route altitude (MEA), approach, and landing under basic VFR.

Answer (B) is correct. *(14 CFR 91.169)*
DISCUSSION: Unless otherwise authorized, no one may include an alternate airport with only a nonprecision approach in an IFR flight plan unless current weather forecasts indicate that, at the ETA at the alternate airport, the ceiling will be at least 800 ft. and 2 SM visibility.
Answer (A) is incorrect. The visibility requirement is 2 SM, not 1 SM. Answer (C) is incorrect. If no instrument approach procedure is available at an airport, the ceiling and visibility minimums are those allowing descent from the MEA, approach, and landing under basic VFR.

62. For aircraft other than helicopters, what minimum weather conditions must be forecast for your ETA at an alternate airport that has a precision approach procedure, with standard alternate minimums, in order to list it as an alternate for the IFR flight?

A. 600-foot ceiling and 2 SM visibility at your ETA.

B. 600-foot ceiling and 2 SM visibility from 2 hours before to 2 hours after your ETA.

C. 800-foot ceiling and 2 SM visibility at your ETA.

Answer (A) is correct. *(14 CFR 91.169)*
DISCUSSION: Unless otherwise authorized, no person may include an alternate airport that has a precision (ILS) approach in an IFR flight plan unless current weather forecasts indicate that at the ETA at the alternate airport the ceiling is at least 600 ft. and visibility is 2 SM.
Answer (B) is incorrect. The alternate airport weather minimums apply to the ETA, not 2 hr. plus or minus. Answer (C) is incorrect. The alternate airport minimums for a nonprecision approach are 800 ft. and 2 SM.

63. For an airplane, determine the weather minimum conditions required at the destination airport to avoid listing an alternate on your IFR flight plan.

A. From 2 hours before to 2 hours after ETA, forecast ceiling 2,000, and visibility 2 and 1/2 miles.

B. From 2 hours before to 2 hours after ETA, forecast ceiling 3,000, and visibility 3 miles.

C. From 1 hour before to 1 hour after ETA, forecast ceiling 2,000, and visibility 3 miles.

Answer (C) is correct. *(14 CFR 91.169)*
DISCUSSION: An alternate airport is not required to be listed on an IFR flight plan if the destination airport has a standard instrument approach procedure available and, for at least 1 hr. before and 1 hr. after the estimated time of arrival, the weather reports or forecasts, or any combination of them, indicate

1. The ceiling will be at least 2,000 ft. above the airport elevation; and
2. The visibility will be at least 3 SM.

Answer (A) is incorrect. The destination weather condition forecast is from 1 hr., not 2 hr., before and after ETA, and the visibility must be at least 3 SM, not 2 1/2 SM. Answer (B) is incorrect. The destination weather condition forecast is from 1 hr., not 2 hr., before and after ETA, and the ceiling must be at least 2,000 ft. AGL, not 3,000 ft. AGL.

64. What are the minimum weather conditions that must be forecast to list an airport as an alternate when the airport has no approved IAP?

A. The ceiling and visibility at ETA, 2,000 feet and 3 miles, respectively.

B. The ceiling and visibility from 2 hours before until 2 hours after ETA, 2,000 feet and 3 miles, respectively.

C. The ceiling and visibility at ETA must allow descent from MEA, approach, and landing, under basic VFR.

Answer (C) is correct. *(14 CFR 91.169)*
DISCUSSION: Unless otherwise authorized, no one may include an alternate airport that has no instrument approach in an IFR flight plan unless current weather forecasts indicate that, at the ETA at the alternate airport, the ceiling and visibility will allow descent from the MEA, approach, and landing under basic VFR.
Answer (A) is incorrect. An alternate must be listed on your IFR flight plan unless the weather at your destination is forecast, from 1 hr. before to 1 hr. after ETA, to have a ceiling of 2,000 ft. and visibility of 3 SM. Answer (B) is incorrect. An alternate must be listed on your IFR flight plan, unless the weather at your destination is forecast, from 1 hr., not 2 hr., before to 1 hr. after ETA, to have at least a 2,000-ft. ceiling and visibility of 3 SM.

65. What standard minimums are required to list an airport as an alternate on an IFR flight plan if the airport has VOR approach only?

A. Ceiling and visibility at ETA, 800 feet and 2 miles, respectively.

B. Ceiling and visibility from 2 hours before until 2 hours after ETA, 800 feet and 2 miles, respectively.

C. Ceiling and visibility at ETA, 600 feet and 2 miles, respectively.

Answer (A) is correct. *(14 CFR 91.169)*
DISCUSSION: Unless otherwise authorized, no person may include an alternate airport that has only a VOR (i.e., nonprecision) approach in an IFR flight plan unless current weather forecasts indicate that at the ETA at the alternate airport the ceiling is at least 800 ft. and visibility is 2 SM.
Answer (B) is incorrect. The alternate airport weather minimums apply to the ETA, not 2 hr. plus or minus. Answer (C) is incorrect. The alternate airport weather minimums for a precision approach, i.e., ILS, are 600 ft. and 2 SM.

66. An airport without an authorized IAP may be included on an IFR flight plan as an alternate, if the current weather forecast indicates that the ceiling and visibility at the ETA will

A. allow for descent from the IAF to landing under basic VFR conditions.

B. be at least 1,000 feet and 1 mile.

C. allow for a descent from the MEA, approach, and a landing under basic VFR conditions.

Answer (C) is correct. *(14 CFR 91.169)*
DISCUSSION: Unless otherwise authorized, no person may include an alternate airport that does not have a standard instrument approach on an IFR flight plan unless current weather forecasts indicate that, at the ETA at the alternate airport, the ceiling and visibility will allow for a descent from the MEA, approach, and landing under basic VFR conditions.
Answer (A) is incorrect. Descent must be possible from the MEA, not the IAF (initial approach fix), under basic VFR conditions. Answer (B) is incorrect. A ceiling of 800 ft., not 1,000 ft., and visibility of 2 SM, not 1 SM, are the standard alternate airport weather minimums at ETA for a nonprecision approach procedure.

67. When an alternate airport is required, what are the weather minimums that must be forecast at the ETA for an alternate airport that has a precision approach procedure?

A. Ceiling 200 feet above the approach minimums and at least 1 statute mile visibility, but not less than the minimum visibility for the approach.

B. 600 foot ceiling and 2 statute miles visibility.

C. Ceiling 200 feet above field elevation and visibility 1 statute mile, but not less than the minimum visibility for the approach.

Answer (B) is correct. *(14 CFR 91.169)*
DISCUSSION: Unless otherwise authorized, no person may include an alternate airport that has a precision (ILS) approach in an IFR flight plan unless current weather forecasts indicate that, at the ETA at the alternate airport, the ceiling is at least 600 ft. and visibility is 2 SM.
Answer (A) is incorrect. The minimum ceiling is 600 ft., not 200 ft. above minimums, and 2 SM, not 1 SM, is the minimum visibility required to list an airport with a precision approach as an alternate. Answer (C) is incorrect. The alternate minimums for airports with precision approaches are 600 ft., not 200 ft., and 2 SM, not 1 SM.

91.171 VOR Equipment Check for IFR Operations

68. What is the maximum tolerance allowed for an operational VOR equipment check when using a VOT?

A. Plus or minus 4°.

B. Plus or minus 6°.

C. Plus or minus 8°.

Answer (A) is correct. *(14 CFR 91.171)*
DISCUSSION: When using a VOT for an operational VOR equipment check, the maximum permissible indicated bearing error is plus or minus 4°.
Answer (B) is incorrect. Plus or minus 6° is the maximum error allowed when using an airborne checkpoint. Answer (C) is incorrect. Plus or minus 8° is not an acceptable error for any type of VOR equipment check.

69. What record shall be made in the aircraft log or other permanent record by the pilot making the VOR operational check?

    A. The date, place, bearing error, and signature.

    B. The date, frequency of VOR or VOT, number of flight hours since last check, and signature.

    C. The date, place, bearing error, aircraft total time, and signature.

Answer (A) is correct. *(14 CFR 91.171)*
    DISCUSSION: Each person making the VOR operational check shall enter the date, place, and bearing error and sign the aircraft log or other record.
    Answer (B) is incorrect. VOR frequency and number of flight hr. since last check are not required. Answer (C) is incorrect. The aircraft's total time is not required.

70. When must an operational check on the aircraft VOR equipment be accomplished when used to operate under IFR?

    A. Within the preceding 10 days or 10 hours of flight time.

    B. Within the preceding 30 days or 30 hours of flight time.

    C. Within the preceding 30 days.

Answer (C) is correct. *(14 CFR 91.171)*
    DISCUSSION: No person may operate a civil aircraft under IFR using the VOR system of radio navigation unless the VOR equipment of that aircraft is maintained, checked, and inspected under an approved procedure, or has been operationally checked within the preceding 30 days and was found to be within the limits of the permissible indicated bearing error.
    Answer (A) is incorrect. It must be checked every 30 days, not 10 days or 10 hr. Answer (B) is incorrect. There is no time requirement regarding hours of flight time.

71. Which data must be recorded in the aircraft log or other appropriate log by a pilot making a VOR operational check for IFR operations?

    A. VOR name or identification, date of check, amount of bearing error, and signature.

    B. Place of operational check, amount of bearing error, date of check, and signature.

    C. Date of check, VOR name or identification, place of operational check, and amount of bearing error.

Answer (B) is correct. *(14 CFR 91.171)*
    DISCUSSION: Each person making the VOR operational check shall enter the date, place, and bearing error and sign the aircraft log or other record.
    Answer (A) is incorrect. The place of operational check rather than the VOR name or identification is required. Answer (C) is incorrect. A signature is required, but the VOR name is not required.

72. Which checks and inspections of flight instruments or instrument systems must be accomplished before an aircraft can be flown under IFR?

    A. VOR within 30 days, altimeter systems within 24 calendar months, and transponder within 24 calendar months.

    B. ELT test within 30 days, altimeter systems within 12 calendar months, and transponder within 24 calendar months.

    C. VOR within 24 calendar months, transponder within 24 calendar months, and altimeter system within 12 calendar months.

Answer (A) is correct. *(14 CFR 91.171, 91.411, 91.413)*
    DISCUSSION: No person may operate a civil aircraft under IFR using the VOR system of radio navigation unless the VOR equipment of that aircraft is maintained, checked, and inspected under an approved procedure, or has been operationally checked within the preceding 30 days and was found to be within the limits of the permissible indicated bearing error. Also, within the preceding 24 calendar months, each altimeter system and transponder must be tested, inspected, and found to comply with the regulations.
    Answer (B) is incorrect. Check and inspection of the altimeter system is required every 24 months, not 12 months, and ELTs must be inspected every 12 months, not tested within 30 days. Answer (C) is incorrect. VORs must be checked within 30 days, not 24 months, and altimeter systems must be inspected within 24 months, not 12 months.

91.173 ATC Clearance and Flight Plan Required

73. When departing from an airport located outside controlled airspace during IMC, you must file an IFR flight plan and receive a clearance before

    A. takeoff.

    B. entering IFR conditions.

    C. entering Class E airspace.

Answer (C) is correct. *(14 CFR 91.173)*
    DISCUSSION: No person may operate an aircraft in controlled airspace under IFR unless (s)he has filed an IFR flight plan and received an appropriate ATC clearance.
    Answer (A) is incorrect. An IFR flight plan and clearance are not required until you enter controlled airspace. Answer (B) is incorrect. An IFR flight plan and clearance are not required until you enter controlled airspace.

74. To operate an aircraft under IFR, a flight plan must have been filed and an ATC clearance received prior to

    A. controlling the aircraft solely by use of instruments.

    B. entering weather conditions in any airspace.

    C. entering controlled airspace.

Answer (C) is correct. *(14 CFR 91.173)*
    DISCUSSION: No person may operate an aircraft in controlled airspace under IFR unless (s)he has filed an IFR flight plan and received an appropriate ATC clearance.
    Answer (A) is incorrect. An IFR flight plan and clearance are not required until you enter controlled airspace. Answer (B) is incorrect. An IFR flight plan and clearance are not required until you enter controlled airspace.

75. To operate under IFR below 18,000 feet, a pilot must file an IFR flight plan and receive an appropriate ATC clearance prior to

    A. entering controlled airspace.

    B. entering weather conditions below VFR minimums.

    C. takeoff.

Answer (A) is correct. *(14 CFR 91.173)*
    DISCUSSION: No person may operate an aircraft in controlled airspace under IFR unless (s)he has filed an IFR flight plan and received an appropriate ATC clearance.
    Answer (B) is incorrect. An IFR flight plan and clearance are not required until you enter controlled airspace. Answer (C) is incorrect. An IFR flight plan and clearance are not required until you enter controlled airspace.

76. Prior to which operation must an IFR flight plan be filed and an appropriate ATC clearance received?

    A. Flying by reference to instruments in controlled airspace.

    B. Entering controlled airspace when IMC exists.

    C. Takeoff when IFR weather conditions exist.

Answer (B) is correct. *(14 CFR 91.173)*
    DISCUSSION: No person may operate an aircraft in controlled airspace when instrument meteorological conditions (IMC) exist unless (s)he has filed an IFR flight plan and received an appropriate ATC clearance.
    Answer (A) is incorrect. You may fly by reference to instruments with a safety pilot in VFR weather conditions without an IFR flight plan or an IFR clearance. Answer (C) is incorrect. An IFR flight plan is not required until you enter controlled airspace.

77. No person may operate an aircraft in controlled airspace under IFR unless he/she files a flight plan

    A. and receives a clearance by telephone prior to takeoff.

    B. prior to takeoff and requests the clearance upon arrival on an airway.

    C. and receives a clearance prior to entering controlled airspace.

Answer (C) is correct. *(14 CFR 91.173)*
    DISCUSSION: No person may operate an aircraft in controlled airspace under IFR unless (s)he has filed an IFR flight plan and received an appropriate ATC clearance.
    Answer (A) is incorrect. It does not matter how the clearance is obtained. Answer (B) is incorrect. A person must file an IFR flight plan and receive clearance before operating in controlled airspace, e.g., a federal airway.

91.177 Minimum Altitudes for IFR Operations

78. Except when necessary for takeoff or landing or unless otherwise authorized by the Administrator, the minimum altitude for IFR flight is

    A. 3,000 feet over all terrain.

    B. 3,000 feet over designated mountainous terrain; 2,000 feet over terrain elsewhere.

    C. 2,000 feet above the highest obstacle over designated mountainous terrain; 1,000 feet above the highest obstacle over terrain elsewhere.

Answer (C) is correct. *(14 CFR 91.177)*
    DISCUSSION: Except when necessary for takeoff or landing, no person may operate an aircraft under IFR below 2,000 ft. above the highest obstacle within a horizontal distance of 4 NM from the course to be flown over designated mountainous terrain, or 1,000 ft. above the highest obstacle within a horizontal distance of 4 NM from the course to be flown over terrain elsewhere.
    Answer (A) is incorrect. The minimum IFR altitude is 2,000 ft. above the highest obstacle over mountainous terrain or 1,000 ft. over the highest obstacle over terrain elsewhere, not 3,000 ft. over all terrain. Answer (B) is incorrect. The minimum IFR altitude is 2,000 ft., not 3,000 ft., above the highest obstacle over mountainous terrain, or 1,000 ft., not 2,000 ft., above the highest obstacle over terrain elsewhere.

79. Unless otherwise prescribed, what is the rule regarding altitude and course to be maintained during an IFR off airways flight over mountainous terrain?

A. 1,000 feet above the highest obstacle within a horizontal distance of 5 NM of course.

B. 2,000 feet above the highest obstacle within a horizontal distance of 4 NM of course.

C. 7,500 feet above the highest obstacle within a horizontal distance of 3 NM of course.

Answer (B) is correct. *(14 CFR 91.177)*

DISCUSSION: If no applicable minimum is prescribed, an altitude of 2,000 feet above the highest obstacle within a horizontal distance of 4 NM from the course to be flown is mandated.

Answer (A) is incorrect. The mandated altitude minimum above obstacles in mountainous terrain is 2,000 feet, not 1,000 feet, and the horizontal distance requirement is 4 NM, not 5 NM. Answer (C) is incorrect. The mandated altitude minimum above obstacles in mountainous terrain is 2,000 feet, not 7,500 feet, and the horizontal distance requirement is 4 NM, not 3 NM.

91.205 Powered Civil Aircraft with Standard Category U.S. Airworthiness Certificates: Instrument and Equipment Requirements

80. What minimum navigation equipment is required for IFR flight?

A. VOR/LOC receiver, transponder, and DME.

B. VOR receiver and, if in ARTS III environment, a coded transponder equipped for altitude reporting.

C. Navigation equipment appropriate to the ground facilities to be used.

Answer (C) is correct. *(14 CFR 91.205)*

DISCUSSION: The minimum navigation equipment requirement for IFR flight is navigation equipment that is appropriate to the ground facilities to be used.

Answer (A) is incorrect. A VOR/LOC receiver and DME are required only if VORTAC stations will be used for navigation and DME fixes need to be identified. If you are using alternative means of navigation (e.g., LORAN), this equipment is not needed. A transponder is not a navigation system. Answer (B) is incorrect. A VOR is required only if using VOR stations for navigation. A transponder is not a navigation system.

81. An aircraft operated during IFR under 14 CFR Part 91 is required to have which of the following?

A. Radar altimeter.

B. Dual VOR system.

C. Gyroscopic direction indicator.

Answer (C) is correct. *(14 CFR 91.205)*

DISCUSSION: An aircraft operated during IFR under FAR Part 91 is required to have a gyroscopic direction indicator (directional gyro or equivalent).

Answer (A) is incorrect. Only a sensitive altimeter, not a radar altimeter, is required. Answer (B) is incorrect. If VOR navigation is to be used, only one, not two, VOR is required under FAR Part 91.

82. Aircraft being operated under IFR are required to have, in addition to the equipment required for VFR and night, at least

A. a slip skid indicator.

B. dual VOR receivers.

C. distance measuring equipment.

Answer (A) is correct. *(14 CFR 91.205)*

DISCUSSION: An aircraft operated under FAR Part 91 under IFR is required to have a slip-skid indicator (e.g., the ball of the turn coordinator).

Answer (B) is incorrect. The requirement is for navigational equipment appropriate to the ground facilities to be used, not necessarily dual VOR receivers. Answer (C) is incorrect. DME is required only above 24,000 ft. MSL when VOR navigational equipment is required.

83. Where is DME required under IFR?

A. At or above 24,000 feet MSL if VOR navigational equipment is required.

B. In positive control airspace.

C. Above 18,000 feet MSL.

Answer (A) is correct. *(14 CFR 91.205)*

DISCUSSION: If VOR navigational equipment is required, no person may operate a U.S.-registered civil aircraft within the 50 states and the District of Columbia, at or above 24,000 ft. MSL (FL 240), unless that aircraft is equipped with approved distance measuring equipment (DME).

Answer (B) is incorrect. If VOR navigational equipment is required, DME is required at or above FL 240, not only in positive control airspace. Positive control airspace is that airspace in which ATC separates all aircraft, e.g., Class A, Class B, Class C. Answer (C) is incorrect. Class A airspace begins at 18,000 ft. MSL, and DME is required at or above FL 240, if VOR navigational equipment is required.

84. To meet the requirements for flight under IFR, an aircraft must be equipped with certain operable instruments and equipment. One of those required is

A. a radar altimeter.

B. a transponder with altitude reporting capability.

C. a clock with sweep second pointer or digital presentation.

Answer (C) is correct. *(14 CFR 91.205)*
DISCUSSION: An aircraft operated under FAR Part 91 under IFR is required to have a clock displaying hours, minutes, and seconds with a sweep-second pointer or digital presentation.
Answer (A) is incorrect. A radio (radar) altimeter is required under some circumstances for Category II operations with decision heights below 150 ft. AGL, not for all flights under IFR. Answer (B) is incorrect. A transponder with altitude encoding capability is required in certain airspace areas, not for all flights under IFR.

91.211 Supplemental Oxygen

85. What is the oxygen requirement for an unpressurized aircraft at 15,000 feet?

A. All occupants must use oxygen for the entire time at this altitude.

B. Crew must start using oxygen at 12,000 feet and passengers at 15,000 feet.

C. Crew must use oxygen for the entire time above 14,000 feet and passengers must be provided supplemental oxygen only above 15,000 feet.

Answer (C) is correct. *(14 CFR 91.211)*
DISCUSSION: No one may operate a U.S. civil aircraft at cabin pressure altitudes above 14,000 ft. MSL unless the required minimum flight crew is provided with and uses supplemental oxygen during the entire flight time at those altitudes. At cabin pressure altitudes above 15,000 ft. MSL, each passenger must be provided with supplemental oxygen.
Answer (A) is incorrect. The required minimum flight crew must use oxygen above 14,000 ft. MSL, and others must be provided with oxygen above 15,000 ft. MSL. Answer (B) is incorrect. The crew must start using oxygen above 14,000 ft. MSL or after 30 min. above 12,500 ft. MSL.

86. What is the maximum IFR altitude you may fly in an unpressurized aircraft without providing passengers with supplemental oxygen?

A. 12,500 feet.

B. 14,000 feet.

C. 15,000 feet.

Answer (C) is correct. *(14 CFR 91.211)*
DISCUSSION: At cabin pressure altitudes above 15,000 ft. MSL, each occupant must be provided with supplemental oxygen.
Answer (A) is incorrect. At cabin pressure altitudes above 12,500 ft. MSL up to and including 14,000 ft. MSL, only the minimum flight crew must use supplemental oxygen for that part of the flight at those altitudes that is more than 30 min. duration. Answer (B) is incorrect. At cabin pressure altitudes above 14,000 ft MSL, only the required minimum flight crew must use supplemental oxygen.

87. What is the maximum cabin pressure altitude at which a pilot can fly for longer than 30 minutes without using supplemental oxygen?

A. 10,500 feet.

B. 12,000 feet.

C. 12,500 feet.

Answer (C) is correct. *(14 CFR 91.211)*
DISCUSSION: No one may operate a U.S. civil aircraft at cabin pressure altitudes above 12,500 ft. MSL up to and including 14,000 ft. MSL unless the required minimum flight crew uses supplemental oxygen for that part of the flight at those altitudes that is of more than 30 min. duration.
Answer (A) is incorrect. Supplemental oxygen is not required at any time at 10,500 ft. Answer (B) is incorrect. Supplemental oxygen is not required at any time at 12,000 ft.

88. If an unpressurized aircraft is operated above 12,500 feet MSL, but not more than 14,000 feet MSL, for a period of 2 hours 20 minutes, how long during that time is the minimum flightcrew required to use supplemental oxygen?

A. 2 hours 20 minutes.

B. 1 hour 20 minutes.

C. 1 hour 50 minutes.

Answer (C) is correct. *(14 CFR 91.211)*
DISCUSSION: No one may operate a U.S. civil aircraft at cabin pressure altitudes above 12,500 ft. MSL up to and including 14,000 ft. MSL unless the required minimum flight crew uses supplemental oxygen for that part of the flight at those altitudes that is of more than 30 min. duration. If the flight lasts 2 hr. and 20 min., the crew must use supplemental oxygen for all but 30 min., or 1 hr. and 50 min.
Answer (A) is incorrect. One may fly for 30 min. without supplemental oxygen between 12,500 ft. MSL and 14,000 ft. MSL. Answer (B) is incorrect. Thirty minutes of flight, not 1 hr., is permitted without supplemental oxygen between 12,500 ft. MSL up to and including 14,000 ft. MSL.

91.215 ATC Transponder and Altitude Reporting Equipment and Use

89. In the 48 contiguous states, excluding the airspace at or below 2,500 feet AGL, an operable coded transponder equipped with Mode C capability is required in all controlled airspace at and above

    A. 12,500 feet MSL.

    B. 10,000 feet MSL.

    C. Flight level (FL) 180.

Answer (B) is correct. *(14 CFR 91.215)*
    DISCUSSION: Unless otherwise authorized or directed by ATC, no person may operate an aircraft in the 48 contiguous states at and above 10,000 ft. MSL, excluding the airspace at or below 2,500 ft. AGL, unless the aircraft is equipped with an operable Mode C transponder.
    Answer (A) is incorrect. This figure pertains to supplemental oxygen, not Mode C, requirements. Answer (C) is incorrect. FL 180 is the floor of Class A airspace.

90. A coded transponder equipped with altitude reporting capability is required in all controlled airspace

    A. at and above 10,000 feet MSL, excluding at and below 2,500 feet AGL.

    B. at and above 2,500 feet above the surface.

    C. below 10,000 feet MSL, excluding at and below 2,500 feet AGL.

Answer (A) is correct. *(14 CFR 91.215)*
    DISCUSSION: Unless otherwise authorized or directed by ATC, no person may operate an aircraft in the 48 contiguous states at and above 10,000 ft. MSL, excluding the airspace at or below 2,500 ft. AGL, unless the aircraft is equipped with an operable Mode C transponder.
    Answer (B) is incorrect. The airspace above 2,500 ft. AGL must also be at or above 10,000 ft. MSL. Answer (C) is incorrect. The limit is at and above, not below, 10,000 ft. MSL.

91. Prior to operating an aircraft not equipped with a transponder in Class B airspace, a request for a deviation must be submitted to the

    A. FAA Administrator at least 24 hours before the proposed operation.

    B. nearest FAA General Aviation District Office 24 hours before the proposed operation.

    C. controlling ATC facility at least 1 hour before the proposed flight.

Answer (C) is correct. *(14 CFR 91.215)*
    DISCUSSION: ATC may authorize deviations on a continuing basis, or for individual flights, for operations of aircraft without a transponder. The request for a deviation must be submitted to the ATC facility having jurisdiction over the airspace concerned at least 1 hr. before the proposed operation.
    Answer (A) is incorrect. A request for a deviation to operate in Class B airspace in an airplane not equipped with a transponder must be submitted to the controlling ATC facility at least 1 hr. before the proposed flight, not to the FAA Administrator at least 24 hr. before the operation. Answer (B) is incorrect. A request for a deviation to operate in Class B airspace in an airplane not equipped with a transponder must be submitted to the controlling ATC facility at least 1 hr. before the proposed flight, not to the nearest FSDO (formerly called GADO) 24 hr. before the proposed operation.

92. When an aircraft is not equipped with a transponder, what requirement must be met before ATC will authorize a flight within Class B airspace?

    A. A request for the proposed flight must be made to ATC at least 1 hour before the flight.

    B. The proposed flight must be conducted when operating under instrument flight rules.

    C. The proposed flight must be conducted in visual meteorological conditions (VMC).

Answer (A) is correct. *(14 CFR 91.215)*
    DISCUSSION: Requests for ATC authorized deviations must be made to the ATC facility having jurisdiction over the concerned airspace. A request for a deviation from the transponder equipment requirement in Class B airspace must be made to the controlling ATC facility at least 1 hr. before the flight.
    Answer (B) is incorrect. You must request a deviation from the transponder equipment requirement from ATC. The requirement is not that the proposed flight be conducted under IFR. Answer (C) is incorrect. You must request a deviation from the transponder equipment requirement from ATC. The requirement is not that the proposed flight be conducted in VMC.

93. If the aircraft's transponder fails during flight within Class B airspace,

    A. the pilot should immediately request clearance to depart the Class B airspace.

    B. ATC may authorize deviation from the transponder requirement to allow aircraft to continue to the airport of ultimate destination.

    C. aircraft must immediately descend below 1,200 feet AGL and proceed to destination.

Answer (B) is correct. *(14 CFR 91.215)*
    DISCUSSION: If an aircraft's transponder fails during flight within Class B airspace, ATC may authorize deviation from the transponder requirement to allow the aircraft to continue to the airport of ultimate destination, including any intermediate stops, or to proceed to a place where suitable repairs can be made, or both.
    Answer (A) is incorrect. ATC can immediately authorize a deviation from the transponder requirement without requiring the pilot to request clearance to depart the Class B airspace area. Answer (C) is incorrect. A pilot may descend only if clearance from ATC is obtained.

91.411 Altimeter System and Altitude Reporting Equipment Tests and Inspections

94. Your aircraft had the static pressure system and altimeter tested and inspected on January 5, of this year, and was found to comply with FAA standards. These systems must be reinspected and approved for use in controlled airspace under IFR by

    A.   January 5, next year.

    B.   January 5, 2 years hence.

    C.   January 31, 2 years hence.

Answer (C) is correct. *(14 CFR 91.411)*
    DISCUSSION: Within the preceding 24 calendar months, each static pressure system, each altimeter instrument, and each automatic pressure altitude reporting system must be tested, inspected, and found to comply with the regulations. The 24-calendar-month period following January of this year begins February 1, this year, and ends on January 31, 2 years hence.
    Answer (A) is incorrect. These tests must be completed every 24 calendar months, not 1 year from the date of the last inspection. Answer (B) is incorrect. These tests must be completed within the preceding 24 calendar months, not 2 years from the date of the last inspection.

95. An aircraft altimeter system test and inspection must be accomplished within

    A.   12 calendar months.

    B.   18 calendar months.

    C.   24 calendar months.

Answer (C) is correct. *(14 CFR 91.411)*
    DISCUSSION: Within the preceding 24 calendar months, each static pressure system, each altimeter instrument, and each automatic pressure altitude reporting system must be tested, inspected, and found to comply with the regulations.
    Answer (A) is incorrect. An annual inspection, not the altimeter system, must be accomplished within the preceding 12 calendar months. Answer (B) is incorrect. The aircraft's altimeter system must be tested and inspected within 24, not 18, calendar months.

96. An aircraft altimeter system test and inspection are required to be accomplished within

    A.   18 calendar months of operating in IMC conditions.

    B.   24 calendar months of operating in IMC conditions.

    C.   24 calendar months of operating under IFR in controlled airspace.

Answer (C) is correct. *(14 CFR 91.411)*
    DISCUSSION: To operate under IFR in controlled airspace, each static pressure system, altimeter instrument, and automatic pressure altitude reporting system must be tested, inspected, and found to comply with the regulations every 24 calendar months.
    Answer (A) is incorrect. Regulation requires an altimeter inspection every 24 calendar months, not every 18 calendar months. Furthermore, the requirement limits operations under IFR in controlled airspace, not just in IMC conditions. Answer (B) is incorrect. The regulation limits operations under IFR in controlled airspace, not just in IMC conditions.

4.4   NTSB Part 830

97. Which publication covers the procedures required for aircraft accident and incident reporting responsibilities for pilots?

    A.   FAR Part 61.

    B.   FAR Part 91.

    C.   NTSB Part 830.

Answer (C) is correct. *(NTSB 830.1)*
    DISCUSSION: NTSB Part 830 contains rules pertaining to the following:

1.   Notification and reporting aircraft accidents and incidents and certain other occurrences in the operation of aircraft when they involve civil aircraft of the U.S. wherever they occur, or foreign civil aircraft when such events occur in the U.S., its territories, or possessions
2.   Reporting aircraft accidents and listed incidents in the operation of aircraft when they involve certain public aircraft
3.   Preservation of aircraft wreckage, mail, cargo, and records involving all civil aircraft in the U.S., its territories, or possessions

    Answer (A) is incorrect. FAR Part 61 concerns certification of pilots, flight instructors, and ground instructors. Answer (B) is incorrect. FAR Part 91 concerns general operating and flight rules.

END OF STUDY UNIT

STUDY UNIT FIVE
AIRPORTS, AIR TRAFFIC CONTROL, AND AIRSPACE

(11 pages of outline)

This study unit contains outlines of major concepts tested; sample test questions and answers regarding airports, air traffic control, and airspace; and an explanation of each answer. The table of contents above lists each subunit within this study unit, the number of questions pertaining to that particular subunit, and the pages on which the outlines and questions begin, respectively.

Recall that the **sole purpose** of this book is to expedite your passing of the FAA pilot knowledge test for the instrument rating. Accordingly, all extraneous material (i.e., topics or regulations not directly tested on the FAA pilot knowledge test) is omitted, even though much more knowledge is necessary to fly safely. This additional material is presented in *Pilot Handbook*, *Aviation Weather and Weather Services*, *FAR/AIM*, and *Instrument Pilot Flight Maneuvers and Practical Test Prep*, available from Gleim Publications, Inc. Order online at www.gleim.com.

5.1 PRECISION INSTRUMENT RUNWAY MARKINGS

1. The figure below depicts a precision instrument runway.

   a. The distance from the runway threshold to the fixed distance marker is 1,000 ft. (distance A).

   b. The distance from the runway threshold to the touchdown zone marker is 500 ft. (distance B).

   c. The distance from the beginning of the touchdown zone marker to the beginning of the fixed distance marker is 500 ft. (distance C).

PRECISION INSTRUMENT RUNWAY

2.   A displaced threshold is a threshold that is not at the beginning of a runway. It is indicated by arrows in the middle of the runway pointing to a broad, solid line across the runway. The remainder of the runway, following the displaced threshold, is the landing portion of the runway.

   a.   The paved area before the displaced threshold is available for taxiing, the landing rollout, and the takeoff of aircraft, but not for landing.

   b.   In the runway diagram below, the approach end of the runway is on the right. Thus, taxiing and takeoff are permitted toward the green threshold lights (marked by the arrow).

Figure 138. – Runway Legend.

3.   Runway end identifier lights (REIL) consist of a pair of synchronized flashing lights, one on each side of the runway threshold facing the approach area.

   a.   REIL permit the rapid and positive identification of a runway surrounded by other lighting, lacking contrast with surrounding terrain, and/or experiencing reduced visibility.

4.   Hydroplaning occurs when an aircraft's tires are separated from the runway by water.

   a.   It usually occurs at high speeds when water is standing on a smooth runway.

5.2 AIRPORT SIGNS AND MARKINGS

1.   Mandatory airport instruction signs have a red background with white lettering. Mandatory instruction signs include

   a.   Runway approach area holding position signs and runway holding position signs

      1)   These signs denote an entrance to a runway from a taxiway or from an intersecting runway.

   b.   No entry signs (example on the next page)

      1)   These signs denote paved areas where aircraft entry is prohibited.

2. Runway holding position markings (hold lines) at the intersection of taxiways and runways consist of four yellow lines, two solid and two dashed, that extend across the width of the taxiway with the dashed lines nearest the runway.

   a. These markings identify where an aircraft is to hold short of the runway.

3. The ILS critical area boundary sign identifies the edge of the ILS critical area.

   a. These signs indicate the area where, when an ILS is in use, aircraft must hold short to prevent blocking or interfering with the ILS glide slope antenna installed at the airport.

   b. These signs have a yellow background and black lines that look like a sideways ladder.

No Entry

RED

YELLOW   Runway Boundary

YELLOW

ILS Critical Area Boundary

4. Direction signs consist of black lettering on a yellow background.

   a. A taxiway directional sign indicates the designation (name) and direction (orientation) of taxiways leading out of an intersection.

   b. A runway exit sign indicates the designation and direction of an exit taxiway from the runway.

5. Destination signs direct pilots to a destination on the airport, such as runways, taxiways, aprons, terminals, FBOs, cargo areas, civil aviation areas, and military areas.

5.3 VISUAL APPROACH SLOPE INDICATOR (VASI)

1. Visual approach slope indicators (VASIs) are a system of lights that provide visual descent information during the approach to a runway.

2. The standard VASI consists of a two-barred tier of lights.

    a. If both light bars appear red, you are below the glide path. Remember this with the mnemonic, "red means dead."

    b. If the far lights (on top visually) appear red and the near lights (on bottom visually) appear white, you are on the glide path.

        1) This glide path is normally set at 3°.

    c. If both light bars appear white, you are above the glide path.

3. Actually, each light bar marks a separate glide path. The far light bar marks a higher glide path than the glide path extended from the nearer light bar. You are between them when you are below the higher glide path and above the lower glide path.

    a. Remember that red over white (if it helps, R before W alphabetically) is the desired sequence.

        1) White over red is impossible.

4. VASIs also may have three light bars, which provide a lower glide path and a higher glide path. The higher glide path marked by the middle and far light bars is intended for use by high cockpit aircraft.

    a. If the nearest light bar is white and the two farther light bars are red, you are on the lower glide path, usually 3°.

    b. If the farthest light bar is red and the two nearer light bars are white, you are on the upper glide path, usually 3.25°.

    c. Above both glide paths, all lights will be white. Below both glide paths, all lights will be red.

5. If all VASI lights appear red as you reach the MDA, you should level off momentarily to intercept the proper glide path.

6. A tricolor VASI is a single light unit projecting three colors visible for 1/2 to 1 mi. in daylight and about 5 mi. at night.

    a. The below glide path indicator is red.
    b. The above glide path indicator is amber.
    c. The on glide path indicator is green.

7. VASI provides only glide path guidance and safe obstruction clearance within ±10° of the extended runway centerline from as far as 4 NM from the runway threshold.

    a. It does not provide information on alignment with the runway.

5.4 PRECISION APPROACH PATH INDICATOR (PAPI)

1. PAPI lights are similar to VASIs, but they are installed in a single row of either two or four lights.

2. The glide path indications are depicted below.

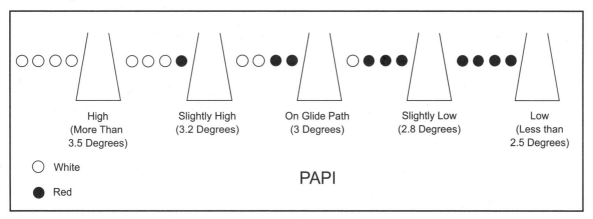

| High (More Than 3.5 Degrees) | Slightly High (3.2 Degrees) | On Glide Path (3 Degrees) | Slightly Low (2.8 Degrees) | Low (Less than 2.5 Degrees) |

○ White
● Red

PAPI

5.5 WAKE TURBULENCE

1. The greatest vortex strength occurs behind heavy, clean, and slow aircraft (e.g., during the takeoff of a jet transport because it has a high gross weight and a high angle of attack).

2. Light quartering tailwinds prolong the hazards of wake turbulence the longest because they move the vortices of preceding aircraft forward to the touchdown zone and hold the upwind vortex on the runway.

    a. A light crosswind of 1 to 5 kt. would result in an upwind vortex tending to remain over the runway.

3. When landing behind a large aircraft on the same runway, stay at or above the other aircraft's final approach flight path and land beyond that airplane's touchdown point.

5.6 COLLISION AVOIDANCE

1. When climbing to an assigned altitude on an airway, use the centerline except to avoid other aircraft when in VFR conditions.

2. During climbs and descents in VFR conditions, execute gentle banks left and right to permit continual scanning of surrounding airspace.

3. When weather conditions permit, i.e., in VFR conditions, you must assume the responsibility to see and avoid other aircraft, regardless of whether operating under IFR or VFR.

4. ADS-B (Automatic Dependent Surveillance-Broadcast) is new technology that allows air traffic controllers (and ADS-B equipped aircraft) to see traffic with more precision. Instead of relying on old radar technology, ADS-B uses highly accurate GPS signals. Because of this, ADS-B works where radar often will not.

    a. This system

        1) Works in remote areas such as mountainous terrain

        2) Functions at low altitudes and even on the ground

        3) Can be used to monitor traffic on the taxiways and runways

        4) Allows air traffic controllers as well as aircraft with certain equipment to receive ADS-B traffic

        5) Provides subscription-free weather information to all aircraft flying over the U.S.

    b. ADS-B will be required in 2020. This system is going to help make our skies safer. For more information, visit www.garmin.com/us/intheair/ads-b.

5.7 IFR FLIGHT PLANNING INFORMATION

1. Every pilot should receive a preflight briefing from a Flight Service Station (FSS), whether by telephone, radio, or personal visit.

    a. The briefing should contain weather advisories and notices about en route airports and other navigational aids.

2. The **Notice to Airmen (NOTAM) System** disseminates time-critical aeronautical information that is temporary in nature or not known in time to publish on charts or in procedural publications.

    a. NOTAMs include airport or primary runway closures, changes in the status of navigational aids, instrument landing systems, radar service availability, and other information that could affect a pilot's decision to make a flight.

3. NOTAMs are grouped into five types:

    a. **NOTAMs (D)**, sometimes called "distant" NOTAMs, include information such as airport or primary runway closures; changes in the status of navigational aids, ILSs, and radar service availability; and other information essential to planned en route, terminal, or landing operations. Also included is information on airport taxiways, aprons, ramp areas, and associated lighting.

    b. **FDC NOTAMs** are issued by the Flight Data Center and contain regulatory information such as amendments to published instrument approach charts and other current aeronautical charts.

    c. **Pointer NOTAMs** reduce total NOTAM volume by pointing to other NOTAMs (D) and FDC NOTAMs rather than duplicating potentially unnecessary information for an airport or NAVAID. They allow pilots to reference NOTAMs that might not be listed under a given airport or NAVAID identifier.

    d. **SAA NOTAMs** are issued when Special Activity Airspace (SAA) will be active outside the published schedule times and when required by the published schedule, although pilots must still check published schedule times for SAA as well as any other NOTAMs for that airspace.

    e. **Military NOTAMs** reference military airports and NAVAIDs and are rarely of any interest to civilian pilots.

4. NOTAMs are disseminated by two means:

    a. The most current data are disseminated via telecommunications. They are included as part of a routine pilot weather briefing given by an FSS specialist.

    b. The *Notices to Airmen Publication*, also known as NTAP (formerly Class II NOTAMs), is published every 28 days. The NTAP contains all current NOTAMs (D) and FDC NOTAMs, except FDC NOTAMs for temporary flight restrictions. Once published, these NOTAMs are not provided during pilot weather briefing unless specifically requested.

5. The best source of airport conditions would be to combine data available from the *Airport/Facility Directory* and NOTAMs (D).

6. **Automatic Terminal Information Service (ATIS)** broadcasts are updated whenever any official weather data are received, regardless of content change or reported values, or when there is a change in other pertinent data, such as active runway, instrument approach in use, etc.

    a. Absence of the sky condition and visibility from the ATIS broadcast specifically implies that the ceiling is more than 5,000 ft. and visibility is more than 5 SM.

7. In Class B, C, D, and E surface areas, operation of an airport beacon during daylight hours usually indicates IFR weather conditions (ground visibility less than 3 SM and/or ceiling less than 1,000 ft.).

5.8 IFR FLIGHT PLAN

1. To operate under instrument flight rules in controlled airspace, you are required to file an IFR flight plan.

    a. The FAA's standard flight plan form appears in Figure 1 below.

<table>
<tr><td colspan="6"></td><td>Form Approved: OMB No. 2120-0034</td></tr>
<tr>
<td rowspan="2">U.S. DEPARTMENT OF TRANSPORTATION
FEDERAL AVIATION ADMINISTRATION

FLIGHT PLAN</td>
<td rowspan="2">(FAA USE ONLY)</td>
<td>☐ PILOT BRIEFING</td>
<td>☐ VNR</td>
<td>TIME STARTED</td>
<td>SPECIALIST INITIALS</td>
</tr>
<tr>
<td colspan="2">☐ STOPOVER</td>
<td></td>
<td></td>
</tr>
</table>

| 1. TYPE

VFR
X IFR
DVFR | 2. AIRCRAFT IDENTIFICATION | 3. AIRCRAFT TYPE/ SPECIAL EQUIPMENT | 4. TRUE AIRSPEED

KTS | 5. DEPARTURE POINT | 6. DEPARTURE TIME
PROPOSED (Z) \| ACTUAL (Z) | 7. CRUISING ALTITUDE |

8. ROUTE OF FLIGHT

| 9. DESTINATION (Name of airport and city) | 10. EST. TIME ENROUTE
HOURS \| MINUTES | 11. REMARKS |

| 12. FUEL ON BOARD
HOURS \| MINUTES | 13. ALTERNATE AIRPORT(S) | 14. PILOTS NAME, ADDRESS & TELEPHONE NUMBER & AIRCRAFT HOME BASE

17. DESTINATION CONTACT/TELEPHONE (OPTIONAL) | 15. NUMBER ABOARD |

| 16. COLOR OF AIRCRAFT | CIVIL AIRCRAFT PILOTS. FAR Part 91 requires you file an IFR flight plan to operate under instrument flight rules in controlled airspace. Failure to file could result in a civil penalty not to exceed $1,000 for each violation (Section 901 of the Federal Aviation Act of 1958, as amended). Filing of a VFR flight plan is recommended as a good operating practice. See also Part 99 for requirements concerning DVFR flight plans. |

FAA Form 7233-1 (8-82)   CLOSE VFR FLIGHT PLAN WITH _____ FSS ON ARRIVAL

Figure 1. – Flight Plan.

2. When you file a composite (part VFR, part IFR) flight plan, you should check both VFR and IFR in block 1. Your IFR flight plan must include all points of transition from one airway to another, fixes defining direct route segments, and the clearance limit fix.

3. In block 3, you are to indicate the aircraft type and special equipment.

    a. After the aircraft type, a slash is followed by a letter indicating the combination of

        1) Usable transponder
        2) DME
        3) Area navigation (RNAV) equipment

    b. Not reported is airborne radar capability.

4. When an IFR flight plan has different altitudes for different legs, you should enter the altitude only for the first leg in block 7.

5. Time en route (block 10) should be based on arrival at the point of first intended landing.

6. The fuel-on-board time (block 12) should be based upon the total usable fuel on board.

7. On composite flight plans for which the first portion of the flight is IFR, the flight plan should be a standard IFR flight plan, including

    a. Points of transition from one airway to another

    b. Fixes defining direct route segments

    c. The clearance limit fix, i.e., the point at which you will begin the VFR portion of the flight

8. When transitioning from VFR to IFR on a composite flight plan, you should contact the nearest FSS to close the VFR portion and request an ATC IFR clearance.

    a. You must obtain an IFR clearance before entering IFR conditions.

9.   IFR flight plans can be canceled only if you are flying in VFR conditions outside Class A airspace.

10. When landing at an airport without a control tower or FSS on the field, the pilot must initiate IFR flight plan cancelation. The pilot may cancel

   a.   By radio while airborne if conditions are VFR
   b.   By radio or telephone as soon as (s)he is on the ground

11. A waypoint on an IFR flight is a predetermined geographical position used for an RNAV route or RNAV instrument approach identification or progress reporting. It is defined relative to a VORTAC position **or** by longitude and latitude; i.e., it does not have to be relative to a VORTAC.

5.9   ATC CLEARANCES

1.   Pilots of airborne aircraft should read back ATC clearances concerning altitude assignments and/or vectors and any part requiring verification.

2.   An abbreviated IFR clearance includes

   a.   Destination airport
   b.   The route of flight, given fix-by-fix or "as filed"
   c.   Initial altitude
   d.   DP (instrument departure procedure) name, number, and/or transition, if appropriate

3.   When a departure clearance from an airport without an operating control tower contains a void time, the pilot must advise ATC as soon as possible (but no later than 30 min. after the void time) if a decision is made NOT to take off.

4.   A cruise clearance assigns a pilot a block of airspace from the minimum IFR altitude up to and including the altitude specified in the cruise clearance.

   a.   Climb and descent within the block are at the discretion of the pilot.

5.10   ATC COMMUNICATION PROCEDURES

1.   You should state your position on the airport when calling the tower for takeoff from a runway intersection (i.e., an intersection other than at the end of the runway).

2.   When flying IFR, the pilot must maintain continuous contact with assigned ATC frequencies.

   a.   All radio frequency changes are made at the direction of ATC.

3.   When climbing or descending per ATC clearance, the pilot should use the optimum rate consistent with the aircraft to 1,000 ft. above or below the assigned altitude and then climb or descend at the rate of between 500 and 1,500 fpm until attaining the assigned altitude.

   a.   It is sufficient to use a cruise climb rather than a maximum angle of climb.
   b.   If you cannot climb or descend at least 500 fpm, you should notify ATC.
   c.   You should lead your turns so that you remain in the center of the airway.

4.   The reports that a pilot must make to ATC without a specific ATC request include

   a.   At all times:

      1)   Inability to climb or descend at a rate of at least 500 fpm
      2)   Change in the average true airspeed at cruising altitude when it varies by more than the greater of 5% or 10 kt. from that filed in your flight plan
      3)   Change from assigned altitude
      4)   Missed approach
      5)   Departure from any assigned holding fix or point
      6)   The time and altitude when reaching holding fix or clearance limit

       7)   Loss of communication or navigation capability or anything else affecting the safety of flight

   b.   When not in radar contact:

      1)   Departure from final approach fix inbound on final approach
      2)   Correction of an estimate which appears to be more than 3 min. in error
      3)   Passage over certain reporting points:

         a)   Compulsory reporting points as marked by solid black triangles on en route charts
         b)   Each fix used in the flight plan to define the route of flight on a direct flight not flown on radials or courses of established airways or routes

5.   Your Mode C transponder should always be set to Mode C and turned ON unless otherwise requested by ATC.

6.   When receiving traffic advisories from ATC, remember that the controller sees only the airplane's direction of travel, not the airplane heading.

   a.   You must adjust traffic reports for any wind correction you are holding.

7.   **Radar contact** means your airplane has been identified on the radar screen and radar flight following will be provided until radar identification is terminated by the controller.

8.   **Resume own navigation** means that you continue to be under ATC radar surveillance but are responsible for your own navigation. No more vectors will be given.

   a.   You are still in radar contact with ATC. Thus, you do not need to make position reports.

9.   **Radar service terminated** means that you are no longer under ATC radar surveillance and must resume position reports at compulsory reporting points.

10.   IFR flights receive separation from all IFR aircraft and participating VFR aircraft operating within the outer area of Class C airspace.

11.   When flying VFR on practice instrument approaches, you must avoid IFR conditions. You do not have an IFR clearance.

12.   While you should comply with all headings and altitudes assigned by ATC, you should feel free to question any assigned altitude or heading believed to be incorrect. The pilot has ultimate responsibility for safe flight.

13.   When ATC requests a specified airspeed, you are expected to maintain the speed plus or minus 10 kt. based upon indicated airspeed.

14.   If you cancel your IFR flight plan 10 mi. from your destination airport (located in Class D airspace), you must establish communications with the tower prior to entering the Class D airspace.

15.   At airports with a part-time control tower and an FSS located on the same airport, the FSS will provide Local Airport Advisory (LAA) service when the control tower is not in operation.

   a.   The FSS provides advisory data on runways, weather, traffic patterns, etc. Advisory data do **not** constitute ATC clearance or other authoritative ATC actions.

   b.   Remember, if ATC is not operating, you must cancel your own flight plan by notifying the FSS.

16.   Pilots never have to accept a controller's clearance, regardless of meteorological conditions.

   a.   A pilot should only accept a LAHSO (Land and Hold Short Operation) clearance provided (s)he feels (s)he can land the plane within the available distance without compromising safety.

17.   **Minimum fuel** is just an advisory to ATC that indicates an emergency situation is possible should any undue delay occur.

5.11 RADIO COMMUNICATION FAILURE

1. In the event of two-way communications failure, ATC will assume the pilot is operating in accordance with FAR 91.185.

    a. As always, pilot judgment is the final determinant of safest flying.

2. According to FAR 91.185, if you lose two-way communications

    a. When you are holding and you receive an expected further clearance (EFC) time, you should leave the holding pattern at the EFC time.

    b. When you are on an IFR flight in VFR weather conditions, you should continue your flight under VFR and land as soon as practicable.

    c. When you are in IFR conditions, you should continue on the route specified in your clearance (for each leg of your flight) at the highest of

        1) The last assigned altitude
        2) Expected altitude per ATC
        3) MEA (minimum en route altitude)

3. When losing radio communications, you should alert ATC by setting your transponder code to 7600.

    a. If you are in an emergency situation, you should set and leave the transponder at 7700.

5.12 NAVIGATION RADIO FAILURE

1. If your DME fails above FL 240, you should notify ATC of the failure and continue to the next airport of intended landing at which repairs or replacement of the equipment can be made.

2. When operating under IFR, you must immediately report to ATC the loss of VOR, TACAN, or LF navigation receiver capability; complete or partial loss of ILS receiver; and/or any impairment of radio communications capability.

5.13 TYPES OF AIRSPACE

1. En Route Low-Altitude Charts show the limits of controlled airspace, military training routes, and special-use airspace.

    a. However, they do not show Class A airspace.

2. Class G (uncontrolled) airspace is airspace where ATC does not control air traffic.

3. Transition areas are Class E airspace and are used to transition between the terminal area and en route flight.

    a. When designated in conjunction with an airport with a prescribed instrument approach, Class E airspace extends upward from 700 ft. AGL.

    b. When designated in conjunction with airway route structures, etc., Class E airspace extends upward from 1,200 ft. AGL.

    c. Both types of transition areas terminate at the base of overlying controlled airspace, i.e., Class A airspace.

4. Class A airspace is from 18,000 ft. MSL to FL 600.

5. Military operations areas (MOA) consist of airspace established for the purpose of separating certain military training activities from IFR traffic.

6. The maximum altitude at which Class G airspace will exist is 14,500 ft. MSL (excluding the airspace less than 1,500 ft. AGL).

7. Generally, the maximum altitude for Class B airspace is 10,000 ft. MSL.

8. The normal lateral limit for Class D airspace is 4 NM.

9.   The normal upper limit of Class D airspace is 2,500 ft. AGL.

10.   Class C airspace consists of controlled airspace within which all aircraft are subject to the operating rules and equipment requirements specified in FAR Part 91.

   a.   Aircraft must be equipped with two-way radio communications and a Mode C transponder.

5.14   AIRPORT DIAGRAM – *AIRPORT FACILITY DIRECTORY (A/FD)*

1.   Airport Diagrams, published in regional booklets, provide information about airports, both VFR and IFR. The *A/FD* Airport Diagram includes information such as runway slope (e.g., 0.3% DOWN) and runway heading (e.g., 003.6°). Review the *A/FD* Airport Diagram illustration below for more information.

A/FD Airport Diagram.

QUESTIONS AND ANSWER EXPLANATIONS: All of the instrument rating knowledge test questions chosen by the FAA for release as well as additional questions selected by Gleim relating to the material in the previous outlines are reproduced on the following pages. These questions have been organized into the same subunits as the outlines. To the immediate right of each question are the correct answer and answer explanation. You should cover these answers and answer explanations while responding to the questions. Refer to the general discussion in the Introduction on how to take the FAA knowledge test.

Remember that the questions from the FAA knowledge test bank have been reordered by topic and organized into a meaningful sequence. Also, the first line of the answer explanation gives the citation of the authoritative source for the answer.

QUESTIONS

5.1 Precision Instrument Runway Markings

1. Which type of runway lighting consists of a pair of synchronized flashing lights, one on each side of the runway threshold?

    A. RAIL.

    B. HIRL.

    C. REIL.

Answer (C) is correct. *(AIM Para 2-1-3)*
    DISCUSSION: Runway end identifier lights (REIL) consist of a pair of synchronized flashing lights, one on each side of the runway threshold.
    Answer (A) is incorrect. RAIL refers to runway alignment indicator lights, which are sequenced flashing lights that are used in combination with other approach lighting systems. Answer (B) is incorrect. HIRL refers to high-intensity runway lights, which are a runway edge light system.

2. The primary purpose of runway end identifier lights, installed at many airfields, is to provide

    A. rapid identification of the approach end of the runway during reduced visibility.

    B. a warning of the final 3,000 feet of runway remaining as viewed from the takeoff or approach position.

    C. rapid identification of the primary runway during reduced visibility.

Answer (A) is correct. *(AIM Para 2-1-3)*
    DISCUSSION: Runway end identifier lights (REIL) are effective for rapid and positive identification of the approach end of a runway that is surrounded by a preponderance of other lighting, lacks contrast with surrounding terrain, and/or has reduced visibility. They are white strobe lights, one on each side of the runway threshold.
    Answer (B) is incorrect. It describes runway remaining lights in the center of the runway, not REIL. Answer (C) is incorrect. REIL of other than the primary runway may be used to help identify the airport. In other words, REIL may be flashing at the end of a runway that is not the primary runway.

3. Which runway marking indicates a displaced threshold on an instrument runway?

    A. Arrows leading to the threshold mark.

    B. Centerline dashes starting at the threshold.

    C. Red chevron marks in the nonlanding portion of the runway.

Answer (A) is correct. *(AIM Para 2-3-3)*
    DISCUSSION: On any runway, a displaced threshold is marked with a series of arrows in the middle of the runway pointing to the threshold mark, which is a solid line across the runway. A displaced threshold is available for taxiing, landing rollout, and takeoff, but not landing.
    Answer (B) is incorrect. It describes the centerline marking of a runway. Answer (C) is incorrect. Chevron marks are usually yellow. They indicate a nonusable portion of the runway that is only available for emergency use (overrun and stopway areas).

4. Under which conditions is hydroplaning most likely to occur?

    A. When rudder is used for directional control instead of allowing the nosewheel to contact the surface early in the landing roll on a wet runway.

    B. During conditions of standing water, slush, high speed, and smooth runway texture.

    C. During a landing on any wet runway when brake application is delayed until a wedge of water begins to build ahead of the tires.

Answer (B) is correct. *(FAA-P-8740-50)*
    DISCUSSION: In hydroplaning, the aircraft tire is separated from the runway by water. It is more apt to happen at higher speeds, with standing water or slush on the runway, and on a runway with a smooth texture.
    Answer (A) is incorrect. The nosewheel cannot hydroplane if it is not put down to the runway surface. Answer (C) is incorrect. Hydroplaning occurs regardless of brake timing.

5. (Refer to Figure 137 below.) What is the distance (A) from the beginning of the runway to the fixed distance marker?

    A. 500 feet.

    B. 1,000 feet.

    C. 1,500 feet.

Answer (B) is correct. *(AIM Para 2-3-3)*
    DISCUSSION: The fixed distance marker on precision instrument runways consists of two heavy lines parallel to the direction of the runway, 1,000 ft. from the runway threshold.
    Answer (A) is incorrect. The six parallel lines (somewhat lighter and narrower than the fixed distance marker) 500 ft. from the threshold of the runway are the touchdown zone marker. Answer (C) is incorrect. The marker at roughly 1,500 ft. from the threshold is the next marker beyond the fixed distance marker, not the fixed distance marker.

6. (Refer to Figure 137 below.) What is the distance (B) from the beginning of the runway to the touchdown zone marker?

    A. 250 feet.

    B. 500 feet.

    C. 750 feet.

Answer (B) is correct. *(AIM Para 2-3-3)*
    DISCUSSION: The distance from the runway threshold to the touchdown zone marker is 500 ft. The touchdown zone marker consists of six lines parallel to the runway.
    Answer (A) is incorrect. There is no standardized marking 250 ft. from the beginning of the runway. Answer (C) is incorrect. There is no standardized marking 750 ft. from the beginning of the runway.

Figure 137. – Precision Instrument Runway.

7. (Refer to Figure 137 above.) What is the distance (C) from the beginning of the touchdown zone marker to the beginning of the fixed distance marker?

    A. 1,000 feet.

    B. 500 feet.

    C. 250 feet.

Answer (B) is correct. *(AIM Para 2-3-3)*
    DISCUSSION: Since the touchdown zone marker is 500 ft. from the runway threshold and the fixed distance marker is 1,000 ft. from the runway threshold, the distance from the beginning of the touchdown zone marker to the beginning of the fixed distance marker is 500 ft. (1,000 – 500).
    Answer (A) is incorrect. This is the distance from the beginning of the runway to the fixed distance marker. Answer (C) is incorrect. This is not a standard distance between runway markings.

8. (Refer to Figure 138 below.) What night operations, if any, are authorized between the approach end of the runway and the threshold lights?

   A. No aircraft operations are permitted short of the threshold lights.

   B. Only taxi operations are permitted in the area short of the threshold lights.

   C. Taxi and takeoff operations are permitted, providing the takeoff operations are toward the visible green threshold lights.

Answer (C) is correct. *(AIM Para 2-3-3)*
   DISCUSSION: On displaced thresholds, runway edge lights appear red when taxiing toward the green threshold lights and white when taxiing away from the threshold to the departure end of the runway. The area behind the displaced runway threshold is available for taxiing, landing rollout, and takeoff of aircraft.
   Answer (A) is incorrect. Overrun areas are areas where only emergency operations are permitted. Overrun areas do not have any runway edge lights. Answer (B) is incorrect. Landing rollout and takeoff operations are also permitted behind displaced thresholds.

Figure 138. – Runway Legend.

5.2 Airport Signs and Markings

9. The "runway hold position" sign denotes

   A. intersecting runways.

   B. an entrance to runway from a taxiway.

   C. an area protected for an aircraft approaching a runway.

Answer (B) is correct. *(AIM Para 2-3-8)*
   DISCUSSION: Runway holding position signs, consisting of white numbering on a red background, are found adjacent to runway holding position markings that are painted on a taxiway or a runway. These signs and markings indicate the point at which aircraft are expected to hold short of a runway if an ATC clearance to proceed onto that runway has not been received at an airport with an operating control tower or without making sure of adequate separation at an airport without an operating control tower. Runway holding position signs therefore denote the entrance to a runway from a taxiway or from an intersecting runway.
   Answer (A) is incorrect. A runway hold position sign is only used to denote an intersecting runway when that runway is used for "Land and Hold Short" operations or as a taxiway. Answer (C) is incorrect. A runway approach area holding position sign, not a runway holding position sign, denotes an area protected for aircraft approaching or departing a runway.

10. (Refer to Figure 51C below.) Which sign indicates you're holding short of the ILS critical area?

A. Top red.

B. Middle yellow.

C. Bottom yellow.

Answer (C) is correct. *(AIM Para 2-3-1)*
DISCUSSION: The ILS critical area sign has a yellow background and black lines drawn that looks like a sideways ladder. This sign identifies the ILS critical area exit boundary. If an aircraft is on this line and instrument approaches are in progress, the ILS signal may be blocked. Do not cross or block this during IMC unless clearance is given.

Answer (A) is incorrect. The top red sign is a mandatory "No Entry" sign. It means "do not go beyond this sign." Answer (B) is incorrect. The middle yellow sign is a runway boundary sign. It is located on taxiways on the back side of certain runway/taxiway holding position signs or runway approach area signs.

RED

*NOTE: This figure can be seen in color on the inside back cover.

YELLOW

YELLOW

Figure 51C. – Airport Signs.

11. (Refer to Figure 51C above.) While clearing an active runway, you are clear of the ILS critical area when you pass which sign?

A. Top red.

B. Middle yellow.

C. Bottom yellow.

Answer (C) is correct. *(AIM Para 2-3-1)*
DISCUSSION: The ILS critical area sign has a yellow background and black lines drawn that looks like a sideways ladder. This sign identifies the ILS critical area exit boundary. If an aircraft is on this line and instrument approaches are in progress, the ILS signal may be blocked. Do not cross or block this during IMC unless clearance is given.

Answer (A) is incorrect. The top red sign is a mandatory "No Entry" sign. It means "do not go beyond this sign." Answer (B) is incorrect. The middle yellow sign is a runway boundary sign. It is located on taxiways on the back side of certain runway/taxiway holding position signs or runway approach area signs.

12. Destination signs indicate

A. The taxiway a pilot is on.

B. The runway a pilot is on.

C. The direction to takeoff runways.

Answer (C) is correct. *(AIM Para 2-3-11)*
DISCUSSION: Destination signs direct pilots to a destination on the airport. These signs can direct pilots to runways, taxiways, aprons, terminals, FBOs, cargo areas, civil aviation areas, and military areas.
Answer (A) is incorrect. Destination signs indicate the direction to a point, not the specific point where the pilot is currently located. Answer (B) is incorrect. Destination signs indicate the direction to a point, not the specific point where the pilot is currently located.

13. (Refer to Figure 94 on page 411.) Mandatory airport instruction signs are designated by having

A. yellow lettering with a black background.

B. white lettering with a red background.

C. black lettering with a yellow background.

Answer (B) is correct. *(AIM Para 2-3-8)*
DISCUSSION: Mandatory airport instruction signs have a red background with white lettering and are used to denote an entrance to a runway or critical area and areas where an aircraft is prohibited from entering.
Answer (A) is incorrect. Yellow lettering on a black background denotes taxiway or runway location signs (where the aircraft is located). Answer (C) is incorrect. Black lettering on a yellow background denotes direction, destination, and information signs.

14. (Refer to Figure 94 on page 411.) What sign is designated by illustration 7?

A. Location sign.

B. Mandatory instruction sign.

C. Direction sign.

Answer (B) is correct. *(AIM Para 2-3-8)*
DISCUSSION: Mandatory instruction signs have a red background with white lettering. The sign designated by illustration 7 (15-APCH) protects the approach to RWY 15 and/or the departure for RWY 33.
Answer (A) is incorrect. Location signs use yellow lettering on a black background. Answer (C) is incorrect. Direction signs use black lettering on a yellow background.

15. (Refer to Figure 94 on page 411.) What colors are runway holding position signs?

A. White with a red background.

B. Red with a white background.

C. Yellow with a black background.

Answer (A) is correct. *(AIM Para 2-3-8)*
DISCUSSION: Runway holding position signs, like other mandatory instruction signs, have white lettering on a red background. Runway holding position signs are located at the holding position on taxiways that intersect a runway or on runways that intersect other runways.
Answer (B) is incorrect. Red lettering on a white background is used on the landing area of a hospital heliport but is not used on any airport signs. Answer (C) is incorrect. Taxiway and runway location signs, not runway holding position signs, have yellow lettering on a black background.

16. (Refer to Figure 94 on page 411.) Hold line markings at the intersection of taxiways and runways consist of four lines that extend across the width of the taxiway. These lines are

A. white, and the dashed lines are nearest the runway.

B. yellow, and the dashed lines are nearest the runway.

C. yellow, and the solid lines are nearest the runway.

Answer (B) is correct. *(AIM Para 2-3-5)*
DISCUSSION: Runway holding position markings on taxiways identify the location where you are supposed to stop when you do not have a clearance to proceed onto the runway. These markings consist of four yellow lines, two solid and two dashed, spaced 6 inches apart and extending across the width of the taxiway, with the dashed lines nearest the runway. The solid lines are always on the side where the aircraft is to hold.
Answer (A) is incorrect. The lines are yellow, not white. Answer (C) is incorrect. Solid lines are always on the holding side, not the runway side.

17. What is the purpose of the runway exit sign?

A. Defines direction and designation of runway when exiting a taxiway.

B. Defines direction and designation of exit taxiway from runway.

C. Defines a mandatory exit point from the runway during Land and Hold Short Operations (LAHSO).

Answer (B) is correct. *(AIM Para 2-3-10)*
DISCUSSION: A runway exit sign defines the direction and designation of an exit taxiway from the runway.
Answer (A) is incorrect. A runway exit sign is positioned on the runway, not on a taxiway. This answer choice describes a runway destination sign. Answer (C) is incorrect. Runway exit signs are not mandatory exit points during Land and Hold Short Operations (LAHSO). This answer choice partially describes runway holding position markings.

18. When exiting the runway, what is the purpose of the runway exit sign?

A. Indicates designation and direction of exit taxiway from runway.

B. Indicates designation and direction of taxiway leading out of an intersection.

C. Indicates direction to take-off runway.

Answer (A) is correct. *(PHAK Chap 13)*
   DISCUSSION: This direction sign has a yellow background with black text, and it defines the direction and designation of an exit taxiway from the runway.
   Answer (B) is incorrect. A taxiway intersection sign is located on a taxiway and denotes proper taxi routes. It does not provide runway exit information. Answer (C) is incorrect. A direction sign indicates the necessary taxi route to get to the end of a specific runway. It does not provide guidance on exiting a runway.

19. A runway exit sign

A. points toward a named taxiway that leads off the runway.

B. designates an intersection of two or more runways.

C. shows the direction to exit from a named taxiway onto a runway.

Answer (A) is correct. *(PHAK Chap 13)*
   DISCUSSION: This direction sign has a yellow background with black text, and it defines the direction and designation of an exit taxiway from the runway.
   Answer (B) is incorrect. A runway intersection sign is a mandatory sign that indicates an area where an airplane must hold. It does not provide guidance on exiting the runway. Answer (C) is incorrect. The runway exit sign indicates the direction to exit from a runway onto a taxiway, not from a taxiway onto a runway.

20. The "No Entry" sign identifies

A. the exit boundary for the runway protected area.

B. an area that does not continue beyond intersection.

C. paved area where aircraft entry is prohibited.

Answer (C) is correct. *(AIM Para 2-3-8)*
   DISCUSSION: No entry signs consist of a white horizontal line surrounded by a white circle on a red background. These signs are posted at points where aircraft entry is prohibited. These signs are typically found on taxiways that are intended to be used in only one direction and at the intersection of vehicle roadways with runways, taxiways, or ramp areas where the roadway may be mistaken for a taxiway or other aircraft movement area.
   Answer (A) is incorrect. A runway boundary sign, not a no entry sign, identifies the boundary of the runway protected area for aircraft leaving the runway. Runway boundary signs consist of a black depiction of a runway holding position marking on a yellow background. Answer (B) is incorrect. A taxiway ending marker sign, not a no entry sign, indicates that a taxiway does not continue beyond the next intersection. Taxiway ending marker signs consist of alternating yellow and black diagonal stripes.

21. "Runway hold position" markings on the taxiway

A. identifies where aircraft hold short of the runway.

B. identifies area where aircraft are prohibited.

C. allows an aircraft permission onto the runway.

Answer (A) is correct. *(AIM Para 2-3-5)*
   DISCUSSION: Runway holding position markings on taxiways identify the location where you are supposed to stop when you do not have an ATC clearance to proceed at an airport with an operating control tower or without making sure of adequate separation at an airport without an operating control tower. These markings consist of four yellow lines, two solid and two dashed, spaced 6 inches apart and extending across the width of the taxiway, with the dashed lines nearest the runway. The solid lines are always on the side where the aircraft is to hold.
   Answer (B) is incorrect. A no entry sign, not a runway hold position marking, identifies an area where aircraft are prohibited. Answer (C) is incorrect. Runway holding position markings indicate that aircraft should hold short of the runway, not taxi onto it, until a clearance to proceed onto the runway is received.

22. When turning onto a taxiway from another taxiway, the "taxiway directional sign" indicates

A. direction to the take-off runway.

B. designation and direction of taxiway leading out of an intersection.

C. designation and direction of exit taxiway from runway.

Answer (B) is correct. *(AIM Para 2-3-10)*
   DISCUSSION: Direction signs consist of black lettering on a yellow background. These signs identify the designations of taxiways leading out of an intersection. An arrow next to each taxiway designation indicates the direction that an aircraft must turn in order to taxi onto that taxiway.
   Answer (A) is incorrect. Outbound destination signs, not direction signs, indicate the direction that must be taken out of an intersection in order to follow the preferred taxi route to a runway. Answer (C) is incorrect. The question specifies that you are turning onto a taxiway from another taxiway, not from a runway.

23. The "ILS critical area boundary" sign identifies the

A. Area where an aircraft is prohibited from entering.

B. Edge of the ILS critical area.

C. Exit boundary for the runway protected area.

Answer (B) is correct. *(PHAK Chap 13)*

DISCUSSION: The ILS critical area boundary sign has a yellow background with two horizontal, parallel black lines and four sets of two vertical, parallel lines connecting the two horizontal lines. This sign is the same as the painted marking representing the ILS critical area boundary. When an ILS is in operation, aircraft must hold at this line and not pass it unless so authorized by ATC so as not to block or interfere with the signal from the ILS glide slope antenna installed at the airport. If taxiing off of a runway, the aircraft is not clear of the ILS critical area until all parts of the aircraft are past this sign and associated painted marking.

Answer (A) is incorrect. It describes the purpose of a no entry sign. Answer (C) is incorrect. It describes the purpose of a runway hold position sign.

24. Within aircraft movement areas, "destination signs" identify the

A. runway on which an aircraft is located.

B. direction to the takeoff runway.

C. entrance to the runway from a taxiway.

Answer (B) is correct. *(AIM Para 2-3-11)*

DISCUSSION: Destination signs help direct you toward other areas of the airport. These signs have a yellow background with black text.

Answer (A) is incorrect. This describes a runway location sign. Answer (C) is incorrect. This describes a holding position sign.

5.3 Visual Approach Slope Indicator (VASI)

25. Which approach and landing objective is assured when the pilot remains on the proper glidepath of the VASI?

A. Continuation of course guidance after transition to VFR.

B. Safe obstruction clearance in the approach area.

C. Course guidance from the visual descent point to touchdown.

Answer (B) is correct. *(AIM Para 2-1-2)*

DISCUSSION: The VASI system provides visual descent guidance and provides safe obstruction clearance within plus or minus 10° of the extended runway centerline from as far as 4 NM from the runway threshold.

Answer (A) is incorrect. VASI does not provide course guidance. Answer (C) is incorrect. VASI does not provide course guidance.

26. (Refer to Figure 134 below.) Unless a higher angle is necessary for obstacle clearance, what is the normal glidepath angle for a 2-bar VASI?

A. 2.75°.

B. 3.00°.

C. 3.25°.

Answer (B) is correct. *(AIM Para 2-1-2)*

DISCUSSION: Two-bar VASI installations provide one visual glide path, which is normally set at 3°. Angles at some locations may be as high as 4.5°, however, to give proper obstacle clearance. This greater angle may necessitate increased runway for landing and rollout of some high-performance airplanes.

Answer (A) is incorrect. The normal glide path angle for a 2-bar VASI is 3°, not 2.75°. Answer (C) is incorrect. This figure is the normal upper glide path provided by a 3-bar VASI.

Figure 134. – 2-BAR VASI.

27. Which of the following indications would a pilot see while approaching to land on a runway served by a 2-bar VASI?

    A. If on the glidepath, the near bars will appear red, and the far bars will appear white.

    B. If departing to the high side of the glidepath, the far bars will change from red to white.

    C. If on the glidepath, both near bars and far bars will appear white.

Answer (B) is correct. *(AIM Para 2-1-2)*
    DISCUSSION: As you move to the high side of a VASI glide slope, the far bar will change from red to white. When you are on the glide slope, the far bar is red. When you are above the glide slope, the far bar is white.
    Answer (A) is incorrect. If you are on the glide slope, the near bars are white, not red, and the far bars are red, not white (the opposite is impossible). Answer (C) is incorrect. If both near and far bars are white, you are above, not on, the glide slope.

28. (Refer to Figure 135 below.) Unless a higher angle is required for obstacle clearance, what is the normal glidepath for a 3-bar VASI?

    A. 2.3°.

    B. 2.75°.

    C. 3.0°.

Answer (C) is correct. *(AIM Para 2-1-2)*
    DISCUSSION: The normal glide path for a 3-bar VASI (the lower glide path) is 3°. The upper glide path is usually a 3.25° slope. Higher-angle glide slopes, up to 4.5°, are used in some places for adequate obstruction clearance.
    Answer (A) is incorrect. This figure is not a VASI glide path angle. Answer (B) is incorrect. This figure is not a VASI glide path angle.

29. (Refer to Figure 135 below.) Which illustration would a pilot observe when on the lower glidepath?

    A. 4.

    B. 5.

    C. 6.

Answer (B) is correct. *(AIM Para 2-1-2)*
    DISCUSSION: On the lower glide path of a 3-bar VASI, the near lights should be white and the middle and far bars should be red, which is illustration 5.
    Answer (A) is incorrect. Illustration 4 indicates that you are below both glide paths. Answer (C) is incorrect. Illustration 6 indicates that you are on the upper glide path.

Figure 135. – 3-BAR VASI.

30. (Refer to Figure 135 above.) Which illustration would a pilot observe if the aircraft is above both glidepaths?

    A. 5.

    B. 6.

    C. 7.

Answer (C) is correct. *(AIM Para 2-1-2)*
    DISCUSSION: If you are above both glide paths on a 3-bar VASI, you will observe that all three rows of lights appear white, which is illustration 7.
    Answer (A) is incorrect. Illustration 5 indicates that you are on the lower glide path. Answer (B) is incorrect. Illustration 6 indicates that you are on the upper glide path.

31. (Refer to Figure 135 above.) Which illustration would a pilot observe if the aircraft is below both glidepaths?

    A. 4.

    B. 5.

    C. 6.

Answer (A) is correct. *(AIM Para 2-1-2)*
    DISCUSSION: If you are below both glide paths on a 3-bar VASI, you will observe that all three rows of lights appear red, which is illustration 4.
    Answer (B) is incorrect. Illustration 5 indicates that you are on the lower glide path. Answer (C) is incorrect. Illustration 6 indicates that you are on the upper glide path.

32. When on the proper glidepath of a 2-bar VASI, the pilot will see the near bar as

   A. white and the far bar as red.

   B. red and the far bar as white.

   C. white and the far bar as white.

Answer (A) is correct. *(AIM Para 2-1-2)*
   DISCUSSION: When you are on the proper glide path of a 2-bar VASI, the near lights will be white and the far lights red.
   Answer (B) is incorrect. White over red is impossible. Answer (C) is incorrect. White over white means you are above, not on, the glide path.

33. Which is a feature of the tricolor VASI?

   A. One light projector with three colors: red, green, and amber.

   B. Two visual glidepaths for the runway.

   C. Three glidepaths, with the center path indicated by a white light.

Answer (A) is correct. *(AIM Para 2-1-2)*
   DISCUSSION: Tricolor VASIs normally consist of a single light unit projecting a three-color visual approach path. The colors are amber (above the glide path), green (on the path), and red (below the path).
   Answer (B) is incorrect. Having two visual glide paths for the runway is a feature of a 3-bar, not tricolor, VASI. Answer (C) is incorrect. It is a nonsense concept; i.e., there is not a three-glide path VASI.

34. If an approach is being made to a runway that has an operating 3-bar VASI and all the VASI lights appear red as the airplane reaches the MDA, the pilot should

   A. start a climb to reach the proper glidepath.

   B. continue at the same rate of descent if the runway is in sight.

   C. level off momentarily to intercept the proper approach path.

Answer (C) is correct. *(AIM Para 2-1-2)*
   DISCUSSION: If all three VASI bars are red, you are beneath both glide paths and should level off momentarily to intercept the proper approach path.
   Answer (A) is incorrect. A climb is not necessary. If you level off you will soon be back on the glide path. Answer (B) is incorrect. You should briefly stop, not continue, your rate of descent to get back on the desired glide path.

35. The middle and far bars of a 3-bar VASI will

   A. both appear white to the pilot when on the upper glidepath.

   B. constitute a 2-bar VASI for using the lower glidepath.

   C. constitute a 2-bar VASI for using the upper glidepath.

Answer (C) is correct. *(AIM Para 2-1-2)*
   DISCUSSION: On 3-bar VASIs, the lower glide path is provided by the near and middle bars at a 3° glide slope. The middle and far bars normally have a 1/4° greater glide slope and are used for the upper glide path.
   Answer (A) is incorrect. When both the middle and far bars are white, the airplane is above both glide paths. Answer (B) is incorrect. The near and middle bars are used for the lower glide path.

36. Tricolor Visual Approach Indicators normally consist of

   A. a single unit, projecting a three-color visual approach path.

   B. three separate light units, each projecting a different color approach path.

   C. three separate light projecting units of very high candle power with a daytime range of approximately 5 miles.

Answer (A) is correct. *(AIM Para 2-1-2)*
   DISCUSSION: Tricolor visual approach indicators consist of a single light unit projecting a three-color visual approach path. The unit has a useful range of 1/2 to 1 mi. in daylight and as much as 5 mi. at night.
   Answer (B) is incorrect. Tricolor visual approach indicators have only one light unit and only one glide path. Answer (C) is incorrect. Tricolor VASIs have only one projecting unit with a daytime range of about 1, not 5, mi.

5.4 Precision Approach Path Indicator (PAPI)

37. (Refer to Figure 136 on page 155.) Which illustration would a pilot observe if the aircraft is "slightly high" (3.2°) on the glidepath?

   A. 8.

   B. 9.

   C. 11.

Answer (B) is correct. *(AIM Para 2-1-2)*
   DISCUSSION: Slightly high on a PAPI is about 3.2°, which is indicated by three white lights out of four. The remaining light is red as in illustration 9.
   Answer (A) is incorrect. Illustration 8 indicates a glide slope that is high, or more than 3.5°. Answer (C) is incorrect. Illustration 11 indicates a glide slope that is slightly low, or about 2.8°.

38. (Refer to Figure 136 below.) An "on glidepath" indication is

A. 8.

B. 10.

C. 11.

Answer (B) is correct. *(AIM Para 2-1-2)*
    DISCUSSION: The precision approach path indicator (PAPI) uses light units similar to the VASI, but they are installed in a single row of either two or four units, rather than bars. If all the light units indicate white, you are above the glide slope. If all indicate red, you are below the glide slope. If two lights indicate red and two lights indicate white, you are on the glide slope, as shown in illustration 10.
    Answer (A) is incorrect. Illustration 8 indicates that you are above the glide slope. Answer (C) is incorrect. Illustration 11 indicates that you are slightly below (2.8°) the glide slope.

39. (Refer to Figure 136 below.) Which illustration depicts a "slightly low" (2.8°) indication?

A. 9.

B. 10.

C. 11.

Answer (C) is correct. *(AIM Para 2-1-2)*
    DISCUSSION: On PAPI, you are slightly (2.8°) below the glide path when three of the four lights indicate red as in illustration 11.
    Answer (A) is incorrect. Illustration 9 indicates that you are slightly (3.2°) above the glide path. Answer (B) is incorrect. Illustration 10 indicates that you are on (3.0°) the glide path.

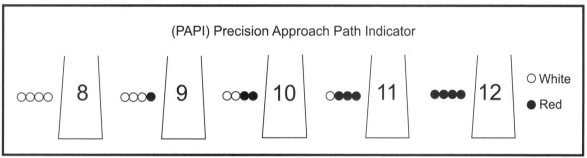

Figure 136. – Precision Approach Path Indicator (PAPI).

40. (Refer to Figure 136 above.) Which illustration would a pilot observe if the aircraft is on a glidepath higher than 3.5°?

A. 8.

B. 9.

C. 11.

Answer (A) is correct. *(AIM Para 2-1-2)*
    DISCUSSION: Higher than the glide path on PAPIs means 3.5° or more, which is indicated by all white lights as in illustration 8.
    Answer (B) is incorrect. Illustration 9 indicates that you are slightly high (3.2°). Answer (C) is incorrect. Illustration 11 indicates that you are slightly low (2.8°).

41. (Refer to Figure 136 above.) Which illustration would a pilot observe if the aircraft is less than 2.5°?

A. 10.

B. 11.

C. 12.

Answer (C) is correct. *(AIM Para 2-1-2)*
    DISCUSSION: On PAPI systems, low is indicated by all red lights as in illustration 12. Low means the aircraft is on a glide slope of less than 2.5°.
    Answer (A) is incorrect. Illustration 10 indicates that you are on the glide path (3.0°). Answer (B) is incorrect. Illustration 11 indicates that you are slightly low (2.8°).

42. (Refer to Figure 136 above.) Which illustration would a pilot observe if the aircraft is far below the glidepath?

A. 10.

B. 11.

C. 12.

Answer (C) is correct. *(AIM Para 2-1-2)*
    DISCUSSION: Illustration 12 shows four red lights, indicating that the aircraft is far below the glidepath. An easy way to remember this is:

    "Red over red, you're dead!" (too low)
    "White over white, you're out of sight!" (too high)
    "Red over white, you're alright!" (on glidepath)

    Answer (A) is incorrect. Illustration 10 shows two white lights and two red lights, indicating the aircraft is on the glidepath, not below it. Answer (B) is incorrect. Illustration 11 shows one white light and three red lights, indicating the aircraft is slightly below the glidepath, not far below it.

5.5 Wake Turbulence

43. What wind condition prolongs the hazards of wake turbulence on a landing runway for the longest period of time?

A. Direct headwind.

B. Direct tailwind.

C. Light quartering tailwind.

Answer (C) is correct. *(AIM Para 7-3-4)*
DISCUSSION: Light quartering tailwinds require maximum caution because they can move the vortices of preceding aircraft forward into the touchdown zone and hold the upwind vortex on the runway.
Answer (A) is incorrect. A direct headwind will permit the vortices to move away from each side of the runway. Answer (B) is incorrect. A direct tailwind will permit the vortices to move away from each side of the runway.

44. Wake turbulence is near maximum behind a jet transport just after takeoff because

A. the engines are at maximum thrust output at slow airspeed.

B. the gear and flap configuration increases the turbulence to maximum.

C. of the high angle of attack and high gross weight.

Answer (C) is correct. *(AIM Para 7-3-3)*
DISCUSSION: The greatest vortex strength occurs when the generating aircraft is heavy, clean, and slow, such as in takeoff climbout. At this time, there is a high gross weight and also a high angle of attack.
Answer (A) is incorrect. Vortices have to do with airflows about the wingtips, not the engines. Answer (B) is incorrect. The gear and flap configuration will change the characteristics of the vortex.

45. What effect would a light crosswind of approximately 7 knots have on vortex behavior?

A. The light crosswind would rapidly dissipate vortex strength.

B. The upwind vortex would tend to remain over the runway.

C. The downwind vortex would tend to remain over the runway.

Answer (B) is the best answer. *(AIM Para 7-3-4)*
DISCUSSION: A light crosswind of 1 to 5 kt. could result in the upwind vortex of a preceding aircraft remaining in the touchdown zone for a period of time. Also, it could hasten the drift of the downwind vortex toward another runway.
NOTE: This is an actual FAA question, and it does not correspond to the windspeed in the referenced *AIM*. This answer choice is the best option available.
Answer (A) is incorrect. Strong, not light, winds would help rapidly dissipate vortex strength. Answer (C) is incorrect. The upwind, not downwind, vortex would tend to remain over the runway in a light crosswind.

46. When landing behind a large jet aircraft, at which point on the runway should you plan to land?

A. If any crosswind, land on the windward side of the runway and prior to the jet's touchdown point.

B. At least 1,000 feet beyond the jet's touchdown point.

C. Beyond the jet's touchdown point.

Answer (C) is correct. *(AIM Para 7-3-6)*
DISCUSSION: When landing behind a large aircraft on the same runway, stay at or above the large aircraft's final approach flight path, and land beyond its touchdown point.
Answer (A) is incorrect. You must land beyond, not prior to, the touchdown point. Answer (B) is incorrect. There is no minimum distance (i.e., 1,000 ft.) that you should land beyond the jet's touchdown point.

5.6 Collision Avoidance

47. Which procedure is recommended while climbing to an assigned altitude on the airway?

A. Climb on the centerline of the airway except when maneuvering to avoid other air traffic in VFR conditions.

B. Climb slightly on the right side of the airway when in VFR conditions.

C. Climb far enough to the right side of the airway to avoid climbing or descending traffic coming from the opposite direction if in VFR conditions.

Answer (A) is correct. *(FAR 91.181)*
DISCUSSION: When climbing to an assigned altitude on an airway, one should use the centerline except to avoid other aircraft when in VFR conditions. This procedure is specified in FAR 91.181, which requires aircraft to operate along the centerline of federal airways.
Answer (B) is incorrect. You are required to maintain the centerline, not remain on the right side, while operating on a federal airway. Answer (C) is incorrect. You are required to maintain the centerline, not remain on the right side, while operating on a federal airway.

48. What is expected of you as pilot on an IFR flight plan if you are descending or climbing in VFR conditions?

A. If on an airway, climb or descend to the right of the centerline.

B. Advise ATC you are in visual conditions and will remain a short distance to the right of the centerline while climbing.

C. Execute gentle banks, left and right, at a frequency which permits continuous visual scanning of the airspace about you.

Answer (C) is correct. *(AIM Para 4-4-14)*
DISCUSSION: During climbs and descents in VFR conditions, pilots should execute gentle banks left and right to permit continual scanning of surrounding airspace.
Answer (A) is incorrect. You are required to maintain, not remain to the right of, the centerline while operating on a federal airway, except when maneuvering to avoid other traffic in VFR conditions. Answer (B) is incorrect. You are not required to advise ATC that you are in visual conditions, but you are required to maintain, not remain to the right of, the centerline while operating on a federal airway, except when maneuvering to avoid other traffic in VFR conditions.

49. When is a pilot on an IFR flight plan responsible for avoiding other aircraft?

A. At all times when not in radar contact with ATC.

B. When weather conditions permit, regardless of whether operating under IFR or VFR.

C. Only when advised by ATC.

Answer (B) is correct. *(FAR 91.113)*
DISCUSSION: When weather conditions permit, regardless of whether an operation is conducted under IFR or VFR, each pilot shall maintain vigilance in order to see and avoid other aircraft.
Answer (A) is incorrect. If weather conditions permit, each pilot is responsible for avoiding other aircraft, whether in radar contact or not. Answer (C) is incorrect. If weather conditions permit, each pilot, not ATC, is responsible for avoiding other aircraft.

50. What responsibility does the pilot in command of an IFR flight assume upon entering VFR conditions?

A. Reporting VFR conditions to ARTCC.

B. Obtaining an amended clearance authorizing VFR flight.

C. Seeing and avoiding other aircraft.

Answer (C) is correct. *(FAR 91.113)*
DISCUSSION: When weather conditions permit, regardless of whether an operation is conducted under IFR or VFR, each pilot shall maintain vigilance in order to see and avoid other aircraft.
Answer (A) is incorrect. VFR conditions are not reported unless so requested by ATC. Answer (B) is incorrect. IFR operating procedures are to be followed on an IFR flight, even when given a clearance for VFR flight, such as a "VFR-on-top" clearance.

5.7 IFR Flight Planning Information

51. The most current en route and destination flight information for planning an instrument flight should be obtained from

A. the ATIS broadcast.

B. the FSS.

C. Notices to Airmen (Class II).

Answer (B) is correct. *(AIM Para 5-1-1)*
DISCUSSION: The FAA urges every pilot to receive a preflight briefing, which may be obtained from a Flight Service Station (FSS) by telephone, radio, or personal visit. The preflight briefing should cover weather, airport, and en route navigation data.
Answer (A) is incorrect. The ATIS (Automatic Terminal Information Service) broadcasts only information pertaining to landing and departing operations at one airport. ATIS does not provide any en route information. Answer (C) is incorrect. *Notices to Airmen Publication* (formerly Class II) is published every 28 days and contains NOTAMs still in effect but not transmitted with weather information. It is only one aspect of a complete flight briefing.

52. What is the purpose of FDC NOTAMs?

A. To provide the latest information on the status of navigation facilities to all FSS facilities for scheduled broadcasts.

B. To issue notices for all airports and navigation facilities in the shortest possible time.

C. To advise of changes in flight data which affect instrument approach procedures (IAP), aeronautical charts, and flight restrictions prior to normal publication.

Answer (C) is correct. *(AIM Para 5-1-3)*
DISCUSSION: FDC (Flight Data Center) NOTAMs are regulatory in nature and issued to establish restrictions to flight or amend charts or published instrument approach procedures. FDC NOTAMs are published as needed and indexed in the *Notices to Airmen Publication*.
Answer (A) is incorrect. NOTAMs (D), not FDC NOTAMs, provide information for the status of navigational facilities. These NOTAMs are appended to the hourly weather reports.
Answer (B) is incorrect. The purpose of NOTAMs (D) is to issue notices for all public-use airports and navigation facilities in the shortest possible time.

53. From what source can you obtain the latest FDC NOTAMs?

A. Notices to Airmen Publication.

B. FAA FSS.

C. Airport/Facility Directory.

Answer (B) is correct. *(AIM Para 5-1-3)*
DISCUSSION: The National Flight Data Center occasionally publishes regulatory changes (either permanent or temporary) in FDC (Flight Data Center) NOTAMs. They are also used to advertise temporary flight restrictions caused by such things as natural disasters, large public events, and other events that may generate congested air traffic. FSSs are required to keep a file of current FDC NOTAMs.
Answer (A) is incorrect. The *Notices to Airmen Publication* is published every 28 days. The FSSs may have more current data. Answer (C) is incorrect. The *Airport/Facility Directory* is only published every 56 days. The *A/FD* includes only permanent changes that were known at the time of publication.

54. Absence of the sky condition and visibility on an ATIS broadcast specifically implies that

A. the ceiling is more than 5,000 feet and visibility is 5 miles or more.

B. the sky condition is clear and visibility is unrestricted.

C. the ceiling is at least 3,000 feet and visibility is 5 miles or more.

Answer (A) is correct. *(AIM Para 4-1-13)*
DISCUSSION: The ATIS broadcast generally includes the latest weather sequence, sky conditions, temperature, dew point, wind direction and velocity, altimeter, runways in use, etc. Absence of the sky condition and visibility on an ATIS broadcast specifically implies that the ceiling is more than 5,000 ft. and visibility is more than 5 SM.
Answer (B) is incorrect. The absence of the sky condition and visibility on an ATIS broadcast implies that ceilings are more than 5,000 ft., not clear, and visibility is 5 SM or more, not unrestricted. Answer (C) is incorrect. The absence of the sky condition on an ATIS broadcast implies a ceiling of more than 5,000 ft., not at least 3,000 ft.

55. The operation of an airport rotating beacon during daylight hours may indicate that

A. the in-flight visibility is less than 3 miles and the ceiling is less than 1,500 feet within Class E airspace.

B. the ground visibility is less than 3 miles and/or the ceiling is less than 1,000 feet in Class B, C, D, or E airspace.

C. an IFR clearance is required to operate within the airport traffic area.

Answer (B) is correct. *(AIM Para 2-1-8)*
DISCUSSION: In Class B, C, D, and E surface areas, operation of an airport beacon during daylight hours often indicates that the ground visibility is less than 3 SM and/or the ceiling is less than 1,000 ft. Pilots should not rely solely on the beacon to indicate weather conditions because there is no regulatory requirement for daylight operation of the airport's rotating beacon.
Answer (A) is incorrect. The operation of an airport rotating beacon during daylight hours at an airport located in Class E airspace may indicate that in-flight visibility (if ground is not reported) is less than 3 SM, and/or the ceiling is less than 1,000 ft., not 1,500 ft. Answer (C) is incorrect. An IFR clearance is required only in controlled airspace when IMC exists, not at an airport that is operating a rotating beacon during the day.

56. Which sources of aeronautical information, when used collectively, provide the latest status of airport conditions (e.g., runway closures, runway lighting, snow conditions)?

A. Aeronautical Information Manual, aeronautical charts, and Distant (D) NOTAMs.

B. Airport Facility Directory and FDC NOTAMs.

C. Airport Facility Directory and Distant (D) NOTAMs.

Answer (C) is correct. *(AIM Para 5-1-3)*
DISCUSSION: The latest status of airport conditions can be determined by using the *Airport/Facility Directory* for items that have been known for some time and distant NOTAMs (D), which contain the most up-to-date data.
Answer (A) is incorrect. The *Aeronautical Information Manual (AIM)* is a source of basic flight information and ATC procedures, not specific airport information, and aeronautical charts do not indicate the latest status of runway conditions. Answer (B) is incorrect. FDC NOTAMs deal with regulatory changes or unusual air traffic congestion, not local airport conditions.

57. When are ATIS broadcasts updated?

A. Every 30 minutes if weather conditions are below basic VFR; otherwise, hourly.

B. Upon receipt of any official weather, regardless of content change or reported values.

C. Only when the ceiling and/or visibility changes by a reportable value.

Answer (B) is correct. *(AIM Para 4-1-13)*
DISCUSSION: ATIS broadcasts are updated upon the receipt of any official weather regardless of content change or reported values. A new recording will also be made when there is a change in other pertinent data such as runway change, instrument approach in use, etc.
Answer (A) is incorrect. The frequency of ATIS updates does not differ under VFR or IFR conditions. Answer (C) is incorrect. The recording will be updated whenever official weather is received, even if there is no change.

58. What information is contained in the Notices to Airmen Publication (NTAP)?

A. Current NOTAM (D) and FDC NOTAMs.

B. Military NOTAMs only.

C. Current NOTAM (D), FDC NOTAMs, and military NOTAMs.

Answer (A) is correct. *(IPH Chap 1)*
DISCUSSION: The *NTAP* contains NOTAMs (D) that are expected to remain in effect for an extended period and FDC NOTAMs that are current at the time of publication.
Answer (B) is incorrect. Military NOTAMs are not published in the *NTAP*. Answer (C) is incorrect. While current NOTAMs (D) and FDC NOTAMs are published in the *NTAP*, military NOTAMs are not.

5.8 IFR Flight Plan

59. When filling out a composite flight plan, you should

A. Check VFR and put additional remarks in block 11.

B. Check both VFR and IFR.

C. Check IFR and put additional comments in block 11.

Answer (B) is correct. *(AIM Para 5-1-7)*
DISCUSSION: When filling out a composite flight plan, you should check both VFR and IFR in block 1 of the flight plan form.
Answer (A) is incorrect. You should check both VFR and IFR in block 1 of the flight plan form. However, it is acceptable to include a note that you are filing a composite flight plan in the remarks section, block 11. Answer (C) is incorrect. You should check both VFR and IFR in block 1 of the flight plan form. However, it is acceptable to include a note that you are filing a composite flight plan in the remarks section, block 11.

60. When filing a composite flight plan where the first portion of the flight is IFR, which fix(es) should be indicated on the flight plan form?

A. All points of transition from one airway to another, fixes defining direct route segments, and the clearance limit fix.

B. Only the fix where you plan to terminate the IFR portion of the flight.

C. Only those compulsory reporting points on the IFR route segment.

Answer (A) is correct. *(AIM Para 5-1-7)*
DISCUSSION: On composite flight plans for which the first portion of the flight is IFR, the flight plan should be a standard IFR flight plan, which includes points of transition from one airway to another, fixes defining direct route segments, and the clearance limit fix.
Answer (B) is incorrect. You have to define the route to get to your clearance limit fix. Answer (C) is incorrect. Compulsory reporting points are not listed on an IFR flight plan unless they define a point of transition, direct route segments, or the clearance limit fix.

61. When may a pilot file a composite flight plan?

A. When requested or advised by ATC.

B. Any time a portion of the flight will be VFR.

C. Any time a landing is planned at an intermediate airport.

Answer (B) is correct. *(AIM Para 5-1-7)*
DISCUSSION: A composite flight plan should be filed whenever VFR operation is specified for one portion of the flight and IFR for another portion.
Answer (A) is incorrect. ATC does not request or advise on the type of flight plan to file other than IFR flight plans required in certain weather conditions and in the positive control area. Answer (C) is incorrect. You are not required to convert a flight plan from or to IFR or VFR when landing is planned at an intermediate airport.

62. What point at the destination should be used to compute estimated time en route on an IFR flight plan?

A. The final approach fix on the expected instrument approach.

B. The initial approach fix on the expected instrument approach.

C. The point of first intended landing.

Answer (C) is correct. *(FAR 91.169)*
DISCUSSION: Estimated time en route on an IFR flight plan should be the time from takeoff at the departure airport to touchdown at the point of first intended landing.
Answer (A) is incorrect. Due to varying weather conditions, runways in use, traffic, etc., there is no way of accurately telling which approach will be used. Answer (B) is incorrect. Due to varying weather conditions, runways in use, traffic, etc., there is no way of accurately telling which approach will be used.

63. (Refer to Figure 1 below.) Which item(s) should be checked in block 1 for a composite flight plan?

   A. VFR with an explanation in block 11.

   B. IFR with an explanation in block 11.

   C. VFR and IFR.

Answer (C) is correct. *(AIM Para 5-1-7)*
   DISCUSSION: If you are filing a composite VFR/IFR flight plan, you should check both VFR and IFR in block 1 of the flight plan. A DVFR flight plan is required for flights through air defense identification zones (ADIZ) for national security reasons.
   Answer (A) is incorrect. Both VFR and IFR should be checked. Answer (B) is incorrect. Both VFR and IFR should be checked.

64. (Refer to Figure 1 below.) Which equipment determines the code to be entered in block 3 as a suffix to aircraft type on the flight plan form?

   A. DME and airborne radar.

   B. DME, transponder, and ADF.

   C. DME, transponder, and RNAV.

Answer (C) is correct. *(AIM Para 5-1-8)*
   DISCUSSION: Block 3 asks for the aircraft type and special equipment. After the aircraft type, a slash is followed by a letter indicating the combination of transponder, DME, and area navigation (RNAV) equipment that you have in the airplane.
   Answer (A) is incorrect. You need not report airborne radar. Answer (B) is incorrect. An ADF is not considered a special type of navigation equipment.

Figure 1. – Flight Plan.

65. (Refer to Figure 1 above.) What information should be entered in block 7 of an IFR flight plan if the flight has three legs, each at a different altitude?

   A. Altitude for first leg.

   B. Altitude for first leg and highest altitude.

   C. Highest altitude.

Answer (A) is correct. *(AIM Para 5-1-8)*
   DISCUSSION: Block 7 of IFR flight plans is for altitude. You should enter only the initial request for altitude. When more than one altitude or flight level is desired along the route of flight, it is best to make subsequent requests direct to the controller.
   Answer (B) is incorrect. Initial, not highest, altitude is to be submitted on your flight plan. Answer (C) is incorrect. Initial, not highest, altitude is to be entered on your flight plan.

66. (Refer to Figure 1 on page 160.) The time entered in block 12 for an IFR flight should be based on which fuel quantity?

A. Total fuel required for the flight.

B. Total usable fuel on board.

C. The amount of fuel required to fly to the destination airport, then to the alternate, plus a 45-minute reserve.

Answer (B) is correct. *(AIM Para 5-1-8)*
DISCUSSION: Block 12 should be filled in with the time at normal cruising speed using total usable fuel on board. It should be computed from the departure point.
Answer (A) is incorrect. Total fuel required for the flight is determined in your flight planning but is not an item that is listed on an IFR flight plan. Answer (C) is incorrect. It describes the IFR fuel requirement.

67. What is a waypoint when used for an IFR flight?

A. A predetermined geographical position used for an RNAV route or an RNAV instrument approach.

B. A reporting point defined by the intersection of two VOR radials.

C. A location on a victor airway which can only be identified by VOR and DME signals.

Answer (A) is correct. *(IFH Chap 9)*
DISCUSSION: A waypoint on an IFR flight is a predetermined geographical position used for an RNAV route or an RNAV instrument approach definition or progress-reporting purposes. It is defined relative to a VORTAC position or in terms of latitude/longitude coordinates.
Answer (B) is incorrect. A point defined by the intersection of two VOR radials is called an intersection, not a waypoint. Answer (C) is incorrect. A location on a victor airway that can be identified only by VOR and DME signals is called a DME fix, not a way point.

68. What is the recommended procedure for transitioning from VFR to IFR on a composite flight plan?

A. Prior to transitioning to IFR, contact the nearest FSS, close the VFR portion, and request ATC clearance.

B. Upon reaching the proposed point for change to IFR, contact the nearest FSS and cancel your VFR flight plan, then contact ARTCC and request an IFR clearance.

C. Prior to reaching the proposed point for change to IFR, contact ARTCC, request your IFR clearance, and instruct them to cancel the VFR flight plan.

Answer (A) is correct. *(AIM Para 5-1-7)*
DISCUSSION: Prior to transitioning from VFR to IFR, you should close the VFR portion with FSS and request ATC clearance. You must remain in VFR weather conditions until operating in accordance with the IFR clearance.
Answer (B) is incorrect. You must obtain an IFR clearance before beginning IFR operations. Answer (C) is incorrect. You should cancel your VFR flight plan with FSS, not ATC.

69. You may cancel an IFR flight plan

A. at any time as long as you advise ATC.

B. only in an emergency.

C. if VMC outside Class A airspace.

Answer (C) is correct. *(AIM Para 5-1-15)*
DISCUSSION: An IFR flight plan may be canceled at any time you are operating in VFR conditions when not in Class A airspace by stating, "Cancel my IFR flight plan," to ATC. Once accepted by ATC, you should change to the appropriate communications frequency, transponder code, and altitude.
Answer (A) is incorrect. You cannot proceed under VFR when IFR conditions exist or when you are flying above FL 180 (i.e., in Class A airspace). Answer (B) is incorrect. ATC will provide needed assistance in emergencies while you are operating under an IFR flight plan.

70. How is your flight plan closed when your destination airport has IFR conditions and there is no control tower or flight service station (FSS) on the field?

A. The ARTCC controller will close your flight plan when you report the runway in sight.

B. You may close your flight plan any time after starting the approach by contacting any FSS or ATC facility.

C. Upon landing, you must close your flight plan by radio or by telephone to any FSS or ATC facility.

Answer (C) is correct. *(AIM Para 5-1-15)*
DISCUSSION: IFR flight plans are automatically closed by ATC if you land at an airport with an operating control tower. However, if operating under an IFR flight plan to an airport with no functioning control tower, you must cancel the IFR flight plan. You may cancel your IFR flight plan while airborne only if weather permits. If your destination airport has IFR conditions and there is no tower or FSS on the field, you should close your IFR flight plan upon landing by radio or telephone to any FSS or ATC facility.
Answer (A) is incorrect. You, not ATC, must close your IFR flight plan at airports without an operating control tower or FSS on the field. Answer (B) is incorrect. When an airport has IFR conditions, you must have IFR clearances until you have safely landed.

5.9 ATC Clearances

71. What response is expected when ATC issues an IFR clearance to pilots of airborne aircraft?

A. Read back the entire clearance as required by regulation.

B. Read back those parts containing altitude assignments or vectors and any part requiring verification.

C. Read-back should be unsolicited and spontaneous to confirm that the pilot understands all instructions.

Answer (B) is correct. *(AIM Para 4-4-6)*
DISCUSSION: Pilots of airborne aircraft should read back those parts of ATC clearances and instructions containing altitude assignments or vectors and any part requiring verification. The read-back serves as a double-check between pilots and ATC and reduces the kinds of communications errors that occur when a number is either misheard or incorrect.
Answer (A) is incorrect. The read-back is an expected procedure, but there is no regulatory requirement to read back an ATC clearance. Only those parts containing altitude assignments or vectors and any part requiring verification, not the entire clearance, should be read back. Answer (C) is incorrect. Only those parts containing altitude assignments or vectors and any part requiring verification, not all instructions, should be read back.

72. Which clearance items are always given in an abbreviated IFR departure clearance? (Assume radar environment.)

A. Altitude, destination airport, and one or more fixes which identify the initial route of flight.

B. Destination airport, altitude, DP Name, Number, and/or Transition, if appropriate.

C. Clearance limit, DP Name, Number, and/or Transition, if appropriate.

Answer (B) is correct. *(AIM Para 5-2-4)*
DISCUSSION: An abbreviated IFR departure clearance will include the destination airport. En route altitude will be stated in the clearance, and the pilot will be advised to expect an assigned or filed altitude within a given time or at a certain point after departure. Any DP (instrument departure procedure) will also be specified by ATC stating the DP name, the current number, and the DP transition name.
Answer (A) is incorrect. The fixes are already included in the flight plan and do not need to be repeated in an abbreviated IFR departure clearance. Answer (C) is incorrect. An en route altitude is always given in an abbreviated IFR departure clearance.

73. Which information is always given in an abbreviated departure clearance?

A. DP or transition name and altitude to maintain.

B. Name of destination airport or specific fix and altitude.

C. Altitude to maintain and code to squawk.

Answer (B) is correct. *(AIM Para 5-2-4)*
DISCUSSION: An abbreviated IFR departure clearance always contains the name of your destination airport or clearance limit; altitude; and, if a DP is to be flown, the DP name, the current number, and the DP transition name.
Answer (A) is incorrect. The destination airport or clearance limit is always given in an abbreviated clearance. Answer (C) is incorrect. The destination airport or clearance limit is always given in an abbreviated clearance.

74. An abbreviated departure clearance "...CLEARED AS FILED..." will always contain the name

A. and number of the STAR to be flown when filed in the flight plan.

B. of the destination airport filed in the flight plan.

C. of the first compulsory reporting point if not in a radar environment.

Answer (B) is correct. *(AIM Para 5-2-4)*
DISCUSSION: An abbreviated IFR departure clearance will include the destination airport. En route altitude will be stated, and the pilot will be advised to expect an assigned or filed altitude by a certain time or at a certain point after departure either separately or as part of a DP. The abbreviated clearance also includes the DP name-number-transition, if appropriate.
Answer (A) is incorrect. A STAR, when filed in a flight plan, is considered a part of the filed route of flight and will not normally be stated in an initial departure clearance. Answer (C) is incorrect. Compulsory reporting points are not given in an abbreviated clearance.

75. When departing from an airport not served by a control tower, the issuance of a clearance containing a void time indicates that

A. ATC will assume the pilot has not departed if no transmission is received before the void time.

B. The pilot must advise ATC as soon as possible, but no later than 30 minutes, of their intentions if not off by the void time.

C. ATC will protect the airspace only to the void time.

Answer (B) is correct. *(AIM Para 5-2-5)*
DISCUSSION: If operating from an airport not served by a control tower, the pilot may receive a clearance containing a provision that, if the flight has not departed by a specific time (void time), the clearance is void. In this situation, the pilot who does not depart prior to the void time must advise ATC of his or her intentions as soon as possible, but no later than 30 min. after the void time.
Answer (A) is incorrect. ATC will assume a departure unless it hears from the pilot. Answer (C) is incorrect. The airspace is protected until ATC hears from the pilot.

76. On the runup pad, you receive the following clearance from ground control:

CLEARED TO THE DALLAS-LOVE AIRPORT AS FILED – MAINTAIN SIX THOUSAND – SQUAWK ZERO SEVEN ZERO FOUR JUST BEFORE DEPARTURE – DEPARTURE CONTROL WILL BE ONE TWO FOUR POINT NINER.

An abbreviated clearance, such as this, will always contain the

A. departure control frequency.

B. transponder code.

C. destination airport and route.

Answer (C) is correct. *(AIM Para 5-2-4)*
DISCUSSION: An IFR departure clearance will always contain the destination airport and the route of flight. The route of flight will either be given fix-by-fix by the controller or "as filed," in which case the route on the IFR flight plan is the assigned route. The statement, "Cleared to the Dallas-Love airport as filed," contains the destination airport and the specific route to be taken (the filed route).
Answer (A) is incorrect. If the abbreviated clearance contains a DP, the departure control frequency may not be given if the frequency is published in the DP. Answer (B) is incorrect. An abbreviated IFR departure clearance will always contain the destination airport and the route of flight, but not the transponder code.

77. What is the significance of an ATC clearance which reads "...CRUISE SIX THOUSAND..."?

A. The pilot must maintain 6,000 until reaching the IAF serving the destination airport, then execute the published approach procedure.

B. It authorizes a pilot to conduct flight at any altitude from minimum IFR altitude up to and including 6,000.

C. The pilot is authorized to conduct flight at any altitude from minimum IFR altitude up to and including 6,000, but each change in altitude must be reported to ATC.

Answer (B) is correct. *(AIM Para 4-4-3)*
DISCUSSION: The term "cruise" in a clearance assigns a pilot a block of airspace from the minimum IFR altitude up to and including the specified altitude (e.g., 6,000 ft. MSL). The pilot may level off at any intermediate altitude within this block of airspace. Climb and descent within the block are to be made at the discretion of the pilot. However, once the pilot starts descent and verbally reports leaving an altitude in the block, (s)he may not return to that altitude without additional ATC clearance.
Answer (A) is incorrect. The pilot need not maintain 6,000 ft. Answer (C) is incorrect. The pilot may change altitude without reporting to ATC.

78. What is the significance of an ATC clearance which reads "...CRUISE SIX THOUSAND..."?

A. The pilot must maintain 6,000 feet until reaching the IAF serving the destination airport, then execute the published approach procedure.

B. Climbs may be made to, or descents made from, 6,000 feet at the pilot's discretion.

C. The pilot may utilize any altitude from the MEA/MOCA to 6,000 feet, but each change in altitude must be reported to ATC.

Answer (B) is correct. *(AIM Para 4-4-3)*
DISCUSSION: The term "cruise" in a clearance assigns a pilot a block of airspace from the minimum IFR altitude up to and including the specified altitude (e.g., 6,000 ft. MSL). The pilot may climb to, level off at, or descend from any intermediate altitude within this block of airspace. Once the pilot starts descent and verbally reports leaving an altitude in the block, however, (s)he may not return to that altitude without additional ATC clearance.
Answer (A) is incorrect. The pilot need not maintain 6,000 ft. Answer (C) is incorrect. The pilot is assigned all the airspace from the minimum IFR altitude to 6,000 ft. MSL and may change altitudes without reporting to ATC.

79. What is the rule for a pilot receiving a "Land and Hold Short Operation (LAHSO) clearance?"

A. The pilot is required to accept the controller's clearance in visual meteorological conditions.

B. The pilot must accept the clearance if the pavement is dry and the stopping distance is adequate.

C. The pilot has the option to accept or reject all LAHSO clearances regardless of the meteorological conditions.

Answer (C) is correct. *(IPH Chap 1)*
DISCUSSION: It is always the pilot's option to accept or reject all LAHSO clearances regardless of the meteorological conditions. Pilots have the option to decline any LAHSO clearance. The pilot should only accept a LAHSO clearance provided the pilot feels (s)he can land the plane within the available distance without compromising safety.
Answer (A) is incorrect. Pilots never have to accept a controller's clearance, regardless of the meteorological conditions. Pilots have the option to decline any LAHSO clearance. A pilot should only accept a LAHSO clearance provided the pilot feels (s)he can land the plan within the available distance, without compromising safety. Answer (B) is incorrect. Pilots never have to accept a controller's clearance, regardless of the runway conditions or stopping distance. Pilots have the option to decline any LAHSO clearance. A pilot should only accept a LAHSO clearance provided the pilot feels (s)he can land the plane within the available distance, without compromising safety.

80. A "CRUISE FOUR THOUSAND FEET" clearance would mean that the pilot is authorized to

A. vacate 4,000 feet without notifying ATC.

B. climb to, but not descend from 4,000 feet, without further ATC clearance.

C. use any altitude from minimum IFR to 4,000 feet, but must report leaving each altitude.

Answer (A) is correct. *(AIM Para 4-4-3)*
DISCUSSION: The term "cruise" in a clearance assigns a pilot a block of airspace from the minimum IFR altitude up to and including the specified altitude (e.g., 4,000 ft. MSL). The pilot may level off at any intermediate altitude within this block of airspace. Climb and descent within the block are to be made at the discretion of the pilot. However, once the pilot starts descent and verbally reports leaving an altitude in the block, (s)he may not return to that altitude without additional ATC clearance.
Answer (B) is incorrect. Any airspace between the minimum IFR altitude and 4,000 ft. MSL may be used without further ATC clearance. Answer (C) is incorrect. Cruise clearances do not require reporting a change in altitude to ATC.

5.10 ATC Communication Procedures

81. When should pilots state their position on the airport when calling the tower for takeoff?

A. When visibility is less than 1 mile.

B. When parallel runways are in use.

C. When departing from a runway intersection.

Answer (C) is correct. *(AIM Para 4-3-10)*
DISCUSSION: You should state your position on the airport when calling the tower for takeoff from a runway intersection. Additionally, you are expected to request from ground control approval for the intersection departure (i.e., a departure from any runway intersection except the end of the runway) prior to taxi.
Answer (A) is incorrect. A pilot is not expected to state his or her position on the airport when calling the tower for takeoff when visibility is less than 1 mile. Answer (B) is incorrect. A pilot is not expected to state his or her position on the airport when calling the tower for takeoff when parallel runways are in use.

82. During a takeoff into IMC with low ceilings, you should contact departure

A. before entering the clouds.

B. when the tower instructs the change.

C. upon reaching the traffic pattern altitude.

Answer (B) is correct. *(AIM Para 5-2-6)*
DISCUSSION: A pilot should not change to the departure control frequency until advised by ATC. Because the pilot maintains continuous contact with assigned ATC frequencies, all frequency changes are at the direction of ATC.
Answer (A) is incorrect. The tower will advise the pilot when to contact departure control, and such contact is not based on whether the aircraft has penetrated the clouds. Answer (C) is incorrect. The tower will advise the pilot when to contact departure control, which may or may not be upon reaching the traffic pattern altitude.

83. When should your transponder be on Mode C while on an IFR flight?

A. Only when ATC requests Mode C.

B. At all times if the equipment has been calibrated, unless requested otherwise by ATC.

C. When passing 12,500 feet MSL.

Answer (B) is correct. *(AIM Para 4-1-19)*
DISCUSSION: If your airplane's transponder is equipped to reply on Mode C, it should be on at all times unless deactivation is directed by ATC.
Answer (A) is incorrect. Mode C should be turned off, not on, only when directed by ATC. Answer (C) is incorrect. Mode C is a requirement anytime you are flying above 10,000 ft. MSL, not 12,500 ft. MSL.

84. What is the recommended climb procedure when a nonradar departure control instructs a pilot to climb to the assigned altitude?

A. Maintain a continuous optimum climb until reaching assigned altitude and report passing each 1,000 foot level.

B. Climb at a maximum angle of climb to within 1,000 feet of the assigned altitude, then 500 feet per minute the last 1,000 feet.

C. Maintain an optimum climb on the centerline of the airway without intermediate level-offs until 1,000 feet below assigned altitude, then 500 to 1,500 feet per minute.

Answer (C) is correct. *(AIM Para 4-4-9)*
DISCUSSION: When ATC clearances are given to descend or climb to a certain altitude, the pilot should use the optimum rate consistent with the operating characteristics of the aircraft to 1,000 ft. above or below the assigned altitude and then attempt to descend or climb at a rate of between 500 and 1,500 fpm until reaching the assigned altitude. Also, on airways, one should climb and descend on the centerline of the airway with no intermediate level-offs.
Answer (A) is incorrect. The pilot is not required to report passing each 1,000 ft. of altitude. Answer (B) is incorrect. One should normally use a cruise climb rather than a maximum angle of climb.

85. To comply with ATC instructions for altitude changes of more than 1,000 feet, what rate of climb or descent should be used?

A. As rapidly as practicable to 500 feet above/below the assigned altitude, and then at 500 feet per minute until the assigned altitude is reached.

B. 1,000 feet per minute during climb and 500 feet per minute during descents until reaching the assigned altitude.

C. As rapidly as practicable to 1,000 feet above/below the assigned altitude, and then between 500 and 1,500 feet per minute until reaching the assigned altitude.

Answer (C) is correct. *(AIM Para 4-4-9)*
DISCUSSION: When ATC clearances are given to descend or climb to a certain altitude, the pilot should use the optimum rate consistent with the operating characteristics of the aircraft to 1,000 ft. above or below the assigned altitude and then attempt to descend or climb at a rate of between 500 and 1,500 fpm until reaching the assigned altitude. Also, one should climb and descend on the centerline of the airway with no intermediate level-offs.
Answer (A) is incorrect. The rate should be between 500 and 1,500 fpm after you are within 1,000 ft., not 500 ft., of the target altitude. Answer (B) is incorrect. The rate of climb and descent should be based upon aircraft capability. Also, when 1,000 ft. above or below the assigned altitude, the pilot should attempt to descend or climb at a rate of between 500 and 1,500 fpm until the assigned altitude is reached.

86. Which report should be made to ATC without a specific request when not in radar contact?

A. Entering instrument meteorological conditions.

B. When leaving final approach fix in bound on final approach.

C. Correcting an E.T.A. any time a previous E.T.A. is in error in excess of 2 minutes.

Answer (B) is correct. *(AIM Para 5-3-3)*
DISCUSSION: The following reports (in addition to those that are made at all times) should be made to ATC without a specific request when not in radar contact:

1. A report when leaving final approach fix inbound on final approach (nonprecision approach) or when leaving the outer marker or fix used in lieu of the outer marker inbound on final approach (precision approach)
2. Position reports over compulsory reporting points
3. A corrected ETA to a reporting point at any time it becomes apparent that an estimate as previously submitted is in error in excess of 3 minutes

Answer (A) is incorrect. A report should be made to ATC whether or not in radar contact anytime you encounter any type of weather conditions that have not been forecast. If IMC were forecast, no report is necessary. Answer (C) is incorrect. A report should be made to ATC when correcting an ETA anytime a previous ETA is in error in excess of 3 min., not 2 min.

87. When ATC has not imposed any climb or descent restrictions and aircraft are within 1,000 feet of assigned altitude, pilots should attempt to both climb and descend at a rate of between

A. 500 feet per minute and 1,000 feet per minute.

B. 500 feet per minute and 1,500 feet per minute.

C. 1,000 feet per minute and 2,000 feet per minute.

Answer (B) is correct. *(AIM Para 4-4-9)*
DISCUSSION: When ATC clearances are given to descend or climb to a certain altitude, the pilot should use the optimum rate consistent with the operating characteristics of the aircraft to 1,000 ft. above or below the assigned altitude and then attempt to descend or climb at a rate of between 500 and 1,500 fpm until reaching the assigned altitude. Also, on airways, one should climb and descend on the centerline of the airway with no intermediate level-offs.
Answer (A) is incorrect. Within 1,000 ft. of the assigned altitude, pilots should attempt to climb/descend at a rate of between 500 and 1,500 fpm, not 1,000 fpm. Answer (C) is incorrect. Within 1,000 ft. of the assigned altitude, pilots should attempt to climb/descend at a rate of between 500 and 1,500 fpm, not 1,000 and 2,000 fpm.

88. What does the ATC term "Radar Contact" signify?

A. Your aircraft has been identified and you will receive separation from all aircraft while in contact with this radar facility.

B. Your aircraft has been identified on the radar display and radar flight-following will be provided until radar identification is terminated.

C. You will be given traffic advisories until advised the service has been terminated or that radar contact has been lost.

Answer (B) is correct. *(P/C Glossary)*
DISCUSSION: The term "radar contact" is used by ATC to inform an aircraft that it is identified on the radar display and that radar flight following will be provided until radar service is terminated. Reporting over compulsory reporting points is not required when an aircraft is in radar contact.
Answer (A) is incorrect. Separation from all aircraft occurs only in Class A, B, and C airspace. Answer (C) is incorrect. Traffic advisory service is provided only to the extent possible. Higher-priority duties take precedence, such as controlling or other limitations, volume of traffic, frequency congestion, or controller workload.

89. For IFR planning purposes, what are the compulsory reporting points when using VOR/DME or VORTAC fixes to define a direct route not on established airways?

    A. Fixes selected to define the route.

    B. There are no compulsory reporting points unless advised by ATC.

    C. At the changeover points.

Answer (A) is correct. *(AIM Para 5-3-2)*
    DISCUSSION: When using VOR/DME or VORTAC fixes to define a direct route not on an established airway, those fixes selected to define the route automatically become compulsory reporting points (when not in radar contact) for the flight.
    Answer (B) is incorrect. On a direct flight, the compulsory reporting points are those fixes used to define the route. Answer (C) is incorrect. Some navigation systems used on direct flights do not require COPs to prevent the loss of navigation guidance, e.g., GPS.

90. During a flight, the controller advises "traffic 2 o'clock 5 miles southbound." The pilot is holding 20° correction for a crosswind from the right. Where should the pilot look for the traffic?

    A. 40° to the right of the aircraft's nose.

    B. 20° to the right of the aircraft's nose.

    C. Straight ahead.

Answer (A) is correct. *(AIM Para 4-1-14)*
    DISCUSSION: ATC issues traffic advisories in terms of the aircraft's course (i.e., ground track), not its heading. Allowance must be made for drift correction or course change made simultaneously with the radar traffic information. Two o'clock is approximately 60° to the right of the aircraft's course. Since the pilot is already holding a 20° right-wind correction, (s)he should look only 40° to the right of the aircraft's nose for the traffic.
    Answer (B) is incorrect. This direction is 40° to the right of the aircraft's track, which is between 1 and 2 o'clock. Answer (C) is incorrect. Straight ahead is 20° (wind correction) to the right of the aircraft's track, which is between 12 and 1 o'clock.

91. If, during a VFR practice instrument approach, Radar Approach Control assigns an altitude or heading that will cause you to enter the clouds, what action should be taken?

    A. Enter the clouds, since ATC authorization for practice approaches is considered an IFR clearance.

    B. Avoid the clouds and inform ATC that altitude/heading will not permit VFR.

    C. Abandon the approach.

Answer (B) is correct. *(AIM Para 4-3-21)*
    DISCUSSION: During a VFR practice instrument approach, you are responsible to comply with basic visual flight rules. Thus, if radar approach assigns an altitude or heading that will cause you to enter the clouds, you must avoid the clouds and inform ATC that that altitude/heading will not permit VFR.
    Answer (A) is incorrect. Pilots may not enter clouds without an IFR clearance. Answer (C) is incorrect. The pilot need only modify, not abandon the approach, to maintain VFR.

92. You have not yet been cleared for the approach, but you are being vectored to the ILS approach course. It is clear that you will pass through the localizer course unless you take action. You should

    A. turn outbound and complete the procedure turn.

    B. continue as assigned and query ATC.

    C. turn inbound and join the final approach course.

Answer (B) is correct. *(AIM Para 5-4-3)*
    DISCUSSION: Normally, you will be informed by ATC when it is necessary to vector across the final approach course for spacing or other reasons. If you have not been cleared for the approach and it becomes evident that you will cross the approach course, you must continue on your assigned heading and question ATC.
    Answer (A) is incorrect. While you are being radar vectored, you are not authorized to make a procedure turn unless cleared by ATC. Answer (C) is incorrect. You must maintain your assigned heading, not turn inbound on the final approach course.

93. What is the pilot in command's responsibility when flying a propeller aircraft within 20 miles of the airport of intended landing and ATC requests the pilot to reduce speed to 160? Pilot complies with speed adjustment.)

    A. Reduce TAS to 160 knots and maintain until advised by ATC.

    B. Reduce IAS to 160 MPH and maintain until advised by ATC.

    C. Reduce IAS to 160 knots and maintain that speed within 10 knots.

Answer (C) is correct. *(AIM Para 4-4-11)*
    DISCUSSION: ATC will express all speed adjustments in terms of knots based on indicated airspeed (IAS) in 10-kt. increments below FL 240. When complying with an ATC speed adjustment to reduce to 160, you should reduce IAS to 160 kt. and maintain that speed within 10 kt.
    Answer (A) is incorrect. ATC speed restrictions are based on indicated airspeed (IAS), not true airspeed (TAS). Answer (B) is incorrect. Airspeeds are given in knots, not MPH.

94. During the en route phase of an IFR flight, the pilot is advised "Radar service terminated." What action is appropriate?

- A. Set transponder to code 1200.
- B. Resume normal position reporting.
- C. Activate the IDENT feature of the transponder to re-establish radar contact.

Answer (B) is correct. *(AIM Para 5-3-2)*
 DISCUSSION: During the en route phase of an IFR flight, if you are advised of "radar service terminated" or "radar contact lost," you should resume normal position reporting as required when not in radar contact.
 Answer (A) is incorrect. You should set the transponder to code 1200 (VFR) only when you cancel your IFR flight plan with ATC and you are instructed to squawk VFR. Answer (C) is incorrect. You should activate the IDENT feature of the transponder only upon the request of ATC.

95. What is meant when departure control instructs you to "resume own navigation" after you have been vectored to a Victor airway?

- A. You should maintain the airway by use of your navigation equipment.
- B. Radar service is terminated.
- C. You are still in radar contact, but must make position reports.

Answer (A) is correct. *(P/C Glossary)*
 DISCUSSION: Assuming you have been vectored to an airway on your intended route of flight, you should maintain your course along the airway by use of your navigation equipment when ATC advises you to resume your own navigation.
 Answer (B) is incorrect. "Resume navigation" means that the radar controller will stop vectoring you, not stop observing you. Answer (C) is incorrect. Position reporting is not required when you are in radar contact with ATC.

96. Upon intercepting the assigned radial, the controller advises you that you are on the airway and to "RESUME OWN NAVIGATION." This phrase means that

- A. You are still in radar contact, but must make position reports.
- B. Radar services are terminated and you will be responsible for position reports.
- C. You are to assume responsibility for your own navigation.

Answer (C) is correct. *(P/C Glossary)*
 DISCUSSION: Assuming you have been vectored to an airway on your intended route of flight, you should maintain your course along the airway by use of your navigation equipment when ATC advises you to resume your own navigation.
 Answer (A) is incorrect. Position reporting is not required when in radar contact. Answer (B) is incorrect. "Resume navigation" means only that the radar controller is going to stop vectoring you, not stop observing you.

97. What service is provided by departure control to an IFR flight when operating from an airport within the outer area of Class C airspace?

- A. Separation from all aircraft.
- B. Position and altitude of all traffic within 2 miles of the IFR pilot's line of flight and altitude.
- C. Separation from all IFR aircraft and participating VFR aircraft.

Answer (C) is correct. *(FAR 91.130)*
 DISCUSSION: In the outer area of Class C airspace, ATC provides an IFR flight with separation from all IFR aircraft and participating VFR aircraft. VFR aircraft participation in the outer area is voluntary.
 Answer (A) is incorrect. An IFR flight is provided traffic advisories and conflict resolution with other IFR aircraft and with only participating VFR aircraft within the outer area of Class C airspace. Answer (B) is incorrect. ATC provides position and altitude of aircraft that may conflict, not position and altitude of all traffic within 2 NM of your line of flight.

98. While on an IFR flight plan, you should notify ATC of a variation in speed when

- A. ground speed changes more than 5 knots.
- B. average TAS changes 10 knots or 5 percent.
- C. ground speed changes 10 MPH or more.

Answer (B) is correct. *(AIM Para 5-3-3)*
 DISCUSSION: There are a number of things a pilot needs to report to ATC without being requested. One is a change in the average TAS at cruising altitude when it varies by 10 kt. or 5% (whichever is greater) from that filed in the flight plan.
 Answer (A) is incorrect. ATC should be notified if TAS, not ground speed, varies more than 10 kt., not 5 kt., or 5%, whichever is greater. Answer (C) is incorrect. ATC should be notified if TAS, not ground speed, varies more than 10 kt., not 10 MPH, or 5%, whichever is greater.

99. Unless otherwise stated, instrument procedures use the standard IFR climb gradient of

    A. 500 feet per minute.

    B. 400 feet per nautical mile.

    C. 200 feet per nautical mile.

Answer (C) is correct. *(IPH Chap 2)*

    DISCUSSION: Instrument procedures design criteria assumes an initial climb of 200 feet per nautical mile for obstacle clearance during a departure procedure.

    Answer (A) is incorrect. Climb gradients are developed as a part of a departure procedure to ensure obstacle protection. The rate of climb is 200 feet per nautical mile. Answer (B) is incorrect. The rate of climb is 200 feet per nautical mile.

100. When are you required to establish communications with the tower (Class D airspace), if you cancel your IFR flight plan 10 miles from the destination?

    A. Immediately after canceling the flight plan.

    B. When advised by ARTCC.

    C. Before entering Class D airspace.

Answer (C) is correct. *(FAR 91.129)*

    DISCUSSION: You must establish two-way radio communication with the tower before entering Class D airspace. Thus, if you cancel your IFR flight plan, you must notify the tower of your position and intentions prior to entering Class D airspace.

    Answer (A) is incorrect. While it is a good operating practice to make an initial call to the tower up to 15 mi. from a Class D airport, it is required only before entering Class D airspace. Answer (B) is incorrect. While ARTCC may advise you to contact the tower when the controller accepts your IFR flight plan cancelation, you are required to contact the tower only prior to entering Class D airspace.

101. If a control tower and an FSS are located on the same airport, which function is provided by the FSS during those periods when the tower is closed?

    A. Automatic closing of the IFR flight plan.

    B. Approach control services.

    C. Airport Advisory Service.

Answer (C) is correct. *(AIM Para 4-1-9)*

    DISCUSSION: An FSS located on an airport will provide Local Airport Advisory (LAA) service at that airport when there is no operating control tower. This service provides arriving and departing aircraft with wind direction and speed, favored runway, altimeter setting, pertinent known traffic, pertinent known field condition, and airport taxi routes and traffic patterns. The information is advisory in nature.

    Answer (A) is incorrect. The pilot must initiate cancelation of the IFR plan if operating IFR to an airport with no functioning control tower. Answer (B) is incorrect. FSS personnel can only issue advisories, not provide ATC services, to pilots.

102. Which service is provided for IFR arrivals by a FSS located on an airport without a control tower?

    A. Automatic closing of the IFR flight plan.

    B. Airport advisories.

    C. All functions of approach control.

Answer (B) is correct. *(AIM Para 4-1-9)*

    DISCUSSION: An FSS located on an airport will provide Local Airport Advisory (LAA) service at that airport if there is no operating control tower. This service provides arriving and departing aircraft with wind direction and speed, favored runway, altimeter setting, pertinent known traffic, pertinent known field condition, and airport taxi routes and traffic patterns. The information is advisory in nature.

    Answer (A) is incorrect. The pilot must initiate cancelation of the IFR plan if operating IFR to an airport with no operating control tower. Answer (C) is incorrect. FSS personnel can issue only advisories, not ATC clearances and instructions, to pilots.

103. What does declaring "minimum fuel" to ATC imply?

    A. Traffic priority is needed to the destination airport.

    B. Emergency handling is required to the nearest usable airport.

    C. Merely an advisory that indicates an emergency situation is possible should any undue delay occur.

Answer (C) is correct. *(AIM Para 5-5-15)*

    DISCUSSION: You should advise ATC of your minimum fuel status when your fuel supply has reached a state in which, upon reaching your destination, you cannot accept any undue delay. Be aware that this is not an emergency situation, but merely an advisory that indicates an emergency situation is possible should any undue delay occur.

    Answer (A) is incorrect. Priority may be issued when declaring an emergency, not when declaring minimum fuel. Answer (B) is incorrect. Minimum fuel advisory is not an emergency situation.

5.11 Radio Communication Failure

104. Which procedure should you follow if you experience two-way communications failure while holding at a holding fix with an EFC time? (The holding fix is not the same as the approach fix.)

A. Depart the holding fix to arrive at the approach fix as close as possible to the EFC time.

B. Depart the holding fix at the EFC time.

C. Proceed immediately to the approach fix and hold until EFC.

Answer (B) is correct. *(FAR 91.185)*
    DISCUSSION: If you experience two-way radio communication failure at a holding fix that is not the same as the approach fix, leave the holding fix at the EFC time and complete the approach.
    Answer (A) is incorrect. You would leave for, not arrive at, the approach fix at the EFC time. Answer (C) is incorrect. You should not leave the holding fix to go to the approach fix until the EFC time.

105. You enter a holding pattern (at a fix that is not the same as the approach fix) with an EFC time of 1530. At 1520 you experience complete two-way communications failure. Which procedure should you follow to execute the approach to a landing?

A. Depart the holding fix to arrive at the approach fix as close as possible to the EFC time and complete the approach.

B. Depart the holding fix at the EFC time, and complete the approach.

C. Depart the holding fix at the earliest of the flight planned ETA or the EFC time, and complete the approach.

Answer (B) is correct. *(FAR 91.185)*
    DISCUSSION: If you experience two-way radio communication failure at a holding fix that is not the same as the approach fix, leave the holding fix at the EFC time and complete the approach.
    Answer (A) is incorrect. You leave for, not arrive at, the approach fix at the EFC time. Answer (C) is incorrect. The EFC time takes precedence over the flight plan ETA.

106. You are in IMC and have two-way radio communications failure. If you do not exercise emergency authority, what procedure are you expected to follow?

A. Set transponder to code 7600, continue flight on assigned route and fly at the last assigned altitude or the MEA, whichever is higher.

B. Set transponder to code 7700 for 1 minute, then to 7600, and fly to an area with VFR weather conditions.

C. Set transponder to 7700 and fly to an area where you can let down in VFR conditions.

Answer (A) is correct. *(FAR 91.185, AIM Para 6-4-2)*
    DISCUSSION: When you lose two-way radio capability, you should alert ATC by changing your transponder to code 7600. If you experience two-way radio communication failure while in IMC, continue your flight on the assigned route and maintain the last assigned altitude or the MEA, whichever is higher.
    Answer (B) is incorrect. The transponder should be set on 7600 at all times, not 7700 for 1 min., and you must maintain your assigned route and altitude (or MEA). If VMC are encountered, continue the flight under VFR and land as soon as practicable. Answer (C) is incorrect. You should set the transponder to 7600. While in IMC, you must maintain your assigned route and altitude (or MEA).

107. What altitude and route should be used if you are flying in IMC and have two-way radio communications failure?

A. Continue on the route specified in your clearance, fly at an altitude that is the highest of last assigned altitude, altitude ATC has informed you to expect, or the MEA.

B. Fly direct to an area that has been forecast to have VFR conditions, fly at an altitude that is at least 1,000 feet above the highest obstacles along the route.

C. Descend to MEA and, if clear of clouds, proceed to the nearest appropriate airport. If not clear of clouds, maintain the highest of the MEA's along the clearance route.

Answer (A) is correct. *(FAR 91.185)*
    DISCUSSION: When you lose two-way radio communication in IMC, continue the flight by the route assigned by the last ATC clearance, by the route that ATC has advised may be expected to be assigned, or by the flight plan. Use the highest of the altitude assigned in the last ATC clearance, the MEA, or the flight level ATC may be expected to assign.
    Answer (B) is incorrect. You should continue the assigned route. Answer (C) is incorrect. You should use the highest of the altitude assigned, the altitude expected to be assigned, or MEA.

108. Which procedure should you follow if, during an IFR flight in VFR conditions, you have two-way radio communications failure?

    A. Continue the flight under VFR and land as soon as practicable.

    B. Continue the flight at assigned altitude and route, start approach at your ETA, or, if late, start approach upon arrival.

    C. Land at the nearest airport that has VFR conditions.

Answer (A) is correct. *(FAR 91.185)*
    DISCUSSION: If a radio failure occurs during an IFR flight in VFR conditions or if VFR conditions are encountered after the failure, the pilot should continue the flight under VFR and land as soon as practicable.
    Answer (B) is incorrect. This procedure applies only if you are in instrument meteorological conditions, not VFR. Answer (C) is incorrect. The pilot retains the prerogative of exercising good judgment and is not required to land at an unauthorized airport or an airport unsuitable for the type of aircraft flown, nor is the pilot required to land only minutes short of the destination.

109. While flying on an IFR flight plan, you experience two-way communications radio failure while in VFR conditions. In this situation, you should continue your flight under

    A. VFR and land as soon as practicable.

    B. IFR and maintain the last assigned route and altitude to your flight plan destination.

    C. VFR and proceed to your flight plan destination.

Answer (A) is correct. *(FAR 91.185)*
    DISCUSSION: If a radio failure occurs during an IFR flight in VFR conditions or if VFR conditions are encountered after the failure, the pilot should continue the flight under VFR and land as soon as practicable.
    Answer (B) is incorrect. This procedure applies only if you are in instrument meteorological conditions, not VFR. Answer (C) is incorrect. You should land as soon as practicable rather than proceeding to your flight plan destination.

5.12 Navigation Radio Failure

110. What action should you take if your DME fails at FL 240?

    A. Advise ATC of the failure and land at the nearest available airport where repairs can be made.

    B. Notify ATC that it will be necessary for you to go to a lower altitude, since your DME has failed.

    C. Notify ATC of the failure and continue to the next airport of intended landing where repairs can be made.

Answer (C) is correct. *(FAR 91.205)*
    DISCUSSION: When required DME fails at or above FL 240, the pilot should notify ATC immediately and may continue operations at and above FL 240 to the next airport of intended landing at which repairs or replacement of the equipment can be made.
    Answer (A) is incorrect. You can continue to your destination, not the nearest airport, and have repairs made there. Answer (B) is incorrect. You need not descend to a lower altitude after you notify ATC. You may continue to operate at or above FL 240.

111. What action should you take if your No. 1 VOR receiver malfunctions while operating in controlled airspace under IFR? Your aircraft is equipped with two VOR receivers. The No. 1 receiver has Omni/Localizer/Glide Slope capability, and the No. 2 receiver has only VOR/Localizer capability.

    A. Report the malfunction immediately to ATC.

    B. Continue the flight as cleared; no report is required.

    C. Continue the approach and request a VOR approach.

Answer (A) is correct. *(FAR 91.187)*
    DISCUSSION: When operating under IFR in controlled airspace, you must immediately report to ATC as soon as practical any malfunctions of navigational, approach, or communication equipment occurring in flight. Each report should include the following:

1. Aircraft identification,
2. Equipment affected,
3. Degree to which the capability of the pilot to operate under IFR in the ATC system is impaired, and
4. Nature and extent of assistance desired from ATC.

    Answer (B) is incorrect. A report to ATC is required. Answer (C) is incorrect. ATC will know that you need a VOR approach if you report the ILS receiver inoperative.

112. What is the procedure when the DME malfunctions at or above 24,000 feet MSL?

A. Notify ATC immediately and request an altitude below 24,000 feet.

B. Continue to your destination in VFR conditions and report the malfunction.

C. After immediately notifying ATC, you may continue to the next airport of intended landing where repairs can be made.

Answer (C) is correct. *(FAR 91.205)*
DISCUSSION: When required DME fails at or above FL 240, the pilot should notify ATC immediately and may continue operations at and above FL 240 to the next airport of intended landing at which repairs or replacement of the equipment can be made.
Answer (A) is incorrect. There is no need to descend to a lower altitude. You may continue to your destination and have repairs made there. Answer (B) is incorrect. You may continue your flight as normal, even under IFR, and make repairs at your destination.

5.13 Types of Airspace

113. Which types of airspace are depicted on the En Route Low Altitude Chart?

A. Limits of controlled airspace, military training routes, and special use airspace.

B. Class A, special use airspace, Class D, and Class E.

C. Special use airspace, Class E, Class D, Class A, Class B, and Class C.

Answer (A) is correct. *(ACL)*
DISCUSSION: En Route Low-Altitude Charts limits of controlled airspace, military training routes, and special use airspace.
Answer (B) is incorrect. Class A airspace is airspace above FL 180. It is not depicted on En Route Low-Altitude Charts. Answer (C) is incorrect. Class A airspace is not depicted on En Route Low-Altitude Charts.

114. Class G airspace is that airspace where

A. ATC does not control air traffic.

B. ATC controls only IFR flights.

C. the minimum visibility for VFR flight is 3 miles.

Answer (A) is correct. *(AIM Para 3-3-1)*
DISCUSSION: Class G airspace is that portion of the airspace that has not been designated as Class A, Class B, Class C, Class D, or Class E. In Class G airspace, ATC has neither the authority nor the responsibility for exercising control over air traffic in any weather condition.
Answer (B) is incorrect. ATC does not control IFR flight in Class G airspace. Answer (C) is incorrect. The minimum visibility for VFR flight is 1 SM, not 3 SM, in Class G airspace during the day when below 10,000 ft. MSL.

115. MOAs are established to

A. prohibit all civil aircraft because of hazardous or secret activities.

B. separate certain military activities from IFR traffic.

C. restrict civil aircraft during periods of high-density training activities.

Answer (B) is correct. *(AIM Para 3-4-5)*
DISCUSSION: MOAs consist of airspace of defined vertical and lateral limits established for the purpose of separating certain military training activities from IFR traffic. When an MOA is in use, nonparticipating IFR traffic may be cleared to fly through if ATC can provide IFR separation. Otherwise, ATC will reroute or restrict nonparticipating IFR traffic.
Answer (A) is incorrect. A prohibited area, not an MOA, prohibits all aircraft for reasons of national security. Answer (C) is incorrect. A restricted area, not an MOA, is used to restrict aircraft during certain periods.

116. The vertical extent of the Class A airspace extends from

A. 18,000 feet to and including FL 450.

B. 18,000 feet to and including FL 600.

C. 12,500 feet to and including FL 600.

Answer (B) is correct. *(AIM Para 3-2-2)*
DISCUSSION: Class A airspace extends from 18,000 ft. MSL to and including FL 600.
Answer (A) is incorrect. FL 450 is the top of the jet routes. Answer (C) is incorrect. The base of Class A airspace is 18,000 ft. MSL, not 12,500 ft. MSL.

117. Which airspace is defined as a transition area when designated in conjunction with an airport which has a prescribed IAP?

A. The Class E airspace extending upward from 700 feet or more above the surface and terminating at the base of the overlying controlled airspace.

B. That Class D airspace extending from the surface and terminating at the base of the continental control area.

C. The Class C airspace extending from the surface to 700 or 1,200 feet AGL, where designated.

Answer (A) is correct. *(AIM Para 3-2-6)*
   DISCUSSION: Transition areas are Class E airspace that extends upward from 700 ft. or more above the surface when designated in conjunction with an airport for which an instrument approach procedure (IAP) has been prescribed. Class E airspace extends up to but does not include 18,000 ft. MSL, i.e., the base of Class A airspace.
   Answer (B) is incorrect. A transition area is classified as Class E, not Class D, airspace. Answer (C) is incorrect. Transition areas are Class E, not Class C, airspace and extend upward from, not to, 700 ft.

118. (Refer to Figure 93 on page 173.) What is the floor of Class E airspace when designated in conjunction with an airway?

A. 700 feet AGL.

B. 1,200 feet AGL.

C. 1,500 feet AGL.

Answer (B) is correct. *(AIM Para 3-2-6)*
   DISCUSSION: The floor of Class E airspace when designated in conjunction with an airway is 1,200 ft. AGL.
   Answer (A) is incorrect. This is the floor of Class E airspace when designated in conjunction with an airport which has an approved IAP, not with an airway. Answer (C) is incorrect. The floor of Class E airspace when designated in conjunction with an airway is 1,200 ft. AGL, not 1,500 ft. AGL.

119. (Refer to Figure 93 on page 173.) Which altitude is the normal upper limit for Class D airspace?

A. 1,000 feet AGL.

B. 2,500 feet AGL.

C. 4,000 feet AGL.

Answer (B) is correct. *(AIM Para 3-2-5)*
   DISCUSSION: Class D airspace extends from the surface up to and including 2,500 ft. AGL.
   Answer (A) is incorrect. This is the normal traffic pattern altitude for piston aircraft, not the ceiling of Class D airspace. Answer (C) is incorrect. This is the upper limit for Class C, not Class D, airspace.

120. (Refer to Figure 93 on page 173.) What is the floor of Class E airspace when designated in conjunction with an airport which has an approved IAP?

A. 500 feet AGL.

B. 700 feet AGL.

C. 1,200 feet AGL.

Answer (B) is correct. *(AIM Para 3-2-6)*
   DISCUSSION: The floor of Class E airspace when designated in conjunction with an airport which has an approved IAP is 700 ft. AGL.
   Answer (A) is incorrect. This is not an altitude that defines airspace. Answer (C) is incorrect. This is the floor of Class E airspace when designated in conjunction with an airway, not an approved IAP.

121. (Refer to Figure 93 on page 173.) Which altitude is the upper limit for Class A airspace?

A. 14,500 feet MSL.

B. 18,000 feet MSL.

C. 60,000 feet MSL.

Answer (C) is correct. *(AIM Para 3-2-2)*
   DISCUSSION: Class A airspace extends from 18,000 ft. MSL to and including 60,000 ft. MSL (i.e., FL 600).
   Answer (A) is incorrect. This is the upper limit for Class G, not Class A, airspace. Answer (B) is incorrect. This is the floor, not the upper limit, of Class A airspace.

122. (Refer to Figure 93 on page 173.) What is the maximum altitude that Class G airspace will exist? (Does not include airspace less than 1,500 feet AGL.)

A. 18,000 feet MSL.

B. 14,500 feet MSL.

C. 14,000 feet MSL.

Answer (B) is correct. *(AIM Para 3-3-1)*
   DISCUSSION: The maximum altitude at which Class G airspace will exist (not including airspace less than 1,500 ft. AGL) is 14,500 ft. MSL.
   Answer (A) is incorrect. This is the floor of Class A airspace, not the maximum altitude at which Class G airspace will exist. Answer (C) is incorrect. This is not an altitude that defines airspace.

123. (Refer to Figure 93 below.) What is generally the maximum altitude for Class B airspace?

A. 4,000 feet MSL.

B. 10,000 feet MSL.

C. 14,500 feet MSL.

Answer (B) is correct. *(AIM Para 3-2-3)*
 DISCUSSION: The maximum altitude for Class B airspace will generally be 10,000 ft. MSL.
 Answer (A) is incorrect. This is not an altitude that defines airspace. Answer (C) is incorrect. This is the maximum altitude at which Class G, not Class B, airspace will exist.

124. (Refer to Figure 93 below.) What are the normal lateral limits for Class D airspace?

A. 8 NM.

B. 5 NM.

C. 4 NM.

Answer (C) is correct. *(AIM Para 3-2-5)*
 DISCUSSION: The normal lateral limit for Class D airspace is approximately 4 NM.
 Answer (A) is incorrect. This distance is not a defined lateral limit of any class of airspace surface area. Answer (B) is incorrect. This distance defines the lateral limit of a Class C, not Class D, surface area.

125. (Refer to Figure 93 below.) What is the floor of Class A airspace?

A. 10,000 feet MSL.

B. 14,500 feet MSL.

C. 18,000 feet MSL.

Answer (C) is correct. *(AIM Para 3-2-2)*
 DISCUSSION: Class A airspace extends from 18,000 ft. MSL up to, and including, FL 600.
 Answer (A) is incorrect. This is the floor of controlled airspace in which a transponder with altitude encoding capability is required, not the floor of Class A airspace. Answer (B) is incorrect. This is a floor of Class E, not Class A, airspace.

Figure 93. – New Airspace Classification.

126. What are the vertical limits of a transition area that is designated in conjunction with an airport having a prescribed IAP?

   A. Surface to 700 feet AGL.

   B. 1,200 feet AGL to the base of the overlying controlled airspace.

   C. 700 feet AGL or more to the base of the overlying controlled airspace.

Answer (C) is correct. *(AIM Para 3-2-6)*
DISCUSSION: Transition areas are controlled airspace extending upward from 700 ft. or more above the surface when designated in conjunction with an airport for which an instrument approach procedure has been prescribed. Transition areas terminate at the base of overlying controlled airspace (i.e., Class A airspace).
   Answer (A) is incorrect. A transition area begins at 700 ft. AGL, not the surface, when it is designated in conjunction with an IAP. Answer (B) is incorrect. Transition areas begin at 1,200 ft. AGL when designated in conjunction with an airway route structure or segment, not with an airport with an instrument approach.

127. What minimum aircraft equipment is required for operation within Class C airspace?

   A. Two-way communications and Mode C transponder.

   B. Two-way communications.

   C. Transponder and DME.

Answer (A) is correct. *(AIM Para 3-2-4)*
DISCUSSION: In Class C airspace, the equipment requirement is an operating two-way communications radio and a Mode C transponder.
   Answer (B) is incorrect. A Mode C transponder is also required. Answer (C) is incorrect. Two-way communications and Mode C capability are also required and DME is not required.

5.14 Airport Diagram – *Airport Facility Directory (A/FD)*

128. (Refer to Figure 162 on page 175.) You are cleared to land on RWY 16L at Eugene Mahlon Sweet Field. As you break out of the clouds, you are lined up with the white lights down the center of the runway, which lets you know that you

   A. are on course and lined up correctly.

   B. are off course.

   C. should recheck the winds prior to landing.

Answer (B) is correct. *(A/FD Airport Diagram Legend)*
DISCUSSION: The description of RWY 16R – 34L in the A/FD shows an entry for "CL," which indicates centerline lighting. The description for RWY 16L – 34R has no such entry. Because you are cleared for RWY 16L, you can deduce that the lights you see are centerline lights for RWY 16R, which indicates that you are off course.
   Answer (A) is incorrect. RWY 16L does not have centerline lighting. However, RWY 16R does have centerline lighting. See the note labeled "CL" in the *A/FD* page for Eugene Mahlon, which indicates centerline lighting for only RWY 16R. Answer (C) is incorrect. You are off course. RWY 16L does not have centerline lighting, and there is insufficient information to suggest you are off course due to winds and should recheck the winds prior to landing. It is more important at this point that you recognize that you are off course and correct accordingly.

OREGON 119

EUGENE

MAHLON SWEET FLD (EUG) 7 NW UTC–8(–7DT) N44°07.48′ W123°12.72′
374 B S4 **FUEL** 100LL, JET A OX 1, 2, 3, 4 TPA—1174(800) Class I, ARFF Index B
NOTAM FILE EUG

RWY 16R–34L: H8009X150 (ASPH–GRVD) S–75, D–200, 2D–400
HIRL CL
   RWY 16R: ALSF2. TDZL. PAPI(P4L)—GA 3.0° TCH 50′.
   RWY 34L: ODALS. VASI(V4L)—GA 3.0° TCH 53′.
RWY 16L–34R: H6000X150 (ASPH–GRVD) S–105, D–175, 2D–240
HIRL
   RWY 16L: MALSR. PAPI(P4L)—GA 3.0° TCH 52′.
   RWY 34R: REIL. PAPI(P4L)—GA 3.0° TCH 50′.

RUNWAY DECLARED DISTANCE INFORMATION
   RWY 16L: TORA–6000 TODA–6000 ASDA–6000 LDA–6000
   RWY 16R: TORA–8009 TODA–8009 ASDA–8009 LDA–8009
   RWY 34L: TORA–8009 TODA–8009 ASDA–8009 LDA–8009
   RWY 34R: TORA–6000 TODA–6000 ASDA–6000 LDA–6000

AIRPORT REMARKS: Attended continuously. Migratory waterfowl and other
birds on and invof arpt. PPR for unscheduled air carrier ops with more
than 30 passenger seats call 541–682–5430. ARFF svcs unavailable
0000–0500 local except PPR 541–682–5430. No access to Rwy 34L
byd Twy A9. Helicopters ldg and departing avoid overflying the airline
passenger terminal and ramp located E of Rwy 16R–34L. Helipad west
of Rwy 16R restricted, PPR phone 541–682–5430. Twys H and K unavailable to acft 21,000 pounds single weight and
40,000 pounds dual gross weight. Terminal apron closed to acft except scheduled air carriers and flights with prior
permission. PAPI Rwy 16R and Rwy 16L and 34R and VASI Rwy 34L opr 24 hrs. When twr clsd HIRL Rwy 16L–34R
and Rwy 16R–34L preset medium ints. When twr clsd ACTIVATE ALSF2 Rwy 16R, ODALS Rwy 34L MALSR Rwy 16L
and REIL Rwy 34R—CTAF.
WEATHER DATA SOURCES: ASOS (541) 461–3114 **HIWAS** 112.9 EUG.
COMMUNICATIONS: CTAF 118.9 **ATIS** 125.225 541–607–4699 **UNICOM** 122.95
   EUGENE RCO 122.3 (MC MINNVILLE RADIO)
Ⓡ **CASCADE APP/DEP CON** 119.6 (340°–159°) 120.25 (160°–339°) (1400–0730Z‡)
Ⓡ **SEATTLE CENTER APP/DEP CON** 125.8 (0730–1400Z‡)
   EUGENE TOWER 118.9 (Rwy 16R– 34L) 124.15 (Rwy 16L– 34R) (1400–0730Z‡) **GND CON** 121.7 **CLNC DEL** 121.7
AIRSPACE: CLASS D svc 1400–0730Z‡ other times CLASS E.
RADIO AIDS TO NAVIGATION: NOTAM FILE EUG.
   EUGENE (H) VORTACW 112.9 EUG Chan 76 N44°07.25′ W123°13.37′ at fld. 364/20E. **HIWAS.**
   ILS/DME 111.75 I–ADE Chan 54(Y) Rwy 16L. Class IE.
   ILS/DME 110.1 I–EUG Chan 38 Rwy 16R. Class IIIE. Unmonitored when ATCT clsd.

FLORENCE

FLORENCE MUNI (6S2) 1 N UTC–8(–7DT) N43°58.97′ W124°06.68′
51 B **FUEL** 100LL, JET A TPA—1051(1000) NOTAM FILE MMV

RWY 15–33: H3000X60 (ASPH) S–12.5 MIRL 0.4% up NW
   RWY 15: Hill. Rgt tfc.
   RWY 33: PAPI(P2L)—GA 3.0° TCH 40′. Trees.

AIRPORT REMARKS: Attended 1630–0030Z‡. Birds, deer and wildlife on and
invof arpt. ACTIVATE MIRL Rwy 15–33—CTAF. PAPI Rwy 33 opr 24
hrs.
WEATHER DATA SOURCES: AWOS–3 118.225 (541) 997–8664.
COMMUNICATIONS: CTAF/UNICOM 122.8
RADIO AIDS TO NAVIGATION: NOTAM FILE OTH.
   NORTH BEND (L) VORTACW 112.1 OTH Chan 58 N43°24.93′
   W124°10.11′ 346° 34.1 NM to fld. 707/18E. **HIWAS.**
   VORTAC unusable:
     012°–087° byd 30 NM blo 5,000′

Figure 162.

129. (Refer to Figure 251 on page 177.) What is the slope of RWY 9?

    A. 0.4% up.

    B. 0.4% down.

    C. 0.3% down.

Answer (B) is correct. *(IPH Chap 1)*
    DISCUSSION: Fig. 251 shows an arrow pointing in the direction of RWY 27 labeled "0.4% UP." That indicates RWY 9, which is the reciprocal of RWY 27, is sloped 0.4% down.
    Answer (A) is incorrect. Fig. 251 shows an arrow pointing in the direction of RWY 27 labeled "0.4% UP." Therefore, RWY 27 has an upslope grade of 0.4%. Answer (C) is incorrect. Fig. 251 shows an arrow pointing in the direction of RWY 36 labeled "0.3% DOWN."

130. (Refer to Figure 251 on page 177.) When lined up for takeoff on runway 4, the compass and heading indicator should read a heading of about

    A. 040°

    B. 050°

    C. 055°

Answer (B) is correct. *(A/FD Airport Diagram Legend)*
    DISCUSSION: Runway 4 includes a notation that reads "048.0°" with an arrow pointing in the direction of the runway alignment. This indicates that the actual alignment of runway 4 is 48°. Of the options offered, 050° is the closest to the correct heading.
    Answer (A) is incorrect. Although runway naming convention would suggest runway 4 is aligned with 040°, there is in fact a considerable amount of leeway in the actual heading. In this case, runway 4 includes a notation that reads "048.0°" with an arrow pointing in the direction of the runway alignment. This indicates that the actual alignment of runway 4 is 48°. Answer (C) is incorrect. Runway 4 includes a notation that reads "048.0°" with an arrow pointing in the direction of the runway alignment. This indicates that the actual alignment of runway 4 is 48°, not 55°.

131. (Refer to Figure 251 on page 177.) When lined up for takeoff on runway 18, the compass and heading indicator should display a heading of about

    A. 180°

    B. 185°

    C. 175°

Answer (B) is correct. *(A/FD Airport Diagram Legend)*
    DISCUSSION: Runway 18 includes a notation that reads "183.6°" in conjunction with an arrow pointing in the direction of the runway alignment. This indicates that the actual heading can be rounded to 184° and could easily display on the compass and heading indicator as about 185°.
    Answer (A) is incorrect. Although runway naming convention would suggest runway 18 is aligned with 180°, there is in fact a considerable amount of leeway in the actual heading. Runway 18 includes a notation that reads "183.6°" in conjunction with an arrow pointing in the direction of the runway alignment. This indicates the actual heading can be rounded to 184° and could easily display on the compass and heading indicator as about 185°. Answer (C) is incorrect. This answer option would be more for a runway 17 with a notation such as "173.6°" with an arrow pointing in the direction of a runway 17.

132. (Refer to Figure 251 on page 177.) When lined up for takeoff on RWY 27, the compass and heading indicator should display a heading of about

    A. 270°

    B. 275°

    C. 265°

Answer (B) is correct. *(A/FD Airport Diagram Legend)*
    DISCUSSION: Runway 27 includes a notation that reads "273.7°" in conjunction with an arrow pointing in the direction of the runway alignment. This indicates that the actual heading can be rounded to 274° and could easily display on the compass and heading indicator as about 275°.
    Answer (A) is incorrect. This would be correct if there was not an indication of "273.7°" with an arrow pointing in the direction of the runway. Answer (C) is incorrect. This answer would be more for a RWY 26 with a heading notation of about "263.7°" and an arrow pointing in the direction of the runway.

Figure 251.

133. (Refer to Figure 154 below.) What is the actual heading of the north runway at Oshkosh/Wittman Regional (OSH) airport?

A. 0.3%.

B. 002.3°.

C. 360°.

Answer (B) is correct. *(A/FD and AIM)*
  DISCUSSION: The actual heading for the north runway is 002.3°, as shown on the right side of RWY 36 in the diagram.
  Answer (A) is incorrect. The indication of a DOWN slope on RWY 36 is 0.3%. Answer (C) is incorrect. The runway number is the whole number nearest one-tenth the magnetic azimuth of the centerline of the runway, measured clockwise from the magnetic north. The north runway is 36, or 360, but the actual heading for this runway is 002.3°, not 360°.

Figure 154. – OshKosh/Wittman Regional (OSH).

STUDY UNIT SIX
HOLDING AND INSTRUMENT APPROACHES

(33 pages of outline)

In 2014, the FAA released an **Addendum A for the *Computer Testing Supplement for Instrument Rating***. This addendum contains over 100 additional figures, including approach plates, approach procedures, departure procedures, A/FD excerpts, etc. The FAA has released some questions referencing certain figures from this addendum. Gleim has included those FAA-released questions and the relevant figures in our instrument rating materials. **However, we have not included any of the addendum figures that do not have FAA-released questions. If you answer all of the questions in the Gleim test bank for the instrument rating, you will be comfortable using the figures in the addendum to answer similar questions on the knowledge test.**

This study unit contains outlines of major concepts tested, sample test questions and answers regarding holding and instrument approaches, and an explanation of each answer. The table of contents above lists each subunit within this study unit, the number of questions pertaining to that particular subunit, and the pages on which the outlines and questions begin, respectively.

6.1 CONTACT AND VISUAL APPROACHES

1. You may request a contact approach if there is 1 SM flight visibility and you can operate clear of clouds to the destination airport.

    a. A contact approach is an alternative to a standard instrument approach procedure (SIAP).

    b. ATC will assign a contact approach only upon request if the reported visibility is at least 1 mile.

2. ATC may assign a visual approach to an airport or authorize you to follow other airplanes for a landing if the approach can be accomplished in VFR.

    a. You must have the airport or the preceding aircraft in sight.

    b. Visual approaches can be assigned by ATC; contact approaches cannot.

    c. On visual approaches, radar service is automatically terminated when the aircraft is instructed to contact the tower.

6.2 LDA AND SDF APPROACHES

1. LDA (localizer-type directional aid) is as useful and accurate as a localizer (3° to 6° course width).

    a. The LDA is very similar to an instrument landing system (ILS), but it usually does not have a glide slope (i.e., it has only a localizer) and is **not** aligned with the runway.

2. SDF (simplified directional facility) has a course width of either 6° or 12°.

    a. SDF approaches may or may not be aligned with a runway (and their courses are wider). SDF does not have a glide slope.

6.3 PRECISION RUNWAY MONITOR (PRM)

1. Precision Runway Monitoring (PRM) is a RADAR system that has a high update rate and is able to monitor approaches to closely spaced parallel runways.

2. Simultaneous close parallel ILS Precision Runway Monitor (PRM) approaches are authorized for use at airports that have parallel runways separated by at least 3,400 ft. and no more than 4,300 ft. They are approved for airports with parallel runways separated by at least 3,000 ft. with an offset localizer (LOC) where the offset angle is at least 2.5° but no more than 3°. Two aircraft can make simultaneous ILS approaches next to each other.

    a. Approval for ILS PRM approaches requires the airport to have a precision runway monitoring system and a final monitor controller who can only communicate with aircraft on the final approach course. The controller is equipped with a monitoring system that tracks the aircraft performance on the final approach segment of the approach. Additionally, two tower frequencies are required to be used, and the controller broadcasts over both frequencies to reduce the chance of instructions being missed.

    b. Pilot training is required for pilots using the PRM system. This training is available for FAR Parts 121 and 135 and general aviation pilots at www.faa.gov/training_testing/training/prm/.

6.4 RUNWAY VISUAL RANGE (RVR)

1. RVR is an instrumentally derived value that represents the horizontal distance the pilot can see down the runway from the approach end.

    a. It is based on the measurement of a transmissometer near the touchdown point of the instrument runway and is reported in hundreds of feet.

2. If RVR is inoperative and cannot be reported, convert the RVR minimum to ground visibility, and use that as the visibility minimum for takeoffs and landings.

    a. Legend 11 on the next page has a chart of RVR/visibility comparable values.

3. The normal ILS visibility minimum is 1/2 SM, which is 2400 RVR.

6.5 MISSED APPROACHES

1. When executing a missed approach prior to the missed approach point (MAP), continue the approach to the MAP at or above the minimum descent altitude (MDA) or decision height (DH) before executing any turns.

2. If you lose visual reference in a circle to land from an instrument approach, you should make a climbing turn toward your landing runway to become established on the missed approach course.

SC-1, 24 FEB 2000   A2

00055
TERMS/LANDING MINIMA DATA

COPTER MINIMA ONLY

CATEGORY	COPTER		
H-176°	680-½	363	(400-½)

Copter Approach Direction   Height of MDA/DH
                                             Above Landing Area (HAL)

No circling minimums are provided

RADAR MINIMA

							Visibility (RVR 100's of feet)		
PAR (c)	10	2.5°/42/1000	ABCDE	195/16	100	(100-¼)			
(d)	28	2.5°/48/1068	ABCDE	187/16	100	(100-¼)			
ASR	10		ABC	560/40	463	(500-¾)	D	560/50	463 (500-1)
			E	580/60	463	(500-1¼)			
	28		AB	600/50	513	(600-1)	C	600/60	513 (600-1¼)
			DE	600-1½	513	(600-1½)			
CIR (b)	10		AB	560-1¼	463	(500-1¼)	C	560-1½	463 (500-1½)
	28		AB	600-1¼	503	(600-1¼)	C	600-1½	503 (600-1½)
	10, 28		DE	660-2	563	(600-2)			

All minimums in parentheses not applicable to Civil Pilots.
Military Pilots refer to appropriate regulations.

Visibility in Statute Miles

Radar Minima:
1. Minima shown are the lowest permitted by established criteria. Pilots should consult applicable directives for their category of aircraft.
2. The circling MDA and weather minima to be used are those for the runway to which the final approach is flown - not the landing runway. In the above RADAR MINIMA example, a category C aircraft flying a radar approach to runway 10, circling to land on runway 28, must use an MDA of 560 feet with weather minima of 500-1½ .

▲ Alternate Minimums not standard. Civil users refer to tabulation. USA/USN/USAF pilots refer to appropriate regulations.

▲ NA Alternate minimums are Not Authorized due to unmonitored facility or absence of weather reporting service.

▼ Take-off Minimums not standard and/or Departure Procedures are published. Refer to tabulation.

AIRCRAFT APPROACH CATEGORIES

Speeds are based on 1.3 times the stall speed in the landing configuration of maximum gross landing weight. An aircraft shall fit in only one category. If it is necessary to maneuver at speeds in excess of the upper limit of a speed range for a category, the minimums for the next higher category should be used. For example, an aircraft which falls in Category A, but is circling to land at a speed in excess of 91 knots, should use the approach Category B minimums when circling to land. See following category limits:

MANEUVERING TABLE

Approach Category	A	B	C	D	E
Speed (Knots)	0-90	91-120	121-140	141-165	Abv 165

RVR/ Meteorological Visibility Comparable Values

The following table shall be used for converting RVR to meteorological visibility when RVR is not reported for the runway of intended operation. Adjustments of landing minima may be required - see Inoperative Components Table.

RVR (feet)	Visibility (statute miles)	RVR (feet)	Visibility (statute miles)
1600	¼	4000	¾
2000	⅜	4500	⅞
2400	½	5000	1
3200	⅝	6000	1¼

TERMS/ ...NDING MINI... DATA

Legend 11. – Instrument Approach Procedures Explanation of Terms.

6.6 ILS SPECIFICATIONS

1. The ILS missed approach should be executed upon arrival at the DH on the glide slope if the visual reference requirements are not met.

2. The normal decision height for a Category I ILS is 200 ft. AGL.

    a. This is the height of the glide slope centerline at the middle marker.

3. The amount of deflection and distance from the localizer and the glide slope for an ILS is presented as Figure 139 below.

    a. A series of questions asks how far you are from the localizer or glide slope centerlines given certain types of deflection on your glide slope indicator. These questions require interpreting Figure 139.

4. The direction of deflection of the localizer and glide slope bar shows where the actual course is located. You should "fly to the needles" or "fly the crosshair" to maintain a perfect course.

    a. When the localizer bar is left of center and the glide slope bar is below center, you are right of the localizer course and above the glide slope course. To correct your course, "fly to the needles." Make a left correction to intercept the localizer centerline and descend to intercept the glide slope centerline.

    b. For each combination of localizer and glide slope deflection, use similar corrective actions.

Figure 139. – Glide Slope and Localizer Illustration.

5. Compass locators, when used for the outer marker (OM) and middle marker (MM) of an ILS, transmit two-letter identification groups.

  a. The outer compass locator (LOM) transmits the first two letters of the localizer identification group.

  b. The middle compass locator (LMM) transmits the last two letters of the localizer identification group.

  c. If the OM and/or MM are not compass locators, there is no two-letter identification transmission.

6. An inner marker (IM) is identified by continual dots at the rate of 6 per second and a flashing white marker beacon.

7. If DME is available on an ILS or localizer approach, the DME/TACAN channel will be indicated in the localizer frequency box on the instrument approach chart.

8. Parallel (dependent) ILS approaches provide aircraft a minimum of 1.5-mi. radar separation diagonally between successive aircraft on the adjacent localizer course.

9. The legend below contains the ILS standard characteristics and terminology.

Legend 28. – ILS Standard Characteristics and Terminology.

6.7 UNUSABLE ILS COMPONENTS

1. ILS components include

    a. Localizer
    b. Glide slope
    c. Outer marker
    d. Middle marker
    e. Approach lights

2. If more than one component is unusable, each minimum is raised to the highest minimum required by any single component that is inoperative.

3. A compass locator or precision approach radar (PAR) may be substituted for an inoperative OM or MM.

    a. An inoperative MM does not change the landing minimums; thus, no substitution is necessary.

4. When installed with the ILS and specified in the approach procedure, DME may be used in lieu of the OM.

5. When the glide slope fails, the ILS reverts to a nonprecision localizer (LOC) approach.

    a. The LOC MDA and visibility minimums will be used.

6. If you are on the glide slope when the ILS fails and a VASI is in sight, you should continue the approach using the VASI and report the malfunction to ATC.

6.8 FLYING THE APPROACH

1. Rate of descent on the glide slope is dependent on the airplane groundspeed because the descent must be constant relative to the distance traveled over the ground.

    a. As groundspeed increases, the descent rate must increase.
    b. As groundspeed decreases, the descent rate must decrease.

2. The approach should be under the stabilized approach concept. Operational experience and research have shown that a descent rate of more than approximately 1,000 feet per minute (fpm) is unacceptable during the final stages of an approach.

3. If the airspeed is too fast and the glide slope and localizer are centered, you should initially reduce power.

4. When you are being vectored for an ILS approach and are about to fly through the localizer, you should maintain your last assigned heading and question ATC rather than deviate from a clearance.

5. If a wind shear changes from a headwind to a tailwind, the airspeed drops, the nose pitches down, and the vertical speed increases. You must initially increase power to resume normal approach speed.

    a. Then power must be reduced as airspeed stabilizes so you can maintain the glide slope due to the increased groundspeed.
    b. The tendency is to go below the glide slope.

6. If a wind shear changes from a tailwind to a headwind (or even to calm), you must decrease your power initially and then increase it once you are through the shear to maintain the glide slope.

    a. The tendency is to go above the glide slope.

7. In tracking the localizer, you should have your drift correction established to maintain the localizer centerline before reaching the outer marker.

   a. Then completion of the approach should be accomplished with heading corrections no greater than 2°.

8. The pilot must maintain a stabilized approach.

   a. A stabilized approach ensures safe operations and is recommended for all aircraft.
   b. The aircraft must be in an approved configuration for landing or circling.

      1) For turbojets, the engines should be spooled up.
      2) The airspeed should be correct for the approach.
      3) The flight path with a descent rate of less than 1,000 feet above the airport or TDZE.
      4) For a straight-in approach in IFR weather conditions, the approach should be stabilized before the FAF and before descending below 1,000 feet AGL.
      5) The descent rate should be less than 1,000 fpm before descending below the following minimum stabilized approach heights.

         a) For a visual approach or straight-in instrument approach in VFR weather conditions, the approach must be stabilized before descending below 500 feet above the airport elevation.
         b) For the final segment of a circling approach maneuver, the approach must be stabilized 500 feet above the airport elevation or at the MDA, whichever is lower.

      6) Once on a stabilized approach and below 500 feet AGL, the bank angle should be less than 15°.

6.9 ASR APPROACHES

1. During airport surveillance radar (ASR) approaches, ATC provides headings, tells when to commence descent to MDA, gives the airplane's position each mile on final from the runway, and indicates arrival at the MAP.

2. Surveillance approaches may be used at airports for which civil radar instrument approach minimums have been published.

3. ATC radar, when approved for approach control service, may be used for course guidance to the final approach, ASR and PAR approaches, and monitoring of nonradar approaches.

4. During a no-gyro approach (i.e., when your gyroscopic instruments have failed), all turns prior to final approach should be made at the standard rate.

   a. After being handed off to the final approach controller, all turns should be at one-half the standard rate.

6.10 SIDE-STEP APPROACHES

1. A side-step approach is an instrument approach to one runway until you can see a parallel runway and "side step" to land on the parallel runway.

2. A side-step approach is used when a pilot (1) executes an approach procedure serving one of two or more parallel runways that are separated by 1,200 ft. or less and then (2) diverts to the other parallel runway using a straight-in approach.

3. Execute a side-step procedure as soon as possible after the runway environment is in sight.

6.11 TIMED APPROACHES FROM HOLDING FIXES

1.   A timed approach is one in which you are cleared to leave the final approach fix or outer marker at a specified future time.

2.   Timed approaches from a holding fix may be executed only under the following conditions:

   a.   A control tower is in operation at the airport where the approach is conducted.

   b.   Direct communication is maintained between pilot and approach control or center until the pilot is instructed to contact tower.

   c.   If more than one missed approach procedure is available, none may require a course reversal; i.e., the missed approach procedure must not take you back to the final approach fix.

   d.   If only one missed approach procedure is available, course reversal is not required and the reported ceiling and visibility must be greater than the highest circling minimum for the IAP.

   e.   When cleared for the approach, the pilot shall not execute a procedure turn.

3.   When making a timed approach from a holding fix at the outer marker, you should adjust the holding pattern to leave the final approach fix inbound at the assigned time.

NOTE: Timed approaches are primarily used in nonradar environments.

6.12 HOLDING

1.   A holding procedure is a predetermined maneuver that keeps aircraft within a specified airspace while awaiting further clearance from ATC.

2.   Holding patterns are racetrack-shaped patterns based on a fix that is a radio navigation facility (VOR or other NAVAID); an intersection of NAVAID bearings, radials, or a DME fix; or a waypoint (GPS or other RNAV equipment).

3.   Holding patterns consist of the following components (note that the fix is always at the end of the inbound leg):

   a.   A **standard pattern** means the turns in the holding pattern are to the right.

   b.   A **nonstandard pattern** means the turns in the holding pattern are to the left.

      1)   ATC will specify in the holding clearance if left turns are to be made.

4.   You enter a holding pattern using one of three procedures as illustrated in the figure below. This illustrates a standard pattern; the same concept is used in a nonstandard pattern.

    a.   Parallel procedure. Fly a parallel holding course as in (a). Turn left and return to the holding fix or intercept the holding course.

    b.   Teardrop procedure. Proceed on an outbound track of 30° or less to the holding course; turn right to intercept the holding course, as in (b).

    c.   Direct entry procedure. Turn right and fly the pattern, as in (c).

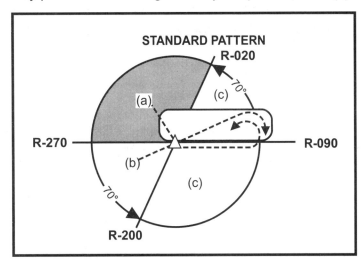

5.   The best way to determine the entry method on the FAA knowledge test is to draw a holding pattern complete with the fix and inbound leg.

    a.   Through the fix, draw the 70° angle such that it intersects the outbound leg at about 1/3 of the outbound leg length.

    b.   Then, slightly shade the (a) area, which is the 110° angle between the extension of the inbound leg and the 70° line.

    c.   The (b) area is the 70° angle between the 70° line and the extension of the inbound leg.

    d.   EXAMPLE: In the previous illustration, the inbound leg to the fix is 270°, and the outbound leg is 090°. If the fix is a VOR station, the following radials define which entry procedure to use:

        R-200 to R-270 -- teardrop procedure
        R-270 to R-020 -- parallel procedure
        R-020 to R-200 -- direct procedure

6.   The timing of the outbound leg begins over or abeam the fix, whichever occurs later.

    a.   If the abeam position cannot be determined, start timing when the turn to outbound is complete (i.e., wings level).

7.   Maximum holding pattern airspeed (IAS) for all aircraft

    a.   From the minimum holding altitude (MHA) through 6,000 ft. -- 200 kt.
    b.   From 6,001 ft. through 14,000 ft. -- 230 kt.
    c.   From 14,001 ft. and above -- 265 kt.

8.   When a holding pattern is used in lieu of a procedure turn, the holding maneuver must still be executed within the time or leg length specified in the profile view on the instrument approach procedure (IAP) chart.

9.   When more than one circuit of the holding pattern is needed to lose altitude or become better established on course, additional circuits can be made at the pilot's discretion only if the pilot advises ATC and ATC approves.

10. The descent gradient during a nonprecision approach is very important. Locate the approach ground speed and time table found in the lower left or right corner of an approach chart (plate) for the appropriate ground speed. Under the ground speed will be the required time to reach the MAP.

   a.   Time (and altitude) establishes the MAP on most nonprecision approaches.

   b.   The key elements one must know are

      1)   Ground speed,
      2)   Altitude descent distance, and
      3)   Time required to reach a point (i.e., MAP).

   c.   EXAMPLE:

      1)   Ground speed is 90 knots.
      2)   We are at the final approach fix (FAF) at 2,000 feet MSL and must descend to the MAP at 600 feet MSL, so we must descend 1,400 feet (2,000 − 600 = 1,400 feet).
      3)   We have to descend 1,400 feet in 2 minutes, 44 seconds.
      4)   Convert seconds of time to a decimal number (44 seconds ÷ 60 = 0.73).
      5)   Add 2 minutes to arrive at 2.73 (minutes).
      6)   Divide distance by time (1,400 ÷ 2.73 = 513 fpm).

11. Some approach plates will have a glide path labeled in degrees near the bottom of the plate in the plan view area. Descent rates can be found on the Rate of Descent Table (Legend 21 on the next page).

   a.   Find the ground speed located across the top of the table.

   b.   Find the angle of descent (or glide path) located from top to bottom on the left side of the table.

   c.   Follow down and across, respectively, and where they meet is the descent rate for that ground speed and descent angle.

6.13 INSTRUMENT APPROACH CHARTS

1.   The questions in this subunit are wide ranging. They are best prepared for by studying the approach chart legends on pages 199 through 211. The questions will not refer you to these legends, but the legends will be available to you in the FAA's *Computer Testing Supplement for Instrument Rating* book. Use them when needed. Remember that approach charts consist of several parts:

   a.   Top and bottom margin identification
   b.   Planview
   c.   Profile view
   d.   Minimums section
   e.   Airport diagram

2.   Initial approach fixes (IAF) identify the beginning of an initial approach segment of an instrument approach procedure and are identified by the letters IAF on the planview of approach charts.

3.   Aircraft approach categories are listed as A, B, C, D, and E based upon 1.3 times the stall speed of the aircraft in the landing configuration at maximum certified gross landing weight (1.3 V_{s0}).

RATE OF DESCENT TABLE

A rate of descent table is provided for use in planning and executing precision descents under known or approximate ground speed conditions. It will be especially useful for approaches when the localizer only is used for course guidance. A best speed, power, altitude combination can be programmed which will result in a stable glide rate and altitude favorable for executing a landing if minimums exist upon breakout. Care should always be exercised so that minimum descent altitude and missed approach point are not exceeded.

ANGLE OF DESCENT (degrees and tenths)	FEET /NM	GROUND SPEED (knots)										
		30	45	60	75	90	105	120	135	150	165	180
2.0	210	105	160	210	265	320	370	425	475	530	585	635
2.5	265	130	200	265	330	395	465	530	595	665	730	795
2.7	287	143	215	287	358	430	501	573	645	716	788	860
2.8	297	149	223	297	371	446	520	594	669	743	817	891
2.9	308	154	231	308	385	462	539	616	693	769	846	923
3.0	318	159	239	318	398	478	557	637	716	796	876	955
3.1	329	165	247	329	411	494	576	658	740	823	905	987
3.2	340	170	255	340	425	510	594	679	764	849	934	1019
3.3	350	175	263	350	438	526	613	701	788	876	963	1051
3.4	361	180	271	361	451	541	632	722	812	902	993	1083
3.5	370	185	280	370	465	555	650	740	835	925	1020	1110
4.0	425	210	315	425	530	635	740	845	955	1060	1165	1270
4.5	475	240	355	475	595	715	835	955	1075	1190	1310	1430
5.0	530	265	395	530	660	795	925	1060	1190	1325	1455	1590
5.5	580	290	435	580	730	875	1020	1165	1310	1455	1600	1745
6.0	635	315	475	635	795	955	1110	1270	1430	1590	1745	1950
6.5	690	345	515	690	860	1030	1205	1375	1550	1720	1890	2065
7.0	740	370	555	740	925	1110	1295	1480	1665	1850	2035	2220
7.5	795	395	595	795	990	1190	1390	1585	1785	1985	2180	2380
8.0	845	425	635	845	1055	1270	1480	1690	1905	2115	2325	2540
8.5	900	450	675	900	1120	1345	1570	1795	2020	2245	2470	2695
9.0	950	475	715	950	1190	1425	1665	1900	2140	2375	2615	2855
9.5	1005	500	750	1005	1255	1505	1755	2005	2255	2510	2760	3010
10.0	1055	530	790	1055	1320	1585	1845	2110	2375	2640	2900	3165
10.5	1105	555	830	1105	1385	1660	1940	2215	2490	2770	3045	3320
11.0	1160	580	870	1160	1450	1740	2030	2320	2610	2900	3190	3480
11.5	1210	605	910	1210	1515	1820	2120	2425	2725	3030	3335	3635
12.0	1260	630	945	1260	1575	1890	2205	2520	2835	3150	3465	3780

Note: For angles 2.7 through 3.4, the left column is labeled VERTICAL PATH ANGLE.

DESCENT TABLE 99028

Legend 21. – Instrument Approach Procedure Charts, Rate-of-Descent Table.

4. The symbol "T" in a point-down black triangle indicates that takeoff minimums are not standard and/or departure minimums are published and you should consult alternative takeoff procedures.

    a. The symbol "A" in a point-up black triangle indicates that nonstandard minimums exist to list the airport as an IFR alternate.

        1) Standard alternate minimums are 800-2 for a nonprecision approach and 600-2 for a precision approach.

5. An airport may not be qualified for alternate use if the NAVAIDs used for the final approach are unmonitored.

6. If there is penetration of the obstacle identification surfaces (OIS), the published visibility for the ILS approach can be no lower than 3/4 SM.

7. The absence of the procedure turn barb on the planview on an approach chart indicates that a procedure turn is not authorized for that approach.

    a. The term NoPT means that there is no procedure turn.

8. A course reversal (procedure turn) is not required (or authorized) when radar vectors are being provided.

9. Minimum safe-sector altitudes are depicted on approach charts. These provide at least 1,000 ft. of obstacle clearance within a 25-NM radius of the navigation facility upon which the procedure is predicated but do not necessarily ensure acceptable navigational signal coverage.

10. Published landing minimums apply when you are making an instrument approach to an airport.

11. If you adhere to the minimum altitudes depicted on the IAP, you can be assured of terrain and obstacle clearance.

12. When being radar-vectored to an instrument approach, you should comply with the last assigned altitude until the airplane is established on a segment of a published route or IAP and you have been cleared for the approach, after which you should continue descents to the listed minimum altitudes.

13. When simultaneous approaches are in progress, each pilot will be advised to monitor the tower frequency to receive advisories and instructions.

14. When straight-in minimums are not published, you can make a straight-in landing if the active runway is in sight, there is sufficient time to make a normal landing, and you have been cleared to land.

15. If you are doing an approach in a category B airplane but maintaining a speed faster than the maximum specified for that category, you should use category C minimums.

16. When an instrument approach procedure involves a procedure turn, the maximum allowable indicated airspeed is 200 kt.

17. When a DME is inoperative, there will be no code tone (identifier) broadcast.

18. On instrument approach segments, the minimum altitudes are indicated on the planview and profile view, which YOU are expected to be able to interpret and specify on the FAA instrument rating knowledge test.

19. When holding patterns exist in lieu of outbound procedure turns, the length of the outbound leg may be indicated as a distance rather than time. This information is given in both the planview and the profile view of the approach chart.

20. On RNAV approaches, the MAP is identified when the TO/FROM indicator changes, which indicates station passage at the MAP waypoint.

   a. On some RNAV approach charts, the distance from the MAP to another more prominent waypoint located along the extended final approach course may be shown in the profile and plan views.

21. RNAV waypoints, when used for an instrument approach, contain boxes in which the latitude and longitude are listed on the first line and the VOR direction and distance are listed on the second line.

22. RNAV approaches require an approved RNAV receiver; no other navigation equipment is specifically required.

23. LDA is as useful and accurate as an ILS localizer but is not part of a complete ILS.

   a. The LDA is not aligned with the runway.

24. On procedure turns, there may be a distance limitation from a NAVAID, and procedural turns should be made entirely on the side of the inbound radial or bearing to which the procedural turn arrow points.

   a. If a teardrop turn is depicted, only a teardrop course reversal can be executed.

25. The airport diagram at the top of the IAP chart contains the following important elevation figures in MSL:

   a. Airport elevation (ELEV)
   b. Touchdown elevation (TDZE)
   c. Threshold elevation (THRE)

26. If you are not able to identify a NAVAID marking a descent to a lower altitude on a nonprecision approach, you cannot descend to the next lower altitude.

27. The MAP of a precision approach is arrival at the DH on the glide slope.

28. The appropriate approach and tower frequencies are indicated at the top of the planview.

29. When a marker beacon receiver becomes inoperative and you cannot identify the MM during an ILS approach, you should use the published minimums.

30. A second VOR receiver may be needed when doing a localizer approach with a final step-down fix to be identified by a VOR radial.

31. Some nonprecision approaches will allow descents to lower altitudes at specified DME distances.

   a. The advantage of DME can be determined by comparing the two MDA values.

32. Use the recommended entry into holding patterns as discussed in the previous subunit.

33. The minimum navigation equipment required for a VOR/DME approach is one VOR receiver and DME.

34. Restrictions to circle-to-land procedures are found below the minimums section of the IAP chart.

35. The height above touchdown (HAT) is the height of the MDA or DH above the touchdown zone. It is the smaller numbers that appear after the MDA or DH.

   a. The numbers in parentheses are military minimums.

36. The minimums section of the approach chart provides the MDA or DH and the visibility (expressed as RVR or SM).

37. When making an LOC approach to the primary airport of the Class B airspace, the aircraft must be equipped with

   a.   Two-way radio communication
   b.   Mode C transponder
   c.   VOR

38. When the glide slope becomes inoperative during an ILS approach, the approach becomes a nonprecision LOC approach.

   a.   The LOC minimums then apply.

39. The final approach fix (FAF) for a precision approach is identified on the approach chart by a lightning bolt (✦).

   a.   The intercept altitude is indicated next to the symbol.

40. On a nonprecision approach, the distance from the FAF to the MAP is indicated below the airport diagram.

41. If a runway has a displaced threshold, the distance available for landing will be shown by a notation in the airport diagram. For example, "Rwy 21 ldg 5957'" signifies that 5,957 ft. of the total length of runway 21 are available for landing.

42. A category C aircraft must use category C minimums, even if using category B approach speed.

43. Legends 10 through 22 (except 16 and 17) concern instrument approaches and are presented on pages 199 through 211.

6.14 DPs AND STARs

1.   DPs (instrument departure procedures), STARs (standard terminal arrival routes), and visual approaches are all routinely assigned by ATC as appropriate.

2.   DPs and STARs are issued to simplify clearance delivery procedures when ATC deems it appropriate, unless you have requested "no DP" or "no STAR" in the remarks section of your flight plan.

   a.   Less desirably, pilots may refuse DPs and STARs when they are part of a clearance.

3.   When a DP requires a minimum climb rate of a specified number of ft. per NM, you may be asked to convert the climb rate into feet per minute.

   a.   Use the Rate of Climb Table in Legend 16 on the following page.
   b.   Another method is first to divide the groundspeed by 60 to get the NM per min. Then multiply NM per min. by the required climb rate per NM to determine climb rate in feet per minute (fpm).

      1)   EXAMPLE: If 200 ft. per NM is required to a specified altitude and your groundspeed is 120 kt., you will be traveling 2 NM/min. (120 NM/60 min.), which will require a minimum climb rate of 400 fpm (200 required ft./NM × 2 NM/min.).

4.   To accept a DP, you must have at least a textual description of it.

5.   Preferred IFR routes are correlated with DPs and STARs and may be defined by airways, jet routes, and direct routes between NAVAIDs.

6.   The departure route description of a DP explains the departure procedures. It also explains the route to be used if communication is lost.

INSTRUMENT TAKEOFF PROCEDURE CHARTS
RATE-OF-CLIMB TABLE
(ft. per min.)

A rate-of-climb table is provided for use in planning and executing takeoff procedures under known or approximate ground speed conditions.

REQUIRED CLIMB RATE (ft. per NM)	GROUND SPEED (KNOTS)						
	30	60	80	90	100	120	140
200	100	200	267	300	333	400	467
250	125	250	333	375	417	500	583
300	150	300	400	450	500	600	700
350	175	350	467	525	583	700	816
400	200	400	533	600	667	800	933
450	225	450	600	675	750	900	1050
500	250	500	667	750	833	1000	1167
550	275	550	733	825	917	1100	1283
600	300	600	800	900	1000	1200	1400
650	325	650	867	975	1083	1300	1516
700	350	700	933	1050	1167	1400	1633

REQUIRED CLIMB RATE (ft. per NM)	GROUND SPEED (KNOTS)					
	150	180	210	240	270	300
200	500	600	700	800	900	1000
250	625	750	875	1000	1125	1250
300	750	900	1050	1200	1350	1500
350	875	1050	1225	1400	1575	1750
400	1000	1200	1400	1600	1700	2000
450	1125	1350	1575	1800	2025	2250
500	1250	1500	1750	2000	2250	2500
550	1375	1650	1925	2200	2475	2750
600	1500	1800	2100	2400	2700	3000
650	1625	1950	2275	2600	2925	3250
700	1750	2100	2450	2800	3150	3500

Legend 16. – Instrument Takeoff Procedure Charts, Rate-of-Climb Table.

7.   Legend 17 concerns DPs (formerly known as SIDs) and STARs.

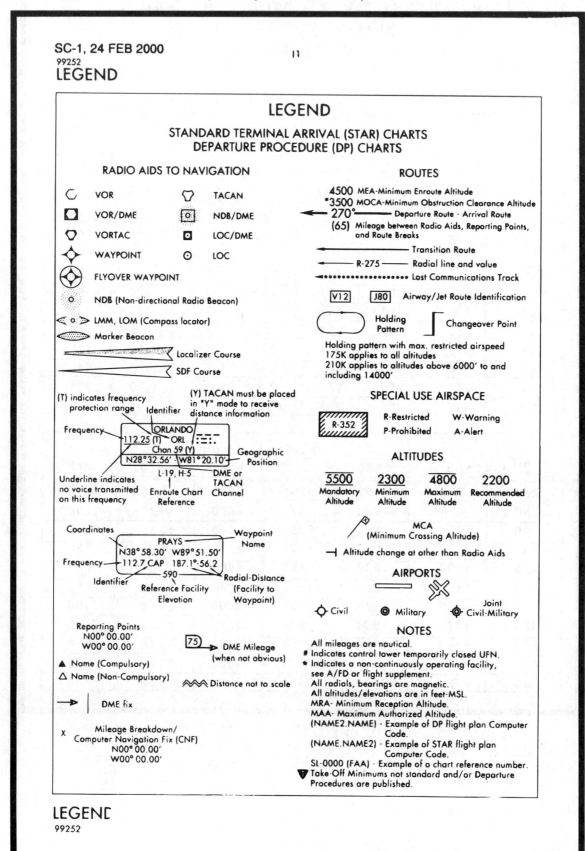

Legend 17. – Standard Arrival/Departure Charts.

6.15 MICROWAVE LANDING SYSTEM AND GPS APPROACHES

1. **Microwave landing system (MLS)** precision approaches provide azimuth, elevation, and distance information.

    a. Additional data, including MLS status, airport conditions, and weather information, is provided through MLS.

    b. A four-letter Morse code identifier, with the first letter being "M," is used to identify a specific interim standard MLS.

    c. The azimuth coverage of the MLS is laterally 40° each side, vertically 15° to 20,000 feet, and a range of 20 NM for front guidance and 7 NM for back guidance.

    d. MLS requires separate airborne equipment to receive and process these signals.

        1) With the advent of more technically advanced means of conducting instrument approaches, MLS systems virtually are no longer used in the United States.

2. Authorization to conduct any GPS approach requires that procedures be established for use in the event that the loss of RAIM capability is predicted to occur.

    a. In such an event, you must rely on other approved navigation equipment.

3. When you are using GPS for navigation and instrument approaches, any required alternate airport must have an approved instrument approach procedure, other than GPS, that is anticipated to be operational and available at the estimated time of arrival (ETA) and that the airplane is equipped to fly.

    a. Handheld GPS systems are not authorized for instrument approaches and are only considered an aid to situational awareness.

4. When shooting a GPS instrument approach, most systems require you to choose to load an approach or load and activate an approach.

    a. EXAMPLE: When ATC tells you to expect a certain approach, select that approach and load it into the flight plan. Once cleared for the approach, it can be activated.

5. There are two modes during an approach that pilots must be aware of:

    a. **Terminal mode** occurs within 30 NM of the destination airport and is used to increase sensitivity. Terminal mode increases the sensitivity on the course deviation indicator (CDI) from 5 NM to 1 NM.

    b. **Approach mode** further increases the sensitivity on the CDI within 2 NM of the final approach waypoint (FAWP) from 1 NM to 0.3 NM.

6. Pilots are commonly vectored by ATC to the final approach course, and many GPS units have a setting that guides a pilot using these vectors along the final approach course. It is commonly referred to as the "vectors-to-final" feature.

7. A fly-over waypoint is depicted on an approach plate's planview as a four-pointed star enclosed in a circle.

    a. A fly-over waypoint precludes any turn until the waypoint is overflown and is followed by either an intercept maneuver of the next flight segment or direct flight to the next waypoint.

    b. This type of waypoint is used to denote a missed approach point, a missed approach holding point, or other specific points in space that must be flown over.

8. If you examine the planview of the approach plate, you will see a box, usually in the lower left corner, that depicts the minimum safe altitude(s) (MSA) for a given segment of the approach coverage area.

    a. This notation gives you an obstacle clearance altitude while also telling you when you may begin descending to the indicated altitude when cleared to a specific waypoint.

9. Baro-VNAV is a navigational system that presents computed vertical guidance based on barometric altitude.

    a. Cold temperatures have a pronounced effect on Baro-VNAV operations because barometric altimeters will substantially over-read in very low temperatures.

    b. For this reason, a minimum temperature limitation is published for each procedure for which Baro-VNAV minimums are published. At this published temperature, the use of Baro-VNAV is not authorized to the LNAV/VNAV DA.

    c. On Figure 152 on the next page, the note "BARO-VNAV NA below –20°C (–5°F)" implies that the approach may not be flown at all using Baro-VNAV when the temperature is below –20°C.

    d. However, Baro-VNAV may be used for approach guidance down to the published LNAV MDA.

    e. A Baro-VNAV approach, along with the traditional LNAV approach, is terminated at the missed approach point (MAP), which is where the missed approach segment begins.

10. The Wide Area Augmentation System (WAAS) is a ground-based enhancement component of the satellite-based GPS navigation system.

    a. This system improves GPS signal accuracy and allows pilots with WAAS-certified equipment to conduct various types of GPS instrument approaches to varying heights above the ground.

        1) A new class of approach procedures that provide vertical guidance but do not meet the more stringent requirements for precision approaches has been developed.

        2) These new procedures are referred to in the general sense as approaches with vertical guidance (APV).

CATEGORY	A	B	C	D
GLS DA		NA		
LNAV/ VNAV DA		3100-¾ 329 (400-¾)		
LNAV MDA	3280-½ 509 (600-½)		3280-1 509 (600-1)	
CIRCLING	3360-1 581 (600-1)	3380-1 601 (700-1)	3400-1¾ 621 (700-1¾)	3400-2 621 (700-2)

Figure 152. – RNAV (GPS) RWY 30, North Plate Regional Airport Lee Bird Field (LBF).

b.   The LNAV approach is a conventional, nonprecision, GPS (RNAV) approach. There is no vertical guidance offered with this approach type.

1)   Some GPS receivers do offer advisory guidance for LNAV approaches. These approaches will appear as "LNAV+V" on your GPS receiver.

2)   Bear in mind that the vertical guidance is only advisory in nature. It will not offer lower approach minimums than what is published for the standard LNAV approach procedure.

3)   The MAP for an LNAV-only approach is the runway threshold, marked as a waypoint on the instrument approach chart with the designation "RW" followed by the runway number.

4)   In some cases, a visual descent point will appear on the profile view of an instrument approach chart, which allows the pilot to continue a descent below the published MDA as long as visual contact with the surface exists and is maintained throughout the descent.

a)   Note that this allowance for a visual descent is only approved for the LNAV approach type.

c.   The LNAV/VNAV approach is a full WAAS-enabled approach that provides vertical guidance using an electronic glide slope indication.

1)   This approach type will offer slightly lower minimums than a traditional LNAV (non-WAAS approach).

2)   Similar to flying an ILS approach, you will see a decision altitude (DA) indicated on the instrument approach chart rather than the MDA seen in an LNAV-only approach procedure.

3)   The missed approach point for an LNAV/VNAV approach is upon reaching the published decision altitude.

d.   When GPS accuracy allows, a localizer performance with vertical guidance (LPV) approach may be created for a given runway. This is a WAAS-enabled approach procedure that offers the lowest descent altitude for any GPS approach procedure, sometimes as low as 200 feet AGL, the same as an ILS approach.

1)   An LPV approach is commonly misinterpreted as a precision approach procedure. Instead, it is an approach with vertical guidance (APV) procedure, just like the other WAAS-enabled approach procedures.

2)   It is flown almost identically to an LNAV/VNAV approach. However, the decision altitude for an LPV approach is usually much lower than the LNAV/VNAV approach.

3)   Like the LNAV/VNAV approach, the missed approach point for an LPV approach is upon reaching the decision altitude (DA) published on the approach chart.

4)   When GPS accuracy is sufficient in a given area but obstacles make vertical navigation unsafe, a localizer performance (LP) approach may be put in place instead of the LPV approach.

e.   Ultimately, the GPS receiver will determine what type of WAAS-enabled approach you can conduct. If the necessary accuracy does not exist for an LPV approach into a given runway, the receiver will default to the next most feature-rich approach procedure.

1)   If your GPS receiver does not complete this function automatically, it will be up to you to determine the navigational accuracy available to you at the time of the approach.

2)   Be sure that you understand the features and capabilities of your GPS before attempting these procedures on your own. We also recommend that you receive specialized instruction on completing WAAS-enabled approaches from a qualified certificated flight instructor.

TERMS ⁄NDING MINI⁄ DATA

<u>IFR LANDING MINIMA</u>

The United States Standard for Terminal Instrument Procedures (TERPS) is the approved criteria for formulating instrument approach procedures. Landing minima are established for six aircraft approach categories (ABCDE and COPTER). In the absence of COPTER MINIMA, helicopters may use the CAT A minimums of other procedures. The standard format for RNAV minima and landing minima portrayal follows:

RNAV MINIMA

CATEGORY	A	B	C	D
GLS PA DA	1382/24 200 (200-½)			
LNAV/ DA VNAV	1500/24 318 (400-½)			1500/40 318 (400-¾)
LNAV MDA	1700/24 518 (600-½)		1700/50 518 (600-1)	1700/60 518 (600-1¼)
CIRCLING	1760-1 578 (600-1)		1760-1½ 578 (600-1½)	1760-2 578 (600-2)

RNAV minimums are dependent on navigation equipment capability, as stated in the applicable AFM or AFMS and as outlined below.

GLS (GLobal Navigation System (GNSS) Landing System)
Must have WAAS (Wide Area Augmentation System) equipment approved for precise approach.
Note: "PA" indicates that the runway environment, i.e., runway markings, runway lights, parallel taxiway, etc., meets precision approach requirements. If the GLS minimums line does not contain "PA", then the runway environment does not support precision requirements.

LNAV/VNAV (Lateral Navigation/Vertical Navigation)
Must have WAAS equipment approved for precision approach, or RNP-0.3 system based on GPS or DME/DME, with an IFR approach approved Baro-VNAV system. Other RNAV approach systems require special approval. Use of Baro-VNAV systems is limited by temperature, i.e., "Baro-VNAV NA below -20 C(-4 F)". (Not applicable if chart is annotated "Baro-VNAV NA".)
NOTE: DME/DME based RNP-0.3 systems may be used only when a chart note indicates DME/DME availability, for example, "DME/DME RNP-0.3 Authorized." Specific DME facilities may be required, for example: "DME/DME RNP-0.3 Authorized. ABC, XYZ required."

LNAV (Lateral Navigation)
Must have IFR approach approved WAAS, GPS, GPS based FMS systems, or RNP-0.3 systems based on GPS or DME/DME. Other RNAV approach systems require special approval.
NOTE: DME/DME based RNP-0.3 systems may be used only when a chart note indicates DME/DME availability, for example, "DME/DME RNP-0.3 Authorized." Specific DME facilities may be required, for example: "DME/DME RNP-0.3 Authorized. ABC, XYZ required."

<u>LANDING MINIMA FORMAT</u>

In this example airport elevation is 1179, and runway touchdown zone elevation is 1152.

TERMS/LANDING MINIMA DATA

A1

Legend 10. – Instrument Approach Procedures Explanation of Terms.

SC-1, 24 FEB 2000   A2

00055
TERMS/LANDING MINIMA DATA

COPTER MINIMA ONLY

CATEGORY	COPTER		
H-176°	680-½	363	(400-½)

Copter Approach Direction   Height of MDA/DH
                                   Above Landing Area (HAL)

No circling minimums are provided

RADAR MINIMA

Visibility
(RVR 100's of feet)

PAR (c)	10	2.5°/42/1000	ABCDE	**195**/16	100	(100-¼)				
(d)	28	2.5°/48/1068	ABCDE	**187**/16	100	(100-¼)				
ASR	10		ABC	**560**/40	463	(500-¾)	D	**560**/50	463	(500-1)
			E	**580**/60	463	(500-1¼)				
	28		AB	**600**/50	513	(600-1)	C	**600**/60	513	(600-1¼)
			DE	**600**-1½	513	(600-1½)				
CIR (b)	10		AB	**560**-1¼	463	(500-1¼)	C	**560**-1½	463	(500-1½)
	28		AB	**600**-1¼	503	(600-1¼)	C	**600**-1½	503	(600-1½)
	10, 28		DE	**660**-2	563	(600-2)				

All minimums in parentheses not applicable to Civil Pilots.
Military Pilots refer to appropriate regulations.

Visibility in Statute Miles

Radar Minima:

1. Minima shown are the lowest permitted by established criteria. Pilots should consult applicable directives for their category of aircraft.
2. The circling MDA and weather minima to be used are those for the runway to which the final approach is flown - not the landing runway. In the above RADAR MINIMA example, a category C aircraft flying a radar approach to runway 10, circling to land on runway 28, must use an MDA of 560 feet with weather minima of 500-1½ .

▲ Alternate Minimums not standard. Civil users refer to tabulation. USA/USN/USAF pilots refer to appropriate regulations.

▲ NA   Alternate minimums are Not Authorized due to unmonitored facility or absence of weather reporting service.

▼ Take-off Minimums not standard and/or Departure Procedures are published. Refer to tabulation.

AIRCRAFT APPROACH CATEGORIES

Speeds are based on 1.3 times the stall speed in the landing configuration of maximum gross landing weight. An aircraft shall fit in only one category. If it is necessary to maneuver at speeds in excess of the upper limit of a speed range for a category, the minimums for the next higher category should be used. For example, an aircraft which falls in Category A, but is circling to land at a speed in excess of 91 knots, should use the approach Category B minimums when circling to land. See following category limits:

MANEUVERING TABLE

Approach Category	A	B	C	D	E
Speed (Knots)	0-90	91-120	121-140	141-165	Abv 165

RVR/ Meteorological Visibility Comparable Values

The following table shall be used for converting RVR to meteorological visibility when RVR is not reported for the runway of intended operation. Adjustments of landing minima may be required - see Inoperative Components Table.

RVR (feet)	Visibility (statute miles)	RVR (feet)	Visibility (statute miles)
1600	¼	4000	¾
2000	⅜	4500	⅞
2400	½	5000	1
3200	⅝	6000	1¼

TERMS/ ʌNDING MINIʌ DATA

Legend 11. – Instrument Approach Procedures Explanation of Terms.

F1

99252
GENERAL INFO

GENERAL INFORMATION

This publication includes Instrument Approach Procedures (IAPs), Departure Procedures (DPs), and Standard Terminal Arrivals (STARs) for use by both civil and military aviation and is issued every 56 days.

STANDARD TERMINAL ARRIVALS AND DEPARTURE PROCEDURES

The use of the associated codified STAR/DP and transition identifiers are requested of users when filing flight plans via teletype and are required for users filing flight plans via computer interface. It must be noted that when filing a STAR/DP with a transition, the first three coded characters of the STAR and the last three coded characters of the DP are replaced by the transition code. Examples: ACTON SIX ARRIVAL, file (AQN.AQN6); ACTON SIX ARRIVAL, EDNAS TRANSITION, file (EDNAS.AQN6). FREEHOLD THREE DEPARTURE, file (FREH3.RBV), FREEHOLD THREE DEPARTURE, ELWOOD CITY TRANSITION, file (FREH3.EWC).

PILOT CONTROLLED AIRPORT LIGHTING SYSTEMS

Available pilot controlled lighting (PCL) systems are indicated as follows:
1. Approach lighting systems that bear a system identification are symbolized using negative symbology, e.g., ⬤, ⬤, ⬤
2. Approach lighting systems that do not bear a system identification are indicated with a negative "⬤" besides the name.
A star (✷) indicates non-standard PCL, consult Directory/Supplement, e.g., ⬤✷
To activate lights use frequency indicated in the communication section of the chart with a ⬤ or the appropriate lighting system identification e.g., UNICOM 122.8 ⬤, ⬤, ⬤

KEY MIKE	FUNCTION
7 times within 5 seconds	Highest intensity available
5 times within 5 seconds	Medium or lower intensity (Lower REIL or REIL-off)
3 times within 5 seconds	Lowest intensity available (Lower REIL or REIL-off)

CHART CURRENCY INFORMATION

FAA procedure amendment number ──────── Amdt 11A 99365 ────────► Date of latest change
                                          Orig 00365

The Chart Date indentifies the Julian date the chart was added to the volume or last revised for any reason. The first two digits indicate the year, the last three digits indicate the day of the year (001 to 365/6) in which the latest addition or change was first published.
The Procedure Amendment Number precedes the Chart Date, and changes any time instrument information (e.g., DH, MDA, approach routing, etc.) changes. Procedure changes also cause the Chart Date to change.

MISCELLANEOUS

✷ Indicates a non-continuously operating facility, see A/FD or flight supplement.
# Indicates control tower temporarily closed UFN.
"Radar required" on the chart indicates that radar vectoring is required for the approach.
Distances in nautical miles (except visibility in statute miles and Runway Visual Range in hundreds of feet). Runway Dimensions in feet. Elevations in feet. Mean Sea Level (MSL). Ceilings in feet above airport elevation. Radials/ bearings/headings/courses are magnetic. Horizontal Datum: Unless otherwise noted on the chart, all coordinates are referenced to North American Datum 1983 (NAD 83), which for charting purposes is considered equivalent to World Geodetic System 1984 (WGS 84).

Legend 12. – General Information.

99140

GENERAL INFO

ABBREVIATIONS

ADF	Automatic Direction Finder
ALS	Approach Light System
ALSF	Approach Light System with Sequenced Flashing Lights
APP CON	Approach Control
ARR	Arrival
ASOS	Automated Surface Observing System
ASR/PAR	Published Radar Minimums at this Airport
ATIS	Automatic Terminal Information Service
AWOS	Automated Weather Observing System
AZ	Azimuth
BC	Back Course
C	Circling
CAT	Category
CCW	Counter Clockwise
Chan	Channel
CLNC DEL	Clearance Delivery
CNF	Computer Navigation Fix
CTAF	Common Traffic Advisory Frequency
CW	Clockwise
DH	Decision Height
DME	Distance Measuring Equipment
DR	Dead Reckoning
ELEV	Elevation
FAF	Final Approach Fix
FM	Fan Marker
FMS	Flight Management System
GCO	Ground Communications Outlet
GPI	Ground Point of Interception
GPS	Global Positioning System
GS	Glide Slope
HAA	Height above Airport
HAL	Height above Landing
HAT	Height above Touchdown
HIRL	High Intensity Runway Lights
IAF	Initial Approach Fix
ICAO	International Civil Aviation Organization
IM	Inner Marker
Intcp	Intercept
INT	Intersection
LDA	Localizer Type Directional Aid
Ldg	Landing
LDIN	Lead in Light System
LIRL	Low Intensity Runway Lights
LOC	Localizer
LR	Lead Radial. Provides at least 2 NM (Copter 1 NM) of lead to assist in turning onto the intermediate/final course.
MALS	Medium Intensity Approach Light System
MALSR	Medium Intensity Approach Light System with RAIL
MAP	Missed Approach Point
MDA	Minimum Descent Altitude
MIRL	Medium Intensity Runway Lights
MLS	Microwave Landing System
MM	Middle Marker
NA	Not Authorized
NDB	Non-directional Radio Beacon
NM	Nautical Mile
NoPT	No Procedure Turn Required (Procedure Turn shall not be executed without ATC clearance)
ODALS	Omnidirectional Approach Light System
OM	Outer Marker
R	Radial
RA	Radio Altimeter setting height
RAIL	Runway Alignment Indicator Lights
RBn	Radio Beacon
RCLS	Runway Centerline Light System
REIL	Runway End Identifier Lights
RNAV	Area Navigation
RNP	Required Navigation Performance
RPI	Runway Point of Intercept(ion)
RRL	Runway Remaining Lights
Rwy	Runway
RVR	Runway Visual Range
S	Straight-in
SALS	Short Approach Light System
SSALR	Simplified Short Approach Light System with RAIL
SDF	Simplified Directional Facility
TA	Transition Altitude
TAC	TACAN
TCH	Threshold Crossing Height (height in feet Above Ground level)
TDZ	Touchdown Zone
TDZE	Touchdown Zone Elevation
TDZ/CL	Touchdown Zone and Runway Centerline Lighting
TDZL	Touchdown Zone Lights
TLv	Transition Level
VASI	Visual Approach Slope Indicator
VDP	Visual Descent Point
VGSI	Visual Glide Slope Indicator
WP/WPT	Waypoint (RNAV)
X	Radar Only Frequency

GENERAL INFO
99140

SW-1, 4 NOV 1999

Legend 13. – Abbreviations.

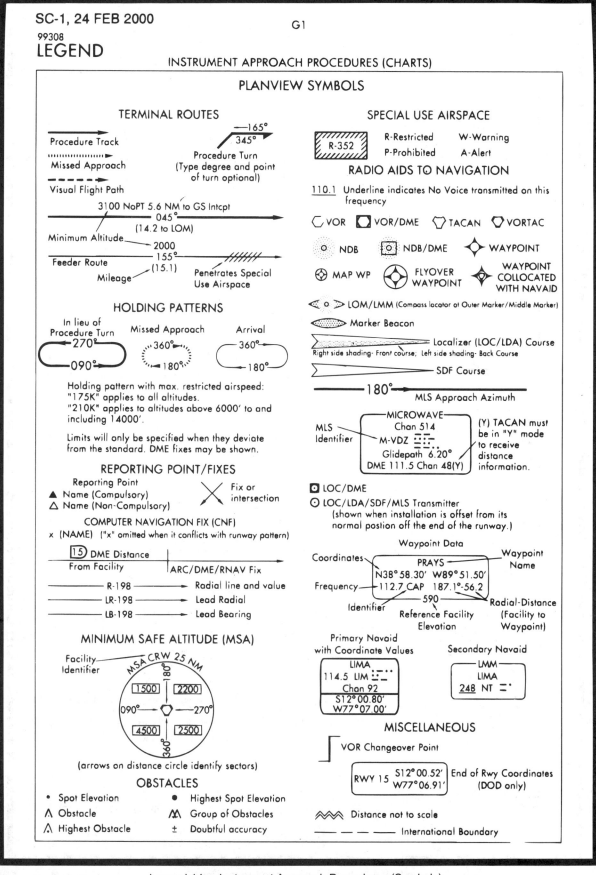

Legend 14. – Instrument Approach Procedures (Symbols).

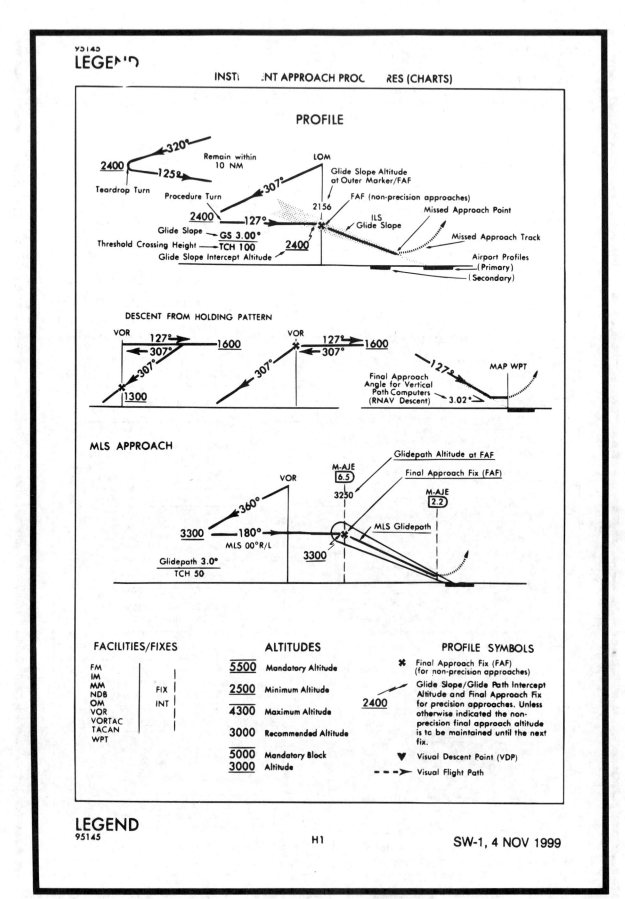

Legend 15. – Instrument Approach Procedures (Profile).

INSTRUMENT TAKEOFF PROCEDURE CHARTS
RATE-OF-CLIMB TABLE
(ft. per min.)

A rate-of-climb table is provided for use in planning and executing takeoff procedures under known or approximate ground speed conditions.

REQUIRED CLIMB RATE (ft. per NM)	GROUND SPEED (KNOTS)						
	30	60	80	90	100	120	140
200	100	200	267	300	333	400	467
250	125	250	333	375	417	500	583
300	150	300	400	450	500	600	700
350	175	350	467	525	583	700	816
400	200	400	533	600	667	800	933
450	225	450	600	675	750	900	1050
500	250	500	667	750	833	1000	1167
550	275	550	733	825	917	1100	1283
600	300	600	800	900	1000	1200	1400
650	325	650	867	975	1083	1300	1516
700	350	700	933	1050	1167	1400	1633

REQUIRED CLIMB RATE (ft. per NM)	GROUND SPEED (KNOTS)					
	150	180	210	240	270	300
200	500	600	700	800	900	1000
250	625	750	875	1000	1125	1250
300	750	900	1050	1200	1350	1500
350	875	1050	1225	1400	1575	1750
400	1000	1200	1400	1600	1700	2000
450	1125	1350	1575	1800	2025	2250
500	1250	1500	1750	2000	2250	2500
550	1375	1650	1925	2200	2475	2750
600	1500	1800	2100	2400	2700	3000
650	1625	1950	2275	2600	2925	3250
700	1750	2100	2450	2800	3150	3500

Legend 16. – Instrument Takeoff Procedure Charts, Rate-of-Climb Table.

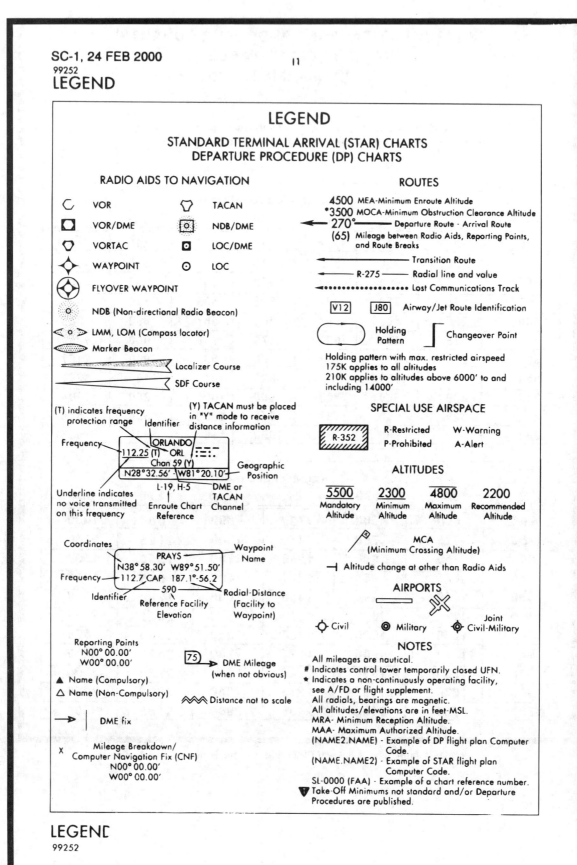

LEGEND

STANDARD TERMINAL ARRIVAL (STAR) CHARTS
DEPARTURE PROCEDURE (DP) CHARTS

RADIO AIDS TO NAVIGATION

VOR
TACAN
VOR/DME
NDB/DME
VORTAC
LOC/DME
WAYPOINT
LOC
FLYOVER WAYPOINT
NDB (Non-directional Radio Beacon)
LMM, LOM (Compass locator)
Marker Beacon
Localizer Course
SDF Course

(T) indicates frequency protection range
Identifier
(Y) TACAN must be placed in "Y" mode to receive distance information
Frequency
ORLANDO
112.25 (T) ORL
Chan 59 (Y)
N28°32.56' W81°20.10'
L-19, H-5
Geographic Position
Underline indicates no voice transmitted on this frequency
Enroute Chart Reference
DME or TACAN Channel

Coordinates
PRAYS
N38°58.30' W89°51.50'
112.7 CAP 187.1°-56.2
590
Waypoint Name
Frequency
Identifier
Reference Facility Elevation
Radial-Distance (Facility to Waypoint)

Reporting Points
N00° 00.00'
W00° 00.00'
▲ Name (Compulsory)
△ Name (Non-Compulsory)

75 DME Mileage (when not obvious)
Distance not to scale

DME fix

X Mileage Breakdown/ Computer Navigation Fix (CNF)
N00° 00.00'
W00° 00.00'

ROUTES

4500 MEA-Minimum Enroute Altitude
*3500 MOCA-Minimum Obstruction Clearance Altitude
270° Departure Route - Arrival Route
(65) Mileage between Radio Aids, Reporting Points, and Route Breaks
Transition Route
R-275 Radial line and value
Lost Communications Track
V12 J80 Airway/Jet Route Identification
Holding Pattern
Changeover Point

Holding pattern with max. restricted airspeed 175K applies to all altitudes 210K applies to altitudes above 6000' to and including 14000'

SPECIAL USE AIRSPACE

R-352
R-Restricted
W-Warning
P-Prohibited
A-Alert

ALTITUDES

5500 2300 4800 2200
Mandatory Altitude Minimum Altitude Maximum Altitude Recommended Altitude

MCA (Minimum Crossing Altitude)
Altitude change at other than Radio Aids

AIRPORTS

◇ Civil ◎ Military ◈ Joint Civil-Military

NOTES

All mileages are nautical.
\# Indicates control tower temporarily closed UFN.
★ Indicates a non-continuously operating facility, see A/FD or flight supplement.
All radials, bearings are magnetic.
All altitudes/elevations are in feet-MSL.
MRA- Minimum Reception Altitude.
MAA- Maximum Authorized Altitude.
(NAME2.NAME) - Example of DP flight plan Computer Code.
(NAME.NAME2) - Example of STAR flight plan Computer Code.
SL-0000 (FAA) - Example of a chart reference number.
▼ Take-Off Minimums not standard and/or Departure Procedures are published.

Legend 17. – Standard Arrival/Departure Charts.

95201
LEGEND

K1

SW-1, 4 NOV 1999

INSTRUMENT APPROACH PROCEDURES (CHARTS)

AIRPORT DIAGRAM/AIRPORT SKETCH

Runways

Hard Surface	Other Than Hard Surface	Stopways, Taxiways, Parking Areas	Displaced Threshold

Closed Runway	Closed Taxiway	Under Construction	Metal Surface	Runway Centerline Lighting

ARRESTING GEAR: Specific arresting gear systems; e.g., BAK-12, MA-1A etc., shown on airport diagrams, not applicable to Civil Pilots. Military Pilots Refer to Appropriate DOD Publications.

uni-directional   bi-directional   Jet Barrier

REFERENCE FEATURES

Buildings...■

Tanks...●

Obstruction..∧

Airport Beacon #.....................................☆

Runway
Radar Reflectors.....................................⊠

Control Tower #.......................................■

\# When Control Tower and Rotating Beacon are co-located, Beacon symbol will be used and further identified as TWR.

Runway length depicted is the physical length of the runway (end-to-end, including displaced thresholds if any) but excluding areas designated as stopways. Where a displaced threshold is shown and/or part of the runway is otherwise not available for landing, an annotation is added to indicate the landing length of the runway; e.g., RWY 13 ldg 5000'.

Runway Weight Bearing Capacity/or PCN Pavement Classification Number is shown as a codified expression.
Refer to the appropriate Supplement/Directory for applicable codes; e.g.,
RWY 14-32 S75, T185, ST175, TT325
PCN 80 F/D/X/U

Helicopter Alighting Areas   Ⓗ ⊞ H ⚠ ⊞

Negative Symbols used to identify Copter Procedures

landing point.................●Ⓗ ⊞ H ▲ ⊞

Runway TDZ elevation...................TDZE 123

←0.3% DOWN

Runway Slope.............................0.8% UP→

(shown when runway slope exceeds 0.3%)

NOTE:
Runway Slope measured to midpoint on runways 8000 feet or longer.

■ U.S. Navy Optical Landing System (OLS) "OLS" location is shown because of its height of approximately 7 feet and proximity to edge of runway may create an obstruction for some types of aircraft.

Approach light symbols are shown in the Flight Information Handbook.

Airport diagram scales are variable.

True/magnetic North orientation may vary from diagram to diagram.

Coordinate values are shown in 1 or ½ minute increments. They are further broken down into 6 second ticks, within each 1 minute increment.

Positional accuracy within ±600 feet unless otherwise noted on the chart.

NOTE:
All new and revised airport diagrams are shown referenced to the World Geodetic System (WGS) (noted on appropriate diagram), and may not be compatible with local coordinates published in FLIP. (Foreign Only)

SCOPE

Airport diagrams are specifically designed to assist in the movement of ground traffic at locations with complex runway/taxiway configurations and provide information for updating Computer Based Navigation Systems (I.E., INS, GPS) aboard aircraft. Airport diagrams are not intended to be used for approach and landing or departure operations. For revisions to Airport Diagrams: Consult FAA Order 7910.4B.

LEGE
95201

Legend 18. – Airport Diagram.

Legend 19. – Approach Lighting Systems.

Legend 20. – Approach Lighting System.

RATE OF DESCENT TABLE

A rate of descent table is provided for use in planning and executing precision descents under known or approximate ground speed conditions. It will be especially useful for approaches when the localizer only is used for course guidance. A best speed, power, altitude combination can be programmed which will result in a stable glide rate and altitude favorable for executing a landing if minimums exist upon breakout. Care should always be exercised so that minimum descent altitude and missed approach point are not exceeded.

ANGLE OF DESCENT (degrees and tenths)	FEET /NM	GROUND SPEED (knots)										
		30	45	60	75	90	105	120	135	150	165	180
2.0	210	105	160	210	265	320	370	425	475	530	585	635
2.5	265	130	200	265	330	395	465	530	595	665	730	795
2.7	287	143	215	287	358	430	501	573	645	716	788	860
2.8	297	149	223	297	371	446	520	594	669	743	817	891
2.9	308	154	231	308	385	462	539	616	693	769	846	923
3.0	318	159	239	318	398	478	557	637	716	796	876	955
3.1	329	165	247	329	411	494	576	658	740	823	905	987
3.2	340	170	255	340	425	510	594	679	764	849	934	1019
3.3	350	175	263	350	438	526	613	701	788	876	963	1051
3.4	361	180	271	361	451	541	632	722	812	902	993	1083
3.5	370	185	280	370	465	555	650	740	835	925	1020	1110
4.0	425	210	315	425	530	635	740	845	955	1060	1165	1270
4.5	475	240	355	475	595	715	835	955	1075	1190	1310	1430
5.0	530	265	395	530	660	795	925	1060	1190	1325	1455	1590
5.5	580	290	435	580	730	875	1020	1165	1310	1455	1600	1745
6.0	635	315	475	635	795	955	1110	1270	1430	1590	1745	1950
6.5	690	345	515	690	860	1030	1205	1375	1550	1720	1890	2065
7.0	740	370	555	740	925	1110	1295	1480	1665	1850	2035	2220
7.5	795	395	595	795	990	1190	1390	1585	1785	1985	2180	2380
8.0	845	425	635	845	1055	1270	1480	1690	1905	2115	2325	2540
8.5	900	450	675	900	1120	1345	1570	1795	2020	2245	2470	2695
9.0	950	475	715	950	1190	1425	1665	1900	2140	2375	2615	2855
9.5	1005	500	750	1005	1255	1505	1755	2005	2255	2510	2760	3010
10.0	1055	530	790	1055	1320	1585	1845	2110	2375	2640	2900	3165
10.5	1105	555	830	1105	1385	1660	1940	2215	2490	2770	3045	3320
11.0	1160	580	870	1160	1450	1740	2030	2320	2610	2900	3190	3480
11.5	1210	605	910	1210	1515	1820	2120	2425	2725	3030	3335	3635
12.0	1260	630	945	1260	1575	1890	2205	2520	2835	3150	3465	3780

(Rows 2.7 through 3.4 are labeled vertically: VERTICAL PATH ANGLE)

DESCENT TABLE 99028

Legend 21. – Instrument Approach Procedure Charts, Rate-of-Descent Table.

INOP COMPONENTS
99084

INOPERATIVE COMPONENTS OR VISUAL AIDS TABLE

Landing minimums published on instrument approach procedure charts are based upon full operation of all components and visual aids associated with the particular instrument approach chart being used. Higher minimums are required with inoperative components or visual aids as indicated below. If more than one component is inoperative, each minimum is raised to the highest minimum required by any single component that is inoperative. ILS glide slope inoperative minimums are published on the instrument approach charts as localizer minimums. This table may be amended by notes on the approach chart. Such notes apply only to the particular approach catergory(ies) as stated. See legend page for description of components indicated below.

(1) ILS, MLS, and PAR

Inoperative Component or Aid	Approach Category	Increase Visibility
ALSF 1 & 2, MALSR, & SSALR	ABCD	1/4 mile

(2) ILS with visibility minimum 0f 1,800 RVR

	Approach Category	Increase Visibility
ALSF 1 & 2, MALSR, & SSALR	ABCD	To 4000 RVR
TDZL RCLS	ABCD	To 2400 RVR
RVR	ABCD	To 1/2 mile

(3) VOR,VOR/DME, VORTAC, VOR (TAC), VOR/DME (TAC), LOC, LOC/DME, LDA, LDA/DME, SDF, SDF/DME, GPS, RNAV,and ASR

Inoperative Visual Aid	Approach Category	Increase Visibility
ALSF 1 & 2, MALSR, & SSALR	ABCD	1/2 mile
SSALS,MALS, & ODALS	ABC	1/4 mile

(4) NDB

ALSF 1 & 2, MALSR, & SSALR	C	1/2 mile
MALS, SSALS, ODALS	ABD	1/4 mile
	ABC	1/4 mile

CORRECTIONS, COMMENTS AND/OR PROCUREMENT

FOR CHARTING ERRORS CONTACT:
National Ocean Service/NOAA
N/ACC1, SSMC-4, Sta. #2335
1305 East-West Highway
Silver Spring, MD 20910-3281
Telephone Toll-Free (800) 626-3677
Internet/E-Mail: Aerochart@NOAA.GOV

FOR CHANGES, ADDITIONS, OR RECOMMENDATIONS ON PROCEDURAL ASPECTS:
Contact Federal Aviation Administration, ATA 110
800 Independence Avenue, SW
Washington, DC 20591
Telephone Toll Free (800) 457-6656

TO PURCHASE CHARTS CONTACT:
National Ocean Service
NOAA, N/ACC3
Distribution Division
Riverdale, MD 20737
Telephone Toll Free (800) 638-8972

Requests for the creation or revisions to Airport Diagrams should be in accordance with FAA Order 7910.4B.

Legend 22. – Inoperative Components or Visual Aids Table.

QUESTIONS

6.1 Contact and Visual Approaches

1. What conditions are necessary before ATC can authorize a visual approach?

A. You must have the preceding aircraft in sight, and be able to remain in VFR weather conditions.

B. You must have the airport in sight or the preceding aircraft in sight, and be able to proceed to, and land in IFR conditions.

C. You must have the airport in sight or a preceding aircraft to be followed, and be able to proceed to the airport in VFR conditions.

Answer (C) is correct. *(AIM Para 5-4-22)*
   DISCUSSION: ATC may authorize airplanes to conduct visual approaches to an airport or to follow another airplane when flight to and landing at the airport can be accomplished in VFR weather. You must have the airport or preceding aircraft in sight before the clearance is issued.
   Answer (A) is incorrect. You can have the airport in sight instead of having the preceding aircraft in sight. Answer (B) is incorrect. You must be able to land in VFR, not IFR, conditions.

2. What are the main differences between a visual approach and a contact approach?

A. The pilot must request a contact approach; the pilot may be assigned a visual approach and higher weather minimums must exist.

B. The pilot must request a visual approach and report having the field in sight; ATC may assign a contact approach if VFR conditions exist.

C. Anytime the pilot reports the field in sight, ATC may clear the pilot for a contact approach; for a visual approach, the pilot must advise that the approach can be made under VFR conditions.

Answer (A) is correct. *(AIM Para 5-4-22)*
   DISCUSSION: Contact approaches can be issued only upon pilot request, but visual approaches may be assigned by ATC. Visual approaches require VFR conditions. Contact approaches require 1 SM flight visibility and the ability to remain clear of clouds.
   Answer (B) is incorrect. ATC may assign visual approaches without pilot request, and ATC cannot issue a contact approach clearance without the pilot's request. Answer (C) is incorrect. ATC cannot issue a contact approach clearance without the pilot's request.

3. Flying clear of clouds on an instrument flight plan, what are the requirements for a contact approach to an airport that has an approved IAP?

A. The controller must determine that the pilot can see the airport at the altitude flown and can remain clear of clouds.

B. The controller must have determined that the visibility was at least 1 mile and be reasonably sure the pilot can remain clear of clouds.

C. The pilot must request the approach, have at least 1 mile visibility, and be reasonably sure of remaining clear of clouds.

Answer (C) is correct. *(AIM Para 5-4-24)*
   DISCUSSION: Pilots operating in accordance with an IFR flight plan, provided they are clear of clouds, who have at least 1 SM flight visibility, and who can reasonably expect to continue to the destination airport in those conditions may request ATC authorization for a contact approach.
   Answer (A) is incorrect. The pilot, not the controller, must determine whether (s)he can reasonably expect to continue to the airport in at least 1 SM flight visibility and clear of clouds. Answer (B) is incorrect. The pilot must request a contact approach; ATC does not solicit or assign contact approaches.

4. A contact approach is an approach procedure that may be used

    A. in lieu of conducting a SIAP.

    B. if assigned by ATC and will facilitate the approach.

    C. in lieu of a visual approach.

Answer (A) is correct. *(AIM Para 5-4-24)*

    DISCUSSION: A contact approach may be requested by the pilot if there is 1 SM flight visibility and the pilot can operate clear of clouds. It is an alternative to a standard instrument approach procedure (SIAP).

    Answer (B) is incorrect. ATC cannot assign a contact approach; pilots must request them. Answer (C) is incorrect. Using a contact approach is not necessary if a visual approach is possible.

5. You arrive at your destination airport on an IFR flight plan. Which is a prerequisite condition for the performance of a contact approach?

    A. A ground visibility of at least 2 SM.

    B. A flight visibility of at least 1/2 NM.

    C. Clear of clouds and at least 1 SM flight visibility.

Answer (C) is correct. *(AIM Para 5-4-24)*

    DISCUSSION: A contact approach may be requested by the pilot if there is 1 SM flight visibility and the pilot can operate clear of clouds.

    Answer (A) is incorrect. The flight, not ground, visibility must be at least 1 SM, not 2 SM. Answer (B) is incorrect. The flight visibility must be at least 1 SM, not 1/2 NM.

6. When is radar service terminated during a visual approach?

    A. Automatically when ATC instructs the pilot to contact the tower.

    B. Immediately upon acceptance of the approach by the pilot.

    C. When ATC advises, "Radar service terminated; resume own navigation."

Answer (A) is correct. *(AIM Para 5-4-23)*

    DISCUSSION: During a visual approach, radar service is automatically terminated without advising the pilot once the pilot has been instructed to contact the tower or change to advisory frequency.

    Answer (B) is incorrect. Approach clearance is given well before radar service is terminated. Answer (C) is incorrect. "Resume own navigation" is generally an en route instruction and is not applicable to approaches.

7. When may you obtain a contact approach?

    A. ATC may assign a contact approach if VFR conditions exist or you report the runway in sight and are clear of clouds.

    B. ATC may assign a contact approach if you are below the clouds and the visibility is at least 1 mile.

    C. ATC will assign a contact approach only upon request if the reported visibility is at least 1 mile.

Answer (C) is correct. *(AIM Para 5-4-24)*

    DISCUSSION: ATC will assign a contact approach only upon pilot request if the pilot is operating clear of clouds, has at least 1 SM flight visibility, and expects to reach the airport and land in those conditions.

    Answer (A) is incorrect. ATC may assign a visual, not a contact, approach if VFR weather conditions exist. ATC may not assign a contact approach. Answer (B) is incorrect. ATC may not assign a contact approach. The pilot must request one.

6.2 LDA and SDF Approaches

8. What are the main differences between the SDF and the localizer of an ILS?

    A. The usable off-course indications are limited to 35° for the localizer and up to 90° for the SDF.

    B. The SDF course may not be aligned with the runway and the course may be wider.

    C. The course width for the localizer will always be 5° while the SDF course will be between 6° and 12°.

Answer (B) is correct. *(AIM Para 1-1-10)*

    DISCUSSION: The approach techniques and procedures used in performance of an SDF instrument approach are essentially identical to those employed to execute a standard localizer approach, except that the SDF course may not be aligned with the runway and the course may be wider, resulting in less precision.

    Answer (A) is incorrect. The off-course indications are limited to 35° for both types of approach. Answer (C) is incorrect. The course width for the localizer is usually between 3° and 6°, and SDF is either 6° or 12° (not between).

9. What is the difference between a Localizer-Type Directional Aid (LDA) and the ILS localizer?

    A. The LDA is not aligned with the runway.

    B. The LDA uses a course width of 6° or 12°, while an ILS uses only 5°.

    C. The LDA signal is generated from a VOR-type facility and has no glide slope.

Answer (A) is correct. *(AIM Para 1-1-9)*
    DISCUSSION: The localizer-type directional aid (LDA) is similar to a localizer but is not part of a complete ILS, and it is not aligned with the runway.
    Answer (B) is incorrect. The LDA uses the same course width as the ILS, i.e., 3° to 6°. The SDF uses 6° or 12°. Answer (C) is incorrect. The LDA is a localizer-type, not VOR-type, signal.

10. How wide is an SDF course?

    A. Either 3° or 6°.

    B. Either 6° or 12°.

    C. Varies from 5° to 10°.

Answer (B) is correct. *(AIM Para 1-1-10)*
    DISCUSSION: The simplified directional facility (SDF) signal is fixed at either 6° or 12° as necessary to provide maximum flyability and optimum course quality.
    Answer (A) is incorrect. Either 3° or 6° is half the course width of an SDF. Answer (C) is incorrect. A course 5° to 10° wide does not relate to ILS, LDA, or SDF.

11. What is a difference between an SDF and an LDA facility?

    A. The SDF course width is either 6° or 12° while the LDA course width is approximately 5°.

    B. The SDF course has no glide slope guidance while the LDA does.

    C. The SDF has no marker beacons while the LDA has at least an OM.

Answer (A) is correct. *(AIM Para 1-1-9)*
    DISCUSSION: The localizer-type directional aid (LDA) is of comparable utility and accuracy as a localizer but is not part of a complete ILS. The LDA usually provides a more precise approach course than the simplified directional facility (SDF) installation, which has a course width of 6° or 12°. The LDA course widths are from 3° to 6°.
    Answer (B) is incorrect. Only some LDA approaches provide glide slope guidance, but this is not a requirement of the system. Answer (C) is incorrect. Both SDF and LDA may have marker beacons.

6.3 Precision Runway Monitor (PRM)

12. A Precision Runway Monitor (PRM) approach may require

    A. simultaneously monitoring two frequencies.

    B. special training to monitor two ILS receivers simultaneously.

    C. tracking performance parameters at the decision point.

Answer (B) is correct. *(IPH Chap 1)*
    DISCUSSION: Approval for an ILS PRM approach requires the airport to have a precision runway monitoring system and a final monitor controller who can only communicate with aircraft on the final approach course. Additionally, two tower frequencies are required to be used and the controller broadcasts over both frequencies to reduce the chance of instructions being missed. Pilot training is also required for pilots using the PRM system.
    Answer (A) is incorrect. There is not a requirement to have two ILS receivers to monitor during a PRM approach. Dual VHF communications receivers are required to be monitored. Answer (C) is incorrect. Tracking performance is done throughout the complete approach, not just at the decision point. This tracking performance is monitored by the controller.

13. Precision Runway Monitoring (PRM) is:

    A. an airborne RADAR system for monitoring approaches to two runways.

    B. a RADAR system for monitoring approaches to closely spaced parallel runways.

    C. a high update rate RADAR system for monitoring multiple aircraft ILS approaches to a single runway.

Answer (B) is correct. *(IPH Chap 1)*
    DISCUSSION: PRM is a RADAR system, which has a high update rate and is able to monitor approaches to closely spaced parallel runways.
    Answer (A) is incorrect. PRM is not an airborne RADAR system; it is a ground-based RADAR system, which has a high update rate and is able to monitor approaches to closely spaced parallel runways. Answer (C) is incorrect. PRM is not for monitoring multiple aircraft ILS approaches to a single runway. PRM is a RADAR system, which has a high update rate and is able to monitor approaches to two closely spaced parallel runways.

6.4 Runway Visual Range (RVR)

14. What does the Runway Visual Range (RVR) value, depicted on certain straight-in IAP Charts, represent?

A. The slant range distance the pilot can see down the runway while crossing the threshold on glide slope.

B. The horizontal distance a pilot should see when looking down the runway from a moving aircraft.

C. The slant visual range a pilot should see down the final approach and during landing.

Answer (B) is correct. *(AWS Sect 2)*
   DISCUSSION: RVR is an instrumentally derived value that represents the horizontal distance the pilot will see down the runway from the approach end. It is based on the measurement of a transmissiometer near the touchdown point of the instrument runway and is reported in hundreds of feet.
   Answer (A) is incorrect. RVR is the horizontal, not slant range, distance the pilot will see down the runway. Answer (C) is incorrect. RVR is the horizontal, not slant range, distance the pilot will see down the runway, not the final approach.

15. The RVR minimums for takeoff or landing are published in an IAP, but RVR is inoperative and cannot be reported for the runway at the time. Which of the following would apply?

A. RVR minimums which are specified in the procedure should be converted and applied as ground visibility.

B. RVR minimums may be disregarded, providing the runway has an operative HIRL system.

C. RVR minimums may be disregarded, providing all other components of the ILS system are operative.

Answer (A) is correct. *(14 CFR 91.175)*
   DISCUSSION: If RVR minimums for takeoff or landing are prescribed in an instrument approach procedure, but RVR is inoperative and cannot be reported for the runway of intended operation, the RVR minimum shall be converted to ground visibility and shall be the visibility minimum for takeoff or landing on that runway.
   Answer (B) is incorrect. RVR minimums must be converted to ground visibility, not disregarded. Answer (C) is incorrect. RVR minimums must be converted to ground visibility, not disregarded.

16. RVR minimums for landing are prescribed in an IAP, but RVR is inoperative and cannot be reported for the intended runway at the time. Which of the following would be an operational consideration?

A. RVR minimums which are specified in the procedures should be converted and applied as ground visibility.

B. RVR minimums may be disregarded, providing the runway has an operative HIRL system.

C. RVR minimums may be disregarded, providing all other components of the ILS system are operative.

Answer (A) is correct. *(14 CFR 91.175)*
   DISCUSSION: If RVR minimums for takeoff or landing are prescribed in an instrument approach procedure, but RVR is inoperative and cannot be reported for the runway of intended operation, the RVR minimum shall be converted to ground visibility and shall be the visibility minimum for takeoff or landing on that runway.
   Answer (B) is incorrect. RVR minimums must be converted to ground visibility, not disregarded. Answer (C) is incorrect. RVR minimums must be converted to ground visibility, not disregarded.

17. If the RVR equipment is inoperative for an IAP that requires a visibility of 2,400 RVR, how should the pilot expect the visibility requirement to be reported in lieu of the published RVR?

A. As a slant range visibility of 2,400 feet.

B. As an RVR of 2,400 feet.

C. As a ground visibility of 1/2 SM.

Answer (C) is correct. *(14 CFR 91.175)*
   DISCUSSION: Refer to Legend 11 on page 181 for a chart of RVR/visibility comparable values. An RVR of 2,400 ft. may be converted to 1/2 SM visibility when the RVR is not reported.
   Answer (A) is incorrect. RVR is a horizontal, not slant range, visibility. Answer (B) is incorrect. RVR cannot be reported if the RVR equipment is inoperative. It must be converted to ground visibility.

18. If the RVR is not reported, what meteorological value should you substitute for 2400 RVR?

A. A ground visibility of 1/2 NM.

B. A slant range visibility of 2,400 feet for the final approach segment of the published approach procedure.

C. A ground visibility of 1/2 SM.

Answer (C) is correct. *(14 CFR 91.175)*
   DISCUSSION: Refer to Legend 11 on page 181 for a chart of RVR/visibility comparable values. An RVR of 2,400 ft. may be converted to 1/2 SM visibility when the RVR is not reported.
   Answer (A) is incorrect. RVR is converted into statute, not nautical, miles. Answer (B) is incorrect. When RVR is not reported, ground visibility, not slant range visibility on approach, is substituted.

6.5 Missed Approaches

19. (Refer to Figure 233 below.) The missed approach point for the DUC RNAV (GPS) RWY 17 (LNAV/VNAV) procedure is

A. 1,903 feet MSL.

B. 300 feet AGL.

C. 0.8 NM from runway threshold.

Answer (A) is correct. *(IPH Chap 4)*
DISCUSSION: The missed approach point is given as the LNAV/VNAV DA on the minimums section of Fig. 233. It is listed as 1,903 feet MSL.
Answer (B) is incorrect. The DA for the LNAV/VNAV approach is 789 feet AGL, not 300 AGL. Answer (C) is incorrect. The distance from TEPCO to a point 1.9 NM from the threshold is 0.8 NM. It is not the missed approach point.

Figure 233.

20. (Refer to Figure 232 below.) During the LOC RWY 35 missed approach at Duncan/Halliburton Field (DUC), what would be the appropriate entry for the holding?

- A. Direct.
- B. Teardrop.
- C. Parallel.

Answer (C) is correct. *(IFH Chap 10)*
    DISCUSSION: Because you will arrive at the fix aligned within approximately 25° of the reciprocal of the inbound hold, a parallel entry is appropriate.
    Answer (A) is incorrect. Upon arrival at the fix, you will be roughly aligned with the reciprocal of the inbound fix, not inbound on the fix itself. A direct entry would be impractical. Answer (B) is incorrect. You will arrive at the fix on a heading of approximately 170°, which nearly aligns with the outbound course of the hold. A teardrop entry would be for an aircraft arriving on a heading of somewhere between 77° and 147°.

Figure 232.

21. (Refer to Figure 152 below.) At what point would a pilot execute the missed approach for the Baro Nav and LNAV approaches at LBF?

A. 3,100 feet DA for Baro NAV, or 1.5 NM from the RWY 30 waypoint for LNAV.

B. 3,280 feet DA for the Baro NAV, or the BEMXI waypoint for the LNAV.

C. 3,100 feet DA for Baro NAV, or RWY 30 waypoint for the LNAV.

Answer (C) is correct. *(IPH Chap 4)*
   DISCUSSION: Fig. 152 shows the DA for the Baro NAV approach is 3,100 feet, and the LNAV approach terminates at the RWY 30 waypoint. It would be appropriate to execute a missed approach from those points.
   Answer (A) is incorrect. Although 3,100 feet is the DA for the Baro NAV approach, 1.5 NM from the RWY 30 waypoint is incorrect. The approach plate indicates the waypoint is 1.5 NM from the threshold, not that it is 1.5 NM from the missed approach point. Answer (B) is incorrect. The LNAV MDA, not the Baro NAV DA, is 3,280 feet.

Figure 152. – RNAV (GPS) RWY 30, North Plate Regional Airport Lee Bird Field (LBF).

22. If an early missed approach is initiated before reaching the MAP, the following procedure should be used unless otherwise cleared by ATC.

A. Proceed to the missed approach point at or above the MDA or DH before executing a turning maneuver.

B. Begin a climbing turn immediately and follow missed approach procedures.

C. Maintain altitude and continue past MAP for 1 minute or 1 mile whichever occurs first.

Answer (A) is correct. *(AIM Para 5-4-21)*
DISCUSSION: When an early missed approach is executed, the pilot should, unless otherwise directed by ATC, fly the IAP as specified on the approach plate to the missed approach point at or above the MDA or DH before executing a turning maneuver.
Answer (B) is incorrect. One should continue to the MAP before executing any turns. Answer (C) is incorrect. One need only continue to, not past, the MAP.

23. If the pilot loses visual reference while circling to land from an instrument approach and ATC radar service is not available, the missed approach action should be to

A. execute a climbing turn to parallel the published final approach course and climb to the initial approach altitude.

B. climb to the published circling minimums then proceed direct to the final approach fix.

C. make a climbing turn toward the landing runway and continue the turn until established on the missed approach course.

Answer (C) is correct. *(AIM Para 5-4-21)*
DISCUSSION: If visual reference is lost while circling to land, the missed approach specified for that particular procedure must be followed. To become established on the prescribed missed approach course, the pilot should make an initial climbing turn toward the landing runway and continue the turn until established on the missed approach course.
Answer (A) is incorrect. The climbing turn should be toward the landing runway; then the pilot should execute the published missed approach procedures. Answer (B) is incorrect. There should be a climbing turn toward the landing runway.

6.6 ILS Specifications

24. If all ILS components are operating and the required visual references are not established, the missed approach should be initiated upon

A. arrival at the DH on the glide slope.

B. arrival at the middle marker.

C. expiration of the time listed on the approach chart for missed approach.

Answer (A) is correct. *(14 CFR 91.175)*
DISCUSSION: The missed approach procedure should be executed upon arrival at the decision height (DH) on the glide slope if the visual reference requirements are not met. Thus, DH on an ILS is the MAP.
Answer (B) is incorrect. The DH rather than the middle marker is the MAP. Answer (C) is incorrect. The time listed on the approach chart for missed approaches is used in conjunction with the localizer for a timed approach if the glide slope fails during the ILS approach; i.e., it is not the primary indicator.

25. If during an ILS approach in IFR conditions, the approach lights are not visible upon arrival at the DH, the pilot is

A. required to immediately execute the missed approach procedure.

B. permitted to continue the approach and descend to the localizer MDA.

C. permitted to continue the approach to the approach threshold of the ILS runway.

Answer (A) is correct. *(14 CFR 91.175)*
DISCUSSION: The missed approach procedure should be executed upon arrival at the decision height (DH) on the glide slope if the visual reference requirements are not met. Thus, the DH on an ILS is the MAP.
Answer (B) is incorrect. The DH is the MAP on an ILS, which is lower than the localizer MDA. Answer (C) is incorrect. The pilot may continue the approach below the DH only if the required visual references (e.g., approach lights) are established.

26. How does a pilot determine if DME is available on an ILS/LOC?

A. IAP indicate DMETACAN channel in LOC frequency box.

B. LOCDME are indicated on en route low altitude frequency box.

C. LOCDME frequencies available in the *Airman's Information Manual.*

Answer (A) is correct. *(IFH Chap 10)*
DISCUSSION: If DME is available on an ILS or localizer approach, the DME/TACAN channel will be indicated in the localizer frequency box on the approach plate.
Answer (B) is incorrect. LOC/DME frequencies are available on approach plates, not en route charts. Answer (C) is incorrect. The *AIM* gives general information on navigation systems, not specific frequencies.

27. (Refer to Figure 140 below, and Figure 139 on page 221.) Which displacement from the localizer and glide slope at the 1.9 NM point is indicated?

A.   710 feet to the left of the localizer centerline and 140 feet below the glide slope.

B.   710 feet to the right of the localizer centerline and 140 feet above the glide slope.

C.   430 feet to the right of the localizer centerline and 28 feet above the glide slope.

Answer (B) is correct. *(AIM Para 1-1-9)*
   DISCUSSION: The airplane is to the right of the localizer and above the glide slope each by 2 dots at 1.9 NM out. Per Fig. 139, 2 dots at 1.9 NM are 140 ft. above the glide slope and 710 ft. to the right of the localizer.
   Answer (A) is incorrect. The airplane is to the right, not left, of the localizer and above, not below, the glide slope. Answer (C) is incorrect. The 430-ft. and 28-ft. deviations are at 1,300 ft., not 1.9 NM.

Figure 140. – OBS, ILS, and GS
Displacement.

28. (Refer to Figure 139 on page 221 and Figure 141 on page 221.) Which displacement from the localizer centerline and glide slope at the 1,300-foot point from the runway is indicated?

A.   21 feet below the glide slope and approximately 320 feet to the right of the runway centerline.

B.   28 feet above the glide slope and approximately 250 feet to the left of the runway centerline.

C.   21 feet above the glide slope and approximately 320 feet to the left of the runway centerline.

Answer (C) is correct. *(AIM Para 1-1-9)*
   DISCUSSION: The airplane is above the glide slope and to the left of the localizer by 1 1/2 dots each at 1,300 ft. out. Per extrapolation and Fig. 139, this displacement is 21 ft. above the glide slope and about 320 ft. to the left of the localizer.
   Answer (A) is incorrect. The airplane is above, not below, the glide slope, and to the left, not right, of the localizer. Answer (B) is incorrect. A length of 28 ft. is 2 dots, and 250 ft. is less than 1 1/4 dots.

29. (Refer to Figure 139 on page 221 and Figure 142 on page 221.) Which displacement from the localizer and glide slope at the outer marker is indicated?

A.   1,550 feet to the left of the localizer centerline and 210 feet below the glide slope.

B.   1,550 feet to the right of the localizer centerline and 210 feet above the glide slope.

C.   775 feet to the left of the localizer centerline and 420 feet below the glide slope.

Answer (A) is correct. *(AIM Para 1-1-9)*
   DISCUSSION: The airplane is below the glide slope by 1 dot and to the left of the localizer by 2 dots at the outer marker. Per Fig. 139, 1 dot on the glide slope is 210 ft. at the outer marker (OM), and 2 dots on the localizer is 1,550 ft.
   Answer (B) is incorrect. The airplane is to the left, not right, of the localizer, and below, not above, the glide slope. Answer (C) is incorrect. At the OM, 775 ft. is 1 dot on the localizer, not the glide slope, and 420 ft. is 2 dots on the glide slope, not the localizer.

Figure 139. – Glide Slope and Localizer Illustration.

Figure 141. – OBS, ILS, and GS Displacement.

Figure 142. – OBS, ILS, and GS Displacement.

30. (Refer to Figures 140, 141, and 142 below.) Which displacement from the localizer centerline and glide slope indicates you are high and to the left of the ILS course?

   A. Figure 140.

   B. Figure 141.

   C. Figure 142.

Answer (B) is correct. *(AIM Para 1-1-9, IFH Chap 7)*
   DISCUSSION: Fig. 141 shows an aircraft that is above the glideslope and to the left of the localizer. A correction downward and to the right would be appropriate.
   Answer (A) is incorrect. Fig. 140 shows an aircraft that is high and to the right of the localizer. Answer (C) is incorrect. Fig. 142 shows an aircraft that is low and to the left of the localizer.

31. (Refer to Figures 140, 141, and 142 below.) Which displacement from the localizer centerline and glide slope indicates you are low and to the left of the ILS course?

   A. Figure 140.

   B. Figure 141.

   C. Figure 142.

Answer (C) is correct. *(IFH Chap 9)*
   DISCUSSION: Fig. 142 shows an above-center glide slope indication and a right-from-center localizer indication. This deflection indicates that you are low and left of the ILS centerline because you are supposed to "fly to the needles" to maintain the proper course. Decrease your rate of descent and make a right correction to intercept the course centerline.
   Answer (A) is incorrect. Fig. 140 indicates that you are above and to the right of the course centerline. Answer (B) is incorrect. Fig. 141 indicates that you are above and to the left of the course centerline.

32. (Refer to Figures 140, 141, and 142 below.) Which displacement from the localizer centerline and glide slope indicates you are high and to the right of the ILS course?

   A. Figure 140.

   B. Figure 141.

   C. Figure 142.

Answer (A) is correct. *(IFH Chap 9)*
   DISCUSSION: Fig. 140 shows a below-center glide slope indication and a left-from-center localizer indication. This deflection indicates that your are above and right of the ILS centerline because you are supposed to "fly to the needles" to maintain the proper course. Increase your rate of descent and make a left correction to intercept the course centerline.
   Answer (B) is incorrect. Fig. 141 indicates that you are above and to the left of the course centerline. Answer (C) is incorrect. Fig. 142 indicates that you are below and to the left of the course centerline.

Figure 140. – OBS, ILS, and GS Displacement.

Figure 141. – OBS, ILS, and GS Displacement.

Figure 142. – OBS, ILS, and GS Displacement.

33. Approximately what height is the glide slope centerline at the MM of a typical ILS?

   A. 100 feet.

   B. 200 feet.

   C. 300 feet.

Answer (B) is correct. *(AIM Para 1-1-9)*
   DISCUSSION: The ILS glide path projection angle is normally 3° above horizontal so it intersects the middle marker (MM) at 200 ft. and the outer marker (OM) at about 1,400 ft. above the touchdown zone elevation (TDZE).
   Answer (A) is incorrect. The glide slope centerline at the inner, not middle, marker on a Category II ILS is at 100 ft. above the TDZE. Answer (C) is incorrect. The glide slope centerline at the MM is usually 200 ft. AGL, not 300 ft.

34. Which range facility associated with the ILS is identified by the last two letters of the localizer identification group?

A. Inner marker.

B. Outer marker.

C. Middle compass locator.

Answer (C) is correct. *(AIM Para 1-1-9)*
DISCUSSION: Compass locators transmit two-letter identification groups. The outer locator transmits the first two letters of the localizer identification group, and the middle locator transmits the last two letters of the localizer identification group.
Answer (A) is incorrect. Marker beacons are not identified by letters when they are not compass locators. Answer (B) is incorrect. Marker beacons are not identified by letters when they are not compass locators.

35. Which indications will a pilot receive where an IM is installed on a front course ILS approach?

A. One dot per second and a steady amber light.

B. Six dots per second and a flashing white light.

C. Alternate dashes and a blue light.

Answer (B) is correct. *(AIM Para 1-1-9)*
DISCUSSION: The inner marker (IM) indicates a point at which an airplane is at a designated decision height (DH) on the glide slope between the middle marker and the landing threshold. It is identified with continual dots keyed at the rate of six dots per second and a white marker beacon.
Answer (A) is incorrect. The middle marker, not the inner marker, has an amber light with 95 dot-dash combinations per minute. Answer (C) is incorrect. The outer marker, not the inner marker, has continuous, not alternate, dashes and a blue light.

36. Which range facility associated with the ILS can be identified by a two-letter coded signal?

A. Middle marker.

B. Outer marker.

C. Compass locator.

Answer (C) is correct. *(AIM Para 1-1-9)*
DISCUSSION: Each compass locator (middle and outer) is identified by a two-letter coded signal.
Answer (A) is incorrect. Marker beacons are not identified by letters when they are not a compass locator. Answer (B) is incorrect. Marker beacons are not identified by letters when they are not a compass locator.

37. Which of the following statements is true regarding Parallel ILS approaches?

A. Parallel ILS approach runway centerlines are separated by at least 4,300 feet and standard IFR separation is provided on the adjacent runway.

B. Parallel ILS approaches provide aircraft a minimum of 1 1/2 miles radar separation between successive aircraft on the adjacent localizer course.

C. Landing minimums to the adjacent runway will be higher than the minimums to the primary runway, but will normally be lower than the published circling minimums.

Answer (B) is correct. *(AIM Para 5-4-14)*
DISCUSSION: Aircraft are afforded a minimum of 1 1/2 mi. radar separation diagonally between successive aircraft on the adjacent localizer course and a minimum 2 1/2 mi. radar separation from aircraft on the same final approach during parallel ILS operations.
Answer (A) is incorrect. Parallel approach runway centerlines are separated by at least 4,300 ft., a minimum of 2 mi. diagonal radar separation is between successive aircraft, not standard IFR separation. Answer (C) is incorrect. A side-step maneuver, not a parallel ILS approach, will have landing minimums to the adjacent runway which are higher than the minimums to the primary runway, but these minimums will normally be lower than the published circling minimums.

6.7 Unusable ILS Components

38. Which pilot action is appropriate if more than one component of an ILS is unusable?

A. Use the highest minimum required by any single component that is unusable.

B. Request another approach appropriate to the equipment that is usable.

C. Raise the minimums a total of that required by each component that is unusable.

Answer (A) is correct. *(AIM Para 1-1-9)*
DISCUSSION: Landing minimums published on instrument approach procedure charts are based upon full operation of all components and the use of visual aids associated with the particular instrument approach chart. Higher visibility minimums are required with inoperative components or visual aids as specified in FAA tables. If more than one component is inoperative, each minimum is raised to the highest minimum required by any single component that is inoperative.
Answer (B) is incorrect. An ILS can be used with some inoperative components. Those inoperative components would increase the approach minimums, but you would not need to request another approach appropriate to the equipment that is usable. Answer (C) is incorrect. It is not cumulative; you need only use the highest minimum required as a result of any one component being unusable.

39. If the ILS outer marker is inoperative, you may substitute

A. a compass locator or precision radar.

B. VOR radials that identify the location.

C. Distant Measuring Equipment (DME).

Answer (A) is correct. *(14 CFR 91.175)*

DISCUSSION: A compass locator or precision radar may be substituted for an inoperative outer or middle marker. Compass locators, precision radar, DME, VOR, or nondirectional fixes authorized in the standard instrument approach or surveillance radar may be substituted for an inoperative outer marker.

Answer (B) is incorrect. VOR radials can be substituted for the outer marker but not the middle marker. Answer (C) is incorrect. DME can be substituted for the outer marker but not the middle marker.

40. Which of these facilities may be substituted for an MM during a complete ILS IAP?

A. Surveillance and precision radar.

B. Compass locator and precision radar.

C. A VOR/DME fix.

Answer (B) is correct. *(14 CFR 91.175)*

DISCUSSION: Compass locators or precision radar may be substituted for the outer or middle marker.

Answer (A) is incorrect. Airport surveillance radar may be substituted for the outer marker but not the middle marker. Answer (C) is incorrect. A VOR/DME fix authorized in the standard instrument approach may only be substituted for the outer marker.

41. What facilities, if any, may be substituted for an inoperative middle marker during an ILS approach without affecting the straight-in minimums?

A. ASR.

B. Substitution not necessary, minimums do not change.

C. Compass locator, PAR, and ASR.

Answer (B) is correct. *(14 CFR 91.175)*

DISCUSSION: Refer to Legend 22 on page 211, Inoperative Components or Visual Aids Table. Note that an inoperative middle marker (MM) is not listed as an inoperative ILS component that would require an increase in the visibility minimum. While a compass locator or PAR may be substituted for an inoperative MM, no substitution is necessary since the landing minimums are not changed.

Answer (A) is incorrect. No substitution is necessary for an inoperative MM since the landing minimums do not change. Answer (C) is incorrect. No substitution is necessary for an inoperative MM since the landing minimums do not change.

42. Which substitution is appropriate during an ILS approach?

A. A VOR radial crossing the outer marker site may be substituted for the outer marker.

B. LOC minimums should be substituted for ILS minimums whenever the glide slope becomes inoperative.

C. DME, when located at the localizer antenna site, should be substituted for either the outer or middle marker.

Answer (B) is correct. *(AIM Para 1-1-9)*

DISCUSSION: When the glide slope becomes inoperative during an ILS approach, the approach can be conducted as a localizer approach and the LOC minimums apply.

Answer (A) is incorrect. A VOR radial must be authorized in the standard approach procedure to be used as a substitute. Answer (C) is incorrect. DME can be substituted for the outer marker, but not the middle marker.

43. A pilot is making an ILS approach and is past the OM to a runway which has a VASI. What action should the pilot take if an electronic glide slope malfunction occurs and the pilot has the VASI in sight?

A. The pilot should inform ATC of the malfunction and then descend immediately to the localizer DH and make a localizer approach.

B. The pilot may continue the approach and use the VASI glide slope in place of the electronic glide slope.

C. The pilot must request an LOC approach, and may descend below the VASI at the pilot's discretion.

Answer (B) is correct. *(14 CFR 91.175)*

DISCUSSION: Once the necessary specified visual requirements, e.g., the VASI, are attained for the intended runway, the pilot may continue the approach and use the VASI in place of the electronic glide slope.

Answer (A) is incorrect. Once the pilot has the necessary visual references, the approach may be continued visually. Answer (C) is incorrect. Once the pilot has the necessary visual references, the approach may be continued visually. Descent below the VASI glide path shall occur only when necessary for a safe landing.

44. Immediately after passing the final approach fix inbound during an ILS approach in IFR conditions, the glide slope warning flag appears. The pilot is

A. permitted to continue the approach and descend to the DH.

B. permitted to continue the approach and descend to the localizer MDA.

C. required to immediately begin the prescribed missed approach procedure.

Answer (B) is correct. *(AIM Para 1-1-9)*
   DISCUSSION: When the glide slope fails, the approach can continue as a nonprecision localizer approach. Accordingly, if the glide slope fails on an ILS approach, the pilot may switch to the localizer approach and descend to the localizer MDA (minimum descent altitude).
   Answer (A) is incorrect. Once the glide slope is inoperative, the localizer may be used only for a nonprecision approach, which uses MDA, not DH. Answer (C) is incorrect. The pilot should execute the missed approach procedure only after reaching the missed approach point.

45. When installed with the ILS and specified in the approach procedures, DME may be used

A. in lieu of the OM.

B. in lieu of visibility requirements.

C. to determine distance from TDZ.

Answer (A) is correct. *(AIM Para 1-1-9)*
   DISCUSSION: When installed with the ILS and specified in the approach procedure, DME may be used in lieu of the outer marker (OM).
   Answer (B) is incorrect. DME has no effect on visibility requirements. Answer (C) is incorrect. Touchdown zone (TDZ) is the first 3,000 ft. of the runway, not a specific point.

6.8 Flying the Approach

46. When passing through an abrupt wind shear which involves a shift from a tailwind to a headwind, what power management would normally be required to maintain a constant indicated airspeed and ILS glide slope?

A. Higher than normal power initially, followed by a further increase as the wind shear is encountered, then a decrease.

B. Lower than normal power initially, followed by a further decrease as the wind shear is encountered, then an increase.

C. Higher than normal power initially, followed by a decrease as the shear is encountered, then an increase.

Answer (B) is correct. *(AC 00-54)*
   DISCUSSION: When an airplane is on the ILS glide slope and there is a change from a tailwind to a headwind, the groundspeed will decrease. During the tailwind, lower-than-normal power will be required. When the wind shear is encountered, even lower power will be required to decrease the spurt in airspeed. Once the wind shifts to a headwind, the airplane will require an increase in power to maintain the necessary groundspeed to stay on the ILS glide slope.
   Answer (A) is incorrect. Initially there is lower-than-normal, not higher-than-normal, power with a tailwind, and when the headwind is encountered, a decrease, not an increase, in power is required. Answer (C) is incorrect. Initially there is lower-than-normal, not higher-than-normal, power with a tailwind.

47. The rate of descent on the glide slope depends on

A. true airspeed.

B. indicated airspeed.

C. ground speed.

Answer (C) is correct. *(IFH Chap 10)*
   DISCUSSION: The rate of descent required to stay on the ILS glide slope depends on the ground speed because the descent must be constant relative to the distance traveled over the ground. Thus, the descent must be decreased if ground speed is decreased.
   Answer (A) is incorrect. The rate of descent is based on ground speed, not true airspeed. Answer (B) is incorrect. The rate of descent is based on ground speed, not indicated airspeed.

48. The rate of descent required to stay on the ILS glide slope

A. must be increased if the ground speed is decreased.

B. will remain constant if the indicated airspeed remains constant.

C. must be decreased if the ground speed is decreased.

Answer (C) is correct. *(IFH Chap 10)*
   DISCUSSION: The rate of descent required to stay on the ILS glide slope is dependent on the ground speed because the descent must be constant relative to the distance traveled over the ground. Thus, the descent must be decreased if ground speed is decreased.
   Answer (A) is incorrect. If ground speed decreases and descent increases, the airplane will go below the glide slope. Answer (B) is incorrect. Ground speed rather than airspeed determines the rate of descent.

49. When tracking in bound on the localizer, which of the following is the proper procedure regarding drift corrections?

A. Drift corrections should be accurately established before reaching the outer marker and completion of the approach should be accomplished with heading corrections no greater than 2°.

B. Drift corrections should be made in 5° increments after passing the outer marker.

C. Drift corrections should be made in 10° increments after passing the outer marker.

Answer (A) is correct. *(IFH Chap 10)*
DISCUSSION: When you are tracking in bound on the localizer, your drift correction should be small and reduced proportionately as the course narrows. By the time you reach the outer marker, your drift correction should be established accurately enough to permit completion of the approach with heading corrections no greater than 2°.
Answer (B) is incorrect. After you pass the outer marker, your drift corrections should be no greater than 2°, not 5°. Answer (C) is incorrect. After you pass the outer marker, your drift corrections should be no greater than 2°, not 10°.

50. During a precision radar or ILS approach, the rate of descent required to remain on the glide slope will

A. remain the same regardless of groundspeed.

B. increase as the groundspeed increases.

C. decrease as the groundspeed increases.

Answer (B) is correct. *(IFH Chap 10)*
DISCUSSION: The rate of descent required to stay on the ILS glide slope is dependent on the groundspeed because the descent must be constant relative to the distance traveled over the ground. Thus, the descent must be increased if groundspeed is increased.
Answer (A) is incorrect. The descent rate varies with the groundspeed. Answer (C) is incorrect. The descent rate must increase, not decrease, as groundspeed increases.

51. What effect will a change in wind direction have upon maintaining a 3° glide slope at a constant true airspeed?

A. When ground speed decreases, rate of descent must increase.

B. When ground speed increases, rate of descent must increase.

C. Rate of descent must be constant to remain on the glide slope.

Answer (B) is correct. *(IFH Chap 10)*
DISCUSSION: The rate of descent required to stay on the ILS glide slope is dependent on the ground speed because the descent must be constant relative to the distance traveled over the ground. Thus, the descent must be increased if ground speed is increased.
Answer (A) is incorrect. If you increase the rate of descent when the ground speed decreases, you will fly below the glide slope. Answer (C) is incorrect. The rate of descent must change with changes in ground speed.

52. While being vectored, if crossing the ILS final approach course becomes imminent and an approach clearance has not been issued, what action should be taken by the pilot?

A. Turn outbound on the final approach course, execute a procedure turn, and inform ATC.

B. Turn inbound and execute the missed approach procedure at the outer marker if approach clearance has not been received.

C. Maintain the last assigned heading and query ATC.

Answer (C) is correct. *(AIM Para 5-4-3)*
DISCUSSION: While being vectored, if you determine that crossing the final approach course is imminent and you have not been informed that you will be vectored across it, you should question the controller. You should not turn inbound on the final approach course unless you have received an approach clearance.
Answer (A) is incorrect. You should maintain the last assigned heading until you receive an amended clearance. When in doubt, query ATC. Answer (B) is incorrect. You should maintain the last assigned heading until you receive an amended clearance. When in doubt, query ATC.

53. (Refer to Figure 133 on page 227.) During a stabilized IMC approach, the pilot should have the aircraft in a landing configuration

A. with engines spooled up before descending below 1,261 ft. MSL.

B. established on the glide slope before descending below 1,791 ft. MSL.

C. descending no greater than 1,000 feet per minute below 1,591 ft. MSL and making bank angles not exceeding 15° below 500 ft. AGL.

Answer (B) is correct. *(IPH Chap 4, AC 120-71A)*
DISCUSSION: An approach should be stabilized before descending below 1,000 feet above the airport or TDZE. Fig. 133 shows a TDZE of 791, meaning you should be configured, stabilized, and established on the glide slope before descending below 1,791 ft. MSL.
Answer (A) is incorrect. There is no requirement to have engines spooled up during an approach, and, in this case, 1,260 units is the decision altitude (DA) for the approach. You should be stabilized and in the landing configuration well before you reach DA on an ILS approach in IMC. Answer (C) is incorrect. Although it is good advice to limit your descent rate and bank angles during an approach, 1,591 ft. MSL is an arbitrary number that has no relevance to this question.

Figure 133. – ILS RWY 9 (RAL).

54. Thrust is managed to maintain IAS, and glide slope is being flown. What characteristics should be observed when a headwind shears to be a constant tailwind?

A. PITCH ATTITUDE: Increases; REQUIRED THRUST: Increased, then reduced; VERTICAL SPEED: Increases; IAS: Increases, then decreases to approach speed.

B. PITCH ATTITUDE: Decreases; REQUIRED THRUST: Increased, then reduced; VERTICAL SPEED: Increases; IAS: Decreases, then increases to approach speed.

C. PITCH ATTITUDE: Increases; REQUIRED THRUST: Reduced, then increased; VERTICAL SPEED: Decreases; IAS: Decreases, then increases to approach speed.

Answer (B) is correct. *(AC 00-54)*
DISCUSSION: When a headwind shears to a tailwind, the airplane's airspeed drops, its nose pitches down, and its vertical speed increases. The power must be increased initially to resume normal approach speed, then reduced as airspeed stabilizes to maintain the glide slope due to the increased groundspeed.
Answer (A) is incorrect. The airspeed decreases, not increases, initially as the headwind shears to a tailwind, causing the pitch to decrease, not increase. Answer (C) is incorrect. The pitch attitude decreases, not increases, due to the decreased airspeed, causing the vertical speed to increase, not decrease. Initially, the thrust must be increased, not decreased, to maintain approach airspeed.

55. The glide slope and localizer are centered, but the airspeed is too fast. Which should be adjusted initially?

A. Pitch and power.

B. Power only.

C. Pitch only.

Answer (B) is correct. *(IFH Chap 10)*
DISCUSSION: If the glide slope and localizer are centered but the airspeed is too fast, you should reduce power initially. Almost immediately, you will then have to make pitch adjustments to compensate for the power adjustment to maintain the glidepath.
Answer (A) is incorrect. Although the pitch and power adjustments must be closely coordinated, the power is actually adjusted first. Answer (C) is incorrect. Adjusting pitch initially would cause you to fly above the glide path.

56. While flying a 3° glide slope, a constant tailwind shears to a calm wind. Which conditions should the pilot expect?

A. Airspeed and pitch attitude decrease and there is a tendency to go below glide slope.

B. Airspeed and pitch attitude increase and there is a tendency to go below glide slope.

C. Airspeed and pitch attitude increase and there is a tendency to go above glide slope.

Answer (C) is correct. *(AC 00-54)*
DISCUSSION: When a constant tailwind shears to a calm wind, the airplane's airspeed increases, its nose pitches up, and it has a tendency to go above the glide slope. The nose pitches up due to the increased lift from the increased airspeed.
Answer (A) is incorrect. The airspeed and pitch increase, not decrease, and there is a tendency to go above, not below, the glide slope. Answer (B) is incorrect. The tendency is to go above, not below, the glide slope.

57. (Refer to Figure 153 on page 229.) For a stabilized approach, the aircraft must be in an approved configuration for landing

A. with the engines spooled up, before descending below 1,768 feet MSL.

B. with the correct speed and on glide path before descending below 1,268 feet MSL.

C. with a descent rate of less than 1,000 fpm below 1,080 feet MSL and bank angles of less than 15° below 500 feet AGL.

Answer (C) is correct. *(IPH)*
DISCUSSION: For turbojets, the airplane must be in an approved configuration for landing or circling, if appropriate, with the engines spooled up and on the correct speed and flight path with a descent rate of less than 1,000 fpm before descending below the following minimum stabilized approach heights:

1. For all straight-in instrument approaches (including contact approaches) in IFR weather conditions, the approach must be stabilized before descending below 1,000 ft. above the airport or TDZE.
2. For visual approaches and straight-in instrument approaches in VFR weather conditions, the approach must be stabilized before descending below 500 ft. above the airport elevation.
3. For the final segment of a circling approach maneuver, the approach must be stabilized 500 ft. above the airport elevation or at the MDA, whichever is lower.

Answer (A) is incorrect. The aircraft should be spooled up before descending below 1,000 ft. above the airport TDZE elevation of 268 ft., not 1,500 ft. above that TDZE elevation. Answer (B) is incorrect. The correct speed should be attained before passing the final approach fix at 2,200 feet. The correct glide path should be attained just after crossing the final approach fix at 2,200 ft. and before the 21 DME fix at 1,140 feet.

Figure 153. – VOR/DME RWY 3, Norridgewock/Central Maine Airport of Norridgewock (OWK).

58. (Refer to Figure 250 below.) For a stabilized approach, the aircraft would be in a configuration for approach or landing and descending at about

A. 480 feet per minute to MDA.

B. 480 feet per nautical mile below 1,580 feet MSL.

C. a descent rate of less than 1,000 fpm below 1,080 feet MSL and bank angles of less than 15° below 500 feet AGL.

Answer (C) is correct. *(IPH Chap 5)*
    DISCUSSION: The airplane must be in an approved configuration for landing or circling, if appropriate, with the engines spooled up, and on the correct speed and flight path with a descent rate of less than 1,000 fpm before descending below the minimum stabilized approach heights.
    Answer (A) is incorrect. The descent rate should be less than 1,000 fpm below 1,080 feet MSL. Answer (B) is incorrect. The descent rate should be less than 1,000 fpm below 1,080 feet MSL.

Figure 250.

59. While flying a 3° glide slope, a headwind shears to a tailwind. Which conditions should the pilot expect on the glide slope?

A. Airspeed and pitch attitude decrease and there is a tendency to go below glide slope.

B. Airspeed and pitch attitude increase and there is a tendency to go above glide slope.

C. Airspeed and pitch attitude decrease and there is a tendency to remain on the glide slope.

Answer (A) is correct. *(AC 00-54)*
DISCUSSION: When a headwind shears to a tailwind, the airplane's airspeed drops, its nose pitches down, and it begins to drop below the glide slope. The airplane will be both slow and power deficient.
Answer (B) is incorrect. Airspeed and pitch decrease, not increase, and there is a tendency to go below, not above, the glide slope. Answer (C) is incorrect. There is a tendency to go below, not remain on, the glide slope.

6.9 ASR Approaches

60. Which information, in addition to headings, does the radar controller provide without request during an ASR approach?

A. The recommended altitude for each mile from the runway.

B. When reaching the MDA.

C. When to commence descent to MDA, the aircraft's position each mile on final from the runway, and arrival at the MAP.

Answer (C) is correct. *(AIM Para 5-4-11)*
DISCUSSION: A surveillance approach (ASR) provides navigation guidance in azimuths (direction) only. The pilot is furnished headings to align the airplane with the extended centerline of the landing runway and will be advised when to commence descent to the MDA and the MAP. In addition, the pilot will be advised of the airplane's position each mile on the final approach from the runway or MAP as appropriate.
Answer (A) is incorrect. The recommended altitude for each mile from the runway is provided only upon request. Answer (B) is incorrect. The controller does not have precise altitude capability.

61. During a "no-gyro" approach and prior to being handed off to the final approach controller, the pilot should make all turns

A. one-half standard rate unless otherwise advised.

B. any rate not exceeding a 30° bank.

C. standard rate unless otherwise advised.

Answer (C) is correct. *(AIM Para 5-4-11)*
DISCUSSION: During "no-gyro" approaches prior to the final approach, all turns should be made at the standard rate unless otherwise advised by ATC.
Answer (A) is incorrect. One-half the standard-rate turn should be used in conjunction with the final approach controller. Answer (B) is incorrect. The turn should be at the standard rate unless otherwise advised.

62. Where may you use a surveillance approach?

A. At any airport that has an approach control.

B. At any airport which has radar service.

C. At airports for which civil radar instrument approach minimums have been published.

Answer (C) is correct. *(AIM Para 5-4-11)*
DISCUSSION: ASR (surveillance) approaches are available at airports for which radar instrument approach minimums have been published and a separate approach chart is available. That is, a surveillance approach must have previously been authorized and established by the FAA for a particular runway at a particular airport prior to its availability.
Answer (A) is incorrect. Specific procedures, minimums, missed approach points, etc., must be established before a surveillance approach can be conducted by ATC. Answer (B) is incorrect. Specific procedures, minimums, missed approach points, etc., must be established before a surveillance approach can be conducted by ATC.

63. How is ATC radar used for instrument approaches when the facility is approved for approach control service?

A. Precision approaches, weather surveillance, and as a substitute for any inoperative component of a navigation aid used for approaches.

B. ASR approaches, weather surveillance, and course guidance by approach control.

C. Course guidance to the final approach course, ASR and PAR approaches, and the monitoring of nonradar approaches.

Answer (C) is correct. *(AIM Para 5-4-3)*
DISCUSSION: Where radar is approved for approach control service, it is used not only to provide course guidance for radar approaches but also to provide vectors in conjunction with published nonradar approaches based on radio NAVAIDs.
Answer (A) is incorrect. Approach control radar is not designed for weather surveillance. Answer (B) is incorrect. Approach control radar is not designed for weather surveillance.

64. After being handed off to the final approach controller during a "no-gyro" surveillance or precision approach, the pilot should make all turns

    A.   one-half standard rate.

    B.   based upon the groundspeed of the aircraft.

    C.   standard rate.

Answer (A) is correct. *(AIM Para 5-4-11)*
    DISCUSSION: After being handed off to the final approach controller on a "no-gyro" surveillance or precision approach, all turns should be at one-half the standard rate.
    Answer (B) is incorrect. The established procedure is to turn at one-half the standard rate regardless of groundspeed. Answer (C) is incorrect. A standard-rate turn should be used on "no-gyro" approaches prior to working with the final approach controller.

6.10 Side-Step Approaches

65. When cleared to execute a published sidestep maneuver for a specific approach and landing on the parallel runway, at what point is the pilot expected to commence this maneuver?

    A.   At the published minimum altitude for a circling approach.

    B.   As soon as possible after the runway or runway environment is in sight.

    C.   At the localizer MDA minimum and when the runway is in sight.

Answer (B) is correct. *(AIM Para 5-4-19)*
    DISCUSSION: Pilots are expected to commence the side-step maneuver as soon as possible after the runway or runway environment is in sight.
    Answer (A) is incorrect. The side-step maneuver should be performed only when the runway environment is in sight. Answer (C) is incorrect. The side-step maneuver should be performed as soon as the runway environment is in sight, which may be before reaching the MDA.

66. Assume this clearance is received:

"CLEARED FOR ILS RUNWAY 07 LEFT APPROACH, SIDE-STEP TO RUNWAY 07 RIGHT."

When would the pilot be expected to commence the side-step maneuver?

    A.   As soon as possible after the runway environment is in sight.

    B.   Any time after becoming aligned with the final approach course of Runway 07 left, and after passing the final approach fix.

    C.   After reaching the circling minimums for Runway 07 right.

Answer (A) is correct. *(AIM Para 5-4-19)*
    DISCUSSION: Pilots are expected to commence the side-step maneuver as soon as possible after the runway or runway environment is in sight.
    Answer (B) is incorrect. The side-step maneuver should be performed as soon as possible but only after the runway or runway environment is in sight. Answer (C) is incorrect. The side-step maneuver should be performed as soon as possible but only after the runway or runway environment is in sight.

6.11 Timed Approaches from Holding Fixes

67. Which of the following conditions is required before "timed approaches from a holding fix" may be conducted?

    A.   If more than one missed approach procedure is available, only one may require a course reversal.

    B.   If more than one missed approach procedure is available, none may require a course reversal.

    C.   Direct communication between the pilot and the tower must be established prior to beginning the approach.

Answer (B) is correct. *(AIM Para 5-4-10)*
    DISCUSSION: Timed approaches from a holding fix may be conducted when a control tower is in operation at the airport of intended landing and direct communications are maintained between the pilot and center approach until switching to the tower. Course reversals are not permitted when more than one missed approach procedure exists.
    Answer (A) is incorrect. No course reversals are permitted on a missed approach procedure if more than one missed approach procedure is available. Answer (C) is incorrect. Prior to beginning the approach, the pilot must be in contact with approach, not the tower.

68. If only one missed approach procedure is available, which of the following conditions is required when conducting "timed approaches from a holding fix"?

A. The pilot must contact the airport control tower prior to departing the holding fix in bound.

B. The reported ceiling and visibility minimums must be equal to or greater than the highest prescribed circling minimums for the IAP.

C. The reported ceiling and visibility minimums must be equal to or greater than the highest prescribed straight in MDA minimums for the IAP.

Answer (B) is correct. *(AIM Para 5-4-10)*
DISCUSSION: If only one missed approach procedure is available, the reported ceiling and visibility must be equal to or greater than the highest prescribed circling minimums for the IAP.
Answer (A) is incorrect. The pilot contacts the tower when so directed by approach or center. Answer (C) is incorrect. The ceiling and visibility minimums must exceed the highest circling, not straight-in, minimums.

69. Prior to conducting "timed approaches from a holding fix," which one of the following is required?

A. The time required to fly from the primary facility to the field boundary must be determined by a reliable means.

B. The airport where the approach is to be conducted must have a control tower in operation.

C. The pilot must have established two-way communications with the tower before departing the holding fix.

Answer (B) is correct. *(AIM Para 5-4-10)*
DISCUSSION: One requirement for timed approaches is that the airport where the approach is to be conducted must have a control tower in operation.
Answer (A) is incorrect. The times to fly from the holding fix to the runway at various groundspeeds are provided on approach plates. Answer (C) is incorrect. The pilot must be in communication with approach or center until told to switch to the tower.

70. When making a "timed approach" from a holding fix at the outer marker, the pilot should adjust the

A. holding pattern to start the procedure turn at the assigned time.

B. airspeed at the final approach fix in order to arrive at the missed approach point at the assigned time.

C. holding pattern to leave the final approach fix inbound at the assigned time.

Answer (C) is correct. *(AIM Para 5-4-10)*
DISCUSSION: The pilot should adjust the holding pattern to leave the final approach fix inbound at the assigned time.
Answer (A) is incorrect. In timed approaches, the pilot will not execute a procedure turn unless cleared to do so by ATC. Answer (B) is incorrect. The assigned time is the departure time from the final approach fix, not the arrival time at the MAP.

6.12 Holding

71. At what point should the timing begin for the first leg outbound in a nonstandard holding pattern?

A. Abeam the holding fix, or wings level, whichever occurs last.

B. When the wings are level at the completion of the 180° turn outbound.

C. When over or abeam the holding fix, whichever occurs later.

Answer (C) is correct. *(IFH Chap 10)*
DISCUSSION: Outbound leg timing begins when over or abeam the holding fix, whichever occurs later. If the abeam position cannot be determined, start timing when the turn to outbound is completed (i.e., wings return to level).
Answer (A) is incorrect. Timing begins on the outbound leg when the wings are level only if the abeam position cannot be determined. Answer (B) is incorrect. The wings may be level before you are abeam the fix.

72. To ensure proper airspace protection while in a holding pattern above 14,000 feet in a propeller-driven airplane, what is the maximum indicated airspeed a pilot should use?

A. 265 knots.

B. 175 knots.

C. 200 knots.

Answer (A) is correct. *(AIM Para 5-3-7)*
DISCUSSION: The maximum indicated airspeed while in a holding pattern above 14,000 ft. in any airplane is 265 kt.
Answer (B) is incorrect. This is a nonstandard maximum airspeed, which is depicted by an icon on the appropriate chart. Answer (C) is incorrect. This is the maximum holding airspeed for an airplane from the MHA through 6,000 ft., not above 14,000 ft.

73. To ensure proper airspace protection while in a holding pattern, what is the maximum airspeed above 14,000 feet for civil turbojet aircraft?

    A. 230 knots.

    B. 265 knots.

    C. 200 knots.

Answer (B) is correct. *(AIM Para 5-3-7)*
    DISCUSSION: For civil turbojets, the maximum indicated airspeed above 14,000 ft. MSL for holding patterns is 265 kt.
    Answer (A) is incorrect. This is the maximum holding airspeed for a civil turbojet from above 6,000 ft. through 14,000 ft., not above 14,000 ft. Answer (C) is incorrect. This is the maximum holding airspeed for a turbojet aircraft from the MHA through 6,000 ft., not above 14,000 ft.

74. (Refer to Figure 112 below.) You arrive at the 15 DME fix on a heading of 350°. Which holding pattern correctly complies with the ATC clearance below, and what is the recommended entry procedure?

"...HOLD WEST OF THE ONE FIVE DME FIX ON THE ZERO NINE ZERO RADIAL OF THE ABC VORTAC, FIVE MILE LEGS, LEFT TURNS..."

    A. 1; teardrop entry.

    B. 1; direct entry.

    C. 2; direct entry.

Answer (B) is correct. *(AIM Para 5-3-7)*
    DISCUSSION: Holding pattern 1 is correct because the holding fix is always at the end of the inbound leg. Draw the 70° line through the fix such that it intersects the outbound leg 1/3 of the leg length from abeam the fix.

Airplane Heading to Fix	Entry
340° to 160°	Direct
160° to 270°	Parallel
270° to 340°	Teardrop

A 350° heading to the fix requires a direct entry, which requires a standard-rate left turn to 270° beginning over the holding fix.
    Answer (A) is incorrect. Approaching the fix on a heading of 350° requires a direct, not teardrop, entry. Answer (C) is incorrect. Holding pattern 2 does not show the holding fix at the end of the inbound leg.

Figure 112. – Holding Entry Procedure.

75. (Refer to Figure 113 on page 235.) You receive this ATC clearance:

"...CLEARED TO THE ABC VORTAC. HOLD WEST ON THE TWO SEVEN ZERO RADIAL..."

What is the recommended procedure to enter the holding pattern?

    A. Parallel only.

    B. Direct only.

    C. Teardrop only.

Answer (B) is correct. *(AIM Para 5-3-7)*
    DISCUSSION: You are cleared to hold west on R-270 with right turns, so you will be south of R-270. Since you are coming in on R-240, you need to make a direct entry.

R-020 to R-090	Teardrop
R-090 to R-200	Parallel
R-200 to R-020	Direct

    Answer (A) is incorrect. A parallel entry is appropriate only on R-090 to R-200. Answer (C) is incorrect. A teardrop entry is appropriate only when coming in on R-020 to R-090.

76. (Refer to Figure 113 below.) You receive this ATC clearance:

"...HOLD EAST OF THE ABC VORTAC ON THE ZERO NINER ZERO RADIAL, LEFT TURNS..."

What is the recommended procedure to enter the holding pattern?

- A. Parallel only.
- B. Direct only.
- C. Teardrop only.

Answer (A) is correct. *(AIM Para 5-3-7)*
   DISCUSSION: You are cleared to hold east of the ABC VORTAC with left turns on R-090. The holding side will be south of R-090, with the holding fix being the VORTAC. Draw the 70° line through the VORTAC on R-340/R-160.

R-270 to R-340	Teardrop
R-340 to R-160	Direct
R-160 to R-270	Parallel

Since you are approaching the VORTAC from the southwest on R-240 (see Fig. 113), you will make a parallel entry.
   Answer (B) is incorrect. A direct entry would be appropriate if you were coming in on R-340 to R-160. Answer (C) is incorrect. A teardrop entry would be appropriate if you were coming in from R-270 to R-340.

77. (Refer to Figure 113 below.) You receive this ATC clearance:

"...CLEARED TO THE ABC VORTAC. HOLD SOUTH ON THE ONE EIGHT ZERO RADIAL..."

What is the recommended procedure to enter the holding pattern?

- A. Teardrop only.
- B. Direct only.
- C. Parallel only.

Answer (B) is correct. *(AIM Para 5-3-7)*
   DISCUSSION: You are cleared to hold south on the 180° radial with right turns, which means you will be to the east of R-180. Since you are coming in from the southwest (R-240), you can make a direct entry.

R-290 to R-360	Teardrop
R-360 to R-110	Parallel
R-110 to R-290	Direct

   Answer (A) is incorrect. A teardrop entry would be appropriate only from R-290 to R-360. Answer (C) is incorrect. A parallel entry would be appropriate only from R-360 to R-110.

Figure 113. – Aircraft Course and DME Indicator.

78. (Refer to Figure 113 above.) You receive this ATC clearance:

"...CLEARED TO THE XYZ VORTAC. HOLD NORTH ON THE THREE SIX ZERO RADIAL, LEFT TURNS..."

What is the recommended procedure to enter the holding pattern?

- A. Parallel only.
- B. Direct only.
- C. Teardrop only.

Answer (C) is correct. *(AIM Para 5-3-7)*
   DISCUSSION: Holding north of the XYZ VORTAC with left turns on R-360 means you are on the east side of the radial. Since you are coming in from the southwest (R-240), you will be making a teardrop entry.

R-180 to R-250	Teardrop
R-250 to R-070	Direct
R-070 to R-180	Parallel

   Answer (A) is incorrect. A parallel approach would be appropriate only if you were coming in between R-070 and R-180. Answer (B) is incorrect. A direct entry is appropriate only between R-250 and R-070.

79. (Refer to Figure 114 below.) A pilot receives this ATC clearance:

"...CLEARED TO THE ABC VORTAC. HOLD WEST ON THE TWO SEVEN ZERO RADIAL..."

What is the recommended procedure to enter the holding pattern?

    A. Parallel or teardrop.

    B. Parallel only.

    C. Direct only.

Answer (C) is correct. *(AIM Para 5-3-7)*
    DISCUSSION: When holding west on the 270° radial, use right turns because left turns were not stated in the clearance. The holding pattern will be to the south of the 270° radial, so the VORTAC (the fix) is at the end of the inbound leg. To determine entry procedures, draw a 70° line through the holding fix such that it crosses through the outbound leg 1/3 of the leg length from abeam the fix.

R-020 to R-090	Teardrop
R-090 to R-200	Parallel
R-200 to R-020	Direct

Since you are approaching the holding fix from the northwest on R-330 of ABC VORTAC (Fig. 114), you will make a direct entry.
    Answer (A) is incorrect. The parallel or teardrop entries are alternatives only when approaching on R-090. Answer (B) is incorrect. The parallel entry is appropriate only when approaching on R-090 to R-200.

Figure 114. – Aircraft Course and DME Indicator.

80. (Refer to Figure 114 above.) A pilot receives this ATC clearance:

"...CLEARED TO THE XYZ VORTAC. HOLD NORTH ON THE THREE SIX ZERO RADIAL, LEFT TURNS..."

What is the recommended procedure to enter the holding pattern?

    A. Teardrop only.

    B. Parallel only.

    C. Direct only.

Answer (C) is correct. *(AIM Para 5-3-7)*
    DISCUSSION: Visualize a 360° radial with left turns. The pattern will be to the east of the radial with the holding fix being the VORTAC. Since you are approaching from the northwest on R-330 of XYZ VORTAC (see Fig. 114), you will be able to make a direct entry.

R-180 to R-250	Teardrop
R-250 to R-070	Direct
R-070 to R-180	Parallel

    Answer (A) is incorrect. If you were approaching on R-180 to R-250, you would make a teardrop entry. Answer (B) is incorrect. If you were approaching on R-070 to R-180, you would fly through the VOR, parallel the holding course, turn right to the holding course, and make an entry.

81. (Refer to Figure 114 above.) A pilot receives this ATC clearance:

"...CLEARED TO THE ABC VORTAC. HOLD SOUTH ON THE ONE EIGHT ZERO RADIAL..."

What is the recommended procedure to enter the holding pattern?

    A. Teardrop only.

    B. Parallel only.

    C. Direct only.

Answer (A) is correct. *(AIM Para 5-3-7)*
    DISCUSSION: If you are holding south on the 180° radial, you will have right turns because left turns are not specified, and you will be on the east side of the radial (to cross the VORTAC at the end of your inbound leg). Draw the 70° line through the VORTAC on R-110/R-290. Since you are inbound on R-330 (Fig. 114), you will make a teardrop entry.

R-290 to R-360	Teardrop
R-360 to R-110	Parallel
R-110 to R-290	Direct

    Answer (B) is incorrect. A parallel entry is appropriate from R-360 to R-110. Answer (C) is incorrect. A direct entry is appropriate from R-110 to R-290.

82. (Refer to Figure 115 below.) You receive this ATC clearance:

"...HOLD WEST OF THE ONE FIVE DME FIX ON THE ZERO NINE ZERO RADIAL OF ABC VORTAC, FIVE MILE LEGS, LEFT TURNS..."

You arrive at the 15 DME fix on a heading of 350°. Which holding pattern correctly complies with these instructions, and what is the recommended entry procedure?

    A. 1; teardrop.

    B. 2; direct.

    C. 1; direct.

Answer (C) is correct. *(AIM Para 5-3-7)*
    DISCUSSION: Holding pattern 1 is correct because the holding fix is always at the end of the inbound leg. Draw the 70° line through the fix such that it intersects the outbound leg 1/3 of the leg length from abeam the fix.

Airplane Heading to Fix	Entry
340° to 160°	Direct
160° to 270°	Parallel
270° to 340°	Teardrop

A 350° heading to the fix requires a direct entry, which requires a standard-rate left turn to 270° beginning over the holding fix.
    Answer (A) is incorrect. Approaching the fix on a heading of 350° requires a direct, not teardrop, entry. Answer (B) is incorrect. Holding pattern 2 does not show the holding fix at the end of the inbound leg.

Figure 115. – DME Fix with Holding Pattern.

83. What timing procedure should be used when performing a holding pattern at a VOR?

    A. Timing for the outbound leg begins over or abeam the VOR, whichever occurs later.

    B. Timing for the inbound leg begins when initiating the turn inbound.

    C. Adjustments in timing of each pattern should be made on the inbound leg.

Answer (A) is correct. *(AIM Para 5-3-7)*
    DISCUSSION: Outbound leg timing begins over or abeam the fix, whichever occurs later. If abeam the position cannot be determined, start timing when the turn to outbound is completed.
    Answer (B) is incorrect. The timing for the inbound leg begins when the inbound turn is completed, not when it is initiated. Answer (C) is incorrect. The timing of the pattern is adjusted by varying the length of the outbound leg. Once inbound, you must fly to the holding fix and cannot adjust the length of the leg.

84. To ensure proper airspace protection while holding at 5,000 feet in a civil aircraft, what is the maximum indicated airspeed a pilot should use?

    A. 230 knots.

    B. 200 knots.

    C. 210 knots.

Answer (B) is correct. *(AIM Para 5-3-7)*
    DISCUSSION: The maximum airspeed in holding patterns for a civil aircraft is 200 kt. from the minimum holding altitude (MHA) through 6,000 ft.
    Answer (A) is incorrect. This is the maximum holding speed from 6,001 ft. through 14,000 ft. Answer (C) is incorrect. This is the maximum holding airspeed from 6,001 ft. through 14,000 ft. where published.

85. Where a holding pattern is specified in lieu of a procedure turn, the holding maneuver must be executed within

A. the 1-minute time limitation or DME distance as specified in the profile view.

B. a radius of 5 miles from the holding fix.

C. 10 knots of the specified holding speed.

Answer (A) is correct. *(AIM Para 5-3-7)*
DISCUSSION: Holding patterns should always be executed within the time or leg length published in the profile view of the IAP.
Answer (B) is incorrect. A radius of 5 mi. for a procedure turn can be specified only for category A or helicopter aircraft. Answer (C) is incorrect. ATC does not specify a holding speed. You need only remain below the maximum allowable holding speed.

86. When more than one circuit of the holding pattern is needed to lose altitude or become better established on course, the additional circuits can be made

A. at pilot's discretion.

B. only in an emergency.

C. only if pilot advises ATC and ATC approves.

Answer (C) is correct. *(AIM Para 5-4-8)*
DISCUSSION: If you are cleared for the approach while in a holding pattern, ATC will not expect you to make any additional circuits in the hold. If you do elect to make additional circuits to lose altitude or become better established on course, it is your responsibility to so advise ATC when you receive your approach clearance.
Answer (A) is incorrect. While you may elect to make additional circuits in the holding pattern, you are required to advise ATC of your intentions. Answer (B) is incorrect. Additional circuits may be made at your discretion; declaring an emergency is not necessary.

87. The standard IFR climb gradient is

A. 500 feet per NM.

B. 400 feet per NM.

C. 200 feet per NM.

Answer (C) is correct. *(IPH Chap 1, FAA Order 8260.3B)*
DISCUSSION: The standard IFR climb gradient is 200 feet per NM.
Answer (A) is incorrect. The standard IFR climb gradient is 200, not 500, feet per NM. Answer (B) is incorrect. The standard IFR climb gradient is 200, not 400, feet per NM.

88. (Refer to Figure 246 on page 239.) Using an average ground speed of 90 knots, what constant rate of descent from 2,000 feet MSL at the FAF would enable the aircraft to arrive at 600 feet MSL at the MAP?

A. 510 feet per minute.

B. 360 feet per minute.

C. 460 feet per minute.

Answer (A) is the best answer. *(IPH Chap 5)*
DISCUSSION: Time establishes the MAP on this approach. With a ground speed of 90 knots, we can see that we need to lose 1,400 feet (2,000 – 600) between the FAF and the MAP in 2 minutes 44 seconds. Convert time to a decimal number. 44 seconds ÷ 60 seconds = 0.73 minute. Add the 2 minutes to arrive at 2.73 minutes. Divide distance by time to find the answer. 1400 ÷ 2.73 = 513 feet per minute. This is the closest and best answer.
Answer (B) is incorrect. We can calculate the correct answer using known values. You must lose 1,400 feet in 2:44 between the FAF and the MAP. Divide distance by time (in decimal form). 1,400 (feet) ÷ 2.73 (minutes) = 513 feet per minute, not 360 feet per minute. Answer (C) is incorrect. We can calculate the correct answer using known values. You must lose 1,400 feet in 2:44 between the FAF and the MAP. Divide distance by time (in decimal form). 1,400 (feet) ÷ 2.73 (minutes) = 513 feet per minute, not 460 feet per minute.

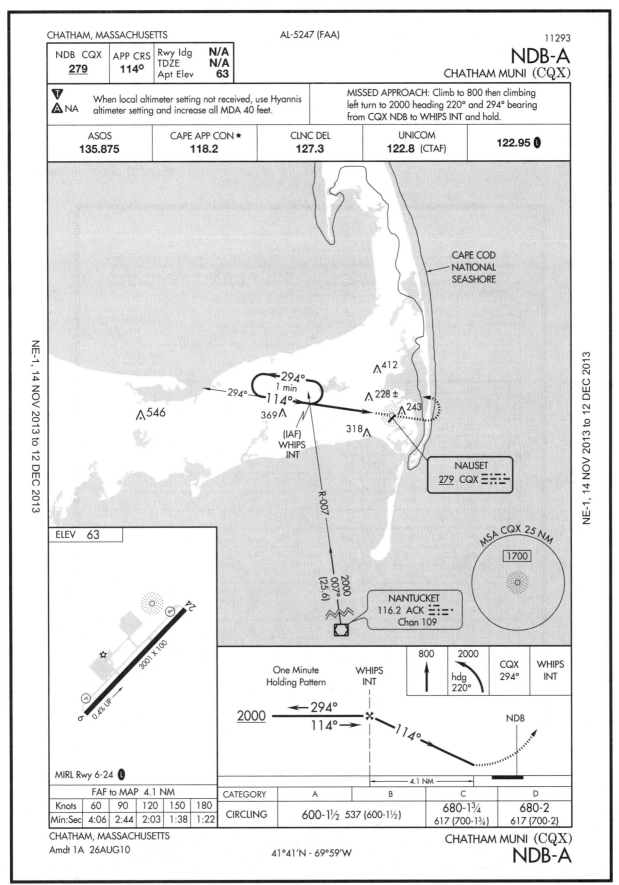

Figure 246.

89. (Refer to Figure 29 on page 241 and Legend 21 below.) What is the approximate rate of descent required (for planning purposes) to maintain the electronic glide slope at 105 knots ground speed?

A. 520 feet per minute.

B. 520 feet per NM.

C. 557 feet per minute.

Answer (C) is correct. *(IPH Chap 5)*
DISCUSSION: Fig. 29 confirms the glide slope is at 3 degrees. On Legend 21, find "3.0" in the left-hand column labeled "Vertical Path Angle." Trace to the right until you find the column for 105 knots ground speed. The correct descent rate for planning purposes is 557 feet per minute.
NOTE: The second column is the only one that lists values in feet per NM. All other columns are in feet per minute.
Answer (A) is incorrect. Planning to maintain a 3.0 degree glide slope at 105 knots ground speed equates to a descent rate of 557, not 520, feet per minute. Answer (B) is incorrect. Planning to maintain a 3.0 degree glide slope at 105 knots ground speed equates to a descent rate of 557 feet per minute, not 520 feet per NM. The second column in Legend 21 is the only one that lists values in feet per NM.

RATE OF DESCENT TABLE

A rate of descent table is provided for use in planning and executing precision descents under known or approximate ground speed conditions. It will be especially useful for approaches when the localizer only is used for course guidance. A best speed, power, altitude combination can be programmed which will result in a stable glide rate and altitude favorable for executing a landing if minimums exist upon breakout. Care should always be exercised so that minimum descent altitude and missed approach point are not exceeded.

ANGLE OF DESCENT (degrees and tenths)	FEET /NM	GROUND SPEED (knots)										
		30	45	60	75	90	105	120	135	150	165	180
2.0	210	105	160	210	265	320	370	425	475	530	585	635
2.5	265	130	200	265	330	395	465	530	595	665	730	795
2.7	287	143	215	287	358	430	501	573	645	716	788	860
2.8	297	149	223	297	371	446	520	594	669	743	817	891
2.9	308	154	231	308	385	462	539	616	693	769	846	923
3.0	318	159	239	318	398	478	557	637	716	796	876	955
3.1	329	165	247	329	411	494	576	658	740	823	905	987
3.2	340	170	255	340	425	510	594	679	764	849	934	1019
3.3	350	175	263	350	438	526	613	701	788	876	963	1051
3.4	361	180	271	361	451	541	632	722	812	902	993	1083
3.5	370	185	280	370	465	555	650	740	835	925	1020	1110
4.0	425	210	315	425	530	635	740	845	955	1060	1165	1270
4.5	475	240	355	475	595	715	835	955	1075	1190	1310	1430
5.0	530	265	395	530	660	795	925	1060	1190	1325	1455	1590
5.5	580	290	435	580	730	875	1020	1165	1310	1455	1600	1745
6.0	635	315	475	635	795	955	1110	1270	1430	1590	1745	1950
6.5	690	345	515	690	860	1030	1205	1375	1550	1720	1890	2065
7.0	740	370	555	740	925	1110	1295	1480	1665	1850	2035	2220
7.5	795	395	595	795	990	1190	1390	1585	1785	1985	2180	2380
8.0	845	425	635	845	1055	1270	1480	1690	1905	2115	2325	2540
8.5	900	450	675	900	1120	1345	1570	1795	2020	2245	2470	2695
9.0	950	475	715	950	1190	1425	1665	1900	2140	2375	2615	2855
9.5	1005	500	750	1005	1255	1505	1755	2005	2255	2510	2760	3010
10.0	1055	530	790	1055	1320	1585	1845	2110	2375	2640	2900	3165
10.5	1105	555	830	1105	1385	1660	1940	2215	2490	2770	3045	3320
11.0	1160	580	870	1160	1450	1740	2030	2320	2610	2900	3190	3480
11.5	1210	605	910	1210	1515	1820	2120	2425	2725	3030	3335	3635
12.0	1260	630	945	1260	1575	1890	2205	2520	2835	3150	3465	3780

Rows 2.7 through 3.4 are enclosed in a box labeled vertically "VERTICAL PATH ANGLE".

DESCENT TABLE 99028

Legend 21.–Instrument Approach Procedure Charts, Rate-of-Descent Table.

Figure 29. – ILS RWY 16 (EUG) and Excerpt from Airport/Facility Directory.

90. (Refer to Figure 247 on page 243 and Legend 21 below.) With a 15 knot headwind while flying the ILS Rwy 9 at RAL with 90 knots, you expect to set power for a

    A. 318 feet per minute rate of descent.

    B. 398 feet per minute rate of descent.

    C. 478 feet per minute rate of descent.

Answer (B) is correct. *(IPH Chap 5)*

    DISCUSSION: Although flying at 90 knots, the 15 knot headwind gives you a ground speed of 75 knots. Fig. 247 verifies the glide slope is 3.0 degrees. Use Legend 21 to find the 3.0 degree vertical path angle, and then move right until that row intersects with the 75 knot ground speed column. You can expect to set power for a 398 foot per minute rate of descent.

    Answer (A) is incorrect. Power set for a 318 feet per minute rate of descent would be appropriate for a 60 knot ground speed. Answer (C) is incorrect. Power set for a 478 feet per minute rate of descent would be appropriate for a 90 knot ground speed.

RATE OF DESCENT TABLE

A rate of descent table is provided for use in planning and executing precision descents under known or approximate ground speed conditions. It will be especially useful for approaches when the localizer only is used for course guidance. A best speed, power, altitude combination can be programmed which will result in a stable glide rate and altitude favorable for executing a landing if minimums exist upon breakout. Care should always be exercised so that minimum descent altitude and missed approach point are not exceeded.

ANGLE OF DESCENT (degrees and tenths)	FEET /NM	GROUND SPEED (knots)										
		30	45	60	75	90	105	120	135	150	165	180
2.0	210	105	160	210	265	320	370	425	475	530	585	635
2.5	265	130	200	265	330	395	465	530	595	665	730	795
2.7	287	143	215	287	358	430	501	573	645	716	788	860
2.8	297	149	223	297	371	446	520	594	669	743	817	891
2.9	308	154	231	308	385	462	539	616	693	769	846	923
3.0	318	159	239	318	398	478	557	637	716	796	876	955
3.1	329	165	247	329	411	494	576	658	740	823	905	987
3.2	340	170	255	340	425	510	594	679	764	849	934	1019
3.3	350	175	263	350	438	526	613	701	788	876	963	1051
3.4	361	180	271	361	451	541	632	722	812	902	993	1083
3.5	370	185	280	370	465	555	650	740	835	925	1020	1110
4.0	425	210	315	425	530	635	740	845	955	1060	1165	1270
4.5	475	240	355	475	595	715	835	955	1075	1190	1310	1430
5.0	530	265	395	530	660	795	925	1060	1190	1325	1455	1590
5.5	580	290	435	580	730	875	1020	1165	1310	1455	1600	1745
6.0	635	315	475	635	795	955	1110	1270	1430	1590	1745	1950
6.5	690	345	515	690	860	1030	1205	1375	1550	1720	1890	2065
7.0	740	370	555	740	925	1110	1295	1480	1665	1850	2035	2220
7.5	795	395	595	795	990	1190	1390	1585	1785	1985	2180	2380
8.0	845	425	635	845	1055	1270	1480	1690	1905	2115	2325	2540
8.5	900	450	675	900	1120	1345	1570	1795	2020	2245	2470	2695
9.0	950	475	715	950	1190	1425	1665	1900	2140	2375	2615	2855
9.5	1005	500	750	1005	1255	1505	1755	2005	2255	2510	2760	3010
10.0	1055	530	790	1055	1320	1585	1845	2110	2375	2640	2900	3165
10.5	1105	555	830	1105	1385	1660	1940	2215	2490	2770	3045	3320
11.0	1160	580	870	1160	1450	1740	2030	2320	2610	2900	3190	3480
11.5	1210	605	910	1210	1515	1820	2120	2425	2725	3030	3335	3635
12.0	1260	630	945	1260	1575	1890	2205	2520	2835	3150	3465	3780

(Left vertical label spanning rows 2.7 through 3.4: VERTICAL PATH ANGLE)

DESCENT TABLE 99028

Legend 21. – Instrument Approach Procedure Charts, Rate-of-Descent Table.

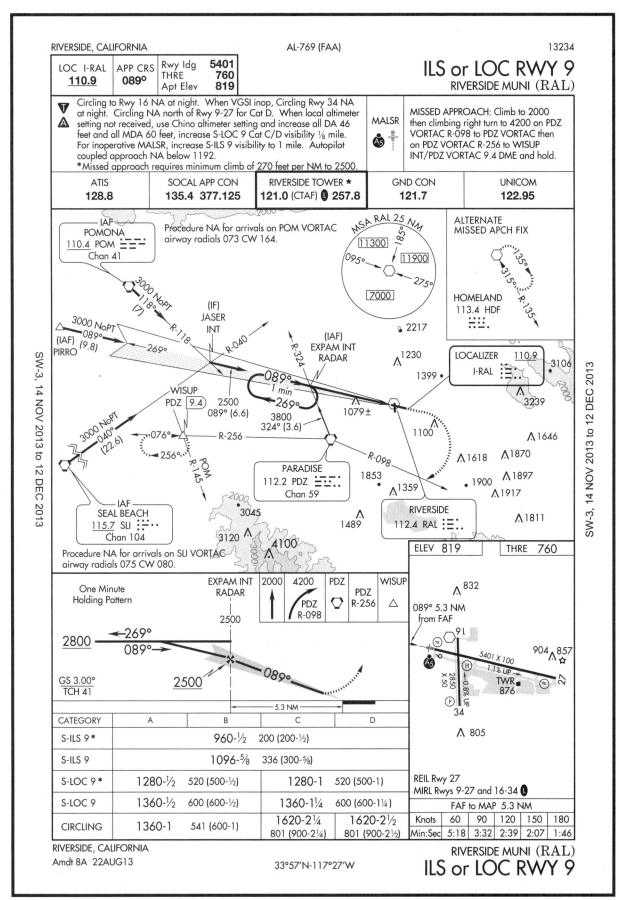

Figure 247.

91. (Refer to Figure 116 below.) You arrive over the 15 DME fix on a heading of 350°. Which holding pattern correctly complies with the ATC clearance below, and what is the recommended entry procedure?

"...HOLD WEST OF THE ONE FIVE DME FIX ON THE TWO SIX EIGHT RADIAL OF THE ABC VORTAC, FIVE MILE LEGS, LEFT TURNS..."

A.   1; teardrop entry.

B.   2; direct entry.

C.   1; direct entry.

Answer (B) is correct. *(AIM Para 5-3-7)*

DISCUSSION: Based on the drawing in image 2, you can cross the fix, then safely turn to the outbound heading (268°) and fly the outbound leg for 5 miles. A left turn inbound will bring you onto the appropriate radial, which you can track inbound to establish yourself in the hold. This procedure describes a direct entry with left turns. Draw the station, the radial, and your position out on paper to better visualize this procedure.

Answer (A) is incorrect. The drawing in image 1 shows a track that leads away from the fix while established on the radial. That is opposite the norm, which has the pilot flying the inbound leg (flying toward the fix) while established on the radial. The entry type is immaterial, since the direction of the hold is incorrect. Answer (C) is incorrect. The drawing in image 1 shows a track that leads away from the fix while established on the radial. That is opposite the norm, which has the pilot flying the inbound leg (flying toward the fix) while established on the radial. The entry type is immaterial, since the direction of the hold is incorrect.

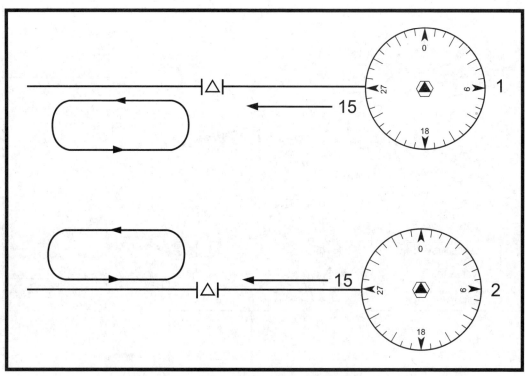

Figure 116. – Holding Entry Procedure.

6.13 Instrument Approach Charts

92. How can an IAF be identified on a Standard Instrument Approach Procedure (SIAP) Chart?

A. All fixes that are labeled IAF.

B. Any fix illustrated within the 10 mile ring other than the FAF or stepdown fix.

C. The procedure turn and the fixes on the feeder facility ring.

Answer (A) is correct. *(AIM P/C Glossary)*
    DISCUSSION: The fixes depicted on Instrument Approach Procedure Charts that identify the beginning of an initial approach segment are the initial approach fixes (IAF). Initial approach fixes are identified by the letters IAF on instrument approach charts. There may be more than one for any given approach.
    Answer (B) is incorrect. IAFs are specifically identified with "IAF." Answer (C) is incorrect. IAFs are specifically identified with "IAF."

93. Which fixes on the IAP Charts are initial approach fixes?

A. Any fix on the en route facilities ring, the feeder facilities ring, and those at the start of arc approaches.

B. Only the fixes at the start of arc approaches and those on either the feeder facilities ring or en route facilities ring that have a transition course shown to the approach procedure.

C. Any fix that is identified by the letters IAF.

Answer (C) is correct. *(AIM P/C Glossary)*
    DISCUSSION: The fixes depicted on Instrument Approach Procedure Charts that identify the beginning of an initial approach segment are the initial approach fixes (IAF). Initial approach fixes are identified by the letters IAF on instrument approach charts. There may be more than one for any given approach.
    Answer (A) is incorrect. IAFs are specifically identified with "IAF." Answer (B) is incorrect. IAFs are specifically identified with "IAF."

94. Aircraft approach categories are based on

A. certificated approach speed at maximum gross weight.

B. 1.3 times the stall speed in landing configuration at maximum gross landing weight.

C. 1.3 times the stall speed at maximum gross weight.

Answer (B) is correct. *(IFH Chap 10)*
    DISCUSSION: IFR approach minimums are specified for various aircraft speed/weight combinations. Speeds are based upon the value of 1.3 times the stall speed of the aircraft in the landing configuration at maximum certified gross landing weight.
    Answer (A) is incorrect. Aircraft do not have certificated approach speeds. Answer (C) is incorrect. Speeds are based on 1.3 times the stall speed in landing configuration at maximum gross landing weight, not just maximum gross weight.

95. How can the pilot determine, for an ILS runway equipped with MALSR, that there may be a penetration of the obstacle identification surfaces (OIS), and care should be taken in the visual segment to avoid any obstacles?

A. The runway has a visual approach slope indicator (VASI.)

B. The published visibility for the ILS is no lower than 3/4 SM.

C. The approach chart has a visual descent point (VDP) published.

Answer (B) is correct. *(IPH Chap 5)*
    DISCUSSION: If there is penetration of the obstacle identification surfaces (OIS), the published visibility for the ILS approach can be no lower than 3/4 SM.
    Answer (A) is incorrect. If there is penetration of the obstacle identification surfaces for a particular approach, the way to determine that is so is to refer to the visibility minimums for the approach. A VASI-equipped runway is not an indication of the penetration of obstacle identification surfaces. Answer (C) is incorrect. If there is penetration of the obstacle identification surfaces for a particular approach, the way to determine that is so is to refer to the visibility minimums for the approach. An approach chart that has a published visual descent point is not an indication of the penetration of obstacle identification surfaces.

Figure 60A. – ILS RWY 4 (HOU).

96. (Refer to Figure 60A on page 246.) What is the elevation of the TDZE for RWY 4?

   A. 70 feet MSL.

   B. 54 feet MSL.

   C. 46 feet MSL.

Answer (C) is correct. *(IFH Chap 10)*
   DISCUSSION: The TDZE (touchdown zone elevation) is the highest elevation in the first 3,000 ft. of the runway on a straight-in landing approach. On an NOS chart, it is marked in the airport diagram near the approach end of the runway. Thus, the TDZE for RWY 4 is 46 ft. MSL.
   Answer (A) is incorrect. This is the elevation of a tower near the approach end of RWY 4. Answer (B) is incorrect. This is the TCH (threshold crossing height) on the ILS RWY 4 approach, i.e., the height at which the airplane's glide slope antenna should cross the runway's threshold on the glide slope.

97. (Refer to Figure 61 below, and Figure 60A on page 246.) Determine your position relative to the PLATS intersection, glide slope, and localizer course.

   A. Past PLATS, below the glide slope, and right of the localizer course.

   B. Approaching PLATS, above the glide slope, and left of the localizer course.

   C. Past PLATS, above the glide slope, and right of the localizer course.

Answer (C) is correct. *(IFH Chap 10)*
   DISCUSSION: The VOR in Fig. 61 is tuned to the localizer. The CDI and glide slope needles show your position is above the glide slope and right of the localizer course. The RMI #2 indicator is tuned to the Scholes VORTAC and shows your position is R-300 (tail of the double needle). Since the PLATS intersection is on R-291, you are northeast of PLATS, or past it on the inbound course.
   Answer (A) is incorrect. The glide slope needle is below center, indicating above, not below, the glide slope. Answer (B) is incorrect. R-300 of Scholes VORTAC is northeast, not southwest, of PLATS, and the CDI is left of center, indicating right, not left, of course.

Figure 61. – RMI and CDI Indicators.

98. (Refer to Figure 74 below, and Figure 80 on page 249.) V$_{YSE}$ is 95 knots. Which aircraft approach category should be used for a circling approach for a landing on RWY 25?

A. B.

B. A.

C. C.

Answer (A) is correct. *(IPH Chap 4, AIM Para 5-4-7)*
DISCUSSION: The Aircraft Information listed in Fig. 74 indicates an aircraft with a V$_{SO}$ of 72 knots. 72 × 1.3 = 93.6. This indicates an approach speed of 94 knots, which corresponds with Category B aircraft that exhibit a speed of 91 knots or more, but less than 121 knots.

Answer (B) is incorrect. Category A indicates aircraft with an approach speed of 91 knots or less. Because 91 knots is less than V$_{YSE}$ for this aircraft, it is an unacceptably slow approach speed. Answer (C) is incorrect. Category C indicates an aircraft flying at 121 knots or more, but not more than 141 knots. With a listed V$_{SO}$ of 72 knots, this aircraft would fly its approach at closer to 94 knots (V$_{SO}$ × 1.3 = approach speed), too slow for Category C.

Form Approved: OMB No. 2120-0034

U.S. DEPARTMENT OF TRANSPORTATION FEDERAL AVIATION ADMINISTRATION **FLIGHT PLAN**	(FAA USE ONLY)	□ PILOT BRIEFING □STOPOVER	□ VNR	TIME STARTED	SPECIALIST INITIALS

1. TYPE	2. AIRCRAFT IDENTIFICATION	3. AIRCRAFT TYPE/ SPECIAL EQUIPMENT	4. TRUE AIRSPEED	5. DEPARTURE POINT	6. DEPARTURE TIME		7. CRUISING ALTITUDE
VFR / X IFR / DVFR	N242T	C310/	160 KTS	HLN	PROPOSED (Z)	ACTUAL (Z)	11000

8. ROUTE OF FLIGHT

STAKK2, V365 BZN, V86

9. DESTINATION (Name of airport and city) LOGAN INTL. AIRPORT (BIL)	10. EST. TIME ENROUTE HOURS / MINUTES	11. REMARKS

12. FUEL ON BOARD HOURS / MINUTES	13. ALTERNATE AIRPORT(S) N/A	14. PILOTS NAME, ADDRESS & TELEPHONE NUMBER & AIRCRAFT HOME BASE / 17. DESTINATION CONTACT/TELEPHONE (OPTIONAL)	15. NUMBER ABOARD 2

16. COLOR OF AIRCRAFT RED/BLACK/WHITE	CIVIL AIRCRAFT PILOTS. FAR Part 91 requires you file an IFR flight plan to operate under instrument flight rules in controlled airspace. Failure to file could result in a civil penalty not to exceed $1,000 for each violation (Section 901 of the Federal Aviation Act of 1958, as amended). Filing of a VFR flight plan is recommended as a good operating practice. See also Part 99 for requirements concerning DVFR flight plans.

FAA Form 7233-1 (8-82)   CLOSE VFR FLIGHT PLAN WITH _____ FSS ON ARRIVAL

AIRCRAFT INFORMATION

MAKE Cessna   MODEL 310R

N 242T   Vso 72

AIRCRAFT EQUIPMENT/STATUS**

**NOTE: X= OPERATIVE   INOP= INOPERATIVE   N/A= NOT APPLICABLE

TRANSPONDER: X (MODE C) X   ILS: (LOCALIZER) X (GLIDE SLOPE) INOP

VOR NO.1 X (NO.2) X   ADF: X   RNAV: N/A

VERTICAL PATH COMPUTER: N/A   DME: X

MARKER BEACON: X (AUDIO) X   (VISUAL) X

Figure 74. – Flight Plan and Aircraft Information.

Figure 80. – VOR/DME RWY 27R and Airport/Facility Directory (BIL).

99. (Refer to Figure 118 below.) During the ILS RWY 12L procedure at DSM, what altitude minimum applies if the glide slope becomes inoperative?

A. 1,420 feet.

B. 1,360 feet.

C. 1,121 feet.

Answer (B) is correct. *(AIM Para 1-1-9)*

DISCUSSION: If the glide slope fails during an ILS approach, the approach can be continued as a nonprecision localizer approach. The MDA for the LOC RWY 12L is 1,360 ft.

Answer (A) is incorrect. This is the circling, not straight-in, MDA for Categories B and C. Answer (C) is incorrect. This is the DH for the ILS, not the MDA for the localizer.

Figure 118. – ILS RWY 12L (DSM).

100. (Refer to Figure 119 below.) The final approach fix for the precision approach is located at

A. DENAY intersection.

B. Glide slope intercept (lightning bolt).

C. ROMEN intersection/locator outer marker.

Answer (B) is correct. *(AIM P/C Glossary)*
DISCUSSION: On a precision approach, the final approach fix is the glide slope intercept point at the published altitude. It is identified on an IAP chart by a lightning bolt.
Answer (A) is incorrect. DENAY INT is an IAF, not the FAF.
Answer (C) is incorrect. ROMEN INT/LOM is the FAF on the LOC 24R, not the ILS 24R, approach.

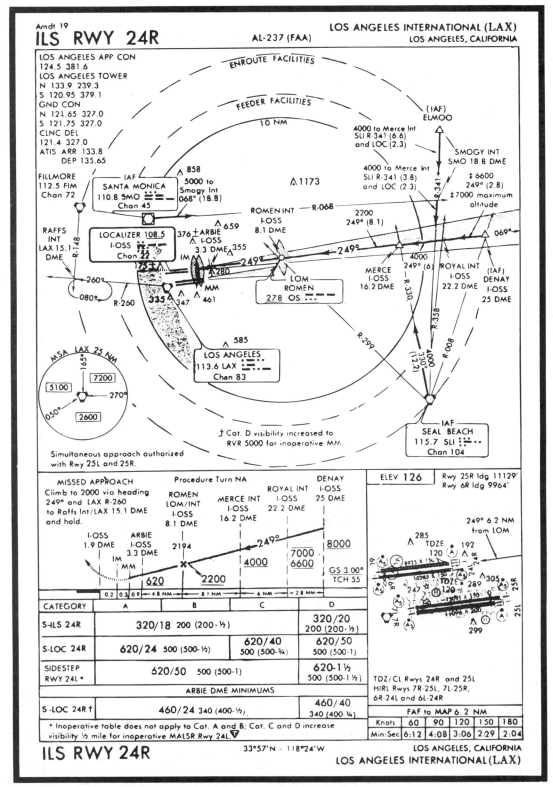

Figure 119. – ILS RWY 24R (LAX).

101. (Refer to Figure 120 below.) The symbol on the plan view of the ILS RWY 35R procedure at DEN represents a minimum safe sector altitude within 25 NM of

- A. Denver VORTAC.
- B. Gandi outer marker.
- C. Denver/Stapleton International Airport.

Answer (A) is correct. *(AIM Para 5-4-5)*
DISCUSSION: Minimum safe altitudes provide obstacle clearance within 25 NM of the specified navigational facility. In Fig. 120, the MSA circle specifies DEN VORTAC.

Answer (B) is incorrect. An MSA for the ILS RWY 35R at DEN is based on Denver VORTAC, not the OM. Answer (C) is incorrect. An MSA will always be based on a navigation facility or a waypoint (GPS or RNAV approach), not an airport.

Figure 120. – ILS RWY 35R (DEN).

102. (Refer to Figure 121 below.) During the ILS RWY 30R procedure at DSM, the minimum altitude for glide slope interception is

A. 2,365 feet MSL.

B. 2,500 feet MSL.

C. 3,000 feet MSL.

Answer (B) is correct. *(AIM P/C Glossary)*
DISCUSSION: The minimum glide slope interception altitude for an ILS is the FAF (marked by a lightning bolt). In Fig. 121, the FAF is 2,500 ft. MSL.

Answer (A) is incorrect. This is the glide slope altitude over the LOM. Answer (C) is incorrect. This is the MSA when south of the LOM.

Figure 121. – ILS RWY 30R (DSM).

103. (Refer to Figure 122 below.) The missed approach point of the ATL S-LOC 8L procedure is located how far from the LOM?

A. 4.8 NM.

B. 5.1 NM.

C. 5.2 NM.

Answer (C) is correct. *(AIM P/C Glossary)*
    DISCUSSION: In Fig. 122, the profile view indicates that CATTA LOM is the FAF for the S-LOC 8L approach, as indicated by the Maltese cross. At the lower right corner of the IAP chart, it indicates that from the FAF (i.e., CATTA LOM) to the MAP is 5.2 NM for the S-LOC 8L approach.
    Answer (A) is incorrect. This is the distance from the LOM to the MM, not the MAP. Answer (B) is incorrect. This is the distance from the LOM to the IM, not the MAP.

Figure 122. – ILS RWY 8L (ATL).

104. (Refer to Figure 123 below.) What minimum navigation equipment is required to complete the VOR/DME-A procedure?

A. One VOR receiver.

B. One VOR receiver and DME.

C. Two VOR receivers and DME.

Answer (B) is correct. *(IFH Chap 10)*
DISCUSSION: Since all of the navigation for the VOR/DME-A approach (Fig. 123) is done from the White Cloud VORTAC, only one VOR receiver is required. DME is also required because it is a VOR/DME approach.

Answer (A) is incorrect. DME is also required because this is a VOR/DME approach. Answer (C) is incorrect. Only one VOR receiver, not two receivers, is required.

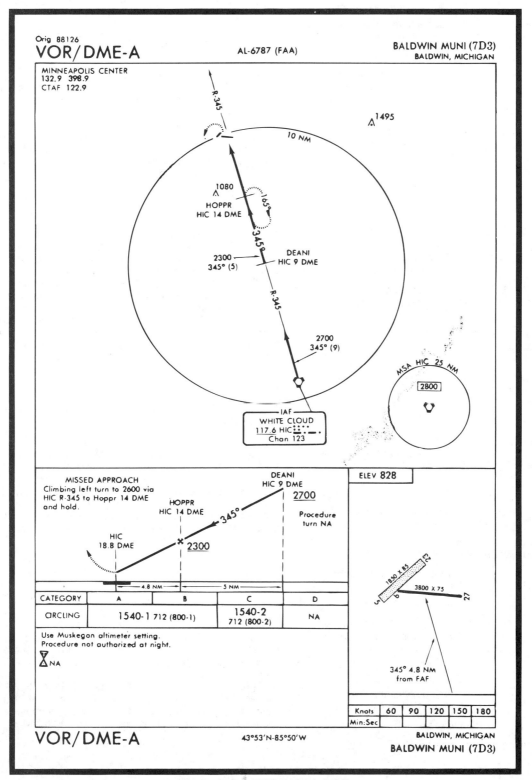

Figure 123. – VOR/DME-A (7D3).

105. The primary reason single pilot operations in reduced visibility on an instrument approach procedure are made more difficult than multicrew operations is that the pilot must

A. continue to fly by instruments while attempting to acquire a visual reference for the runway.

B. multitask, coordinating the operation of the flight controls, avionics, and radio equipment.

C. manage a more complex aircraft than those commonly used in multicrew operations.

Answer (A) is correct. *(IPH Chap 5)*
DISCUSSION: Single pilot IFR operations are more complicated than multicrew operations because the pilot flying is responsible for both the instrument reference and visual reference tasks associated with an instrument approach.
Answer (B) is incorrect. A single pilot operating in instrument conditions must multitask the operation of the flight controls, avionics, and radio during all phases of flight, not just the instrument approach procedure. Answer (C) is incorrect. Multicrew operations generally involve more complex aircraft than those used in single pilot operations.

106. When making an instrument approach at the selected alternate airport, what landing minimums apply?

A. Standard alternate minimums (600-2 or 800-2).

B. The IFR alternate minimums listed for that airport.

C. The landing minimums published for the type of procedure selected.

Answer (C) is correct. *(14 CFR 91.175)*
DISCUSSION: Published landing minimums always apply when making an instrument approach to an airport.
Answer (A) is incorrect. Alternate minimums refer to the minimum forecast weather allowable to list an airport as an alternate on the flight plan. Answer (B) is incorrect. Alternate minimums refer to the minimum forecast weather allowable to list an airport as an alternate on the flight plan.

107. What obstacle clearance and navigation signal coverage is a pilot assured with the Minimum Sector Altitudes depicted on the IAP charts?

A. 1,000 feet and acceptable navigation signal coverage within a 25 NM radius of the navigation facility.

B. 1,000 feet within a 25 NM radius of the navigation facility but not acceptable navigation signal coverage.

C. 500 feet and acceptable navigation signal coverage within a 10 NM radius of the navigation facility.

Answer (B) is correct. *(AIM Para 5-4-5)*
DISCUSSION: Minimum sector altitudes are depicted on approach charts and provide at least 1,000 ft. of obstacle clearance within a 25-NM radius of the navigation facility upon which the procedure is predicated. These altitudes are for emergency use only and do not necessarily assure acceptable navigational signal coverage.
Answer (A) is incorrect. Minimum sector altitudes do not guarantee acceptable signal coverage. Answer (C) is incorrect. Minimum sector altitudes do not guarantee acceptable signal coverage, and they provide 1,000 ft., not 500 ft., of obstacle clearance.

108. (Refer to Figure 124 on page 257.) What options are available concerning the teardrop course reversal for LOC RWY 35 approach to Duncan/Halliburton Field?

A. If a course reversal is required, only the teardrop can be executed.

B. The point where the turn is begun and the type and rate of turn are optional.

C. A normal procedure turn may be made if the 10 DME limit is not exceeded.

Answer (A) is correct. *(AIM Para 5-4-9)*
DISCUSSION: When a procedure turn track is specified for the LOC RWY 35 approach, the turn must be flown exactly as depicted. Thus, only the teardrop can be executed.
Answer (B) is incorrect. The turn must be begun at a point such that the aircraft remains within 10 NM of the VOR, and the procedure turn must be a teardrop. Answer (C) is incorrect. The procedure turn must be a teardrop.

109. (Refer to Figure 124 on page 257.) The point on the teardrop procedure where the turn in bound (LOC RWY 35) Duncan/Halliburton, is initiated is determined by

A. DME and timing to remain within the 10-NM limit.

B. Timing for a 2 minute maximum.

C. Estimating ground speed and radius of turn.

Answer (A) is correct. *(AIM Para 5-4-9)*
DISCUSSION: The pilot may use DME and/or timing to determine his or her position, and may turn inbound at his or her discretion as long as (s)he remains within 10 NM of Duncan VOR.
Answer (B) is incorrect. The only maximum limit on the procedure turn is 10 NM from the VOR. Answer (C) is incorrect. Estimating ground speed and radius of turn is only part of what is required. The pilot must also remain within 10 NM.

Figure 124. — LOC RWY 35, Duncan, Oklahoma.

110. During an instrument precision approach, terrain and obstacle clearance depends on adherence to

    A. minimum altitude shown on the IAP.

    B. terrain contour information.

    C. natural and man-made reference point information.

Answer (A) is correct. *(AIM Para 5-4-5)*
    DISCUSSION: A pilot adhering to the altitudes, flight paths, and weather minimums depicted on the IAP chart is assured of terrain and obstruction clearance.
    Answer (B) is incorrect. The design of IAPs takes terrain and obstacle clearance into account. Answer (C) is incorrect. During instrument approaches, instrument, not visual, reference points are used to assure terrain and obstacle clearance.

111. While being radar vectored, an approach clearance is received. The last assigned altitude should be maintained until

    A. reaching the FAF.

    B. advised to begin descent.

    C. established on a segment of a published route or IAP.

Answer (C) is correct. *(AIM Para 5-4-7)*
    DISCUSSION: When an approach clearance is received, the last assigned altitude should be maintained until the aircraft is established on a segment of a published route or IAP. Then published altitudes apply.
    Answer (A) is incorrect. Published altitudes may be used as soon as the aircraft is on a published route, which should be before the FAF. Answer (B) is incorrect. When ATC issues an approach clearance, descent to published altitudes is left to the discretion of the pilot.

112. When being radar vectored for an ILS approach, at what point may you start a descent from your last assigned altitude to a lower minimum altitude if cleared for the approach?

    A. When established on a segment of a published route or IAP.

    B. You may descend immediately to published glide slope interception altitude.

    C. Only after you are established on the final approach unless informed otherwise by ATC.

Answer (A) is correct. *(AIM Para 5-4-7)*
    DISCUSSION: When you are cleared for the approach while being radar vectored, you must maintain your last assigned altitude until the airplane is established on a segment of a published route or IAP. Then use the published altitude to descend within each succeeding route or approach segment.
    Answer (B) is incorrect. You must wait to descend until you are on part of the published procedure. Answer (C) is incorrect. You should follow prescribed altitudes whenever you are on a segment of a published route or IAP.

113. If the plan view on an approach chart does not include a procedure turn barb, that means

    A. a procedure turn is not authorized.

    B. you should fly a teardrop entry.

    C. a racetrack-type turn is required.

Answer (A) is correct. *(AIM Para 5-4-8)*
    DISCUSSION: The absence of the procedure turn barb in the planview indicates that a procedure turn is not authorized for that approach.
    Answer (B) is incorrect. The absence of a procedure turn barb indicates that all, not just teardrop-type, procedure turns are not authorized. Answer (C) is incorrect. The absence of a procedure turn barb indicates that all, not just racetrack-type, procedure turns are not authorized.

114. (Refer to Figure 125 on page 259.) If your aircraft was cleared for the ILS RWY 17R at Lincoln Municipal and crossed the Lincoln VOR at 5,000 feet MSL, at what point in the teardrop could a descent to 3,000 feet commence?

    A. As soon as intercepting LOC in bound.

    B. Immediately.

    C. Only at the point authorized by ATC.

Answer (B) is correct. *(AIM Para 5-4-9)*
    DISCUSSION: The profile view of the IAP chart shows a descent to 3,000 ft. upon crossing LNK VORTAC outbound. Published altitudes apply when you are on a published route or procedure and have been cleared for the approach.
    Answer (A) is incorrect. A descent to 3,000 ft. may begin when you are LNK VORTAC out bound, not LOC in bound. Answer (C) is incorrect. Published altitudes apply when you are on a published route or procedure and have been cleared for the approach.

115. (Refer to Figure 125 on page 259.) If cleared for an S-LOC 17R approach at Lincoln Municipal from over TOUHY, it means the flight should

    A. land straight in on runway 17R.

    B. comply with straight-in landing minimums.

    C. begin final approach without making a procedure turn.

Answer (C) is correct. *(AIM Para 5-4-9)*
    DISCUSSION: When the symbol NoPT is shown, as in Fig. 125 on the transition from TOUHY, a procedure turn is not authorized.
    Answer (A) is incorrect. The pilot may request clearance to land on another runway, if desired. Answer (B) is incorrect. Circling minimums should be used if landing on another runway is desired.

Figure 125. – ILS RWY 17R, Lincoln, Nebraska.

116. When simultaneous approaches are in progress, how does each pilot receive radar advisories?

A. On tower frequency.

B. On approach control frequency.

C. One pilot on tower frequency and the other on approach control frequency.

Answer (A) is correct. *(AIM Para 5-4-14)*
DISCUSSION: When simultaneous approaches are in progress, each pilot will be advised to monitor the tower frequency to receive advisories and instructions.
Answer (B) is incorrect. Pilots will receive radar advisories on tower, not approach control, frequency. Answer (C) is incorrect. Both pilots will receive radar advisories on tower frequency.

117. When may a pilot make a straight-in landing, if using an IAP having only circling minimums?

A. A straight-in landing may not be made, but the pilot may continue to the runway at MDA and then circle to land on the runway.

B. The pilot may land straight-in if the runway is the active runway and (s)he has been cleared to land.

C. A straight-in landing may be made if the pilot has the runway in sight in sufficient time to make a normal approach for landing, and has been cleared to land.

Answer (C) is correct. *(IFH Chap 10)*
DISCUSSION: When the normal rate of descent or the runway alignment factor of 30° is exceeded, a straight-in minimum is not published, and a circling minimum applies. Even without published straight-in minimums, the pilot may land straight-in if (s)he has the active runway in sight in sufficient time to make a normal landing and has been cleared to land.
Answer (A) is incorrect. A straight-in landing may be made if it is the appropriate runway. Answer (B) is incorrect. The pilot must also have sufficient time to make a normal approach for a landing.

118. (Refer to Figure 126 on page 261.) What landing minimums apply for a 14 CFR Part 91 operator at Dothan, AL using a category C aircraft during a circling LOC 31 approach at 120 knots? (DME available.)

A. MDA 860 feet MSL and visibility 2 SM.

B. MDA 860 feet MSL and visibility 1 and 1/2 SM.

C. MDA 720 feet MSL and visibility 3/4 SM.

Answer (B) is correct. *(IFH Chap 10)*
DISCUSSION: Although the aircraft is circling at 120 kt. (which is Category B), it is a Category C aircraft, and the higher category applies. Thus, the circling minimums (with an operative DME) are 860 ft. MSL and 1 1/2 SM.
Answer (A) is incorrect. The minimum visibility for Category D, not C, is 2 SM. Answer (C) is incorrect. The Category D straight-in, not Category C circling, minimums are 720 ft. and 3/4 SM.

119. (Refer to Figure 126 on page 261.) If cleared for a straight-in LOC approach from over OALDY, it means the flight should

A. land straight in on runway 31.

B. comply with straight-in landing minimums.

C. begin final approach without making a procedure turn.

Answer (C) is correct. *(AIM Para 5-4-9)*
DISCUSSION: When the symbol NoPT is shown, as in Fig. 126 on the transition from OALDY, a procedure turn is not authorized.
Answer (A) is incorrect. The pilot may request clearance to land on another runway, if desired. Answer (B) is incorrect. Circling minimums should be used if landing on another runway is desired.

120. (Refer to Figure 126 on page 261.) What is the ability to identify the RRS 2.5 stepdown fix worth in terms of localizer circle-to-land minimums for a category C aircraft?

A. Decreases MDA by 20 feet.

B. Decreases visibility by 1/2 SM.

C. Without the stepdown fix, a circling approach is not available.

Answer (A) is correct. *(IFH Chap 10)*
DISCUSSION: The MDA without DME is 880 ft. and with DME is 860 ft. Thus, DME decreases the MDA by 20 ft.
Answer (B) is incorrect. Visibility minimums remain the same, regardless of DME. Answer (C) is incorrect. Circling is authorized without DME.

Figure 126. – ILS RWY 31, Dothan, Alabama.

121. An airport may not be qualified for alternate use if

A. the airport has AWOS-3 weather reporting.

B. the airport is located next to a restricted or prohibited area.

C. the NAVAIDS used for the final approach are unmonitored.

Answer (C) is correct. *(IPH Chap 2)*
   DISCUSSION: Not all airports can be used as an alternate. An airport may not be qualified for alternate use if the NAVAIDs used for the final approach are unmonitored.
   Answer (A) is incorrect. An airport can qualify for alternate use if the airport has AWOS-3 weather reporting. An airport may not qualify for alternate use if the NAVAIDs used for final approach are unmonitored. Answer (B) is incorrect. An airport can qualify for alternate use if the airport is located next to a restricted or prohibited area. An airport may not qualify for alternate use if the NAVAIDs used for final approach are unmonitored.

122. During an instrument approach, under what conditions, if any, is the holding pattern course reversal not required?

A. When radar vectors are provided.

B. When cleared for the approach.

C. None, since it is always mandatory.

Answer (A) is correct. *(AIM Para 5-4-8)*
   DISCUSSION: A course reversal (procedure turn) is not required when radar vectors are being provided.
   Answer (B) is incorrect. A course reversal may be required when cleared for a full approach. Answer (C) is incorrect. A course reversal is not mandatory when radar vectors are provided.

123. (Refer to Figure 128 on page 263.) What type entry is recommended for the missed approach holding pattern depicted on the VOR RWY 36 approach chart for Price/Carbon County Airport?

A. Direct only.

B. Teardrop only.

C. Parallel only.

Answer (A) is correct. *(AIM Para 5-3-7)*
   DISCUSSION: On the missed approach to VOR RWY 36, the pilot makes a climbing right turn via PUC R-127 to 8,100 ft. and then a right turn directly to the PUC VOR and to 9,000 ft. Since the aircraft will be approaching PUC VOR from the south, a direct entry will be appropriate.
   Answer (B) is incorrect. A teardrop entry would be appropriate only if coming in from the northwest. Answer (C) is incorrect. A parallel entry would be appropriate only from the northeast.

124. (Refer to Figure 128 on page 263.) At which points may you initiate a descent to the next lower minimum altitude when cleared for the VOR RWY 36 approach, from the PUC R-095 IAF (DME operative)?

A. Start descent from 8,000 when established on final, from 7,500 when at the 4 DME fix, and from 6,180 when landing requirements are met.

B. Start descent from 8,000 when established on the PUC R-186, from 6,400 at the 4 DME fix, and from 6,180 when landing requirements are met.

C. Start descent from 8,000 at the R-127, from 6,400 at the LR-127, from 6,180 at the 4 DME fix.

Answer (B) is correct. *(IFH Chap 10)*
   DISCUSSION: When cleared for the VOR RWY 36 approach with DME, maintain 8,000 ft. on the 10 DME arc until established on R-186, when you may begin descent to 6,400 ft. At the 4 DME fix, you may descend from 6,400 to 6,180 ft., which is the MDA with an operative DME. With the runway environment in sight, at or before the MAP, you may descend below 6,180 ft.
   Answer (A) is incorrect. The minimum altitude once you are established outbound on the procedure turn is 7,500 ft. when executing the VOR RWY 36 approach from the PUC IAF. Answer (C) is incorrect. You may start your descent from 8,000 ft. when established on R-186, not R-127, from 6,400 ft. at the 4 DME fix, and from 6,180 ft. only with the runway environment in sight, at or before the MAP.

125. (Refer to Figure 128 on page 263.) What is the purpose of the 10,300 MSA on the Price/Carbon County Airport Approach Chart?

A. It provides safe clearance above the highest obstacle in the defined sector out to 25 NM.

B. It provides an altitude above which navigational course guidance is assured.

C. It is the minimum vector altitude for radar vectors in the sector southeast of PUC between 020° and 290° magnetic bearing to PUC VOR.

Answer (A) is correct. *(AIM Para 5-4-5)*
   DISCUSSION: The MSA in PUC sector R-110 to R-200 at 10,300 ft. provides safe clearance above the highest obstacle plus 1,000 ft. in the defined sector out to 25 NM.
   Answer (B) is incorrect. Navigational course guidance is not assured by the MSA. Answer (C) is incorrect. MSA gives a safe clearance altitude, not a minimum vector altitude.

Figure 128. – VOR RWY 36 (PUC).

126. (Refer to Figure 129 on page 265.) What indication should you get when it is time to turn in bound while in the procedure turn at LABER?

A.   4 DME miles from LABER.

B.   10 DME miles from the MAP.

C.   12 DME miles from LIT VORTAC.

Answer (A) is correct. *(AIM Para 5-3-7)*
   DISCUSSION: The "4 NM" at the perpendicular line across the end of the outbound leg of the holding pattern southeast of LABER means the turn in bound should begin when 4 DME is indicated from LABER waypoint.
   Answer (B) is incorrect. The distance from LABER to the MAP is 10 NM. Answer (C) is incorrect. No 12-NM distance is shown from LIT.

127. (Refer to Figure 129 on page 265.) What is the recommended descent angle for the RNAV RWY 36 approach?

A.   2.12°.

B.   2.52°.

C.   2.82°.

Answer (C) is correct. *(IAP)*
   DISCUSSION: The profile view of the RNAV RWY 36 instrument approach procedure indicates a descent angle of 2.82°.
   Answer (A) is incorrect. The profile view of the RNAV RWY 36 instrument approach procedure indicates a descent angle of 2.82°, not 2.12°. Answer (B) is incorrect. The profile view of the RNAV RWY 36 instrument approach procedure indicates a descent angle of 2.82°, not 2.52°.

128. (Refer to Figure 129 on page 265.) How should the missed approach point be identified when executing the RNAV RWY 36 approach at Adams Field?

A.   When the TO-FROM indicator changes.

B.   Upon arrival at 760 feet on the glidepath.

C.   When time has expired for 5 NM past the FAF.

Answer (A) is correct. *(IFH Chap 10)*
   DISCUSSION: The MAP is a waypoint and is identified when the TO-FROM indicator changes, which indicates station passage at the waypoint; i.e., you have arrived at the MAP and the visual references are not there, so you must execute a missed approach.
   Answer (B) is incorrect. You will be at 760 ft. on a RWY 36 approach for approximately 1 1/2 NM before reaching the MAP. Answer (C) is incorrect. On the RNAV RWY 36 approach, the MAP is identified by a waypoint, not by the time from the FAF.

129. (Refer to Figure 129 on page 265.) What minimum airborne equipment is required to be operative for RNAV RWY 36 approach at Adams Field?

A.   An approved RNAV receiver that provides both horizontal and vertical guidance.

B.   A transponder and an approved RNAV receiver that provides both horizontal and vertical guidance.

C.   Any approved RNAV receiver.

Answer (C) is correct. *(IFH Chap 10)*
   DISCUSSION: An approved RNAV receiver is required for RNAV approaches. Area navigation, when approved by the FAA, is sufficient to conduct RNAV approaches. Area navigation simply moves the location of VORs based upon internal circuitry.
   Answer (A) is incorrect. RNAV receivers with vertical guidance are not required for RNAV approaches. Answer (B) is incorrect. RNAV receivers with vertical guidance are not required for RNAV approaches.

130. (Refer to Figure 129 on page 265.) What type of entry is recommended to the missed approach holding pattern if the inbound heading is 050°?

A.   Direct.

B.   Parallel.

C.   Teardrop.

Answer (C) is correct. *(AIM Para 5-3-7)*
   DISCUSSION: Extend the 222° radial from BENDY. If you are coming in on a 050° heading, you are on R-230. The teardrop approach should be used because you are north of R-222.
   Answer (A) is incorrect. A direct entry would be from R-292 to R-112. Answer (B) is incorrect. The parallel entry would be from R-112 to R-222.

131. (Refer to Figure 129 on page 265.) What is the position of LABER relative to the reference facility?

A.   316°, 24.3 NM.

B.   177°, 10 NM.

C.   198°, 8 NM.

Answer (C) is correct. *(IFH Chap 10)*
   DISCUSSION: The LABER waypoint is referenced on the Little Rock VOR. On the IAP chart, it is shown in the bottom line of the information box, "113.9 LIT 198.0°-8," which is 198° and 8 NM.
   Answer (A) is incorrect. This choice has to do with the no procedure turn approach from the Pine Bluff VORTAC. Answer (B) is incorrect. LABER is 177° and 10 NM from the MAP.

Figure 129. – RNAV RWY 36 (LIT).

132. (Refer to Figure 242 below, and Legend 21 on page 267.) You have been cleared for the RNAV (GPS) RWY 36 approach to LIT. At a groundspeed of 105 knots, what are the vertical descent angle and rate of descent on final approach?

A. 2.82 degrees and 524 feet per minute.

B. 3.00 degrees and 557 feet per minute.

C. 4.00 degrees and 550 feet per nautical mile.

Answer (B) is correct. *(IPH Chap 1)*
DISCUSSION: Refer to Fig. 242 and see that the notation in the profile view of the approach confirms the approach angle is 3.00 degrees. To confirm the second portion of the answer, refer to Legend 21, the rate-of-descent table. On the left side of the chart, locate the angle of descent of 3.00 degrees. Move to the right until under the column for the airspeed of 105 knots. The rate of descent will be 557 feet per minute.

Answer (A) is incorrect. The profile view in Fig. 242, under and to the right of KAGBE, shows 3.00 degrees as the approach angle, not 2.82 degrees. Answer (C) is incorrect. The profile view in Fig. 242, under and to the right of KAGBE, shows 3.00 degrees as the approach angle, not 4.00 degrees.

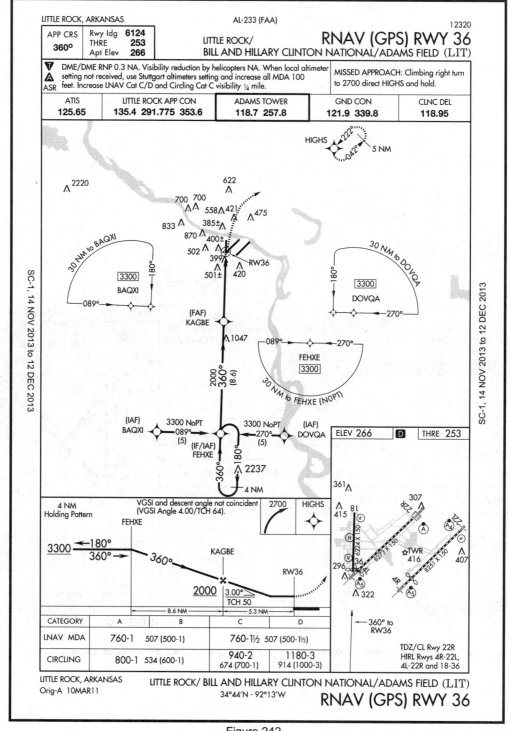

Figure 242.

RATE OF DESCENT TABLE

A rate of descent table is provided for use in planning and executing precision descents under known or approximate ground speed conditions. It will be especially useful for approaches when the localizer only is used for course guidance. A best speed, power, altitude combination can be programmed which will result in a stable glide rate and altitude favorable for executing a landing if minimums exist upon breakout. Care should always be exercised so that minimum descent altitude and missed approach point are not exceeded.

ANGLE OF DESCENT (degrees and tenths)		FEET /NM	GROUND SPEED (knots)										
			30	45	60	75	90	105	120	135	150	165	180
2.0		210	105	160	210	265	320	370	425	475	530	585	635
2.5		265	130	200	265	330	395	465	530	595	665	730	795
VERTICAL PATH ANGLE	2.7	287	143	215	287	358	430	501	573	645	716	788	860
	2.8	297	149	223	297	371	446	520	594	669	743	817	891
	2.9	308	154	231	308	385	462	539	616	693	769	846	923
	3.0	318	159	239	318	398	478	557	637	716	796	876	955
	3.1	329	165	247	329	411	494	576	658	740	823	905	987
	3.2	340	170	255	340	425	510	594	679	764	849	934	1019
	3.3	350	175	263	350	438	526	613	701	788	876	963	1051
	3.4	361	180	271	361	451	541	632	722	812	902	993	1083
3.5		370	185	280	370	465	555	650	740	835	925	1020	1110
4.0		425	210	315	425	530	635	740	845	955	1060	1165	1270
4.5		475	240	355	475	595	715	835	955	1075	1190	1310	1430
5.0		530	265	395	530	660	795	925	1060	1190	1325	1455	1590
5.5		580	290	435	580	730	875	1020	1165	1310	1455	1600	1745
6.0		635	315	475	635	795	955	1110	1270	1430	1590	1745	1950
6.5		690	345	515	690	860	1030	1205	1375	1550	1720	1890	2065
7.0		740	370	555	740	925	1110	1295	1480	1665	1850	2035	2220
7.5		795	395	595	795	990	1190	1390	1585	1785	1985	2180	2380
8.0		845	425	635	845	1055	1270	1480	1690	1905	2115	2325	2540
8.5		900	450	675	900	1120	1345	1570	1795	2020	2245	2470	2695
9.0		950	475	715	950	1190	1425	1665	1900	2140	2375	2615	2855
9.5		1005	500	750	1005	1255	1505	1755	2005	2255	2510	2760	3010
10.0		1055	530	790	1055	1320	1585	1845	2110	2375	2640	2900	3165
10.5		1105	555	830	1105	1385	1660	1940	2215	2490	2770	3045	3320
11.0		1160	580	870	1160	1450	1740	2030	2320	2610	2900	3190	3480
11.5		1210	605	910	1210	1515	1820	2120	2425	2725	3030	3335	3635
12.0		1260	630	945	1260	1575	1890	2205	2520	2835	3150	3465	3780

DESCENT TABLE 99028

Legend 21. – Instrument Approach Procedure Charts, Rate-of-Descent Table.

133. On a nonprecision approach what is the maximum acceptable descent rate during the final stages of the approach (below 1,000 ft. AGL)?

A. 1,000 fpm.

B. 1,000 fpm to 500 AGL, then 500 fpm.

C. 500 fpm.

Answer (A) is correct. *(IPH Chap 5)*
   DISCUSSION: According to research, human perceptual limitations allow for a maximum rate of descent of 1,000 fpm in the final stages of the approach, regardless of the type of aircraft being flown. Descents greater than 1,000 fpm on the final stages of the approach are not permitted.
   Answer (B) is incorrect. The maximum rate of descent below 1,000 feet AGL is 1,000 fpm, but this descent rate does not change at 500 feet AGL. Answer (C) is incorrect. The maximum rate of descent below 1,000 feet AGL is 1,000 fpm, not 500 fpm.

134. (Refer to Figure 130 on page 269.) How does an LDA facility, such as the one at Roanoke Regional, differ from a standard ILS approach facility?

A. The LOC is wider.

B. The LOC is offset from the runway.

C. The GS is unusable beyond the MM.

Answer (B) is correct. *(AIM Para 1-1-9)*
   DISCUSSION: LDA (localizer-type directional aid) has utility and accuracy comparable to a localizer but is not part of a complete ILS. The LDA is not aligned with the runway.
   Answer (A) is incorrect. The LOC in an LDA is similar in width to the localizer in an ILS. Answer (C) is incorrect. The note in the profile view of Fig. 130 states that the glide slope is unusable inside, not beyond, the MM.

135. (Refer to Figure 130 on page 269.) What are the procedure turn restrictions on the LDA RWY 6 approach at Roanoke Regional?

A. Remain within 10 NM of CLAMM INT and on the north side of the approach course.

B. Remain within 10 NM of the airport on the north side of the approach course.

C. Remain within 10 NM of the outer marker on the north side of the approach course.

Answer (A) is correct. *(IFH Chap 10)*
   DISCUSSION: In the IAP chart, the profile view indicates in its upper left corner: "Remain within 10 NM." That means 10 NM from the final approach fix, which is the CLAMM INT on the Callahan NDB. The procedure turn also indicates right turn outbound, which means that one must remain on the north side of the approach course.
   Answer (B) is incorrect. The 10-NM ring is around the FAF, not the airport. Answer (C) is incorrect. The 10-NM ring is around the FAF, not the outer marker.

136. (Refer to Figure 130 on page 269.) What are the restrictions regarding circle to land procedures for LDA RWY/GS 6 approach at Roanoke Regional?

A. Circling to runway 24 not authorized.

B. Circling not authorized NW of RWY 6-24.

C. Visibility increased 1/2 mile for circling approach.

Answer (B) is correct. *(IFH Chap 10)*
   DISCUSSION: In the remarks section of the IAP chart, it is noted that circling is not authorized (NA) northwest of RWY 6-24 and to RWY 15.
   Answer (A) is incorrect. Circling to runway 15, not 24, is not authorized. Answer (C) is incorrect. The minimum circling visibility goes up 1/4 to 3/4 SM, depending on aircraft category.

137. (Refer to Figure 130 on page 269.) At what minimum altitude should you cross CLAMM intersection during the S-LDA 6 approach at Roanoke Regional?

A. 4,200 MSL.

B. 4,182 MSL.

C. 2,800 MSL.

Answer (A) is correct. *(IFH Chap 10)*
   DISCUSSION: On the final approach using the S-LDA 6 approach, you presumably do not have glide slope capability (otherwise you will use S-LDA/GS 6). Thus, the minimum altitude at CLAMM is 4,200 ft. MSL (see the note at 4,500 glide slope interception altitude).
   Answer (B) is incorrect. The GS altitude at CLAMM is 4,182 ft. Answer (C) is incorrect. The minimum altitude after CLAMM and prior to SKIRT OM is 2,800 ft.

138. (Refer to Figure 130 on page 269.) How should the pilot identify the missed approach point for the S-LDA GS 6 approach to Roanoke Regional?

A. Arrival at 1,540 feet on the glide slope.

B. Arrival at 1.0 DME on the LDA course.

C. Time expired for distance from OM to MAP.

Answer (A) is correct. *(IFH Chap 10)*
   DISCUSSION: Since the S-LDA/GS 6 is a precision approach (due to the electronic glide slope), the MAP is arrival at decision height (1,540 ft. for Categories A, B, and C aircraft) on the glide slope.
   Answer (B) is incorrect. The MAP on the LDA, not LDA GS, approach is 1.3 DME, not 1.0 DME. Answer (C) is incorrect. Precision approaches do not provide for time expiration to the MAP, other than as a backup.

Figure 130. – LDA RWY 6 (ROA).

139. (Refer to Figure 131 on page 271.) What determines the MAP for the straight-in VOR/DME RNAV RWY 4R approach at BOS?

    A.   RULSY way point.

    B.   .5 NM to RULSY way point.

    C.   2.5 NM to RULSY at 840 feet MSL.

Answer (B) is correct. *(ACL)*
    DISCUSSION: The missed approach point (MAP) is identified by "MAP WP" in the profile view of the VOR/DME RNAV RWY 4R approach into BOS. The notation "0.5 NM from RULSY WP" above the missed approach point means that the missed approach point is located 0.5 NM from RULSY waypoint. Therefore, the missed approach procedure should begin when 0.5 NM remains before reaching RULSY waypoint.
    Answer (A) is incorrect. The missed approach point is located 0.5 NM from RULSY waypoint, not at RULSY waypoint. Answer (C) is incorrect. A distance of 2.5 NM to RULSY waypoint at 840 ft. MSL is the visual descent point, indicated by the heavy "V" in the profile view, not the missed approach point.

140. (Refer to Figure 131 on page 271.) The control tower at BOS reports "tall vessels" in the approach area. What are the VOR/DME RNAV RWY 4R straight-in approach minimums for Category A aircraft?

    A.   840/40

    B.   890/24

    C.   890/40

Answer (A) is correct. *(IFH Chap 10)*
    DISCUSSION: There is a note in the second line of information at the top of the VOR/DME RNAV RWY 4R approach chart which states that category A aircraft making the straight-in approach must increase the visibility minimums to RVR 4,000 when the control tower reports tall vessels in the approach area. No adjustments to the MDA are required, so the minimums are 840 ft. MSL and RVR 4,000.
    Answer (B) is incorrect. The visibility minimums must be increased to RVR 4,000, and there is no 890 ft. MSL MDA for the VOR/DME RNAV RWY 4R approach at BOS. Answer (C) is incorrect. There is no 890 ft. MSL MDA for the VOR/DME RNAV RWY 4R approach at BOS.

141. (Refer to Figure 131 on page 271.) Other than VOR/DME RNAV, what additional navigation equipment is required to conduct the VOR/DME RNAV RWY 4R approach at BOS?

    A.   None.

    B.   VNAV.

    C.   Transponder with altitude encoding and Marker Beacon.

Answer (A) is correct. *(IFH Chap 10)*
    DISCUSSION: No additional equipment is required to conduct the VOR/DME RNAV RWY 4R approach at Boston. All approach waypoints, including the missed approach waypoint, the missed approach holding waypoint, and the minimum safe altitude (MSA) circle center waypoint, require the use of just the VOR/DME RNAV equipment.
    Answer (B) is incorrect. Vertical navigation (VNAV) equipment may be used if available, but it is not required. If it is available and is used, the profile view of the approach chart shows a 3.00° descent angle. The visual descent point shown 2 miles from the missed approach waypoint on the profile view of the chart is not a mandatory descent point and is based on distance from the runway at the MDA of 840 ft. MSL, not on vertical navigation. Answer (C) is incorrect. Even though a transponder with altitude encoding (Mode C) would normally be required to operate in the Boston Class B airspace, it is not required equipment to conduct any instrument approach procedure. In addition, no marker beacon is shown on the instrument approach chart; therefore, none is required.

142. (Refer to Figure 131 on page 271.) During a missed approach from the VOR/DME RNAV RWY 4R approach at BOS, what course should be flown to the missed approach holding way point?

    A.   036°.

    B.   Runway heading.

    C.   033°.

Answer (C) is correct. *(IFH Chap 10)*
    DISCUSSION: In the upper right corner of Fig. 131, just under "Boston, Massachusetts," there is a missed approach procedure information box. It reads, "MISSED APPROACH: Climb to 3000 via 033° track to WAXEN WP and hold." Also, on the profile view just above the MAP WP, the data box shows a climb to 3,000 feet on a track of 033° to WAXEN.
    Answer (A) is incorrect. The missed approach procedure is fly to WAXEN via the 033° track (course), not 036°, which is the final approach course. Answer (B) is incorrect. The missed approach procedure is fly to WAXEN via the 033° track (course), not via runway heading.

143. (Refer to Figure 131 below.) What is the landing distance available for the VOR/DME RNAV RWY 4R approach at BOS?

- A. 7,000 ft.
- B. 8,850 ft.
- C. 10,005 ft.

Answer (B) is correct. *(ACL)*

    DISCUSSION: In the upper right corner of the airport diagram, there is a notation that says "Rwy 4R ldg 8850'." This notation signifies that the runway length available for landing is 8,850 ft.; the remainder of the 10,005 ft. runway length is a displaced threshold.

    Answer (A) is incorrect. This is the length of runway 9-27, not the available landing distance on runway 4R. Answer (C) is incorrect. This is the total length of runway 4R, not the runway length available for landing.

Figure 131. – VOR/DME RNAV RWY 4R.

144. (Refer to Figure 133 on page 273.) How should a pilot reverse course to get established on the inbound course of the ILS RWY 9, if radar vectoring or the three IAFs are not utilized?

A. Execute a standard 45° procedure turn toward Seal Beach VORTAC or Pomona VORTAC.

B. Make an appropriate entry to the depicted holding pattern at Swan Lake OM/INT.

C. Use any type of procedure turn, but remain within 10 NM of Riverside VOR.

Answer (B) is correct. *(AIM Para 5-4-9)*
DISCUSSION: If you do not use radar vectoring or the three IAFs for the ILS RWY 9 approach, you should make an appropriate entry into the depicted holding pattern at the Swan Lake outer marker/intersection.
Answer (A) is incorrect. To execute a standard 45° procedure turn toward Seal Beach VORTAC or Pomona VORTAC is a nonsense statement. Answer (C) is incorrect. The depicted holding pattern is the only type of course reversal authorized for the ILS RWY 9 approach.

145. (Refer to Figure 133 on page 273.) What type of entry is recommended for the missed approach holding pattern at Riverside Municipal?

A. Direct.

B. Parallel.

C. Teardrop.

Answer (A) is correct. *(IFH Chap 10)*
DISCUSSION: To enter the holding pattern on the missed approach for ILS RWY 9, use a direct entry because you will arrive at the holding fix (PDZ VORTAC) in the direction of the holding pattern. Thus, at PDZ VORTAC, you will make a right turn to a heading of 078° (direct entry).
Answer (B) is incorrect. A parallel entry would be made from the northwest. Answer (C) is incorrect. A teardrop entry would be made from the southwest.

146. (Refer to Figure 133 on page 273.) What action should the pilot take if the marker beacon receiver becomes inoperative during the S-ILS 9 approach at Riverside Municipal?

A. Substitute SWAN LAKE INT for the OM and surveillance radar for the MM.

B. Raise the DH 100 feet (50 feet for the OM and 50 feet for the MM).

C. Substitute SWAN LAKE INT for the OM and use published minimums.

Answer (C) is correct. *(IFH Chap 10)*
DISCUSSION: The OM has a compass locator, which is an acceptable substitute. An inoperative MM does not require any adjustment to be made to the published minimums (see Legend 22 on page 211).
Answer (A) is incorrect. You can substitute SWAN LAKE INT for the OM, but no substitute is required for the MM. Answer (B) is incorrect. You can substitute SWAN LAKE INT for the OM, but no substitute is necessary for the MM. Thus, the DH will be as published on the IAP, not raised 100 ft.

147. (Refer to Figure 133 on page 273.) Why are two VOR/LOC receivers recommended to obtain an MDA of 1,160 when making an S-LOC 9 approach to Riverside Municipal?

A. To obtain R-327 of PDZ when on the localizer course.

B. In order to identify Riverside VOR.

C. To utilize the published stepdown fix.

Answer (C) is correct. *(IFH Chap 10)*
DISCUSSION: Two VOR/localizer receivers are necessary to identify the step-down fix at Agnes INT. One VOR is set on the localizer, and the other is set to Paradise VOR (R-032). The MDA for the S-LOC 9 approach is 1,260 ft. until Agnes INT, after which a descent to 1,160 ft. is permitted.
Answer (A) is incorrect. R-327 of PDZ can be determined when on the localizer through the Swan Lake NDB. Answer (B) is incorrect. The Riverside VOR is not used in the S-LOC 9 approach.

148. (Refer to Figure 133 on page 273.) What is the minimum altitude descent procedure if cleared for the S-ILS 9 approach from Seal Beach VORTAC?

A. Descend and maintain 3,000 to JASER INT, descend to and maintain 2,500 until crossing SWAN LAKE, descend and maintain 1,260 until crossing AGNES, and to 991 (DH) after passing AGNES.

B. Descend and maintain 3,000 to JASER INT, descend to 2,800 when established on the LOC course, intercept and maintain the GS to 991 (DH).

C. Descend and maintain 3,000 to JASER INT, descend to 2,500 while established on the LOC course inbound, intercept and maintain the GS to 991 (DH).

Answer (C) is correct. *(IFH Chap 10)*
DISCUSSION: From Seal Beach VORTAC, descend to 3,000 ft. to Jaser INT, then descend to 2,500 ft. on the localizer inbound, and then descend on the glide slope to the decision height of 991 ft.
Answer (A) is incorrect. A height of 2,500 ft. is maintained until the glide slope, and the ILS glide slope is flown down to 991 ft. Answer (B) is incorrect. When on the localizer, you should descend to 2,500 ft., not 2,800 ft., until intercepting the glide slope.

Figure 133. – ILS RWY 9 (RAL).

149. When the approach procedure involves a procedure turn, the maximum speed should not be greater than

    A. 180 knots IAS.

    B. 200 knots IAS.

    C. 250 knots IAS.

Answer (B) is correct. *(AIM Para 5-4-9)*
    DISCUSSION: When the approach procedure involves a procedure turn, a maximum speed of not greater than 200 kt. IAS should be observed, and the turn should be executed within the distance specified in the profile view.
    Answer (A) is incorrect. The maximum speed that should be used is 200 kt., not 180 kt. Answer (C) is incorrect. The maximum speed that should be used is 200 kt., not 250 kt.

150. (Refer to Figure 152 on page 275.) VOYQU is a

    A. fly-over waypoint.

    B. fly-over final approach waypoint.

    C. fly-by waypoint.

Answer (C) is correct. *(IPH Chap 2)*
    DISCUSSION: VOYQU is a fly-by waypoint as defined by the four-pointed star symbol that identifies it on Fig. 152.
    Answer (A) is incorrect. A fly-over waypoint is represented by a four-pointed star enclosed within a circle. The symbol for VOYQU is a four-pointed star, which is the symbol for a fly-by waypoint. Answer (B) is incorrect. A fly-over waypoint is represented by a four-pointed star enclosed within a circle. A final approach waypoint is noted as such on instrument approach procedures. The symbol for VOYQU is a four-pointed star, which is the symbol for a fly-by waypoint, which in this case is not identified as a final approach waypoint, making this answer selection incorrect on both counts.

151. (Refer to Figure 152 on page 275.) Which points are designated as fly-over waypoints?

    A. The Missed Approach Point and BEMXI.

    B. The Missed Approach Point and AGHAN.

    C. AJCIZ and BEMXI.

Answer (B) is correct. *(IPH Chap 2)*
    DISCUSSION: Both the missed approach point (RW30) and AGHAN are depicted as four-pointed stars enclosed by a circle, the symbol for a fly-over waypoint.
    Answer (A) is incorrect. BEMXI is a fly-by waypoint, symbolized by a four-pointed star. A fly-over waypoint would be the same symbol enclosed by a circle, as is the case with RW30 and AGHAN. Answer (C) is incorrect. Both AJCIZ and BEMXI are fly-by waypoints, symbolized by a four-pointed star. A fly-over waypoint would be the same symbol enclosed by a circle, as is the case with RW30 and AGHAN.

152. (Refer to Figure 152 on page 275.) You are 27 NM out at 7,000 feet on heading 300° on the RNAV (GPS) RWY 30 approach to LBF approaching AJCIZ. You are cleared for the approach. You should

    A. Descend to 4,800 feet inbound to AJCIZ, descend to 4,600 feet in the procedure turn, descend to 4,400 feet at BEMXI, and complete the approach.

    B. Descend to 4,600 feet in the procedure turn at AJCIZ, descend to 4,400 feet at BEMXI, and complete the approach.

    C. Descend to 4,600 feet, do not perform the procedure turn at AJCIZ, descend to 4,400 feet at BEMXI, and complete the approach.

Answer (C) is correct. *(IPH Chap 5)*
    DISCUSSION: Fig. 152 indicates you may descend below 4,800 feet within 30 NM of AJCIZ with no procedure turn when on a heading of 300°. Although there is a possibility you may be asked to hold at AJCIZ, this allows you to descend to 4,600 feet to AJCIZ, then descend to 4,400 feet at BEMXI and complete the approach.
    Answer (A) is incorrect. The "NoPT" notation on Fig. 152 translates to "no procedure turn" when arriving on a course between 027° and 207°, which you are. It also notes in the profile that you can descend to 4,600 feet, not 4,800 feet, when inside 30 NM of AJCIZ. Answer (B) is incorrect. The "NoPT" notation on Fig. 152 translates to "no procedure turn" when arriving on a course between 027° and 207°. You are arriving on a course of 300°.

153. (Refer to Figure 152 on page 275.) SUXYO is defined as which of the following?

    A. Fly-over waypoint.

    B. Initial approach waypoint.

    C. Fly-to waypoint.

Answer (B) is correct. *(IPH Chap 2, AIM Para 5-4-1)*
    DISCUSSION: The SUXYO waypoint is a fly-by waypoint, as indicated on the instrument approach chart by a four-point star. It is also an initial approach fix, as indicated by the letters "IAF" above its designation on the chart.
    Answer (A) is incorrect. SUXYO is an initial approach fix, thus making it a fly-by waypoint, as a fly-over waypoint is not required. Answer (C) is incorrect. Waypoints exist in two forms, fly-over and fly-by, not fly-to.

Figure 152. – RNAV (GPS) RWY 30, North Plate Regional Airport Lee Bird Field (LBF).

154. (Refer to Figure 187 below.) When the MALSR are NOTAM'd out of service, what are the minimums for a category B airplane LPV approach?

A. 2400 RVR.

B. 5500 RVR.

C. 4500 RVR.

Answer (C) is correct. *(IFH Chap 8)*

DISCUSSION: See the note in the upper left-hand corner of the approach plate, which stipulates increased minimums for inoperative MALSR. It increases LPV minimums for all categories to 4500 RVR.

Answer (A) is incorrect. The note in the upper left-hand corner of the approach plate increases LPV minimums for all categories to 4500 RVR, not 2400 RVR. Answer (B) is incorrect. The note in the upper left-hand corner of the approach plate increases LPV minimums for all categories to 4500 RVR, not 5500 RVR. That higher value is established for LNAV category approaches, not LPV approaches.

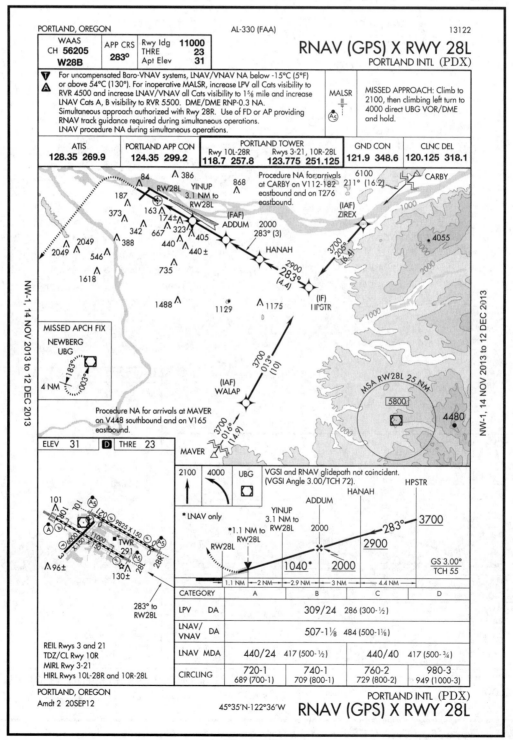

Figure 187.

155. (Refer to Figure 210 below.) What is the THRE elevation for RWY 6?

A. 173 feet MSL.

B. 200 feet AGL.

C. 270 feet MSL.

Answer (A) is correct. *(IAP Chart)*
    DISCUSSION: The instrument approach procedure (IAP) has the THRE (threshold) elevation located in the upper right corner of the airport diagram block. The THRE 173 is the threshold elevation of 173 feet MSL.
    Answer (B) is incorrect. The altitude minimum for the ILS approach, not the threshold elevation, is 200 feet AGL.
    Answer (C) is incorrect. The threshold elevation is labeled on the IAP chart as THRE 173.

Figure 210.

156. (Refer to Figure 217 below.) During the approach to DSM before you can begin the ILS RWY 13 procedure, the glide slope fails and you are cleared for the LOC RWY 13 at DSM. What altitude minimum applies?

A. 1,420 feet.

B. 1,380 feet.

C. 1,121 feet.

Answer (B) is correct. *(AIM Para 1-1-9, IAP Chart)*
DISCUSSION: You are cleared for the LOC RWY 13 at DSM. At the bottom of the IAP chart under the heading "CATEGORY," you will see S-LOC 13 in the second line. To the right of that indicates the minimums for a straight-in, localizer approach to runway 13. The minimum altitude is indicated as 1,380 feet.

Answer (A) is incorrect. The minimum altitude for a circling to land procedure for runway 13 is 1,420 feet. Answer (C) is incorrect. The minimum altitude for an ILS approach for runway 13 is 1,121 feet.

Figure 217.

157. (Refer to Figure 221 below.) The final approach fix for the ILS RWY 24R is located at

A. MERCE intersection.

B. Glide Slope Intercept (lightning bolt).

C. JETSA intersection.

Answer (B) is correct. *(IPH Chap 4)*

DISCUSSION: The final approach fix for an ILS approach is indicated on an instrument approach procedure by a lightning bolt symbol. This is also the point of glide slope intercept.

Answer (A) is incorrect. The MERCE intersection is an initial fix (indicated by the "IF" notation), not the final approach fix. Answer (C) is incorrect. The Maltese cross symbol indicates that JETSA is the final approach fix for the nonprecision localizer approach, not for the precision ILS approach.

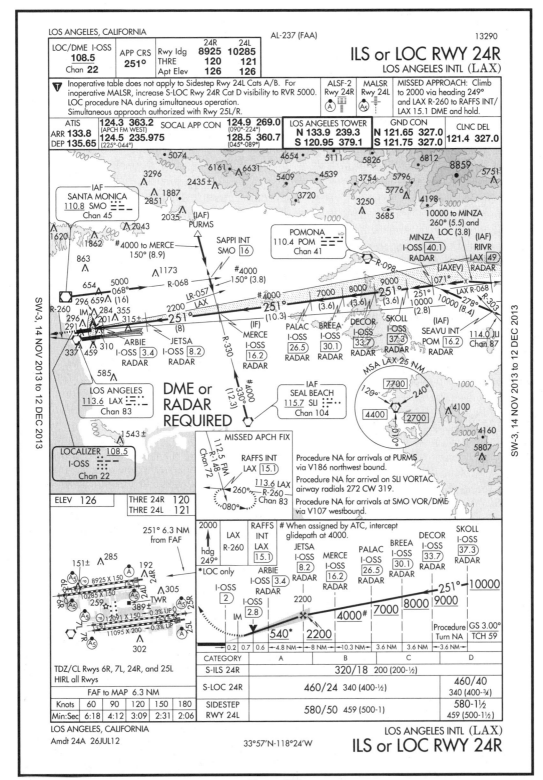

Figure 221.

158. Which procedure should be followed by a pilot who is circling to land in a Category B airplane, but is maintaining a speed 5 knots faster than the maximum specified for that category?

    A. Use the approach minimums appropriate for Category C.

    B. Use Category B minimums.

    C. Use Category D minimums since they apply to all circling approaches.

Answer (A) is correct. *(IFH Chap 10)*
    DISCUSSION: If it is necessary to maneuver at speeds in excess of the upper limit of the speed range for any category, the minimums for the next higher category should be used.
    Answer (B) is incorrect. A pilot should use minimums for the category appropriate to the approach speed being used. Answer (C) is incorrect. Category D minimums do not necessarily apply to all circling approaches.

159. Under the stabilized approach concept, what is the maximum acceptable descent rate during the final stages of an approach?

    A. 1,000 fpm for either precision or nonprecision approaches.

    B. 1,200 fpm above 1,000 feet AGL and 500 fpm below 1,000 feet AGL for all approaches.

    C. 1,000 fpm for precision and 1,200 fpm for nonprecision approaches.

Answer (A) is correct. *(IPH Chap 4, AC 120-71A)*
    DISCUSSION: Operational experience and research have shown that a descent rate of greater than approximately 1,000 fpm is unacceptable during the final stages of an approach.
    Answer (B) is incorrect. It has been found that a descent of 1,000 feet per minute in the final stages of an approach is the maximum allowable rate. This limitation is due to human perceptual limitations. There is no recommended limitation of 500 fpm below 1,000 feet AGL. Answer (C) is incorrect. The maximum acceptable descent rate for the final stages of precision and nonprecision approaches is identical. It has been established as 1,000 fpm, as a safety restriction due to the limitations of human perceptions.

160. What does the symbol T within a black triangle in the minimums section of the IAP for a particular airport indicate?

    A. Takeoff minimums are 1 mile for aircraft having two engines or less and 1/2 mile for those with more than two engines.

    B. Instrument takeoffs are not authorized.

    C. Takeoff minimums are not standard and/or departure procedures are published.

Answer (C) is correct. *(ACL)*
    DISCUSSION: The symbol in the question indicates that takeoff minimums are not standard and/or departure procedures are published, and one should consult the alternate takeoff procedures. Takeoff minimums apply to operations under Parts 121, 125, 127, 129, and 135, i.e., operations other than Part 91.
    Answer (A) is incorrect. It gives the standard minimums for takeoff when there is a published instrument approach. Answer (B) is incorrect. The alternate takeoff procedures will indicate if instrument takeoffs are not authorized.

161. (Refer to Figure 228 on page 281.) The missed approach point for the LOC RWY 31 procedure is

    A. 2:33 from PECAT.

    B. 200 feet AGL.

    C. 1,081 feet MSL.

Answer (A) is correct. *(IPH Chap 4)*
    DISCUSSION: On some nonprecision approaches, the missed approach point (MAP) is given as a fixed distance with an associated time from the final approach fix (FAF) to the MAP based on the groundspeed of the aircraft. A table (timing block) on the lower left-hand side of Fig. 228 shows the distance in NM from the FAF to the MAP and the time it takes at specific groundspeeds. Under the 120 knots speed is the time of 2:33 from PECAT to the MAP. Pilots must determine the approximate groundspeed and time based on the approach speed and true airspeed of their aircraft and the current winds along the final approach course. A clock or stopwatch should be started at the FAF of an approach requiring this method. Many nonprecision approaches designate a specific fix as the MAP. These can be identified by a course (LOC or VOR) and DME, a cross radial from a VOR, or a GPS waypoint.
    Answer (B) is incorrect. A MAP of 200 feet AGL is even lower than the DA for the ILS (274 feet AGL), which is a precision approach. The MAP for this nonprecision approach is 553 feet AGL (1,360 feet MSL). Answer (C) is incorrect. A height of 1,081 feet MSL is the DA for the ILS approach, not the MAP for the nonprecision localizer approach.

Figure 228.

162. (Refer to Figure 227 below.) Refer to the DEN ILS RWY 35R procedure. The FAF intercept altitude is

- A. 7,080 feet MSL.
- B. 7,977 feet MSL.
- C. 8,000 feet MSL.

Answer (C) is correct. *(IPH Chap 5)*
DISCUSSION: The glide slope intercept altitude at the FAF (lightning bolt) is 8,000 feet MSL.
Answer (A) is incorrect. The minimum altitude for the nonprecision approaches, excluding the LECET-fix minimum altitude, is 7,080 feet MSL. Answer (B) is incorrect. The altitude at the FAF is 7,977 feet MSL.

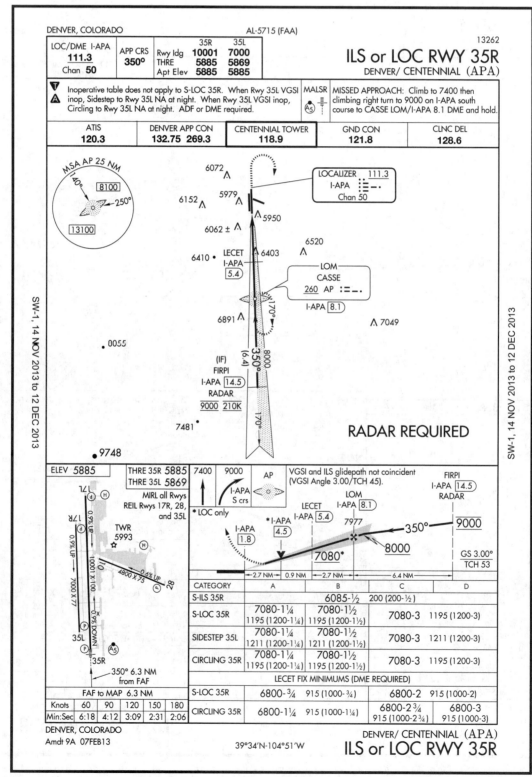

Figure 227.

163. (Refer to Figure 240 below.) If the DME at PUC airport is inoperative, the airborne DME will

A. continuously indicate "99" as the mileage.

B. enter "search" mode but fail to lock on.

C. not transmit a coded identification audio tone.

Answer (C) is correct. *(AIM Para 1-1-7)*

DISCUSSION: When a DME is inoperative, the code tone (identifier) will not be broadcast, although a signal may still be received.

Answer (A) is incorrect. The airborne DME will give no indication if the DME is inoperative. Answer (B) is incorrect. The airborne DME may be inoperative.

Figure 240.

164. (Refer to Figure 230 below.) The minimum safe altitude (MSA) for the VOR/DME or GPS-A at 7D3 is geographically centered at what position?

A. DEANI intersection.

B. WHITE CLOUD VOR/DME.

C. MAJUB intersection.

Answer (B) is correct. *(AIM Para 5-4-5)*

DISCUSSION: Minimum safe altitudes provide obstacle clearance within 25 NM of the specified navigational facility. In Fig. 230, the MSA circle specifies WHITE CLOUD VOR/DME.

Answer (A) is incorrect. DEANI intersection is the point of descent to the final approach fix. Answer (C) is incorrect. An MSA will always be based on a navigation facility or a waypoint (GPS or RNAV approach), not an intersection.

Figure 230.

165. (Refer to Figure 231 below, and Figure 230 on page 284.) You plan to fly to Baldwin for Christmas. What minimum equipment is required for the VOR/DME or GPS-A procedure, and can you complete the flight?

A. One VOR receiver; yes, the trip will be fun.

B. One VOR receiver and one DME receiver; no flight though, the airport is closed.

C. Two VOR receivers; yes, but no fuel is available because the airport is unattended.

Answer (B) is correct. *(IFH Chap 8)*
  DISCUSSION: Note in the Airport Remarks section of the A/FD page (Fig. 231) that the airport is closed November through April.
  Answer (A) is incorrect. The flight cannot be completed. The airport is closed November through April, as noted in the Airport Remarks in Fig. 231. Answer (C) is incorrect. Only one VOR receiver is required, not two, and the flight cannot take place as the Airport Remarks in Fig. 231 stipulate the airport is closed November through April.

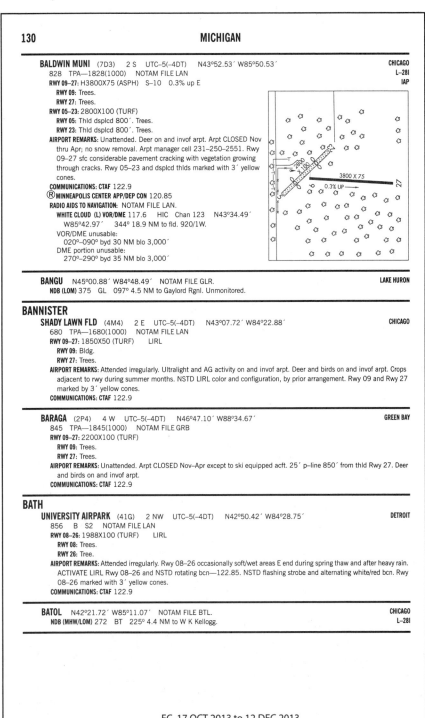

Figure 231.

166. (Refer to Figure 244 below.) At what minimum altitude should you cross RAMKE intersection during the S-LDA RWY 6 approach at ROA?

A. 2,720 MSL.

B. 4,300 MSL.

C. 1,780 MSL.

Answer (B) is correct. *(IPH Chaps 4, 8 (IAP Legend))*
DISCUSSION: The profile view of the approach includes a Maltese cross at RAMKE and a notation of 4,300 feet MSL. That is the minimum altitude you should cross the intersection.

Answer (A) is incorrect. The S-LDA 6 approach minimum is 2,720 feet MSL. Answer (C) is incorrect. The SKIRT minimum for the S-LDA 6 approach is 1,780 MSL.

Figure 244.

**Page
Intentionally
Left Blank**

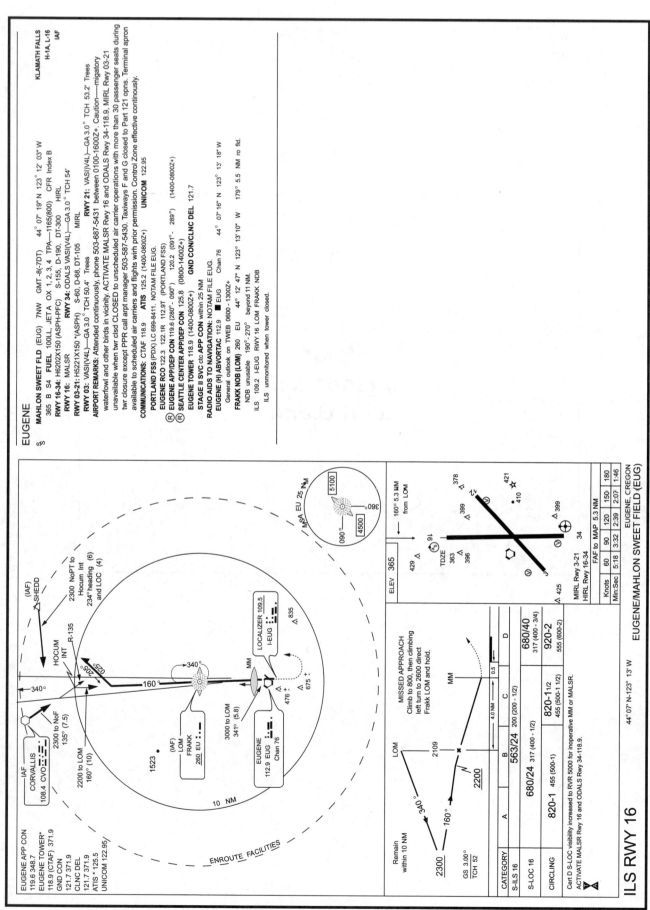

Figure 29. – ILS RWY 16 (EUG) and Excerpt from Airport/Facility Directory.

167. (Refer to Figure 29 on page 288.) During the final approach, as you reach the outer marker, ATC advises that the middle marker is out of service. You should

    A. Increase the ILS minimums by 50 feet to 613 feet.

    B. Increase the LOC minimums by 50 feet to 730 feet.

    C. Continue the approach as planned.

Answer (C) is correct. *(IFH Chap 8)*
    DISCUSSION: The middle marker is not a required component of the ILS or the localizer approach. You may continue your approach to the minimums published in the approach procedure.
    Answer (A) is incorrect. The middle marker is not a required component of the ILS approach. No action is required should it be out of service. You do not need to increase the approach minimums as a result. Answer (B) is incorrect. The middle marker is not a required component of the localizer approach. No action is required should it be out of service. You do not need to increase the approach minimums as a result.

6.14 DPs and STARs

168. Which of the following statements regarding STARs is most accurate?

    A. STARs facilitate the transition between the departure procedure and en route portion of the flight.

    B. STARs facilitate the transition between the en route portion of the flight and the instrument approach procedure.

    C. STARs can be planned for use by aircraft with RNAV capability, subject to any limitations or requirements noted on en route charts in applicable Advisory Circulars, or by NOTAM.

Answer (B) is correct. *(AIM Para 5-4-1)*
    DISCUSSION: STARs facilitate the transition between the en route portion of the flight and the instrument approach procedure.
    Answer (A) is incorrect. STARs facilitate the transition between the en route portion of the flight and the instrument approach, not the departure procedure and en route portion of the flight. Answer (C) is incorrect. RNAV routes, not STARs, can be planned for use by aircraft with RNAV capability, subject to any limitations or requirements noted on en route charts or in applicable Advisory Circulars, or by NOTAM.

169. What action is recommended if a pilot does not wish to use an instrument departure procedure?

    A. Advise clearance delivery or ground control before departure.

    B. Advise departure control upon initial contact.

    C. Enter "No DP" in the REMARKS section of the IFR flight plan.

Answer (C) is correct. *(AIM Para 5-2-6)*
    DISCUSSION: A pilot who does not possess an instrument departure procedure (DP) chart or does not wish to use a DP should advise ATC by indicating "No DP" in the remarks section of the flight plan.
    Answer (A) is incorrect. Verbal requests are less desirable than entering "No DP" in the flight plan. Answer (B) is incorrect. Verbal requests are less desirable than entering "No DP" in the flight plan.

170. A particular instrument departure procedure requires a minimum climb rate of 210 feet per NM to 8,000 feet. If you climb with a ground speed of 140 knots, what is the rate of climb required in feet per minute?

    A. 210

    B. 450

    C. 490

Answer (C) is correct. *(IPH Chap 1)*
    DISCUSSION: Divide GS by time to find NM per minute. 140 (knots) ÷ 60 (seconds) = 2.33 NM per minute. Multiply the number of NM covered in a minute by the required number of feet per NM to find feet per minute. 2.33 (NM per minute) × 210 (feet per NM) = 489.3 feet per minute.
    Answer (A) is incorrect. The number of feet we need to climb is 210 per nautical mile, not the number of feet per minute. Answer (B) is incorrect. Although close, 450 feet per minute is slightly short of the required 490 feet per minute we would need to climb for this departure procedure.

Figure 86. – CDI and OBS Indicators.

171. (Refer to Figure 86 above, and Figure 85 on page 291.) Which combination of indications confirm that you are approaching WAGGE intersection slightly to the right of the LOC centerline on departure?

    A. 1 and 3.

    B. 1 and 4.

    C. 2 and 3.

Answer (C) is correct. *(IFH Chap 10)*
    DISCUSSION: If you are flying out on the back course, you have front course indications. Therefore, if you are to the right of the localizer centerline, you will get a left needle deflection, such as in 2 (see Figs. 85 and 86). To determine whether you are at WAGGE INT, visualize yourself flying out on Squaw Valley R-062 (113.2). If you were north of the radial, you would get a right needle deflection such as in 3.
    Answer (A) is incorrect. Illustration 1 would mean you are left, not right, of the localizer centerline. Answer (B) is incorrect. Illustration 1 would mean you are left, not right, of the localizer centerline. Also, a left needle deflection on 113.2 (as in 4) would mean that you were south of R-062 and would thus be beyond WAGGE INT.

172. (Refer to Figure 85 on page 291.) What route should you take if cleared for the Washoe Two Departure and your assigned route is V6?

    A. Climb on the LOC south course to WAGGE where you will be vectored to V6.

    B. Climb on the LOC south course to cross WAGGE at 9,000, turn left and fly direct to FMG VORTAC and cross at or above 10,000, and proceed on FMG R-241.

    C. Climb on the LOC south course to WAGGE, turn left and fly direct to FMG VORTAC. If at 10,000 turn left and proceed on FMG R-241; if not at 10,000 enter depicted holding pattern and climb to 10,000 before proceeding on FMG R-241.

Answer (A) is correct. *(AIM Para 5-2-6)*
    DISCUSSION: The instructions on Fig. 85 for the Washoe Two Departure are to "climb via Reno localizer south course to WAGGE INT for radar vector to assigned route."
    Answer (B) is incorrect. It describes the lost communication procedure. Answer (C) is incorrect. It describes the lost communication procedure.

(VECTOR) (WASH2.WAGGE) 91094
WASHOE TWO DEPARTURE SL-346 (FAA)

RENO CANNON INTL
RENO, NEVADA

ATIS
124.35 277.2
CLNC DEL
124.9 343.9
GND CON
121.9
RENO DEP CON
NE-SW 119.2 325.8

MUSTANG
117.9 FMG
Chan 126
N39°31.88'–W119°39.30'

LOCALIZER 110.9
I-RNO
Chan 46

R-041

221°

041°

V200-392   R-241

R-167

R-218

164°

V6

V165

13

SQUAW VALLEY
113.2 SWR
Chan 79

R-062

R-192

BACK COURSE

344°

WAGGE
N39°15.72'
W119°46.13'
L-2, 5

V28-113

MINIMUM CROSSING ALTITUDES
AT FMG VORTAC
South V165, 10000
Southwest V28-113, 10500
Southwest V200-392, 10000
Southwest V6, 12000

NOTE: Minimum climb rate at 400'
per NM to 9000' required.

NOTE: Chart not to scale.

DEPARTURE ROUTE DESCRIPTION

<u>TAKE-OFF RUNWAYS 16L/R:</u> Climb via I-RNO Localizer south course to WAGGE
INT then via radar vectors to assigned route.
<u>LOST COMMUNICATIONS:</u> If not in contact with departure control within one
minute after takeoff, or if communications are lost before reaching 9000', continue
climb via I-RNO localizer south course to WAGGE INT, turn left, proceed direct
FMG VORTAC. Cross FMG VORTAC at or above MCA, thence via assigned route
or climb in holding pattern northeast on FMG R-041, left turns to cross FMG
VORTAC at or above MCA for assigned route.

WASHOE TWO DEPARTURE
(VECTOR) (WASH2.WAGGE)

RENO. NEVADA
RENO CANNON INTL

Figure 85. – WASHOE TWO DEPARTURE.

173. (Refer to Figure 85 on page 293.) What procedure should be followed if communications are lost before reaching 9,000 feet?

A. At 9,000, turn left direct to FMG VORTAC, then via assigned route if at proper altitude; if not, climb in holding pattern until reaching the proper altitude.

B. Continue climb to WAGGE INT, turn left direct to FMG VORTAC, then if at or above MCA, proceed on assigned route; if not, continue climb in holding pattern until at the proper altitude.

C. Continue climb on LOC course to cross WAGGE INT at or above 9,000, turn left direct to FMG VORTAC to cross at 10,000 or above, and continue on assigned course.

Answer (B) is correct. *(AIM Para 5-2-6)*
DISCUSSION: The Lost Communications section under the departure route description states, "...if communications are lost before reaching 9,000 ft., continue climb via I-RNO localizer south course to WAGGE INT, turn left proceed direct FMG VORTAC. Cross FMG VORTAC at or above MCA, thence via assigned route or climb in holding pattern northeast on FMG R-041, left turns to cross FMG VORTAC at or above MCA for assigned route."
Answer (A) is incorrect. You are to turn left to FMG VORTAC at WAGGE, irrespective of altitude. Answer (C) is incorrect. There is no requirement to cross WAGGE INT at 9,000 ft.

174. (Refer to Figure 85 on page 293 and Legend 16 below.) Of the following, which is the minimum acceptable rate of climb (feet per minute) to 9,000 feet required for the WASH2 WAGGE departure at a GS of 150 knots?

A. 750 feet per minute.

B. 825 feet per minute.

C. 1,000 feet per minute.

Answer (C) is correct. *(ACL)*
DISCUSSION: The required climb rate is 400 ft./NM (Fig. 85). Use Legend 16. Required climb rate (ft. per NM) is found on the left, and groundspeed (kt.) is found on the top. Locate 400 ft. per NM and move right to the 150-kt. groundspeed column to determine a 1,000-fpm rate of climb.
Answer (A) is incorrect. This rate of climb at a groundspeed of 150 kt. results in a climb of 300, not 400, ft. per NM. Answer (B) is incorrect. This is the rate of climb at approximately 125 kt., not 150 kt., that results in a climb of 400 ft. per NM.

INSTRUMENT TAKEOFF PROCEDURE CHARTS
RATE-OF-CLIMB TABLE
(ft. per min.)

A rate-of-climb table is provided for use in planning and executing takeoff procedures under known or approximate ground speed conditions.

REQUIRED CLIMB RATE (ft. per NM)	GROUND SPEED (KNOTS)						
	30	60	80	90	100	120	140
200	100	200	267	300	333	400	467
250	125	250	333	375	417	500	583
300	150	300	400	450	500	600	700
350	175	350	467	525	583	700	816
400	200	400	533	600	667	800	933
450	225	450	600	675	750	900	1050
500	250	500	667	750	833	1000	1167
550	275	550	733	825	917	1100	1283
600	300	600	800	900	1000	1200	1400
650	325	650	867	975	1083	1300	1516
700	350	700	933	1050	1167	1400	1633

REQUIRED CLIMB RATE (ft. per NM)	GROUND SPEED (KNOTS)					
	150	180	210	240	270	300
200	500	600	700	800	900	1000
250	625	750	875	1000	1125	1250
300	750	900	1050	1200	1350	1500
350	875	1050	1225	1400	1575	1750
400	1000	1200	1400	1600	1700	2000
450	1125	1350	1575	1800	2025	2250
500	1250	1500	1750	2000	2250	2500
550	1375	1650	1925	2200	2475	2750
600	1500	1800	2100	2400	2700	3000
650	1625	1950	2275	2600	2925	3250
700	1750	2100	2450	2800	3150	3500

Legend 16.–Instrument Takeoff Procedure Charts, Rate-of-Climb Table.

175. (Refer to Figure 85 below.) What is the minimum rate climb per NM to 9,000 feet required for the WASH2 WAGGE Departure?

A. 400 feet.

B. 750 feet.

C. 875 feet.

Answer (A) is correct. *(AIM Para 5-2-6)*
DISCUSSION: The right-hand side of the WASH2 Departure (Fig. 85) states, "NOTE: Minimum climb rate of 400' per NM to 9000' required."

Answer (B) is incorrect. The required minimum rate of climb is 400 ft. per NM, not 750 ft. per NM. Answer (C) is incorrect. The required minimum rate of climb is 400 ft. per NM, not 875 ft. per NM.

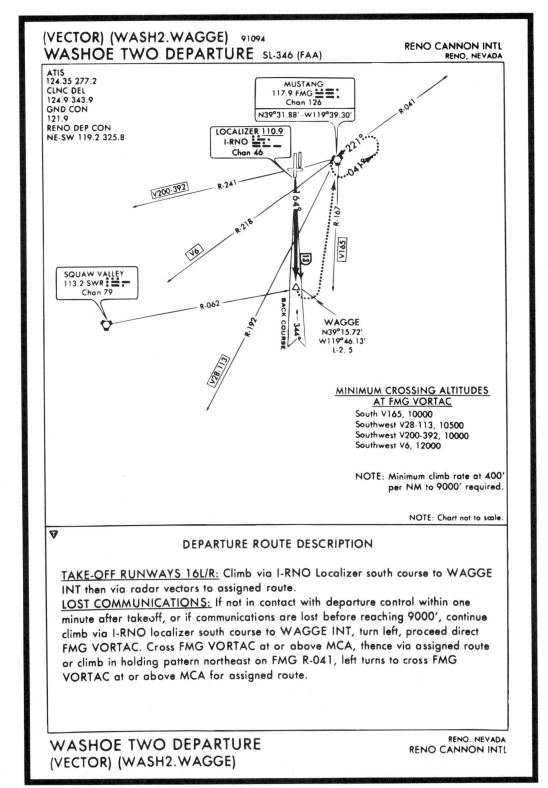

Figure 85. – WASHOE TWO DEPARTURE.

176. Which procedure applies to instrument departure procedures?

- A. Instrument departure clearances will not be issued unless requested by the pilot.
- B. The pilot in command must accept an instrument departure procedure when issued by ATC.
- C. If an instrument departure procedure is accepted, the pilot must possess a textual or graphic description.

Answer (C) is correct. *(AIM Para 5-2-6)*
DISCUSSION: Once an instrument departure procedure (DP) is accepted, the presumption by ATC is that the pilot possesses a textual description of the DP.

Answer (A) is incorrect. Pilots operating from locations with DPs may expect ATC clearances containing a DP. Answer (B) is incorrect. You must reject a DP clearance if you do not have a text of the DP or if it is otherwise unacceptable.

177. (Refer to Figure 174 below, and Figure 175 on page 295.) At which point does the JEN.JEN9 arrival begin?

- A. INK VOR.
- B. GLEN ROSE VORTAC.
- C. FEVER intersection.

Answer (B) is correct. *(IPH Chap 4)*
DISCUSSION: Fig. 174 shows three feeder routes that converge at JEN, the identifier for the GLEN ROSE VORTAC. The arrival descriptions included in Fig. 175 all conclude at the JEN VORTAC, then proceed from there. The approach starts at that point, the GLEN ROSE VORTAC.

Answer (A) is incorrect. INK VOR establishes the beginning of one of three feeder routes to the arrival; it is not the arrival itself. Answer (C) is incorrect. FEVER is the first intersection listed along the arrival; it is not the origination point of the arrival.

Figure 174.

(JEN.JEN9) 09351

GLEN ROSE NINE ARRIVAL   ST-6039 (FAA)   DALLAS-FT. WORTH, TEXAS

SC-2, 14 NOV 2013 to 12 DEC 2013

SC-2, 14 NOV 2013 to 12 DEC 2013

ARRIVAL DESCRIPTION

ABILENE TRANSITION (ABI.JEN9): From over ABI VORTAC via R-099 to GEENI INT, then via JEN R-267 to JEN VORTAC. Thence. . . .

CENTEX TRANSITION (CWK.JEN9): From over CWK VORTAC via CWK R-321 and AGJ R-142 to AGJ VORTAC, then via AGJ R-350 to JUMBO INT, then via JEN R-197 to JEN VORTAC. Thence . . . .

JUMBO TRANSITION (JUMBO.JEN9): From over JUMBO INT via JEN R-197 to JEN VORTAC. Thence . . . .

SAN ANTONIO TRANSITION (SAT.JEN9): From over SAT VORTAC via SAT R-359 to JUMBO INT, then via JEN R-197 to JEN VORTAC. Thence . . . .

WACO TRANSITION (ACT.JEN9): From over ACT VORTAC via ACT R-305 and JEN R-128 to JEN VORTAC. Thence. . . .

WINK TRANSITION (INK.JEN9): From over INK VORTAC via INK R-071 and TQA R-254 to TQA VOR/DME, then via TQA R-082 to GEENI INT, then via JEN R-267 to JEN VORTAC. Thence. . . .

. . . . ALL AIRCRAFT: From over JEN VORTAC via JEN R-039, thence . . . .

ALL AIRCRAFT LANDING NORTH: To CURLE INT, expect vectors to final approach course.

JETS LANDING SOUTH: To DELMO, depart DELMO heading 355°.

For /E, /F, /G and /R (RNP 2.0) EQUIPMENT SUFFIXED AIRCRAFT: From over DELMO WP direct TEVON WP, expect vector to final approach course prior to TEVON WP. If not received by TEVON fly present heading.

NON TURBOJETS LANDING SOUTH: To CURLE INT, depart CURLE heading 010° for vectors to final approach course.

AIRCRAFT LANDING DAL, ADS, TKI: To DELMO INT, depart DELMO via FUZ R-171 to FUZ VORTAC then FUZ R-064 to HURBS INT, expect vectors to final approach course.

GLEN ROSE NINE ARRIVAL   DALLAS-FT. WORTH, TEXAS
(JEN.JEN9) 09351

Figure 175.

178. Preferred IFR routes beginning with a fix, indicate that departing aircraft will normally be routed to the fix by

    A. the established airway(s) between the departure airport and the fix.

    B. an instrument departure procedure (DP), or radar vectors.

    C. direct route only.

Answer (B) is correct. *(P/C Glossary)*
    DISCUSSION: Preferred IFR routes are correlated with DPs and STARs and may be defined by airways, jet routes, and direct routes between NAVAIDs. Thus, preferred routes beginning with a fix indicate that the departing traffic will normally be routed to the fix via a DP or radar vectors.
    Answer (A) is incorrect. Established airways may not exist between the airport and the fix, and other methods may be more efficient and effective. Answer (C) is incorrect. A direct route may not be appropriate due to obstructions or traffic flows.

179. (Refer to Figure 208 below, and Figure 209 on page 297.) At which location or condition does the STELA.STELA1 arrival begin?

    A. ALB VORTAC.

    B. CANAN intersection.

    C. STELA intersection.

Answer (B) is correct. *(IPH Chap 4)*
    DISCUSSION: Fig. 208 shows three feeder routes that converge at CANAN intersection, with a single approach flowing from that point. Each of the arrival route descriptions included in Fig. 209 lead to CANAN before moving into the arrival itself. CANAN intersection is the starting point of the arrival procedure.
    Answer (A) is incorrect. Although the ALBANY VOR feeds into the STELA.STELA1 arrival, it does not include traffic from two additional feeder routes. Answer (C) is incorrect. STELA intersection establishes a holding fix along the route of the arrival procedure, but it is not the start of the arrival procedure.

Figure 208.

STELA ONE ARRIVAL
WINDSOR LOCKS, CONNECTICUT

ARRIVAL ROUTE DESCRIPTION

<u>ALBANY TRANSITION (ALB.STELA1):</u> From over ALB VORTAC via ALB R-147 to CANAN INT. Thence. . . .
<u>AUDIL TRANSITION (AUDIL.STELA1):</u> From over AUDIL INT via RKA R-306 to RKA VOR/DME, then via RKA R-099 to CANAN INT. Thence. . . .
<u>CAMBRIDGE TRANSITION (CAM.STELA1):</u> From over CAM VOR/DME via CAM R-203 to CANAN INT. Thence. . . .
<u>HANCOCK TRANSITION (HNK.STELA1):</u> From over HNK VOR/DME via HNK R-060 to SWEDE INT, then via RKA R-099 to CANAN INT. Thence. . . .
<u>WILET TRANSITION (WILET.STELA1):</u> From over WILET INT via RKA R-292 to RKA VOR/DME, then via RKA R-099 TO CANAN INT. Thence. . . .

<u>KBDL and KHFD ARRIVALS:</u> From over CANAN INT via ALB R-147 to TOMES INT. Expect radar vectors to final approach course prior to TOMES INT.

<u>KBAF, KCEF and KORH ARRIVALS:</u> From over CANAN INT via ALB R-147 to MOLDS INT. Then via BAF R-295 to BAF VORTAC. Expect radar vectors to final approach course prior to BAF VORTAC.

NE-1, 14 NOV 2013 to 12 DEC 2013

NE-1, 14 NOV 2013 to 12 DEC 2013

Figure 209.

180. Which is true regarding the use of an instrument departure procedure chart?

    A. The use of instrument departure procedures is mandatory.

    B. To use an instrument departure procedure, the pilot must possess at least the textual description of the approved procedure.

    C. To use an instrument departure procedure, the pilot must possess both the textual and graphic form of the approved procedure.

Answer (B) is correct. *(AIM Para 5-2-6)*
    DISCUSSION: Use of an instrument departure procedure (DP) requires that the pilot have at least the textual description of the procedure.
    Answer (A) is incorrect. Use of a DP is never mandatory. Answer (C) is incorrect. A pilot need only possess the textual form of the DP.

181. Which is true regarding STARs?

    A. STARs are used to separate IFR and VFR traffic.

    B. STARs are established to simplify clearance delivery procedures.

    C. STARs are used at certain airports to decrease traffic congestion.

Answer (B) is correct. *(AIM Para 5-4-1)*
    DISCUSSION: A STAR's purpose is to simplify clearance delivery procedures.
    Answer (A) is incorrect. STARs do not pertain to VFR traffic. Answer (C) is incorrect. STARs are used to decrease radio, not traffic, congestion.

182. Which clearance procedures may be issued by ATC without prior pilot request?

    A. DP's, STAR's, and contact approaches.

    B. Contact and visual approaches.

    C. DP's, STAR's, and visual approaches.

Answer (C) is correct. *(AIM Para 5-4-24)*
    DISCUSSION: DPs, STARs, and visual approaches are all routinely assigned by ATC as appropriate. Contact approaches must be requested by the pilot and made in lieu of a standard or special instrument approach.
    Answer (A) is incorrect. Contact approaches must be requested by the pilot. Answer (B) is incorrect. Contact approaches must be requested by the pilot.

183. ATC can issue a STAR

    A. to all pilots wherever STARs are available.

    B. only if the pilot requests a STAR in the "Remarks" section of the flight plan.

    C. when ATC deems it appropriate, unless the pilot requests "No STAR."

Answer (C) is correct. *(AIM Para 5-4-1)*
    DISCUSSION: Pilots of IFR civil aircraft destined to locations for which STARs have been published may be issued a clearance containing a STAR whenever ATC deems it appropriate. The pilot should notify ATC if (s)he does not wish to use a STAR by placing "No STAR" in the remarks section of the flight plan or by the less desirable method of verbally stating the request to ATC.
    Answer (A) is incorrect. STARs are not mandatory to ATC or pilots. Answer (B) is incorrect. Pilot request is necessary to avoid, not obtain, STARs.

184. (Refer to Figure 216 on page 299.) If you take off from RWY 34L, or RWY 34R with minimum weather, which of the following is the minimum acceptable rate of climb (feet per minute) to 8,700 feet required for the RENO6.RENO departure at a GS of 150 knots?

    A. 960 feet per minute.

    B. 1,200 feet per minute.

    C. 430 feet per minute.

Answer (B) is correct. *(IPH Chap 1, IAP Climb/Descent Table)*
    DISCUSSION: A note on Fig. 216 stipulates a 480 foot per NM climb for aircraft taking off from Runways 34L and 34R. Our GS is 150 knots. Divide GS by time to find NM per minute (150 knots ÷ 60 seconds = 2.5 NM per minute). Multiply feet per NM by number of NM per minute to find the answer (480 feet per NM × 2.5 NM per minute = 1,200 feet per minute). This can also be found on the climb/descent table found in any IAP booklet. Look under the column ft/NM. Follow it down to 480, then across to the right until under the column 150, and find 1,195 feet per minute.
    Answer (A) is incorrect. The actual requirement is 1,200, not 960, feet per minute. Answer (C) is incorrect. A 480 foot per NM climb for aircraft taking off from Runways 34L and 34R is required. At a ground speed of 150 knots, 430 feet per minute is far too low a value to meet the requirement.

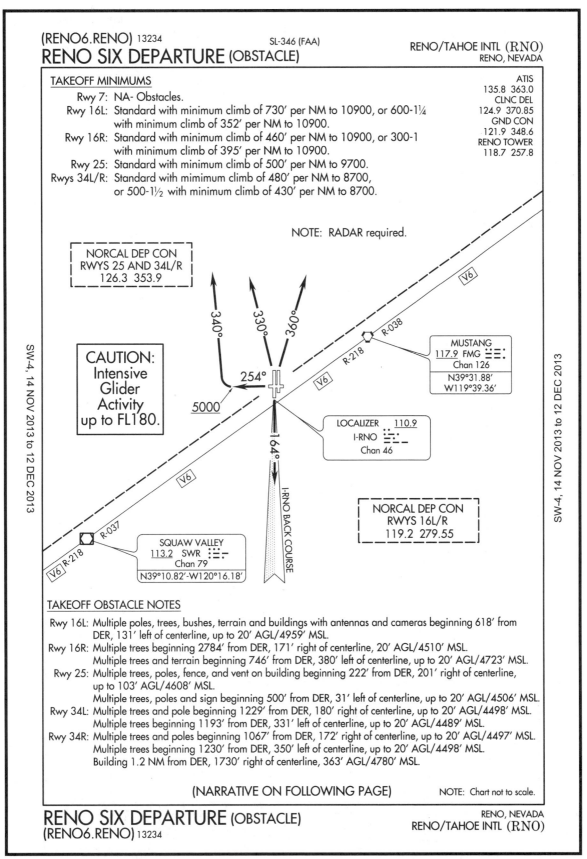

(RENO6.RENO) 13234
SL-346 (FAA)
RENO/TAHOE INTL (RNO)
RENO, NEVADA

RENO SIX DEPARTURE (OBSTACLE)

TAKEOFF MINIMUMS

ATIS
135.8 363.0
CLNC DEL
124.9 370.85
GND CON
121.9 348.6
RENO TOWER
118.7 257.8

Rwy 7: NA- Obstacles.
Rwy 16L: Standard with minimum climb of 730' per NM to 10900, or 600-1¼ with minimum climb of 352' per NM to 10900.
Rwy 16R: Standard with minimum climb of 460' per NM to 10900, or 300-1 with minimum climb of 395' per NM to 10900.
Rwy 25: Standard with minimum climb of 500' per NM to 9700.
Rwys 34L/R: Standard with mimimum climb of 480' per NM to 8700, or 500-1½ with minimum climb of 430' per NM to 8700.

NOTE: RADAR required.

NORCAL DEP CON
RWYS 25 AND 34L/R
126.3 353.9

MUSTANG
117.9 FMG
Chan 126
N39°31.88'
W119°39.36'

CAUTION:
Intensive
Glider
Activity
up to FL180.

254°
5000

LOCALIZER 110.9
I-RNO
Chan 46

164°
I-RNO BACK COURSE

NORCAL DEP CON
RWYS 16L/R
119.2 279.55

SQUAW VALLEY
113.2 SWR
Chan 79
N39°10.82'-W120°16.18'

SW-4, 14 NOV 2013 to 12 DEC 2013

TAKEOFF OBSTACLE NOTES

Rwy 16L: Multiple poles, trees, bushes, terrain and buildings with antennas and cameras beginning 618' from DER, 131' left of centerline, up to 20' AGL/4959' MSL.
Rwy 16R: Multiple trees beginning 2784' from DER, 171' right of centerline, 20' AGL/4510' MSL.
Multiple trees and terrain beginning 746' from DER, 380' left of centerline, up to 20' AGL/4723' MSL.
Rwy 25: Multiple trees, poles, fence, and vent on building beginning 222' from DER, 201' right of centerline, up to 103' AGL/4608' MSL.
Multiple trees, poles and sign beginning 500' from DER, 31' left of centerline, up to 20' AGL/4506' MSL.
Rwy 34L: Multiple trees and pole beginning 1229' from DER, 180' right of centerline, up to 20' AGL/4498' MSL.
Multiple trees beginning 1193' from DER, 331' left of centerline, up to 20' AGL/4489' MSL.
Rwy 34R: Multiple trees and poles beginning 1067' from DER, 172' right of centerline, up to 20' AGL/4497' MSL.
Multiple trees beginning 1230' from DER, 350' left of centerline, up to 20' AGL/4498' MSL.
Building 1.2 NM from DER, 1730' right of centerline, 363' AGL/4780' MSL.

(NARRATIVE ON FOLLOWING PAGE)

NOTE: Chart not to scale.

RENO SIX DEPARTURE (OBSTACLE)
(RENO6.RENO) 13234

RENO, NEVADA
RENO/TAHOE INTL (RNO)

Figure 216.

185. (Refer to Figure 211 below.) For takeoff on RWY 9 using an average groundspeed of 140 knots, what minimum rate of climb would meet the required minimum rate of climb as specified on the instrument departure procedure?

A. 830 feet per minute.

B. 415 feet per minute.

C. 970 feet per minute.

Answer (C) is correct. *(IPH Chap 1)*

DISCUSSION: Fig. 211 provides takeoff minimums for RWY 9 that stipulate a minimum climb of 415 feet per NM. Divide GS (140 knots) by time (60 seconds) to find the number of NM per minute (140 ÷ 60 = 2.33 NM per minute). Multiply the number of NM per minute (2.33) by the number of feet per NM (415) required to find the feet per minute (2.33 × 415 = 966.9, which can be rounded to 967). The best answer is 970 feet per minute.

Answer (A) is incorrect. The rate of climb is 970, not 830, feet per minute. Answer (B) is incorrect. The number 415 is the feet per NM required for aircraft climbing out on this departure; it is not the number of feet per minute required.

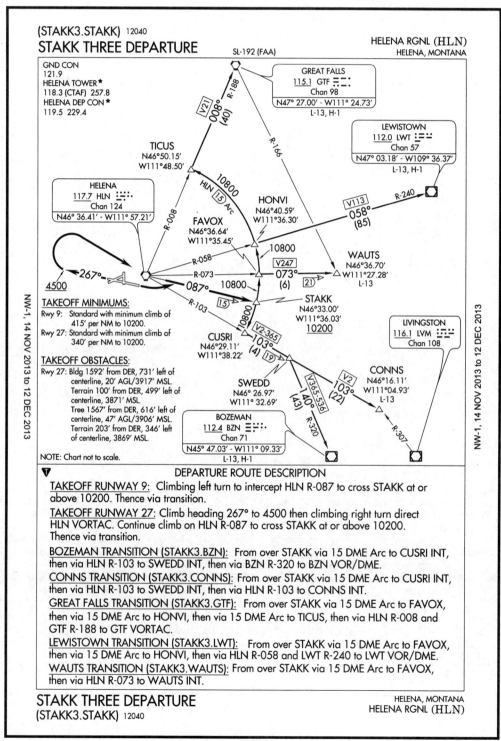

Figure 211.

6.15 Microwave Landing System and GPS Approaches

186. On a GPS with WAAS capability, what is the significance of "LNAV+V" being displayed?

    A. Approved vertical guidance to descend to the decision height is provided to the pilot.

    B. Advisory vertical guidance is provided as an aid to the pilot during the descent to the runway.

    C. Advisory vertical guidance is provided to the pilot that must be used in lieu of published step-down fixes on the instrument approach.

Answer (B) is correct. *(AIM Para 1-1-20)*
    DISCUSSION: LNAV+V is not an approach type; rather, it provides advisory vertical guidance that may be used in lieu of the published step-down fixes on the IAP.
    Answer (A) is incorrect. LNAV+V offers advisory, not approved, vertical guidance. Answer (C) is incorrect. LNAV+V offers advisory vertical guidance that may, not must, be used in lieu of the published step-down fixes on the IAP.

187. When flying a GPS approach procedure, what effect will overriding an automatically selected sensitivity have?

    A. No effect.

    B. Cancel the approach mode annunciation.

    C. Initiate a descent to MDA.

Answer (B) is correct. *(IFH Chap 2)*
    DISCUSSION: Overriding an automatically selected sensitivity during an approach cancels the approach mode annunciation.
    Answer (A) is incorrect. Overriding an automatically selected sensitivity during an approach has the effect of canceling the approach mode annunciation. Answer (C) is incorrect. Overriding an automatically selected sensitivity during an approach cancels the approach mode annunciation. A missed approach will be required, not a descent to MDA.

188. When proper RAIM sensitivity is not available, manually resetting sensitivity to 0.3 NM will

    A. Not automatically change the RAIM sensitivity on some receivers.

    B. Automatically change settings to approach mode.

    C. Allow the approach to continue in terminal sensitivity.

Answer (A) is correct. *(IFH Chap 2)*
    DISCUSSION: When the proper RAIM sensitivity is not available and the CDI sensitivity does not automatically change to 0.3 NM, manually setting CDI sensitivity does not automatically change the RAIM sensitivity on some receivers.
    Answer (B) is incorrect. Manually resetting the sensitivity to 0.3 NM will not automatically initiate approach mode sensitivity. Answer (C) is incorrect. An instrument approach cannot continue with terminal sensitivity. However, manually setting CDI sensitivity does not automatically change the RAIM sensitivity on some receivers.

189. Microwave landing systems provide what information?

    A. Azimuth, elevation, and distance information.

    B. Azimuth, elevation, and traffic avoidance information.

    C. Azimuth, weather conditions, and traffic avoidance information.

Answer (A) is correct. *(AAH Chap 3)*
    DISCUSSION: Microwave landing system (MLS) precision approaches provide azimuth, elevation, and distance information.
    Answer (B) is incorrect. Traffic avoidance is not a characteristic or feature of MLS. Answer (C) is incorrect. Traffic avoidance is not a characteristic or feature of MLS.

190. What international Morse Code identifier is used to identify a specific interim standard microwave landing system?

    A. A two letter Morse Code identifier preceded by the Morse Code for the letters "IM".

    B. A four letter Morse Code identifier preceded by the Morse Code for the letter "M".

    C. A three letter Morse Code identifier preceded by the Morse Code for the letters "ML".

Answer (B) is correct. *(AIM Para 1-1-11)*
    DISCUSSION: MLS identification is a four-character alphabetic designation starting with the letter "M," transmitted in international Morse Code at least 6 times per minute.
    Answer (A) is incorrect. The identifier letter is the single character "M," which is followed by three other letters. Answer (C) is incorrect. The identifier letter is the single character "M," which is followed by three other letters.

191. If Receiver Autonomous Integrity Monitoring (RAIM) is not available prior to beginning a GPS approach, the pilot should

    A. use a navigation or approach system other than GPS for an approach.

    B. continue to the MAP and hold until the satellites are recaptured.

    C. continue the approach, expecting to recapture the satellites before reaching the FAF.

Answer (A) is correct. *(AIM Para 1-1-19)*
    DISCUSSION: RAIM outages may occur due to an insufficient number of satellites or due to unsuitable satellite geometry, which causes the error in the position solution to become too large. If RAIM is not available when setting up a GPS approach, you must select another type of navigation and approach system other than GPS.
    Answer (B) is incorrect. If RAIM is not available when setting up a GPS approach, you should select another type of navigation and approach system. You should not fly to the MAP and hold. Additionally, there is no holding pattern at the MAP. Answer (C) is incorrect. If RAIM is not available when setting up a GPS approach, you should select another type of navigation and approach system. If RAIM failure occurs while you are setting up the GPS approach or conducting a GPS approach, you must not continue the approach hoping that RAIM will become available before the FAF.

192. During a WAAS GPS approach, you receive an LNAV+V annunciation on the GPS display. You should

    A. descend to LNAV approach minimums using the barometric altimeter to comply with altitude restrictions, referencing advisory vertical guidance as an aid.

    B. not descend any further, proceed to the missed approach point, and execute the missed approach.

    C. descend to LNAV/VNAV approach minimums, while closely monitoring the vertical guidance for anomalies.

Answer (A) is correct. *(AC 90-107)*
    DISCUSSION: The barometric altimeter remains the primary altitude reference instrument, even when the LNAV+V annunciation appears. This vertical guidance feature is advisory in nature and has not been approved for vertical guidance as those found on LNAV/VNAV or LPV approaches.
    Answer (B) is incorrect. You may continue your descent using the barometric altimeter as your primary altitude reference instrument. Answer (C) is incorrect. You may only descend to the LNAV approach minimums, not to the lower LNAV/VNAV minimums.

193. When using GPS for navigation and instrument approaches, any required alternate airport must have

    A. an approved operational instrument approach procedure other than GPS.

    B. authorization to fly approaches under IFR using GPS avionics systems.

    C. a GPS approach that is anticipated to be operational and available at the ETA.

Answer (A) is correct. *(AIM Para 1-1-19)*
    DISCUSSION: When you are using GPS for navigation and instrument approaches, any required alternate airport must have an approved instrument approach procedure, other than GPS, which is anticipated to be operational and available at the estimated time of arrival (ETA) and which the airplane is equipped to fly.
    Answer (B) is incorrect. Authorization to fly approaches under IFR using GPS avionics systems requires that the GPS unit and installation meet FAA standards and receive FAA approval. Answer (C) is incorrect. Any required alternate airport must have an approved instrument approach procedure other than GPS, not a GPS approach, that is anticipated to be operational and available at the ETA.

194. (Refer to Figure 238 on page 303.) If cleared for the RNAV (GPS) RWY 28 approach (Lancaster/Fairfield) over APE VORTAC, what will ATC expect of you?

    A. Proceed to CASER, use the S-28 LOC 1620-1 minimums.

    B. Proceed straight in from FAIRF, descend after FAIRF.

    C. Proceed direct to FAIRF and execute the parallel entry depicted on the instrument approach procedure.

Answer (B) is correct. *(IPH Chaps 4 and 5)*
    DISCUSSION: From APE, you would fly to NUMDE, which is an initial approach fix, then proceed to FAIRF and track inbound on the approach, descending as appropriate. Note the "NoPT" listed on the route from NUMDE to FAIRF. This means no procedure turn is necessary when flying the approach along this route.
    Answer (A) is incorrect. There is no CASER and there are no 1620 approach minimums for this RNAV (not an S-LOC) approach. Answer (C) is incorrect. You would not proceed direct to FAIRF; you would instead fly from APE to NUMDE, which is an initial approach fix, then proceed to FAIRF and track inbound on the approach, descending as appropriate.

Figure 238.

195. (Refer to Figure 152 on page 305.) You are established on the RNAV (GPS) RWY 30 approach and lose RAIM functionality after passing BEMXI. You should

    A. Climb to 4,400 feet, continue to the missed approach point, and then fly the missed approach as published.

    B. Initiate a climb to 4,700 feet, continue to the missed approach point, and then fly the missed approach as published.

    C. Continue the approach using circling minimums.

Answer (B) is correct. *(IFH Chap 2)*
    DISCUSSION: A pilot who loses RAIM once established on the approach should climb to the altitude specified on the missed approach procedure, continue to the missed approach point, and then fly the missed approach as published or as instructed by ATC.
    Answer (A) is incorrect. The pilot should climb to 4,700 feet, not 4,400 feet. Answer (C) is incorrect. The pilot would not continue the approach; instead, (s)he would initiate a climb to 4,700 feet, continue to the missed approach point, and then fly the missed approach as published or as instructed by ATC.

196. (Refer to Figure 152 on page 305.) When flying the LNAV/VNAV approach, the missed approach point (MAP) would be indicated by reaching

    A. an altitude of 3,100 feet.

    B. a distance of 1.5 NM to RW30.

    C. the RW30 waypoint.

Answer (C) is correct. *(IFH Chap 7)*
    DISCUSSION: The missed approach point for LNAV/VNAV approaches is usually designed to coincide with the runway threshold. In this example, the waypoint "RW30" represents the runway threshold for Runway 30.
    Answer (A) is incorrect. An altitude of 3,100 feet is the decision altitude, not the missed approach point, for the LNAV/VNAV approach. Answer (B) is incorrect. The visual descent point (VDP) is 1.5 nautical miles from the threshold for Runway 30. This is not the missed approach point.

197. (Refer to Figure 152 on page 305.) Which of the following best describes BEMXI?

    A. The missed approach point (MAP).

    B. The initial approach fix (IAF).

    C. The final approach fix (FAF).

Answer (C) is correct. *(IFH Chap 2)*
    DISCUSSION: The Maltese cross in the profile view and the letters "FAF" above its designation on the plan view defines BEMXI as the FAF.
    Answer (A) is incorrect. The MAP on a GPS approach procedure is usually the runway threshold, indicated by "RW" and the runway number. This can be identified on both the plan and profile views of the approach chart. Answer (B) is incorrect. The IAFs on a GPS approach procedure are usually depicted in a straight line forming the cross of a "T" shape. They also have the letters "IAF," not "FAF," above their designations on the plan view of the instrument approach chart.

198. (Refer to Figure 152 on page 305.) The correct GPS entry when told by ATC to "expect the GPS approach to runway 30" is

    A. load and activate the approach.

    B. to select the vectors-to-final approach setting.

    C. only load the approach.

Answer (C) is correct. *(AAH Chap 3)*
    DISCUSSION: When ATC tells you to expect a certain approach, select that approach and load it into the flight plan. Once cleared for the approach, it can be activated.
    Answer (A) is incorrect. A pilot should not activate an approach when only told to expect a certain approach. Answer (B) is incorrect. The vectors-to-final feature guides a pilot using vectors along the final approach course as directed by ATC.

199. (Refer to Figure 152 on page 305.) At what point is the pilot authorized to descend below 5,200 feet when cleared to the SUXYO waypoint from the West?

    A. 24 NM from AJCIZ.

    B. 24 NM from SUXYO.

    C. 30 NM from SUXYO.

Answer (B) is correct. *(IPH Chap 5)*
    DISCUSSION: The minimum safe altitude (MSA) that can be flown over SUXYO is 4,600 feet. If you examine the planview of the approach plate, you will see 4,900 in a box above SUXYO and a curved line to the left (or west) of SUXYO. This means that, within 24 NM of SUXYO between 117° and 027°, a pilot can descend to 4,900 feet. To the left (or west) of the box containing 4,900, you will find another box with 5,200. To the left of this box, you will see a curved line indicating that within 30 NM to SUXYO and between 117° and 027°, a pilot can descend to 5,200 feet. Therefore, a pilot can descend to 5,200 feet within 30 NM of SUXYO and can then descend below 5,200 feet to a MSA of 4,900 feet when (s)he is within 24 NM of SUXYO.
    Answer (A) is incorrect. The question asks about SUXYO, not AJCIZ. Answer (C) is incorrect. According to the approach plate, you can descend to, but not below, 5,200 feet at 30 NM from SUXYO. Once you are within 24 NM from SUXYO, you can descend to, but not below, 4,900 feet.

Figure 152. – RNAV (GPS) RWY 30, North Plate Regional Airport Lee Bird Field (LBF).

200. (Refer to Figure 152 on page 307.) What waypoints are designated as fly-over waypoints?

    A. FAF and AGHAN.

    B. Missed approach and AGHAN.

    C. Missed approach and the IAFs.

Answer (B) is correct. *(IPH Chap 5)*
    DISCUSSION: A fly-over waypoint is depicted on an approach plate's planview as a four-pointed star enclosed in a circle. Moreover, a fly-over waypoint precludes any turn until the waypoint is overflown and is followed by either an intercept maneuver of the next flight segment or direct flight to the next waypoint. This type of waypoint is used to denote a missed approach point, a missed approach holding point, or other specific points in space that must be flown over. Both the missed approach waypoint and AGHAN are designated by a four-pointed star enclosed in a circle and are, therefore, fly-over waypoints.
    Answer (A) is incorrect. The FAF point is designated by a four-pointed star but is not enclosed in a circle. Thus, the FAF is a fly-by waypoint, which is a waypoint designed to allow you to anticipate and begin your turn prior to reaching the waypoint, thus providing smoother transitions. Answer (C) is incorrect. The FAF point is designated by a four-pointed star but is not enclosed in a circle. Thus, the FAF is a fly-by waypoint, which is a waypoint designed to allow you to anticipate and begin your turn prior to reaching the waypoint, thus providing smoother transitions.

201. (Refer to Figure 152 on page 307.) Why is there a note stating a temperature limitation for executing this approach with BARO-VNAV equipment?

    A. The descent gradient exceeds the maximum standard of 400-foot per Nautical Mile at low temperatures.

    B. The decision altitude and final approach segment height above obstacles or terrain is unsafe when temperatures are lower than charted.

    C. The missed approach climb gradient exceeds the airplane maximum standard of 40 to 1 at low temperatures.

Answer (B) is correct. *(IPH Chap 5)*
    DISCUSSION: Considering the pronounced effect of cold temperatures, which cause barometric altimeters to substantially over-read, BARO-VNAV operations become unsafe and so a minimum temperature limitation is published for each procedure for which BARO-VNAV minimums are published. This temperature represents the airport temperature below which the use of BARO-VNAV is not authorized to the LNAV/VNAV DA. The note "BARO-VNAV NA below -20°C (-5°F)" implies that the approach may not be flown at all using BARO-VNAV when the temperature is below -20°C. However, BARO-VNAV may be used for approach guidance down to the published LNAV MDA.
    Answer (A) is incorrect. Cold temperatures will not effect the descent gradient indicated by barometric instruments, only the absolute altitude indicated is subject to error. Answer (C) is incorrect. The climb gradient indicated by barometric instruments is not affected by variations in temperature, only the absolute altitude reading is subject to error.

202. (Refer to Figure 152 on page 307.) How do you recognize the missed approach point on the LNAV/VNAV approach?

    A. At the RW30 waypoint.

    B. At the Decision Altitude (DA) for the LPV portion of this approach.

    C. Arrival at the LNAV/VNAV Decision Altitude (DA).

Answer (C) is correct. *(IPH Chap 4, IFH Chaps 7 and 8)*
    DISCUSSION: The LNAV/VNAV DA is published as the missed approach point for the precision approach RNAV GPW RWY 30.
    Answer (A) is incorrect. RW30 is the location of the runway threshold, not the missed approach point. Answer (B) is incorrect. There is no LPV portion for this approach. Note that there are no LPV minimums listed.

Figure 152. – RNAV (GPS) RWY 30, North Platte Regional Airport Lee Bird Field (LBF).

203. The missed approach for the BARO-VNAV and LNAV is initiated at the

    A. decision height.

    B. missed approach point.

    C. final approach fix.

Answer (B) is correct. *(IAP)*
    DISCUSSION: The BARO-VNAV and LNAV approaches are terminated at the missed approach point, which is where the missed approach segment begins.
    Answer (A) is incorrect. There is no decision height published for BARO-VNAV and LNAV approaches. Answer (C) is incorrect. The final approach fix is where the final approach and descent to the runway begins. The missed approach point is where the missed approach segment begins.

204. Which of the following is true concerning GPS approaches?

    A. Handheld GPS receivers are approved in emergency situations.

    B. Terminal mode occurs within 20 NM of the destination airport.

    C. In approach mode, the sensitivity on the CDI changes from 1 NM to 0.3 NM.

Answer (C) is correct. *(AAH Chap 3)*
    DISCUSSION: Approach mode increases the sensitivity on the CDI within 2 NM of the airport from 1 NM to 0.3 NM.
    Answer (A) is incorrect. Handheld receivers are not approved for GPS approaches. They may be referenced in both normal and emergency situations as an aid to situational awareness. Answer (B) is incorrect. Terminal mode occurs within 30 NM of the destination airport, not 20 NM.

205. (Refer to Figure 249 on page 309.) Which type of waypoint is the AGHAN fix?

    A. Computer navigation fix (CNF).

    B. Fly-over waypoint.

    C. Fly-by waypoint.

Answer (C) is correct. *(AIM Para 1-1-18)*
    DISCUSSION: The AGHAN waypoint is not contained within a circle. This indicates a fly-by waypoint.
    Answer (A) is incorrect. CNFs are points used to define the navigational track for an airborne computer system. These include unnamed DME fixes, beginning and ending points of DME arcs, and sensor final approach fixes on some GPS overlay approaches. Answer (B) is incorrect. A fly-over waypoint is symbolized by a waypoint symbol contained within a circle. RW30 is a fly-over waypoint. AGHAN's symbology does not include that circle, so it is a fly-by waypoint.

206. (Refer to Figure 249 on page 309.) You are flying the RNAV(GPS) RWY 30 approach to LBF, over BEMXI, and you receive a RAIM error. You should

    A. Continue to the missed approach point while climbing to 4,900 feet, and then execute the missed approach instructions.

    B. Continue the approach, but descend no lower than the circling minimums.

    C. Continue the approach to published minimums, but complete the approach in 2 minutes or less.

Answer (A) is correct. *(AIM Para 1-1-18)*
    DISCUSSION: If a RAIM failure occurs after the final approach waypoint, the missed approach should be executed immediately. BEMXI is the FAWP on this approach. Climb to 4,900 feet as indicated in the missed approach procedure and fly direct to AGHAN where you will hold.
    Answer (B) is incorrect. Circling minimums do not apply in this situation as the correct response is to execute a missed approach due to a RAIM failure. Answer (C) is incorrect. In this situation, you may not continue to the published approach minimums. You must immediately perform a missed approach due to a RAIM failure.

207. (Refer to Figure 249 on page 309.) At what point is the pilot authorized to descend below 5,300 feet when cleared to the AJCIZ waypoint from the west?

    A. 15 NM from the waypoint.

    B. 6 NM past the waypoint.

    C. 30 NM from the waypoint.

Answer (A) is correct. *(IPH Chap 9, AIM Para 5-4-4)*
    DISCUSSION: When arriving from the west, the IAP shows pilots must maintain at least 5,300 feet between 30 NM and 15 NM from AJCIZ. Within 15 NM from AJCIZ, they may descend to 4,700 feet. This is indicated on the IAP with 5,300 inside the box between the 30 NM line to the 15 NM line near AJCIZ. From the 15 NM line to AJCIZ is 4,700 feet, as indicated on the IAP with 4,700 inside the box.
    Answer (B) is incorrect. The profile view shows that pilots are expected to be at 4,700 feet, not 5,300 feet, when arriving at AJCIZ for an additional 6 NM. Pilots must maintain at least 5,300 feet between 30 NM and 15 NM from AJCIZ. Within 15 NM from AJCIZ, they may descend to 4,700 feet. Answer (C) is incorrect. Pilots must maintain at least 5,300 feet between 30 NM and 15 NM from AJCIZ. Only when they are within 15 NM from AJCIZ, may they descend to 4,700 feet.

Figure 249.

208. Your onboard GPS-based FMS/RNAV unit is IFR certified under TSO-C129 or TSO-C196. Your destination is below minimums for the GPS RNAV approach and you proceed to your filed alternate. You know that

A. GPS units certified under TSO-C129 or TSO-C196 are not authorized for alternate approach requirements; subsequently, you must use an approach procedure based on ground-based NAVAIDs.

B. once diverted to the alternate airport, you may fly a GPS-based approach as long as there is an operational ground-based NAVAID and appropriate airborne receiver for use as a backup.

C. if your aircraft is equipped with a second TSO-C129 certified GPS as a backup in place of a ground-based NAVAID receiver, you may complete the approach even if the IAP is based on ground-based NAVAIDs.

Answer (B) is correct. *(AIM Para 1-1-19)*
DISCUSSION: Any required alternate airport must have an approved instrument approach procedure other than GPS, which is anticipated to be operational and available at the estimated time of arrival and which the aircraft is equipped to fly.

Answer (A) is incorrect. Before a GPS unit can be used for instrument approaches, it has to be authorized by TSO-C129 or TSO-C196. Answer (C) is incorrect. For flight planning purposes, any approved alternate airport must have an approved instrument approach procedure other than GPS.

END OF STUDY UNIT

STUDY UNIT SEVEN
AEROMEDICAL FACTORS

(3 pages of outline)

This study unit contains outlines of major concepts tested, sample test questions and answers regarding aeromedical factors, and an explanation of each answer. The table of contents above lists each subunit within this study unit, the number of questions pertaining to that particular subunit, and the pages on which the outlines and questions begin, respectively.

Recall that the **sole purpose** of this book is to expedite your passing of the FAA pilot knowledge test for the instrument rating. Accordingly, all extraneous material (i.e., topics or regulations not directly tested on the FAA pilot knowledge test) is omitted, even though much more knowledge is necessary to fly safely. This additional material is presented in *Pilot Handbook*, *Aviation Weather and Weather Services*, *FAR/AIM*, and *Instrument Pilot Flight Maneuvers and Practical Test Prep*, available from Gleim Publications, Inc. Order online at www.gleim.com.

7.1 HYPOXIA AND HYPERVENTILATION

1. Hypoxia results from a lack of oxygen in the bloodstream and causes a lack of clear thinking, fatigue, euphoria, and, shortly thereafter, unconsciousness.

2. The following are four types of hypoxia based on their causes:

   a. **Hypoxic hypoxia** is a result of insufficient oxygen available to the body as a whole.

      1) EXAMPLE: Reduction of partial pressure at high altitude, a blocked airway, or drowning

   b. **Hypemic hypoxia** occurs when the blood is not able to take up and transport a sufficient amount of oxygen to the cells in the body. The result is oxygen deficiency in the blood rather than a lack of inhaled oxygen.

      1) EXAMPLE: Carbon monoxide poisoning

   c. **Stagnant hypoxia** results when oxygen-rich blood in the lungs is not moving.

      1) EXAMPLE: Shock, reduced circulation due to extreme cold, or pulling excessive Gs in flight

   d. **Histotoxic hypoxia** is the inability of cells to effectively use oxygen.

      1) EXAMPLE: Impairment due to alcohol and drugs

3. Symptoms of hypoxia include an initial feeling of euphoria but lead to more serious concerns such as headache, delayed reaction time, visual impairment, tunnel vision, bluing of fingernails and lips (cyanosis), and eventual unconsciousness.

   a. Symptoms of hypoxia are difficult to detect before the pilot's reactions are affected.

4. The correct response to counteracting feelings of hypoxia is to lower altitude or use supplemental oxygen.

5. Hyperventilation occurs when an excessive amount of air is breathed into the lungs at an excessive rate.

   a. EXAMPLE: When one becomes excited as a result of stress, fear, or anxiety

b.   Ways to overcome hyperventilation include

1)   Placing a paper bag over your nose and mouth and breathing into it,
2)   Talking aloud, and
3)   Slowing the breathing rate.

7.2 SPATIAL DISORIENTATION

1.   Spatial disorientation (sometimes called vertigo) is a state of temporary confusion resulting from misleading information sent to the brain by various sensory organs.

2.   The best way to overcome the effects of spatial disorientation is to rely on the airplane instruments and ignore body (kinesthetic) signals.

3.   The nervous system often interprets centrifugal force as vertical movement, i.e., rising or falling.

4.   Coriolis illusion is caused by an abrupt head movement in a prolonged constant-rate turn.

a.   This can cause spatial disorientation.

5.   An abrupt change from a climb to straight-and-level flight can create the illusion of tumbling backwards.

6.   A rapid acceleration during takeoff can create the illusion of being in a nose-up attitude.

7.   False horizon is an illusion that is caused by a sloping cloud formation, an obscured horizon, or a dark scene spread with ground lights and stars.

8.   The vestibular system in the inner ear is responsible for most of the illusions leading to spatial disorientation. The vestibular sense (motion sensing) can confuse the pilot.

7.3 VISION AND VISUAL ILLUSION

1.   Pilots should adapt their eyes for night flying by avoiding bright white lights for 30 min. prior to flight.

a.   Thereafter, white light must be avoided because it will cause temporary night blindness and impair night vision adaptation.

2.   The most effective way to scan for other aircraft in daylight is to use a series of short, regularly spaced eye movements that bring successive areas of the sky into your central vision field.

a.   Each movement should not exceed 10°, and each area should be observed for at least 1 second to enable detection.

b.   Only a very small center area of the eye has the ability to send clear, sharply focused messages to the brain. All other areas provide less detail.

c.   At night, however, the eyes are most effective at seeing objects off center. Accordingly, pilots should scan slowly back and forth to facilitate off-center viewing.

3.   Haze can also create the illusion of being a greater distance from the runway, resulting in the pilot's flying a lower-than-normal approach.

4.   A narrower-than-usual runway may create the illusion that the airplane is higher than it actually is.

a.   This illusion results in a lower-than-normal approach.
b.   A wider-than-usual runway creates the opposite illusion and problem.

5.   An upward-sloping runway may create the illusion that the airplane is at a higher-than-actual altitude.

a.   This illusion results in a lower-than-normal approach.
b.   A downward-sloping runway creates the opposite illusion and problem.

7.4 FATIGUE

1. Fatigue is one of the most treacherous hazards to flight safety.

2. The nature of fatigue is such that pilots may not be aware they are feeling the effects of fatigue until after serious errors have been committed.

3. Fatigue can be either acute (short-term) or chronic (long-term).

QUESTIONS AND ANSWER EXPLANATIONS: All of the instrument rating knowledge test questions chosen by the FAA for release as well as additional questions selected by Gleim relating to the material in the previous outlines are reproduced on the following pages. These questions have been organized into the same subunits as the outlines. To the immediate right of each question are the correct answer and answer explanation. You should cover these answers and answer explanations while responding to the questions. Refer to the general discussion in the Introduction on how to take the FAA knowledge test.

Remember that the questions from the FAA knowledge test bank have been reordered by topic and organized into a meaningful sequence. Also, the first line of the answer explanation gives the citation of the authoritative source for the answer.

QUESTIONS

7.1 Hypoxia and Hyperventilation

1. Why is hypoxia particularly dangerous during flights with one pilot?

A. Night vision may be so impaired that the pilot cannot see other aircraft.

B. Symptoms of hypoxia may be difficult to recognize before the pilot's reactions are affected.

C. The pilot may not be able to control the aircraft even if using oxygen.

Answer (B) is correct. *(AIM Para 8-1-2)*
   DISCUSSION: Hypoxia symptoms are gradual, and a pilot may not recognize the symptoms before his or her reactions are affected. Because the symptoms of hypoxia vary with the individual, having two pilots increases the chance of detection before pilot reactions are affected.
   Answer (A) is incorrect. Hypoxia, which is a lack of sufficient oxygen, affects all mental and physical activity, not just night vision. Answer (C) is incorrect. Hypoxia will not occur if supplemental oxygen is used properly.

2. What action should be taken if hyperventilation is suspected?

A. Breathe at a slower rate by taking very deep breaths.

B. Consciously breathe at a slower rate than normal.

C. Consciously force yourself to take deep breaths and breathe at a faster rate than normal.

Answer (B) is correct. *(AIM Para 8-1-3)*
   DISCUSSION: Hyperventilation occurs when abnormally large amounts of air are breathed in and out of the lungs. Early symptoms of hyperventilation and hypoxia are similar and include dizziness, drowsiness, tingling of the fingers and toes, and sensation of body heat. If hyperventilation is suspected, you should consciously breathe at a slower rate than normal.
   Answer (A) is incorrect. Taking deep breaths will only aggravate hyperventilation. Answer (C) is incorrect. Taking deep breaths and breathing at a faster rate than normal is the cause, not the cure, of hyperventilation.

3. If you experience tunnel vision and cyanosis, you may have the symptoms of

A. hypoxia.

B. hyperventilation.

C. carbon monoxide poisoning.

Answer (A) is correct. *(PHAK Chap 16)*
   DISCUSSION: The common symptoms of hypoxia include bluing of the fingernails and lips (cyanosis), headache, delayed reaction time, impaired judgment, euphoria, visual impairment, drowsiness, lightheadedness or dizziness, tingling in the fingers and toes, and numbness. If it becomes worse, tunnel vision begins.
   Answer (B) is incorrect. Hyperventilation is caused by breathing too rapidly. This leads to abnormal loss of carbon dioxide from the blood. Answer (C) is incorrect. The symptoms of carbon monoxide (CO) poisoning include blurred thinking and vision, uneasiness, dizziness, and tightness across the forehead, followed by headache and loss of muscle power. CO is a colorless, odorless gas produced by all combustion engines.

4. Which is not a type of hypoxia?

A. Histotoxic.

B. Hypoxic.

C. Hypertoxic.

Answer (C) is correct. *(PHAK Chap 16)*
DISCUSSION: There is no such thing as hypertoxic hypoxia. The four types of hypoxia are histotoxic, hypoxic, hypemic, and stagnant hypoxia.
Answer (A) is incorrect. The four types of hypoxia are histotoxic, hypoxic, hypemic, and stagnant hypoxia. Answer (B) is incorrect. The four types of hypoxia are histotoxic, hypoxic, hypemic, and stagnant hypoxia.

5. Which of the following is a correct response to counteract the feelings of hypoxia in flight?

A. Promptly descend altitude.

B. Increase cabin air flow.

C. Avoid sudden inhalations.

Answer (A) is correct. *(PHAK Chap 16)*
DISCUSSION: The correct response to counteract feelings of hypoxia is to lower altitude or use supplemental oxygen if the aircraft is so equipped.
Answer (B) is incorrect. Increasing the amount of air flowing inside an aircraft will not help counteract hypoxia. Because of the reduction of partial pressure at higher altitudes, there is less oxygen in the air to draw from. Answer (C) is incorrect. Breathing deeply or suddenly will not counteract feelings of hypoxia.

6. Carbon monoxide poisoning, common in flying as a result of an exhaust leak, is considered what type of hypoxia?

A. Hypemic.

B. Histotoxic.

C. Hypoxic.

Answer (A) is correct. *(PHAK Chap 16)*
DISCUSSION: Carbon monoxide poisoning is an example of hypemic hypoxia in that it creates an oxygen deficiency in the blood.
Answer (B) is incorrect. An example of histotoxic hypoxia, the inability of cells to effectively use oxygen, would be an impairment due to drugs or alcohol. Answer (C) is incorrect. An example of hypoxic hypoxia, a deficiency of oxygen to the body as a whole, would include drowning or a blocked airway.

7. Hyperventilation occurs when

A. an insufficient amount of air is breathed into the lungs.

B. there is a lack of oxygen in the bloodstream.

C. an excessive amount of air is breathed into the lungs.

Answer (C) is correct. *(PHAK Chap 16)*
DISCUSSION: Hyperventilation occurs when an excessive amount of air is breathed into the lungs.
Answer (A) is incorrect. An excessive, not insufficient, amount of air in the lungs is defined as hyperventilation. Answer (B) is incorrect. Hypoxia is a lack of oxygen in the bloodstream.

8. A corrective action to overcome symptoms of hyperventilation is to

A. take quick, deep breaths.

B. lower altitude immediately.

C. slow the breathing rate.

Answer (C) is correct. *(PHAK Chap 16)*
DISCUSSION: Slowing the breathing rate, placing a paper bag over your mouth and nose and breathing into it, or talking aloud are all ways to overcome hyperventilation.
Answer (A) is incorrect. Taking quick, deep breaths will further irritate and increase the feelings of hyperventilation. Answer (B) is incorrect. Lowering the altitude will not have an effect on hyperventilation or its causes.

7.2 Spatial Disorientation

9. The sensations which lead to spatial disorientation during instrument flight conditions

A. are frequently encountered by beginning instrument pilots, but never by pilots with moderate instrument experience.

B. occur, in most instances, during the initial period of transition from visual to instrument flight.

C. must be suppressed and complete reliance placed on the indications of the flight instruments.

Answer (C) is correct. *(AIM Para 8-1-5)*
DISCUSSION: In instrument flight conditions, the only way to prevent spatial disorientation is by visual reference to and reliance on the flight instruments.
Answer (A) is incorrect. Pilots with moderate and even extensive instrument experience can experience spatial disorientation. Answer (B) is incorrect. Spatial disorientation can occur at any time outside visual references are lost. This can happen on a clear day flying in VMC or in IMC.

10. Which system is most likely responsible for a pilot suffering spatial disorientation?

    A. Cardiopulmonary system.

    B. Autokinesis system.

    C. Vestibular system.

Answer (C) is correct. *(IFH Chap 5)*
    DISCUSSION: Spatial disorientation is caused by conflicting signals sent to the brain by the vestibular system and the pilot's eyes.
    Answer (A) is incorrect. The cardiopulmonary system is not responsible for spatial disorientation. Answer (B) is incorrect. Autokinesis is a form of visual illusion that leads to disorientation; it is not a system of the human body.

11. A pilot is more subject to spatial disorientation if

    A. kinesthetic senses are ignored.

    B. eyes are moved often in the process of cross-checking the flight instruments.

    C. body signals are used to interpret flight attitude.

Answer (C) is correct. *(AIM Para 8-1-5)*
    DISCUSSION: Spatial disorientation is a state of temporary confusion resulting from misleading information being sent to the brain by various sensory organs. Thus, the pilot should ignore sensations of muscles and inner ear and kinesthetic senses (those which sense motion).
    Answer (A) is incorrect. Spatial disorientation is prevented/overcome by ignoring the kinesthetic senses. Answer (B) is incorrect. Spatial disorientation is prevented/overcome by using and trusting the flight instruments.

12. Which procedure is recommended to prevent or overcome spatial disorientation?

    A. Reduce head and eye movements to the extent possible.

    B. Rely on the kinesthetic sense.

    C. Rely on the indications of the flight instruments.

Answer (C) is correct. *(AIM Para 8-1-5)*
    DISCUSSION: To overcome the effect of spatial disorientation, pilots should rely entirely on the indications of the flight instruments.
    Answer (A) is incorrect. Although rapid head movements should be avoided, eye movement is necessary for proper scanning of the flight instruments. Answer (B) is incorrect. The kinesthetic sense is creating the problem; i.e., it should be ignored.

13. How can an instrument pilot best overcome spatial disorientation?

    A. Rely on kinesthetic sense.

    B. Use a very rapid cross-check.

    C. Read and interpret the flight instruments, and act accordingly.

Answer (C) is correct. *(IFH Chap 3)*
    DISCUSSION: To overcome spatial disorientation, the IFR pilot should read and interpret the flight instruments and ignore all the body senses.
    Answer (A) is incorrect. The kinesthetic sense is what causes the problem; i.e., it should be ignored. Answer (B) is incorrect. The flight instruments should be read and understood in a deliberate manner, not in haste or panic.

14. How can an instrument pilot best overcome spatial disorientation?

    A. Use a very rapid cross-check.

    B. Properly interpret the flight instruments and act accordingly.

    C. Avoid banking in excess of 30°.

Answer (B) is correct. *(IFH Chap 3)*
    DISCUSSION: To overcome spatial disorientation, the IFR pilot should read and interpret the flight instruments and ignore all the body senses.
    Answer (A) is incorrect. The flight instruments should be read and understood in a deliberate manner, not in haste or panic. Answer (C) is incorrect. Spatial disorientation can also occur in bank angles less than 30°.

15. Abrupt head movement during a prolonged constant rate turn in IMC or simulated instrument conditions can cause

    A. pilot disorientation.

    B. false horizon.

    C. elevator illusion.

Answer (A) is correct. *(AIM Para 8-1-5)*
    DISCUSSION: An abrupt head movement in a prolonged constant-rate turn that has ceased stimulating the motion sensing system can create the illusion of rotation or movement in an entirely different axis. This illusion is called the Coriolis illusion and can lead to spatial disorientation.
    Answer (B) is incorrect. A false horizon is an illusion caused by sloping cloud formations, an obscured horizon, a dark scene spread with ground lights and stars, or certain geometric patterns of ground light. This illusion creates the impression of not being aligned correctly with the actual horizon and can also lead to spatial disorientation. Answer (C) is incorrect. An elevator illusion is caused by an abrupt upward vertical acceleration, usually by an updraft. This illusion can also lead to spatial disorientation.

16. A rapid acceleration during takeoff can create the illusion of

A. spinning in the opposite direction.

B. being in a noseup attitude.

C. diving into the ground.

Answer (B) is correct. *(AIM Para 8-1-5)*
DISCUSSION: A rapid acceleration during takeoff can create the illusion of being in a nose-up attitude. The disoriented pilot will push the airplane into a nose-low, or dive, attitude. This is called a somatogravic illusion.
Answer (A) is incorrect. A proper recovery from a spin that has ceased stimulating the motion sensing system (i.e., inner ear) can create the illusion of spinning in the opposite direction. This is known as a graveyard spin. Answer (C) is incorrect. A rapid deceleration or an abrupt downward vertical acceleration (usually caused by a downdraft) can cause the illusion of a nose-down, or dive, attitude.

17. An abrupt change from climb to straight-and-level flight can create the illusion of

A. tumbling backwards.

B. a noseup attitude.

C. a descent with the wings level.

Answer (A) is correct. *(AIM Para 8-1-5)*
DISCUSSION: An abrupt change from climb to straight-and-level flight can create the illusion of tumbling backwards. The disoriented pilot will push the airplane abruptly into a nose-low attitude, possibly intensifying this illusion, which is called an inversion illusion.
Answer (B) is incorrect. A rapid acceleration during takeoff can create an illusion of being in a nose-up attitude. This is called a somatogravic illusion. Answer (C) is incorrect. An observed loss of altitude during a coordinated constant-rate turn that has ceased stimulating the motion sensing system (i.e., inner ear) can create the illusion of being in a descent with the wings level. This illusion is called a graveyard spiral.

18. A sloping cloud formation, an obscured horizon, and a dark scene spread with ground lights and stars can create an illusion known as

A. elevator illusions.

B. autokinesis.

C. false horizons.

Answer (C) is correct. *(AIM Para 8-1-5)*
DISCUSSION: A sloping cloud formation, an obscured horizon, a dark scene spread with ground lights and stars, and certain geometric patterns of ground light can create an illusion known as false horizons. The disoriented pilot will place the airplane in a dangerous attitude.
Answer (A) is incorrect. Elevator illusions are caused by abrupt upward or downward vertical accelerations, usually by updrafts and downdrafts. These lead to illusions of being in a climb or descent. Answer (B) is incorrect. At night, a static light will appear to move about when stared at for many seconds, creating an illusion known as autokinesis.

19. Abrupt head movement during a prolonged constant rate turn in IMC or simulated instrument conditions can cause

A. Coriolis illusion.

B. elevator illusion.

C. inversion illusion.

Answer (A) is correct. *(AIM Para 8-1-5)*
DISCUSSION: An abrupt head movement in a prolonged constant-rate turn that has ceased stimulating the motion sensing system can create the illusion of rotation or movement in an entirely different axis. This illusion is called the Coriolis illusion and can lead to spatial disorientation.
Answer (B) is incorrect. An elevator illusion is caused by an abrupt upward vertical acceleration, usually by an updraft. This illusion can also lead to spatial disorientation. Answer (C) is incorrect. An inversion illusion is caused by an abrupt change from climb to straight and level flight, which can create the illusion of tumbling backwards. The disoriented pilot will push the aircraft abruptly into a nose low attitude, possibly intensifying this illusion.

20. The sensory system responsible for most of the illusions leading to spatial disorientation is the

A. visual system.

B. vestibular system.

C. postural system.

Answer (B) is correct. *(IFH Chap 3, AIM Para 8-1-5)*
DISCUSSION: The sensory system responsible for most of the illusions leading to spatial disorientation is the vestibular system. The vestibular sense (motion sensing by the inner ear) can confuse the pilot.
Answer (A) is incorrect. Although visual illusions can cause spatial disorientation, the system responsible for most of the illusions leading to spatial disorientation is the vestibular system. Pilots use their visual system to monitor the flight instruments to help prevent spatial disorientation caused by the vestibular system. Answer (C) is incorrect. The postural system involves signals from the skin, muscles, and joints going to the brain. They are not responsible for the majority of illusions leading to spatial disorientation.

21. Without visual aid, a pilot often interprets centrifugal force as a sensation of

A. rising or falling.

B. turning.

C. motion reversal.

Answer (A) is correct. *(IFH Chap 3)*
   DISCUSSION: Nerves in tendons and muscles, including shifting of abdominal muscles, often incorrectly interpret centrifugal force as vertical movement, i.e., rising or falling.
   Answer (B) is incorrect. Centrifugal force is caused by turning but is often misinterpreted as rising or falling. Answer (C) is incorrect. Centrifugal force is caused by turning, not motion reversal.

22. Pilots should take care when retrieving charts or dropped objects in the cockpit to avoid

A. Autokinesis.

B. False horizon.

C. Coriolis illusion.

Answer (C) is correct. *(IFH Chap 5)*
   DISCUSSION: The Coriolis illusion is created by rapid head movements. Pilots should take care when retrieving items like charts or dropped objects in the cockpit and ensure a proper instrument cross check is maintained.
   Answer (A) is incorrect. Autokinesis is the result of staring at an object, not rapid head movement. Answer (B) is incorrect. The false horizon illusion is the result of confusing a sloping cloud formation or shapes on the ground with the horizon.

23. While making prolonged constant-rate turns under IFR conditions, an abrupt head movement can create the illusion of rotation on an entirely different axis. This is known as

A. Coriolis illusion.

B. autokinesis.

C. the leans.

Answer (A) is correct. *(AIM Para 8-1-5)*
   DISCUSSION: An abrupt head movement in a prolonged constant-rate turn that has ceased stimulating the motion sensing system can create the illusion of rotation or movement in an entirely different axis. This illusion is called the Coriolis illusion and can lead to spatial disorientation.
   Answer (B) is incorrect. Autokinesis is a night-flying illusion. In the dark, a static light will appear to move about when stared at for many seconds. The disoriented pilot will lose control of the aircraft in attempting to align it with the light. Answer (C) is incorrect. The leans are caused by an abrupt correction of a banked attitude that has been entered too slowly.

7.3 Vision and Visual Illusion

24. To preserve night vision, the most appropriate cockpit lighting is

A. Reducing the interior lighting intensity to a minimum level.

B. The use of regular white light, such as a flashlight, will not impair night adaptation.

C. Increase the interior intensity to slightly above the outside level.

Answer (A) is correct. *(AIM Para 8-1-6)*
   DISCUSSION: In darkness, vision becomes more sensitive to light, making it possible for the pilot to see distant objects. A pilot can achieve a moderate degree of this dark adaptation within 20 min. under dim red cockpit lighting. White cockpit lighting is required for map and instrument reading, especially when operating under IFR. To maintain some night vision, the interior lighting intensity is to be kept at a minimum level.
   Answer (B) is incorrect. After a pilot's eyes have become adapted to darkness, the pilot must avoid exposing them to any bright white light, which would cause temporary night blindness and impair night adaptation. Answer (C) is incorrect. To maintain some night vision, the interior light intensity should be less than the outside level.

25. What effect does haze have on the ability to see traffic or terrain features during flight?

A. Haze causes the eyes to focus at infinity, making terrain features harder to see.

B. The eyes tend to overwork in haze and do not detect relative movement easily.

C. Haze creates the illusion of being a greater distance than actual from the runway, and causes pilots to fly a lower approach.

Answer (C) is correct. *(AIM Para 8-1-5)*
   DISCUSSION: Haze can create the illusion of being at a greater distance from the runway and often causes pilots to fly a lower approach.
   Answer (A) is incorrect. Haze may cause the condition known as empty-field myopia. This condition results when the pilot has nothing specific to focus on outside the airplane and the eyes relax and focus at a range of about 10 to 30 ft., not infinity. Answer (B) is incorrect. In haze, the eyes tend to relax, not overwork, thus causing empty-field myopia, or looking without seeing.

26. Which statement is correct regarding the use of cockpit lighting for night flight?

A. Reducing the lighting intensity to a minimum level will eliminate blind spots.

B. The use of regular white light, such as a flashlight, will impair night adaptation.

C. Coloration shown on maps is least affected by the use of direct red lighting.

Answer (B) is correct. *(AIM Para 8-1-6)*
DISCUSSION: After a pilot's eyes have become adapted to darkness, the pilot must avoid exposing them to any bright white light, which would cause temporary night blindness and impair night adaptation.
Answer (A) is incorrect. The minimum level of cockpit lighting may be insufficient to read maps, gauges, etc. Answer (C) is incorrect. The colors on maps can be severely distorted when using a red light.

27. Which technique should a pilot use to scan for traffic to the right and left during straight-and-level flight?

A. Systematically focus on different segments of the sky for short intervals.

B. Concentrate on relative movement detected in the peripheral vision area.

C. Continuous sweeping of the windshield from right to left.

Answer (A) is correct. *(AIM Para 8-1-6)*
DISCUSSION: The most effective way to scan for other aircraft during daylight is to use a series of short, regularly spaced eye movements that bring successive areas of the sky into your central vision field. Only a very small center area of the eye has the ability to send clear, sharply focused messages to the brain. All other areas provide less detail.
Answer (B) is incorrect. The peripheral areas do not send sharply focused messages to the brain. Peripheral vision is more effective at night. Answer (C) is incorrect. Concentration for at least 1 second is needed for each 10° sector.

28. Due to visual illusion, when landing on a narrower-than-usual runway, the aircraft will appear to be

A. higher than actual, leading to a lower-than-normal approach.

B. lower than actual, leading to a higher-than-normal approach.

C. higher than actual, leading to a higher-than-normal approach.

Answer (A) is correct. *(AIM Para 8-1-5)*
DISCUSSION: A narrower-than-usual runway may create the illusion that the aircraft is higher than actual, resulting in a lower-than-normal approach.
Answer (B) is incorrect. Wider, not narrower, runways give a lower-than-actual altitude illusion. Answer (C) is incorrect. A higher-than-actual altitude illusion results in a lower-than-usual, not higher-than-usual, approach.

29. What visual illusion creates the same effect as a narrower-than-usual runway?

A. An upsloping runway.

B. A wider-than-usual runway.

C. A downsloping runway.

Answer (A) is correct. *(AIM Para 8-1-5)*
DISCUSSION: Both a narrower-than-usual runway and an upsloping runway may create the illusion that the airplane is at a higher altitude than it actually is. The pilot will fly a lower approach and risk striking obstructions or landing short.
Answer (B) is incorrect. A wider-than-usual runway may create the illusion that the aircraft is at a lower altitude than it actually is, and the unknowing pilot may land hard or overshoot the runway. Answer (C) is incorrect. A downsloping runway may create the illusion that the aircraft is at a lower altitude than it actually is, and the unknowing pilot may land hard or overshoot the runway.

7.4 Fatigue

30. Why is fatigue hazardous to flight safety?

A. The pilot hurries to get done in order to rest.

B. Fatigue may not be apparent to a pilot until serious errors are made (an impaired pilot is a dangerous pilot).

C. The pilot is lazy and rushes to get done quickly.

Answer (B) is correct. *(IFH Chap 3, AIM Para 8-1-1)*
DISCUSSION: Fatigue is one of the most treacherous hazards to flight safety because it may not become apparent to a pilot until serious errors are made.
Answer (A) is incorrect. The risk is not found in the pilot hurrying, but rather the risk is found in the diminished cognitive power that fatigue introduces to the situation, sometimes causing pilots to make serious errors before they realize how fatigued they are. Answer (C) is incorrect. The risk is not found in the pilot being lazy or rushing to complete a series of tasks, but rather the risk is found in the diminished cognitive power that fatigue introduces to the situation, sometimes causing pilots to make serious errors before they realize how fatigued they are.

END OF STUDY UNIT

STUDY UNIT EIGHT
AVIATION WEATHER

(9 pages of outline)

This study unit contains outlines of major concepts tested, sample test questions and answers regarding aviation weather, and an explanation of each answer. The table of contents above lists each subunit within this study unit, the number of questions pertaining to that particular subunit, and the pages on which the outlines and questions begin, respectively.

Recall that the **sole purpose** of this book is to expedite your passing of the FAA pilot knowledge test for the instrument rating. Accordingly, all extraneous material (i.e., topics or regulations not directly tested on the FAA pilot knowledge test) is omitted, even though much more knowledge is necessary to fly safely. This additional material is presented in *Pilot Handbook, Aviation Weather and Weather Services, FAR/AIM,* and *Instrument Pilot Flight Maneuvers and Practical Test Prep,* available from Gleim Publications, Inc. Order online at www.gleim.com.

8.1 CAUSES OF WEATHER

1. Every physical process of weather is accompanied by, or is the result of, heat exchanges.

2. Unequal heating of the Earth's surface causes differences in pressure and, thus, altimeter settings.

   a. On weather maps, the lines drawn to connect points of equal pressure show pressure contours called **isobars**.

3. Three of the forces at work on winds are discussed below.

   a. The pressure gradient force causes wind to flow from an area of high pressure to one of low pressure.

      1) This flow is thus perpendicular to the isobars.

   b. Coriolis force deflects winds to the right in the Northern Hemisphere. Coriolis force is a result of the Earth's rotation.

      1) The Coriolis force is at a right angle to wind direction and directly proportional to wind speed. Its effect is more forceful at greater altitudes (above approximately 2,000 ft. AGL) because surface winds are slowed by friction.

      2) It deflects winds so strongly that they flow parallel to isobars.

   c. Friction with the Earth's surface weakens the wind.

      1) Since these winds are slower, they are less affected by Coriolis force. The pressure gradient becomes stronger than Coriolis force, and the wind flows across, rather than parallel to, the isobars.

      2) Friction is what causes winds to be greater at higher altitudes than at the surface.

4.   An **air mass** is an extensive body of air having uniform moisture and temperature properties.

5.   The average height of the layer of the Earth's atmosphere called the **troposphere** is about 37,000 ft. in mid-latitudes. It varies between approximately 25,000 ft. at the poles to 65,000 ft. at the equator.

6.   The boundary between the troposphere and the stratosphere is the thin layer called the **tropopause**.

    a.   Temperature and wind vary greatly in the vicinity of the tropopause.
    b.   It is associated with an abrupt change in the temperature lapse rate.

7.   The **stratosphere** is the layer of atmosphere above the tropopause.

    a.   It is characterized by low moisture content and absence of clouds.
    b.   It has relatively small changes in temperature with an increase in altitude.

8.   The **jet stream** is a narrow, disjointed, wandering "river" of maximum winds.

    a.   It moves with pressure ridges and troughs in the upper atmosphere near the tropopause.
    b.   It blows from a generally westerly direction and, by definition, has a speed of 50 kt. or more.
    c.   The jet stream is normally weaker and farther north in the summer.
    d.   The jet stream is normally stronger and farther south in the winter.

9.   A **front** is the zone of transition between two air masses of different temperature, humidity, and wind.

    a.   There is always a change in wind when you fly across a front.
    b.   The threat of low-level wind shear occurs just before the warm front passes the airport.
    c.   With a cold front, the most critical period for wind shear occurs just as or just after the cold front passes the airport.

10.   Frontal waves and cyclones (and areas of low pressure) usually form in slow-moving cold fronts or in stationary fronts.

11.   Squall lines usually develop ahead of a cold front.

8.2 STABILITY OF AIR MASSES

1.   The **lapse rate** is a measure of how much temperature decreases (or possibly increases) with an increase in altitude. This is the actual temperature change associated with increases in altitude and sometimes is referred to as the **ambient lapse rate**.

    a.   In contrast to the ambient or actual lapse rate is the **adiabatic lapse rate**. The adiabatic, or "expansional cooling" lapse rate, is the temperature decrease due only to expansion of air as it rises. The adiabatic lapse rate means no heat gain or loss -- just a decrease in temperature because of expansion.

        1)   The dry adiabatic lapse rate is 3°C per 1,000 ft.
        2)   The adiabatic lapse rate varies from about 1.1°C to 2.8°C based on moisture content of the air.
        3)   The average adiabatic lapse rate is 2°C per 1,000 ft.

2.   The ambient lapse rate can thus be used by pilots to determine the stability of air masses.

    a.   The greater the ambient lapse rate (more than 2°C per 1,000 ft.) and the higher the humidity, the more unstable the air -- and the more thunderstorms can be expected.
    b.   Moist air is less stable than dry air because it cools adiabatically at a slower rate, which means that moist air must rise higher before its temperature cools to that of the air around it (i.e., cumulus build-up).

3. Cloud formation after lifting is determined by the stability of the air before lifting.

 a. Turbulence and clouds with vertical development (cumuliform) result when unstable air rises (due to convective currents).

 b. Moist, stable air moving up a mountain slope produces stratiform clouds as it cools.

 1) Unstable air moving up a mountain slope produces clouds with extensive vertical development.

4. When a cold air mass moves over a warm surface, heating from below provides unstable lifting action, giving rise to cumuliform clouds, turbulence, and good visibility.

5. The growth rate of precipitation is enhanced by upward air currents carrying water droplets upward where condensation increases droplet size.

6. Stable air characteristics

 a. Stratiform clouds and fog
 b. Smooth air
 c. Continuous (steady) precipitation
 d. Fair-to-poor visibility in haze and smoke

7. Unstable air characteristics

 a. Cumuliform clouds
 b. Turbulent air
 c. Showery precipitation
 d. Good visibility

8.3 TEMPERATURE INVERSIONS

1. Normally, temperature decreases as altitude increases. A temperature inversion occurs when temperature increases as altitude increases.

2. Temperature inversions usually result in a stable layer of warm air below the inversion.

3. A temperature inversion often develops near the ground on clear, cool nights when the wind is light.

 a. It is caused by terrestrial radiation.

4. Smooth air with restricted visibility (due to fog, haze, or low clouds) is usually found beneath a low-level temperature inversion.

8.4 TEMPERATURE, DEW POINT, AND FOG

1. When the temperature-dew point spread is 3°C (5°F) or less and decreasing, you should expect fog and/or low clouds.

2. Air temperature largely determines how much water vapor can be held by the air.

 a. **Dew point** is the temperature at which the air will be saturated with moisture, i.e., 100% humidity.

3. Frost forms when the temperature of the collecting surface (e.g., the airplane) is below the dew point of the surrounding air and the dew point is below freezing (0°C or 32°F).

4. Water vapor becomes visible as it condenses into clouds, fog, or dew.

 a. **Evaporation** is the conversion of liquid water to water vapor.
 b. **Sublimation** is the conversion of ice to water vapor or water vapor to ice.

5. **Radiation fog** is most likely to occur when there is a clear sky, little or no wind, and a small temperature-dew point spread over a land surface (especially low, flatland areas).

    a. As the ground cools rapidly due to radiation, the air close to the surface cools more quickly than slightly higher air.

        1) This is the most frequent type of surface-based temperature inversion.

    b. As the air reaches its dew point, radiation fog forms.

6. **Advection fog** forms as a result of moist air condensing as it moves over a colder surface (i.e., water or ground).

    a. It requires wind to force the movement.

    b. Advection fog is most likely to occur in coastal areas, when air moves inland from the coast in winter.

7. **Upslope fog** results from warm, moist air being cooled as it is forced up sloping terrain.

8. **Precipitation-induced fog** results from warm fronts (warmer air over cooler air), i.e., when warm rain or drizzle falls through the cooler air.

    a. Evaporation from the precipitation saturates the cooler air, causing fog.

9. Fog can also form easily in industrial areas where combustion pollution provides a high concentration of condensation nuclei (tiny particles on which moisture can condense as the air cools).

8.5 CLOUDS

1. Clouds are divided into four families based on their height:

    a. High clouds (consist of ice crystals and do not pose an icing threat)
    b. Middle clouds
    c. Low clouds
    d. Clouds with extensive vertical development

2. Lifting action, unstable air, and moisture are the ingredients for the formation of cumulonimbus clouds.

    a. Fair weather cumulus clouds form in convective currents and often indicate turbulence at and below the cloud level.
    b. Nimbus means rain cloud.
    c. Towering cumulus is an early stage of cumulonimbus.
    d. The greatest turbulence is in cumulonimbus clouds (thunderstorms).

3. Standing lenticular altocumulus clouds (ACSL) are almond or lens-shaped and form on the crests of waves created by barriers in the wind flow (e.g., on the leeward side of a mountain).

    a. The presence of these clouds indicates very strong turbulence.

8.6 THUNDERSTORMS

1. Thunderstorms have three phases in their life cycle:

    a. **Cumulus** -- the building stage of a thunderstorm when there are continuous updrafts
    b. **Mature** -- the time of greatest intensity when there are both updrafts and downdrafts (causing severe wind shear and turbulence)

        1) The commencing of rain on the Earth's surface indicates the beginning of the mature stage of a thunderstorm.

    c. **Dissipating** -- characterized predominantly by downdrafts; i.e., the phase of the storm raining itself out

2. A thunderstorm, by definition, always has lightning, because lightning causes thunder.

   a. Lightning strikes are most common when operating with an outside air temperature (OAT) of between −5°C and +5°C.

3. Thunderstorms are produced by cumulonimbus clouds. They form when there is

   a. Sufficient water vapor
   b. An unstable lapse rate
   c. An initial upward boost (i.e., a lifting action) to start the process

4. Thunderstorms produce wind shear turbulence, a hazardous and invisible phenomenon, particularly for airplanes landing and taking off.

   a. If a thunderstorm is penetrated, a pilot should fly straight ahead, set power for recommended turbulence penetration airspeed, and attempt to maintain a level attitude.

5. The most severe thunderstorm conditions (heavy hail, destructive winds, tornadoes, etc.) are generally associated with squall line thunderstorms.

   a. A **squall line** is a nonfrontal, narrow band of thunderstorms usually ahead of a cold front.

6. A **squall** (not squall line) is defined as a sudden increase in wind speed of at least 16 kt., the speed rising to 22 kt. or more and lasting at least 1 min.

7. Embedded thunderstorms are obscured because they occur in very cloudy conditions or thick haze layers.

8. Airborne weather-avoidance radar detects only precipitation drops. It does not detect minute cloud droplets (i.e., clouds and fog).

   a. Thus, airborne weather-avoidance radar provides no assurance of avoiding instrument weather conditions.

8.7 ICING

1. Structural icing requires two conditions:

   a. Flight through visible moisture
   b. The temperature at freezing or below

2. Freezing rain usually causes the greatest accumulation of structural ice.

   a. Freezing rain indicates that temperatures are above freezing at some higher altitude.
   b. Supercooled Large Droplets (SLD) can accrue even if SLD droplets are not being observed at the surface.

      1) A visible symptom of supercooled water droplets is a buildup of ice forward of an unheated propeller spinner, but not extending back past the blades.

3. Ice pellets are caused when rain droplets freeze at a higher altitude; i.e., freezing rain exists above.

4. Heavy, wet snow indicates the temperature is above freezing at your altitude.

   a. Snow that is heavy and wet formed above you but is on the verge of melting.

5. Frost on wings disrupts the airflow over the wings, causing early airflow separation and resulting in a loss of lift. It should be removed before flight is attempted.

   a. Small patches of ice or frost can result in localized, asymmetrical stalls on the wing, which can then result in roll control problems during liftoff.
   b. The only way to ensure the wing is free of critical ice is to perform a tactile inspection. This type of inspection is valuable for detecting critical ice. By physically touching the surface, any fine contaminants not easily visible can be detected.

6.   Test data indicate that ice, snow, or frost having a thickness and roughness similar to medium or coarse sandpaper on the leading edge and upper surface of a wing can reduce wing lift by as much as 30% and increase drag by 40%.

    a.   When ice does accumulate, it is harder to remove from the upper surface of the wing than the leading edge. Generally speaking, smooth ice on top of the wing is more dangerous than heavy accumulated icing on the leading edge.

7.   With a standard (average) temperature lapse rate of 2°C per 1,000 ft., the freezing level can be determined by knowing the current temperature and elevation.

    a.   EXAMPLE: At a field elevation of 1,350 ft. MSL, the temperature is +8°C. To reach the freezing level, the temperature must drop 8°C. Thus the freezing level is 4,000 ft. (8°C ÷ 2°C/1,000 ft.) above field elevation, or 5,350 ft. MSL (1,350 + 4,000).

8.   When conditions favoring the formation of ice are present, pilots should check for ice accumulation prior to flight by using a flashlight to scan the surface of the airframe and watch for light reflections.

    a.   Ice on the surface of the wing is virtually undetectable and causes a reduction in lift over the wing.

    b.   Narrow objects tend to pick up ice that is visually detectable. Ice accumulation on the air temperature probe or on a pitot tube (of a high-wing airplane) would be the first area that the pilot would observe ice buildup.

9.   Ice tends to accumulate on small and narrow parts of the aircraft before others. The most susceptible surface of the airframe to accumulate icing is the tailplane due to its position being outside the visual range as well as its thin, simple shape.

    a.   A tailplane stall as the result of ice accumulation is most likely to occur during the extension of the flaps to the landing position. Thus, tailplane stalls due to icing are mostly likely during the approach and landing phase of flight.

    b.   Any of the following symptoms, occurring singly or in combination, may be a warning of tailplane icing:

        1)   Elevator control pulsing, oscillations, or vibrations

        2)   Abnormal nose-down trim change

        3)   Any other unusual or abnormal pitch anomalies (possibly resulting in pilot induced oscillations)

        4)   Reduction or loss of elevator effectiveness

        5)   Sudden change in elevator force (control would move nose-down if unrestrained)

        6)   Sudden uncommanded nose-down pitch

    c.   To recover from a tailplane stall, you should retract the flaps to the last safe position and increase power only to the extent that you compensate for the loss of lift created from retracting the flaps.

        1)   Over-increasing the power can aggravate and deepen a tailplane stall in some aircraft.

10.   Another serious result of icing is uncommanded roll due to ice accumulation forward of the ailerons.

    a.   The following procedures apply if you experience roll upset while flying in icing conditions:

        1)   Reduce the angle of attack (AOA) by increasing airspeed or extending wing flaps to the first setting if at or below the flaps extend speed (V_{FE}). If in a turn, roll wings level.

        2)   Set appropriate power and monitor the airspeed/AOA. A controlled descent is a vastly better alternative than an uncontrolled descent.

    3)   If flaps are extended, do not retract them unless it can be determined that the upper surface of the airfoil is clear of ice, because retracting the flaps will increase the AOA at a given airspeed.

    4)   Verify that wing ice protection is functioning normally and symmetrically by visual observation of the left and right wing. If not, follow manufacturer's instructions.

11.   If you detect icing accumulation in flight, especially if the aircraft is not equipped with a deicing system, you should leave the area of precipitation, if you are able, or fly to an altitude where the ambient temperature is above freezing.

    a.   Be aware that warmer temperatures are not always found at lower altitudes. In the case of a temperature inversion, for instance, warmer air will be above rather than below.

12.   In an aircraft equipped with a pneumatic deicing system, the appropriate technique for removing ice is to operate the pneumatic deicing system several times.

    a.   This technique will clear accumulated ice as well as residual ice left behind between system cycles.

    b.   The FAA recommends that the deicing system be activated at the first indication of icing rather than after any significant amount of ice is allowed to accumulate.

    1)   Because some residual ice continues to adhere between pneumatic boot system cycles, the wing is never entirely "clean."

    2)   The amount of residual ice increases as airspeed and/or temperature decrease due to the more favorable conditions for ice accumulation associated with these conditions.

    3)   At airspeeds typical of small airplanes, it may take many boot cycles to effectively shed the ice.

13.   Supercooled Large Droplets (SLD) are supercooled droplets with a diameter greater than 50 micrometers (0.05 mm). SLD conditions include freezing drizzle drops and freezing raindrops.

    a.   Ice may become visible on the upper or lower surface of the wing, aft of the active part of the deicing boots. Pilots should look for irregular or jagged lines of ice or for pieces of ice shedding off the airplane. During night operations, adequate illumination should be used to observe all areas. On most airplanes, the last inch of the deicing boot is inactive.

    b.   Vigilance for SLD ice accretions should be exercised when flying into or over areas reporting precipitation at the surface, such as rain, freezing rain, sleet, ice pellets, drizzle, freezing drizzle, or snow, where temperatures are near freezing.

    c.   Pilots should be aware that SLD could occur aloft without any SLD precipitation on the surface.

    d.   Current weather information can miss SLD, so it is important to know and watch for cues on the airplane.

14.   Pilots may consider periodically disengaging the autopilot and hand flying the airplane when operating in icing conditions.

    a.   If this is not desirable due to cockpit workload levels, pilots should monitor the autopilot closely for abnormal trim, trim rate, or airplane attitude.

    b.   As ice builds up on aircraft without auto-throttles, the autopilot will attempt to hold altitude without regard for airspeed, leading to a potential stall situation.

8.8 WIND SHEAR

1. **Wind shear** is any change in wind velocity (speed and/or direction).

    a.   If the change is abrupt and of more than slight magnitude, it can be an extreme hazard to flight.

    b.   A characteristic of low-level wind shear associated with a low-level temperature inversion is an increase in airspeed during climbout and while on approach.

        1)   To reduce the risk of inadvertent stalls, pilots are advised to improve their awareness of normal climbout pitch attitude and to put less emphasis on strict airspeed control.

2. Wind shear can occur at any level in the atmosphere and be horizontal and/or vertical; i.e., it occurs wherever adjacent air flows in different directions and/or at different speeds.

3. Wind shear is an atmospheric condition that may be associated with a low-level temperature inversion, a jet stream, or a frontal zone.

4. **Light turbulence** momentarily causes slight, erratic changes in altitude and/or attitude.

5. **Severe turbulence** and wind shear may be found on all sides of a thunderstorm, including directly beneath it and as much as 20 mi. laterally.

6. Hazardous wind shear is commonly encountered near the ground during periods of strong temperature inversion and near thunderstorms.

    a.   Expect wind shear in a temperature inversion whenever wind speed at 2,000 to 4,000 ft. AGL is 25 kt. or more.

    b.   When going through the inversion, allow airspeed to go above normal climb and approach speed.

8.9 MICROBURSTS

1. Microbursts are small-scale intense downdrafts that, on reaching the surface, spread outward in all directions from the downdraft center. This causes the presence of both vertical and horizontal wind shears that can be extremely hazardous to all types and categories of aircraft, especially at low altitudes.

2. Parent clouds producing microburst activity can be any of the low or middle layer convective cloud types.

    a.   Microbursts commonly occur within the heavy rain portion of thunderstorms but also occur in much weaker, benign-appearing convective cells that have little or no precipitation reaching the ground.

3. The life cycle of a microburst as it descends in a convective rain shaft is illustrated below.

    a.   "T" is the time the microburst strikes the ground.

4. Characteristics of microbursts include

    a. Size. The microburst downdraft is typically less than 1 mi. in diameter as it descends from the cloud base to about 1,000-3,000 ft. above the ground.

        1) In the transition zone near the ground, the downdraft changes to a horizontal outflow that can extend to approximately 2 1/2 mi. in diameter.

    b. Intensity. The downdrafts can be as strong as 6,000 fpm.

        1) Horizontal winds near the surface can be as strong as 45 kt., resulting in a 90-kt. shear (headwind to tailwind change for a traversing aircraft) across the microburst.

        2) These strong horizontal winds occur within a few hundred feet of the ground.

    c. Visual signs. Microbursts can be found almost anywhere there is convective activity.

        1) They may be embedded in heavy rain associated with a thunderstorm or in light rain in benign-appearing virga.

        2) When there is little or no precipitation at the surface accompanying the microburst, a ring of blowing dust may be the only visual clue of its existence.

    d. Duration. An individual microburst will seldom last longer than 15 min. from the time it strikes the ground until dissipation.

        1) An important consideration for pilots is that the microburst intensifies for about 5 min. after it strikes the ground, with the maximum-intensity winds lasting approximately 2 to 4 min.

        2) Once microburst activity starts, multiple microbursts in the same general area are not uncommon and should be expected.

        3) Sometimes microbursts are concentrated into a line structure, and under these conditions, activity may continue for as long as an hour.

5. Microburst wind shear may create a severe hazard for aircraft within 1,000 ft. of the ground, particularly during the approach to landing and landing and takeoff phases.

    a. The aircraft may encounter a headwind (performance increasing) followed by a downdraft and tailwind (both performance decreasing), possibly resulting in terrain impact.

    b. See Figure 13 below.

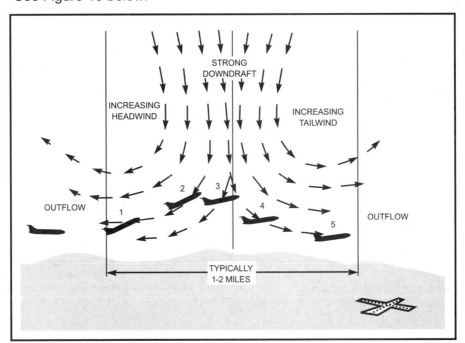

Figure 13. – Microburst Section Chart.

QUESTIONS AND ANSWER EXPLANATIONS: All of the instrument rating knowledge test questions chosen by the FAA for release as well as additional questions selected by Gleim relating to the material in the previous outlines are reproduced on the following pages. These questions have been organized into the same subunits as the outlines. To the immediate right of each question are the correct answer and answer explanation. You should cover these answers and answer explanations while responding to the questions. Refer to the general discussion in the Introduction on how to take the FAA knowledge test.

Remember that the questions from the FAA knowledge test bank have been reordered by topic and organized into a meaningful sequence. Also, the first line of the answer explanation gives the citation of the authoritative source for the answer.

QUESTIONS

8.1 Causes of Weather

1. The primary cause of all changes in the Earth's weather is

    A. variation of solar energy received by the Earth's regions.

    B. changes in air pressure over the Earth's surface.

    C. movement of the air masses.

Answer (A) is correct. *(AvW Chap 2)*
    DISCUSSION: Every physical process of weather is accompanied by, or is the result of, a heat exchange. Unequal solar heating of the Earth's surface causes differences in air pressure, which result in all changes in the Earth's weather.
    Answer (B) is incorrect. Changes in air pressure are a result of varying temperatures. Answer (C) is incorrect. Movement of air masses (wind) is a result of varying temperatures and pressures.

2. Which force, in the Northern Hemisphere, acts at a right angle to the wind and deflects it to the right until parallel to the isobars?

    A. Centrifugal.

    B. Pressure gradient.

    C. Coriolis.

Answer (C) is correct. *(AvW Chap 4)*
    DISCUSSION: Coriolis force is a result of the Earth's rotation. As the wind moves perpendicular to the isobars (from high to low pressure), it is apparently deflected to the right in the Northern Hemisphere, until it is moving parallel to the isobars. This effect is most pronounced above 2,000 ft. AGL.
    Answer (A) is incorrect. Centrifugal force is a force that acts outwardly on any object moving in a curved path. Answer (B) is incorrect. Pressure gradient causes the wind to move perpendicular to the isobars. The wind is then deflected by Coriolis force.

3. What relationship exists between the winds at 2,000 feet above the surface and the surface winds?

    A. The winds at 2,000 feet and the surface winds flow in the same direction, but the surface winds are weaker due to friction.

    B. The winds at 2,000 feet tend to parallel the isobars while the surface winds cross the isobars at an angle toward lower pressure and are weaker.

    C. The surface winds tend to veer to the right of the winds at 2,000 feet and are usually weaker.

Answer (B) is correct. *(AvW Chap 4)*
    DISCUSSION: Generally, winds near the surface are weaker than those aloft due to the friction between the Earth's surface and the wind. Also, because they are slower, winds near the surface are less affected by the Coriolis force. The pressure gradient forces are thus stronger near the surface, and the winds cross the isobars at an angle instead of flowing parallel to them.
    Answer (A) is incorrect. The Coriolis force is less at the surface, so surface winds flow in a direction different from those aloft. Answer (C) is incorrect. The winds aloft veer to the right of surface winds, not the opposite.

4. Winds at 5,000 feet AGL on a particular flight are southwesterly while most of the surface winds are southerly. This difference in direction is primarily due to

    A. a stronger pressure gradient at higher altitudes.

    B. friction between the wind and the surface.

    C. stronger Coriolis force at the surface.

Answer (B) is correct. *(AvW Chap 4)*
    DISCUSSION: Southerly winds at the surface will become southwesterly winds at 5,000 ft. because the Coriolis force deflects winds aloft to the right. This force has less effect on surface winds which have been slowed by friction with the Earth's surface.
    Answer (A) is incorrect. The pressure differentials are approximately uniform through the altitudes. Answer (C) is incorrect. The Coriolis force at the surface is weaker with slower wind speed.

5. What causes surface winds to flow across the isobars at an angle rather than parallel to the isobars?

A. Coriolis force.

B. Surface friction.

C. The greater density of the air at the surface.

Answer (B) is correct. *(AvW Chap 4)*
   DISCUSSION: Generally, winds near the surface are weaker than those aloft due to the friction between the Earth's surface and the wind. Also, because they are slower, winds near the surface are less affected by the Coriolis force. The pressure gradient forces are thus stronger near the surface, and the winds cross the isobars at an angle instead of flowing parallel to them.
   Answer (A) is incorrect. The Coriolis force is directly proportional to wind speed. At higher altitudes (above 2,000 to 3,000 ft. AGL), winds not slowed by surface friction are so deflected by the Coriolis force that they flow parallel to the isobars, not across them. Answer (C) is incorrect. The greater air density at the surface has little effect on the relationship of winds to the isobars.

6. An air mass is a body of air that

A. has similar cloud formations associated with it.

B. creates a wind shift as it moves across the Earth's surface.

C. covers an extensive area and has fairly uniform properties of temperature and moisture.

Answer (C) is correct. *(AvW Chap 8)*
   DISCUSSION: An air mass is an extensive body of air within which the conditions of temperature and moisture in a horizontal plane are essentially uniformly distributed. Generally, an air mass takes on the properties of the large area it overlies.
   Answer (A) is incorrect. An air mass may have cloud formations or it may be clear and dry. Answer (B) is incorrect. Changes in wind, temperature, etc., indicate a frontal zone between two air masses.

7. A characteristic of the stratosphere is

A. an overall decrease of temperature with an increase in altitude.

B. a relatively even base altitude of approximately 35,000 feet.

C. relatively small changes in temperature with an increase in altitude.

Answer (C) is correct. *(AvW Chap 1)*
   DISCUSSION: The stratosphere is the atmospheric layer above the tropopause. It is the band of altitude from about 7 to 22 mi. It is characterized by a slight average increase in temperature from base to top and thus is very stable. It also has a low moisture content and an absence of clouds.
   Answer (A) is incorrect. There is a slight increase, not decrease, in temperature with increase in altitude. Answer (B) is incorrect. The base of the stratosphere is considerably higher at the equator than at the poles.

8. A jet stream is defined as wind of

A. 30 knots or greater.

B. 40 knots or greater.

C. 50 knots or greater.

Answer (C) is correct. *(AvW Chap 13)*
   DISCUSSION: The jet stream is a roughly horizontal stream of wind of 50 kt. or more (by definition) concentrated within a narrow band embedded in the westerly winds in the high troposphere. It occurs in an area of intensified pressure gradients. A second or even third jet stream may form at one time, and these may not be continuous.
   Answer (A) is incorrect. A jet stream, by definition, is a wind of 50 kt., not 30 kt., or greater. Answer (B) is incorrect. A jet stream, by definition, is a wind of 50 kt., not 40 kt., or greater.

9. The average height of the troposphere in the middle latitudes is

A. 20,000 feet.

B. 25,000 feet.

C. 37,000 feet.

Answer (C) is correct. *(AvW Chap 1)*
   DISCUSSION: In the mid-latitudes, the average height of the troposphere is about 37,000 ft. It is 25,000 to 30,000 ft. at the poles and 55,000 to 65,000 ft. at the equator. It is generally higher in summer than in winter.
   Answer (A) is incorrect. The average height of the troposphere is 25,000 to 30,000 ft. at the poles, not the mid-latitudes. Answer (B) is incorrect. The average height of the troposphere is 25,000 to 30,000 ft. at the poles, not the mid-latitudes.

10. The strength and location of the jet stream is normally

A. stronger and farther north in the winter.

B. weaker and farther north in the summer.

C. stronger and farther north in the summer.

Answer (B) is correct. *(AvW Chap 13)*
   DISCUSSION: In the mid-latitudes, the wind speed in the jet stream averages considerably less in the summer than in the winter. Also, the jet stream shifts farther north in summer than in winter.
   Answer (A) is incorrect. The jet stream is usually farther south, not north, in winter. Answer (C) is incorrect. The jet stream is usually weaker, not stronger, in summer.

11. Which feature is associated with the tropopause?

A. Absence of wind and turbulent conditions.

B. Absolute upper limit of cloud formation.

C. Abrupt change in temperature lapse rate.

Answer (C) is correct. *(AvW Chap 13)*
   DISCUSSION: The tropopause is the transition layer of atmosphere between the troposphere (surface to about 7 to 22 mi.) and the stratosphere. A characteristic of the tropopause is that there is an abrupt change in the temperature lapse rate, i.e., the rate at which temperature decreases with height.
   Answer (A) is incorrect. There are usually very strong winds in the tropopause. These create narrow zones of wind shear, which may generate hazardous turbulence. Answer (B) is incorrect. Clouds may form above the tropopause even though there is little moisture in the stratosphere.

12. Which weather phenomenon is always associated with the passage of a frontal system?

A. A wind change.

B. An abrupt decrease in pressure.

C. Clouds, either ahead or behind the front.

Answer (A) is correct. *(AvW Chap 8)*
   DISCUSSION: Whenever a front passes, a wind shift will always occur. This discontinuity may be in direction, speed, or both.
   Answer (B) is incorrect. The pressure and/or temperature may not change significantly as a weak front passes. Answer (C) is incorrect. Some fronts do not contain enough moisture to produce clouds. Therefore, clouds are not always associated with a frontal system.

13. Which is a characteristic of low-level wind shear as it relates to frontal activity?

A. With a warm front, the most critical period is before the front passes the airport.

B. With a cold front, the most critical period is just before the front passes the airport.

C. Turbulence will always exist in wind-shear conditions.

Answer (A) is correct. *(PHAK Chap 11)*
   DISCUSSION: Wind shear associated with a warm front occurs above an airport before the front passes the airport. A warm front is warmer air overtaking colder air.
   Answer (B) is incorrect. Cold front wind shear occurs just as or just after the front passes rather than before it passes. Answer (C) is incorrect. Wind shear can sometimes occur with no forewarning from turbulence.

14. Frontal waves normally form on

A. slow moving cold fronts or stationary fronts.

B. slow moving warm fronts and strong occluded fronts.

C. rapidly moving cold fronts or warm fronts.

Answer (A) is correct. *(AvW Chap 8)*
   DISCUSSION: Frontal waves and cyclones (areas of low pressure) usually form in slow-moving cold fronts or in stationary fronts.
   Answer (B) is incorrect. Frontal waves are usually not associated with warm fronts or occluded fronts. Answer (C) is incorrect. Frontal waves usually form on slow-moving, not rapidly moving, cold fronts and not on warm fronts.

15. Where do squall lines most often develop?

A. In an occluded front.

B. In a cold air mass.

C. Ahead of a cold front.

Answer (C) is correct. *(AvW Chap 11)*
   DISCUSSION: A squall line is a nonfrontal band of active thunderstorms that sometimes develops ahead of a cold front.
   Answer (A) is incorrect. Squall lines are usually associated with a fast-moving cold front. Answer (B) is incorrect. They occur ahead of the cold front, not behind the front in the cold air.

16. When compared to winds at the surface, winds at 2,000 feet are

A. higher due to friction.

B. higher and go at right angles to the isobars due to friction.

C. higher because they move from an area of higher pressure to lower pressure.

Answer (A) is correct. *(AvW)*
   DISCUSSION: Friction between the wind and the terrain surface slows the wind. The rougher the terrain, the greater the frictional effect.
   Answer (B) is incorrect. Although the winds are higher at 2,000 feet than they are at the surface, friction does not cause them to cross the isobars at right angles. It is the pressure gradient that forces the winds to cross the isobars in search of lower pressure. Answer (C) is incorrect. Although the winds at altitude are higher and do seek lower pressure, it is the action of friction at the surface that slows the winds at the surface. The rougher the terrain, the greater the frictional effect.

8.2 Stability of Air Masses

17. Which are characteristics of an unstable cold air mass moving over a warm surface?

   A. Cumuliform clouds, turbulence, and poor visibility.

   B. Cumuliform clouds, turbulence, and good visibility.

   C. Stratiform clouds, smooth air, and poor visibility.

Answer (B) is correct. *(AvW Chap 8)*
    DISCUSSION: When a cold air mass moves over a warm surface, the warm air near the surface rises and creates an unstable situation. These convective currents give rise to cumuliform clouds, turbulence, and good visibility.
    Answer (A) is incorrect. Unstable air lifts and blows haze away, resulting in good, not poor, visibility. Answer (C) is incorrect. Unstable conditions produce cumuliform rather than stratiform clouds. Also, the air is turbulent, and visibility is good.

18. What are the characteristics of stable air?

   A. Good visibility, steady precipitation, and stratus-type clouds.

   B. Poor visibility, intermittent precipitation, and cumulus-type clouds.

   C. Poor visibility, steady precipitation, and stratus-type clouds.

Answer (C) is correct. *(AvW Chap 8)*
    DISCUSSION: Stable air is air that is still or moving horizontally but not vertically. As a result, the pollutants hang in the air and visibility is poor. Also, stable air forms stratus-type clouds since the air is moving in layers. Relatedly, precipitation spreads out over a wide area and is relatively steady.
    Answer (A) is incorrect. The visibility is poor rather than good in stable air. Answer (B) is incorrect. The precipitation is steady, and the clouds are stratiform.

19. What type clouds can be expected when an unstable air mass is forced to ascend a mountain slope?

   A. Layered clouds with little vertical development.

   B. Stratified clouds with considerable associated turbulence.

   C. Clouds with extensive vertical development.

Answer (C) is correct. *(AvW Chap 6)*
    DISCUSSION: Unstable air has a greater lapse rate. Because the air above is much colder than the air below, the lower (warmer) air tends to rise very easily. When an unstable air mass is forced to ascend up a mountain slope, it will probably continue to ascend beyond the mountain slope. Once the air expands and cools to the dew point, cumulus clouds will form with considerable vertical development. Any unstable air mass movement will usually result in turbulence as well.
    Answer (A) is incorrect. Layered clouds are associated with stable air. Answer (B) is incorrect. Stratified clouds are associated with stable air and no turbulence.

20. Which is a characteristic of stable air?

   A. Fair weather cumulus clouds.

   B. Stratiform clouds.

   C. Unlimited visibility.

Answer (B) is correct. *(AvW Chap 8)*
    DISCUSSION: Stratiform clouds, i.e., layer-type clouds, characteristically form in stable air. A stable atmosphere resists any upward or downward displacement, so clouds tend to lie horizontally instead of developing vertically.
    Answer (A) is incorrect. Cumulus clouds indicate unstable conditions. Answer (C) is incorrect. Restricted, not unlimited, visibility near the ground is an indication of stable air.

21. The general characteristics of unstable air are

   A. good visibility, showery precipitation, and cumuliform-type clouds.

   B. good visibility, steady precipitation, and stratiform-type clouds.

   C. poor visibility, intermittent precipitation, and cumuliform-type clouds.

Answer (A) is correct. *(AvW Chap 8)*
    DISCUSSION: Unstable air is moving vertically and usually produces cumulus clouds. The precipitation from cumulus clouds is showery. The lifting associated with unstable air generally clears smoke and other pollution away; thus, visibility is relatively good.
    Answer (B) is incorrect. Unstable air generally has showery, not steady, precipitation and cumulus, not stratiform, clouds. Answer (C) is incorrect. Unstable air generally has good, not poor, visibility.

22. What type of clouds will be formed if very stable moist air is forced up slope?

   A. First stratified clouds and then vertical clouds.

   B. Vertical clouds with increasing height.

   C. Stratified clouds with little vertical development.

Answer (C) is correct. *(AvW Chap 6)*
    DISCUSSION: Even when being forced up slope, stable air forms stratus-type clouds. This is because the air resists any further upward movement.
    Answer (A) is incorrect. There would be vertical clouds if the air were unstable rather than stable. Answer (B) is incorrect. There would be vertical clouds if the air were unstable rather than stable.

23. Steady precipitation, in contrast to showers, preceding a front is an indication of

A. stratiform clouds with moderate turbulence.

B. cumuliform clouds with little or no turbulence.

C. stratiform clouds with little or no turbulence.

Answer (C) is correct. (AvW Chap 8)
DISCUSSION: Steady precipitation is a characteristic of stable air because of its lack of lifting action. Also characteristic are stratiform clouds with relatively little turbulence.
Answer (A) is incorrect. Stable air has little or no turbulence. Answer (B) is incorrect. Stratiform rather than cumuliform clouds form in stable air.

24. What enhances the growth rate of precipitation?

A. Advective action.

B. Upward currents.

C. Cyclonic movement.

Answer (B) is correct. (AvW Chap 5)
DISCUSSION: The growth rate of precipitation is enhanced by upward currents, which carry moisture particles to cooler levels. The particles grow in size and weight (due to condensation) until the atmosphere can no longer hold them (saturation point) and they fall as precipitation.
Answer (A) is incorrect. Advective action usually refers to the horizontal transport of atmospheric properties by wind, such as warm advection (warm land air moving out over colder water). Answer (C) is incorrect. Cyclonic movement refers to the counterclockwise movement around a low-pressure area.

25. Which of the following combinations of weather producing variables would likely result in cumuliform-type clouds, good visibility, rain showers, and possible clear-type icing in clouds?

A. Unstable, moist air, and no lifting mechanism.

B. Stable, dry air, and orographic lifting.

C. Unstable, moist air, and orographic lifting.

Answer (C) is correct. (AvW Chap 6)
DISCUSSION: Cumuliform clouds, good visibility, and showery rain are produced as unstable, moist air is lifted into higher, cooler regions. When the lifting is the result of movement over terrain (e.g., up a mountain slope), it is called orographic lifting. Clear icing is formed from large drops, such as those found in cumuliform clouds.
Answer (A) is incorrect. Without a lifting mechanism, there would be no vertical development of clouds to result in showery rain and icing in clouds. Answer (B) is incorrect. Stable conditions result in stratiform rather than cumuliform clouds, and dry air does not result in showery rain or icing even when lifted.

26. What determines the structure or type of clouds which form as a result of air being forced to ascend?

A. The method by which the air is lifted.

B. The stability of the air before lifting occurs.

C. The amount of condensation nuclei present after lifting occurs.

Answer (B) is correct. (AvW Chap 6)
DISCUSSION: The structure of clouds is determined by the stability of the air before it is lifted. If unstable, the clouds will have vertical development. If stable, the clouds will be horizontal, i.e., stratiform.
Answer (A) is incorrect. The stability of the air, not the lifting mechanism, determines the type of cloud formations. Answer (C) is incorrect. Condensation nuclei encourage the formation of rain droplets or ice but have no effect on the type of cloud formations.

27. Stability can be determined from which measurement of the atmosphere?

A. Low-level winds.

B. Ambient lapse rate.

C. Atmospheric pressure.

Answer (B) is correct. (AvW Chap 6)
DISCUSSION: The ambient lapse rate is the actual rate of decrease in temperature with height. A great decrease in temperature as altitude increases encourages warm air from below to rise and creates an unstable air mass. Lifting is inhibited by lesser or very small temperature decreases with altitude (i.e., a low lapse rate).
Answer (A) is incorrect. Stability refers to vertical air movement, not horizontal air movement. Answer (C) is incorrect. Atmospheric pressure is a measure of the weight or downward force of air and does not affect air stability.

28. What are some characteristics of unstable air?

A. Nimbostratus clouds and good surface visibility.

B. Turbulence and poor surface visibility.

C. Turbulence and good surface visibility.

Answer (C) is correct. (AvW Chap 8)
DISCUSSION: The lifting tendency of unstable air creates turbulence and clears the surface air of clouds, dust, and other pollution.
Answer (A) is incorrect. Stratus clouds are characteristic of stable, not unstable, air. Answer (B) is incorrect. Poor surface visibility is a characteristic of stable, not unstable, air.

29. Unsaturated air flowing up slope will cool at the rate of approximately (dry adiabatic lapse rate)

A. 3°C per 1,000 feet.

B. 2°C per 1,000 feet.

C. 2.5°C per 1,000 feet.

Answer (A) is correct. *(AvW Chap 6)*
  DISCUSSION: The dry adiabatic lapse rate signifies a prescribed rate of expansional cooling or compressional heating. The dry adiabatic rate is 3°C for each 1,000 ft. Note that this rate differs from the average normal lapse rate of 2°C for each 1,000 ft. of altitude. The average lapse rate does NOT occur in dry air, but rather in air with "average" humidity.
  Answer (B) is incorrect. This amount is the standard lapse rate in stable air. Answer (C) is incorrect. This amount is the rate at which the temperature and dew point converge in a convective current of unsaturated air.

8.3 Temperature Inversions

30. What feature is associated with a temperature inversion?

A. A stable layer of air.

B. An unstable layer of air.

C. Air mass thunderstorms.

Answer (A) is correct. *(AvW Chaps 2 and 6)*
  DISCUSSION: A temperature inversion is defined as an increase in temperature with height; i.e., the lapse rate is less than standard. The cooler air stays near the surface, and there is little or no vertical movement.
  Answer (B) is incorrect. Instability occurs when the temperature decreases, not increases as in a temperature inversion, with an increase in height, and the warmer air continues to rise. Answer (C) is incorrect. Air mass thunderstorms result from instability. They do not occur when there is a temperature inversion.

31. Which weather conditions should be expected beneath a low-level temperature inversion layer when the relative humidity is high?

A. Smooth air and poor visibility due to fog, haze, or low clouds.

B. Light wind shear and poor visibility due to haze and light rain.

C. Turbulent air and poor visibility due to fog, low stratus-type clouds, and showery precipitation.

Answer (A) is correct. *(AvW Chap 2)*
  DISCUSSION: A temperature inversion is an increase in temperature as altitude increases; normally temperature decreases with increases in altitude. In an inversion, warm air rises to its own temperature and forms a stable layer of air. A low-level inversion results in poor visibility by trapping fog, smoke, dust, etc., in low levels of the atmosphere.
  Answer (B) is incorrect. Wind shear may be expected within, not beneath, a low-level temperature inversion. Answer (C) is incorrect. An inversion forms a stable layer of air, thus making it smooth, not turbulent, and causing steady, not showery, precipitation.

32. A common type of ground or surface based temperature inversion is that which is produced by

A. warm air being lifted rapidly aloft in the vicinity of mountainous terrain.

B. the movement of colder air over warm air, or the movement of warm air under cold air.

C. ground radiation on clear, cool nights when the wind is light.

Answer (C) is correct. *(AvW Chap 2)*
  DISCUSSION: A temperature inversion means the temperature becomes warmer rather than cooler with increases in altitude. A ground- or surface-based temperature inversion is produced when the air near the surface is cooled faster than the overlying air as a result of radiation of heat on a clear, still night. The air very close to the surface is thus cooler than the air a few hundred feet above.
  Answer (A) is incorrect. When warm air is lifted, unstable, not stable, air is the result. Answer (B) is incorrect. A temperature inversion consists of warm air over colder air, not colder over warm.

33. A temperature inversion will normally form only

A. in stable air.

B. in unstable air.

C. when a stratiform layer merges with a cumuliform mass.

Answer (A) is correct. *(AvW Chap 2)*
  DISCUSSION: In a temperature inversion, warm air overlies colder air; i.e., the lapse rate is inverted. By definition, this is a stable condition since there is no lifting action.
  Answer (B) is incorrect. Unstable air has colder air above warm air. Answer (C) is incorrect. A merger of stratus and cumulus clouds is associated with an occluded front, not necessarily a temperature inversion.

8.4 Temperature, Dew Point, and Fog

34. Which conditions are favorable for the formation of radiation fog?

    A. Moist air moving over colder ground or water.

    B. Cloudy sky and a light wind moving saturated warm air over a cool surface.

    C. Clear sky, little or no wind, small temperature/dew point spread, and over a land surface.

Answer (C) is correct. *(AvW Chap 12)*
    DISCUSSION: Conditions favorable for radiation fog are a clear sky, little or no wind, and a small temperature-dew point spread. The fog forms as terrestrial radiation cools the ground. The air near the ground is cooled to dew point, and fog forms.
    Answer (A) is incorrect. Advection fog, not radiation fog, forms when moist air moves over colder ground or water. The sky may be cloudy over advection fog. Answer (B) is incorrect. Advection fog, not radiation fog, forms when moist air moves over colder ground or water. The sky may be cloudy over advection fog.

35. What situation is most conducive to the formation of radiation fog?

    A. Warm, moist air over low, flatland areas on clear, calm nights.

    B. Moist, tropical air moving over cold, offshore water.

    C. The movement of cold air over much warmer water.

Answer (A) is correct. *(AvW Chap 12)*
    DISCUSSION: Conditions favorable for radiation fog are a clear sky, little or no wind, and a small temperature-dew point spread. The fog forms as terrestrial radiation cools the ground. The air close to the surface cools more quickly than the slightly higher air. The air near the ground is cooled to dew point, and fog forms.
    Answer (B) is incorrect. Advection fog forms as a result of warm air moving over a colder surface. Answer (C) is incorrect. Steam fog forms when cold air moves over a warmer surface.

36. The most frequent type of ground- or surface-based temperature inversion is that produced by

    A. radiation on a clear, relatively still night.

    B. warm air being lifted rapidly aloft in the vicinity of mountainous terrain.

    C. the movement of colder air under warm air, or the movement of warm air over cold air.

Answer (A) is correct. *(AvW Chap 2)*
    DISCUSSION: An inversion often develops near the ground on clear, cool nights when the wind is light. The ground radiates heat and cools much faster than the overlying air. Air in contact with the ground becomes cold, while the temperature a few hundred feet above changes very little. Thus, temperature increases with height.
    Answer (B) is incorrect. It describes orographic lifting. Answer (C) is incorrect. It describes a cold front and a warm front, respectively.

37. What types of fog depend upon a wind in order to exist?

    A. Steam fog and down slope fog.

    B. Precipitation-induced fog and ground fog.

    C. Advection fog and up slope fog.

Answer (C) is correct. *(AvW Chap 12)*
    DISCUSSION: Up slope fog forms as a result of moist, stable air being cooled as it moves up a sloping terrain. Advection fog forms when moist air is blown over a cold surface, decreasing the moist air's temperature to its dew point. Thus, both up slope fog and advection fog depend on air moving from one area to another; i.e., they depend on wind.
    Answer (A) is incorrect. Down slope fog is a nonsense term. Answer (B) is incorrect. Precipitation fog forms when warm rain or drizzle falls through cool air, and ground fog requires little or no wind.

38. Which weather condition can be expected when moist air flows from a relatively warm surface to a colder surface?

    A. Increased visibility.

    B. Convective turbulence due to surface heating.

    C. Fog.

Answer (C) is correct. *(AvW Chap 12)*
    DISCUSSION: When moist air flows from a relatively warm surface to a colder surface, the warm, moist air is cooled to its dew point, and advection fog is produced.
    Answer (A) is incorrect. Fog forms, which decreases, not increases, visibility. Answer (B) is incorrect. The surface cools the air, resulting in stable air with little or no convective turbulence.

39. Fog is usually prevalent in industrial areas because of

    A. atmospheric stabilization around cities.

    B. an abundance of condensation nuclei from combustion products.

    C. increased temperatures due to industrial heating.

Answer (B) is correct. *(AvW Chap 12)*
    DISCUSSION: Fog often forms in industrial areas because the combustion products leave dust in the air on which water can condense. These particles are called condensation nuclei.
    Answer (A) is incorrect. Cities, per se, have no effect on air stability. Answer (C) is incorrect. The amount of heat that factories release into the air is not significant in the formation of fog.

40. In what localities is advection fog most likely to occur?

A. Coastal areas.

B. Mountain slopes.

C. Level inland areas.

Answer (A) is correct. *(AvW Chap 12)*
 DISCUSSION: Advection fog forms when moist air moves over colder ground or water. This type of fog is thus most common along coastal areas. During the winter, advection fog over the central and eastern United States results when moist air from the Gulf of Mexico spreads northward over cold ground.
 Answer (B) is incorrect. Mountain slopes are required for upslope, not advection, fog. Answer (C) is incorrect. Level inland areas will most likely produce radiation, not advection, fog.

41. In which situation is advection fog most likely to form?

A. An air mass moving inland from the coast in winter.

B. A light breeze blowing colder air out to sea.

C. Warm, moist air settling over a warmer surface under no-wind conditions.

Answer (A) is correct. *(AvW Chap 12)*
 DISCUSSION: Advection fog forms when moist air moves over colder ground or water. This type of fog is most likely to form when an air mass moves from the warmer water inland from the coast in winter. As the air moves over the cooler land, it cools to the dew point and forms advection fog.
 Answer (B) is incorrect. Colder air blowing out to sea results in steam, not advection, fog. Answer (C) is incorrect. Warm, moist air settling over a warmer surface would not cool, so fog would not form.

42. Under which condition does advection fog usually form?

A. Moist air moving over colder ground or water.

B. Warm, moist air settling over a cool surface under no-wind conditions.

C. A land breeze blowing a cold air mass over a warm water current.

Answer (A) is correct. *(AvW Chap 12)*
 DISCUSSION: Advection fog forms when moist air moves over colder ground or water. The moist air is cooled to the dew point, and fog forms.
 Answer (B) is incorrect. Radiation fog, not advection fog, forms when warm, moist air settles over a cool surface under no-wind conditions. Answer (C) is incorrect. Steam fog, not advection fog, forms when a land breeze blows a cold air mass over a warm water current.

43. The amount of water vapor which air can hold largely depends on

A. relative humidity.

B. air temperature.

C. stability of air.

Answer (B) is correct. *(AvW Chap 5)*
 DISCUSSION: Air temperature largely determines how much water vapor can be held by the air. Warm air, which is less dense, can hold more water vapor than cold air.
 Answer (A) is incorrect. Relative humidity is the ratio of the existing amount of water vapor in the air at a given temperature to the maximum amount that could be held at that temperature. Answer (C) is incorrect. Air stability is related to the temperature lapse rate, not moisture.

44. To which meteorological condition does the term "dew point" refer?

A. The temperature to which air must be cooled to become saturated.

B. The temperature at which condensation and evaporation are equal.

C. The temperature at which dew will always form.

Answer (A) is correct. *(AvW Chap 5)*
 DISCUSSION: Dew point refers to the temperature to which air must be cooled to become saturated by the water vapor in the air. Dew point, when related to air temperature in aviation weather reports, reveals how close the air is to saturation and possible cloud, fog, or precipitation formation.
 Answer (B) is incorrect. Condensation (vapor to water) occurs at low temperatures, and evaporation (water to vapor) occurs at high temperatures. Answer (C) is incorrect. The formation of dew depends on relative humidity and the temperature of the collecting surface.

45. Clouds, fog, or dew will always form when

A. water vapor condenses.

B. water vapor is present.

C. the temperature and dew point are equal.

Answer (A) is correct. *(AvW Chap 5)*
 DISCUSSION: As water vapor condenses, it becomes visible as clouds, fog, or dew.
 Answer (B) is incorrect. Some water vapor is usually present, but it does not necessarily form clouds, fog, or dew. Answer (C) is incorrect. Even at 100% humidity (when the dew point equals actual temperature), water vapor may not condense if sufficient condensation nuclei are not present.

46. Which conditions result in the formation of frost?

A. The temperature of the collecting surface is at or below freezing and small droplets of moisture are falling.

B. When dew forms and the temperature is below freezing.

C. Temperature of the collecting surface is below the dewpoint of surrounding air and the dewpoint is colder than freezing.

Answer (C) is correct. *(AvW Chap 5)*
DISCUSSION: If the air temperature drops below the dew point, the air becomes more dense and can no longer hold the water vapor. The water vapor will condense to form visible moisture. Frost will form only if the temperature of the collecting surfaces is below the dew point of the surrounding air AND the dew point is below freezing.
Answer (A) is incorrect. The dew point must also be below freezing and droplets of moisture are not necessary. Answer (B) is incorrect. The formation of dew is not required. The dew point of surrounding air must be below freezing, and the temperature of the collecting surface must be less than the dew point.

8.5 Clouds

47. What are the four families of clouds?

A. Stratus, cumulus, nimbus, and cirrus.

B. Clouds formed by updrafts, fronts, cooling layers of air, and precipitation into warm air.

C. High, middle, low, and those with extensive vertical development.

Answer (C) is correct. *(AvW Chap 7)*
DISCUSSION: For identification purposes, clouds are divided into four "families" based on their height range. The families are high clouds, middle clouds, low clouds, and clouds with extensive vertical development.
Answer (A) is incorrect. It describes cloud formation and characteristic. Answer (B) is incorrect. It describes the way various clouds are formed.

48. Which family of clouds is least likely to contribute to structural icing on an aircraft?

A. Low clouds.

B. High clouds.

C. Clouds with extensive vertical development.

Answer (B) is correct. *(AvW Chaps 7, 10)*
DISCUSSION: High clouds are least likely to contribute to structural icing since they usually consist entirely of ice crystals. Since ice is already frozen, it will not freeze onto the structural surface of the airplane.
Answer (A) is incorrect. Low clouds can contain supercooled water, which freezes on contact with the airplane. Answer (C) is incorrect. Clouds with extensive vertical development can contain supercooled water, which freezes on contact with the airplane.

49. The presence of standing lenticular altocumulus clouds is a good indication of

A. a jetstream.

B. very strong turbulence.

C. heavy icing conditions.

Answer (B) is correct. *(AvW Chaps 7, 9)*
DISCUSSION: When stable air crosses a mountain barrier, it tends to flow in layers. The barrier may set up waves in these layers, which remain stationary while the wind blows rapidly through them. Wave crests extend well above the highest mountain tops. Under each wave crest is a rotary circulation, which can create very violent turbulence. Crests of the standing waves may be marked by stationary lens-shaped clouds known as standing lenticular clouds.
Answer (A) is incorrect. The jet stream flows around the world at high altitudes and at varying latitudes. Answer (C) is incorrect. Standing lenticular clouds occur at varying temperatures, not only below freezing.

50. Standing lenticular clouds, in mountainous areas, indicate

A. an inversion.

B. unstable air.

C. turbulence.

Answer (C) is correct. *(AvW Chaps 7, 9)*
DISCUSSION: The "waves" generated as wind flows across a mountain barrier may form standing lenticular clouds at the crest of each wave. Their presence indicates very strong turbulence, and they should be avoided.
Answer (A) is incorrect. Stratus, not standing lenticular, clouds indicate stable air which may be the result of a temperature inversion. Answer (B) is incorrect. Cumulus, not standing lenticular, clouds indicate unstable air.

51. The suffix "nimbus", used in naming clouds, means a

    A. cloud with extensive vertical development.

    B. rain cloud.

    C. dark massive, towering cloud.

Answer (B) is correct. *(AvW Chap 7)*
    DISCUSSION: The prefix "nimbo" or the suffix "nimbus" means raincloud. For example, stratified clouds from which rain is falling are called nimbostratus clouds. A heavy, swelling, cumulus-type cloud which produces precipitation is called a cumulonimbus cloud.
    Answer (A) is incorrect. The prefix "cumulo," not the suffix "nimbus," denotes a cloud with extensive vertical development. Answer (C) is incorrect. It specifies a cumulonimbus cloud, not any nimbus cloud.

52. A high cloud is composed mostly of

    A. ozone.

    B. condensation nuclei.

    C. ice crystals.

Answer (C) is correct. *(AvW Chap 7)*
    DISCUSSION: The high cloud family is cirriform. It includes cirrus, cirrocumulus, and cirrostratus clouds. They are composed almost entirely of ice crystals. Their bases range from 16,500 ft. to 45,000 ft.
    Answer (A) is incorrect. Ozone is an unstable form of oxygen. The heaviest concentrations are in the stratosphere, not in clouds. Answer (B) is incorrect. Condensation nuclei are the small particles in the air onto which water vapor condenses or sublimates.

53. Which clouds have the greatest turbulence?

    A. Towering cumulus.

    B. Cumulonimbus.

    C. Altocumulus castellanus.

Answer (B) is correct. *(AvW Chap 7)*
    DISCUSSION: Cumulonimbus clouds are thunderstorms and the ultimate manifestation of instability. They are huge vertically developed clouds with dense, billowy tops often crowned with thick veils of dense cirrus, called the "anvil." Nearly the entire spectrum of flying hazards is contained in these clouds, including violent turbulence.
    Answer (A) is incorrect. Towering cumulus clouds are only a preliminary stage of the cumulonimbus cloud. Answer (C) is incorrect. Altocumulus castellanus is a middle-level convective cloud which indicates rough turbulence with some icing, but thunderstorms are far more turbulent.

54. Fair weather cumulus clouds often indicate

    A. turbulence at and below the cloud level.

    B. poor visibility.

    C. smooth flying conditions.

Answer (A) is correct. *(AvW Chap 7)*
    DISCUSSION: Fair weather cumulus clouds form in convective currents and are characterized by relatively flat bases and dome-shaped tops. They indicate a shallow layer of instability, some turbulence, and no significant icing.
    Answer (B) is incorrect. The instability producing the cumulus clouds provides good, not poor, visibility. Answer (C) is incorrect. The instability producing the cumulus clouds creates some turbulence, not smooth conditions.

8.6 Thunderstorms

55. When is an airplane most likely to be struck by lightning?

    A. OAT greater than 0°C.

    B. Independent of OAT.

    C. OAT between –5°C and +5°C.

Answer (C) is correct. *(AIM Para 7-1-28)*
    DISCUSSION: The greatest probability of a lightning strike occurs when flying with an outside air temperature (OAT) of between –5°C and +5°C. Lightning strikes with aircraft are extremely rare but can occur whenever you operate near a thunderstorm, even if you are in the clear.
    Answer (A) is incorrect. The probability of a lightning strike is the greatest with an OAT of between –5°C and +5°C. Answer (B) is incorrect. The probability of a lightning strike does increase in a specific OAT range (–5°C and +5°C).

56. What are the requirements for the formation of a thunderstorm?

    A. A cumulus cloud with sufficient moisture.

    B. A cumulus cloud with sufficient moisture and an inverted lapse rate.

    C. Sufficient moisture, an unstable lapse rate, and a lifting action.

Answer (C) is correct. *(AvW Chap 11)*
    DISCUSSION: For a thunderstorm to form, the air must have sufficient water vapor, an unstable lapse rate, and an initial upward lifting action to start the storm process in motion. Surface heating, converging winds, sloping terrain, a frontal surface, or any combination of these can provide the lift.
    Answer (A) is incorrect. A lifting action is also required for formation of a thunderstorm. Answer (B) is incorrect. A lifting action and an unstable, not inverted, lapse rate are required for the formation of a thunderstorm.

57. What is an indication that downdrafts have developed and the thunderstorm cell has entered the mature stage?

    A. The anvil top has completed its development.

    B. Precipitation begins to fall from the cloud base.

    C. A gust front forms.

Answer (B) is correct. *(AvW Chap 11)*
    DISCUSSION: The mature stage of a thunderstorm is signaled when rain begins falling at the surface. This means that the downdrafts have developed sufficiently to carry water all the way through the thunderstorm.
    Answer (A) is incorrect. An anvil top does not necessarily develop over every thunderstorm. Answer (C) is incorrect. Gust front is a nonsense term.

58. Which procedure is recommended if a pilot should unintentionally penetrate embedded thunderstorm activity?

    A. Reverse aircraft heading or proceed toward an area of known VFR conditions.

    B. Reduce airspeed to maneuvering speed and maintain a constant altitude.

    C. Set power for recommended turbulence penetration airspeed and attempt to maintain a level flight attitude.

Answer (C) is correct. *(AvW Chap 11)*
    DISCUSSION: If a thunderstorm is penetrated, you should always attempt to maintain a constant attitude at or below the maneuvering or turbulence penetration speed recommended for the airplane. Note that the airspeed cannot always be kept constant, but the power can be set so that you will be operating generally at or below the maneuvering speed.
    Answer (A) is incorrect. A straight course will probably take you out of the storm most quickly. Also, turning maneuvers increase stresses on the aircraft. Answer (B) is incorrect. Maintaining a constant airspeed (V_A) in updrafts and downdrafts may be impossible. It is best to set power so you will operate at or below V_A. Also, attempting to maintain constant altitude, not attitude, increases the stress on the airplane.

59. Which thunderstorms generally produce the most severe conditions, such as heavy hail and destructive winds?

    A. Warm front.

    B. Squall line.

    C. Air mass.

Answer (B) is correct. *(AvW Chap 11)*
    DISCUSSION: A squall line is a nonfrontal narrow band of active thunderstorms. It often contains severe, steady-state thunderstorms and presents the single most intense weather hazard to airplanes.
    Answer (A) is incorrect. Warm fronts indicate stable air, which does not usually produce thunderstorms. Answer (C) is incorrect. An air mass thunderstorm is the least severe type of thunderstorm.

60. Which weather phenomenon is always associated with a thunderstorm?

    A. Lightning.

    B. Heavy rain showers.

    C. Supercooled raindrops.

Answer (A) is correct. *(AvW Chap 11)*
    DISCUSSION: A thunderstorm, by definition, has lightning, because lightning causes the thunder. Lightning is the discharge of electricity generated by thunderstorms.
    Answer (B) is incorrect. Hail may occur instead of heavy rain showers. Answer (C) is incorrect. Supercooled raindrops may not occur if the lifting process does not extend above the freezing level.

61. During the life cycle of a thunderstorm, which stage is characterized predominately by downdrafts?

    A. Cumulus.

    B. Dissipating.

    C. Mature.

Answer (B) is correct. *(AvW Chap 11)*
    DISCUSSION: Thunderstorms have three stages in their life cycle: cumulus, mature, and dissipating. In the dissipating stage, the storm is characterized by downdrafts as the storm rains itself out.
    Answer (A) is incorrect. The cumulus stage is the building stage characterized by updrafts. Answer (C) is incorrect. The mature stage has both updrafts and downdrafts, which create strong wind shears.

62. If squalls are reported at your destination, what wind conditions should you anticipate?

A. Sudden increases in wind speed of at least 16 knots rising to 22 knots or more, lasting for at least 1 minute.

B. Peak gusts of at least 35 knots for a sustained period of 1 minute or longer.

C. Rapid variation in wind direction of at least 20° and changes in speed of at least 10 knots between peaks and lulls.

Answer (A) is correct. *(AvW Glossary)*
   DISCUSSION: A squall is a sudden increase in wind speed by at least 16 kt., rising to 22 kt. or more, and lasting for at least 1 min. In contrast, a wind gust is a brief increase in wind with a variation between peaks and lulls of at least 10 kt. Note that these definitions involve variations in wind speed, not wind direction.
   Answer (B) is incorrect. A squall is a sudden increase in wind speed of at least 16 kt., rising to a peak of 22 kt. or more, not a peak gust of at least 35 kt. lasting for at least 1 min. Answer (C) is incorrect. Squalls refer to changes in wind speed, not direction. Additionally, the wind is reported as gusty when there are changes in speed of at least 10 kt. between peaks and lulls.

63. What is indicated by the term "embedded thunderstorms"?

A. Severe thunderstorms are embedded within a squall line.

B. Thunderstorms are predicted to develop in a stable air mass.

C. Thunderstorms are obscured by massive cloud layers and cannot be seen.

Answer (C) is correct. *(AvW Chap 11)*
   DISCUSSION: The term "embedded thunderstorms" means that the storms are embedded in clouds or thick haze layers and cannot be seen.
   Answer (A) is incorrect. A squall line consists of severe thunderstorms which can usually be seen. Answer (B) is incorrect. Thunderstorms do not usually occur in stable air masses.

64. Which weather phenomenon signals the beginning of the mature stage of a thunderstorm?

A. The start of rain at the surface.

B. Growth rate of cloud is maximum.

C. Strong turbulence in the cloud.

Answer (A) is correct. *(AvW Chap 11)*
   DISCUSSION: The mature stage of a thunderstorm is indicated when rain begins falling at the surface. This means that downdrafts have developed sufficiently to carry water all the way through the thunderstorm.
   Answer (B) is incorrect. Maximum growth rate occurs in the first or cumulus stage. Answer (C) is incorrect. Strong turbulence can occur in all stages.

65. The use of airborne weather-avoidance radar

A. provides no assurance of avoiding instrument weather conditions.

B. assures the avoidance of hail.

C. allows you to fly safely between echoes.

Answer (A) is correct. *(AvW Chap 11)*
   DISCUSSION: Weather-avoidance radar provides information on precipitation based on echo returns. Avoiding the heaviest areas of precipitation will often (not always) keep you out of the greatest turbulence. Radar does not show water vapor. Thus, clouds and fog, i.e., instrument weather conditions, are not indicated.
   Answer (B) is incorrect. Intense thunderstorms can often hurl hail for miles. Answer (C) is incorrect. Visual sighting of storms is not assured, because clouds and fog are not shown by radar. This could be detrimental to safety.

8.7 Icing

66. In which meteorological environment is aircraft structural icing most likely to have the highest rate of accumulation?

A. Cumulonimbus clouds.

B. High humidity and freezing temperature.

C. Freezing rain.

Answer (C) is correct. *(AvW Chap 10)*
   DISCUSSION: The condition most favorable for very hazardous icing is the presence of many large, supercooled water drops (i.e., freezing rain). The heaviest icing will usually be found at altitudes at or slightly above the freezing level where the temperature is never more than a few degrees below freezing.
   Answer (A) is incorrect. Icing does not necessarily occur in thunderstorms due to the large variation in temperature in thunderstorms. Answer (B) is incorrect. Visible moisture, not just high humidity, must be present for icing.

67. Test data indicate that ice, snow, or frost having a thickness and roughness similar to medium or coarse sandpaper on the leading edge and upper surface of an airfoil can

    A.   reduce lift by as much as 50 percent and increase drag by as much as 50 percent.

    B.   increase drag and reduce lift by as much as 25 percent.

    C.   reduce lift by as much as 30 percent and increase drag by 40 percent.

Answer (C) is correct. *(AC 120-58)*
    DISCUSSION: Test data indicate that ice, snow, or frost formations having a thickness and surface roughness similar to medium or coarse sandpaper on the leading edge and upper surface of an airfoil can reduce lift by as much as 30% and increase drag by 40%. These changes in lift and drag significantly increase stall speed, reduce controllability, and alter aircraft flight characteristics.
    Answer (A) is incorrect. Ice, snow, or frost having a thickness or roughness similar to medium or coarse sandpaper on the leading edge and upper surface of an airfoil can reduce lift by as much as 30%, not 50%, and increase drag by 40%, not 50%. Answer (B) is incorrect. Ice, snow, or frost having a thickness or roughness similar to medium or coarse sandpaper on the leading edge and upper surface of an airfoil can reduce lift by as much as 30%, not 25%, and increase drag by 40%, not 25%.

68. Which precipitation type normally indicates freezing rain at higher altitudes?

    A.   Snow.

    B.   Hail.

    C.   Ice pellets.

Answer (C) is correct. *(AvW Chap 5)*
    DISCUSSION: Ice pellets normally indicate that rain droplets are freezing at a higher altitude. Warmer air above exists from which rain is falling and freezing on the way down, as it enters cooler air (i.e., freezing rain exists above).
    Answer (A) is incorrect. Snow indicates that the temperature of the air above you is well below freezing. Answer (B) is incorrect. Hail indicates instability of the air aloft where supercooled droplets above the freezing level begin to freeze. Once a drop has frozen, other drops latch onto it, and the hailstone grows.

69. What visual clue would alert a pilot to the presence of large supercooled water droplets?

    A.   Formation of a glossy, transparent ice.

    B.   Loss of RPM or manifold pressure due to induction icing.

    C.   Entering an area of fog.

Answer (A) is correct. *(IFH Chap 6)*
    DISCUSSION: The formation of glossy, transparent ice slowly freezing on the surface of the aircraft is a visual clue to the presence of supercooled water droplets.
    Answer (B) is incorrect. Induction icing is the result of visible moisture not supercooled water. Answer (C) is incorrect. Fog does indicate the presence of visible moisture but not the presence of supercooled water droplets.

70. When large supercooled water droplets (SLD) are present in temperatures below +5°C, outside air temperature, what type of icing would be expected to form?

    A.   Ice that is glossy, clear, or translucent.

    B.   Thick, clumpy ice, that has a milky white color.

    C.   Induction ice.

Answer (A) is correct. *(IFH Chap 6)*
    DISCUSSION: When large supercooled water droplets are encountered in temperatures below +5°C OAT, pilots should expect to see glossy, clear, or translucent ice. This ice accumulates quickly and is very dangerous if prompt action is not taken to leave the icing conditions and/or activate any deicing equipment that is present on the aircraft.
    Answer (B) is incorrect. Pilots should expect glossy, clear, or translucent ice, not ice that is clumpy with a milky white color. Answer (C) is incorrect. Supercooled water droplets are not required for induction icing, which may occur whenever the aircraft is operating in areas of visible moisture.

71. Which of the following would be an accurate description of supercooled large droplets (SLD)?

    A.   Subfreezing water drops greater than 40 microns located in or below clouds.

    B.   Subfreezing water drops greater than 50 microns located in or below clouds.

    C.   Subfreezing water drops greater than 50 microns at the surface.

Answer (B) is correct. *(IFH Chap 6)*
    DISCUSSION: Supercooled large droplets (SLD) are drops of subfreezing water that are 50 microns or greater in size. When present, these droplets will be found in or below clouds.
    Answer (A) is incorrect. Supercooled large droplets are 50, not 40, microns or greater. Answer (C) is incorrect. Supercooled large droplets appear in or below clouds, not at the surface.

72. What is an operational consideration if you fly into rain which freezes on impact?

A. You have flown into an area of thunderstorms.

B. Temperatures are above freezing at some higher altitude.

C. You have flown through a cold front.

Answer (B) is correct. *(AvW Chap 10)*
DISCUSSION: Rain that freezes on impact is called freezing rain. If rain falls through freezing air, it will usually form supercooled water droplets, i.e., freezing rain. It indicates that temperatures somewhere above the airplane are above freezing.
Answer (A) is incorrect. Freezing rain does not necessarily indicate the presence of thunderstorms. Answer (C) is incorrect. Freezing rain does not necessarily indicate the presence of cold fronts.

73. What temperature condition is indicated if wet snow is encountered at your flight altitude?

A. The temperature is above freezing at your altitude.

B. The temperature is below freezing at your altitude.

C. You are flying from a warm air mass into a cold air mass.

Answer (A) is correct. *(AvW Chap 5)*
DISCUSSION: If snow is wet at your altitude, you are in above-freezing temperatures because the snow has started to melt.
Answer (B) is incorrect. The wet snow indicates the temperature is above freezing, not below freezing, at your altitude. Answer (C) is incorrect. The temperature is lower above you but not necessarily in front of you.

74. The presence of ice pellets at the surface is evidence that

A. there are thunderstorms in the area.

B. a cold front has passed.

C. there is freezing rain at a higher altitude.

Answer (C) is correct. *(AvW Chap 5)*
DISCUSSION: Ice pellets form as a result of rain freezing at a higher altitude. Rain droplets cool as they fall from a warmer layer through air with a temperature below freezing.
Answer (A) is incorrect. Thunderstorms do not necessarily cause ice pellets. Answer (B) is incorrect. Cold fronts do not necessarily cause ice pellets.

75. Why is frost considered hazardous to flight operation?

A. Frost changes the basic aerodynamic shape of the airfoil.

B. Frost decreases control effectiveness.

C. Frost causes early airflow separation resulting in a loss of lift.

Answer (C) is correct. *(AvW Chap 10)*
DISCUSSION: Frost spoils the smooth flow of air, thus causing a slowing of the airflow. This causes early airflow separation over the affected airfoil, resulting in a loss of lift. A heavy coat of hard frost will cause a 5 to 10% increase in stall speed. Even a small amount of frost on airfoils may prevent an aircraft from becoming airborne at normal takeoff speed.
Answer (A) is incorrect. Frost is very thin. It does not change the airfoil shape as structural icing does. Answer (B) is incorrect. Frost has no bearing on control effectiveness, only airfoil lift.

76. If the air temperature is +8°C at an elevation of 1,350 feet and a standard (average) temperature lapse rate exists, what will be the approximate freezing level?

A. 3,350 feet MSL.

B. 5,350 feet MSL.

C. 9,350 feet MSL.

Answer (B) is correct. *(AvW Chap 2)*
DISCUSSION: The decrease of temperature with altitude is defined as the lapse rate. The standard lapse rate is 2°C per 1,000 ft. To reach the freezing level, you must have a drop of 8°C. Thus the freezing level is 4,000 ft. (8/2 × 1,000 ft.) up, or 5,350 ft. MSL (1,350 + 4,000).
Answer (A) is incorrect. It represents a standard lapse rate of 4° per 1,000 ft. Answer (C) is incorrect. It represents a standard lapse rate of 1° per 1,000 ft.

77. A pilot who experiences tailplane icing on the approach should

A. notify ATC and request vectors to final.

B. disengage the autopilot and retract flaps.

C. add flaps and engage the autopilot.

Answer (B) is correct. *(AC 91-74A)*
DISCUSSION: Since pilots using an autopilot are not feeling the subtle but constant changes in the flight controls, they are less likely to be aware of ice accumulation on the tail section of the aircraft. Any time tailplane icing is suspected, the autopilot should be deactivated and the flaps should be retracted to the last safe setting.
Answer (A) is incorrect. While pilots should notify ATC upon encountering icing conditions, if the situation permits, the most correct answer to this question would be disconnecting the autopilot and retracting the flaps to the last safe setting. Answer (C) is incorrect. The autopilot should be disengaged, not engaged, and flaps should be retracted to the last safe position, not extended further.

78. What happens to residual ice that remains after deice boots are inflated and shed ice?

A. Residual ice increases with a decrease in airspeed or temperature.

B. Residual ice remains the same until the aircraft exits icing conditions.

C. Residual ice decreases with a decrease in airspeed or temperature.

Answer (A) is correct. *(AC 91-74A)*
DISCUSSION: The FAA recommends that the deicing system be activated at the first indication of icing. Because some residual ice continues to adhere between pneumatic boot system cycles, the wing is never entirely "clean." The amount of residual ice increases as airspeed and/or temperature decrease due to the more favorable conditions for ice accumulation associated with these conditions. At airspeeds typical of small airplanes, it may take many boot cycles to effectively shed the ice.
Answer (B) is incorrect. Residual ice left behind between deicing system cycles will increase in magnitude if either airspeed or temperature decrease due to the more favorable conditions for ice accumulation associated with these conditions. Answer (C) is incorrect. The amount of residual ice increases, not decreases, as airspeed and/or temperature decrease due to the more favorable conditions for ice accumulation associated with these conditions.

79. On which surface of the aircraft could a pilot generally expect to see the first sign of ice accumulation?

A. Pitot tube.

B. Wing.

C. Propeller.

Answer (A) is correct. *(IFH Chap 6)*
DISCUSSION: The smaller the surface, the more likely that surface is to pick up ice. Pitot tubes, being small protrusions into the airstream, are often the first parts of the aircraft to pick up ice.
Answer (B) is incorrect. The pitot tube will show evidence of icing prior to the wings. Answer (C) is incorrect. The pitot tube will show evidence of icing prior to the propeller.

80. What types of surfaces are most likely to see the first signs of ice accumulation?

A. Large wide areas.

B. Small narrow areas.

C. Areas made from metal.

Answer (B) is correct. *(IFH Chap 6)*
DISCUSSION: Small narrow areas, like a pitot tube, are much more likely to accumulate ice.
Answer (A) is incorrect. Large wide areas will accumulate ice after the accumulation has begun on small narrow areas. Answer (C) is incorrect. Portions of the aircraft that are metallic are no more likely to accumulate ice than nonmetal surfaces.

81. While flying a standard instrument departure procedure (DP) you encounter icing conditions and the autopilot is engaged, you should

A. continue the flight with the autopilot engaged.

B. increase the indicated airspeed setting for the autopilot.

C. disengage the autopilot.

Answer (C) is correct. *(AC 91-74A)*
DISCUSSION: Since pilots using an autopilot are not feeling the subtle but constant changes in the flight controls, they are less likely to be aware of ice accumulation on the surface of the aircraft. When icing conditions are encountered, the autopilot should be disengaged.
Answer (A) is incorrect. The autopilot should be disengaged whenever operating in real or forecast icing conditions.
Answer (B) is incorrect. The autopilot should be disengaged whenever operating in real or forecast icing conditions. While airspeed should be increased, it should be accomplished using manual control, not the autopilot.

82. The most susceptible surface of the aircraft for ice accumulation is the

A. windshield.

B. main wing.

C. tailplane.

Answer (C) is correct. *(IFH Chap 4)*
DISCUSSION: On most aircraft the tailplane is not visible to the pilot, who therefore cannot observe how well it has been cleared of ice by any deicing system. Both the main wings and the windshield are in plain view of the pilot, making awareness of ice accumulation more obvious. As well, the thinness of the tailplane over the main wings and its simple shape compared to the windshield make it a more efficient ice collector.
Answer (A) is incorrect. The windshield, while a good collector of ice, is directly in the pilot's line of sight making the pilot's awareness of windshield icing much greater. As well, the simple shape of the tailplane makes it a slightly more efficient collector of ice than the windshield. Answer (B) is incorrect. The main wings are visible by the pilot while the tailplane is not. This makes it much easier for the pilot to notice ice accumulation on the wings. As well, the thinness of the tailplane over the main wings make it a more efficient ice collector.

83. If you detect icing accumulation in flight, especially if the aircraft is not equipped with a deicing system, you should

A. move to a higher altitude.

B. leave the area of precipitation, if able, or fly to an altitude where the temperature is above freezing.

C. fly to an area with liquid precipitation.

Answer (B) is correct. *(IFH Chap 10)*
DISCUSSION: Regardless of the level of anti-ice or deice protection offered by the aircraft, the first course of action should be to leave the area of visible moisture. This might mean descending to an altitude below the cloud bases, climbing to an altitude that is above the cloud tops, or turning to a different course. If this is not possible, then the pilot must move to an altitude where the temperature is above freezing.
Answer (A) is incorrect. The best action is to leave the area of precipitation, but, if that is not possible, the pilot should move to an altitude where the temperature is above freezing. Only during a temperature inversion would that be a higher altitude; usually it means descending to a lower altitude. Answer (C) is incorrect. Areas of liquid precipitation do not necessarily equate to areas where the temperature is above freezing. Freezing rain is an excellent example of liquid precipitation that is incredibly hazardous.

84. When conditions favoring the formation of ice are present, pilots should check for ice accumulation prior to flight. The best way to do this is by

A. using a flashlight and watching for light reflection.

B. running your hand along all control surfaces.

C. using ice detection lights.

Answer (A) is correct. *(IFH Chap 11)*
DISCUSSION: Because ice, particularly clear ice, is difficult to detect on the aircraft's surface, you can shine a flashlight along all visible surfaces of the aircraft and watch for light reflections. This would be an indication of ice on the aircraft's surface.
Answer (B) is incorrect. Physically inspecting the control surfaces is a good tactic, but you should not limit your scan merely to the aircraft's control surfaces as the skin can and will collect ice as well. Additionally, T-tail designs may make a physical inspection of the related control surfaces difficult. Answer (C) is incorrect. Ice detection lights are useful for checking for ice accumulation at night, but they are used during flight, not during the preflight inspection.

85. To recover from a tailplane stall brought on by ice accumulation, the pilot should

A. retract the flaps and increase power, but only to compensate for the reduction in lift.

B. Decrease power and maintain a speed below V_A.

C. extend the flaps and reduce power to slow the aircraft.

Answer (A) is correct. *(IFH Chap 4)*
DISCUSSION: When a tailplane stall occurs, the pilot should immediately return the flaps to the previously selected position. Tailplane stalls are aggravated by an increase in flap extension. You will need to increase power to compensate for the reduction in lift caused by raising the flaps, but be careful to not increase power too drastically because an increase in airspeed can also aggravate a tailplane stall.
Answer (B) is incorrect. This procedure is appropriate for an encounter with moderate to severe turbulence, not a recovery from a tailplane stall. Answer (C) is incorrect. Extending the flaps during a tailplane stall with make the stall worse. Flaps should be retracted to their previous position and power should be increased, not reduced, to compensate for the loss in lift created by the retraction.

86. Tailplane icing can be detected by a(n)

A. increase in elevator effectiveness.

B. gradual uncommanded nose-up pitch.

C. sudden uncommanded nose-down pitch.

Answer (C) is correct. *(IFH Chap 4)*
DISCUSSION: A sudden uncommanded nose-down pitch is a symptom of tailplane icing that has caused a tailplane stall. The correct pilot reaction, unlike in a main wing stall, is to apply full aft-control pressure along with a reduction of the wing flaps to the last safe position.
Answer (A) is incorrect. A decrease, not an increase, in rudder effectiveness is a symptom of tailplane icing. Answer (B) is incorrect. A sudden, not gradual, uncommanded nose-down, not nose-up, pitch is indicative of tailplane icing accumulation that has caused a tailplane stall.

87. Tailplane icing can be detected by

A. elevator control pulsing, oscillations, or vibrations.

B. a gradual uncommanded reduction in engine power.

C. an increase in elevator effectiveness.

Answer (A) is correct. *(IFH Chap 4)*

DISCUSSION: Elevator control pulsing, oscillations, or vibrations as well as any other unusual or abnormal pitch anomalies (possibly resulting in pilot induced oscillations) are indicative of tailplane ice accumulation. If installed, anti-ice equipment should be activated. If no anti-ice system is installed or if the accumulation is not sufficiently combated by the anti-ice system, the pilot should exit icing conditions immediately.

Answer (B) is incorrect. A gradual uncommanded reduction in engine power is indicative of induction icing, not tailplane icing. Answer (C) is incorrect. A decrease, not an increase, in elevator effectiveness is a symptom of tailplane icing.

88. In an aircraft equipped with a pneumatic deicing system, the appropriate technique for removing ice is to

A. operate the pneumatic deicing system several times.

B. operate the pneumatic deicing system once.

C. confirm that ice has accumulated prior to engaging the pneumatic boots.

Answer (A) is correct. *(IFH Chap 4)*

DISCUSSION: To clear accumulated ice as well as residual ice that may be left between cycles, you should operate a pneumatic deicing system several times.

Answer (B) is incorrect. To clear accumulated ice as well as residual ice that may be left between cycles, you should operate a pneumatic deicing system several times, not just once. Answer (C) is incorrect. While this technique was formerly accepted as a rule of thumb, current advisory guidance recommends that deicing systems be activated at the first indication of icing rather than after any significant amount has accumulated.

89. A tailplane stall as the result of ice accumulation is most likely to occur during

A. cruise flight.

B. approach and landing.

C. an instrument holding pattern.

Answer (B) is correct. *(AC 23.143)*

DISCUSSION: An ice-contaminated tailplane stall typically occurs either while extending the wing trailing edge flaps to the landing position or with the flaps already extended to that position when operating in, or departing from, icing conditions. Since flaps are normally only extended to the landing position during final approach to landing, tailplane stalls as the result of ice accumulation are most common in this phase of flight.

Answer (A) is incorrect. Ice contaminated tailplane stalls are most common when the flaps are extended to the landing position, not during cruise flight. Answer (C) is incorrect. Ice-contaminated tailplane stalls are most common when the flaps are extended to the landing position, not during an instrument holding pattern.

90. With regards to icing, which is true?

A. Heavy icing on the leading edge is not as bad as light icing on the upper surface.

B. Smooth ice on the upper surface will not cause any problems.

C. Light icing is more of a problem than heavy icing.

Answer (A) is correct. *(AC 91-74A)*

DISCUSSION: Ice on the leading edge, while seemingly more dangerous, can be removed using deicing systems. Ice on the upper surface is much more difficult to clear from the structure, thus making it more dangerous.

Answer (B) is incorrect. Smooth ice on the upper surface will disrupt laminar flow of the air across the upper wing surface, and it is much more difficult to remove than ice buildup on the leading edge. Answer (C) is incorrect. Light icing is generally less of a problem aerodynamically than heavy icing. Light icing is slightly more difficult to remove with most deicing systems, but it is considered less of an immediate threat than heavy icing.

91. Which of the following is true about icing?

A. Small patches of ice sparsely distributed on the upper surface of the wing can cause asymmetrical stalls that result in roll control issues on takeoff.

B. Small areas of light snow or ice on the upper surface of the wing pose little or no threat to loss of lift.

C. Light ice on the surface of the wing is less of a concern than large accumulation on the leading edge of the wing.

Answer (A) is correct. *(AC 91-74A)*

DISCUSSION: The disrupted airflow caused by icing accumulation on the upper wing surface can create isolated, asymmetrical stalls, which can cause roll upset in any phase of flight, but especially high-lift phases of flight such as the takeoff climb.

Answer (B) is incorrect. Trace icing or frost on the upper surface of the wing can destroy as much as 30% of total lift, making it a significant danger in flight. Answer (C) is incorrect. Ice on the leading edge, while seemingly more dangerous, can be removed using deicing systems. Ice on the upper surface is much more difficult to clear from the structure, thus making it more dangerous.

92. Should you experience uncommanded roll due to icing forward of the ailerons, the most appropriate response is to

    A. begin a steady climb.

    B. retract the flaps in increments and employ available ice removal equipment.

    C. reduce the angle of attack by increasing airspeed or extending flaps to the first setting.

Answer (C) is correct. *(AC 91-74A)*
    DISCUSSION: If you encounter uncommanded roll due to ice accumulation, you must reduce the angle of attack. You can do this by increasing forward airspeed or extending flaps to the first position, provided you are below maximum flap extension speed.
    Answer (A) is incorrect. In the case of uncommanded roll, you should decrease the angle of attack on the wing; thus, climbing is a poor choice. Answer (B) is incorrect. While you should employ any ice protection equipment available, you should not retract the flaps, regardless of their level of extension, during uncommanded roll as this will actually increase the angle of attack. However, if you can verify that the upper surface of the wing is clear of ice, you may retract the flaps if necessary. Bear in mind this is the exception to the rule.

93. Should you experience buffeting or vibrations after extending the flaps upon exiting or during icing conditions, the most likely reason is

    A. incipient tailplane stall.

    B. aerodynamic stall due to increased angle of attack.

    C. aerodynamic instability due to ice accumulation forward of the ailerons.

Answer (A) is correct. *(AC 91-74A)*
    DISCUSSION: Elevator control pulsing, oscillations, or vibrations as well as any other unusual or abnormal pitch anomalies (possibly resulting in pilot-induced oscillations) are indicative of tailplane ice accumulation and the potential for a tailplane stall. You should retract the flaps to the last safe setting in this situation.
    Answer (B) is incorrect. Buffeting after the extension of flaps, especially when in icing conditions, is characteristic of an incipient tailplane stall, not an aerodynamic stall. Answer (C) is incorrect. Uncommanded roll, not buffeting or vibrations, would accompany aerodynamic instability due to ice accumulation forward of the ailerons.

94. The best technique for using deicing boots is to

    A. use them immediately upon visual detection of any ice.

    B. allow ice to build first to reduce likelihood of "ice bridging."

    C. cycle several times after exiting to obtain a completely clean wing.

Answer (A) is correct. *(IFH Chap 4)*
    DISCUSSION: The FAA recommends that the deicing system be activated at the first indication of icing.
    Answer (B) is incorrect. In times past, the FAA did recommend delaying activation of deicing boots until a significant amount of ice built up on the surface. Due to the dangers associated with tailplane icing, however, the FAA now recommends that deicing boots be activated at the first indication of ice. Answer (C) is incorrect. Some residual ice continues to adhere between pneumatic boot system cycles, so the wing is never entirely "clean." The amount of residual ice increases as airspeed and/or temperature decrease due to the more favorable conditions for ice accumulation associated with these conditions.

95. The proper use of deicing boots should include

    A. activation of the system at the first indication of icing and the continued cycling of the boots after leaving icing conditions to ensure any residual ice has been removed.

    B. activation of the system at the first indication of icing and the one cycle of the boots after leaving icing conditions to ensure any residual ice has been removed.

    C. discontinue the use of the boots upon exiting icing conditions.

Answer (A) is correct. *(IFH Chap 4)*
    DISCUSSION: The deicing boots should be activated at the first sign of ice accumulation and should be cycled multiple times upon leaving icing conditions to ensure any residual ice has been removed.
    Answer (B) is incorrect. The deicing boots should be cycled multiple times upon leaving icing conditions, not just once, to ensure any residual ice has been removed. Answer (C) is incorrect. The deicing boots should be cycled multiple times upon leaving icing conditions to ensure any residual ice has been removed.

96. How should deicing boots be used after exiting flight in icing conditions?

    A. It is no longer necessary to operate the boots after leaving icing conditions.

    B. You should continue to cycle the boots several times to remove residual ice left behind after normal boot operation.

    C. Only continue to cycle the boots if you are concerned you may still be accumulating ice.

Answer (B) is correct. *(AC 91-74A)*
    DISCUSSION: Some residual ice continues to adhere between pneumatic boot system cycles. The amount of residual ice increases as airspeed and/or temperature decrease due to the more favorable conditions for ice accumulation associated with these conditions. At airspeeds typical of small airplanes, it may take many boot cycles to effectively shed the ice.
    Answer (A) is incorrect. Residual ice lingers after normal boot system operation. You should continue to operate the boots until all possible residual ice is removed. Answer (C) is incorrect. Once you leave conditions favorable for icing conditions, you will not accumulate further ice. However, boots should still be operated after leaving icing conditions to remove residual ice left behind after normal boot system cycles.

97. Test data indicates that ice, snow, or frost having a thickness and roughness similar to medium or coarse sandpaper on the leading edge and upper surface of an airfoil can

    A. increase drag and reduce lift by as much as 40 percent.

    B. reduce lift by as much as 40 percent and increase drag by 30 percent.

    C. reduce lift by as much as 30 percent and increase drag by 40 percent.

Answer (C) is correct. *(AC 120-58, page 4)*
    DISCUSSION: Lift has been shown to be reduced by as much as 30 percent, while drag may be increased by up to 40 percent when ice, snow, or thick frost is present on the leading edge and upper surface of the wing.
    Answer (A) is incorrect. Although the increase of drag can be as high as 40 percent, the reduction of lift has only been shown to be 30 percent, which is substantially less than this answer choice suggests. Answer (B) is incorrect. The values have been reduced in this answer choice. Actual lift reduction has been shown to be lower, at 30 percent, while the increase in drag is higher, at 40 percent.

98. During or after flight in icing conditions, vibration or buffeting that follows, but was not evident prior to, flap deployment is

    A. an aerodynamic instability due to ice buildup forward of the ailerons but aft of the deicer boots.

    B. an incipient tailplane stall as a result of negative tailplane angle after flap deployment.

    C. an aerodynamic wing stall due to increased angle of attack as a result of flap deployment.

Answer (B) is correct. *(AC 91-74A)*
    DISCUSSION: Tailplane stall is most common when extending the flaps to the landing position, but it can occur with any extension of flaps. A vibration that occurs after flap extension is a warning signal of an impending tailplane stall.
    Answer (A) is incorrect. This condition would likely result in uncommanded roll due to ice accumulation forward of the ailerons. It is not an indication of a tailplane stall. Answer (C) is incorrect. Pilots may assume that a normal wing stall is occurring, but attempting to recover from a potential wing stall by applying down-elevator pressure will only aggravate the likely tailplane stall condition.

99. Which is true concerning aircraft icing?

    A. Small, almost imperceptible amounts of ice on the wing's upper surface cause the same aerodynamic penalties as much larger and more visible accumulations.

    B. Ice accumulation on the wing's leading edge that conforms to the wing contour generally results in little performance degradation.

    C. Small amounts of ice on the wing's surface usually result in correspondingly less performance degradation than larger amounts.

Answer (C) is the best answer. *(AC 91-74A)*
    DISCUSSION: Light icing is generally less of a problem aerodynamically than heavy icing. Light icing is slightly more difficult to remove with most deicing systems, but it is considered less of an immediate threat than heavy icing.
    Answer (A) is incorrect. While this statement can be true, it is not always true. Answer (B) is incorrect. Icing that follows the wing contour is generally clear ice, which is extremely hazardous to flight.

100. Where would you see the first sign of ice buildup?

    A. The pitot tube.

    B. The leading edge of the wing.

    C. The windshield.

Answer (A) is correct. *(AC 91-74A)*
    DISCUSSION: Small extensions from the aircraft structure are generally the best visual indicators of ice accumulation. The pitot tube can be a good visually-identifiable structure in a high-wing airplane.
    Answer (B) is incorrect. Ice accumulation on the leading edge of the wing can be difficult to determine, especially if the ice follows the general contour of the wing. Also, ice accumulation will begin to build on smaller aircraft structures before building on larger ones. Answer (C) is incorrect. While immediately in front of the pilot, ice accumulation on the windshield often begins after accumulation on smaller structures on the airplane.

101. Roll upsets caused by ice accumulation forward of the ailerons can be remedied by

   A. retracting the flaps to decrease the angle of attack at a given airspeed and maintaining a level pitch attitude.

   B. reducing the angle of attack by increasing airspeed or extending wing flaps to the first setting and rolling wings level.

   C. decreasing engine power and maintaining a nose-low pitch attitude to dampen the rolling tendency of the wing tips.

Answer (B) is correct. *(AC 91-74A)*
   DISCUSSION: Roll upsets are common during uneven ice accumulation on the wings. Because this ice accumulation builds forward of the ailerons and behind the deicing boots, it is often very difficult to remove. Reducing the angle of attack and increasing airspeed will assist you in maintaining positive control of the airplane.
   Answer (A) is incorrect. You should increase airspeed to assist with roll control while also rolling the wings back to the level position. Answer (C) is incorrect. You should increase airspeed and maintain a level attitude, not begin a descent with a nose-low attitude.

102. When using deicing boots, the pilot should

   A. wait for a 1/4-inch to 1/2-inch layer of ice to form before cycling the boots to avoid ice bridging.

   B. deactivate the deicing system immediately after exiting the known icing conditions.

   C. activate the deicing system at the first indication of icing and do so in accordance with the manufacturer's guidance.

Answer (C) is correct. *(AC 91-74A)*
   DISCUSSION: Due to the immediate and serious effects of ice accumulation, the FAA and manufacturer's guidance recommend that operators activate deicing boots at the first indication of ice accumulation.
   Answer (A) is incorrect. While formerly accepted as correct procedure, modern research has shown that ice bridging is rare to non-existent in modern boot designs. Answer (B) is incorrect. Even though the aircraft has departed from icing conditions, there may still be residual ice accumulation on the aircraft. Boot operations should be continued after exiting icing conditions to ensure that accumulated ice is removed.

103. If you experience icing during an approach, you should

   A. extend maximum flaps and keep the autopilot engaged.

   B. retract the flaps as necessary and disengage the autopilot.

   C. fly the airplane manually to the final approach fix and then engage the autopilot.

Answer (B) is correct. *(AC 91-74A)*
   DISCUSSION: While the autopilot can help reduce pilot workload, it also disconnects the pilot from the control-loading effects of icing accumulation. In icing conditions, pilots should maintain manual control of the airplane. Also, flaps should be retracted, as necessary, to prevent a potential tailplane stall.
   Answer (A) is incorrect. Pilots should avoid extending flaps in known icing conditions. If the autopilot is engaged, it should be disconnected to allow the pilot to maintain control of the airplane. Answer (C) is incorrect. If the autopilot is engaged, it should be disconnected to allow the pilot to maintain control of the airplane.

104. On the initial climbout after takeoff with the autopilot engaged, you encounter icing conditions. In this situation, it is recommended that

   A. the airspeed mode be disconnected.

   B. the vertical speed mode be disconnected.

   C. the autopilot be set to maintain a specific attitude.

Answer (B) is the best answer. *(AC 91-74A)*
   DISCUSSION: While the pilot should strongly consider disengaging the autopilot altogether, workload permitting, the vertical speed mode should definitely be disconnected to prevent stalls due to ice accumulation.
   Answer (A) is incorrect. While most general aviation autopilots do not feature an airspeed hold mode, this mode is less dangerous than vertical speed hold. However, operation in airspeed hold mode should also be discontinued in icing conditions. Answer (C) is incorrect. It is not safe to stop a climb during takeoff, especially considering obstacles and terrain. In addition, there is less chance of exiting the icing conditions at an altitude where there is known ice accumulation.

105. How can you be sure the wing is free of critical ice?

   A. Visually inspect the wing, giving special attention to the leading edge.

   B. Inspect with a light source, especially if the wing is painted white.

   C. Conduct a tactile inspection as well as a visual inspection.

Answer (C) is correct. *(AC 91-74A)*
   DISCUSSION: The only way to be sure that the wing is free from ice accumulation is to perform a tactile, or touch, inspection as well as a visual inspection.
   Answer (A) is incorrect. A visual inspection is part of the overall process of ensuring the wing is free of ice accumulation, but a tactile inspection should also be completed. Answer (B) is incorrect. A visual inspection with a light source is a good technique, but a visual inspection should accompany a tactile inspection as well.

106. What type of icing should be expected when you encounter supercooled large droplets (SLD) that splash or splatter on impact at temperatures below +5°C OAT?

A. Ice that appears wet or visibly moist.

B. Ice that builds on the propeller spinner but forward of the blades.

C. Ice that forms on the wing aft of the active part of the deicing boots.

Answer (C) is correct. *(AC 91-74A)*
DISCUSSION: You can think of SLD-caused icing as "aft icing" in that it generally occurs aft of where normal icing forms. SLD icing is common aft of the active portion of deicing boots due to run-back caused after the SLD impact the leading edge of the wing.
Answer (A) is incorrect. Due to the "fast-freeze" nature of SLD icing, you should expect this type of icing to be unusually extensive and solid. Answer (B) is incorrect. SLD icing forms aft of the impact site. SLD icing will not build forward from the point of impact, but aft.

107. Which is true regarding Supercooled Large Droplets (SLD) and their accumulation?

A. SLD can accrue aloft even if the droplets are not being observed at the surface.

B. SLD will not accrue even in visible moisture if the OAT is above 0°C.

C. SLD will not accrue even in freezing drizzle because of smaller size droplets.

Answer (A) is correct. *(AC 91-74A)*
DISCUSSION: Pilots should be aware that SLD can occur aloft even if no SLD precipitation is evident at the surface.
Answer (B) is incorrect. Nearly all aircraft icing occurs in supercooled clouds where outside air temperatures are below 0°C. Answer (C) is incorrect. Water droplets larger than 50 micrometers (diameter), which includes freezing drizzle and freezing rain aloft, characterize SLD icing conditions.

108. Ice tends to accumulate first on parts of the plane that are

A. small and narrow.

B. outside the wind stream.

C. thick and big.

Answer (A) is correct. *(AC 91-74A)*
DISCUSSION: Small and narrow objects are the best collectors of droplets and ice up rapidly.
Answer (B) is incorrect. Although the type of ice that forms varies depending on the atmospheric and flight conditions, small and narrow parts tend to accumulate ice first, not parts that are outside the wind stream. Answer (C) is incorrect. Although the type of ice that forms varies depending on the atmospheric and flight conditions, small and narrow parts tend to accumulate ice first, not thick and big parts.

109. After cycling of the deicing boots, residual ice will

A. increase as the airspeed or temperature decreases.

B. decrease as the airspeed decreases or the temperature increases.

C. remain constant until leaving the icing conditions.

Answer (A) is correct. *(AC 91-74A)*
DISCUSSION: The amount of residual ice increases as the airspeed or temperature decreases. Consequently, the FAA recommends that deicing systems be activated at the first indication of icing. Residual ice continues to adhere between pneumatic boot system cycles, meaning the wing is never entirely clean.
Answer (B) is incorrect. The amount of residual ice increases as airspeed or temperature decreases. It does not decrease as the airspeed decreases. Answer (C) is incorrect. Residual ice does not remain constant until the aircraft leaves the icing conditions. The amount of residual ice actually increases as airspeed or temperature decreases.

110. Which is true about ice formation on a wing surface?

A. Ice or frost formation on a wing's upper surface will have no effect on takeoff performance as long as formations are distributed sparsely.

B. Ice or frost formation on a wing surface can result in localized, asymmetrical stalls on the wing resulting in roll control problems during lift off.

C. Small ice or frost formation on a wing's upper surface is not as serious as a large accumulation of ice on the wing's leading edge.

Answer (B) is correct. *(AC 91-74A, NTSB Safety Alert SA-06)*
DISCUSSION: The NTSB has found that small patches of ice or frost can result in localized, asymmetrical stalls on the wing, which can result in roll control problems during lift off.
Answer (A) is incorrect. Sparsely distributed ice formations can still pose a threat to the safety of flight. Answer (C) is incorrect. Any icing on an airfoil has the potential to be a factor in the safety of flight.

111. Which of the following is true about icing characteristics?

A. Ice on the front and back of the airplane wing is easy to see from the pilot's position.

B. Ice is virtually undetectable when clear and may appear wet.

C. Ice on the surface of the wing is virtually undetectable and causes a reduction in lift over the wing.

Answer (C) is correct. *(AC 91-74A, NTSB Safety Alert SA-06)*
DISCUSSION: Virtually imperceptible amounts of ice on the aircraft wing's upper surface can result in significant performance degradation.
Answer (A) is incorrect. Ice is not always easy to see, and virtually imperceptible amounts of ice on the aircraft wing's upper surface can result in significant performance degradation. Answer (B) is incorrect. Clear ice can be difficult to spot due to its general conformity to the upper surface of the wing, but it is not virtually undetectable, especially when aided by a light source that can help identify the presence of icing.

112. What is true regarding ice accumulations on a wing surface?

A. A thin layer of ice on a wing's upper surface will result in little performance degradation if the ice is relatively smooth.

B. Small, visually imperceptible amounts of ice on a wing's surface during takeoff can result in significant performance degradation.

C. Frost, snow, and rime ice is easily detectable on a white upper wing surface, while clear ice is difficult to detect.

Answer (B) is correct. *(AC 91-74A, NTSB Safety Alert SA-06)*
DISCUSSION: Virtually imperceptible amounts of ice on a wing's upper surface can result in significant performance degradation.
Answer (A) is incorrect. Ice of any kind can cause significant performance issues. Answer (C) is incorrect. Fine particles of ice, even if they are the size of a grain of table salt and distributed as sparsely as one particle per square centimeter over a wing's upper surface, can destroy enough lift to prevent an airplane from taking off. The dangers of ice's imperceptibility is not limited to clear ice.

113. Where will the pilot first notice an accumulation of ice?

A. On the leading edge of the wing.

B. On the propeller.

C. On the air temperature probe.

Answer (C) is correct. *(AC 91-74A)*
DISCUSSION: Small, narrow objects tend to pick up ice that is visually detectable. Strategically located protuberances may also serve as ice indicators. The air temperature probe is an excellent example of this.
Answer (A) is incorrect. Small, narrow objects tend to pick up ice that is visually detectable. Strategically located protuberances may also serve as ice indicators. The leading edge of the wing is neither small and narrow nor a protuberance. Although ice may be visible there at some point, it is not where the pilot is likely to see the first signs of ice accumulation. Answer (B) is incorrect. The propeller is spinning far too quickly for the pilot to visually identify early signs of ice on it.

114. Where is airplane icing most difficult to identify?

A. On the wing's leading edge.

B. On the flat upper wing surface.

C. On the trailing edge of the wing.

Answer (B) is correct. *(AC 91-74A)*
DISCUSSION: Ice accumulation on the wing's upper surface may be very difficult to detect from the cockpit, cabin, or front or back of the wing. Additionally, frost, snow, and rime ice may be very difficult to detect on a white upper wing surface.
Answer (A) is incorrect. The leading edge is easily accessible while on the ground and is usually visible from the cockpit or cabin in flight. Conversely, ice accumulation on the wing's upper surface may be very difficult to detect from the cockpit, cabin, or front or back of the wing. Additionally, frost, snow, and rime ice may be very difficult to detect on a white upper wing surface. Answer (C) is incorrect. Well before ice appears on the trailing edge of the wing, it will have been evident elsewhere. However, ice accumulation on the wing's upper surface may be very difficult to detect from the cockpit, cabin, or front or back of the wing. Additionally, frost, snow, and rime ice may be very difficult to detect on a white upper wing surface.

115. A generally recommended practice for autopilot usage during cruise flight in icing conditions is

    A. having the autopilot continuously engaged while monitoring the system for abnormal trim, trim rate, or attitude.

    B. periodically disengaging the autopilot and hand flying the airplane.

    C. periodically disengaging and immediately reengaging the altitude hold function.

Answer (A) is correct. *(AC 91-74A)*
    DISCUSSION: If cockpit workloads do not permit the pilot to hand fly the aircraft, pilots should monitor the autopilot closely for abnormal trim, trim rate, or airplane attitude while cruising on autopilot in icing conditions.
    Answer (B) is incorrect. Although it may be desirable to disengage the autopilot and hand fly the aircraft, cockpit workload may not allow for the option. In such cases, pilots should monitor the autopilot closely for abnormal trim, trim rate, or airplane attitude while cruising on autopilot in icing conditions. Answer (C) is incorrect. As ice accretes on aircraft without auto-throttles, the autopilot will attempt to maintain altitude without regard for airspeed. This can lead to a potential stall situation. If cockpit workloads do not permit the pilot to hand fly the aircraft, pilots should monitor the autopilot closely for abnormal trim, trim rate, or airplane attitude while cruising on autopilot in icing conditions.

8.8 Wind Shear

116. What is an important characteristic of wind shear?

    A. It is an atmospheric condition that is associated exclusively with zones of convergence.

    B. The Coriolis phenomenon in both high- and low-level air masses is the principal generating force.

    C. It is an atmospheric condition that may be associated with a low-level temperature inversion, a jet stream, or a frontal zone.

Answer (C) is correct. *(AvW Chap 9)*
    DISCUSSION: Wind shear can occur at any level where winds are blowing in different directions or at different speeds. It is an atmospheric condition associated with low-level temperature inversions, the jet stream, or a frontal zone.
    Answer (A) is incorrect. Zones of convergence are low-pressure areas. Wind shear can occur in highs as well as lows. Answer (B) is incorrect. The Coriolis force is the deflective force of the Earth's rotation, which affects all wind flows, not just wind shear.

117. A pilot reporting turbulence that momentarily causes slight, erratic changes in altitude and/or attitude should report it as

    A. light turbulence.

    B. moderate turbulence.

    C. light chop.

Answer (A) is correct. *(AWS Sect 14)*
    DISCUSSION: Light turbulence is defined as a disturbed air flow that momentarily causes slight erratic changes in altitude and/or attitude.
    Answer (B) is incorrect. Moderate turbulence is more intense. It is sufficient to cause changes in altitude, but the pilot maintains control throughout. Answer (C) is incorrect. Light chop means slight or moderate, rapid, and somewhat rhythmic bumpiness without appreciable changes in altitude or attitude.

118. What is an important characteristic of wind shear?

    A. It is primarily associated with the lateral vortices generated by thunderstorms.

    B. It usually exists only in the vicinity of thunderstorms, but may be found near a strong temperature inversion.

    C. It may be associated with either a wind shift or a wind speed gradient at any level in the atmosphere.

Answer (C) is correct. *(AvW Chap 9)*
    DISCUSSION: Wind shear can occur at any level where winds are blowing in different directions or at different speeds.
    Answer (A) is incorrect. Wind shear is found in conditions other than thunderstorm turbulence, e.g., mountain waves, fronts, etc. Answer (B) is incorrect. Wind shear is found in conditions other than thunderstorm turbulence, e.g., mountain waves, fronts, etc.

119. Where can wind shear associated with a thunderstorm be found? Choose the most complete answer.

A. In front of the thunderstorm cell (anvil side) and on the right side of the cell.

B. In front of the thunderstorm cell and directly under the cell.

C. On all sides of the thunderstorm cell and directly under the cell.

Answer (C) is correct. *(AvW Chap 11)*
   DISCUSSION: Wind shear associated with thunderstorms may be found on all sides of the thunderstorm cell, including directly beneath it and as much as 20 mi. laterally.
   Answer (A) is incorrect. Wind shear may be found on all sides and beneath the thunderstorm cell. Answer (B) is incorrect. Wind shear may be found on all sides and beneath the thunderstorm cell.

120. Where does wind shear occur?

A. Exclusively in thunderstorms.

B. Wherever there is an abrupt decrease in pressure and/or temperature.

C. With either a wind shift or a wind speed gradient at any level in the atmosphere.

Answer (C) is correct. *(AvW Chap 9)*
   DISCUSSION: Wind shear can occur at any level where winds are blowing in different directions (wind shift) or at different speeds (a wind speed gradient).
   Answer (A) is incorrect. Wind shear is also caused by barriers to wind flow, occurs behind and below airplanes generating lift, etc. Answer (B) is incorrect. Wind shear is the result of wind change, not a change in temperature or pressure, per se.

121. Hazardous wind shear is commonly encountered near the ground

A. during periods when the wind velocity is stronger than 35 knots.

B. during periods when the wind velocity is stronger than 35 knots and near mountain valleys.

C. during periods of strong temperature inversion and near thunderstorms.

Answer (C) is correct. *(AvW Chap 9)*
   DISCUSSION: Thunderstorms produce hazardous wind shear near the ground. Wind shear during temperature inversions is also hazardous when at low levels as it affects aircraft approaching and departing airports.
   Answer (A) is incorrect. Any wind, not only wind shear, is hazardous when in excess of 35 kt. Answer (B) is incorrect. Wind shear usually occurs on the leeward side of mountains, not in valleys.

122. When a climb or descent through an inversion or wind shear zone is being performed, the pilot should be alert for which of the following changes in airplane performance?

A. A sudden change in airspeed.

B. A sudden surge of thrust.

C. A fast rate of climb and slow rate of descent.

Answer (A) is correct. *(AC 00-6A)*
   DISCUSSION: Airspeed changes should be expected during flight through inversions due to the change in air pressure. In wind shear zones, airspeed changes are due to the change in direction and speed of the air flow aloft.
   Answer (B) is incorrect. A sudden surge of thrust would be consistent with a microburst encounter, but not necessarily with an encounter through a temperature inversion or a wind shear zone. Answer (C) is incorrect. A fast rate of climb and a slow rate of descent would be observed when flying in an updraft or thermal column, but not necessarily with an encounter through a temperature inversion or a wind shear zone.

123. Which is a characteristic of low-level wind shear as it relates to low-level temperature inversions?

A. It allows airspeed to go above normal climb and approach speed.

B. The pilot can ignore the possibilities of wind shear since all winds must always be light for this phenomenon to occur.

C. The shear zone condition exists when upper-level winds are reported 5 to 10 knots.

Answer (A) is correct. *(AC 00-6A)*
   DISCUSSION: Especially during takeoff and approach, be alert for airspeed fluctuations at the most critical period when passing through the temperature inversion. These fluctuations may be the first indications of wind shear. Pilots are advised to improve their awareness of normal climbout pitch attitude and to put less emphasis on strict airspeed control.
   Answer (B) is incorrect. Wind shear does not occur exclusively in low-wind conditions. In fact, wind variations can result from topographical conditions, temperature inversions, sea breezes, and frontal systems. Answer (C) is incorrect. There is no limitation that restricts wind shear to situations where upper-level winds are reported at 5 to 10 knots. Low-level wind shear is very dangerous and requires pilot awareness to deal with the issue safely. Especially during takeoff and approach, be alert for airspeed fluctuations. These fluctuations may be the first indications of wind shear. Pilots are advised to improve their awareness of normal climbout pitch attitude and to put less emphasis on strict airspeed control.

8.9   Microbursts

124. (Refer to Figure 13 on page 353.) When penetrating a microburst, which aircraft will experience an increase in performance without a change in pitch or power?

   A.   3.

   B.   2.

   C.   1.

Answer (C) is correct. *(AIM Para 7-1-27)*
DISCUSSION: Refer to Fig. 13 and note that, as the airplane at point 1 approaches the microburst, it will experience an increasing headwind and increasing performance.
Answer (A) is incorrect. At point 3, the airplane is experiencing a strong downdraft. Answer (B) is incorrect. At point 2, the airplane is experiencing a decreasing headwind component.

125. (Refer to Figure 13 on page 353.) The aircraft in position 3 will experience which effect in a microburst encounter?

   A.   Decreasing headwind.

   B.   Increasing tailwind.

   C.   Strong downdraft.

Answer (C) is correct. *(AIM Para 7-1-27)*
DISCUSSION: At point 3 in Fig. 13, the airplane is experiencing a strong downdraft as it is approaching the center of the microburst.
Answer (A) is incorrect. At point 2, not 3, the airplane encounters decreasing headwind. Answer (B) is incorrect. At point 5, the airplane encounters an increasing tailwind that may result in an extreme situation as pictured, i.e., just before impact.

126. (Refer to Figure 13 on page 353.) How will the aircraft in position 4 be affected by a microburst encounter?

   A.   Performance increasing with a tailwind and updraft.

   B.   Performance decreasing with a tailwind and downdraft.

   C.   Performance decreasing with a headwind and downdraft.

Answer (B) is correct. *(AIM Para 7-1-27)*
DISCUSSION: In Fig. 13, point 4 represents decreased performance as a result of both the windshear shift from a headwind to a tailwind and a strong downdraft.
Answer (A) is incorrect. Performance decreases at point 4 due to the tailwind and a downdraft, not an updraft. Answer (C) is incorrect. The performance decreases as a result of the tailwind, not headwind.

127. (Refer to Figure 13 on page 353.) If involved in a microburst encounter, in which aircraft positions will the most severe downdraft occur?

   A.   4 and 5.

   B.   2 and 3.

   C.   3 and 4.

Answer (C) is correct. *(AIM Para 7-1-27)*
DISCUSSION: In Fig. 13, the most severe downdrafts occur at the center of the microburst, which are indicated by points 3 and 4.
Answer (A) is incorrect. Point 5 has significantly less downdraft even though it has considerably more tailwind. Answer (B) is incorrect. Point 2 has not so significant a downdraft as 3 and 4, but it contains significant headwind even though it is decreasing.

128. (Refer to Figure 13 on page 353.) What effect will a microburst encounter have upon the aircraft in position 4?

   A.   Strong tailwind.

   B.   Strong updraft.

   C.   Significant performance increase.

Answer (A) is correct. *(AIM Para 7-1-27)*
DISCUSSION: At point 4 in Fig. 13, the airplane is encountering a strong tailwind in addition to a strong downdraft.
Answer (B) is incorrect. There are no updrafts in microbursts, only downdrafts. Answer (C) is incorrect. The significance in performance increase occurs at point 1, not 4, where there is an increase in headwind.

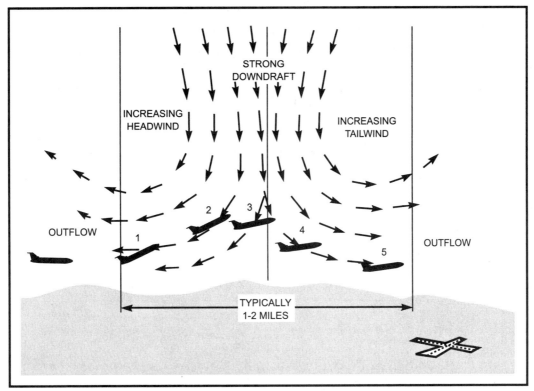

Figure 13. – Microburst Section Chart.

129. An aircraft that encounters a headwind of 45 knots, within a microburst, may expect a total shear across the microburst of

A. 40 knots.

B. 80 knots.

C. 90 knots.

Answer (C) is correct. *(AIM Para 7-1-27)*
DISCUSSION: If a headwind in a microburst is 45 kt., the wind will be going in the opposite direction on the other side of the microburst at presumably the same 45 kt., resulting in a wind shear between the headwind and tailwind of 90 kt.
Answer (A) is incorrect. The total wind shear expected across a microburst is twice the initial headwind, e.g., 45 kt. × 2 = 90 kt., not 40 kt. Answer (B) is incorrect. The total wind shear expected across a microburst is twice the initial headwind, e.g., 45 kt. × 2 = 90 kt., not 80 kt.

130. Maximum downdrafts in a microburst encounter may be as strong as

A. 8,000 feet per minute.

B. 7,000 feet per minute.

C. 6,000 feet per minute.

Answer (C) is correct. *(AIM Para 7-1-27)*
DISCUSSION: Downdrafts in a microburst can be as strong as 6,000 fpm. Horizontal winds near the surface can be as strong as 45 kt., resulting in a 90-kt. wind shear. The strong horizontal winds occur within a few hundred feet of the ground.
Answer (A) is incorrect. Maximum downdrafts are usually 6,000 fpm, not 8,000 fpm. Answer (B) is incorrect. Maximum downdrafts are usually 6,000 fpm, not 7,000 fpm.

131. What is the expected duration of an individual microburst?

A. Two minutes with maximum winds lasting approximately 1 minute.

B. One microburst may continue for as long as 2 to 4 hours.

C. Seldom longer than 15 minutes from the time the burst strikes the ground until dissipation.

Answer (C) is correct. *(AIM Para 7-1-27)*
DISCUSSION: An individual microburst will seldom last longer than 15 min. from the time it strikes ground until dissipation. The horizontal winds continue to increase during the first 5 min. with maximum-intensity winds lasting approximately 2 to 4 min.
Answer (A) is incorrect. Microbursts last 15, not 2 min., and maximum winds last 2 to 4 min., not 1 min. Answer (B) is incorrect. The maximum winds last 2 to 4 min., not 2 to 4 hr., and the microburst is usually limited to about 15 min.

END OF STUDY UNIT

❝ Just for the record I previously used only Gleim study guides for my instrument, commercial, and instructor tests, with first time high passing scores on all of them! Thanks again! You can quote me and my belief that the Gleim Study Guides are the best in the industry. ❞

Jay Rickmeyer

❝ Your courses are incredible. I tried "the other guys" and made them send me my money back after completion. ❞

HRSIII

❝ Keep up the fabulous work; your customer awareness is exemplary! I am a committed Gleim customer. ❞

Ken Norris

❝ I have used the Gleim flight training products for private, instrument, commercial, and multi-engine. They have been very thorough in preparing me for my testing. My wife will use their instrument course as she adds on this rating. ❞

David

❝ I passed the FAA exam successfully (88%) a few weeks ago. Many thanks to you. Your online learning program was an essential tool to success. Thank you 1000x. The ATP kit is very good because it allows needed transfer of knowledge in a very efficient & structural way. ❞

Michel Mesmaekers

What our customers are saying

STUDY UNIT NINE
AVIATION WEATHER SERVICES

(11 pages of outline)

This study unit contains outlines of major concepts tested, sample test questions and answers regarding aviation weather services, and an explanation of each answer. The table of contents above lists each subunit within this study unit, the number of questions pertaining to that particular subunit, and the pages on which the outlines and questions begin, respectively.

Recall that the **sole purpose** of this book is to expedite your passing of the FAA pilot knowledge test for the instrument rating. Accordingly, all extraneous material (i.e., topics or regulations not directly tested on the FAA pilot knowledge test) is omitted, even though much more knowledge is necessary to fly safely. This additional material is presented in *Pilot Handbook*, *Aviation Weather and Weather Services*, *FAR/AIM*, and *Instrument Pilot Flight Maneuvers and Practical Test Prep*, available from Gleim Publications, Inc. Order online at www.gleim.com.

Authors' note: The NWS continually evaluates and updates the products that it produces for aviation. In this fluid environment, it is difficult for the FAA to maintain current figures and questions. Since the sole purpose of this book is to expedite your passing the FAA knowledge test, the outline covers only what is on the test. For up-to-date information, see the Gleim *Aviation Weather and Weather Services* book, Part III, "Aviation Weather Services," beginning on page 209.

9.1 IN-FLIGHT WEATHER ADVISORIES

1. The Hazardous Inflight Weather Advisory Service (HIWAS) is a continuous broadcast over selected VORs of in-flight weather advisories, i.e., SIGMETs, convective SIGMETs, AIRMETs, severe weather forecast alerts (AWW), and center weather advisories.

2. AIRMETs are issued on a scheduled basis every 6 hr., with unscheduled amendments issued as required.

   a. An AIRMET is valid for 6 hr.

3. A SIGMET advises of nonconvective activity that is potentially hazardous to all aircraft.

4. SIGMETs are issued when the following phenomena occur or are expected to occur:

   a. Severe icing not associated with thunderstorms

   b. Severe or extreme turbulence or clear air turbulence (CAT) not associated with thunderstorms

   c. Duststorms, sandstorms, or volcanic ash lowering surface or in-flight visibilities to below 3 SM

   d. Volcanic eruption

5.   Pilots of IFR flights seeking ATC in-flight weather avoidance assistance should keep in mind that ATC radar limitations and frequency congestion may limit the controller's capability to provide this service.

9.2 AVIATION ROUTINE WEATHER REPORT (METAR)

1.   Aviation routine weather reports (METARs) are actual weather observations at the time indicated on the report. There are two types of reports.

   a.   METAR is an hourly routine observation (scheduled).
   b.   SPECI is a special METAR observation (unscheduled).

2.   Following the type of report are the elements listed below:

   a.   The four-letter ICAO station identifier.
   b.   Date and time of report. It is appended with a "Z" to denote Coordinated Universal Time (UTC).
   c.   Modifier (as required).
   d.   Wind.
   e.   Visibility.
   f.   Runway visual range (as required).
   g.   Weather phenomena.
   h.   Sky conditions.

      1)   The ceiling is the lowest broken or overcast layer, or vertical visibility into an obscuration.
      2)   Cloud bases are reported with three digits in hundreds of feet AGL.

         a)   EXAMPLE: OVC007 means overcast cloud layer at 700 ft. AGL.

      3)   Total obscurations are reported in the format "VVhhh" with "VV" meaning vertical visibility and "hhh" being the vertical visibility in hundreds of feet.

         a)   EXAMPLE: VV008 means vertical visibility of 800 ft.

   i.   Temperature-dew point.
   j.   Altimeter.
   k.   Remarks (RMK).

      1)   RAE42SNB42 means rain ended at 42 min. past the hour and snow began at 42 min. past the hour.

3.   EXAMPLE: METAR KAUS 301651Z 12008KT 4SM –RA HZ BKN010 BKN023 OVC160 21/17 A3005 RMK RAB25

   a.   METAR is a routine weather observation.
   b.   KAUS is Austin, TX.
   c.   301651Z means the observation was taken on the 30th day at 1651 UTC (or Zulu).
   d.   12008KT means the wind is from 120° true at 8 kt.
   e.   4SM means the visibility is 4 statute miles.
   f.   –RA HZ means light rain and haze.
   g.   BKN010 BKN023 OVC160 means broken cloud layers at 1,000 ft. and 2,300 ft. and an overcast cloud layer at 16,000 ft.
   h.   21/17 means the temperature is 21°C and the dew point is 17°C.
   i.   A3005 means the altimeter setting is 30.05 in. of Hg.
   j.   RMK RAB25 means remarks, rain began at 25 min. past the hour.

9.3 PILOT WEATHER REPORTS (PIREPs)

1. PIREPs are transmitted in the format illustrated below.

UUA/UA	Type of report: URGENT (UUA) - Any PIREP that contains any of the following weather phenomena: tornadoes, funnel clouds, or waterspouts; severe or extreme turbulence, including clear air turbulence (CAT); severe icing; hail; low-level wind shear (LLWS) (pilot reports air speed fluctuations of 10 knots or more within 2,000 feet of the surface); any other weather phenomena reported which are considered by the controller to be hazardous, or potentially hazardous, to flight operations. ROUTINE (UA) - Any PIREP that contains weather phenomena not listed above, including low-level wind shear reports with air speed fluctuations of less than 10 knots.
/OV	Location: Use VHF NAVAID(s) or an airport using the three- or four-letter location identifier. Position can be over a site, at some location relative to a site, or along a route. Ex: /OV KABC; /OV KABC090025; /OV KABC045020-DEF; /OV KABC-KDEF
/TM	Time: Four digits in UTC. Ex: /TM 0915
/FL	Altitude/Flight level: Three digits for hundreds of feet with no space between FL and altitude. If not known, use UNKN. Ex: /FL095; /FL310; /FLUNKN
/TP	Aircraft type: Four digits maximum; if not known, use UNKN. Ex: /TP L329; /TP B737; /TP UNKN
/SK	Sky cover: Describes cloud amount, height of cloud bases, and height of cloud tops. If unknown, use UNKN. Ex: /SK SCT040-TOP080; /SK BKNUNKN-TOP075; /SK BKN-OVC050-TOPUNKN; /SK OVCUNKN-TOP085
/WX	Flight visibility and weather: Flight visibility (FV) is reported first. Use standard METAR weather symbols. Intensity (– for light, no qualifier for moderate, and + for heavy) shall be coded for all precipitation types except ice crystals and hail. Ex: /WX FV05SM –RA; /WX FV01 SN BR; /WX RA
/TA	Temperature (Celsius): If below zero, prefix with an "M." Temperature should also be reported if icing is reported. Ex: /TA 15; /TA M06
/WV	Wind: Direction from which the wind is blowing coded in tens of degrees using three digits. Directions of less than 100 degrees shall be preceded by a zero. The wind speed shall be entered as a two- or three-digit group immediately following the direction, coded in whole knots using the hundreds, tens, and units digits. Ex: /WV 27045KT; /WV 280110KT
/TB	Turbulence: Use standard contractions for intensity and type (CAT or CHOP when appropriate). Include altitude only if different from FL. Ex: /TB EXTRM; /TB OCNL LGT-MDT BLO 090; /TB MOD-SEV CHOP 080-110
/IC	Icing: Describe using standard intensity and type contractions. Include altitude only if different from FL. Ex: /IC LGT-MDT RIME; /IC SEV CLR 028-045
/RM	Remarks: Use free form to clarify the report putting hazardous elements first. Ex: /RM LLWS – 15 KT SFC-030 DURGC RY 22 JFK

2. EXAMPLE: UA /OV OKC 063064/TM 1522/FL080/TP C172/TA –04/WV 245040/TB LGT/RM IN CLR.

DECODED: Pilot report, 64 NM on the 063° radial from Oklahoma City VOR at 1522 UTC (or Z), flight level 8,000 ft., type of aircraft is a Cessna 172, outside air temperature is –4°C, wind 245° at 40 kt., light turbulence, remarks are that the pilot is in clear skies.

9.4 WEATHER DEPICTION CHART

1. The weather depiction chart is computer-prepared from both manual and automated METARs.

    a. A reporting station is depicted on the chart by a circle called a station circle.
    b. Automated stations are identified by a bracket ( ]) to the right of the station circle.

2. Station circle data

    a. Total sky cover is shown by the amount of shading of the station circle.
    b. Cloud height above ground level (AGL) is entered under the station circle in hundreds of feet.

        1) If the total sky cover is broken, overcast, or obscured, the cloud height is the ceiling.

    c. Weather and obstruction-to-vision symbols are entered to the left of the station circle.

        1) Some may be entered above the station circle for readability.

    d. When visibility is 5 SM or less, it is entered to the left of the weather or obstructions to visibility.

    e. EXAMPLES:

          means overcast sky, ceiling 500 ft., continuous rain (slight at time of observation), and visibility greater than 6 SM.

          means overcast sky, ceiling 1,500 ft., continuous rain (heavy at time of observation), and visibility 1/2 SM.

3. The chart shows observed ceiling and visibility by categories as follows:

    a. IFR -- Ceilings less than 1,000 ft. and/or visibility less than 3 SM is shown by a hatched area outlined by a smooth line.
    b. MVFR (marginal VFR) -- Ceilings 1,000 to 3,000 ft. inclusive and/or visibility 3 to 5 SM inclusive is shown by a nonhatched area outlined by a smooth line.
    c. VFR -- Ceilings greater than 3,000 ft. and visibility greater than 5 SM are not outlined.

9.5 TERMINAL AERODROME FORECAST (TAF)

1. Terminal aerodrome forecasts (TAFs) are weather forecasts for selected airports throughout the country. They are a source of weather to expect at your destination airport at your ETA.

    a. The forecast is for a geographical area within a 5-SM radius of the airport's center.

        1) **VC** (vicinity) is used to refer to weather expected to occur between a 5- to 10-SM radius of the airport.

2. The elements of a TAF are listed below:

    a. Type of report

        1) TAF is a routine forecast.
        2) TAF AMD is an amended forecast.

    b. ICAO station identifier
    c. Date and time the forecast is actually prepared
    d. Valid period of the forecast

e. Forecast meteorological conditions. This is the body of the forecast and includes the following:

1) Wind

a) **VRB** means that the wind direction is forecast to fluctuate due to convective activity or low wind speeds (3 kt. or less).

2) Visibility

a) **P6SM** means the forecast visibility is greater than 6 SM.

3) Weather

4) Sky condition

5) Optional data (wind shear)

a) Wind shear in a TAF is a forecast of nonconvective low-level wind shear (up to 2,000 ft. AGL) and is forecast only when wind shear is expected.

b) EXAMPLE: **WS005/27050KT** means low-level wind shear at 500 ft. AGL, wind 270° true at 50 kt.

9.6 AVIATION AREA FORECAST (FA)

1. The VFR Clouds and Weather (VFR CLDS/WX) section of the aviation area forecast (FA) contains a 12-hr. specific forecast followed by a 6-hr. categorical outlook giving a total forecast period of 18 hr.

a. The VFR CLDS/WX section is usually several paragraphs long and is broken down by states or well-known geographical areas.

b. The specific forecast section covers an area the size of several states (an area greater than 3,000 sq. mi.) and gives a general description of clouds and weather that are significant to VFR flight operations.

2. In the categorical outlook of an FA, the contraction **WND** is included if the winds, sustained or gusty, are expected to be 20 kt. or greater.

9.7 WIND AND TEMPERATURE ALOFT FORECAST (FB)

1. Forecast winds and temperatures, provided at specified altitudes for specific locations in the United States, are presented in table form.

2. A four-digit group (used when temperatures are not forecast) shows wind direction with reference to **true** north and the wind speed in **knots**.

a. The first two digits indicate wind direction after a zero is added.

b. The next two digits indicate the wind speed.

3. A six-digit group includes the forecast temperature aloft.

a. The last two digits indicate the temperature in degrees Celsius.

b. Plus or minus is indicated before the temperature, except at higher altitudes (above 24,000 ft. MSL) where it is always below freezing.

c. The ISA (International Standard Atmosphere) temperature is 15°C at the surface with a standard lapse rate of 2°C per 1,000 ft.

4. When the wind speed is less than 5 kt., the forecast is coded **9900**, which means that the wind is light and variable.

5. Note that at some of the lower levels the wind and temperature information is omitted.

a. Winds aloft are not forecast for levels within 1,500 ft. of the station elevation.

b. No temperatures are forecast for the 3,000-ft. level or for a level within 2,500 ft. of the station elevation.

6.   If the wind speed is forecast to be 100 to 199 kt., the forecaster adds 50 to the direction and subtracts 100 from the speed. To decode, you must do the reverse: subtract 50 from the direction and add 100 to the speed.

    a.   EXAMPLE: If the forecast for the 39,000-ft. level appears as **731960**, subtract 50 from 73 and add 100 to 19. The wind would be 230° at 119 kt. with a temperature of –60°C (above 24,000 ft.).

    b.   It is easy to know when the coded direction has been increased by 50. Coded direction (in tens of degrees) normally ranges from 01 (010)° to 36 (360°). Any coded direction with a numerical value greater than 36 indicates a wind of 100 kt. or greater. The coded direction for winds of 100 to 199 kt. thus ranges from 51 to 86.

7.   If the wind speed is forecast to be 199 kt. or more, the wind group is coded as 199 kt.; e.g., **7799** is decoded 270° at 199 kt. or more.

8.   EXAMPLES: Decode these FD winds and temperatures:

Coded	Decoded
9900+00	Winds light and variable, temperature 0°C
2707	270° at 7 kt.
850552	85 – 50 = 35; 05 + 100 = 105
	350° at 105 kt., temperature –52°C

9.8 LOW-LEVEL SIGNIFICANT WEATHER PROG

1.   Low-level prognostic charts contain four charts (panels) of conditions forecast to exist at a valid time shown on the chart.

    a.   The two upper panels forecast significant weather from the surface up to 24,000 ft.: one for 12 hr. and the other for 24 hr. from the time of issuance.

    b.   The two lower panels forecast surface conditions: one for 12 hr. and the other for 24 hr. from the time of issuance.

    c.   See Figure 18 on the next page.

2.   The top panels show

    a.   Ceilings less than 1,000 ft. and/or visibility less than 3 SM (IFR) indicated by a solid line around the area

    b.   Ceilings 1,000 to 3,000 ft. and/or visibility 3 to 5 SM (MVFR) indicated by a scalloped line around the area

    c.   Moderate or greater turbulence indicated by a broken line around the area

        1)   Altitudes "up to" are above a line; e.g., <u>120</u> is up to 12,000 ft.
        2)   Altitudes "down to" are below a line; e.g., $\overline{90}$ is down to 9,000 ft.

    d.   Freezing levels indicated by a dashed line corresponding to the height of the freezing level

3.   The bottom panels show location of

    a.   Highs, lows, fronts

    b.   Other areas of significant weather

Figure 18. – U.S. Low-Level Significant Weather Prognostic Charts.

4.   The following symbols are used on "prog" charts:

a.   Standard weather symbols

b.   Significant weather symbols

9.9 SEVERE WEATHER OUTLOOK CHART

1.   The severe weather outlook chart is a 48-hr. outlook for thunderstorm activity presented in two panels.

2.   The left-hand panel covers the first 24-hr. period beginning at 1200Z (12Z) and depicts areas of possible general and severe thunderstorm activity in the continental U.S.

a.   A line with an arrowhead delineates an area of probable thunderstorm activity located to the right of the line when facing in the direction of the arrow.

b. If severe thunderstorm activity is expected in an area, that area is labeled with a risk category.

  1) **SLGT** means that there is a slight risk of severe thunderstorms; they are expected to cover 2% to 5% of the area.

  2) **MDT** means that there is a moderate risk of severe thunderstorms; they are expected to cover 6% to 10% of the area.

  3) **HIGH** means that there is a high risk of severe thunderstorms; they are expected to cover more than 10% of the area.

c. If general (i.e., non-severe) thunderstorm activity is expected in an area, that area is not labeled with a risk category.

  1) **NO SVR TSTMS FCST** means that the chart depicts no forecast areas of severe thunderstorms.

3. The right-hand panel covers the following day beginning at 1200Z and is similar to the left-hand panel, except that it is issued less frequently.

4. The severe weather outlook chart is strictly for advanced planning. It alerts all interests to the possibility of future storm development.

9.10 MISCELLANEOUS CHARTS AND FORECASTS

1. PIREPs, AIRMETs, and SIGMETs reflect the most accurate information on current and forecast icing conditions.

a. The rate of icing accumulation (trace, light, moderate, severe) determines how icing is reported in a PIREP or to ATC when asked to report your icing conditions.

  1) The type of icing (rime, clear, mixed) may or may not be reported in the remarks section, but this does not impact the way icing is reported in the PIREP icing group.

2. From constant pressure charts, you can approximate the observed temperature, wind, and temperature-dew point spread along your proposed route.

3. A convective outlook (AC) describes the prospects for general thunderstorm activity during the following 24-hr. period.

a. Areas in which there is a high, moderate, or slight risk of severe thunderstorms are included as well as areas where thunderstorms may approach severe limits.

4. The surface analysis chart depicts actual frontal positions, pressure patterns, temperature, dew point, wind, weather, and obstructions to vision at the valid time of the chart.

5. A severe weather watch bulletin (WW) is unscheduled and is issued as required.

9.11 HIGH-LEVEL SIGNIFICANT WEATHER PROG

1. The U.S. High-Level Significant Weather Prognostic Chart encompasses airspace from above 24,000 ft. to 60,000 ft. pressure altitude (FL 240 to FL 600).

2. Tropopause heights are depicted in hundreds of feet MSL, which may be presented by a five-sided polygon or a small rectangular block.

a. The five-sided polygon indicates areas of high and low tropopause heights.

b. The rectangular block indicates the tropopause height in areas that have a very flat tropopause slope.

c.   Note that, in Figure 20 below, which is out of date, all heights are given as flight levels, not hundreds of feet MSL.

Figure 20. – High-Level Significant Weather Prognostic Chart.

3.   The height and maximum wind speed of jet streams having a core speed of 80 kt. or greater are shown as a solid line with arrowheads indicating the flow direction.

    a.   The height is given as a flight level (FL).

    b.   The maximum core wind velocity is depicted by a shaft with a pennant equal to 50 kt. and a feather, or barb, equal to 10 kt.

        1)   EXAMPLE: ▲▲ ||| ____   means a maximum core speed of 130 kt.

4.   Areas of forecast moderate or greater turbulence are enclosed by bold, dashed lines.

    a.   The enclosed area includes all turbulence not caused by thunderstorms or convective activity (thunderstorms imply turbulence).

    b.   Areas are labeled with the appropriate turbulence symbol(s) and the vertical extent in hundreds of feet MSL.

5.   Small scalloped lines enclose areas of expected cumulonimbus development. "CB" denotes cumulonimbus.

    a.   CB refers to the occurrence or expected occurrence of an area of widespread cumulonimbus clouds or cumulonimbus clouds along a line with little or no space between the individual clouds, or cumulonimbus clouds embedded in cloud layers or concealed by haze or dust.

b. CB bases below 24,000 ft. (FL 240) are shown as XXX.

   1) CB tops are expressed in hundreds of feet MSL.

   2) The term "below 24,000 ft." (FL 240) is used because phenomena that extend beyond the lower limit of the High-Level Significant Weather Prognostic Chart are found on the Low-Level Significant Weather Prognostic Chart, the upper limit of which is 24,000 ft. pressure altitude (FL 240).

6. EXAMPLES:

Moderate to severe turbulence, below 24,000 feet to 33,000 feet (for turbulence below 24,000 feet, see low-level prog)

Moderate turbulence, from 35,000 feet to above upper limit of the prog

Embedded cumulonimbus, less than 1/8 coverage, bases below 24,000 feet, tops 42,000 feet

Embedded cumulonimbus, 1/8 to 4/8 coverage, bases below 24,000 feet, tops 52,000 feet

Cumulonimbus, 5/8 to 8/8 coverage, bases below 24,000 feet, tops 33,000 feet

9.12 OBSERVED WINDS ALOFT CHART

1. Arrows with pennants and barbs show wind direction and speed.

   a. Wind direction is drawn to the nearest 10°, with the second digit of the coded direction entered at the outer end of the arrow.

      1) To determine wind direction, obtain the general direction from the arrow and then use the digit to determine the direction to the nearest 10°.

      2) For example, wind from the northwest with a digit of "3" at the end of the arrow indicates 330°.

   b. Wind speed is indicated by the sum of three symbols: A half barb is 5 kt., a full barb is 10 kt., and a pennant is 50 kt.

2. Temperature is in whole degrees Celsius for each forecast point and is entered above and to the right of the station circle.

3. EXAMPLES:

wind 290° at 50 kt. (represented by one pennant), temperature -48° C

wind 230° at 35 kt. (represented by three and one-half barbs), temperature -47° C

QUESTIONS AND ANSWER EXPLANATIONS: All of the instrument rating knowledge test questions chosen by the FAA for release as well as additional questions selected by Gleim relating to the material in the previous outlines are reproduced on the following pages. These questions have been organized into the same subunits as the outlines. To the immediate right of each question are the correct answer and answer explanation. You should cover these answers and answer explanations while responding to the questions. Refer to the general discussion in the Introduction on how to take the FAA knowledge test.

Remember that the questions from the FAA knowledge test bank have been reordered by topic and organized into a meaningful sequence. Also, the first line of the answer explanation gives the citation of the authoritative source for the answer.

QUESTIONS

9.1 In-Flight Weather Advisories

1. AIRMETs are issued on a scheduled basis every

  A. 15 minutes after the hour only.

  B. 15 minutes until the AIRMET is canceled.

  C. six hours.

Answer (C) is correct. *(AWS Sect 6)*
  DISCUSSION: AIRMETs are issued on a scheduled basis every 6 hr., with unscheduled amendments issued as required.
  Answer (A) is incorrect. AIRMETs are issued on a scheduled basis every 6 hr., not every 15 min. past the hour. Answer (B) is incorrect. AIRMETs are issued on a scheduled basis every 6 hr., not every 15 min. until the AIRMET is canceled.

2. The Hazardous Inflight Weather Advisory Service (HIWAS) is a continuous broadcast over selected VORs of

  A. SIGMETs, CONVECTIVE SIGMETs, AIRMETs, Severe Weather Forecast Alerts (AWW), and Center Weather Advisories.

  B. SIGMETs, CONVECTIVE SIGMETs, AIRMETs, Wind Shear Advisories, and Severe Weather Forecast Alerts (AWW).

  C. Wind Shear Advisories, Radar Weather Reports, SIGMETs, CONVECTIVE SIGMETs, AIRMETs, and Center Weather Advisories (CWA).

Answer (A) is correct. *(AWS Sect 6)*
  DISCUSSION: The Hazardous Inflight Weather Advisory Service (HIWAS) is a continuous broadcast service over selected VORs of in-flight weather advisories, i.e., SIGMETs, convective SIGMETs, AIRMETs, severe weather forecast alerts (AWW), and center weather advisories (CWA).
  Answer (B) is incorrect. A runway wind shear advisory would be given to arriving and departing aircraft by a tower controller, not the HIWAS. Answer (C) is incorrect. Radar weather reports would be available from Flight Watch (FSS), not the HIWAS.

3. Which meteorological condition is issued in the form of a SIGMET (WS)?

  A. Widespread sand or dust storms affecting at least 3,000 square miles or an area deemed to have a significant effect on the safety of aircraft operations.

  B. Moderate icing.

  C. Sustained winds of 30 knots or greater at the surface.

Answer (A) is correct. *(AWS Sect 6)*
  DISCUSSION: SIGMETs warn of weather considered potentially hazardous to all categories of aircraft. SIGMETs are forecasts of tornadoes, lines of thunderstorms, embedded thunderstorms, large hail, severe and extreme turbulence, severe icing, and widespread sandstorms and snowstorms.
  Answer (B) is incorrect. Moderate icing is issued in the form of an AIRMET, not a SIGMET. Answer (C) is incorrect. Sustained winds of 30 knots or greater at the surface are issued in the form of an AIRMET, not a SIGMET.

4. Pilots of IFR flights seeking ATC in-flight weather avoidance assistance should keep in mind that

  A. ATC radar limitations and, frequency congestion may limit the controllers capability to provide this service.

  B. circumnavigating severe weather can only be accommodated in the en route areas away from terminals because of congestion.

  C. ATC Narrow Band Radar does not provide the controller with weather intensity capability.

Answer (A) is correct. *(AIM Para 7-1-15)*
  DISCUSSION: The controllers' primary function is to provide safe separation between aircraft. Any additional service, such as weather avoidance, can be provided only to the extent it does not interfere with the primary function. Unfortunately, the separation workload is usually greater when weather disrupts the normal flow of traffic.
  Answer (B) is incorrect. Controllers can provide weather circumnavigation in terminal areas when workload permits. Answer (C) is incorrect. ATC narrowband radar is replacing digitized radar weather displays in ARTCC facilities to provide even better measurement of precipitation density.

5. SIGMETs are issued as a warning of weather conditions potentially hazardous

A. particularly to light aircraft.

B. to all aircraft.

C. only to light aircraft operations.

Answer (B) is correct. *(AWS Sect 6)*

DISCUSSION: SIGMETs warn of weather considered potentially hazardous to all categories of aircraft. SIGMETs contain information on severe turbulence, severe icing, dust storms, sand storms, and volcanic ash.

Answer (A) is incorrect. SIGMETs apply to all aircraft. Answer (C) is incorrect. AIRMETs, not SIGMETs, apply to light aircraft.

6. What is the maximum forecast period for AIRMETs?

A. Two hours.

B. Four hours.

C. Six hours.

Answer (C) is correct. *(AWS Sect 6)*

DISCUSSION: The maximum forecast period for AIRMETs is 6 hr. If conditions persist beyond 6 hr., the AIRMET must be updated and reissued.

Answer (A) is incorrect. Convective SIGMETs, not AIRMETs, are valid for up to 2 hr. Answer (B) is incorrect. SIGMETs, not AIRMETs, are valid for up to 4 hr.

7. Which meteorological condition is issued in the form of a SIGMET (WS)?

A. Widespread sand or dust storms lowering visibility to less than 3 miles.

B. Moderate icing.

C. Sustained winds of 30 knots or greater at the surface.

Answer (A) is correct. *(AWS Sect 6)*

DISCUSSION: SIGMETs are issued for severe and extreme turbulence; severe icing; and widespread dust storms, sandstorms, or volcanic ash lowering visibility below 3 SM.

Answer (B) is incorrect. Moderate icing is issued in the form of an AIRMET, not a SIGMET. Answer (C) is incorrect. Sustained winds of 30 kt. or greater at the surface are issued in the form of an AIRMET, not a SIGMET.

8. SIGMETs are issued as a warning of weather conditions potentially hazardous

A. particularly to large commercial operators.

B. to all aircraft regardless of size or operating environment.

C. particularly to light aircraft.

Answer (B) is correct. *(FAA AC 00-45G Change 1, Chap 6)*

DISCUSSION: SIGMETs warn of weather considered potentially hazardous to all categories of aircraft.

Answer (A) is incorrect. SIGMETs are issued to warn of weather conditions that present a potential hazard to all aircraft, not just large commercial operators. SIGMETs can include potential hazards such as severe turbulence, severe icing, dust and/or sand storms, and volcanic ash. Answer (C) is incorrect. The potential hazards included in SIGMETs are of a severity that can affect the safety of flight for any aircraft, not only light aircraft. These can include potential hazards such as severe turbulence, severe icing, dust and/or sand storms, and volcanic ash.

9.2 Aviation Routine Weather Report (METAR)

9. Interpret the remarks section of METAR surface report for KBNA.

METAR KBNA 211250Z 33018KT 290V260 1/2SM R31/2700FT +SN BLSNFG VV008 00/M03 A2991 RMK RAE42SNB42

A. The wind is variable from 290° to 360°.

B. Heavy blowing snow and fog on runway 31.

C. Rain ended 42 past the hour, snow began 42 past the hour.

Answer (C) is correct. *(AWS Sect 3)*

DISCUSSION: The contraction RMK follows the altimeter in the body and precedes remarks. RMK RAE42SNB42 means remarks follow, rain ended 42 min. past the hour (RAE42), and snow began 42 min. past the hour (SNB42).

Answer (A) is incorrect. The remarks section indicates that rain ended 42 min. past the hour and snow began 42 min. past the hour, not that the wind is variable from 290° to 360°. Answer (B) is incorrect. The remarks section indicates that rain ended 42 min. past the hour and snow began 42 min. past the hour, not that there is heavy blowing snow and fog on Rwy 31.

10. A ceiling is defined as the height of the

A. highest layer of clouds or obscuring phenomena aloft that covers over 6/10 of the sky.

B. lowest layer of clouds that contributed to the overall overcast.

C. lowest layer of clouds or obscuring phenomena aloft that is reported as broken or overcast.

Answer (C) is correct. *(AWS Sect 3)*
DISCUSSION: For aviation purposes, the ceiling is the lowest broken or overcast layer, or vertical visibility into an obscuration.
Answer (A) is incorrect. The ceiling is the base of the lowest, not highest, broken or overcast layer. Answer (B) is incorrect. The lowest layer of clouds must be broken or overcast, not simply a contributor to the overall overcast.

11. The reporting station originating this Aviation Routine Weather Report has a field elevation of 620 feet. If the reported sky cover is one continuous layer, what is its thickness (tops of OVC are reported at 6,500 feet)?

METAR KMDW 121856Z AUTO 32005KT 1 1/2SM +RA BR OVC007 17/16 A2980

A. 5,180 feet.

B. 5,800 feet.

C. 5,880 feet.

Answer (A) is correct. *(AWS Sect 3)*
DISCUSSION: The sky cover for KMDW is reported as a ceiling of 700 ft. AGL, overcast (OVC007). The field elevation is 620 ft. MSL; thus, the base of the overcast layer is 1,320 ft. MSL (700 + 620). The tops of the overcast are reported at 6,500 ft.; thus, the thickness of the overcast layer is 5,180 ft. (6,500 – 1,320).
Answer (B) is incorrect. This would be the thickness of the sky cover if the field elevation were 0 ft., not 620 ft. Answer (C) is incorrect. This is the height above ground of the tops of the overcast layer, not the thickness of the overcast layer.

12. The station originating the following weather report has a field elevation of 1,300 feet MSL. From the bottom of the overcast cloud layer, what is its thickness (tops of OVC are reported at 3,800 feet)?

SPECI KOKC 2228Z 28024G36KT 3/4SM BKN008 OVC020 28/23 A3000

A. 500 feet.

B. 1,700 feet.

C. 2,500 feet.

Answer (A) is correct. *(AWS Sect 3)*
DISCUSSION: The question is to determine the thickness of the overcast layer at KOKC. The SPECI reported the base of the overcast cloud layer at 2,000 ft. AGL (OVC020). The field elevation is 1,300 ft. MSL; thus, the base of the overcast layer is 3,300 ft. MSL (2,000 + 1,300). The tops of the overcast layer are reported at 3,800 ft. MSL; thus, the thickness of the overcast cloud layer is 500 ft. (3,800 – 3,300).
Answer (B) is incorrect. This is the distance from the base of the broken (BKN), not overcast (OVC), cloud layer to the top of the overcast. Answer (C) is incorrect. This is the height above the ground of the tops of the overcast, not the thickness of the overcast layer.

13. What significant sky condition is reported in this METAR observation?

METAR KBNA 1250Z 33018KT 290V360 1/2SM R31/2700FT +SN BLSNFG VV008 00/M03 A2991 RMK RERAE42SNB42

A. Runway 31 ceiling is 2,700 feet.

B. Sky is obscured with vertical visibility of 800 feet.

C. Measured ceiling is 300 feet overcast.

Answer (B) is correct. *(AWS Sect 3)*
DISCUSSION: The sky condition follows the weather element. At KBNA, the sky cover is reported as VV008, which means the sky is obscured (indefinite ceiling) with a vertical visibility of 800 feet.
Answer (A) is incorrect. Runway 31 RVR, not ceiling, is 2,700 ft. Answer (C) is incorrect. The observation 00/M03 means the temperature is 0°C and the dew point is –3°C, not that there is a measured ceiling of 300 ft. overcast.

9.3 Pilot Weather Reports (PIREPs)

14. Interpret this PIREP.

MRB UA/OV MRB/TM 1430/FL 060/TP C182/SK
BKN BL /WX RA/TB MDT.

A. Ceiling 6,000 feet intermittently below
   moderate thundershowers; turbulence
   increasing westward.

B. FL 60,000, intermittently below clouds;
   moderate rain, turbulence increasing with the
   wind.

C. At 6,000 feet; between layers; moderate
   turbulence; moderate rain.

Answer (C) is correct. *(AWS Sect 3)*
   DISCUSSION: The PIREP decodes as follows: pilot report,
over Martinsburg, WV, at 1430 UTC, flight level is 6,000 ft., type
of aircraft is a Cessna 182, and sky condition is broken with the
pilot reporting between layers in moderate rain and moderate
turbulence.
   Answer (A) is incorrect. The flight level, not the ceiling, is
6,000 ft., and TB MDT means moderate turbulence, not
thundershowers. Answer (B) is incorrect. The flight level is
6,000 ft., not 60,000 ft., and BL means between layers, not below
clouds.

15. Which response most closely interprets the
following PIREP?

UA/OV OKC 063064/TM 1522/FL080/TP C172/TA
–04 /WV245040/TB LGT/RM IN CLR.

A. 64 nautical miles on the 63 degree radial from
   Oklahoma City VOR at 1522 UTC, flight level
   8,000 ft. Type of aircraft is a Cessna 172.

B. Reported by a Cessna 172, turbulence and
   light rime icing in climb to 8,000 ft.

C. 63 nautical miles on the 64 degree radial from
   Oklahoma City, thunderstorm and light rain at
   1522 UTC.

Answer (A) is correct. *(AWS Sect 3)*
   DISCUSSION: The PIREP decodes as follows: pilot report,
64 NM on the 063° radial from Oklahoma City VOR at 1522 UTC,
flight level is 8,000 ft., type of aircraft is a Cessna 172, outside air
temperature is –4°C, wind is from 245° at 40 kt. with light
turbulence, remarks are that the pilot is in clear skies.
   Answer (B) is incorrect. TB LGT RM IN CLR means light
turbulence (remark) in clear, not turbulence and rime icing in
climb. Answer (C) is incorrect. OKC 063064 means the aircraft
was located 64 NM, not 63 NM, on the 063° radial, not the
064° radial. Additionally, there is no report of thunderstorm and
rain.

9.4 Weather Depiction Chart

16. (Refer to Figure 4 on page 371.) The Weather Depiction Chart in the area of northwestern Wyoming indicates

    A. overcast with scattered rain showers.

    B. 1,000-foot ceilings and visibility 3 miles or more.

    C. 500-foot ceilings and continuous rain, less than 3 miles visibility.

Answer (C) is correct. *(AWS Sect 5)*
    DISCUSSION: The station circle in northwestern Wyoming indicates an overcast sky (darkened circle), 500-ft. ceiling ("5" under the circle), and continuous rain (two dots over circle). The station circle is in a shaded area, which indicates IFR with ceiling less than 1,000 ft. and/or visibility less than 3 SM.
    Answer (A) is incorrect. The chart provides data only from observation stations. Rain showers would be reported as intermittent, not scattered. Intermittent showers (moderate intensity at time of observation) would be shown as two vertical, not horizontal, dots. Answer (B) is incorrect. The station in Wyoming is reporting a ceiling of 500 ft., not 1,000 ft., and since visibility is not shown, it is interpreted to mean greater than 6 SM, not 3 SM or more.

17. (Refer to Figure 4 on page 371.) The Weather Depiction Chart indicates the heaviest precipitation is occurring in

    A. north central Florida.

    B. north central Minnesota.

    C. central South Dakota.

Answer (B) is correct. *(AWS Sect 5)*
    DISCUSSION: The heaviest precipitation is occurring in north central Minnesota. The station near the southern edge of the shaded area has four dots in a diamond shape above the circle, which means continuous rain (not freezing), heavy at the time of observation.
    Answer (A) is incorrect. No precipitation is reported for north central Florida. Answer (C) is incorrect. No precipitation is reported for central South Dakota.

18. (Refer to Figure 4 on page 371.) What is the meaning of a bracket ( ]) plotted to the right of the station circle on a weather depiction chart?

    A. The station represents the en route conditions within a 50 mile radius.

    B. The station is an automated observation location.

    C. The station gives local overview of flying conditions for a six-hour period.

Answer (B) is correct. *(AWS Sect 5)*
    DISCUSSION: Data for the weather depiction chart come from the observations reported by both manual and automated observation locations. The automated stations are denoted by a bracket ( ]) plotted to the right of the station circle.
    Answer (A) is incorrect. A bracket to the right of the station circle means the station is an automated site. The chart does not provide en route conditions between stations. Answer (C) is incorrect. A bracket to the right of the station circle means that the station is an automated site, not that the station gives a local overview of flying conditions for a 6-hr. period.

Figure 4. – Weather Depiction Chart.

9.5 Terminal Aerodrome Forecast (TAF)

19. From which primary source should you obtain information regarding the weather expected to exist at your destination at your estimated time of arrival?

    A. Weather Depiction Chart.

    B. Radar Summary and Weather Depiction Chart.

    C. Terminal Aerodrome Forecast.

Answer (C) is correct. *(AWS Sect 7)*
    DISCUSSION: A terminal aerodrome forecast (TAF) is a concise statement of the expected meteorological conditions at an airport during a specified period (usually 24 hr.). Thus, a TAF contains information regarding the expected weather at the destination airport at the ETA.
    Answer (A) is incorrect. A weather depiction chart is a national weather map of observed, not forecast, weather at the time specified on the chart. It is useful for flight planning to get a broad overview of the observed conditions. Answer (B) is incorrect. The radar summary chart is obsolete. It provided an indication of observed, not forecast, weather. A weather depiction chart is a national weather map of observed, not forecast, weather at a specific time. It is useful for flight planning but does not provide specific information about a particular destination.

20. Use the TAF to determine the wind shear forecast.

TAF
KCVG 231051Z 231212 12012KT 4SM –RA BR OVC008
  WS005/27050KT TEMPO 1719 1/2SM –RA FG
FM1930 09012KT 1SM –DZ BR VV003 BECMG 2021
  5SM HZ=

    A. Wind shear from the surface to 500 feet AGL from 270° at 50 KT.

    B. Wind shear at 500 feet MSL from 270° at 50 KT.

    C. Wind shear at 500 feet AGL from 270° at 50 KT.

Answer (C) is correct. *(AIM Para 7-1-31)*
    DISCUSSION: Wind shear in a TAF is a forecast of nonconvective low-level wind shear (up to 2,000 ft. AGL) and is entered after the sky condition when wind shear is expected. The wind shear forecast for KCVG is coded as **WS005/27050KT**, which means low-level wind shear at 500 ft. AGL, wind from 270° true at 50 kt.
    Answer (A) is incorrect. The height of the wind shear (WS005) is 500 ft. AGL, not from the surface to 500 ft. AGL. Answer (B) is incorrect. The height of the wind shear (WS005) is 500 ft. AGL, not 50 ft. MSL.

21. What is the forecast wind at 1800Z in the following TAF?

KMEM 091740Z 1818 00000KT 1/2SM RAFG OVC005=

    A. Calm.

    B. Unknown.

    C. Not recorded.

Answer (A) is correct. *(AWS Sect 7)*
    DISCUSSION: In the TAF for KMEM, the forecast wind at 1800Z is coded as 00000KT, which means a calm wind.
    Answer (B) is incorrect. The forecast wind at 1800Z is 00000KT, which means a calm, not unknown, wind. Answer (C) is incorrect. The forecast wind at 1800Z is 00000KT, which means a calm wind, not an unrecorded wind.

22. When the visibility is greater than 6 SM on a TAF it is

    A. expressed as 6PSM.

    B. expressed as P6SM.

    C. omitted from the report.

Answer (B) is correct. *(AWS Sect 7)*
    DISCUSSION: When the forecast visibility is greater than 6 SM, it will be coded as P6SM.
    Answer (A) is incorrect. Forecast visibility greater than 6 SM will be coded as P6SM, not 6PSM. Answer (C) is incorrect. Forecast visibility greater than 6 SM will be coded as P6SM. It is not omitted from the report.

23. Which weather product is a concise statement of the expected weather for an airport's runway complex?

    A. Area Forecast (FA).

    B. Weather Depiction Charts.

    C. Terminal Aerodrome Forecast (TAF).

Answer (C) is correct. *(AWS Sect 7)*
    DISCUSSION: A terminal aerodrome forecast (TAF) is a concise statement of the expected meteorological conditions at an airport during a specified period (usually 24 hr.). Thus, a TAF contains information regarding the expected weather at the destination airport at the ETA.
    Answer (A) is incorrect. An area forecast (FA) is a forecast of general weather conditions over an area the size of several states, not for a specific airport. The FA is used if the destination airport does not have a TAF. Answer (B) is incorrect. Weather depiction charts are national weather maps of observed weather at a specific time. They are useful for flight planning but do not provide specific information about a particular destination airport.

24. A "VRB" wind entry in a Terminal Aerodrome Forecast (TAF) will be indicated when the wind is

A. 3 knots or less.

B. 6 knots or less.

C. 9 knots or less.

Answer (A) is correct. *(AWS Sect 7)*
DISCUSSION: A "VRB" wind entry in a TAF indicates that the wind direction is forecast to fluctuate due to convective activity or low wind speeds of 3 kt. or less.
Answer (B) is incorrect. A "VRB" wind entry in a TAF indicates that the wind direction is forecast to fluctuate due to convective activity or low wind speeds of 3 kt., not 6 kt., or less. Answer (C) is incorrect. A "VRB" wind entry in a TAF indicates that the wind direction is forecast to fluctuate due to convective activity or low wind speeds of 3 kt., not 9 kt., or less.

25. The body of a Terminal Aerodrome Forecast (TAF) covers a geographical proximity within a

A. 5 nautical mile radius of the center of an airport.

B. 5 statute mile radius from the center of an airport runway complex.

C. 5 to 10 statute mile radius from the center of an airport runway complex.

Answer (B) is correct. *(AWS Sect 7)*
DISCUSSION: The Terminal Aerodrome Forecast (TAF) is a concise statement of the expected meteorological conditions at an airport during a specified period (usually 24 hr.). The TAF covers a geographic area within a 5-SM radius of the airport's center.
Answer (A) is incorrect. The TAF covers a geographic area within a 5-SM radius of the airport's center, not a 5-NM radius. Answer (C) is incorrect. The TAF covers a geographic area within a 5 SM radius of the airport's center, not 5 to 10 statute miles. The letters VC in the TAF describe conditions that will occur within the vicinity of the airport (5 to 10 SM), not at the airport, and will be used only with FG (fog), SH (showers), or TS (thunderstorms).

9.6 Aviation Area Forecast (FA)

26. Area forecasts generally include a forecast period of 18 hours and cover a geographical

A. terminal area.

B. area less than 3,000 square miles.

C. area the size of several states.

Answer (C) is correct. *(AWS Sect 7)*
DISCUSSION: Area forecasts (FA) generally include a total forecast period of 18 hr. and cover a geographical area the size of several states.
Answer (A) is incorrect. A TAF, not an FA, will forecast conditions at a terminal area. Answer (B) is incorrect. An FA forecast covers an area greater than, not less than, 3,000 sq. mi. and gives a general description of clouds and weather that are significant to VFR operations.

27. "WND" in the categorical outlook in the Aviation Area Forecast means that the wind during that period is forecast to be

A. Sustained surface wind speed of 6 knots or greater.

B. Sustained surface wind speed of 15 knots or greater.

C. Sustained surface wind speed of 20 knots or greater.

Answer (C) is correct. *(AWS Sect 7)*
DISCUSSION: WND in the categorical outlook in the aviation area forecast (FA) means that the winds, sustained or gusty, are expected to be 20 kt. or greater during that period.
Answer (A) is incorrect. WND means the winds are expected to be at least 20 kt., not 6 kt., or stronger. Answer (B) is incorrect. WND means the winds are expected to be at least 20 kt., not 15 kt., or stronger.

9.7 Wind and Temperature Aloft Forecast (FB)

28. A station is forecasting wind and temperature aloft at FL 390 to be 300° at 200 knots; temperature –54°C. How would this data be encoded in the FB?

A. 300054

B. 809954

C. 309954

Answer (B) is correct. *(AWS Sect 7)*
DISCUSSION: At FL 390, a 300° wind at 200 kt. is encoded as 809954. Note that the first two digits are the direction. The second two digits are velocity. Wind speeds of 200 kt. or greater are coded as 99 for the speed, and 50 is added to the two-digit direction code. Here, the direction is 80 for 300°. The temperature is the last two digits, and minus signs are omitted above 24,000 ft. MSL.
Answer (A) is incorrect. It indicates winds from 300° at 0 kt. However, when forecast speed is less than 5 kt., the code is 9900 for wind direction and speed. Answer (C) is incorrect. It indicates a 99-kt. wind speed from 300°.

29. (Refer to Figure 2 below.) What approximate wind direction, speed, and temperature (relative to ISA) should a pilot expect when planning for a flight over ALB at FL 270?

    A. 270° magnetic at 97 knots; ISA –4°C.

    B. 260° true at 110 knots; ISA +5°C.

    C. 275° true at 97 knots; ISA +4°C.

Answer (C) is correct. *(AWS Sect 7)*
    DISCUSSION: For conditions at FL 270 over ALB in Fig. 2, you must interpolate between values at FL 240 and FL 300. First, decode the two given flight levels:

	FL 240	= 270°	at	77 kt.	and	–28°C
	FL 300	= 280°	at	118 kt.	and	–42°C
Difference	=	10°		41 kt.		–14°C

Interpolation for each value gives

    FL 270 = 275° at 97 kt. and –35°C

Finally, note that the answer asks for ISA (standard temperature). At 2° per 1,000 ft., ISA would be 54°C (27 × 2) less than surface standard of 15°C. Thus, at FL 270, the standard temperature is 15° – 54° = –39°C. The –35°C forecast temperature is ISA + 4°C.
    Answer (A) is incorrect. Winds aloft are always given in true, not magnetic, direction. Answer (B) is incorrect. Interpolating between 270° and 280° results in 275°, not 260°.

30. (Refer to Figure 2 below.) What approximate wind direction, speed, and temperature (relative to ISA) should a pilot expect when planning for a flight over PSB at FL 270?

    A. 260° magnetic at 93 knots; ISA +7°C.

    B. 280° true at 113 knots; ISA +3°C.

    C. 255° true at 93 knots; ISA +6°C.

Answer (C) is correct. *(AWS Sect 7)*
    DISCUSSION: For conditions at FL 270 over PSB in Fig. 2, you must interpolate between values at FL 240 and FL 300. First, decode the two given flight levels:

	FL 240	= 230°	at	68 kt.	and	–26.0°C
	FL 300	= 280°	at	119 kt.	and	–39.0°C
Difference	=	50°		51 kt.		–13.0°C

Interpolation for each value gives

    FL 270 = 255° at 93 kt. and –33°C

Finally, to compare the temperature to standard, subtract the lapse rate at FL 270 [(27,000 ÷ 1,000) × 2° = 54°] from surface standard of 15°C to get FL 270 standard of –39°C. The forecast temperature of about –33°C at FL 270 is thus 6°C warmer than standard.
    Answer (A) is incorrect. Winds aloft are always given in true, not magnetic, direction. Answer (B) is incorrect. Interpolating between 230° and 280° results in 255°, not 280°.

31. (Refer to Figure 2 below.) What approximate wind direction, speed, and temperature (relative to ISA) should a pilot expect when planning for a flight over EMI at FL 270?

    A. 265° true; 100 knots; ISA +3°C.

    B. 270° true; 110 knots; ISA +5°C.

    C. 260° magnetic; 100 knots; ISA –5°C.

Answer (A) is correct. *(AWS Sect 7)*
    DISCUSSION: For conditions at FL 270 over EMI in Fig. 2, you must interpolate between values at FL 240 and FL 300. First, decode the two given flight levels:

	FL 240	= 280°	at	91 kt.	and	–30.0°C
	FL 300	= 250°	at	110 kt.	and	–41.0°C
Difference	=	30°		19 kt.		–11.0°C

Interpolation for each value gives approximately

    FL 270 = 265° at 100 kt. and –36°C

Finally, to compare the temperature to standard, subtract the lapse rate at FL 270 [(27,000 ÷ 1,000) × 2° = 54°] from surface standard of 15°C to get FL 270 standard of –39°C. The forecast temperature of about –36°C at FL 270 is thus 3°C warmer than standard.
    Answer (B) is incorrect. Interpolating between 250° and 280° results in 265°, not 270°. Answer (C) is incorrect. Winds aloft are given in true, not magnetic, direction.

VALID 141200Z FOR USE 0900-1500Z. TEMPS NEG ABV 24000

FT	3000	6000	9000	12000	18000	24000	30000	34000	39000
EMI	2807	2715-07	2728-10	2842-13	2867-21	2891-30	751041	771150	780855
ALB	0210	9900-07	2714-09	2728-12	2656-19	2777-28	781842	760150	269658
PSB		1509+04	2119+01	2233-04	2262-14	2368-26	781939	760850	780456
STL	2308	2613+02	2422-03	2431-08	2446-19	2461-30	760142	782650	760559

Figure 2. – Winds and Temperatures Aloft Forecast.

32. How much colder than standard temperature is the forecast temperature at 9,000 feet, as indicated in the following excerpt from the Wind and Temperature Aloft Forecast?

FT	6000	9000
	0737-04	1043-10

    A. 3°C.

    B. 10°C.

    C. 7°C.

Answer (C) is correct. *(AWS Sect 7)*
    DISCUSSION: At 9,000 ft., the forecast temperature is –10°C. Standard temperature is 15°C at sea level with a lapse rate of 2°C per 1,000 ft., which would bring the standard temperature to –3°C at 9,000 ft. (15° – 18°). Therefore, the forecast temperature of –10°C is 7° colder than the standard temperature of –3°C.
    Answer (A) is incorrect. Standard temperature at 9,000 ft. is –3°C, not –7°C. Answer (B) is incorrect. Standard temperature at 9,000 ft. is –3°C, not 0°C.

33. What wind direction and speed is represented by the entry 9900+00 for 9,000 feet, on a Wind and Temperature Aloft Forecast (FB)?

    A. Light and variable; less than 5 knots.

    B. Vortex winds exceeding 200 knots.

    C. Light and variable; less than 10 knots.

Answer (A) is correct. *(AWS Sect 7)*
    DISCUSSION: The entry 9900 in a winds and temperatures aloft forecast indicates light and variable winds. The air temperature on the Celsius scale is +00.
    Answer (B) is incorrect. An example of the code for winds over 200 kt. would be 7099, for 200° at 199 kt. or greater. Answer (C) is incorrect. Light and variable means less than 5 kt., not 10 kt.

34. When is the wind group at one of the forecast altitudes omitted at a specific location or station in the Wind and Temperature Aloft Forecast (FB)? When the wind

    A. is less than 5 knots.

    B. is less than 10 knots.

    C. at the altitude is within 1,500 feet of the station elevation.

Answer (C) is correct. *(AWS Sect 7)*
    DISCUSSION: No winds are forecast within 1,500 ft. of the station elevation. No temperatures are forecast for the 3,000-ft. MSL or for a level within 2,500 ft. of station elevation.
    Answer (A) is incorrect. When forecast wind speed is less than 5 kt., the code 9900 is used for direction and velocity. Answer (B) is incorrect. When forecast wind speed is less than 5 kt., not 10 kt., the code 9900 is used for direction and velocity.

35. When is the temperature at one of the forecast altitudes omitted at a specific location or station in the Wind and Temperature Aloft Forecast (FB)?

    A. When the temperature is standard for that altitude.

    B. For the 3,000-foot altitude (level) or when the level is within 2,500 feet of station elevation.

    C. Only when the winds are omitted for that altitude (level).

Answer (B) is correct. *(AWS Sect 7)*
    DISCUSSION: No temperatures are forecast for the 3,000-ft. level or for a level within 2,500 ft. of station elevation. No winds are forecast within 1,500 ft. of the station elevation.
    Answer (A) is incorrect. Temperatures are reported whether standard or not. Answer (C) is incorrect. The winds are omitted within 1,500 ft. of the ground and temperatures are omitted within 2,500 ft. of the ground.

36. Which values are used for winds aloft forecasts?

    A. Magnetic direction and knots.

    B. Magnetic direction and MPH.

    C. True direction and knots.

Answer (C) is correct. *(AWS Sect 7)*
    DISCUSSION: Winds aloft are forecast in true direction and knots.
    Answer (A) is incorrect. True, not magnetic, direction is used. Answer (B) is incorrect. True, not magnetic, direction and knots, not MPH, are used.

37. Decode the excerpt from the Winds and Temperature Aloft Forecast (FB) for OKC at 39,000 feet.

FT	3000	9000	12000	24000	39000
OKC	9900	2018+00	2130-06	2361-30	830558

    A. Wind 130° at 50 knots, temperature –58°C.

    B. Wind 330° at 105 knots, temperature –58°C.

    C. Wind 330° at 205 knots, temperature –58°C.

Answer (B) is correct. *(AWS Sect 7)*
    DISCUSSION: At OKC at 39,000 ft., the 83 for wind direction means that 100 kt. have been deducted from the wind speed and 50 added to the wind direction. Thus, the wind speed is 105 kt. Also, subtract 50 from the first two-digit code for direction to get 330°. Above 24,000 ft., the temperatures are always negative.
    Answer (A) is incorrect. Wind 130° at 50 kt. and temperature –58°C would be 135058. Answer (C) is incorrect. Wind 330° at 205 kt. and temperature –58°C would be 839958.

9.8 Low-Level Significant Weather Prog

38. The Low-Level Significant Weather Prognostic Chart depicts weather conditions

   A. that are forecast to exist at a valid time shown on the chart.

   B. as they existed at the time the chart was prepared.

   C. that existed at the time shown on the chart which is about 3 hours before the chart is received.

Answer (A) is correct. *(AWS Sect 8)*
   DISCUSSION: Prognostic charts show conditions as they are forecast to be at the valid time for the chart. The charts are issued four times daily.
   Answer (B) is incorrect. The low-level prog chart consists of 12- and 24-hr. forecasts. Answer (C) is incorrect. Prognostic charts look to the future; they do not report the past.

39. (Refer to Figure 18 on page 377.) The chart symbols shown in the Gulf of Mexico at 12Z and extending into AL, GA, SC, and northern FL indicate a

   A. hurricane.

   B. tropical storm.

   C. tornado originating in the Gulf of Mexico.

Answer (A) is correct. *(AWS Sect 8)*
   DISCUSSION: The SFC PROG chart at 1200Z is on the lower right panel. The symbol shown in the Gulf of Mexico and extending into AL, GA, SC, and northern FL indicates a hurricane and associated precipitation.
   Answer (B) is incorrect. The symbol in the Gulf of Mexico indicates a hurricane. A tropical storm symbol would have the center circle whitened, not open. Answer (C) is incorrect. The symbol in the Gulf of Mexico indicates a hurricane, not a tornado. Additionally, tornadoes are not forecast on a prog chart.

40. (Refer to Figure 18 on page 377.) The U.S. Low Level Significant Weather Surface Prog Chart at 00Z indicates that northwestern Colorado and eastern Utah can expect

   A. moderate or greater turbulence from the surface to FL 240.

   B. moderate or greater turbulence above FL 240.

   C. no turbulence is indicated.

Answer (A) is correct. *(AWS Sect 8)*
   DISCUSSION: The 12-hr. significant weather prog (SFC-400MB) chart at 0000Z is on the upper left panel. Northwestern Colorado and eastern Utah are enclosed by a long, dashed line, which indicates moderate or greater turbulence. The number 240/ (shown in northwestern WY with an arrow) and the symbols above mean moderate-to-severe turbulence from the surface to FL 240 (24,000 ft. MSL).
   Answer (B) is incorrect. Forecast turbulence from the surface to above FL 240 would be depicted as /SFC, not 240/. Answer (C) is incorrect. No turbulence is forecast for central Colorado, but it is indicated for northwestern Colorado.

41. (Refer to Figure 18 on page 377.) The 24-Hour Low Level Significant Weather Prog at 12Z indicates that southwestern Virginia will likely experience

   A. ceilings less than 1,000 feet, visibility less than 3 miles.

   B. clear sky and visibility greater than 6 miles.

   C. ceilings 1,000 to 3,000 feet and visibility 3 to 5 miles.

Answer (A) is correct. *(AWS Sect 8)*
   DISCUSSION: The 24-hr. significant weather prognostic chart (SFC-400MB) is on the upper right panel. Southwestern Virginia is enclosed by a solid line, which indicates a forecast of IFR with ceilings less than 1,000 ft. and/or visibility less than 3 SM.
   Answer (B) is incorrect. The low-level significant weather prognostic chart does not show areas of clear skies, only areas of ceilings above 3,000 ft., by not being enclosed by solid or scalloped lines. Answer (C) is incorrect. Forecast ceilings of 1,000 to 3,000 ft. inclusive and/or visibility 3 to 5 SM inclusive are indicated by an area enclosed by a scalloped, not solid, line.

42. (Refer to Figure 18 on page 377.) A planned low altitude flight from northern Florida to southern Florida at 00Z is likely to encounter

   A. intermittent rain or rain showers, moderate turbulence, and freezing temperatures above 8,000 feet.

   B. showery precipitation, thunderstorms/rain showers covering half or more of the area.

   C. showery precipitation covering less than half the area, no turbulence below 18,000 feet, and freezing temperatures above 12,000 feet.

Answer (B) is correct. *(AWS Sect 8)*
   DISCUSSION: The SFC PROG at 0000Z is on the lower left panel. The Florida peninsula is in a shaded area surrounded by a dash-dot line. The dash-dot line means showery precipitation, and the shading means the precipitation covers half or more of the area. The type of precipitation is depicted in north Florida. The triangle with the dot over it means rain showers, and the symbol resembling an "R" with an arrow means thunderstorms.
   Answer (A) is incorrect. Intermittent precipitation would be indicated by a solid line, not a dash-dot line. Answer (C) is incorrect. Showery precipitation covering less than half the area is depicted by a dash-dot line with no shading. The Florida peninsula has shading, which means precipitation covering half or more, not less, of the area.

Figure 18. – U.S. Low-Level Significant Weather Prognostic Charts.

43. A prognostic chart depicts the conditions

    A. existing at the surface during the past 6 hours.

    B. which presently exist from the 1,000-millibar through the 700-millibar level.

    C. forecast to exist at a specific time in the future.

Answer (C) is correct. *(AWS Sect 8)*
    DISCUSSION: Prognostic charts show conditions as they are forecast to be at the valid time (UTC or Zulu) for the chart. The charts are issued four times daily.
    Answer (A) is incorrect. Prognostic charts relate to the future, not the past. Answer (B) is incorrect. Prognostic charts relate to the future, not the present.

44. (Refer to Figure 5 below.) What is the meaning of the symbol depicted as used on the U.S. Low-Level Significant Weather Prognostic Chart?

    A. Showery precipitation (e.g., rain showers) embedded in an area of continuous rain covering half or more of the area.

    B. Continuous precipitation (e.g., rain) covering half or more of the area.

    C. Showery precipitation (e.g., thunderstorms/rain showers) covering half or more of the area.

Answer (A) is correct. *(AWS Sect 8)*
    DISCUSSION: The dot over the triangle in Fig. 5 indicates showery precipitation. The two heavy, solid dots indicate continuous rain. The shaded area indicates that more than one-half of the area is obscured.
    Answer (B) is incorrect. The dot over the triangle indicates showery precipitation within the area of continuous precipitation. Answer (C) is incorrect. Thunderstorms are indicated by an R with an arrow on the leg.

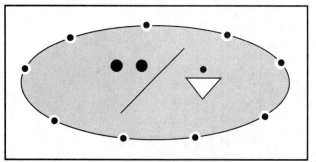

Figure 5. – Symbol Used on Low-Level Significant Weather Prognostic Chart.

45. Which meteorological conditions are depicted by a prognostic chart?

    A. Conditions existing at the time of the observation.

    B. Interpretation of weather conditions for geographical areas between reporting stations.

    C. Conditions forecast to exist at a specific time shown on the chart.

Answer (C) is correct. *(AWS Sect 8)*
    DISCUSSION: Prognostic charts show conditions as they are forecast to be at the valid time for the chart. The charts are issued four times daily.
    Answer (A) is incorrect. Prognostic charts relate to the future, not the present. Answer (B) is incorrect. Prognostic charts relate to the future, not the present.

9.9 Severe Weather Outlook Chart

46. (Refer to Figure 9 on page 379.) The Severe Weather Outlook Chart, which is used primarily for advance planning, provides what information?

    A. An 18-hour categorical outlook with a 48-hour valid time for severe weather watch, thunderstorm lines, and of expected tornado activity.

    B. A preliminary 12-hour outlook for severe thunderstorm activity and probable convective turbulence.

    C. A 24-hour severe weather outlook for possible thunderstorm activity.

Answer (C) is correct. *(AWS Sect 9)*
    DISCUSSION: A severe weather outlook chart is presented in two panels. The left panel covers the first 24-hr. period beginning at 1200Z and depicts areas of possible thunderstorm activity. The right panel covers the following day beginning at 1200Z and contains the same information as the left panel.
    Answer (A) is incorrect. A severe weather outlook chart is valid for 48 hr. and does not have an 18-hr. categorical outlook. Additionally, this chart depicts areas of possible thunderstorm activity, not severe weather watch areas, lines of thunderstorms, or tornado activity. Answer (B) is incorrect. The severe weather outlook chart is a 48-hr., not 12-hr., outlook for possible general thunderstorm activity as well as severe thunderstorms, not convective turbulence.

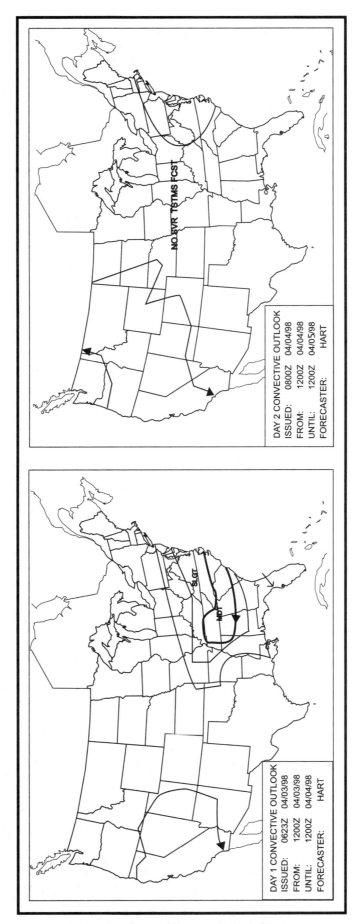

Figure 9. – Severe Weather Outlook Charts.

47. (Refer to Figure 9 on page 381.) The Severe Weather Outlook Chart depicts

    A. areas forecast to have thunderstorms.

    B. areas of forecast, severe or extreme turbulence, and areas of severe icing for the next 24 hours.

    C. areas of general thunderstorm activity (excluding severe) by the use of hatching on the chart.

Answer (A) is correct. *(AWS Sect 9)*
    DISCUSSION: The severe weather outlook chart is a 48-hr. outlook for thunderstorm activity, presented in two panels.
    Answer (B) is incorrect. Areas of forecast severe or extreme turbulence for the next 24 hr. can be found on the significant weather panel of the significant weather prog, not the severe weather outlook chart. Answer (C) is incorrect. An area of possible general thunderstorm activity is shown to the right of a line with an arrowhead (when facing in the direction of the arrow), not a hatched area.

48. (Refer to Figure 9 on page 381.) Using the DAY 2 CONVECTIVE OUTLOOK, what type of thunderstorms, if any, may be encountered on a flight from Montana to central California?

    A. Moderate risk area, surrounded by a slight risk area, of possible severe turbulence.

    B. None.

    C. General.

Answer (C) is correct. *(AWS Sect 9)*
    DISCUSSION: The Day 2 Convective Outlook is the right panel of Fig. 9. On a severe weather outlook chart, a heavy line with an arrowhead indicates an area of thunderstorm activity to the right of the line when facing in the direction of the arrow. A flight from Montana to central California would pass to the right of the two heavy lines that are shown in the western U.S. General thunderstorm activity is expected within this area because it is not labeled with a severe thunderstorm risk category, and because the notation "NO SVR TSTMS FCST" indicates that no areas of severe thunderstorm activity are forecast on the Day 2 Convective Outlook panel.
    Answer (A) is incorrect. The Day 1, not Day 2, Convective Outlook indicates a moderate risk area, surrounded by a slight risk area, of possible severe thunderstorms, not turbulence. Answer (B) is incorrect. Areas where no thunderstorm activity is forecast are shown to the left, not right, of the heavy lines on the Day 2 Convective Outlook panel of Fig. 9, when facing in the direction of the arrow.

49. (Refer to Figure 9 on page 381.) What type of thunderstorm activity is expected over Montana on April 4th at 0800Z?

    A. None.

    B. General.

    C. A slight risk of severe thunderstorms.

Answer (A) is correct. *(AWS Sect 92)*
    DISCUSSION: The thunderstorm activity forecast for April 4 at 0800Z is shown on the Day 1 Convective Outlook panel of Fig. 9, which is valid from 1200Z on April 3 to 1200Z on April 4. On a severe weather outlook chart, a heavy line with an arrowhead indicates an area of thunderstorm activity to the right of the line when facing in the direction of the arrow. Montana is not situated to the right of any lines on the Day 1 Convective Outlook panel. Therefore, no thunderstorm activity is expected over Montana on April 4 at 0800Z.
    Answer (B) is incorrect. Areas where thunderstorm activity is forecast are shown to the right of the lines on a Convective Outlook chart when facing in the direction of the arrow. Montana is not situated to the right of any lines on the Day 1 Convective Outlook panel, meaning that no thunderstorm activity is forecast. Answer (C) is incorrect. Areas where thunderstorm activity is forecast are shown to the right of the lines on a Convective Outlook chart when facing in the direction of the arrow. Montana is not situated to the right of any lines on the Day 1 Convective Outlook panel, meaning that no thunderstorm activity is forecast.

50. (Refer to Figure 9 on page 381.) The Severe Weather Outlook Chart depicts

    A. areas of probable severe thunderstorms by the use of single hatched areas on the chart.

    B. areas of forecast, severe or extreme turbulence, and areas of severe icing for the next 24 hours.

    C. areas of general thunderstorm activity (excluding severe) by the use of hatching on the chart.

Answer (A) is correct. *(AWS Sect 9)*
    DISCUSSION: The severe weather outlook chart is a 48-hr. outlook for thunderstorm activity, presented in two panels. The hatched area indicates possible severe thunderstorms.
    NOTE: This question refers to an old version of the severe weather outlook chart. The current chart does not use hatched areas to indicate severe thunderstorms. Expect the FAA to revise this question in the future.
    Answer (B) is incorrect. Areas of forecast severe or extreme turbulence for the next 24 hr. can be found on the significant weather panel of the significant weather prog, not the severe weather outlook chart. Answer (C) is incorrect. An area of possible general thunderstorm activity is shown to the right of a line with an arrowhead (when facing in the direction of the arrow), not a hatched area.

Figure 9. – Severe Weather Outlook Charts.

9.10   Miscellaneous Charts and Forecasts

51. A pilot planning to depart at 1100Z on an IFR flight is particularly concerned about the hazard of icing. What sources reflect the most accurate information on icing conditions (current and forecast) at the time of departure?

    A. Low-Level Significant Weather Prognostic Chart, and the Area Forecast.

    B. The Area Forecast, and the Freezing Level Chart.

    C. Pilot weather reports (PIREPs), AIRMETs, and SIGMETs.

Answer (C) is correct. *(AWS Sects 3 and 6)*
    DISCUSSION: Pilot reports (PIREPs) can reflect the most current icing conditions for a specific area, including type and intensity. AIRMET Zulu is for icing and freezing levels for a specified time and normally an outlook. A SIGMET is issued for areas of severe icing.
    Answer (A) is incorrect. Low-level sig weather prog charts do not forecast icing conditions but do forecast freezing levels, and an area forecast does not provide any information on icing conditions. Answer (B) is incorrect. A freezing-level chart cannot be used to determine current or forecast icing conditions, and an area forecast does not provide any information on icing conditions.

52. What determines how icing is reported on a PIREP?

    A. Type of ice.

    B. Thickness of ice.

    C. Rate of accumulation.

Answer (C) is correct. *(AWS Sect 3)*
    DISCUSSION: Icing intensities are classified based on the rate of icing accumulation.
    Answer (A) is incorrect. The type of icing accumulation can be listed in the PIREP remarks, but not in the the primary icing group. Answer (B) is incorrect. The thickness of ice would likely not be reported in a PIREP since that information doesn't provide direct information to pilots on what conditions to expect. As well, it is usually very difficult for a pilot to accurately estimate the thickness of the accumulated ice.

53. What conclusion(s) can be drawn from a 500-millibar Constant Pressure Chart for a planned flight at FL 180?

    A. Winds aloft at FL 180 generally flow across the height contours.

    B. Observed temperature, wind, and temperature/dew point spread along the proposed route can be approximated.

    C. Upper highs, lows, troughs, and ridges will be depicted by the use of lines of equal pressure.

Answer (B) is correct. *(AWS Sect 5)*
    DISCUSSION: From a constant pressure analysis chart, you can approximate the observed temperature, wind, and temperature/dew point spread along a proposed route.
    Answer (A) is incorrect. The winds usually flow parallel to, not across, the height contours. Answer (C) is incorrect. Heights of the specified pressure for each station are depicted via solid lines called contours to give a height pattern. The contours depict high height centers and low height centers, not highs and lows.

54. What flight planning information can a pilot derive from constant pressure charts?

    A. Clear air turbulence and icing conditions.

    B. Levels of widespread cloud coverage.

    C. Winds and temperatures aloft.

Answer (C) is correct. *(AWS Sect 5)*
    DISCUSSION: Constant pressure charts provide information about the observed temperature, wind, and temperature/dew point spread along your proposed route.
    Answer (A) is incorrect. Clear air turbulence is shown on the low-level prog chart. Answer (B) is incorrect. Areas and levels of widespread cloud coverage are shown on the weather depiction and surface analysis charts.

55. Which weather forecast describes prospects for an area coverage of both severe and general thunderstorms during the following 24 hours?

    A. Terminal Aerodrome Forecast.

    B. Convective outlook.

    C. Radar Summary Chart.

Answer (B) is correct. *(AWS Sect 6)*
    DISCUSSION: The convective outlook (AC) describes the prospects for general thunderstorm activity during the following 24 hr. Areas with a high, moderate, or slight risk of severe thunderstorms are included, as well as areas where thunderstorms may approach severe limits.
    Answer (A) is incorrect. A terminal aerodrome forecast (TAF) is a statement of expected conditions around an airport, not a forecast of thunderstorms only. Answer (C) is incorrect. The radar summary chart is obsolete. It depicted observed radar returns, which showed precipitation intensity, at the time shown on the chart. It provided an indication of observed, not forecast, severe and general thunderstorms.

56. The Surface Analysis Chart depicts

A. actual pressure systems, frontal locations, cloud tops, and precipitation at the time shown on the chart.

B. frontal locations and expected movement, pressure centers, cloud coverage, and obstructions to vision at the time of chart transmission.

C. actual frontal positions, pressure patterns, temperature, dew point, wind, weather, and obstructions to vision at the valid time of the chart.

Answer (C) is correct. *(AWS Sect 5)*
DISCUSSION: The surface analysis chart provides the locations of pressure systems, dew points, wind, and obstructions to vision at the valid time of the chart.
Answer (A) is incorrect. The surface analysis chart does not depict cloud tops. Answer (B) is incorrect. Expected movement of weather systems is not depicted. This chart depicts current conditions at the time of issuance.

57. What information is provided by a Convective Outlook (AC)?

A. It describes areas of probable severe icing and severe or extreme turbulence during the next 24 hours.

B. It provides prospects of both general and severe thunderstorm activity during the following 24 hours.

C. It indicates areas of probable convective turbulence and the extent of instability in the upper atmosphere (above 500 MB).

Answer (B) is correct. *(AWS Sect 6)*
DISCUSSION: The convective outlook describes the prospects for general thunderstorm activity during the following 24 hours. Areas with a high, moderate, or slight risk of severe thunderstorms are included, as well as areas where thunderstorms may approach severe limits.
Answer (A) is incorrect. Areas of severe or extreme turbulence are forecast in the significant weather prog charts, not in an AC. Additionally, icing is not specifically forecast but is implied in clouds and precipitation above the freezing level. Answer (C) is incorrect. Areas of probable convective turbulence and with the extent of instability above 500 mb/hPa (18,000 ft. MSL) are depicted by the contraction "CB" in a high-level significant weather prog, not an AC.

58. What does a Convective Outlook (AC) describe for a following 24-hr. period?

A. General thunderstorm activity.

B. A severe weather watch bulletin.

C. When forecast conditions are expected to continue beyond the valid period.

Answer (A) is correct. *(AWS Sect 6)*
DISCUSSION: A convective outlook (AC) describes the prospects for general thunderstorm activity during the following 24 hours.
Answer (B) is incorrect. A severe weather watch bulletin is a separate product. An AC forecasts general thunderstorm activity for the following 24 hr., while a severe weather watch bulletin is issued as necessary to define areas of possible severe thunderstorms or tornado activity. Answer (C) is incorrect. An AC is a forecast of thunderstorm activity for the following 24-hr. period, not a statement of forecast conditions that are expected to continue beyond the valid period.

59. When are severe weather watch bulletins (WW) issued?

A. Every 12 hours as required.

B. Every 24 hours as required.

C. Unscheduled and issued as required.

Answer (C) is correct. *(AWS Sect 6)*
DISCUSSION: A severe weather watch bulletin (WW) defines areas of possible severe thunderstorms or tornado activity. WWs are unscheduled and are issued as required by the National Severe Storm Forecast Center.
Answer (A) is incorrect. Severe weather watch bulletins are unscheduled and are issued as required, not every 12 hr. as required. Answer (B) is incorrect. Severe weather watch bulletins are unscheduled and are issued as required, not every 24 hr. as required.

60. If you encounter in-flight icing and ATC asks you to report your conditions, what are the official reportable icing values that you are expected to use?

A. Light, moderate, severe, extreme.

B. Trace, light, moderate, severe.

C. Few, light, moderate, severe.

Answer (B) is correct. *(AC 00-45G)*
DISCUSSION: These values classify icing intensities according to their operational effects on aircraft. When a pilot gives a PIREP, icing is reported as trace, light, moderate, or severe. These are the same icing values a pilot should give to ATC if asked to report icing conditions.
Answer (A) is incorrect. The term "extreme" is a precipitation intensity level used with radar and satellite imagery such as Doppler radar, not a report term given to ATC. Answer (C) is incorrect. The term "few" is used in describing the level of cloud coverage and is not an icing value.

9.11 High-Level Significant Weather Prog

61. (Refer to Figure 7 on page 385.) What information is indicated by arrow A?

    A. The height of the tropopause in meters above sea level.

    B. The height of the existing layer of CAT.

    C. The height of the tropopause in hundreds of feet above MSL.

Answer (C) is correct. *(AWS Sect 8)*
    DISCUSSION: On the U.S. High-Level Significant Weather Prognostic Chart, Fig. 7, tropopause heights are depicted in rectangular boxes in hundreds of feet MSL, i.e., 260, 300, 340, 390, 450, and 530. As you look at the map, you can see how the tropopause height varies around the center.
    Answer (A) is incorrect. The height is in hundreds of feet, not meters. Answer (B) is incorrect. Areas of clear air turbulence (CAT) are bounded by heavy dashed lines.

62. (Refer to Figure 7 on page 385.) What weather conditions are predicted within the area indicated by arrow C?

    A. Light turbulence at FL 370 within the area outlined by dashes.

    B. Moderate turbulence at 35,000 feet MSL.

    C. Moderate to severe CAT has been reported at FL 320.

Answer (B) is correct. *(AWS Sect 8)*
    DISCUSSION: The letter C points to a banana-shaped oval area outlined by a heavy dashed line. About an inch west-northwest of the letter C, there is a symbol composed of a single "mountain peak," or upside-down V, over the number 350, which is separated from 3 Xs by a horizontal line. This symbol indicates that moderate turbulence is forecast in the outlined area from 35,000 ft. MSL to below the lower limit of the chart (24,000 ft. MSL).
    Answer (A) is incorrect. Moderate, not light, turbulence is forecast within the area outlined by dashes. Answer (C) is incorrect. No clear air turbulence (CAT) has been reported by this chart, which is a forecast product, not an observation of existing weather; and the relevant area has moderate, not moderate to severe, CAT forecast from 35,000 ft. MSL to below the lower limit of the chart (24,000 ft. MSL).

63. (Refer to Figure 7 on page 385.) What weather conditions are depicted within the area indicated by arrow B?

    A. Light to moderate turbulence at and above 37,000 feet MSL.

    B. Moderate turbulence from below 24,000 feet MSL to 37,000 feet MSL.

    C. Moderate to severe CAT is forecast to exist at FL 370.

Answer (B) is correct. *(AWS Sect 8)*
    DISCUSSION: On the U.S. High-Level Significant Weather Prognostic Chart, arrow B on Fig. 7 refers to an area bounded by heavy dashed lines, which indicate moderate turbulence. The XXX beneath the line means the base is below FL 240 (the lower limit of all high-level progs), and the 370 means the top of the forecast CAT, FL 370.
    Answer (A) is incorrect. The turbulence is moderate, not light to moderate. Answer (C) is incorrect. The turbulence is moderate, not moderate to severe.

64. (Refer to Figure 7 on page 385.) What weather conditions are depicted within the area indicated by arrow E?

    A. Frequent embedded thunderstorms, less than 1/8 coverage, and tops at FL 370.

    B. Frequent lightning in thunderstorms at FL 370.

    C. Occasional cumulonimbus, 1/8 tp 4/8 coverage, bases below 24,000 feet MSL and tops at 40,000 feet MSL.

Answer (C) is correct. *(AWS Sect 8)*
    DISCUSSION: Arrow E on Fig. 7 points to an area indicating occasional (OCNL), i.e., 1/8 to 4/8, coverage of cumulonimbus clouds and thunderstorms. They are from below FL 240 to FL 400.
    Answer (A) is incorrect. The thunderstorms are not embedded. Also, there is 5/8 to 8/8 area coverage (FRQ). Answer (B) is incorrect. The high-level prog does not indicate lightning.

65. (Refer to Figure 7 on page 385.) Interpret the weather conditions depicted within the area indicated by arrow F.

    A. 2/8 to 6/8 coverage, occasional embedded thunderstorms, tops at FL 540.

    B. 1/8 to 4/8 coverage, occasional embedded thunderstorms, maximum tops at 51,000 feet MSL.

    C. Occasionally embedded cumulonimbus, bases below 25,000 feet with tops to 48,000 feet.

Answer (C) is correct. *(AWS Sect 8)*
    DISCUSSION: The scalloped area on Fig. 7 to which arrow F points shows occasional (1/8 to 4/8) embedded cumulonimbus clouds from below 25,000 ft. (XXX) to 48,000 ft. (480).
    Answer (A) is incorrect. The coverage codes include ISOL (to 1/8), OCNL (1/8 to 4/8), and FRQ (5/8 to 8/8), not 2/8 to 6/8, and the tops are forecast to be at 48,000 ft. (480), not FL 540. Answer (B) is incorrect. The tops are forecast to be at 48,000 ft. (480), not 51,000 ft. MSL.

Figure 7. – High-Level Significant Weather Prognostic Chart.

Figure 7. – High-Level Significant Weather Prognostic Chart.

66. (Refer to Figure 7 on page 386.) What weather conditions are depicted within the area indicated by arrow D?

A. Forecast isolated thunderstorms, tops at FL 440, more than 1/8 coverage.

B. Existing isolated cumulonimbus clouds, tops above 43,000 feet with less than 1/8 coverage.

C. Forecast isolated embedded cumulonimbus clouds with tops at 43,000 feet MSL, and less than 1/8 coverage.

Answer (C) is correct. *(AWS Sect 8)*
   DISCUSSION: Arrow D on the High-Level Significant Weather Prognostic (forecast) Chart points to an area of forecast isolated embedded cumulonimbus clouds with tops at 43,000 feet MSL. The term isolated means less than 1/8 coverage. Approximately 1 inch southwest of the letter D, just off the southern Cuban coast, is the notation "ISOL EMBD CB," and just to the right of this is the notation "430" over a line with 3 Xs under it, meaning that the cumulonimbus clouds extend from 43,000 to below the lower limit of the chart (24,000 feet MSL). There is a thin, heavy line going from these notations due north along the 80°W meridian of longitude to the arrow coming from the letter D.
   Answer (A) is incorrect. The chart notations indicate tops at 43,000 feet, not 44,000 feet, and isolated means less than 1/8 coverage, not more than 1/8 coverage. Answer (B) is incorrect. The High-Level Significant Weather Prognostic Chart depicts forecast, not existing, conditions, and the notations indicate CB tops at, not above, 43,000 feet MSL.

67. (Refer to Figure 7 on page 386.) The symbol on the U.S. HIGH-LEVEL SIGNIFICANT WEATHER PROG, indicated by arrow G, represents the

A. wind direction at the tropopause (300°).

B. height of the tropopause.

C. height of maximum wind shear (30,000 feet).

Answer (B) is correct. *(AWS Sect 8)*
   DISCUSSION: Arrow G points to a rectangular box with a number inside it. On the U.S. High-Level Significant Weather Prognostic Chart, the number inside this symbol indicates the height of the tropopause in hundreds of feet. The box at arrow G has "300," which means the height of the tropopause is 30,000 ft., or FL 300.
   Answer (A) is incorrect. The "300" is the height of the tropopause in hundreds of feet (30,000 ft.), not the wind direction at the tropopause. Answer (C) is incorrect. The "300" is the height of the tropopause, not the height of the maximum wind shear, in hundreds of feet (30,000 ft.).

68. (Refer to Figure 7 on page 386.) The area indicated by arrow H indicates

A. light turbulence below 34,000 feet.

B. isolated embedded cumulonimbus clouds with bases below FL 180 and tops at FL 340.

C. moderate turbulence at and below 34,000 feet.

Answer (C) is correct. *(AWS Sect 8)*
   DISCUSSION: Arrow H points to an area surrounded by heavy dashed lines. Inside that area is a symbol composed of a single "mountain peak," or upside-down V, shown above the number 340, which is separated from three Xs by a horizontal line. This symbol indicates that moderate turbulence is forecast in the outlined area from 34,000 ft. to below the lower limit of the chart (24,000 ft.).
   Answer (A) is incorrect. An area outlined by heavy dashed lines indicates forecast moderate or greater, not light, clear air turbulence. Answer (B) is incorrect. Isolated embedded cumulonimbus clouds with bases below 24,000 ft., not FL 180, and tops at 25,000 ft., not FL 340, are forecast in the area (enclosed by scalloped lines) which appears approximately 1 inch below the letter H.

69. (Refer to Figure 20 on page 389.) What is the maximum wind velocity forecast in the jet stream shown on the High Level Significant Weather Prognostic Chart over Canada?

A. 80 knots.

B. 103 knots.

C. 130 knots.

Answer (C) is correct. *(AWS Sect 8)*
DISCUSSION: The forecast jet streams having a core speed of 80 kt. or greater are shown on the high-level significant weather prog as a solid line with arrowheads indicating the flow direction. The forecast maximum core wind velocity is depicted by a shaft with each pennant (solid triangle) equal to 50 kt. and each feather (single line) equal to 10 kt. The maximum core speed forecast for the jet stream over Canada is 130 kt. (2 pennants + 3 feathers = 130 kt.)

Answer (A) is incorrect. The presence of the line depicting the jet stream indicates that the minimum core speed is 80 kt., but the maximum core speed is depicted by a shaft with pennants and/or feathers. Over Canada, the maximum speed is forecast at 130 kt. Answer (B) is incorrect. Each feather on the shaft indicates 10 kt., not 1 kt., of wind speed. Thus, the maximum core speed of the jet stream over Canada is 130 kt., not 103 kt.

70. (Refer to Figure 12 below, and Figure 20 on page 389.) What is the height of the tropopause over Kentucky?

A. FL 300 sloping to FL400 feet MSL.

B. FL 340.

C. FL 390.

Answer (B) is correct. *(AWS Sect 8)*
DISCUSSION: Over the state of Kentucky is a five-sided polygon which has 340 over a letter "L." This indicates a low tropopause height of 34,000 ft. The chart legend states "All heights in flight level."

Answer (A) is incorrect. The area enclosed by a dashed line centered over Virginia, not Kentucky, is forecasting an area of moderate clear air turbulence (CAT) from FL 300 to FL 400, not a sloping tropopause. Answer (C) is incorrect. FL 390 is the height of the tropopause surrounding Kentucky (indicated by numerous occurrences of "FL 390" inside rectangles), not over Kentucky, where a low tropopause height of FL 340 is indicated by "FL 340 L" inside a five-sided polygon.

Figure 12. – Observed Winds Aloft for 34,000 Feet.

Figure 20. – High-Level Significant Weather Prognostic Chart.

9.12 Observed Winds Aloft Chart

71. (Refer to Figure 12 on page 391.) What is the approximate wind direction and velocity at 34,000 feet (see arrow C)?

    A. 290°/50 knots.

    B. 330°/50 knots.

    C. 090°/48 knots.

Answer (A) is correct. *(AWS Sect 7)*
    DISCUSSION: Refer to arrow C in Fig. 12 (in Oregon) for Portland. The line is from the northwest with a 9 next to it, which means 290°. On the line is a solid triangle, or pennant, which means 50 kt. Thus, the wind is from 290° at 50 kt.
    Answer (B) is incorrect. The 9 next to a northwest line means 290°, not 330°. Answer (C) is incorrect. The 9 next to a northwest line means 290°, not 090°.

72. (Refer to Figure 12 on page 391.) The wind direction and velocity on the Observed Winds Aloft Chart (see arrow A) is indicated from the

    A. northeast at 35 knots.

    B. northwest at 47 knots.

    C. southwest at 35 knots. ·

Answer (C) is correct. *(AWS Sect 7)*
    DISCUSSION: Refer to arrow A in Fig. 12 (in southern Ohio). A line from the southwest with a 3 next to it = 230°. On the line are three 10-kt. symbols and one 5-kt. symbol, indicating wind velocity of 35 kt. Thus, the wind is from 230° at 35 kt.
    Answer (A) is incorrect. The line, and thus the wind, is from the southwest, not the northeast. Answer (B) is incorrect. The line, and thus the wind, is from the southwest, not the northwest.

73. (Refer to Figure 12 on page 391.) What is the approximate wind direction and velocity at CVG at 34,000 feet (see arrow A)?

    A. 040°/35 knots.

    B. 097°/40 knots.

    C. 230°/35 knots.

Answer (C) is correct. *(AWS Sect 7)*
    DISCUSSION: Refer to arrow A in Fig. 12 (in southern Ohio). A line from the southwest with a 3 next to it = 230°. On the line are three 10-kt. symbols and one 5-kt. symbol, indicating wind velocity of 35 kt. Thus, the wind is from 230° at 35 kt.
    Answer (A) is incorrect. The line, and thus the wind, is from the southwest, not the northeast. Answer (B) is incorrect. The line, and thus the wind, is from the southwest, not the east.

74. (Refer to Figure 12 on page 391.) What is the approximate wind direction and velocity at BOI (see arrow B)?

    A. 270°/55 knots.

    B. 250°/95 knots.

    C. 080°/95 knots.

Answer (B) is correct. *(AWS Sect 7)*
    DISCUSSION: Refer to arrow B in Fig. 12 (in Idaho). The line plotted is from the west-southwest with a 5 by it. We can easily see the wind is from the west. The small number helps narrow down the direction by providing the 10th degree; in this case, it is 250°. Adding the 50-kt. symbol with four 10-kt. symbols and one 5-kt. symbol, the wind velocity is 95 kt. Thus, the wind is from 250° at 95 kt.
    Answer (A) is incorrect. The line has a 5 next to it, indicating 250°, not 270°. Answer (C) is incorrect. The line, and thus the wind, is from the west-southwest, not the east.

Figure 12. – Observed Winds Aloft for 34,000 Feet.

END OF STUDY UNIT

STUDY UNIT TEN
IFR EN ROUTE

(2 pages of outline)

In 2014, the FAA released an **Addendum A for the *Computer Testing Supplement for Instrument Rating***. This addendum contains over 100 additional figures, including approach plates, approach procedures, departure procedures, A/FD excerpts, etc. The FAA has released some questions referencing certain figures from this addendum. Gleim has included those FAA-released questions and the relevant figures in our instrument rating materials. **However, we have not included any of the addendum figures that do not have FAA-released questions. If you answer all of the questions in the Gleim test bank for the instrument rating, you will be comfortable using the figures in the addendum to answer similar questions on the knowledge test.**

This study unit contains outlines of major concepts tested, sample test questions and answers regarding IFR en route, and an explanation of each answer. The table of contents above lists each subunit within this study unit, the number of questions pertaining to that particular subunit, and the pages on which the outlines and questions begin, respectively.

10.1 MINIMUM IFR ALTITUDES

1. **Minimum reception altitude (MRA)** is the lowest altitude at which an intersection can be determined.

2. **Minimum obstruction clearance altitude (MOCA)** ensures acceptable navigational signal coverage only within 22 NM (25 SM) of a VOR.

    a. ATC may assign the MOCA as an assigned altitude when certain special conditions exist and when the airplane is within 22 NM of a VOR.

3. **Minimum en route altitude (MEA)** is the lowest published altitude between radio fixes that ensures acceptable navigational signal coverage and meets obstacle clearance requirements between those fixes.

    a. It is the minimum altitude to cross a fix beyond which a higher minimum applies.

4. MOCA and all other minimum IFR altitudes guarantee obstruction clearance in nonmountainous areas by providing at least 1,000 ft. of vertical distance from the highest obstruction 4 NM either side of the center of the airway to be flown.

    a. In mountainous areas, 2,000 ft. of vertical distance is provided.

5. Routes designed to serve aircraft operating from 18,000 ft. MSL up to and including FL 450 are referred to as jet routes or "J" routes.

10.2 VFR-ON-TOP

1. VFR-on-top operations can be conducted only after a pilot has received a VFR-on-top clearance to operate in VFR conditions.

NOTE: The pilot must request a VFR-on-top clearance.

2. VFR-on-top must comply with the appropriate VFR cruising altitudes as prescribed in FAR 91.159, which is based upon magnetic courses.

    a. 000° through 179° -- odd 1,000 ft. plus 500 ft.
    b. 180° through 359° -- even 1,000 ft. plus 500 ft.

3.   VFR-on-top must be conducted at an altitude above the minimum IFR altitude.

4.   VFR-on-top is conducted such that both VFR and IFR rules apply.

5.   A clearance "to VFR-on-top" is authorization to fly through cloud layers to VFR conditions on top.

6.   VFR-on-top operations are specifically prohibited in Class A airspace.

7.   In VFR-on-top clearances, you must provide the same reports to ATC that are required for any other IFR flight, and you must adhere to any ATC clearances.

10.3   IFR EN ROUTE CHART INTERPRETATION

1.   The sample knowledge test questions in this subunit are wide ranging. They are best prepared for by studying the legends for En Route Low-Altitude Charts.

    a.   Legend 25 is presented below.

    b.   Legends 23 and 24 are presented in color on pages 412 and 413.

    c.   Some questions require application of previously covered topics, such as interpretation of VOR indicators.

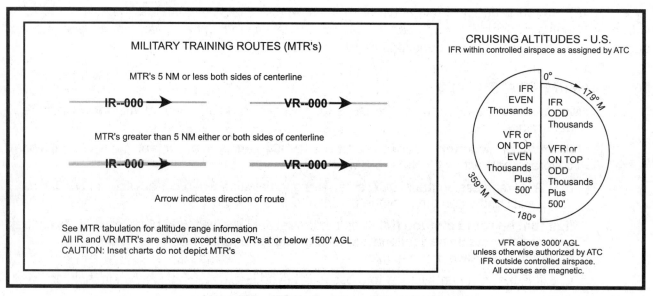

Legend 25. – IFR En Route Low Altitude (U.S.).

QUESTIONS AND ANSWER EXPLANATIONS: All of the instrument rating knowledge test questions chosen by the FAA for release as well as additional questions selected by Gleim relating to the material in the previous outlines are reproduced on the following pages. These questions have been organized into the same subunits as the outlines. To the immediate right of each question are the correct answer and answer explanation. You should cover these answers and answer explanations while responding to the questions. Refer to the general discussion in the Introduction on how to take the FAA knowledge test.

Remember that the questions from the FAA knowledge test bank have been reordered by topic and organized into a meaningful sequence. Also, the first line of the answer explanation gives the citation of the authoritative source for the answer.

QUESTIONS

10.1 Minimum IFR Altitudes

1. What is the definition of MEA?

A. The lowest published altitude which meets obstacle clearance requirements and assures acceptable navigational signal coverage.

B. The lowest published altitude which meets obstacle requirements, assures acceptable navigational signal coverage, two-way radio communications, and provides adequate radar coverage.

C. An altitude which meets obstacle clearance requirements, assures acceptable navigation signal coverage, two-way radio communications, adequate radar coverage, and accurate DME mileage.

Answer (A) is correct. *(AIM P/C Glossary)*
DISCUSSION: The minimum en route altitude (MEA) is the lowest published altitude between radio fixes that ensures acceptable navigational signal coverage and meets the obstacle clearance requirements between those fixes.
Answer (B) is incorrect. By definition, the MEA does not ensure either two-way radio communications or adequate radar coverage. Answer (C) is incorrect. By definition, the MEA is the lowest published, not any, altitude that meets obstacle clearance requirements and ensures acceptable navigation signal coverage. It does not provide for either two-way radio communications or adequate radar coverage.

2. The lowest published altitude which meets obstacle clearance requirements and assures acceptable navigational signal coverage is the

A. MEA.

B. MRA.

C. MOCA.

Answer (A) is correct. *(AIM P/C Glossary)*
DISCUSSION: The MEA (minimum en route altitude) is the lowest published altitude between radio fixes that ensures acceptable navigational signal coverage and meets obstacle clearance requirements between those fixes.
Answer (B) is incorrect. The MRA (minimum reception altitude) is the lowest altitude at which an intersection can be identified. It is usually higher than the MEA. Answer (C) is incorrect. The MOCA (minimum obstruction clearance altitude) only guarantees acceptable navigational signal coverage and meets obstacle clearance requirements when within 22 NM of a NAVAID, not along an entire route that takes the aircraft more than 22 NM from a NAVAID.

3. Reception of signals from an off-airway radio facility may be inadequate to identify the fix at the designated MEA. In this case, which altitude is designated for the fix?

A. MRA.

B. MCA.

C. MOCA.

Answer (A) is correct. *(AIM P/C Glossary)*
DISCUSSION: MRA (minimum reception altitude) is the lowest altitude at which an intersection can be determined. It is the altitude assigned for a fix when the MEA will not provide adequate reception of an off-airway radio facility (NAVAID) identifying the fix.
Answer (B) is incorrect. MCA (minimum crossing altitude) is the lowest altitude at a fix at which an aircraft must cross when proceeding in the direction of a higher MEA. Answer (C) is incorrect. The MOCA (minimum obstruction clearance altitude) is the lowest published altitude in effect between radio fixes on VOR airways, off-airway routes, or route segments that meets obstacle clearance requirements for the entire route segment and that ensures acceptable navigation signal coverage only within 22 NM of a VOR.

4. Reception of signals from a radio facility, located off the airway being flown, may be inadequate at the designated MEA to identify the fix. In this case, which altitude is designated for the fix?

A. MOCA.

B. MRA.

C. MCA.

Answer (B) is correct. *(AIM P/C Glossary)*
DISCUSSION: MRA (minimum reception altitude) is the lowest altitude at which an intersection can be determined. It is the altitude assigned for a fix when the MEA will not provide adequate reception of an off-airway radio facility (NAVAID) identifying the fix.
Answer (A) is incorrect. The MOCA (minimum obstruction clearance altitude) is the lowest published altitude in effect between radio fixes on VOR airways, off-airway routes, or route segments that meets obstacle clearance requirements for the entire route segment and that ensures acceptable navigation signal coverage only within 22 NM of a VOR. Answer (C) is incorrect. MCA (minimum crossing altitude) is the lowest altitude at a fix at which an aircraft must cross when proceeding in the direction of a higher MEA.

5. ATC may assign the MOCA when certain special conditions exist, and when within

   A. 22 NM of a VOR.

   B. 25 NM of a VOR.

   C. 30 NM of a VOR.

Answer (A) is correct. *(AIM P/C Glossary)*
   DISCUSSION: MOCA (minimum obstruction clearance altitude) is the lowest published altitude in effect between radio fixes on VOR airways, off-airway routes, or route segments that meets obstacle clearance requirements for the entire route segment and that ensures acceptable navigational signal coverage only within 22 NM of a VOR. Thus, ATC may assign the MOCA as an assigned altitude, but only within 22 NM of a VOR.
   Answer (B) is incorrect. The MOCA provides acceptable navigational signal coverage only within 25 SM, not 25 NM, of a VOR. Answer (C) is incorrect. ATC may assign the MOCA as an assigned altitude only within 22 NM, not 30 NM.

6. Acceptable navigational signal coverage at the MOCA is assured for a distance from the VOR of only

   A. 12 NM.

   B. 22 NM.

   C. 25 NM.

Answer (B) is correct. *(AIM P/C Glossary)*
   DISCUSSION: MOCA (minimum obstruction clearance altitude) is the lowest published altitude in effect between radio fixes on VOR airways, off-airway routes, or route segments that meets obstacle clearance requirements for the entire route segment and that ensures acceptable navigational signal coverage only within 22 NM of a VOR. Thus, ATC may assign the MOCA as an assigned altitude, but only within 22 NM of a VOR.
   Answer (A) is incorrect. Acceptable navigational signal coverage at the MOCA is ensured for a distance from the VOR of 22 NM, not 12 NM. Answer (C) is incorrect. Acceptable navigational signal coverage at the MOCA is ensured for a distance from the VOR of 22 NM, not 25 NM.

7. Military training routes (MTR) above 1,500 feet are depicted on

   A. IFR Planning Charts.

   B. IFR Low Altitude En Route Charts.

   C. IFR High Altitude En Route Charts.

Answer (B) is correct. *(AIM Para 3-5-2)*
   DISCUSSION: IFR En Route Low-Altitude Charts depict all IFR and VFR MTRs (IR and VR routes) that accommodate operations above 1,500 ft. AGL.
   Answer (A) is incorrect. The U.S. IFR/VFR Planning Chart does not depict MTRs. The DOD Area Planning Chart depicts all MTRs, not only those above 1,500 ft. AGL. Answer (C) is incorrect. IFR En Route High-Altitude Charts cover altitudes at and above 18,000 ft. MSL; generally, MTRs are established below 10,000 ft. MSL.

8. The altitude that provides acceptable navigational signal coverage for the route, and meets obstacle clearance requirements is the minimum:

   A. obstacle clearance altitude.

   B. reception altitude.

   C. enroute altitude.

Answer (C) is correct. *(AIM P/C Glossary)*
   DISCUSSION: The MEA (minimum en route altitude) is the lowest published altitude between radio fixes that ensures acceptable navigational signal coverage and meets obstacle clearance requirements between those fixes.
   Answer (A) is incorrect. The MOCA (minimum obstruction clearance altitude) only guarantees acceptable navigational signal coverage and meets obstacle clearance requirements when within 22 NM of a NAVAID, not along an entire route that takes the aircraft more than 22 NM from a NAVAID. Answer (B) is incorrect. The MRA (minimum reception altitude) is the lowest altitude at which an intersection can be identified. It is usually higher than the MEA.

9. Which condition is guaranteed for all of the following altitude limits: MAA, MCA, MRA, MOCA, and MEA? (Non-mountainous area.)

   A. Adequate navigation signals.

   B. Adequate communications.

   C. 1,000-foot obstacle clearance.

Answer (C) is correct. *(AIM P/C Glossary)*
   DISCUSSION: The MAA, MCA, MRA, MOCA, and MEA meet the minimum obstacle clearance requirements. In non-mountainous areas, 1,000 ft. above the highest obstacle is guaranteed within a horizontal distance of 4 NM from the course to be flown.
   Answer (A) is incorrect. The MOCA ensures acceptable navigational signals only within 22 NM of a VOR. Answer (B) is incorrect. The minimum IFR altitudes do not guarantee adequate communications coverage.

10. If no MCA is specified, what is the lowest altitude for crossing a radio fix, beyond which a higher minimum applies?

A. The MEA at which the fix is approached.

B. The MRA at which the fix is approached.

C. The MOCA for the route segment beyond the fix.

Answer (A) is correct. *(FAR 91.177)*
DISCUSSION: If no MCA (minimum crossing altitude) is specified, the lowest altitude for crossing a radio fix beyond which a higher minimum IFR altitude exists is the MEA at which the fix is approached. A climb must be initiated to a higher minimum immediately after passing the point beyond which that minimum altitude applies.
Answer (B) is incorrect. If a higher minimum altitude exists after the fix and a higher altitude is needed to identify a fix, usually an MCA, not an MRA, is established at that fix. Answer (C) is incorrect. If there is no MCA, the higher minimum altitude does not apply until immediately after passing the fix.

11. In the case of operations over an area designated as a mountainous area, no person may operate an aircraft under IFR below 2,000 feet above the highest obstacle within a horizontal distance of

A. 3 SM from the course flown.

B. 4 SM from the course flown.

C. 4 NM from the course flown.

Answer (C) is correct. *(FAR 91.177)*
DISCUSSION: In the case of operations over an area designated as a mountainous area where no other minimum altitude is prescribed, no person may operate an aircraft under IFR below 2,000 ft. above the highest obstacle within a horizontal distance of 4 NM from the course to be flown.
Answer (A) is incorrect. The horizontal distance is 4 NM, not 3 SM, from the course flown. Answer (B) is incorrect. The horizontal distance is 4 NM, not SM, from the course flown.

12. In the case of operations over an area designated as a mountainous area where no other minimum altitude is prescribed, no person may operate an aircraft under IFR below an altitude of

A. 500 feet above the highest obstacle.

B. 1,000 feet above the highest obstacle.

C. 2,000 feet above the highest obstacle.

Answer (C) is correct. *(FAR 91.177)*
DISCUSSION: In the case of operations over an area designated as a mountainous area where no other minimum altitude is prescribed, no person may operate an aircraft under IFR below 2,000 ft. above the highest obstacle within a horizontal distance of 4 NM from the course to be flown.
Answer (A) is incorrect. No person may operate an aircraft under IFR below an altitude of 2,000 ft., not 500 ft., above the highest obstacle in a mountainous area. Answer (B) is incorrect. No person may operate an aircraft under IFR below an altitude of 1,000 ft. above the highest obstacle in a nonmountainous, not mountainous, area.

13. MEA is an altitude which assures

A. obstacle clearance, accurate navigational signals from more than one VORTAC, and accurate DME mileage.

B. a 1,000-foot obstacle clearance within 2 miles of an airway and assures accurate DME mileage.

C. acceptable navigational signal coverage and meets obstruction clearance requirements.

Answer (C) is correct. *(AIM P/C Glossary)*
DISCUSSION: The minimum en route altitude (MEA) is the lowest published altitude between radio fixes that ensures acceptable navigational signal coverage and meets the obstacle clearance requirements between those fixes.
Answer (A) is incorrect. Only one VORTAC is needed at a time to provide acceptable coverage, and DME is not a required navigational signal. Answer (B) is incorrect. The clearance is within 4 NM, not 2 mi., and there is no assurance of DME coverage.

14. Unless otherwise specified on the chart, the minimum en route altitude along a jet route is

A. 18,000 feet MSL.

B. 24,000 feet MSL.

C. 10,000 feet MSL.

Answer (A) is correct. *(FAR 71.33)*
DISCUSSION: Each designated jet route consists of a direct course for navigating from 18,000 ft. MSL up to and including FL 450 between the navigational aids and intersections specified for that route. Thus, the MEA along a jet route is 18,000 ft. MSL.
Answer (B) is incorrect. This amount (FL 240) is the minimum altitude at which DME is required when navigating by VOR, not the MEA for a jet route. Answer (C) is incorrect. This amount is the minimum altitude at which aircraft are required to operate the transponder on Mode C, not the MEA for a jet route.

10.2 VFR-on-Top

15. Under which of the following circumstances will ATC issue a VFR restriction to an IFR flight?

    A. Whenever the pilot reports the loss of any navigational aid.

    B. When it is necessary to provide separation between IFR and special VFR traffic.

    C. When the pilot requests it.

Answer (C) is correct. *(AIM Para 4-4-7)*
    DISCUSSION: VFR-on-top is an ATC authorization for an IFR aircraft to operate in VFR conditions at any appropriate VFR altitude. ATC may not authorize VFR-on-top operations unless the pilot requests the clearance to operate in VFR conditions.
    Answer (A) is incorrect. A pilot would report only a malfunction of navigation equipment, not a loss of any navigational aid, to ATC. Answer (B) is incorrect. Special VFR traffic would be found near an airport in Class B, C, or D airspace or Class E airspace designated for an airport that is currently experiencing IMC. Thus, ATC would not issue a VFR restriction to an IFR flight.

16. What altitude may a pilot on an IFR flight plan select upon receiving a VFR-on-Top clearance?

    A. Any altitude at least 1,000 feet above or 1,000 feet below the meteorological condition.

    B. Any appropriate VFR altitude at or above the MEA in VFR weather conditions.

    C. Any VFR altitude appropriate for the direction of flight at least 500 feet above the meteorological condition.

Answer (B) is correct. *(AIM Para 4-4-7)*
    DISCUSSION: When operating in VMC with an ATC authorization to "maintain VFR-on-top/maintain VFR conditions," pilots on IFR flight plans are required to

1. Fly at the appropriate VFR altitude;
2. Comply with the VFR visibility and distance from clouds criteria; and
3. Comply with instrument flight rules that are applicable to the flight, i.e., minimum IFR altitudes, position reporting, course to be flown, adherence to ATC clearances, etc.

    Answer (A) is incorrect. After receiving a VFR-on-top clearance, the pilot may select any appropriate VFR altitude at or above the minimum IFR altitude in VMC, not only 1,000 ft. above or below the meteorological condition. This may be above, below, between layers, or in areas where there is no meteorological obscuration. Answer (C) is incorrect. After receiving a VFR-on-top clearance, the pilot may select any appropriate VFR altitude at or above the minimum IFR altitude in VMC, not only 500 ft. above the meteorological condition. This may be above, below, between layers, or in areas where there is no meteorological obscuration.

17. Which rules apply to the pilot in command when operating on a VFR-on-Top clearance?

    A. VFR only.

    B. VFR and IFR.

    C. VFR when "in the clear" and IFR when "in the clouds."

Answer (B) is correct. *(AIM Para 4-4-7)*
    DISCUSSION: When operating in VMC with an ATC authorization to "maintain VFR-on-top/maintain VFR conditions," pilots on IFR flight plans are required to

1. Fly at the appropriate VFR altitude;
2. Comply with the VFR visibility and distance from clouds criteria; and
3. Comply with instrument flight rules that are applicable to the flight, i.e., minimum IFR altitudes, position reporting, course to be flown, adherence to ATC clearances, etc.

    Answer (A) is incorrect. An ATC clearance to operate VFR-on-top does not imply cancelation of the IFR flight plan. Answer (C) is incorrect. A VFR-on-top clearance is issued when the pilot is in VMC and must remain in VMC unless the VFR-on-top clearance is canceled. It does not allow a pilot to fly in IMC.

18. Which ATC clearance should instrument-rated pilots request in order to climb through a cloud layer or an area of reduced visibility and then continue the flight VFR?

    A. To VFR on Top.

    B. Special VFR to VFR Over-the-Top.

    C. VFR Over-the-Top.

Answer (A) is correct. *(AIM Para 4-4-7)*
    DISCUSSION: Pilots desiring to climb through a cloud, haze, smoke, or other meteorological formation and then either cancel their IFR flight plan or operate VFR-on-top may request an ATC clearance to climb to VFR-on-top.
    Answer (B) is incorrect. A special VFR clearance is issued only in Class B, C, or D airspace or Class E airspace designated for an airport, and the pilot must remain clear of clouds, not climb through them. Answer (C) is incorrect. It is VFR-on-top, not VFR-over-the-top.

19. When can a VFR-on-Top clearance be assigned by ATC?

    A. Only upon request of the pilot when conditions are indicated to be suitable.

    B. Any time suitable conditions exist and ATC wishes to expedite traffic flow.

    C. When VFR conditions exist, but there is a layer of clouds below the MEA.

Answer (A) is correct. *(AIM Para 4-4-7)*
    DISCUSSION: ATC may assign a VFR-on-top clearance only when the pilot requests such a clearance, and the flight must be conducted in VFR weather conditions.
    Answer (B) is incorrect. ATC can issue a VFR-on-top clearance only upon a pilot's, not ATC's, request. Answer (C) is incorrect. ATC can issue a VFR-on-top clearance only upon a pilot's request; clearance is not based only on the meteorological conditions.

20. When must a pilot fly at a cardinal altitude plus 500 feet on an IFR flight plan?

    A. When flying above 18,000 feet in VFR conditions.

    B. When flying in VFR conditions above clouds.

    C. When assigned a VFR-on-Top clearance.

Answer (C) is correct. *(AIM Para 4-4-7)*
    DISCUSSION: VFR-on-top clearances are flown at VFR altitudes, which are even or odd thousand-foot intervals plus 500 ft. This is in contrast to IFR altitudes that are at even or odd thousand-foot intervals. Cardinal altitude means 1,000-ft. intervals, e.g., 3,000, 4,000, etc.
    Answer (A) is incorrect. VFR-on-top is not permitted in Class A airspace, which is from 18,000 ft. MSL to and including FL 600. Answer (B) is incorrect. A pilot on an IFR flight plan uses VFR altitudes only when assigned a VFR-on-top clearance.

21. Where are VFR-on-Top operations prohibited?

    A. In Class A airspace.

    B. During off-airways direct flights.

    C. When flying through Class B airspace.

Answer (A) is correct. *(AIM Para 4-4-7)*
    DISCUSSION: ATC will not authorize VFR or VFR-on-top operations in Class A airspace.
    Answer (B) is incorrect. VFR-on-top operations during off-airway direct flights are not prohibited. Answer (C) is incorrect. VFR-on-top operations within Class B airspace are permitted.

22. What minimums must be considered in selecting an altitude when operating with a VFR-on-Top clearance?

    A. At least 500 feet above the lowest MEA, or appropriate MOCA, and at least 1,000 feet above the existing meteorological condition.

    B. At least 1,000 feet above the lowest MEA, appropriate MOCA, or existing meteorological condition.

    C. Minimum IFR altitude, minimum distance from clouds, and visibility appropriate to altitude selected.

Answer (C) is correct. *(AIM Para 4-4-7)*
    DISCUSSION: When operating in VMC with an ATC authorization to "maintain VFR-on-top/maintain VFR conditions," pilots on IFR flight plans are required to

1. Fly at the appropriate VFR altitude;
2. Comply with the VFR visibility and distance from clouds criteria; and
3. Comply with instrument flight rules that are applicable to the flight, i.e., minimum IFR altitudes, position reporting, course to be flown, adherence to ATC clearances, etc.

    Answer (A) is incorrect. You must be at or above, not a specified distance from, the minimum IFR altitude, and while on a VFR-on-top clearance, you may operate above, below, or between layers of, not only above, the existing meteorological condition. Answer (B) is incorrect. You must be at or above, not a specified distance from, the minimum IFR altitude, and while on a VFR-on-top clearance, you may operate above, below, or between layers of, not only above, the existing meteorological condition.

23. When operating under IFR with a VFR-On-Top clearance, what altitude should be maintained?

    A. An IFR cruising altitude appropriate to the magnetic course being flown.

    B. A VFR cruising altitude appropriate to the magnetic course being flown and as restricted by ATC.

    C. The last IFR altitude assigned by ATC.

Answer (B) is correct. *(AIM Para 4-4-7)*
    DISCUSSION: When operating in VMC with an ATC authorization to maintain VFR-on-top/maintain VFR conditions, pilots on IFR flight plans are required to

1. Fly at the appropriate VFR altitude;
2. Comply with the VFR visibility and distance from clouds criteria; and
3. Comply with instrument flight rules that are applicable to the flight, i.e., minimum IFR altitudes, position reporting, course to be flown, adherence to ATC clearances, etc.

    Answer (A) is incorrect. Pilots operating with a VFR-on-top clearance should maintain a VFR, not an IFR, cruising altitude appropriate to the magnetic course being flown. Answer (C) is incorrect. Pilots operating with a VFR-on-top clearance should maintain a VFR, not an IFR, cruising altitude.

24. In which airspace is VFR-on-Top operation prohibited?

A. Class B airspace.

B. Class E airspace.

C. Class A airspace.

Answer (C) is correct. *(AIM Para 4-4-7)*
  DISCUSSION: ATC will not authorize VFR or VFR-on-top operations in Class A airspace.
  Answer (A) is incorrect. VFR-on-top operations are permitted, not prohibited, in Class B airspace. Answer (B) is incorrect. VFR-on-top operations are permitted, not prohibited, in Class E airspace.

25. What reports are required of a flight operating on an IFR clearance specifying VFR on Top in a nonradar environment?

A. The same reports that are required for any IFR flight.

B. All normal IFR reports except vacating altitudes.

C. Only the reporting of any unforecast weather.

Answer (A) is correct. *(AIM Para 4-4-7)*
  DISCUSSION: When on a VFR-on-top clearance, you must comply with instrument flight rules that are applicable to the flight, e.g., minimum flight altitudes, position reporting, radio communications, course to be flown, adherence to ATC communications, etc.
  Answer (B) is incorrect. All normal IFR reports are required when operating on a VFR-on-top clearance. You should advise ATC prior to any altitude change to ensure the exchange of accurate traffic information. Answer (C) is incorrect. All IFR reports, not only unforecast weather, must be made while operating on a VFR-on-top clearance.

26. When on a VFR-on-Top clearance, the cruising altitude is based on

A. true course.

B. magnetic course.

C. magnetic heading.

Answer (B) is correct. *(FAR 91.159)*
  DISCUSSION: While operating under a VFR-on-top clearance, you must fly at the appropriate VFR altitude, which is based on magnetic course.
  Answer (A) is incorrect. VFR cruising altitudes are based on magnetic, not true, course. Answer (C) is incorrect. VFR cruising altitudes are based on magnetic course, not heading.

27. You have filed an IFR flight plan with a VFR-on-Top clearance in lieu of an assigned altitude. If you receive this clearance and fly a course of 180°, at what altitude should you fly? (Assume VFR conditions.)

A. Any IFR altitude which will enable you to remain in VFR conditions.

B. An odd thousand-foot MSL altitude plus 500 feet.

C. An even thousand-foot MSL altitude plus 500 feet.

Answer (C) is correct. *(FAR 91.159)*
  DISCUSSION: When operating in VMC with a VFR-on-top clearance, you must fly at the appropriate VFR cruising altitude. On a magnetic course of 180° through 359°, an even thousand-foot MSL altitude plus 500 ft. must be flown.
  Answer (A) is incorrect. On VFR-on-top, one uses VFR, not IFR, altitudes. Answer (B) is incorrect. Odd thousand-foot altitudes plus 500 ft. are for a magnetic course of 0° through 179°, not 180°.

28. What cruising altitude is appropriate for VFR on Top on a westbound flight below 18,000 feet?

A. Even thousand-foot levels.

B. Even thousand-foot levels plus 500 feet, but not below MEA.

C. Odd thousand-foot levels plus 500 feet, but not below MEA.

Answer (B) is correct. *(FAR 91.159)*
  DISCUSSION: When operating in VMC with a VFR-on-top clearance, you must fly at the appropriate VFR cruising altitude but not below the minimum IFR altitude (e.g., MEA). On a magnetic course of 180° through 359° (i.e., westbound), an even thousand-foot MSL altitude plus 500 ft. must be flown.
  Answer (A) is incorrect. An even thousand-foot level is an IFR, not VFR, cruising altitude for a westbound flight. VFR-on-top clearances must maintain VFR altitudes. Answer (C) is incorrect. An odd thousand-foot level plus 500 ft. is for eastbound, not westbound, flight or a magnetic course from 0° to 179°.

29. If, while in Class E airspace, a clearance is received to "maintain VFR conditions on top," the pilot should maintain a VFR cruising altitude based on the direction of the

A. true course.

B. magnetic heading.

C. magnetic course.

Answer (C) is correct. *(FAR 91.159)*
  DISCUSSION: While operating under a VFR-on-top clearance, you must fly at the appropriate VFR cruising altitude, which is based on magnetic course.
  Answer (A) is incorrect. VFR cruising altitudes are based on magnetic, not true, course. Answer (B) is incorrect. VFR cruising altitudes are based on magnetic course, not heading.

30. You are flying on an IFR flight plan at 5,500 feet with a VFR-on-top clearance when you encounter icing. You know there is clear air above and you request 9,500 feet from ATC. They deny the request, but give you 7,500 feet. Are you still VFR-on-top?

    A. Yes, you are still IFR with a VFR-on-top clearance.

    B. No, you are now VFR.

    C. No, your VFR-on-top clearance has been canceled.

Answer (A) is correct. *(AIM Para 5-5-13)*
    DISCUSSION: While flying on an IFR flight plan and cleared for VFR-on-top, a pilot has latitude to change altitude as necessary to maintain VFR visibility and distance from clouds criteria. The pilot reports those altitude changes to ATC, or ATC assigns another altitude.
    Answer (B) is incorrect. VFR-on-top is not automatically canceled due to an altitude change. The pilot must maintain a VFR cruising altitude and inform ATC of altitude changes, but the VFR-on-top clearance remains valid until the pilot cancels it, provided that aircraft remains in VFR conditions. Answer (C) is incorrect. VFR-on-top is not automatically canceled due to an altitude change. The pilot must cancel VFR-on-top.

31. You encounter structural icing on an IFR flight plan at 7,000 feet. Your request for 9,000 feet is rejected by ATC. You request VFR-on-top at 7,500 feet, which is granted. What must you do with your IFR flight plan?

    A. Comply only with VFR rules.

    B. Cancel it.

    C. Continue as planned.

Answer (C) is correct. *(AIM Para 5-5-13)*
    DISCUSSION: A pilot may request VFR-on-top and, if granted, must comply with both visual and instrument flight rules. However, granting VFR-on-top does not cancel or invalidate an IFR flight plan, nor does it suggest the pilot can ignore instrument flight rules while flying VFR-on-top.
    Answer (A) is incorrect. A pilot may request VFR-on-top and, if granted, must comply with both visual and instrument flight rules while operating VFR-on-top. The pilot must cancel VFR-on-top when VFR rules can no longer be maintained. Answer (B) is incorrect. A pilot may request VFR-on-top and, if granted, must comply with both visual and instrument flight rules. However, granting VFR-on-top does not cancel or invalidate an IFR flight plan. The pilot can continue without canceling his or her IFR flight plan.

32. ATC has approved your request for VFR-on-top while on an IFR clearance. Therefore, you

    A. should set your transponder to code 1200.

    B. must fly appropriate IFR altitudes.

    C. must fly appropriate VFR altitudes.

Answer (C) is correct. *(AIM Para 4-4-8)*
    DISCUSSION: When operating in VFR conditions with an ATC authorization to "maintain VFR-on-top, maintain VFR conditions," pilots on IFR flight plans must fly at the appropriate VFR altitudes and are still on filed IFR flight plans.
    Answer (A) is incorrect. Transponder code 1200 is for VFR operations only and not for IFR flights. Answer (B) is incorrect. VFR-on-top is an IFR clearance to operate in VFR conditions; therefore, pilots must fly at the appropriate VFR altitudes. Aircraft that are on an IFR flight plans flying in VMC without a VFR-on-top clearance must maintain IFR altitudes.

10.3 IFR En Route Chart Interpretation

33. In the event of two-way radio communications failure while operating on an IFR clearance in VFR conditions, the pilot should continue

    A. by the route assigned in the last ATC clearance received.

    B. the flight under VFR and land as soon as practical.

    C. the flight by the most direct route to the fix specified in the last clearance.

Answer (B) is correct. *(FAR 91.185)*
    DISCUSSION: If two-way radio communications fail while operating in VFR conditions, or if VFR conditions are encountered after the failure, each pilot shall continue the flight under VFR and land as soon as practicable.
    Answer (A) is incorrect. If the failure occurs in IFR, not VFR, conditions, and VFR conditions are not encountered after the failure, each pilot shall continue the flight by the route assigned in the last ATC clearance received. Answer (C) is incorrect. One continues the last route assigned by ATC if in IFR, not the most direct route to the next fix.

34. (Refer to Figure 87 on page 424.) Where is the VOR COP when flying east on V306 from Daisetta to Lake Charles?

    A. 50 NM east of DAS.

    B. 40 NM east of DAS.

    C. 30 NM east of DAS.

Answer (C) is correct. *(AIM Para 5-3-6)*
    DISCUSSION: On Fig. 87, when flying east on V306 from Daisetta to Lake Charles, the VOR changeover point (COP) is indicated by the symbol "⌐," and the mileages are given to each VORTAC station. The COP is 30 NM east of Daisetta and 50 NM west of Lake Charles.
    Answer (A) is incorrect. The COP is 50 NM west, not east, of Lake Charles, not DAS. Answer (B) is incorrect. The midway point, not the prescribed COP, is 40 NM.

35. (Refer to Figure 87 on page 424 and Legend 23 on page 412.) What is indicated by the localizer course symbol at Jefferson County Airport?

    A. A published LDA localizer course with voice capability.

    B. A published ILS localizer course, which has an additional navigation function.

    C. A published SDF localizer course with back course capabilities.

Answer (B) is correct. *(ACL)*
    DISCUSSION: When a localizer course symbol is shown on a en route low-altitude chart, this indicates that the published ILS localizer has a navigation function in addition to course guidance. The localizer at Jefferson County Airport, which is located near the center of Fig. 87, is used to define PORTZ and MARSA intersections.
    Answer (A) is incorrect. ILS course symbols, not LDA, are shown as depicted to indicate an additional navigation function. Answer (C) is incorrect. ILS course symbols, not SDF, are shown as depicted to indicate an additional navigation function.

36. (Refer to Figure 87 on page 424 and Legend 23 on page 412.) Why is the localizer back course at Jefferson County Airport depicted?

    A. The back course is not aligned with a runway.

    B. The back course has a glide slope.

    C. The back course has an additional navigation function.

Answer (C) is correct. *(ACL)*
    DISCUSSION: Jefferson County Airport in Beaumont, TX is located near the center of Fig. 87. The extended localizer course symbol shown there applies to this question. This symbol indicates that there is a published ILS localizer course with an additional navigation function. The arrow is further identified (on the chart) as the back course. The back course is used to identify both PORTZ and MARSA intersections.
    Answer (A) is incorrect. The back course symbol suggests an ILS localizer front course, which is always aligned with the runway. Answer (B) is incorrect. A LOC back course never has a glide slope.

37. (Refer to Figure 87 on page 424 and Legend 24 on page 413.) Where is the VOR changeover point on V20 between Beaumont and Hobby?

    A. Halfway point.

    B. MOCKS intersection.

    C. Anahuac Beacon.

Answer (A) is correct. *(AIM Para 5-3-6)*
    DISCUSSION: In Fig. 87, V20 connects Beaumont (BPT) VORTAC and Hobby (HUB) VORTAC. Note that HUB VORTAC is west of Ellington VOR and is not shown on the chart. The changeover point (COP) is located midway between BPT and HUB, which is 34 NM. When the COP is **not** located at the midway point, the symbol "⌐" is used, and the mileage to each NAVAID is given.
    Answer (B) is incorrect. MOCKS INT is 25 NM from BPT, and the halfway point is 34 NM. Answer (C) is incorrect. Anahuac Beacon is not on the airway.

38. (Refer to Figure 58 on page 403.) On which frequencies could you communicate with the Montgomery County FSS while on the ground at College Station?

    A. 122.65, 122.2, 122.1, 113.3.

    B. 122.65, 122.2.

    C. 118.5, 122.65, 122.2.

Answer (B) is correct. *(A/FD)*
    DISCUSSION: Fig. 58 is an excerpt from an *A/FD* for Easterwood Field located at College Station, TX. Locate the **Communications** heading for information on frequencies. There is a College Station RCO to communicate with the Montgomery County FSS on frequencies 122.65 and 122.2 only.
    Answer (A) is incorrect. The frequency 122.1 is not available at College Station to contact the Montgomery County FSS. College Station VORTAC operates on frequency 113.3, but under **Radio Aids to Navigation**, the "W" after VORTAC means that no voice is transmitted on this frequency. Answer (C) is incorrect. The frequency 118.5 is the tower/CTAF, not FSS, frequency.

39. (Refer to Figure 58 on page 403.) Which indications on the VOR receivers and DME at the Easterwood Field VOR receiver checkpoint would meet the regulatory requirement for this flight?

	VOR No. 1	TO/FROM	VOR No. 2	TO/FROM	DME
A.	097°	FROM	101°	FROM	3.3
B.	097°	TO	096°	TO	3.2
C.	277°	FROM	280°	FROM	3.3

Answer (A) is correct. *(FAR 91.171)*
    DISCUSSION: The bottom portion of Fig. 58 lists the VOR receiver checkpoints. Locate College Station (Easterwood Field) to determined that the checkpoint is on the ground (on west edge of parking ramp), the azimuth from the VORTAC is 097° (i.e., R-097), and the distance is 3.2 NM from the VORTAC. On the R-097, you want the CDI needle centered with an OBS setting of 097° FROM or 277° TO the station, with the acceptable error of ±4°. Thus, the acceptable VOR indications are 097° FROM and 101° FROM the station.
    Answer (B) is incorrect. The magnetic azimuth (i.e., radial) from the station at the ground checkpoint is 097°, which results in a TO, not FROM, indication with the OBS set to 097°. Answer (C) is incorrect. The magnetic azimuth (i.e., radial) from the station at the ground checkpoint is 097°, which results in a TO, not FROM, indication with the OBS set to 277°.

140   **TEXAS**

COLLEGE STATION

EASTERWOOD FLD   (CLL)   3 SW   UTC–6(–5DT)   30°35′18″N 96°21′49″W   **HOUSTON**

320   B   S4   FUEL 100LL, JET A   OX 2   ARFF Index A   **H-2K, 5B, L-17A**

RWY 16-34: H7000X150 (ASPH–GRVD)   S-70, D-90, DT-150   MIRL   **IAP**

     RWY 16: VASI(V4R)—GA 3.0°TCH 51′. Tree.   RWY 34: MALSR.

RWY 10-28: H5160X150 (CONC)   S-27, D-50, DT-87   MIRL

     RWY 10: VASI(V4L)—GA 3.0°TCH 50′. Tree.   RWY 28: REIL VASI(V4L)—GA 3.0° TCH 54′. Tree.

RWY 04-22: H5149X150 (CONC)   S-27, D-50, DT-87

     RWY 04: Tree.   RWY 22: Tree.

AIRPORT REMARKS: Attended 1200-0500Z‡. CAUTION: deer on rwys. CAUTION: Rwy 10-28 taxiway B and taxiway E have uneven surfaces. Birds on and in vicinity of arpt. MIRL Rwy 10–28 preset medium ints when twr clsd, to increase ints and ACTIVATE MIRL Rwy 16–34 and MALSR Rwy 34—CTAF. CLOSED to unscheduled air carrier ops with more than 30 passenger seats except 24 hours PPR call, arpt manager 409-845-4811. Rwy 04-22 day VFR ops only. Itinerant acft park North of twr, overnight parking fee. Ldg fee scheduled FAR 135 and all FAR 121 ops. For fuel after hours PPR call 409–845-4811/823 –0690 or ctc Texas A and M University police 409–845-2345; late ngt fee. Rwy 16-34 grvd except south 200′. Rwy 04-22 deteriorating and vegetation growing through cracks. NOTE: See SPECIAL NOTICE—Simultaneous Operations on Intersecting Runways.

COMMUNICATIONS: CTAF 118.5   ATIS 126.85 (1200-0400Z‡)   UNICOM 122.95

     MONTGOMERY COUNTY FSS (CXO) TF 1-800-WX-BRIEF. NOTAM FILE CLL.

     COLLEGE STATION RCO 122.65 122.2 (MONTGOMERY COUNTY FSS).

Ⓡ HOUSTON CENTER APP/DEP CON: 120.4

     TOWER: 118.5 (1200-0400Z‡) (VFR only)   GND CON: 121.7

RADIO AIDS TO NAVIGATION: NOTAM FILE CLL. VHF/DF ctc FSS

     COLLEGE STATION (L) VORTACW 113.3   CLL   Chan 80   30°36′17″N 96°25′13″W   100° 3.1 NM to fld. 370/08E. HIWAS.

     ROWDY NDB (LOM) 260   CL   30°29′36″N 96°20′16″W   341° 5.9 NM to fld.

     ILS 111.7 I-CLL Rwy 34 LOM ROWDY NDB. ILS unmonitored when twr closed.

COLLEGE STATION   30°36′17″N 96°25′13″W   NOTAM FILE CLL.   **HOUSTON**

     (L) VORTACW 113.3   CLL   Chan 80   100° 3.1 NM to Easterwood Fld. 370/08E. HIWAS.   **H-2K, 5B, L-17A**

     RCO 122.65 122.2 (MONTGOMERY COUNTY FSS)

VOR RECEIVER CHECK   259

TEXAS

VOR RECEIVER CHECK POINTS

Facility Name (Arpt Name)	Freq/Ident	Type Check Pt. Gnd. AB/ALT	Azimuth from Fac. Mag	Dist. from Fac. N.M.	Check Point Description
Abilene (Abilene Regional)	113.7/ABI	A/2800	047	10.1	Over silos in center of Ft Phantom Lake.
Alice (Alice International)	114.5/ALI	G	270	0.5	On twy N of hangar.
Amarillo (Amarillo Internationl)	117.2/AMA	G	210	4.5	On east runup pad Rwy 22.
Austin (Robert Mueller Muni)	114.6/AUS	G	118	0.6	On runup area on twy to Rwy 31L.
Beaumont (Jefferson County)	114.5/BPT	G	310	1.0	On runup area for Rwy 12
Big Spring (Big Spring McMahon-Wrinkle)	114.3/BGS	A/3500	107	10.5	Over red and white water tank.
Borger (Hutchinson Co)	108.6/BGD	G	175	6.7	On intersecting twy in front of terminal.
Brownsville (Brownsville/South Padre Island Intl)	116.3/BRO	G	248	3.2	On NE corner of parking ramp.
Brownwood (Brownwood Muni)	108.6/BWD	A/2600	169	6.2	Over rotating bcn.
Childress (Childress Muni)	117.6/CDS	G	353	3.7	At intersection of edge of ramp at center twy.
College Station (Easterwood Field)	113.3/CLL	G	097	3.2	On W edge of parking ramp
Corpus Christi (Corpus Christi Intl)	115.5/CRP	A/1100	187	7.5	Over grain elevator.
Corpus Christi (San Patricio County)	115.5/CRP	A/1000	318	9.5	Over rotating beacon on arpt.
Daisetta (Liberty Muni)	116.9/DAS	A/1200	195	7.5	Over hangar S of arpt.
Dalhart (Dalhart Muni)	112.0/DHT	G	170	3.9	On SE corner of main ramp.
Eagle Lake (Eagle Lake)	116.4/ELA	A/1200	180	4.5	Over water tank 0.4 NM SW

Figure 58. – Excerpts from Airport/Facility Directory.

40. (Refer to Figure 64 below.) The course deviation indicator (CDI) is centered. Which indications on the No. 1 and No. 2 VOR receivers over the Lafayette Regional Airport would meet the requirements for the VOR receiver check?

	VOR No. 1	TO/FROM	VOR No. 2	TO/FROM
A.	162°	TO	346°	FROM
B.	160°	FROM	162°	FROM
C.	341°	FROM	330°	FROM

Answer (A) is correct. *(FAR 91.171)*
DISCUSSION: The top portion of Fig. 64 lists the VOR receiver checkpoints. Locate Lafayette (Lafayette Regional) to determine that the checkpoint is an airborne checkpoint at 1,000 ft. over the rotating beacon and the azimuth from the VORTAC is 340° (i.e., R-340). On the R-340, you want the CDI needle centered with an OBS setting of 340° FROM or 160° TO the station, with an acceptable error of ±6°. Thus, acceptable VOR indications are 162° TO and 346° FROM the station.
Answer (B) is incorrect. The magnetic azimuth (i.e., radial) from the station at the checkpoint is 340°, which results in a TO, not FROM, indication with the OBS set to 160° and 162°. Answer (C) is incorrect. The No. 2 VOR OBS of 330° is greater than 6° difference from the 340° azimuth from the VORTAC.

LOUISIANA

VOR RECEIVER CHECK POINTS

Facility Name (Arpt Name)	Freq/Ident	Type Check Pt. Gnd AB/ALT	Azimuth from Fac. Mag	Dist. from Fac. N.M.	Check Point Description
Baton Rouge (Baton Rouge Metro, Ryan)	116.5/BTR	A/1500	063	7.7	Over water tank W side of arpt.
Downtown	108.6/DTN	A/1500	290	10	Over white water tower.
Esler (Esler Regional)	108.8/ESF	G	151	3.5	On ramp in front of admin bldg.
Hammond (Hammond Muni)	109.6/HMU	G	342	.6	On twy W side app end Rwy 18.
Lafayette (Lafayette Regional)	110.8/LFT	A/1000	340	25	Over rotating beacon.
Lake Charles (Lake Charles Muni)	113.4/LCH	A/1000	253	6.2	Over rotg bcn on atct.
Monroe (Monroe Muni)	117.2/MLU	G	209	0.9	On ramp SE of atct.
Natchez (Concordia Parish)	110.0/HEZ	A/1000	247	10.5	Over hangar NW end of field.
New Orleans (Lakefront)	113.2/MSY	A/1000	081	7.7	Over lakefront atct.
Ruston	112.8/RSN	A/2000	343	14	Over hwy & RR crossing at Dubash.
Shreveport (Shreveport Downtown)	108.6/DTN	G	307	.5	On runup area N side of rwy 14.
Shreveport (Shreveport Regional)	117.4/SHV	A/1200	175	19.3	Over old terminal building.
Tibby (Thibodaux Muni)	112.0/TBD	A/1000	006	5.0	Over railroad bridge off apch end rwy 26.
	112.0/TBD	A, 1000	117	10 0	Over intersection of rwys 17-35 and 12-30

LAFAYETTE REGIONAL (LFT) 2 SE   GMT–6(–5DT)   30°12′14″N 91°59′16″W   **HOUSTON**
42 B S4 FUEL 100LL, JET A   OX 1   CFR Index B   **H-4F, L-17C**
RWY 03-21: H7651X150 (ASPH-GRVD)   S-75, D-170, DT-290   HIRL   **IAP**
   RWY 03: REIL. VASI(V4L)—GA 3.0°TCH 35′. Tree.
   RWY 21: MALSR. VASI(V4L)—GA 3.0°TCH 44′. Tree.
RWY 10-28: H5401X150 (ASPH)   S-85, D-110, DT-175   MIRL
   RWY 10: REIL (out of svc indefinitely). VASI(V4L)—GA 3.0° TCH 35.33′. Tree.
   RWY 28: REIL. VASI(V4L)—GA 3.0° TCH 55′. Thld dspicd 202′. Tree.
RWY 01-19: H5069X150 (ASPH)   S-25, D-45
   RWY 01: VASI(V4R)—GA 3.0°TCH 50′. Tree.
AIRPORT REMARKS: Attended continuously. Rwy 01-19 closed to air carriers. ACTIVATE MALSR Rwy 21—118.5.
COMMUNICATIONS: CTAF 118.5   ATIS 120.5 Opr 1200-0500Z‡   UNICOM 122.95
   LAFAYETTE FSS (LFT) on arpt. 122.35, 122.2, 122.1R, 110.8T LD 318-233-4952 NOTAM FILE LFT.
Ⓡ APP/DEP CON 121.1 (011°-190°) 124.0 (191°-010°) (1200-0400Z‡)
   HOUSTON CENTER APP/DEP CON 133.65 (0400-1200Z‡)
   TOWER 118.5, 121.35 (Helicopter ops) (1200-0400Z‡)   GND CON 121.8   CLNC DEL 125.55
   STAGE III ctc APP CON within 25 NM below 7000′
RADIO AIDS TO NAVIGATION: NOTAM FILE LFT. VHF/DF ctc LAFAYETTE FSS
   (L) VORTAC 110.8   LFT   Chan 45   30°08′45″N 91°59′00″W   344°3.0 NM to fld. 40/06E
   LAFFS NDB (LOM) 375   LF   30°17′21″N 91°54′29″W   215° 5.8 NM to fld
   LAKE MARTIN NDB (MHW) 362   LKM   30°11′33″N 91°52′58″W   270°5.2 NM to fld
   ILS/DME 109.5 I-LFT Chan 32 Rwy 21 LOM LAFFS NDB. Unmonitored when twr clsd.
   ASR

Figure 64. – Excerpt from Airport/Facility Directory.

41. (Refer to Figure 65 on page 421.) Which point would be the appropriate VOR COP on V552 from the LFT to the TBD VORTACs?

    A. CLYNT intersection.

    B. HATCH intersection.

    C. 34 DME from the LFT VORTAC.

Answer (C) is correct. *(AIM Para 5-3-6)*
    DISCUSSION: The changeover point (COP) is located midway between the navigation facilities for straight route segments, unless the COP symbol (⌐) is depicted on the route, in which case the indicated location is the COP. Since no COP symbol appears on V552 from LFT VORTAC (middle left) to TBD VORTAC (lower right), in Fig. 65, the COP is at the midway point. Since the leg is 68 NM, the COP would be at 34 DME from LFT VORTAC.
    Answer (A) is incorrect. CLYNT INT is only about 1/4, not 1/2, the distance from LFT to TBD VORTACs. Answer (B) is incorrect. HATCH INT is 5 NM before the COP at 34 NM (i.e., midway point between the LFT and TBD VORTACs).

42. (Refer to Figure 66 below, and Figure 65 on page 421.) What is your position relative to GRICE intersection?

    A. Right of V552 and approaching GRICE intersection.

    B. Right of V552 and past GRICE intersection.

    C. Left of V552 and approaching GRICE intersection.

Answer (A) is correct. *(IFH Chap 9)*
    DISCUSSION: GRICE INT is located at the lower middle portion of Fig. 65 along V552; it is the intersection of V552 and the localizer course to Harry P. Williams Mem. Airport. Your No. 1 VOR (Fig. 66) is tuned to the TBD VORTAC with an OBS setting of 116E TO the station. If you are flying toward TBD VORTAC on V552 (R-296), a left CDI deflection indicates that you are to the right of V552. Your No. 2 VOR is tuned to the I-PTN localizer course. If you are flying inbound on the localizer, a left CDI needle deflection indicates that you are to the right of the localizer course. Thus, you are right of V552 and approaching GRICE INT.
    Answer (B) is incorrect. If you were past GRICE INT, you would be to the left of the localizer; thus, the CDI needle would have a right, not left, deflection. Answer (C) is incorrect. If you were to the left of V552, the CDI needle would have a right, not left, deflection.

FREQ	OBS	
112.0	116	TO

FREQ	OBS	
108.3	236	/ / / / / /

Figure 66. – CDI and OBS Indicators.

43. (Refer to Figure 67 below, and Figure 65 on page 421.) What is the significance of the symbol at GRICE intersection?

    A. It signifies a localizer-only approach is available at Harry P. Williams Memorial.

    B. The localizer has an additional navigation function.

    C. GRICE intersection also serves as the FAF for the ILS approach procedure to Harry P. Williams Memorial.

Answer (B) is correct. *(ACL)*
    DISCUSSION: The large localizer symbol from Harry P. Williams Memorial to GRICE INT (Fig. 65) indicates that the localizer has a navigation function in addition to course guidance. In this case, the localizer's navigational function is to identify GRICE INT.
    Answer (A) is incorrect. The localizer symbol indicates the availability of an ILS, not an LOC only, approach. Answer (C) is incorrect. GRICE INT is identified by the localizer course. The FAF on an ILS is the interception of the glide slope, not an intersection.

Figure 67. – Localizer Symbol.

44. (Refer to Figure 87 on page 424.) While holding at the 10 DME fix east of LCH for an ILS approach to RWY 15 at Lake Charles Muni Airport, ATC advises you to expect clearance for the approach at 1015. At 1000 you experience two-way radio communications failure. Which procedure should be followed?

    A. Squawk 7600 and listen on the LOM frequency for instructions from ATC. If no instructions are received, start your approach at 1015.

    B. Squawk 7700 for 1 minute, then 7600. After 1 minute, descend to the minimum final approach fix altitude. Start your approach at 1015.

    C. Squawk 7600; plan to begin your approach at 1015.

Answer (C) is correct. *(AIM Para 6-4-1)*
    DISCUSSION: Upon radio failure, the transponder should be set to 7600. Since the expected clearance for the approach was 1015, you should plan to begin your approach at 1015.
    Answer (A) is incorrect. There is no LOM shown on the chart at Lake Charles Muni. Answer (B) is incorrect. You should not squawk 7700 unless you are in an emergency situation, and you should hold at your altitude until the time necessary to begin your approach at 1015.

45. (Refer to Figure 87 on page 424.) At STRUT intersection headed eastbound, ATC instructs you to hold west on the 10 DME fix west of LCH on V306, standard turns. What entry procedure is recommended?

    A. Direct.

    B. Teardrop.

    C. Parallel.

Answer (A) is correct. *(AIM Para 5-3-7)*
    DISCUSSION: You are instructed to hold west at the 10 DME fix west of LCH VORTAC on V306. Since you are at STRUT int., flying eastbound on V306, you should make a direct entry to a heading of 265°. Since the direction of turn was not specified, you should make right turns, which is a standard holding pattern.
    Answer (B) is incorrect. A teardrop entry may be used if you are instructed to hold east, not west, of the 10 DME fix. Answer (C) is incorrect. A parallel entry may be used if you are instructed to hold east, not west, of the 10 DME fix.

46. (Refer to Figure 87 on page 424.) Which VHF frequencies, other than 121.5, can be used to receive De Ridder FSS in the Lake Charles area?

    A. 122.1, 126.4.

    B. 123.6, 122.65.

    C. 122.2, 122.3.

Answer (C) is correct. *(ACL)*
    DISCUSSION: The Lake Charles VORTAC communication box is located in the upper right of Fig. 87. The available frequencies are shown above the box, and the controlling FSS (De Ridder) is shown below the box. All FSSs normally use frequency 122.2 and emergency 121.5, which are not shown. Note the thin line box indicates that other frequencies at the controlling FSS are available; however, altitude and terrain may determine their reception. On top of the box is frequency 122.3. Thus, you can receive De Ridder FSS on the VHF frequencies (other than 121.5) of 122.2 and 122.3.
    Answer (A) is incorrect. Neither 122.1 nor 126.4 is an available frequency to receive De Ridder FSS. Answer (B) is incorrect. These figures are not available frequencies to receive De Ridder FSS.

47. (Refer to Figure 87 on page 424 and Figure 88 on page 407.) What is your position with reference to FALSE intersection (V222) if your VOR receivers indicate as shown?

    A. South of V222 and east of FALSE intersection.

    B. North of V222 and east of FALSE intersection.

    C. South of V222 and west of FALSE intersection.

Answer (A) is correct. *(IFH Chap 9)*
    DISCUSSION: Note: In this edition of the test, Fig. 88 was not updated; thus VOR No. 2 incorrectly shows an OBS setting of 139 instead of 142.
    Your No. 1 VOR (Fig. 88) is tuned to the BPT VORTAC, Fig. 87, with an OBS setting of 264. If you are flying outbound (FROM) BPT on V222 (R-264), a right deflection indicates that V222 is to the right of your location. Thus, you are to the south of V222. Your No. 2 VOR is tuned to the DAS VORTAC with an OBS setting of 142. If you are flying outbound (FROM) DAS on R-142, a right deflection would mean that R-142 is to the right of your location. Thus, you are to the east of R-142. FALSE INT is the intersection of V222 (BPT R-264) and DAS R-142; you are presently to the south of V222 and east of FALSE INT.
    Answer (B) is incorrect. To be north of V222 would be indicated by a left, not right, CDI deflection in the No. 1 VOR. Answer (C) is incorrect. To be north of V222 and west of FALSE INT would be indicated by a left, not right, CDI deflection on both No. 1 and No. 2 VORs.

Figure 88. – CDI and OBS Indicators.

48. (Refer to Figure 89 on page 425.) When flying from Milford Municipal to Bryce Canyon via V235 and V293, what minimum altitude should you be at when crossing Cedar City VOR?

A. 11,400 feet.

B. 12,000 feet.

C. 13,000 feet.

Answer (B) is correct. *(ACL)*
DISCUSSION: In Fig. 89, CDC VOR has a flag with an "X" inside to indicate an MCA (minimum crossing altitude). The MCA is indicated above the CDC communication box. When flying east on V293 to Bryce Canyon, you must cross CDC at a minimum altitude of 12,000 ft. (V293 12000E).
Answer (A) is incorrect. This is the MCA when flying south on V235. Answer (C) is incorrect. This is the MEA for V293 east of CDC.

49. (Refer to Figure 89 on page 425.) What VHF frequencies are available for communications with Cedar City FSS?

A. 123.6, 121.5, 108.6, and 112.8.

B. 122.2, 121.5, 122.6, and 112.1.

C. 122.2, 121.5, 122.0, and 123.6.

Answer (B) is correct. *(ACL)*
DISCUSSION: Cedar City communication box (left center of Fig. 89) is a shadow box, which indicates an FSS. On top of the box is frequency 122.6. Additionally, VHF frequencies 122.2 and 121.5 are available at all FSSs. Frequency 122.1 is used by pilots to contact Cedar City FSS in the vicinity of Milford (MLF), and the FSS would transmit (pilots receive) on the MLF VORTAC frequency 112.1.
Answer (A) is incorrect. The figure of 123.6 is not listed above any communication boxes controlled by Cedar City FSS and both CDC and BCE VORTACs are underlined, which means there is no voice on that frequency. Answer (C) is incorrect. The figures of 122.0 and 123.6 are not listed above any communication boxes controlled by Cedar City FSS.

50. (Refer to Figure 89 on page 425.) What are the oxygen requirements for an IFR flight northeast bound from Bryce Canyon on V382 at the lowest appropriate altitude in an unpressurized aircraft?

A. The required minimum crew must be provided and use supplemental oxygen for that part of the flight of more than 30 minutes.

B. The required minimum crew must be provided and use supplemental oxygen for that part of the flight of more than 30 minutes, and the passengers must be provided supplemental oxygen.

C. The required minimum crew must be provided and use supplemental oxygen, and all occupants must be provided supplemental oxygen for the entire flight above 15,000 feet.

Answer (C) is correct. *(FAR 91.211)*
DISCUSSION: At cabin pressure altitudes above 14,000 ft. MSL, the required minimum flight crew must be provided with and use supplemental oxygen during the entire flight time at those altitudes. Additionally, each occupant must be provided with supplemental oxygen at cabin pressure altitudes above 15,000 ft. MSL. The MEA for V382 is 16,000 ft. MSL.
Answer (A) is incorrect. The requirement that the required minimum crew be provided with and use supplemental oxygen for that part of the flight of more than 30 minutes describes the oxygen requirements when at cabin pressure altitudes above 12,500 ft. MSL up to and including 14,000 ft. MSL, not at 16,000 ft. MSL. Answer (B) is incorrect. The requirement that the required minimum crew be provided with and use supplemental oxygen for that part of the flight of more than 30 minutes describes the oxygen requirements when at cabin pressure altitudes above 12,500 ft. MSL up to and including 14,000 ft. MSL, not at 16,000 ft. MSL.

51. (Refer to Figure 89 on page 425.) What is the ARTCC discrete frequency at the COP on V208 southwest bound from HVE to PGA VOR/DME?

A. 122.1

B. 122.4

C. 133.6

Answer (C) is correct. *(ACL)*
DISCUSSION: The COP on V208 southwest bound to PGA VOR/DME from HVE VORTAC is indicated by the symbol "⌐", and the mileages are given to each VOR station. The COP is 61 NM northeast of PGA and 35 NM southwest of HVE. Notice the ragged line (see Legend 24 on page 413) south of HVE VORTAC, which is the symbol that divides Salt Lake City ARTCC to the north and Denver ARTCC to the south. Thus, the COP is in Salt Lake City ARTCC airspace. To the right of HVE VORTAC is a box indicating that Salt Lake City ARTCC uses an RCO at Hanksville on a discrete frequency of 133.6.
Answer (A) is incorrect. This frequency is shown above the communications boxes at MLF, HVE, and PGA VORs and is used for communicating with FSSs, not the ARTCC. Answer (B) is incorrect. This frequency is shown in the remote communications outlet (RCO) boxes at Bullfrog Basin and Cal Black Memorial Airports and is used for communicating with Cedar City FSS, not the ARTCC.

52. (Refer to Figure 89 on page 425.) What type airspace exists above Bryce Canyon Airport from the surface to 1,200 feet AGL?

A. Class D.

B. Class E.

C. Class G.

Answer (C) is correct. *(ACL, AIM Para 3-3-1)*
DISCUSSION: Bryce Canyon Airport symbol is brown in color, which means it does not have a published IAP. The airport is not indicated to be in Class B or C airspace but does lie below a federal airway (the white area to either side of and along V8). Federal airways are Class E airspace and, unless otherwise specified, extend upward from 1,200 ft. AGL to, but not including, 18,000 ft. MSL. Bryce Canyon is not a Class D airport (indicated by D following the airport name). Class E surface areas are not shown on En Route Low-Altitude Charts. However, since Bryce Canyon has no IAP, we can assume that no Class E surface area is associated with the airport. Therefore, Class G airspace extends from the surface upward to 1,200 ft. AGL, the floor of the federal airway.
Answer (A) is incorrect. Class D airports are indicated by a D following the airport name. Answer (B) is incorrect. Federal airways normally extend upward from 1,200 ft. AGL, not from the surface.

53. (Refer to Figure 90 below, and Figure 89 on page 425.) What is your relationship to the airway while en route from BCE VORTAC to HVE VORTAC on V8?

A. Left of course on V8.

B. Left of course on V382.

C. Right of course on V8.

Answer (A) is correct. *(IFH Chap 9)*
DISCUSSION: Your No. 1 VOR (Fig. 90) is tuned to the BCE VORTAC with a OBS setting of 033° FROM the station. This is the course for V382, which is north of V8 in Fig. 89. The CDI is deflected to the left, which indicates you are to the right of V382. Your No. 2 VOR is tuned to the HVE VORTAC with an OBS setting of 046° TO the station, which is the inbound course on V8. The CDI is deflected to the right, which means you are to the left of course on V8. Thus, you are located to the right of V382 and to the left of V8 while en route from BCE VORTAC to HVE VORTAC.
Answer (B) is incorrect. If you were left of V382, you would have a right, not left, CDI deflection on NAV No. 1. Answer (C) is incorrect. If you were right of V8, you would have a left, not right, CDI deflection on NAV No. 2.

Figure 90. – CDI/OBS Indicators.

54. (Refer to Figure 91 on page 426.) What are the two limiting cruising altitudes useable on V343 for a VFR-on-Top flight from DBS VORTAC to RANEY intersection?

    A. 14,500 and 16,500 feet.

    B. 15,000 and 17,000 feet.

    C. 15,500 and 17,500 feet.

Answer (C) is correct. *(FAR 91.159)*
    DISCUSSION: In Fig. 91, a flight from DBS VORTAC to RANEY intersection on V343 has an MEA of 15,000 ft. A flight with a clearance of VFR-on-top will operate at appropriate VFR cruising altitudes, at or above the minimum IFR altitude. On a magnetic course of 008°, you must be at an odd thousand-foot altitude plus 500 ft. Thus, a VFR-on-top flight is limited to only 15,500 ft. and 17,500 ft. You cannot operate VFR in Class A airspace, i.e., 18,000 ft. MSL to FL 600.
    Answer (A) is incorrect. The appropriate VFR-on-top altitudes for a magnetic course of 008° are odd, not even, thousand-foot altitudes plus 500 ft. Also, 14,500 ft. is below the MEA. Answer (B) is incorrect. VFR-on-top altitudes are cardinal (1,000, 2,000, etc.) plus 500 ft.

55. (Refer to Figure 91 on page 426.) What should be the approximate elapsed time from BZN VOR to DBS VORTAC, if the wind is 24 knots from 260° and your intended TAS is 185 knots? (VAR 17°E.)

    A. 33 minutes.

    B. 37 minutes.

    C. 39 minutes.

Answer (C) is correct. *(PHAK Chap 15)*
    DISCUSSION: First convert your wind from 260° true to 243° magnetic because of the 17°E variation. Then place the 243 below the true index on the wind side of your flight computer and mark the wind speed of 24 kt. up from the grommet (center hole). Then place your magnetic course of 186° under the true index. Next, slide the scale so that the pencil mark is on the 185-kt. TAS and note that the grommet is at 171 kt., which is the groundspeed.
    On the computer side, put 171 kt. on the outer scale under the true index. Locate 111 NM on the outer scale and read the time below on the inner scale, which is approximately 39 min.
    Answer (A) is incorrect. This is the approximate time going north from DBS VORTAC to BZN VOR, not from BZN VOR to DBS VORTAC. Answer (B) is incorrect. This is the approximate time from BZN VOR to DBS VORTAC using the wind direction of 260°, not the magnetic wind direction of 243°.

56. (Refer to Figure 91 on page 426.) Southbound on V257, at what time should you arrive at DBS VORTAC if you crossed over CPN VORTAC at 0850 and over DIVID intersection at 0854?

    A. 0939

    B. 0943

    C. 0947

Answer (B) is correct. *(PHAK Chap 15)*
    DISCUSSION: CPN VORTAC is on the left side of the chart about 1 1/2 in. down from the top. Going south on V257, DIVID INT is 9 NM from CPN VORTAC. Use your flight computer to determine the groundspeed. Locate 9 on the outer scale and place 4 on the minute scale under the 9. The groundspeed is read over the index, which is 135 kt.
    From DIVID to DLN VORTAC is 39 NM; then from DLN VORTAC to DBS VORTAC is 71 NM, or a total of 110 NM. To determine the time, place 135 kt. over the index of your flight computer and locate 110 NM on the outer scale; the time is read below on the minute scale, which is 49 min. from DIVID INT to DBS VORTAC. Thus, your ETA at DBS VORTAC is 0943 (0854 + 49).
    Answer (A) is incorrect. The 49 min. is added to the time you crossed DIVID INT (0854), not the time you crossed CPN VORTAC (0850). Answer (C) is incorrect. The distance from CPN VORTAC to DIVID INT (9 NM) must be subtracted from the 48 NM between CPN VORTAC and DLN VORTAC.

57. (Refer to Figure 91 on page 426.) When flying northbound IFR flight on V257, what is the minimum crossing altitude at DBS VORTAC?

    A. 7,500 feet.

    B. 8,600 feet.

    C. 11,100 feet.

Answer (B) is correct. *(ACL)*
    DISCUSSION: DBS VORTAC is at the center of the large compass rose in the lower left of Fig. 91. At DBS VORTAC, there is a flag with an "X" inside that indicates an MCA. The MCA is indicated next to the VORTAC symbol. When flying north on V257, you must cross DBS VORTAC at a minimum altitude of 8,600 ft. (V21-257 8600N).
    Answer (A) is incorrect. This is the MEA on V257 south of DBS VORTAC. Answer (C) is incorrect. This is the MOCA on V21-257 northwest of DBS VORTAC.

58. (Refer to Figure 91 on page 426.) What are the oxygen requirements for an IFR flight eastbound on V520 from DBS VORTAC in an unpressurized aircraft at the MEA?

A. The required minimum crew must be provided and use supplemental oxygen for that part of the flight of more than 30 minutes.

B. The required minimum crew must be provided and use supplemental oxygen for that part of the flight of more than 30 minutes, and the passengers must be provided supplemental oxygen.

C. The required minimum crew must be provided and use supplemental oxygen.

Answer (C) is correct. *(FAR 91.211)*
DISCUSSION: On Fig. 91, when going eastbound from DBS VORTAC on V520, the MEA is 15,000 ft. MSL. At cabin pressure altitudes above 14,000 ft. MSL, the flight crew must be provided and use supplemental oxygen for the entire flight. At cabin pressure altitudes above 15,000 ft. MSL, the passengers must be provided with supplemental oxygen.
Answer (A) is incorrect. The required minimum crew must be provided and use supplemental oxygen for that part of the flight of more than 30 min. at cabin pressure altitudes above 12,500 ft. MSL up to and including 14,000 ft. MSL. Answer (B) is incorrect. The required minimum crew must be provided and use supplemental oxygen at all times, not only that part of the flight of more than 30 min., at cabin pressure altitudes above 14,000 ft. MSL. Passengers must be provided supplemental oxygen at cabin pressure altitudes above, not at, 15,000 ft. MSL.

59. (Refer to Figure 91 on page 426.) Where should you change VOR frequencies when en route from DBS VORTAC to JAC VOR/DME on V520?

A. 35 NM from DBS VORTAC.

B. 60 NM from DBS VORTAC.

C. 60 NM from JAC VOR/DME.

Answer (B) is correct. *(AIM Para 5-3-6)*
DISCUSSION: When flying from DBS VORTAC to JAC VOR/DME on V520 (Fig. 91), notice that very close to the JAC VOR/DME is a VOR changeover point symbol (⌐), which is 60 NM from the DBS VORTAC.
Answer (A) is incorrect. In this case, the changeover point (COP) is not located at the midway point; the COP is marked by the symbol "⌐", and mileage is given to the VORs. Answer (C) is incorrect. The COP is located 10 NM, not 60 NM, from JAC VOR/DME.

60. (Refer to Figure 91 on page 426.) What lighting is indicated on the chart for Jackson Hole Airport?

A. Lights on prior request.

B. No lighting available.

C. Pilot controlled lighting.

Answer (C) is correct. *(ACL)*
DISCUSSION: The Jackson Hole Airport is located at the lower right of Fig. 91. The "L" indicates that Jackson Hole Airport has night lighting. The circle indicates pilot-controlled lighting.
Answer (A) is incorrect. An asterisk would indicate lighting on request or in operation for only part of the night. Answer (B) is incorrect. If no lighting were available, there would be a "–" after the airport elevation.

61. (Refer to Figure 91 on page 426.) What is the minimum crossing altitude at SABAT intersection when eastbound from DBS VORTAC on V298?

A. 8,300 feet.

B. 11,100 feet.

C. 13,000 feet.

Answer (B) is correct. *(ACL)*
DISCUSSION: SABAT INT is located east of DBS VORTAC on V298 at the lower middle area in Fig. 91. There is a flag with an "X" in it, which indicates an MCA at SABAT. Underneath the SABAT is the MCA, which is 11,100 ft. when eastbound on V298 (V298 11100E).
Answer (A) is incorrect. This is the MOCA between DBS VORTAC and SABAT INT (*8300). Answer (C) is incorrect. This is the MEA when eastbound on V298 between DBS VORTAC and SABAT INT.

62. (Refer to Figure 91 on page 426 and Legend 23 on page 412.) What is the function of the Great Falls RCO (Yellowstone vicinity)?

A. Long range communications outlet for Great Falls Center.

B. Remote communications outlet for Great Falls FSS.

C. Satellite remote controlled by Salt Lake Center with limited service.

Answer (B) is correct. *(ACL)*
DISCUSSION: The Great Falls RCO communication box is located in the center of the chart, in Fig. 91, just above the DBS VORTAC box. An arrow points to a symbol ⊙, which indicates an FSS remote communications outlet. Thus, Great Falls RCO is a remote communications outlet for Great Falls FSS on 122.45 MHz.
Answer (A) is incorrect. The center for that area is Salt Lake City, not Great Falls, as indicated by the ARTCC RCO box above the Great Falls RCO box. Answer (C) is incorrect. Great Falls RCO is just an antenna site for an FSS that extends the communication range for the controlling FSS (e.g., Great Falls FSS), not ARTCC (e.g., Salt Lake Center).

END OF STUDY UNIT

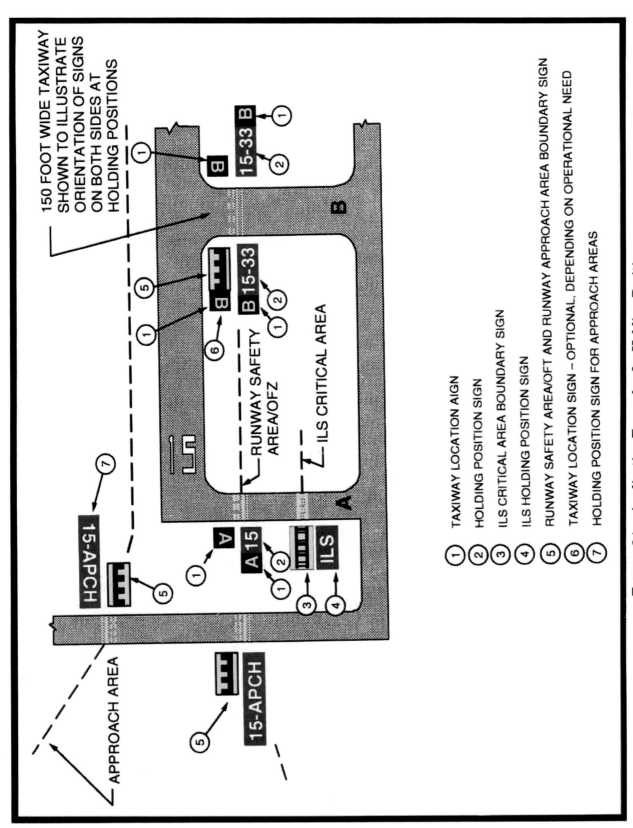

FIGURE 94.—Application Examples for Holding Positions.

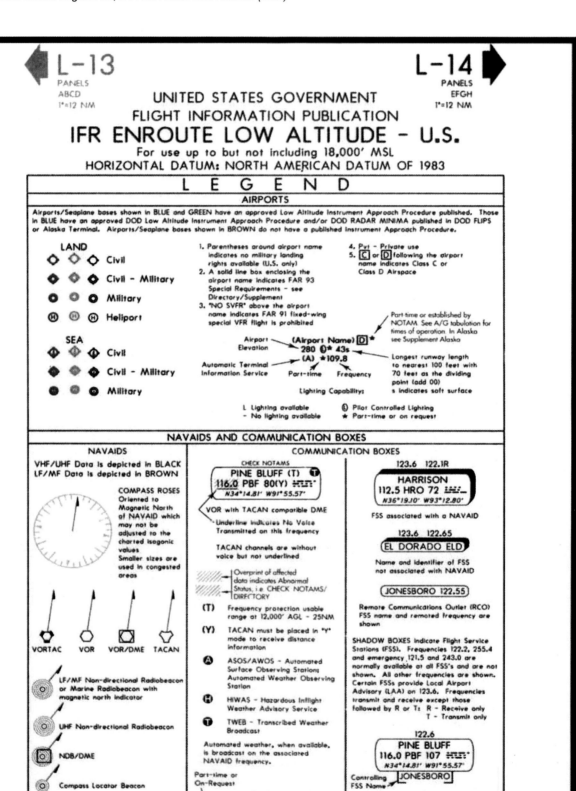

LEGEND 23.—IFR En Route Low Altitude (U.S.).

LEGEND 24.—IFR En Route Low Altitude (U.S.).

FIGURE 24.—En Route Low-Altitude Chart Segment.

FIGURE 31.—En Route Low-Altitude Chart Segment.

FIGURE 34.—En Route Chart.

FIGURE 40.—En Route Chart Segment.

FIGURE 47.—En Route Chart Segment.

FIGURE 53.—En Route Chart Segment.

FIGURE 59.—En Route Chart Segment.

FIGURE 65.—En Route Chart Segment.

FIGURE 71.—En Route Chart Segment.

FIGURE 78.—En Route Chart Segment.

FIGURE 87.—En Route Chart Segment.

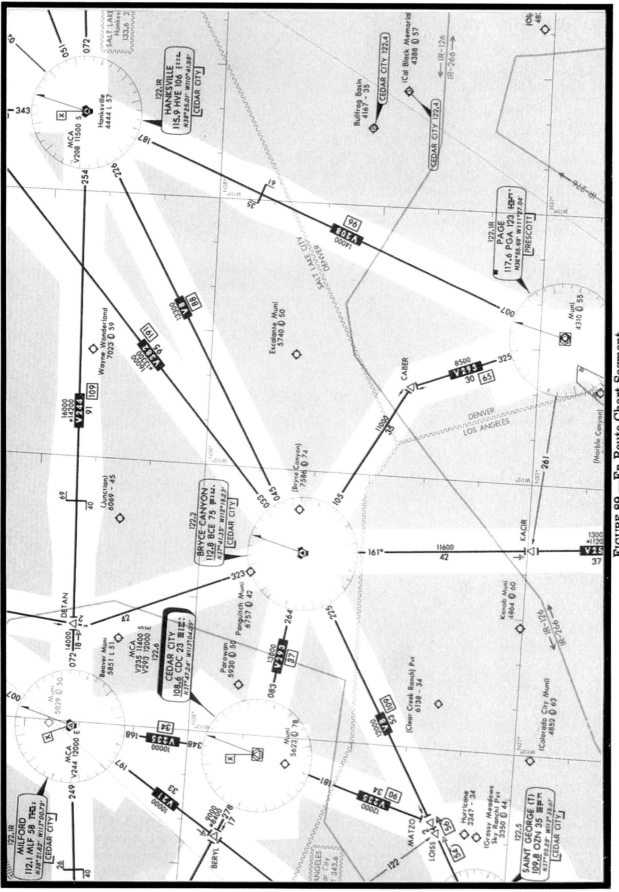

FIGURE 89.—En Route Chart Segment.

FIGURE 91.—En Route Chart Segment.

STUDY UNIT ELEVEN
IFR FLIGHTS

(4 pages of outline)

In 2014, the FAA released an **Addendum A for the *Computer Testing Supplement for Instrument Rating***. This addendum contains over 100 additional figures, including approach plates, approach procedures, departure procedures, A/FD excerpts, etc. The FAA has released some questions referencing certain figures from this addendum. Gleim has included those FAA-released questions and the relevant figures in our instrument rating materials. **However, we have not included any of the addendum figures that do not have FAA-released questions. If you answer all of the questions in the Gleim test bank for the instrument rating, you will be comfortable using the figures in the addendum to answer similar questions on the knowledge test.**

This study unit contains over 100 sample test questions and answers regarding eight IFR flights and an explanation of each answer. The table of contents above lists the individual trips within this study unit, the number of questions pertaining to that particular trip, and the page on which the trip begins.

Note that there are two helicopter trips in the FAA instrument rating test bank. We do not believe it is appropriate to ask helicopter questions on the instrument rating (airplane) knowledge test. However, nine of the questions included in these two helicopter trips are generic to IFR flight, i.e., could apply to you in an airplane. Examples are questions regarding en route charts and the *A/FD*. These questions will appear in other study units as appropriate, e.g., Study Unit 10, "IFR En Route."

The following provides you with a list of the eight IFR trips. The departure and destination airports are listed, followed by the question numbers that relate to that trip.

1. Grand Junction, CO, to Durango, CO (Questions 1-8)
2. Medford, OR, to Eugene, OR (Questions 9-21)
3. Yakima, WA, to Portland, OR (Questions 22-39)
4. Santa Barbara, CA, to Paso Robles, CA (Questions 40-51)
5. Hot Springs, AR, to Dallas, TX (Questions 52-64)
6. Big Spring, TX, to Fort Worth, TX (Questions 65-78)
7. W. Milford, NJ, to Windsor Locks, CT (Questions 79-93)
8. Helena, MT, to Billings, MT (Questions 94-109)

Each trip provides you with the following types of data:

1. Partially completed IFR flight plan
2. Aircraft model and equipment status sheet
3. Partially completed flight log
4. DPs and STARs
5. Appropriate *Airport/Facility Directory* excerpts
6. Instrument approach chart(s)
7. En route low-altitude chart

The questions cover the following topics:

1.   Equipment code to put in block 3 of your IFR flight plan

AIRCRAFT EQUIPMENT SUFFIXES

SUFFIX	AIRCRAFT EQUIPMENT SUFFIXES
	NO DME
/X	No transponder
/T	Transponder with no Mode C
/U	Transponder with Mode C
	DME
/D	No transponder
/B	Transponder with no Mode C
/A	Transponder with Mode C
	TACAN ONLY
/M	No transponder
/N	Transponder with no Mode C
/P	Transponder with Mode C
	AREA NAVIGATION (RNAV)
/Y	LORAN, VOR/DME, or INS with no transponder
/C	LORAN, VOR/DME, or INS, transponder with no Mode C
/I	LORAN, VOR/DME, or INS, transponder with Mode C
	ADVANCED RNAV WITH TRANSPONDER AND MODE C (If an aircraft is unable to operate with a transponder and/or Mode C, it will revert to the appropriate code listed above under Area Navigation.)
/E	Flight Management System (FMS) with en route, terminal, and approach capability. Equipment requirements are: (a) Dual FMS which meets the specifications of AC 25-15, Approval of Flight Management Systems in Transport Category Airplanes; AC 20-129, Airworthiness Approval of Vertical Navigation (VNAV) Systems for use in the U.S. NAS and Alaska; AC 20-130A, Airworthiness Approval of Navigation or Flight Management Systems Integrating Multiple Navigation Sensors; or equivalent criteria as approved by Flight Standards. (b) A flight director and autopilot control system capable of following the lateral and vertical FMS flight path. (c) At least dual inertial reference units (IRU's). (d) A database containing the waypoints and speed/altitude constraints for the route and/or procedure to be flown that is automatically loaded into the FMS flight plan. (e) An electronic map. (U.S. and U.S. territories only unless otherwise authorized.)
/F	A single FMS with en route, terminal, and approach capability that meets the equipment requirements of /E, (a) through (d), above. (U.S. and U.S. territories only unless otherwise authorized.
/G	Global Positioning System (GPS)/Global Navigation Satellite System (GNSS) equipped aircraft with en route and terminal capability
/R	Required Navigational Performance (Denotes capability to operate in RNP designated airspace and routes)
/W	Reduced Vertical Separation Minima (RVSM)

Legend 26. – Aircraft Equipment Suffixes.

2.   Calibrated airspeed (CAS) to maintain true airspeed (TAS) indicated in the flight plan

    a.   On your flight computer, put air temperature (given in question) over the flight altitude (given in the IFR flight plan). On the outer scale, find TAS; CAS is on the inner scale.

3.   Time to complete the flight (time en route for block 10 of the IFR flight plan)

    a.   This question requires you to complete the flight log, which involves wind triangle computations (on your manual or electronic flight computer).

        1)   Note: If filing a composite flight plan, check both VFR and IFR boxes in block 11.

        2)   Note: Fuel quantities listed in block 12 of your flight plan should include total usable fuel, measured in hours.

4.   Composite flights (IFR and VFR) should be entered in block 1 of the flight plan.

    a.   When planning to fly in both IFR and VFR conditions, both VFR and IFR blocks should be selected in block 1 of the flight plan.

5.   Fuel quantity should be entered in block 12 of the flight plan.

    a.   Total usable fuel should always be entered in block 12 of the flight plan.

6.   Interpretation of VOR, RMI, HSI, and GS/LOC indicators to determine position relative to a position specified on a particular approach, DP, STAR, or en route chart

    a.   These interpretations are covered in Study Unit 3, "Navigation Systems."

7.   Interpretation of appropriate procedures, minimum altitude, and other restrictions on instrument approach charts

    a.   Please see the instrument approach chart legends (on pages 199 through 211) in Study Unit 6, "Holding and Instrument Approaches."

    b.   The formula for converting feet per nautical mile to feet per minute is

$$\frac{GS \times FT/NM}{60} = FPM$$

8.   Interpretation of appropriate procedures, minimum altitude, and other restrictions on low-altitude en route charts

    a.   See the IFR en route chart legends. Legend 25 appears on page 394 in Study Unit 10, "IFR En Route." Legends 23 and 24 are provided in color on pages 412 and 413.

9.   Interpretation of DPs and STARs

    a.   A careful reading of the DP or STAR usually provides the correct answer, especially in conjunction with the DP/STAR Legend 17 reproduced on page 194 in Study Unit 6.

10. Calculating climbs and descents

    a.   When calculating rates of climb or descent, specifically be aware of whether you are seeking feet per minute or feet per nautical mile.

    b.   If a climb or descent is specified in feet per nautical miles, calculate the required feet per minute as follows:

        1)   Find ground speed.

        2)   Find distance.

        3)   120 knot groundspeed equates to 2 NM per minute. A 90 knot groundspeed equates to 1.5 NM per minute.

        4)   To achieve a climb or descent of 435 feet per NM at 120 knots groundspeed (2 NM per minute), 435 feet per NM × 2 NM per minute = 870 feet per minute.

        5)   To achieve a climb or descent of 435 feet per NM at 90 knots groundspeed (1.5 NM per minute), 435 feet per NM × 1.5 NM per minute = 652.5 feet per minute.

    c.   If the rate of descent is given in feet per NM but to be solved in feet per minute, calculate the required rate as follows:

        1)   Find your groundspeed.

        2)   Find the altitude to be lost or gained.

        3)   Find the distance between two points where the climb or descent must occur.

        4)   Divide distance by altitude to find feet per NM. For example, 750 feet ÷ 3NM = 250 feet per nautical mile.

        5)   Divide groundspeed by 60 (minutes per hour) to find NM per minute. 120 knots ÷ 60 minutes = 2 NM per minute. 90 knots ÷ 60 minutes = 1.5 NM per minute.

        6)   Multiply speed per minute × rate per NM to arrive at feet per minute. 1.5 NM per minute × 250 feet per NM = 375 feet per minute. 2 NM per minute × 250 feet per NM = 500 feet per minute.

11. Calculating a DME arc

a. Find the degrees from the beginning waypoint or intersection to start the arc, then go to the radial to start the final approach course. For example, if we start on R-251 and go to R-333 (333 – 251 = 82), on a 15 DME arc, it would look like this:

$$Distance\ of\ arc = \frac{\#\ of\ degrees\ \times\ DME\ arc}{60}$$

$$Distance\ of\ arc = \frac{82\ \times\ 15}{60} = 20.5\ NM$$

QUESTIONS AND ANSWER EXPLANATIONS: All of the instrument rating knowledge test questions chosen by the FAA for release as well as additional questions selected by Gleim relating to the material in the previous outlines are reproduced on the following pages. These questions have been organized into the same subunits as the outlines. To the immediate right of each question are the correct answer and answer explanation. You should cover these answers and answer explanations while responding to the questions. Refer to the general discussion in the Introduction on how to take the FAA knowledge test.

Remember that the questions from the FAA knowledge test bank have been reordered by topic and organized into a meaningful sequence. Also, the first line of the answer explanation gives the citation of the authoritative source for the answer.

QUESTIONS
11.1 GJT to DRO

Questions 1 through 8 pertain to an IFR flight from Walker Field, Grand Junction, Colorado, to Durango-La Plata County Airport, Durango, Colorado, and return to Grand Junction.

The route of flight is given in block 8 on the flight plan portion of Figs. 21 and 21A on pages 431 and 432. Information that pertains to your aircraft is given on the bottom portion of Figs. 21 and 21A. The partially completed flight planning log is given in Figs. 22 and 22A on page 433.

The figures provided for this flight are listed below and are presented throughout the sequence of questions, except for Fig. 24, which is provided in color on page 414.

Fig.	Page	
21	431	Flight Plan and Aircraft Information (GJT-DRO)
21A	432	Flight Plan and Aircraft Information (DRO-GJT)
22	433	Flight Planning Log (GJT-DRO)
22A	435	Flight Planning Log (DRO-GJT)
23	436	Grand Junction Nine Departure (JNC9.JNC)
24	414	En Route Low-Altitude Chart Segment
25	437	ILS/DME RWY 2 (DRO)
26	438	ILS RWY 11 (GJT)

---

1. (Refer to Figure 21 on page 431, Figure 22 on page 433, and Figure 24 on page 414.) If the average fuel consumption is 17.5 GPH, how much fuel would you use on the flight between Grand Junction, CO and Durango, CO?

A. 17 gallons.

B. 20 gallons.

C. 25 gallons.

Answer (B) is correct. *(IFH Chap 10)*
DISCUSSION: Complete the flight log by computing the fuel consumption at 17.5 GPH.

	Time	Fuel (gal.)
HERRM INT.	:24:00G	7.0
MANCA INT.	:26:10	7.5
Approach and landing	:18:30G	5.5
Total	1:08:40	20.0

G = Given

Answer (A) is incorrect. This amount of fuel would require an average fuel consumption of 15 GPH, not 17.5 GPH. Answer (C) is incorrect. This amount of fuel would require an average fuel consumption of approximately 22 GPH, not 17.5 GPH.

2. (Refer to Figure 21 below, Figure 22 on page 433, and Figure 24 on page 414.) (Refer to the FD excerpt below, and use the wind entry closest to the flight planned altitude.) Determine the time to be entered in block 10 of the flight from GJT to DRO.

Route of flight .... Figure 21
Flight log & MAG VAR .... Figure 22
En route chart .... Figure 24

FT	12,000	18,000
FNM	2408-05	2208-21

A. 1 hour 08 minutes.

B. 1 hour 03 minutes.

C. 58 minutes.

Answer (A) is correct. *(IFH Chap 10)*
DISCUSSION: Complete the flight log for GJT to DRO (Fig. 22). Note that the wind has been interpolated for you from the figures for 12,000 and 18,000 ft. Calculate groundspeed for the cruise portion of the trip using the wind side of the flight computer. Remember to convert wind direction to magnetic direction first; i.e., 230° − 14°E var. = 216° at 8 kt. Then compute ETE for each leg.

	Distance	MC	Wind (Mag)	Ground-speed	Time
HERRM INT.	X	151°G	216/8G	X	:24:00G
MANCA INT.	75	151°G	216/8G	172	:26:10
Approach and Landing	X	92°G	216/8G	X	:18:30G
					1:08:40

G = Given

Answer (B) is incorrect. An ETE of 1 hr. 3 min. requires a TAS of 223 kt., not 175 kt. Answer (C) is incorrect. An ETE of 58 min. requires a TAS of approximately 293 kt., not 175 kt.

Form Approved: OMB No. 2120-0034

U.S. DEPARTMENT OF TRANSPORTATION FEDERAL AVIATION ADMINISTRATION	(FAA USE ONLY)	☐ PILOT BRIEFING	☐ VNR	TIME STARTED	SPECIALIST INITIALS
FLIGHT PLAN		☐ STOPOVER			

1. TYPE	2. AIRCRAFT IDENTIFICATION	3. AIRCRAFT TYPE/ SPECIAL EQUIPMENT	4. TRUE AIRSPEED	5. DEPARTURE POINT	6. DEPARTURE TIME		7. CRUISING ALTITUDE
VFR					PROPOSED (Z)	ACTUAL (Z)	
X IFR DVFR	N123RC	T210N/	175 KTS	GJT			15,000

8. ROUTE OF FLIGHT

JNC9, JNC, V187, MANCA, V211

9. DESTINATION (Name of airport and city)	10. EST. TIME ENROUTE		11. REMARKS
	HOURS	MINUTES	
DRO			

12. FUEL ON BOARD		13. ALTERNATE AIRPORT(S)	14. PILOT'S NAME, ADDRESS & TELEPHONE NUMBER & AIRCRAFT HOME BASE	15. NUMBER ABOARD
HOURS	MINUTES			
4	30	GJT	17. DESTINATION CONTACT/TELEPHONE (OPTIONAL)	2

16. COLOR OF AIRCRAFT	CIVIL AIRCRAFT PILOTS. FAR Part 91 requires you file an IFR flight plan to operate under instrument flight rules in controlled airspace. Failure to file could result in a civil penalty not to exceed $1,000 for each violation (Section 901 of the Federal Aviation Act of 1958, as amended). Filing of a VFR flight plan is recommended as a good operating practice. See also Part 99 for requirements concerning DVFR flight plans.
RED/WHITE/BLUE	

FAA Form 7233-1 (8-82)   CLOSE VFR FLIGHT PLAN WITH _____ FSS ON ARRIVAL

AIRCRAFT INFORMATION

MAKE Cessna   MODEL T210N

N 123RC   Vso 58 __

AIRCRAFT EQUIPMENT/STATUS**

**NOTE: X= OPERATIVE   INOP=INOPERATIVE   N/A= NOT APPLICABLE

TRANSPONDER: X (MODE C) X ILS: (LOCALIZER) X (GLIDE SLOPE) X

VOR NO.1 X (NO.2) X ADF: X RNAV: X

VERTICAL PATH COMPUTER: N/A   DME: X

MARKER BEACON: X (AUDIO) X   (VISUAL) X

Figure 21. – Flight Plan and Aircraft Information.

3. (Refer to Figure 21A below, Figure 21 on page 431, Figure 22 on page 433, Figure 23 on page 436, and Figure 24 on page 414.) What fuel would be consumed on the flight between Grand Junction Co. and Durango, Co. if the average fuel consumption is 15 GPH?

A. 17 gallons.

B. 20 gallons.

C. 25 gallons.

Answer (A) is correct. *(IFH Chap 10)*
DISCUSSION: Complete the flight log by computing the fuel consumption at 15 GPH.

	Time	Fuel (gal.)
HERRM INT.	:24:00G	6.0
MANCA INT.	:26:10	6.5
Approach and landing	:18:30G	4.6
Total	1:08:40	17.1

G = Given

Answer (B) is incorrect. This amount of fuel would require an average fuel consumption of 17.5 GPH, not 15 GPH. Answer (C) is incorrect. This amount of fuel would require an average fuel consumption of approximately 22 GPH, not 15 GPH.

Figure 21A. – Flight Plan and Aircraft Information.

4. (Refer to Figure 22 below, and Figure 24 on page 414.) For planning purposes, what would be the highest MEA on V187 between Grand Junction, Walker Airport, and Durango, La Plata Co. Airport?

A. 12,000 feet.

B. 15,000 feet.

C. 16,000 feet.

Answer (B) is correct. *(ACL)*
    DISCUSSION: The highest MEA along the route is 15,000 ft. MSL along V187 between HERRM INT. and MANCA INT.
    Answer (A) is incorrect. The MEA between JNC and HERRM INT. is 12,000 ft. MSL, but it is not the highest. Answer (C) is incorrect. There is no MEA of 16,000 ft. MSL along any part of this route.

FLIGHT LOG

GRAND JUNCTION (GJT) TO DURANGO (DRO)

CHECK POINTS		ROUTE		WIND	SPEED-KTS		DIST	TIME		FUEL	
FROM	TO	ALTITUDE	COURSE	TEMP	TAS	GS	NM	LEG	TOT	LEG	TOT
GJT	JNC	JNC9JNC CLIMB		230 08				✕			
	HERRM	V187 15,000	151°		175			:24:0			
	MANCA	V187	151°								
APPROACH & LANDING		V211 DESENT	092°					:18:30			
	DRO										

OTHER DATA:
    NOTE: TAKEOFF RUNWAY 29.
            MAG VAR, 14° E.

FLIGHT SUMMARY

TIME	FUEL (LB)	
		EN ROUTE
		RESERVE
		MISSED APPR.
		TOTAL

Figure 22. – Flight Planning Log.

5. (Refer to Figure 24 on page 414.) While passing near the CORTEZ VOR, southbound on V187, contact is lost with Denver Center. You should attempt to reestablish contact with Denver Center on

A. 133.425 MHz.

B. 122.1 MHz and receive on 108.4 MHz.

C. 122.35 MHz.

Answer (A) is correct. *(ACL)*
    DISCUSSION: To the northwest of the Cortez VOR and south of Dove Creek VORTAC is a box with serrated edges. This box shows the frequency for Denver Center in the Cortez VOR area as 133.425.
    Answer (B) is incorrect. A frequency of 122.1 is not shown on the chart, and 108.4 is the frequency for the Cortez VOR, not Denver Center. Additionally, 108.4 is underlined, indicating that the VOR has no voice capability (i.e., that there would be nothing to receive on 108.4). Answer (C) is incorrect. This is the frequency you would use to contact Denver Flight Service when in the vicinity of the Durango VOR, not Denver Center.

6. (Refer to Figure 24 on page 414.) What is the MOCA between JNC and MANCA intersection on V187?

A. 10,900 feet MSL.

B. 12,000 feet MSL.

C. 13,700 feet MSL.

Answer (C) is correct. *(ACL)*
DISCUSSION: The MOCA (minimum obstruction clearance altitude) appears with an asterisk under the MEA on V187. It is 13,700 ft. MSL.
Answer (A) is incorrect. This is the MEA, not MOCA, between MANCA and RIZAL intersections. Answer (B) is incorrect. This is the MEA, not MOCA, between JNC and HERRM INT.

7. (Refer to Figure 24 on page 414.) At what point should a VOR changeover be made from JNC VOR to MANCA intersection southbound on V187?

A. 36 NM south of JNC.

B. 52 NM south of JNC.

C. 74 NM south of JNC.

Answer (B) is correct. *(AIM Para 5-3-6)*
DISCUSSION: The VOR changeover point is depicted on V187, south of HERRM INT. and depicts the mileage between the VORTAC stations. It shows the COP as being 52 NM south of JNC.
Answer (A) is incorrect. The COP is depicted as 52 NM, not 36 NM, south of JNC. Answer (C) is incorrect. The COP is depicted as 52 NM, not 74 NM, south of JNC.

8. (Refer to Figure 21 on page 431, Figure 21A on page 432, Figure 22 on page 433, Figure 22A on page 435, Figure 23 on page 436, Figure 24 on page 414, Figure 25 on page 437, and Figure 26 on page 438.) After departing GJT and arriving at Durango Co.-La Plata Co. Airport, you are unable to land because of weather. How long can you hold over DRO before departing for return flight to the alternate, Grand Junction Co., Walker Field Airport?

Total usable fuel on board, 68 gallons.
Average fuel consumption 15 GPH.
Wind and velocity at 16,000, 2308–16°.

A. 1 hour 33 minutes.

B. 1 hour 37 minutes.

C. 1 hour 42 minutes.

Answer (A) is correct. *(IFH Chap 10)*
DISCUSSION: To solve this problem, you must calculate times en route and fuel consumption for both trips (GJT-DRO and DRO-GJT), add 45-min. reserve, and subtract the total fuel used from 68 gal.
First, complete the flight log for each trip (Figs. 22 and 22A). Calculate groundspeed for the cruise portions of each trip using the wind side of the flight computer. Remember to convert wind direction to magnetic direction first; i.e., 230° − 14°E var. = 216° at 8 kt. Then compute ETE for each leg and fuel consumption for each trip using the slide rule side of the computer.

GJT to DRO

	Distance	MC	Ground-speed	Time	Fuel (gal.)
HERRM INT.	X	X	X	:24:00G	6.0
MANCA INT.	75	151°	172	:26:10	6.5
Approach and Landing	X	X	X	:18:30G	4.6
				1:08:40	17.1

G = Given

DRO to GJT

	Distance	MC	Ground-speed	Time	Fuel (gal.)
MANCA INT.	X	X	X	:14:30G	3.6
HERRM INT.	75	333°	177	:25:21	6.3
JNC	35	331°	177	:11:52	3.0
Approach and Landing	X	X	X	:12:00G	3.0
				1:03:43	15.9

G = Given

	Fuel (gal.)
GJT-DRO	17.1
DRO-GJT	15.9
45-min. reserve	11.3
Total	44.3

With 68 gal. usable fuel, 23.7 gal. (68 − 44.3) would be available to hold at DRO. At 15-GPH fuel consumption, this would be approximately 1 hr. 34 min. of fuel.
Answer (B) is incorrect. To be able to hold for 1 hr. 37 min. would require an average fuel consumption of approximately 14.8 GPH, not 15 GPH. Answer (C) is incorrect. To be able to hold for 1 hr. 42 min. would require an average fuel consumption of approximately 14.5 GPH, not 15 GPH.

FLIGHT LOG

DURANGO (DRO) TO GRAND JUNCTION, WALKER FIELD (GJT)

CHECK POINTS		ROUTE		WIND	SPEED-KTS		DIST	TIME		FUEL	
FROM	TO	ALTITUDE	COURSE	TEMP	TAS	GS	NM	LEG	TOT	LEG	TOT
DRO	MANCA	V211 CLIMB	272°	230 08				:14:30			
	HERRM	V187 16,000	333°		174						
	JNC	V187	331°								
APPROACH & LANDING		DESCENT						:12:00			
	GJT										

OTHER DATA:
NOTE: MAG. VAR. 14° E.

FLIGHT SUMMARY

TIME	FUEL (LB)	
		EN ROUTE
		RESERVE
		MISSED APPR.
		TOTAL

Figure 22A. – Flight Planning Log.

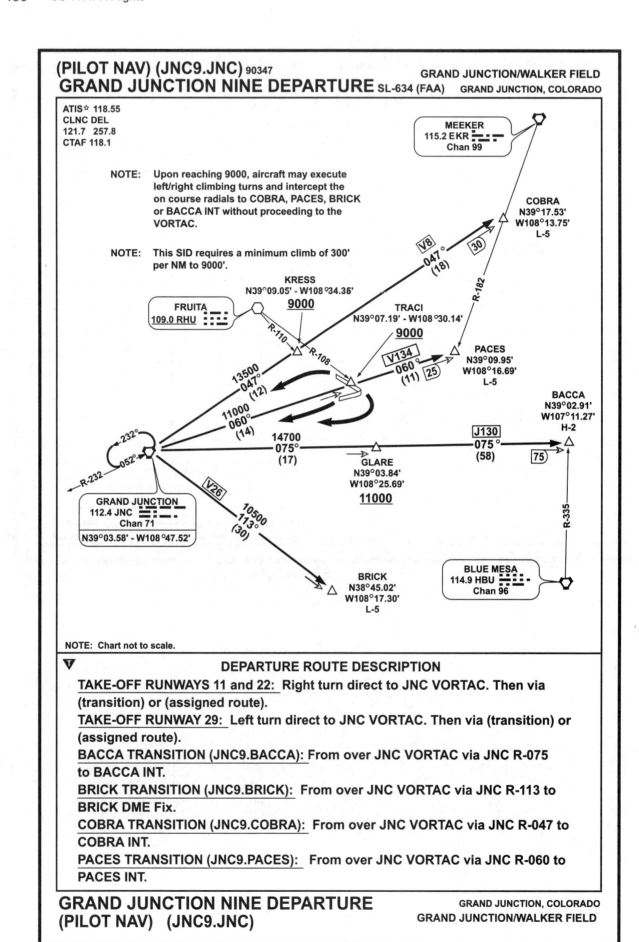

Figure 23. – Grand Junction Nine Departure (JNC9.JNC).

Figure 25. – ILS/DME RWY 2.

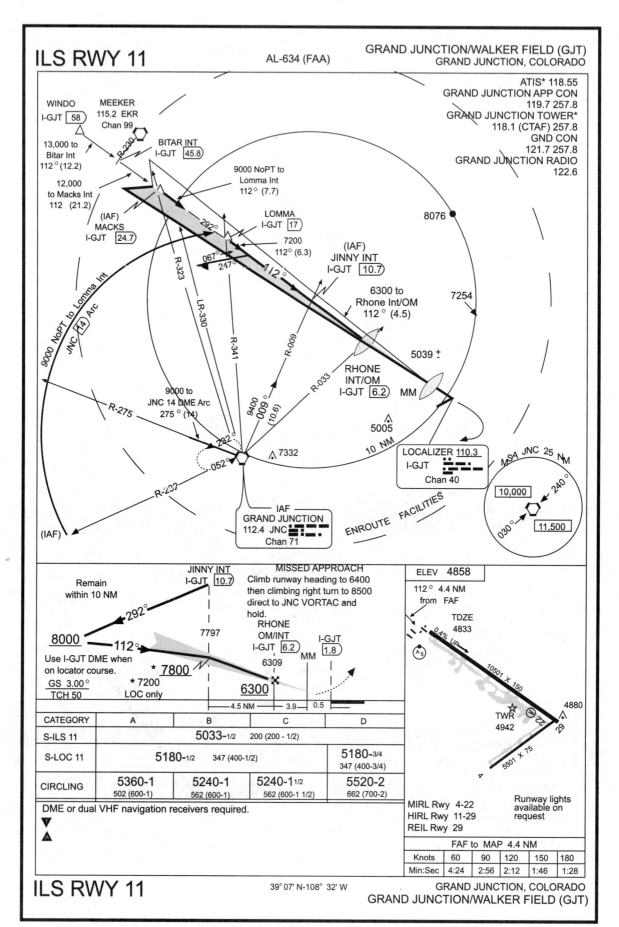

Figure 26. – ILS RWY 11.

11.2 MFR to EUG

Questions 9 through 21 pertain to an IFR flight from Medford-Jackson County Airport, Medford, Oregon, to the Mahlon Sweet Field, Eugene, Oregon.

The route of flight is given in block 8 on the flight plan portion of Fig. 27 on page 440. Information that pertains to your aircraft is given on the bottom portion of Fig. 27. The partially completed flight planning log is given in Fig. 28 on page 441.

The figures provided for this flight are listed below and are presented throughout the sequence of questions, except for Fig. 31, which is provided in color on page 415.

9. (Refer to Figure 27 on page 440, Figure 28 on page 441, Figure 29 on page 444, Figure 30 on page 445, and Figure 31 on page 415.) (Refer to the FD excerpt below, and use the wind entry closest to the flight planned altitude.) Determine the time to be entered in block 10 of the flight plan.

Route of flight ....Figs. 27, 28, 29, 30, & 31
Flight log & MAG VAR .... Fig. 28
GNATS ONE DEPARTURE
  and Excerpt from AFD ....Fig. 30

FT	3000	6000	9000
OTH	0507	2006+03	2215–05

A. 1 hour 10 minutes.

B. 1 hour 15 minutes.

C. 1 hour 20 minutes.

Answer (C) is correct. *(IFH Chap 10)*

DISCUSSION: To determine the estimated time en route to be entered in block 10, you must complete the flight planning log in Fig. 28.

Compute the distance from MERLI intersection to MOURN intersection. First, compute the distance traveled on the OED 15 DME from R-251 (MERLI) to R-333. The number of degrees of the arc is 82° (333 − 251). Use the following general rule to find the distance traveled on the arc:

$$Dist.\ of\ arc = \frac{\#\ of\ deg.\ \times\ DME\ arc}{60}$$

$$Dist.\ of\ arc = \frac{82\ \times\ 15}{60} = 20.5\ NM$$

Next, add the 16 NM on R-333 from the 15 DME arc to MOURN, which is 36.5 (20.5 + 16). Given an average groundspeed of 135 kt., the time is 16 min. 13 sec.

For the next three legs, you need to compute the wind triangle on either your flight computer or your electronic computer to determine the groundspeed as given in the table below.

Remember that winds are given in true direction and must be converted to magnetic. Fig. 28 shows a variation of 20°E. Use the wind at 9,000 ft. because that is closest to the flight planned altitude of 8,000 ft. 220° − 20°E var. = 200° at 15 kt.

	Distance	MC	Wind (Mag)	Ground-speed	Time
MERLI INT.	X	X	X	X	:11:00G
MOURN INT.	37	X	X	135G	:16:13
RBG VOR	19	287°G	200/15	153	:07:26
OTH VORTAC	38	272°G	200/15	149	:15:12
EUG VORTAC	59	026°G	200/15	170	:20:50
Approach and Landing	X	X	X	X	:10:00G
					1:20:41

G = Given

Answer (A) is incorrect. An ETE of 1 hr. 10 min. requires a TAS of approximately 200 kt., not 155 kt. Answer (B) is incorrect. An ETE of 1 hr. 15 min. requires a TAS of 180 kt., not 155 kt.

10. (Refer to Figure 27 below, and Legend 26 on page 428.) What aircraft equipment code should be entered in block 3 of the flight plan?

A. T.

B. U.

C. A.

Answer (C) is correct. *(AIM Para 5-1-8)*
DISCUSSION: In block 3 of the flight plan, you enter the designation of the aircraft followed by a slash (/) and a letter for the equipment code. The bottom portion of Fig. 27 indicates you have a transponder with Mode C and DME, which requires code A. (See Legend 26.)

Answer (A) is incorrect. T indicates only a transponder with no encoding capability and no DME. Answer (B) is incorrect. U indicates a transponder with encoding capability but no DME.

					Form Approved: OMB No. 2120-0034		

U.S. DEPARTMENT OF TRANSPORTATION
FEDERAL AVIATION ADMINISTRATION

FLIGHT PLAN

(FAA USE ONLY)   ☐ PILOT BRIEFING   ☐ VNR   TIME STARTED   SPECIALIST INITIALS

☐ STOPOVER

1. TYPE	2. AIRCRAFT IDENTIFICATION	3. AIRCRAFT TYPE/ SPECIAL EQUIPMENT	4. TRUE AIRSPEED	5. DEPARTURE POINT	6. DEPARTURE TIME		7. CRUISING ALTITUDE
VFR / X IFR / DVFR	N132SM	C 182/	155 KTS	MFR	PROPOSED (Z)	ACTUAL (Z)	8,000

8. ROUTE OF FLIGHT

GNATS1,   MOURN,   V121 EUG

9. DESTINATION (Name of airport and city)	10. EST. TIME ENROUTE		11. REMARKS
MAHLON/ SWEET FEILD, EUGENE, OR.	HOURS	MINUTES	INSTRUMENT TRAINING FLIGHT

12. FUEL ON BOARD		13. ALTERNATE AIRPORT(S)	14. PILOT'S NAME, ADDRESS & TELEPHONE NUMBER & AIRCRAFT HOME BASE	15. NUMBER ABOARD
HOURS	MINUTES	N/R	17. DESTINATION CONTACT/TELEPHONE (OPTIONAL)	

16. COLOR OF AIRCRAFT

CIVIL AIRCRAFT PILOTS. FAR Part 91 requires you file an IFR flight plan to operate under instrument flight rules in controlled airspace. Failure to file could result in a civil penalty not to exceed $1,000 for each violation (Section 901 of the Federal Aviation Act of 1958, as amended). Filing of a VFR flight plan is recommended as a good operating practice. See also Part 99 for requirements concerning DVFR flight plans.

FAA Form 7233-1 (8-82)   CLOSE VFR FLIGHT PLAN WITH _____ FSS ON ARRIVAL

AIRCRAFT INFORMATION

MAKE Cessna   MODEL 182

N 132SM   V$_{so}$ 57

AIRCRAFT EQUIPMENT/STATUS**

**NOTE: X= OPERATIVE   INOP= INOPERATIVE   N/A= NOT APPLICABLE

TRANSPONDER: X (MODE C) X   ILS: (LOCALIZER) X (GLIDE SLOPE) N/A

VOR NO.1 X (NO.2) X   ADF: X   RNAV: N/A

VERTICAL PATH COMPUTER: NA   DME: X

MARKER BEACON: (AUDIO) INOP (VISUAL) Inop.

Figure 27. – Flight Plan and Aircraft Information.

11. (Refer to Figure 31 on page 415.) What minimum navigation equipment is required en route on V448 to identify MOPIO?

    A. One VOR receiver.

    B. Two VOR receivers and DME.

    C. One VOR receiver and DME.

Answer (C) is correct. *(ACL)*
    DISCUSSION: MOPIO is located on the OED 316° radial at 17 NM DME. An operational VOR receiver and DME would be required to identify MOPIO.
    Answer (A) is incorrect. An operational DME would also be required, in addition to an operational VOR receiver, to identify MOPIO. Answer (B) is incorrect. Only one VOR receiver is required to identify MOPIO.

12. (Refer to Figure 28 below, and Figure 27 on page 440.) What CAS must be used to maintain the filed TAS at the flight planned altitude if the outside air temperature is –5°C?

    A. 134 KCAS.

    B. 139 KCAS.

    C. 142 KCAS.

Answer (B) is correct. *(PHAK Chap 15)*
    DISCUSSION: In the center of the computer side of your flight computer, on the right side, put the air temperature of –5°C over the altitude of 8,000 ft. (given in block 7 of the flight plan). On the outer scale, find TAS of 155 (from block 4), which is over calibrated airspeed (CAS) on the inner scale of 139 KCAS.
    Answer (A) is incorrect. Maintaining 134 KCAS would result in a TAS of 150 kt., not 155 kt. Answer (C) is incorrect. Maintaining 142 KCAS would result in a TAS of 158 kt., not 155 kt.

FLIGHT LOG

MEDFORD - JACKSON CO. AIRPORT TO HAHLON/SWEET FIELD, EUGENE, OR.

CHECK POINTS		ROUTE	COURSE	WIND	SPEED-KTS		DIST	TIME		FUEL	
FROM	TO	ALTITUDE		TEMP	TAS	GS	NM	LEG	TOT	LEG	TOT
MFR	MERLI	GNATS1 CLIMB	270°		155			:11:0			
	MOURN	V121 8000	333°			AVER. 135					
	RGB	V121 8000	287°								
	OTH	V121 8000	272°								
	EUG	APPROACH DESCENT	026°								
APPROACH & LANDING								:10:0			
	SWEET FIELD										

OTHER DATA:	FLIGHT SUMMARY		
NOTE:	TIME	FUEL (LB)	
MAG. VAR. 20° E.			EN ROUTE
AVERAGE G.S. 135 KTS. FOR GNATS 1			RESERVE
DEPARTURE CLIMB.			MISSED APPR.
			TOTAL

Figure 28. – Flight Planning Log.

13. (Refer to Figure 27 on page 440 and Figure 30 on page 445.) To which maximum service volume distance from the OED VORTAC should you expect to receive adequate signal coverage for navigation at the flight planned altitude?

    A. 100 NM.

    B. 80 NM.

    C. 40 NM.

Answer (C) is correct. *(AIM Para 1-1-8)*
    DISCUSSION: The flight plan in Fig. 27 shows a planned altitude of 8,000 ft. OED VORTAC is an H-type (high altitude) as indicated in the *A/FD* in Fig. 30 by (H) ABVORTAC in the first line of **Radio Aids to Navigation**. For such VORTACs, the altitude and range boundaries are from 1,000 ft. AGL up to and including 14,500 ft. AGL at distances out to 40 NM.
    Answer (A) is incorrect. This applies to 14,500 ft. AGL up to 18,000 ft. AGL, and from 45,000 ft. AGL up to 60,000 ft. AGL. Answer (B) is incorrect. This is not given as a range for VORs.

14. (Refer to Figure 30A below, and Figure 30 on page 445.) What is your position relative to GNATS intersection and the instrument departure routing?

    A. On departure course and past GNATS.

    B. Right of departure course and past GNATS.

    C. Left of departure course and have not passed GNATS.

Answer (B) is correct. *(IFH Chap 9)*
    DISCUSSION: On the RMI, the fat needle is tuned to the OED VOR (113.6). The tail of the needle is on 224°, which means that the airplane is on R-224. Accordingly, the airplane is past GNATS (which is on R-216). The thin needle is tuned to the VIOLE LMM (356). The tail of the needle is on 280°, which means that the airplane is on the 280° MB FROM. Thus, the airplane is to the right of the departure course (which is the 270° MB FROM).
    Answer (A) is incorrect. The ADF needle indicates the 280° MB FROM, which is right of, not on, the departure course. Answer (C) is incorrect. The ADF needle indicates the 280° MB FROM, which is right, not left, of the departure course, and the VOR needle indicates R-24, which is past, not approaching, GNATS.

Figure 30A. – RMI Indicator.

15. (Refer to Figure 30 on page 445.) During the arc portion of the instrument departure procedure (GNATS1.MOURN), a left crosswind is encountered. Where should the bearing pointer of an RMI be referenced relative to the wing-tip to compensate for wind drift and maintain the 15 DME arc?

    A. Behind the right wing-tip reference point.

    B. On the right wing-tip reference point.

    C. Behind the left wing-tip reference point.

Answer (A) is correct. *(IFH Chap 9)*
    DISCUSSION: Normally when flying a DME arc, the RMI needle will point exactly to 090° or 270° in wind-free conditions. Given a crosswind from the left, you will have to make a correction to the left, which will mean that the needle is behind the right wing while on an arc to the right.
    Answer (B) is incorrect. It will be on the right wingtip only when there is no wind. Answer (C) is incorrect. The VOR is to the right and the RMI points directly to the VOR.

16. (Refer to Figure 30 on page 445.) Using an average groundspeed of 120 knots, what minimum rate of climb must be maintained to meet the required climb rate (feet per NM) to 4,100 feet as specified on the instrument departure procedure?

    A. 400 feet per minute.

    B. 500 feet per minute.

    C. 800 feet per minute.

Answer (C) is correct. *(ACL)*
    DISCUSSION: The instrument departure procedure in Fig. 30 has a note which indicates a minimum climb of 400 ft. per NM to 4,100 ft. To convert this to a rate of climb (fpm), use the formula

$$\frac{GS \times FT/NM}{60} = FPM = \frac{120 \times 400}{60} = \frac{48,000}{60} = 800 \; FRM$$

or use Legend 16 on page 193. Find the 400 ft. per NM column on the left margin and move right to the 120-kt. groundspeed column to determine a rate of climb of 800 fpm.
    Answer (A) is incorrect. A 400 fpm rate of climb at an average groundspeed of 120 kt. would result in a climb rate of 200 ft. per NM, not 400 ft. per NM. Answer (B) is incorrect. A 500 fpm rate of climb at an average groundspeed of 120 kt. would result in a climb rate of 250 ft. per NM, not 400 ft. per NM.

17. (Refer to Figure 30 on page 445.) Which restriction to the use of the OED VORTAC would be applicable to the (GNATS1.MOURN) departure?

A. R-333 beyond 30 NM below 6,500 feet.

B. R-210 beyond 35 NM below 8,500 feet.

C. R-251 within 15 NM below 6,100 feet.

Answer (A) is correct. *(ACL)*
DISCUSSION: On Fig. 30, in the *A/FD* under the **Radio Aids to Navigation** for the OED VORTAC, the VORTAC is listed as being unusable in certain segments. For example, it indicates that radials 280° to 345° are not usable below 6,500 ft. beyond 30 NM. This includes R-333.
Answer (B) is incorrect. There is no restriction to R-210. Answer (C) is incorrect. The restriction to R-251 is beyond 25 NM, not within 15 NM.

18. (Refer to Figure 29 on page 444.) What is the TDZ elevation for RWY 16 on Eugene/Mahlon Sweet Field?

A. 363 feet MSL.

B. 365 feet MSL.

C. 396 feet MSL.

Answer (A) is correct. *(ACL)*
DISCUSSION: On the IAP chart, the TDZE is shown in the airport diagram near the approach end of the landing runway. The TDZE for RWY 16 at EUG is 363 ft.
Answer (B) is incorrect. This is the airport elevation. Answer (C) is incorrect. This is the height of an obstacle to the right of the approach end of RWY 16.

19. (Refer to Figure 29 on page 444 and Legend 21 on page 267.) Using a groundspeed of 90 knots on the ILS final approach course, what rate of descent should be used as a reference to maintain the ILS glide slope?

A. 415 feet per minute.

B. 480 feet per minute.

C. 555 feet per minute.

Answer (B) is correct. *(IFH Chap 1)*
DISCUSSION: The profile view of the NOS chart shows a glide slope (GS) angle of 3.00°. Legend 21 gives rates of descent based on various glide slope angles and groundspeeds. Find the 3.0° glide slope at the left margin and move right to the 90-kt. groundspeed column to determine a rate of descent of 480 fpm.
Answer (A) is incorrect. This is the rate of descent required for a glide slope between 2.5° and 3.0°, not a 3.0° glide slope. Answer (C) is incorrect. This is the required rate of descent at 90 kt. on a 3.5°, not 3.0°, glide slope.

20. (Refer to Figure 162 on page 446.) What are the hours of operation (local standard time) of the control tower at Eugene/Mahlon Sweet Field?

A. 0800 - 2130

B. 0730 - 1400

C. 0600 - 2330

Answer (C) is correct. *(AIM Para 4-2-12)*
DISCUSSION: The A/FD entry for Eugene Mahlon Sweet Field reads, "UTC – 8 (-7DT)." This indicates the field is 8 hours behind Zulu Time during standard time and 7 hours behind during Daylight Savings Time. The Eugene Tower entry shows the tower is in operation between 1400 and 0730Z. 1400 – 0800 = 0600 local standard time. If we back up 8 hours from 0730Z, that equates to 2330 local standard. The tower at Eugene Mahlon Sweet Field operates from 0600 – 2330 local standard time.
Answer (A) is incorrect. Local standard time of 0800 is 6 hours behind 1400 Zulu, not 8 hours as specified in the upper portion of the Mahlon Sweet Field entry. The correct opening time for the tower would be 1400Z – 0800 = 0600 local standard time. Answer (B) is incorrect. Local standard time of 0730 + 0800 variance from Zulu Time equals 1530 Zulu time, not 1400 Zulu as stipulated in the Eugene Tower entry. The correct opening time for Eugene Tower would be 1400Z – 0800 = 0600 local standard time.

21. (Refer to Figure 163 on page 447 and Figure 164 on page 448.) Using an average ground speed of 120 knots and taking off on Runway 14, what minimum rate of climb must be maintained to meet the required climb rate (in feet per NM) to 4,800 feet as specified on the instrument departure procedures?

A. 435 feet per minute

B. 500 feet per minute

C. 1,000 feet per minute

Answer (C) is correct. *(IPH Chap 2)*
DISCUSSION: The Takeoff Minimums note in the lower left corner of Fig. 163 stipulates "a minimum climb of 435' per NM to 4,800." Note this is feet per NM, not feet per minute. With a ground speed of 120 knots, you are covering 2 NM per minute. 2 × 435 = 870 feet per minute to achieve 435 feet per nautical mile. This leaves the answer option of 1,000 feet per minute as the best answer of those available, even though it is higher than the actual minimum rate of climb required. This can also be interpolated by using the chart in Legend 16 on page 193.
Answer (A) is incorrect. When traveling at a ground speed of 120 knots, 435 feet per minute equates to 218 feet per NM. That rate is well below the specified minimum requirement to 4,800 feet. Answer (B) is incorrect. When traveling at a ground speed of 120 knots, 500 feet per minute equates to only 250 feet per NM. The GNATS SIX departure stipulates a minimum of 435 feet per NM.

Figure 29. – ILS RWY 16 (EUG) and Excerpt from Airport/Facility Directory.

Figure 30. – GNATS One Departure and Excerpt from Airport/Facility Directory.

OREGON   119

EUGENE

MAHLON SWEET FLD (EUG)   7 NW   UTC–8(–7DT)   N44°07.48′ W123°12.72′   KLAMATH FALLS
   374   B S4   **FUEL** 100LL, JET A   OX 1, 2, 3, 4   TPA—1174(800)   Class I, ARFF Index B   H–1B, L–1B
   NOTAM FILE EUG   IAP, AD
RWY 16R–34L: H8009X150 (ASPH–GRVD)   S–75, D–200, 2D–400
   HIRL   CL
   RWY 16R: ALSF2. TDZL. PAPI(P4L)—GA 3.0° TCH 50′.
   RWY 34L: ODALS. VASI(V4L)—GA 3.0° TCH 53′.
RWY 16L–34R: H6000X150 (ASPH–GRVD)   S–105, D–175, 2D–240
   HIRL
   RWY 16L: MALSR. PAPI(P4L)—GA 3.0° TCH 52′.
   RWY 34R: REIL. PAPI(P4L)—GA 3.0° TCH 50′.
RUNWAY DECLARED DISTANCE INFORMATION
   RWY 16L:TORA–6000   TODA–6000   ASDA–6000   LDA–6000
   RWY 16R:TORA–8009   TODA–8009   ASDA–8009   LDA–8009
   RWY 34L:TORA–8009   TODA–8009   ASDA–8009   LDA–8009
   RWY 34R:TORA–6000   TODA–6000   ASDA–6000   LDA–6000

AIRPORT REMARKS: Attended continuously. Migratory waterfowl and other
   birds on and invof arpt. PPR for unscheduled air carrier ops with more
   than 30 passenger seats call 541–682–5430. ARFF svcs unavailable
   0000–0500 local except PPR 541–682–5430. No access to Rwy 34L
   byd Twy A9. Helicopters ldg and departing avoid overflying the airline
   passenger terminal and ramp located E of Rwy 16R–34L. Helipad west
   of Rwy 16R restricted, PPR phone 541–682–5430. Twys H and K unavailable to acft 21,000 pounds single weight and
   40,000 pounds dual gross weight. Terminal apron closed to acft except scheduled air carriers and flights with prior
   permission. PAPI Rwy 16R and Rwy 16L and 34R and VASI Rwy 34L opr 24 hrs. When twr clsd HIRL Rwy 16L–34R
   and Rwy 16R–34L preset medium ints. When twr clsd ACTIVATE ALSF2 Rwy 16R, ODALS Rwy 34L MALSR Rwy 16L
   and REIL Rwy 34R—CTAF.
WEATHER DATA SOURCES: ASOS (541) 461–3114 **HIWAS** 112.9 EUG.
COMMUNICATIONS: CTAF 118.9 **ATIS** 125.225 541–607–4699 **UNICOM** 122.95
   EUGENE RCO 122.3 (MC MINNVILLE RADIO)
Ⓡ **CASCADE APP/DEP CON** 119.6 (340°–159°) 120.25 (160°–339°) (1400–0730Z‡)
Ⓡ **SEATTLE CENTER APP/DEP CON** 125.8 (0730–1400Z‡)
   EUGENE TOWER 118.9 (Rwy 16R– 34L) 124.15 (Rwy 16L– 34R) (1400–0730Z‡) **GND CON** 121.7 **CLNC DEL** 121.7
AIRSPACE: CLASS D svc 1400–0730Z‡ other times CLASS E.
RADIO AIDS TO NAVIGATION: NOTAM FILE EUG.
   EUGENE (H) VORTACW 112.9   EUG   Chan 76   N44°07.25′ W123°13.37′   at fld. 364/20E.   **HIWAS.**
   ILS/DME 111.75 I–ADE Chan 54(Y) Rwy 16L. Class IE.
   ILS/DME 110.1 I–EUG Chan 38 Rwy 16R. Class IIIE. Unmonitored when ATCT clsd.

FLORENCE

FLORENCE MUNI (6S2)   1 N   UTC–8(–7DT)   N43°58.97′ W124°06.68′   KLAMATH FALLS
   51   B **FUEL** 100LL, JET A   TPA—1051(1000)   NOTAM FILE MMV   L–1A
RWY 15–33: H3000X60 (ASPH)   S–12.5   MIRL   0.4% up NW
   RWY 15: Hill. Rgt tfc.
   RWY 33: PAPI(P2L)—GA 3.0° TCH 40′. Trees.
AIRPORT REMARKS: Attended 1630–0030Z‡. Birds, deer and wildlife on and
   invof arpt. ACTIVATE MIRL Rwy 15–33—CTAF. PAPI Rwy 33 opr 24
   hrs.

WEATHER DATA SOURCES: AWOS–3 118.225 (541) 997–8664.
COMMUNICATIONS: CTAF/UNICOM 122.8
RADIO AIDS TO NAVIGATION: NOTAM FILE OTH.
   NORTH BEND (L) VORTACW 112.1   OTH   Chan 58   N43°24.93′
      W124°10.11′   346° 34.1 NM to fld. 707/18E.   **HIWAS.**
   VORTAC unusable:
      012°–087° byd 30 NM blo 5,000′

Figure 162.

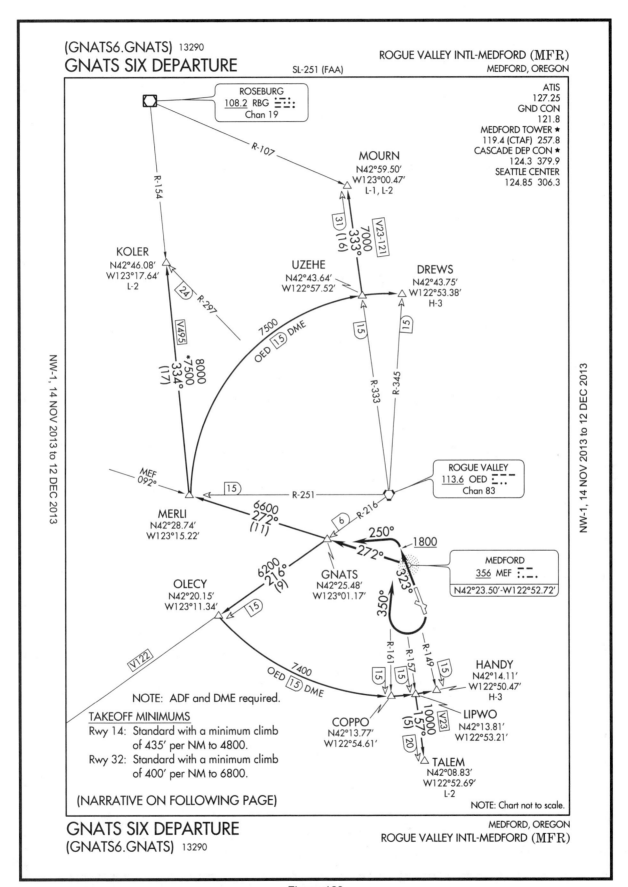

(GNATS6.GNATS) 13290
GNATS SIX DEPARTURE
SL-251 (FAA)

ROGUE VALLEY INTL-MEDFORD (MFR)
MEDFORD, OREGON

ROSEBURG
108.2 RBG
Chan 19

ATIS
127.25
GND CON
121.8
MEDFORD TOWER ★
119.4 (CTAF) 257.8
CASCADE DEP CON ★
124.3 379.9
SEATTLE CENTER
124.85 306.3

R-107

MOURN
N42°59.50'
W123°00.47'
L-1, L-2

R-154

31 (16) 333° 7000 V23-121

KOLER
N42°46.08'
W123°17.64'
L-2

24 R-297

UZEHE
N42°43.64'
W122°57.52'

DREWS
N42°43.75'
W122°53.38'
H-3

V495 334° (17) 8000 *7500

7500 OED 15 DME

15

15

R-333

R-345

MEF
092°

15 R-251

ROGUE VALLEY
113.6 OED
Chan 83

MERLI
N42°28.74'
W123°15.22'

6600
272°
(11)

6 R-216

250°

272°

1800

323°

MEDFORD
356 MEF
N42°23.50'-W122°52.72'

OLECY
N42°20.15'
W123°11.34'

6200
216°
(9)

GNATS
N42°25.48'
W123°01.17'

350°

15

V122

7400 OED 15 DME

R-161

R-157

R-149

HANDY
N42°14.11'
W122°50.47'
H-3

NOTE: ADF and DME required.

15

15

15

LIPWO
N42°13.81'
W122°53.21'

TAKEOFF MINIMUMS
Rwy 14: Standard with a minimum climb
of 435' per NM to 4800.
Rwy 32: Standard with a minimum climb
of 400' per NM to 6800.

COPPO
N42°13.77'
W122°54.61'

10000 157° (5)

V23

20

TALEM
N42°08.83'
W122°52.69'
L-2

(NARRATIVE ON FOLLOWING PAGE)

NOTE: Chart not to scale.

GNATS SIX DEPARTURE
(GNATS6.GNATS) 13290

MEDFORD, OREGON
ROGUE VALLEY INTL-MEDFORD (MFR)

NW-1, 14 NOV 2013 to 12 DEC 2013

NW-1, 14 NOV 2013 to 12 DEC 2013

Figure 163.

(GNATS6.GNATS) 13290
GNATS SIX DEPARTURE
SL-251 (FAA)

ROGUE VALLEY INTL-MEDFORD (MFR)
MEDFORD, OREGON

NW-1, 14 NOV 2013 to 12 DEC 2013

NW-1, 14 NOV 2013 to 12 DEC 2013

DEPARTURE ROUTE DESCRIPTION

<u>TAKEOFF RUNWAY 14:</u> Climbing right turn on heading 350° to intercept bearing 272° from MEF NDB to GNATS INT. Thence . . . .

<u>TAKEOFF RUNWAY 32:</u> Climb on heading 323° to 1800 then climbing left turn on heading 250° to intercept bearing 272° from MEF NDB to GNATS INT. Thence . . . .

. . . . via (transition) or (assigned route). Maintain 11000 or assigned lower altitude.

<u>COPPO TRANSITION (GNATS6.COPPO):</u> From over GNATS INT via OED VORTAC R-216 to OLECY DME, then via the OED VORTAC 15 DME Arc CCW to COPPO DME.

<u>DREWS TRANSITION (GNATS6.DREWS):</u> From over GNATS INT via MEF NDB 272° to MERLI INT, then via the OED VORTAC 15 DME Arc CW to DREWS DME.

<u>HANDY TRANSITION (GNATS6.HANDY):</u> From over GNATS INT via the OED VORTAC R-216 to OLECY DME, then via the OED VORTAC 15 DME Arc CCW to HANDY DME.

<u>KOLER TRANSITION (GNATS6.KOLER):</u> From over GNATS INT via MEF NDB 272° to MERLI INT, then via RBG VOR/DME R-154 to KOLER INT.

<u>MOURN TRANSITION (GNATS6.MOURN):</u> From over GNATS INT via MEF NDB 272° to MERLI INT, then via the OED VORTAC 15 DME Arc CW to UZEHE DME, then via OED VORTAC R-333 to MOURN INT.

<u>TALEM TRANSITION (GNATS6.TALEM):</u> From over GNATS INT via OED VORTAC R-216 to OLECY DME, then via the OED VORTAC 15 DME Arc CCW to LIPWO DME, then via OED VORTAC R-157 to TALEM DME.

GNATS SIX DEPARTURE
(GNATS6.GNATS) 13290

MEDFORD, OREGON
ROGUE VALLEY INTL-MEDFORD (MFR)

Figure 164.

11.3 YKM to PDX

Questions 22 through 39 pertain to an IFR flight from Yakima Air Terminal, Yakima, Washington, to the Portland International Airport, Portland, Oregon.

The route of flight is given in block 8 on the flight plan portion of Fig. 44 on page 450. Information that pertains to your aircraft is given on the bottom portion of Fig. 44. The partially completed flight planning log is given in Fig. 45 on page 451.

The figures provided for this flight are listed below and are presented throughout the sequence of questions, except for Fig. 47, which is provided in color on page 418.

Fig.	Page	
44	450	Flight Plan and Aircraft Information
45	451	Flight Planning Log
46	453	GROMO Two Departure and Excerpt from Airport/Facility Directory
47	418	En Route Chart Segment
48	452	CDI – NAV 1
49	455	LOC/DME RWY 21 (PDX)
188	457	[title not provided by FAA]

22. (Refer to Figure 47 on page 418.) En route on V112 from BTG VORTAC to LTJ VORTAC, the minimum altitude crossing Gymme intersection is

A. 6,400 feet.

B. 6,500 feet.

C. 7,000 feet.

Answer (C) is correct. *(FAR 91.177)*

DISCUSSION: When no minimum crossing altitude (MCA) is specified, e.g., at GYMME intersection, the intersection may be crossed at or above the preceding MEA. Since the MEA along V112 eastbound is 7,000 ft., GYMME may be crossed no lower than 7,000 ft.

Answer (A) is incorrect. This is the MOCA, not the MEA, along V112. Answer (B) is incorrect. This is the MEA west of GYMME when westbound, not eastbound.

23. (Refer to Figure 47 on page 418.) When en route on V448 from YKM VORTAC to BTG VORTAC, what minimum navigation equipment is required to identify ANGOO intersection?

A. One VOR receiver.

B. One VOR receiver and DME.

C. Two VOR receivers.

Answer (A) is correct. *(IFH Chap 10)*

DISCUSSION: To identify ANGOO INT., only one VOR receiver is required. It is important to establish yourself on V448 and maintain heading while you orient yourself to LTJ VORTAC R-330. Your position checks and tuning will need to be done quickly and accurately.

Answer (B) is incorrect. Since ANGOO INT. can be determined by cross radials, only one VOR receiver is required; a DME is not. Answer (C) is incorrect. Only one VOR receiver, not two, is required to identify ANGOO INT.

24. (Refer to Figure 47 on page 418.) En route on V468 from BTG VORTAC to YKM VORTAC, the minimum altitude at TROTS intersection is

A. 7,100 feet.

B. 10,000 feet.

C. 11,500 feet.

Answer (C) is correct. *(FAR 91.177)*

DISCUSSION: TROTS intersection (45 NM northeast of BTG VORTAC on V468 in Fig. 47) shows a minimum crossing altitude (MCA) of 11,500 ft. when northeastbound on V468.

Answer (A) is incorrect. This is the MOCA along V468, not the MCA at TROTS. Answer (B) is incorrect. This is the MEA before TROTS, not the MCA at TROTS.

25. (Refer to Figure 44 on page 450 and Legend 26 on page 428.) What aircraft equipment code should be entered in block 3 of the flight plan?

A. A.

B. C.

C. I.

Answer (C) is correct. *(AIM Para 5-1-8)*

DISCUSSION: In block 3 of the flight plan, you enter the designation of the aircraft followed by a slash (/) and a letter for an equipment mode. Fig. 44 indicates the airplane has a transponder with Mode C and RNAV, which requires code I. (See Legend 26.)

Answer (A) is incorrect. A indicates Mode C transponder and DME but no RNAV. Answer (B) is incorrect. C indicates RNAV and a transponder with no altitude encoding capability.

26. (Refer to Figure 44 below.) What CAS must be used to maintain the filed TAS at the flight planned altitude if the outside air temperature is +5°C?

   A. 147 KCAS.

   B. 150 KCAS.

   C. 154 KCAS.

Answer (A) is correct. *(PHAK Chap 15)*
   DISCUSSION: In the center of the slide rule side of your flight computer, on the right side, put the air temperature of +5°C over the altitude of 12,000 ft. (given in block 7 of the flight plan). On the outer scale, find TAS of 180 kt. (from block 4), which is over calibrated airspeed (CAS) on the inner scale of 147 KCAS.
   Answer (B) is incorrect. Maintaining 150 KCAS would result in a TAS of 185 kt., not 180 kt. Answer (C) is incorrect. Maintaining 154 KCAS would result in a TAS of 190 kt., not 180 kt.

Form Approved: OMB No. 2120-0034

U.S. DEPARTMENT OF TRANSPORTATION
FEDERAL AVIATION ADMINISTRATION

FLIGHT PLAN

(FAA USE ONLY)   ☐ PILOT BRIEFING   ☐ VNR   TIME STARTED   SPECIALIST INITIALS

☐ STOPOVER

1. TYPE	2. AIRCRAFT IDENTIFICATION	3. AIRCRAFT TYPE/ SPECIAL EQUIPMENT	4. TRUE AIRSPEED	5. DEPARTURE POINT	6. DEPARTURE TIME		7. CRUISING ALTITUDE
VFR					PROPOSED (Z)	ACTUAL (Z)	
X IFR	N3678A	PA31/	180 KTS	YKM			12000
DVFR							

8. ROUTE OF FLIGHT

GROMO 2, HITCH, V468 BTG, DIRECT

9. DESTINATION (Name of airport and city)	10. EST. TIME ENROUTE		11. REMARKS
	HOURS	MINUTES	
PORTLAND INTL. AIRPORT PDX			INSTRUMENT TRAINING FLIGHT

12. FUEL ON BOARD		13. ALTERNATE AIRPORT(S)	14. PILOT'S NAME, ADDRESS & TELEPHONE NUMBER & AIRCRAFT HOME BASE	15. NUMBER ABOARD
HOURS	MINUTES			
		N/A	17. DESTINATION CONTACT/TELEPHONE (OPTIONAL)	2

16. COLOR OF AIRCRAFT	CIVIL AIRCRAFT PILOTS. FAR Part 91 requires you file an IFR flight plan to operate under instrument flight rules in controlled airspace. Failure to file could result in a civil penalty not to exceed $1,000 for each violation (Section 901 of the Federal Aviation Act of 1958, as amended). Filing of a VFR flight plan is recommended as a good operating practice. See also Part 99 for requirements concerning DVFR flight plans.
GOLD/WHITE	

FAA Form 7233-1 (8-82)   CLOSE VFR FLIGHT PLAN WITH _____ FSS ON ARRIVAL

AIRCRAFT INFORMATION

MAKE Piper   **MODEL** PA-31

N 3678A   **V**so 77

AIRCRAFT EQUIPMENT/STATUS**

**NOTE: X= OPERATIVE   INOP= INOPERATIVE   N/A= NOT APPLICABLE
TRANSPONDER: X (MODE C) X ILS: (LOCALIZER) X (GLIDE SLOPE) X
VOR NO.1 X (NO.2) X ADF: X RNAV: X
VERTICAL PATH COMPUTER: N/A DME: X
MARKER BEACON: X (AUDIO) INOP   (VISUAL) X

Figure 44. – Flight Plan and Aircraft Information.

27. (Refer to Figure 45 below, Figure 44 on page 450, Figure 46 on page 453, and Figure 47 on page 418.) Determine the time to be entered in block 10 of the flight plan. (Refer to the FD excerpt below, and use the wind entry closest to the flight planned altitude.)

Route of flight .... Figs. 44, 45, 46, & 47
Flight log & MAG VAR .... Fig. 45
GROMO TWO DEPARTURE
  and Excerpt from AFD .... Fig. 46

FT	3000	6000	9000	12000
YKM	1615	1926+12	2032+08	2035+05

A. 54 minutes.

B. 1 hour 02 minutes.

C. 1 hour 07 minutes.

Answer (B) is correct. *(IFH Chap 10)*
  DISCUSSION: To determine estimated time en route to be entered in block 10, you must complete the flight planning log in Fig. 45. Using the wind side of your flight computer, determine groundspeeds as given in the table below.
  Remember that winds are given in true direction and must be converted to magnetic. Fig. 45 indicates a variation of 20°E. 200° − 20°E var. = 180° at 35 kt.
  The distance from BTG VORTAC to PDX is not given. It may be estimated at 10 NM by comparing it to other airway segments of similar length.

	Distance	MC	Wind (Mag)	Ground-speed	Time
HITCH INT.	X	X	X	X	:10:00G
VOR COP	37	206°	180/35	148	:15:00
BTG VORTAC	53	234°	180/35	157	:20:15
PDX	10	160°	180/35	147	:04:05
Approach and Landing	X	X	X	X	:13:00G
					1:02:20

G = Given

Answer (A) is incorrect. An ETE of 54 min. requires a TAS of 220 kt., not 180 kt. Answer (C) is incorrect. An ETE of 1 hr. 7 min. requires a TAS of approximately 165 kt., not 180 kt.

FLIGHT LOG

YAKIMA AIR TERMINAL TO PORTLAND, INTL.

CHECK POINTS		ROUTE		WIND	SPEED-KTS		DIST	TIME		FUEL	
FROM	TO	ALTITUDE	COURSE	TEMP	TAS	GS	NM	LEG	TOT	LEG	TOT
YKM	HITCH	GROMO 2 CLIMB	206°					:10.			
	VOR C.O.P.	V468 12,000	206°		180						
	BTG	V468 12,000	234°								
	PDX	DIRECT	160°								
APPROACH & LANDING								:13.			
	PDX AIRPORT										

OTHER DATA:				FLIGHT SUMMARY	
NOTE:	MAG. VAR. 20° E.		TIME	FUEL (LB)	
					EN ROUTE
					RESERVE
					MISSED APPR.
					TOTAL

Figure 45. – Flight Planning Log.

28. (Refer to Figure 46 on page 453 and Legend 16 on page 292.) Using an average ground speed of 140 knots, what minimum indicated rate of climb must be maintained to meet the required climb rate (feet per NM) to 6,300 feet as specified on the instrument departure procedure?

    A.   350 feet per minute.

    B.   583 feet per minute.

    C.   816 feet per minute.

Answer (C) is correct. *(ACL)*
    DISCUSSION: The DP in Fig. 46 has a note which indicates a minimum climb of 350 ft. per NM to 6,300 ft. To convert this to a rate of climb (fpm), use Legend 16. Find the 350 ft. per NM column on the left margin and move right to the 140-kt. groundspeed column to determine a rate of climb of 816 fpm.
    Answer (A) is incorrect. A 350 fpm climb rate at a groundspeed of 60 kt., not 140 kt., would result in a climb rate of 350 ft. per NM. Answer (B) is incorrect. A 583 fpm climb rate at an average groundspeed of 140 kt. would result in 250 ft. per NM, not 350 ft. per NM.

29. (Refer to Figure 48 below, and Figure 46 on page 453.) What is your position relative to the 9 DME ARC and the 206° radial of the instrument departure procedure?

    A.   On the 9 DME arc and approaching R-206.

    B.   Outside the 9 DME arc and past R-206.

    C.   Inside the 9 DME arc and approaching R-206.

Answer (A) is correct. *(IFH Chap 9)*
    DISCUSSION: The HSI shows that you are currently on a 130° heading, thus flying in a southeasterly direction. The OBS selector is set on R-206, and a left deflection is indicated. This means you are west and north of R-206. (If you were flying out the R-206 with a left deflection, you would turn left to intercept.) You are approaching R-206 because you are flying in a southeasterly direction. The DME indicates 9 NM out, so you are on the 9 DME arc.
    Answer (B) is incorrect. You are on, not outside, the arc and approaching, not past, R-206. Answer (C) is incorrect. You are on, not inside, the arc.

Figure 48. – CDI - NAV 1.

30. (Refer to Figure 46 on page 453.) What are the hours of operation (local time) of the ATIS for the Yakima Air Terminal when daylight savings time is in effect?

    A.   0500 to 2100 local.

    B.   0600 to 2200 local.

    C.   0700 to 2300 local.

Answer (B) is correct. *(ACL)*
    DISCUSSION: The hours of operation of the ATIS at Yakima Air Terminal are listed on Fig. 46 in the *A/FD* on the **Communications** line at ATIS. It operates from 1400Z to 0600Z. Note that the ‡ symbol indicates that, during periods of daylight savings time, effective hours of operation are 1 hr. earlier than those shown (i.e., standard time). For example, the ATIS will begin operation at 6:00 a.m. local time, regardless of whether daylight savings time is in effect. Thus, you should always use the standard conversion; e.g., GMT-8 = 0600-2200 local.
    Answer (A) is incorrect. You must subtract 8 hr., not 9 hr., from Zulu to convert to local time. Answer (C) is incorrect. You must always use the standard, not daylight, conversion.

Figure 46. – GROMO Two Departure and Excerpt from Airport/Facility Directory.

31. (Refer to Figure 44 on page 450 and Figure 49 on page 455.) What is the MDA and visibility criteria for a straight-in LOC/DME RWY 21 approach at Portland International?

    A.   1,100 ft. MSL; visibility 1 SM.

    B.   680 ft. MSL; visibility 1 SM.

    C.   680 ft. MSL; visibility 1 NM.

Answer (B) is correct. *(ACL)*
    DISCUSSION: Refer to Fig. 44 to determine the aircraft category. V_{S0} is 77 kt.; thus, 1.3 V_{S0} is 100.1 kt., which puts the airplane in Category B. The minimums for the LOC/DME RWY 21 approach, Category B, are 680 ft. MSL and one statute mile visibility.
    Answer (A) is incorrect. The minimum altitude after crossing ROBOT FAF, but before reaching the 4 DME fix on the localizer is 1,100 ft. MSL. Answer (C) is incorrect. Visibility minimums are given in statute miles, not nautical miles.

32. (Refer to Figure 49 on page 455.) What determines the MAP on the LOC/DME RWY 21 approach at Portland International Airport?

    A.   I-GPO 1.2 DME.

    B.   5.8 NM from ROBOT FAF.

    C.   160° radial of BTG VORTAC.

Answer (A) is correct. *(ACL)*
    DISCUSSION: The MAP on the LOC/DME RWY 21 approach is the 1.2 DME fix on the localizer (I-GPO).
    Answer (B) is incorrect. While the MAP is located 5.8 NM from ROBOT FAF, the MAP is the 1.2 DME fix on the localizer. Answer (C) is incorrect. The 160° radial of BTG VORTAC is part of the missed approach procedure, not the missed approach point (MAP).

33. (Refer to Figure 49 on page 455.) You have been cleared to the CREAK intersection via the BTG 054° radial at 7,000 ft. Approaching CREAK, you are cleared for the LOC/DME RWY 21 approach to PDX. Descent to procedure turn altitude should not begin prior to

    A.   completion of the procedure turn, and established on the localizer.

    B.   intercepting the glide slope.

    C.   CREAK outbound.

Answer (C) is correct. *(ACL)*
    DISCUSSION: CREAK intersection is an initial approach fix, identified by the letters IAF. It is the fix at which the procedure turn should begin. Because you were cleared to CREAK intersection at an altitude of 7,000 ft., you should remain at that altitude until you reach the intersection. Since you have been cleared for the approach, you may then turn to the northeast and track the localizer outbound (the first portion of the procedure turn) while descending to the minimum procedure turn altitude of 5,700 ft. MSL.
    Answer (A) is incorrect. You should be at the procedure turn altitude (5,700 ft. MSL) at or before the completion of the procedure turn. Descent to the first step-down fix minimum altitude (not the procedure turn altitude) should begin after completion of the procedure turn and when established on the localizer (if you are past CREAK intersection). Answer (B) is incorrect. The LOC/DME RWY 21 approach has no glide slope. Additionally, descent to the procedure turn altitude may begin after crossing CREAK intersection.

34. (Refer to Figure 49 on page 455.) With a ground speed of 120 knots, approximately what minimum rate of descent will be required between I-GPO 7 DME fix (ROBOT) and the I-GPO 4 DME fix?

    A.   1,200 fpm.

    B.   500 fpm.

    C.   800 fpm.

Answer (C) is correct. *(ACL)*
    DISCUSSION: The LOC/DME RWY 21 approach chart does not provide descent angle information, so you must calculate the required rate of descent. From the chart, you can see that the 7 DME fix and the 4 DME fix off I-GPO are 3 NM apart. If your ground speed is 120 kt., you will cover 2 NM every minute. Thus, it will take you 1.5 minutes to cover 3 NM. The minimum altitude at ROBOT is 2,300 ft. MSL, and the minimum altitude at the 4 DME fix is 1,100 ft. MSL, a difference of 1,200 ft. Therefore, you must lose 1,200 ft. of altitude in 1.5 minutes, which requires a descent rate of 800 fpm (1,200 ÷ 1.5 = 800).
    Answer (A) is incorrect. A 1,200-fpm descent rate would be required if your ground speed were 180 kt., not 120 kt. Answer (B) is incorrect. A 500-fpm descent rate would be required if your ground speed were 75 kt., not 120 kt.

35. (Refer to Figure 49 on page 455.) What is the usable runway length for landing on runway 21 at PDX?

    A.   7,900 ft.

    B.   7,000 ft.

    C.   5,957 ft.

Answer (C) is correct. *(ACL)*
    DISCUSSION: In the upper right corner of the airport diagram, there is a notation that says "Rwy 21 ldg 5957'." This notation signifies that the runway length available for landing is 5,957 ft.; the remainder of the 7,000 ft. runway length is a displaced threshold.
    Answer (A) is incorrect. This is not a runway length or runway length available for landing at Portland International (PDX). Answer (B) is incorrect. This is the total length of runway 21, not the runway length available for landing.

Figure 49. – LOC/DME RWY 21 (PDX).

36. (Refer to Figure 188 on page 457.) With a ground speed of 120 knots, approximately what minimum rate of descent will be required between I-GPO 7.3 DME fix (HUDUT) and the I-GPO 4.1 DME fix?

    A. 320 fpm.

    B. 740 fpm.

    C. 510 fpm.

Answer (B) is correct. *(IPH Chap 3)*

    DISCUSSION: To solve this problem, you need to know the distance to be traveled between the two fixes and the amount of altitude that must be lost. You also need to know how long it will take your aircraft to cover that distance. The distance to be traveled is 3.2 NM (7.3 – 4.1 = 3.2). The amount of altitude that must be lost is 1180 feet, descending from 2,300 feet at 7.3 DME to 1,120 feet at 4.1 DME (2,300 – 1,120 = 1,180 feet). With a ground speed of 120 knots, you can calculate the time available. 3.2 NM ÷ 120 knots = 0.026 hours. 0.026 hours × 60 (minutes per hour) = 1.5999 minutes, which you can round to 1.6 minutes. 1180 feet ÷ 1.6 minutes = 737.5 feet per minute. The closest available answer is 740 feet per minute.

    Answer (A) is incorrect. The descent rate of 320 feet per minute is less than half of what you would need to reach the 4.1 DME fix at the correct altitude. Answer (C) is incorrect. A descent rate of 510 feet per minute is insufficient to reach the 4.1 DME fix at the correct altitude.

37. (Refer to Figure 188 on page 457.) With a ground speed of 120 knots, approximately what minimum rate of descent will be required between I-GPO 11.3 DME fix (COVDU) and the I-GPO 7.3 DME fix?

    A. 320 feet per minute.

    B. 600 feet per minute.

    C. 710 feet per minute.

Answer (B) is correct. *(IPH Chap 5)*

    DISCUSSION: Fig. 188 shows an altitude loss of 1,200 feet between I-GPO 11.3 DME and 7.3 DME. The aircraft must lose 1,200 feet while traveling 4 miles. Divide distance by speed to find time. 4 NM ÷ 120 knots = 0.033 (hours) × 60 (minutes) = 2 minutes. Divide altitude to lose by time to arrive at fpm. 1,200 feet ÷ 2 minutes = 600 feet per minute.

    Answer (A) is incorrect. The required descent rate would be 600, not 320, feet per minute. Answer (C) is incorrect. The required descent rate would be 600, not 710, feet per minute.

38. (Refer to Figure 188 on page 457.) When conducting the LOC/DME RWY 21 approach at PDX, what is the Minimum Safe Altitude (MSA) while maneuvering between the BTG VORTAC and CREAK intersection?

    A. 3,500 feet MSL.

    B. 5,700 feet MSL.

    C. 6,200 feet MSL.

Answer (C) is correct. *(ACL)*

    DISCUSSION: The circle in the northwest corner of the planview of the LOC/DME RWY 21 approach into PDX indicates that the minimum safe sector altitudes for this approach are based on the BTG VORTAC. The circle also indicates that the minimum safe sector altitude in the area between the 120° and 300° radials in a clockwise direction is 6,200 ft. MSL. Because CREAK intersection lies in this area, the minimum safe altitude for maneuvering between BTG VORTAC and CREAK intersection is 6,200 ft. MSL.

    Remember, MSA altitudes are for emergency use only and may differ from published minimum altitudes on the IAP chart.

    Answer (A) is incorrect. This is the minimum safe sector altitude in the area between the 120° and 300° radials in a counterclockwise direction. CREAK intersection, which is defined by the intersection of the 054° radial of the BTG VORTAC and the localizer, is not in this area. Answer (B) is incorrect. This is the minimum altitude for flying the charted feeder route, not maneuvering, between BTG VORTAC and CREAK intersection.

39. (Refer to Figure 188 on page 457.) When conducting a missed approach from the LOC/DME RWY 21 approach at PDX, what is the Minimum Safe Altitude (MSA) while maneuvering between the runway and BTG VORTAC?

    A. 4,200 feet MSL.

    B. 3,500 feet MSL.

    C. 6,200 feet MSL.

Answer (A) is correct. *(ACL)*

    DISCUSSION: According to the missed approach instructions, the pilot should perform a climbing right turn to 4,200 ft. en route to the BTG VORTAC.

    Answer (B) is incorrect. While the published MSA for a course between the runway and the VORTAC is 3,500 ft., you should always use the highest altitude applicable to a given flight segment, in this case, the missed approach instructions of 4,200 ft. Answer (C) is incorrect. An MSA of 6,200 ft. would apply to flight between the 120° radial and the 300° radial of the BTG VORTAC, an area to the northeast of the course described.

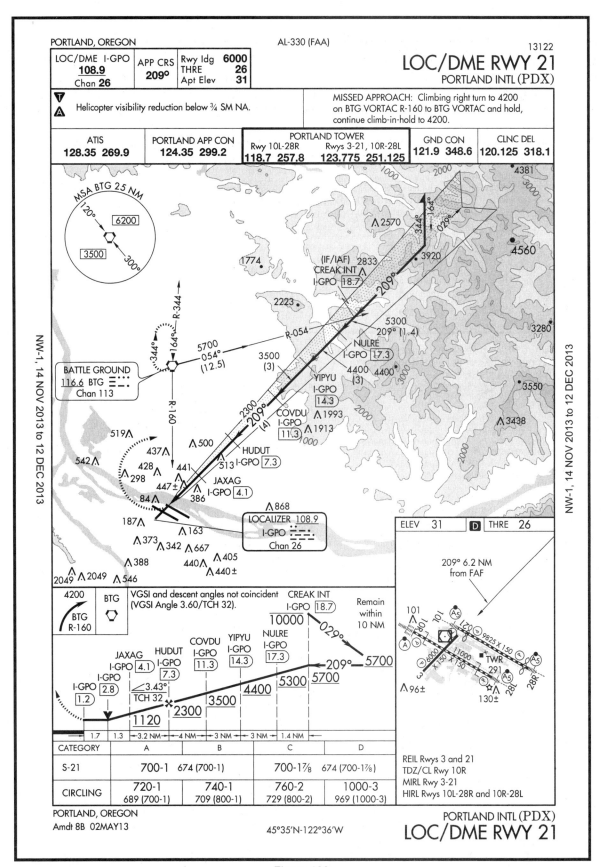

Figure 188.

11.4 SBA to PRB

Questions 40 through 51 pertain to an IFR flight from Santa Barbara Municipal Airport, Santa Barbara, California, to the Paso Robles Municipal Airport, Paso Robles, California.

The route of flight is given in block 8 on the flight plan portion of Fig. 50 on page 460. Information that pertains to your aircraft is given on the bottom portion of Fig. 50. The partially completed flight planning log is given in Fig. 51 on page 461.

The figures provided for this flight are listed below and are presented throughout the sequence of questions, except for Fig. 53, which is provided in color on page 419.

Fig.	Page	
50	460	Flight Plan and Aircraft Information
51	461	Flight Planning Log
52	463	HABUT One Departure and Excerpt from Airport/Facility Directory
53	419	En Route Chart Segment
54	462	RMI and CDI Indicators
55	459	VOR/DME-B (PRB)
189	465	[title not provided by FAA]
192	466	[title not provided by FAA]

40. (Refer to Figure 55 on page 459.) Using an average ground speed of 90 knots, what constant rate of descent from 2,400 feet MSL at the 6 DME fix would enable the aircraft to arrive at 2,000 feet MSL at the FAF?

A. 200 feet per minute.

B. 400 feet per minute.

C. 600 feet per minute.

Answer (A) is correct. *(ACL)*

DISCUSSION: The profile view of the IAP chart shows the distance from the 6 DME fix to the FAF to be 3 NM. At 90 kt. (1 1/2 NM per min.), this distance would be traveled in 2 min. To descend from 2,400 ft. to 2,000 ft. (400 ft.) in 2 min. would require a descent rate of 200 fpm.

Answer (B) is incorrect. This rate would require an average groundspeed of 180 kt., not 90 kt. Answer (C) is incorrect. This rate would require an average groundspeed of 270 kt., not 90 kt.

41. (Refer to Figure 55 on page 459.) As a guide in making range corrections, how many degrees of relative bearing change should be used for each one-half-mile deviation from the desired arc?

A. 2° to 3°.

B. 5° maximum.

C. 10° to 20°.

Answer (C) is correct. *(IFH Chap 10)*

DISCUSSION: As a guide in making corrections when tracking DME arcs, turn 10° to 20° toward the arc for each 1/2 NM that you are off the desired arc.

Answer (A) is incorrect. You should make 10° to 20° corrections, not 2° to 3°, for each 1/2-NM deviation. Answer (B) is incorrect. There is no maximum; the amount of correction should be proportional to the amount of error.

42. (Refer to Figure 55 on page 459.) Under which condition should a missed approach procedure be initiated if the runway environment (Paso Robles Municipal Airport) is not in sight?

A. After descending to 1,440 feet MSL.

B. After descent to 1,440 feet or reaching the 1 NM DME, whichever occurs first.

C. When you reach the established missed approach point and determine the visibility is less than 1 mile.

Answer (C) is correct. *(FAR 91.175)*

DISCUSSION: The missed approach point is the point prescribed in each instrument approach procedure at which a missed approach procedure shall be executed if the required visual reference has not been sighted or the flight visibility is less than visibility prescribed in the IAP. The MAP for VOR/DME-B is the PRB VORTAC. Thus, when you reach the VORTAC and you determine the visibility is less than 1 SM, you must execute the missed approach procedure.

Answer (A) is incorrect. The MAP is PRB VORTAC, not arrival at the MDA. Answer (B) is incorrect. The MAP is PRB VORTAC, not arrival at the MDA or the 1 DME fix.

Figure 55. – VOR/DME-B (PRB).

43. (Refer to Figure 50 below, and Legend 26 on page 428.) What aircraft equipment code should be entered in block 3 of the flight plan?

A. I.

B. T.

C. U.

Answer (A) is correct. *(AIM Para 5-1-8)*
DISCUSSION: In block 3 of the flight plan, you enter the designation of the aircraft followed by a slash (/) and a letter for the equipment code. Fig. 50 indicates the airplane has a transponder with Mode C and RNAV, which requires Code I. (See Legend 26.)

Answer (B) is incorrect. A T indicates only a transponder with no Mode C. Answer (C) is incorrect. A U indicates a transponder with Mode C, but no DME.

Form Approved: OMB No. 2120-0034

U.S. DEPARTMENT OF TRANSPORTATION FEDERAL AVIATION ADMINISTRATION **FLIGHT PLAN**	(FAA USE ONLY)	☐ PILOT BRIEFING ☐ STOPOVER	☐ VNR	TIME STARTED	SPECIALIST INITIALS

1. TYPE	2. AIRCRAFT IDENTIFICATION	3. AIRCRAFT TYPE/ SPECIAL EQUIPMENT	4. TRUE AIRSPEED	5. DEPARTURE POINT	6. DEPARTURE TIME		7. CRUISING ALTITUDE
VFR / **X** IFR / DVFR	N2468	A36/	158 KTS	SBA	PROPOSED (Z)	ACTUAL (Z)	8000

8. ROUTE OF FLIGHT

HABUTI GVO, V27 MQO, V113 PRB

9. DESTINATION (Name of airport and city) PASO ROBLES MUNI PRB	10. EST. TIME ENROUTE HOURS / MINUTES	11. REMARKS IFR TRAINING FLIGHT

12. FUEL ON BOARD HOURS / MINUTES	13. ALTERNATE AIRPORT(S) N/A	14. PILOTS NAME, ADDRESS & TELEPHONE NUMBER & AIRCRAFT HOME BASE 17. DESTINATION CONTACT/TELEPHONE (OPTIONAL)	15. NUMBER ABOARD 2

16. COLOR OF AIRCRAFT GOLD/WHITE	CIVIL AIRCRAFT PILOTS. FAR Part 91 requires you file an IFR flight plan to operate under instrument flight rules in controlled airspace. Failure to file could result in a civil penalty not to exceed $1,000 for each violation (Section 901 of the Federal Aviation Act of 1958, as amended). Filing of a VFR flight plan is recommended as a good operating practice. See also Part 99 for requirements concerning DVFR flight plans.

FAA Form 7233-1 (8-82)   CLOSE VFR FLIGHT PLAN WITH _____ FSS ON ARRIVAL

AIRCRAFT INFORMATION

MAKE Beechcraft   MODEL A-36

N 2468   V$_{so}$ 52

AIRCRAFT EQUIPMENT/STATUS**

**NOTE: X= OPERATIVE   INOP= INOPERATIVE   N/A= NOT APPLICABLE
TRANSPONDER: X (MODE C) X ILS: (LOCALIZER) X (GLIDE SLOPE) X
VOR NO. 1 X (NO. 2) X ADF: X RNAV: X
VERTICAL PATH COMPUTER: N/A DME: X
MARKER BEACON: X (AUDIO) X (VISUAL) INOP

Figure 50. – Flight Plan and Aircraft Information.

44. (Refer to Figure 51 below, Figure 50 on page 460, Figure 52 on page 463, and Figure 53 on page 419.) Determine the time to be entered in block 10 of the flight plan. (Refer to the FD excerpt below, and use the wind entry closest to the flight planned altitude.)

Route of flight........................... Figs. 50, 51, 52, & 53
Flight log and MAG VAR.................................. Fig. 51
HABUT ONE DEPARTURE
  and Excerpt from AFD.................................. Fig. 52

FT	3000	6000	9000
SBA	0610	2115+05	2525+00

A. 43 minutes.

B. 46 minutes.

C. 51 minutes.

Answer (C) is correct. *(IFH Chap 10)*
   DISCUSSION: To determine the estimated time en route to be entered in block 10, you must complete the flight planning log in Fig. 51. Using the wind side of your flight computer, determine groundspeeds as given in the table below.
   Remember that winds are given in true direction and must be converted to magnetic. Fig. 51 shows a variation of 16°E. Use the wind at 9,000 ft. (which is closest to the planned altitude of 8,000 ft.): 250° − 16°E var. = 234° at 25 kt.

	Distance	MC	Wind (Mag)	Ground-speed	Time
HABUT INT.	X	X	X	X	:08:00G
GVO VORTAC	6.4	343°	234/25	164	:02:20
MSO VORTAC	54	307°	234/25	149	:21:45
PRB VORTAC	26	358°	234/25	171	:09:07
Approach and Landing	X	X	X	X	:10:00G
					:51:12

G = Given

   Answer (A) is incorrect. An ETE of 43 min. requires a TAS of approximately 205 kt., not 158 kt. Answer (B) is incorrect. An ETE of 46 min. requires a TAS of approximately 185 kt., not 158 kt.

FLIGHT LOG
SANTA BARBARA MUNI TO PASO ROBLES MUNI

CHECK POINTS		ROUTE		WIND		SPEED-KTS		DIST	TIME		FUEL	
FROM	TO	ALTITUDE	COURSE	TEMP		TAS	GS	NM	LEG	TOT	LEG	TOT
SBA	HABUT	HABUT 1 CLIMB	253°						:08:00			
	GVO	163' R 8000	343°			158						
	MQO	V27 8000	306°									
	PRB	V113	358°									
APPROACH & LANDING		DESCENT							:10:00			
	PRB AIRPORT											

OTHER DATA:
   NOTE: MAG. VAR. 16° E.

FLIGHT SUMMARY

TIME	FUEL (LB)	
		EN ROUTE
		RESERVE
		MISSED APPR.
		TOTAL

Figure 51. – Flight Planning Log.

45. (Refer to Figure 50 on page 460.) What CAS must be used to maintain the filed TAS at the flight planned altitude? (Temperature 0°C.)

    A. 136 KCAS.

    B. 140 KCAS.

    C. 147 KCAS.

Answer (B) is correct. *(PHAK Chap 15)*
    DISCUSSION: In the center of the slide rule side of your flight computer, on the right side, put the air temperature of 0°C over the altitude of 8,000 ft. (given in block 7 of flight plan). On the outer scale, find TAS of 158 kt. (from block 4), which is over CAS on the inner scale of 140 KCAS.
    Answer (A) is incorrect. Maintaining 136 KCAS would result in a TAS of 154 kt., not 158 kt. Answer (C) is incorrect. Maintaining 147 KCAS would result in a TAS of 168 kt., not 158 kt.

46. (Refer to Figure 54 below, and Figure 52 on page 463.) What is the aircraft's position relative to the HABUT intersection? (The VOR-2 is tuned to 116.5.)

    A. South of the localizer and past the GVO R-163.

    B. North of the localizer and approaching the GVO R-163.

    C. South of the localizer and approaching the GVO R-163.

Answer (B) is correct. *(IFH Chap 9)*
    DISCUSSION: On the RMI (Fig. 54), VOR-2 is tuned to 116.5, which is the GVO VORTAC, and the tail indicates that the airplane is on R-130, which means it is to the east of HABUT INT. The VOR is tuned to 110.3, which is the localizer, and you are flying outbound on the front course (our heading is 240 as shown by the RMI). This means there is a reverse sensing indicated, and the airplane is to the north or right of the localizer as flying outbound.
    Answer (A) is incorrect. When you are flying outbound on the front course, there is reverse sensing, so you are north, not south, of the localizer. Since you are on R-130 from GVO, you are approaching, not past, R-163. Answer (C) is incorrect. When you are flying outbound on the front course, there is reverse sensing, so you are north, not south, of the localizer.

Figure 54. – RMI and CDI Indicators.

47. (Refer to Figure 52 on page 463 and Legend 16 on page 292.) Using an average ground speed of 100 knots, what minimum rate of climb would meet the required minimum climb rate per NM as specified by the instrument departure procedure?

    A. 425 feet per minute.

    B. 580 feet per minute.

    C. 642 feet per minute.

Answer (C) is correct. *(ACL)*
    DISCUSSION: The DP on Fig. 52 has a note that indicates a minimum climb rate of 385 ft. per NM to 6,000 ft. To convert this to a rate of climb (fpm), use Legend 16. Since 385 ft. per NM is not listed on the left margin, use 350 and 400 and interpolate between them. Move right to the 100-kt. groundspeed column to see a rate of climb between 583 and 667 fpm, but closer to 667. By interpolation, the minimum rate of climb required would be 642 fpm.
    Answer (A) is incorrect. A 425-fpm climb rate at an average groundspeed of 100 kt. would result in a climb rate of 255 ft. per NM, not 385 ft. per NM. Answer (B) is incorrect. A 580-fpm climb rate at an average groundspeed of 100 kt. would result in a climb rate of approximately 350 ft. per NM, not 385 ft. per NM.

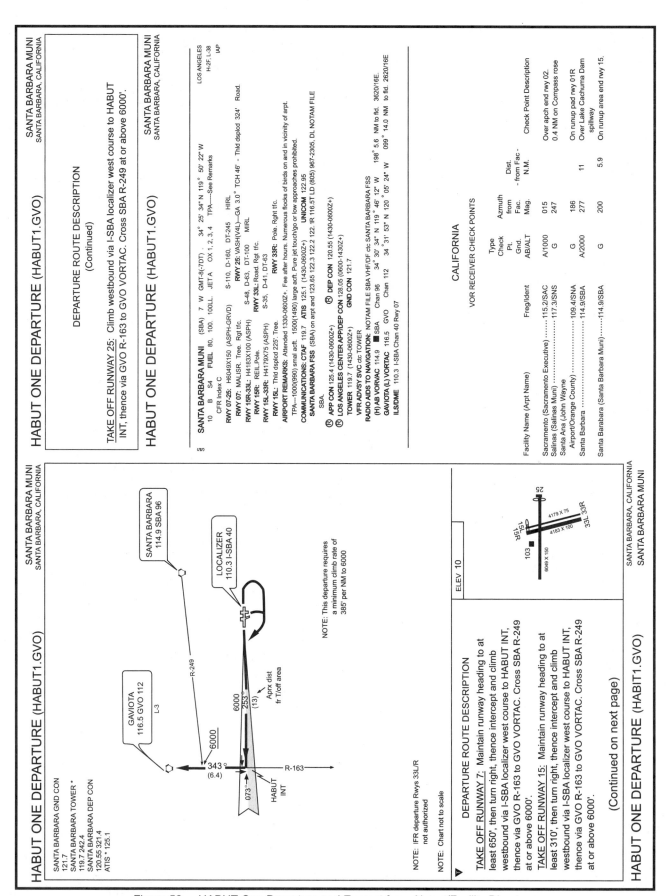

Figure 52. – HABUT One Departure and Excerpt from Airport/Facility Directory.

48. (Refer to Figure 53 on page 419.) Where is the VOR COP on V27 between the GVO and MQO VORTACs?

A. 20 DME from GVO VORTAC.

B. 20 DME from MQO VORTAC.

C. 30 DME from SBA VORTAC.

Answer (A) is correct. *(ACL)*
DISCUSSION: When going north from GVO VORTAC to MQO VORTAC, there is a VOR changeover point (COP) 20 NM northwest of GVO VORTAC and 34 NM southeast of MQO VORTAC.
Answer (B) is incorrect. The COP is 20 NM from GVO, not MQO. Answer (C) is incorrect. SBA is Santa Barbara localizer, which is not on V27.

49. (Refer to Figure 53 on page 419.) What is indicated by the inverse "H" symbol in the radio aids to navigation box for SAN MARCUS VORTAC?

A. VOR with TACAN compatible DME.

B. The availability of HIWAS.

C. The VOR has a high altitude SSV Class Designation.

Answer (B) is correct. *(ACL)*
DISCUSSION: The inverse "H" symbol in the upper right corner of the VOR communication box indicates the availability of HIWAS (Hazardous Inflight Weather Advisory Service).
Answer (A) is incorrect. The VORTAC symbol itself indicates TACAN-compatible DME. Answer (C) is incorrect. The "H" symbol indicates availability of HIWAS, not the SSV Class Designation.

50. (Refer to Figure 189 on page 465.) Using an average ground speed of 90 knots, what minimum rate of climb would meet the required minimum climb rate per NM as specified by the instrument departure procedure?

A. 578 feet per minute.

B. 543 feet per minute.

C. 642 feet per minute.

Answer (A) is correct. *(IPH Chap 2)*
DISCUSSION: A note included with the instrument departure procedure specifies a minimum climb of 385 feet per NM. With an average ground speed of 90 knots, your aircraft is covering 1.5 miles per minute. 385 feet per NM × 1.5 miles per minute = 577.5 feet per minute as your minimum rate of climb that will meet the minimum feet per NM value as specified in the procedure. This can also be interpolated by using the chart in Legend 16 on page 193.
Answer (B) is incorrect. At an average ground speed of 90 knots, 543 feet per minute is less than 385 feet per NM. Your aircraft is covering 1.5 miles per minute. 385 feet per NM × 1.5 miles per minute = 577.5 feet per minute as your minimum rate of climb that will meet the minimum feet per NM value as specified in the procedure. Answer (C) is incorrect. Although 642 feet per minute exceeds the minimum of 385 feet per NM, it is not the minimum rate of climb necessary.

51. (Refer to Figure 192 on page 466.) Using an average ground speed of 90 knots, what constant rate of descent from 3,100 feet MSL at the 6 DME fix would enable the aircraft to arrive at 2,400 feet MSL at the FAF?

A. 350 feet per minute.

B. 400 feet per minute.

C. 450 feet per minute.

Answer (A) is correct. *(IPH Chap 3)*
DISCUSSION: The distance between the 6 DME fix and the FAF (ILSIC) is 3 NM. The altitude lost will be 700 feet (3,100 feet − 2,400 feet = 700 feet). Your aircraft must lose 700 feet in 3 NM. At 90 knots, your aircraft will cover 1.5 NM per minute or 3 NM in 2 minutes. 700 feet ÷ 2 minutes = 350 feet per minute.
Answer (B) is incorrect. Losing 400 feet for 2 minutes would equate to an 800-foot altitude loss, putting you 100 feet below the glideslope. Answer (C) is incorrect. Losing 450 feet for 2 minutes would equate to a 900-foot altitude loss, putting you 200 feet below the glideslope.

Figure 189.

Figure 192.

11.5 HOT to ADS

Questions 52 through 64 pertain to an IFR flight from Hot Springs Memorial Field, Hot Springs, Arkansas, to the Dallas/Addison Airport, Dallas, Texas.

The route of flight is given in block 8 on the flight plan portion of Fig. 32 on page 469. Information that pertains to your aircraft is given on the bottom portion of Fig. 32. The partially completed flight planning log is given in Fig. 33 on page 468.

The figures provided for this flight are listed below and are presented throughout the sequence of questions, except for Fig. 34, which is provided in color on page 416.

Fig.	Page	
32	469	Flight Plan and Aircraft Information
33	468	Flight Planning Log
34	416	En Route Chart
34A	470	Airport/Facility Directory (HOT)
35	472	En Route Chart Segment and Blue Ridge Three Arrival
35A	473	Blue Ridge Three Arrival Description
36	468	Excerpt from Airport/Facility Directory
36A	475	RNAV RWY 33 (ADS)
37	473	CDI and RMI – NAV 1 and NAV 2
167	476	[title not provided by FAA]
168	477	[title not provided by FAA]
171	471	[title not provided by FAA]
174	478	[title not provided by FAA]
175	479	[title not provided by FAA]

52. (Refer to Figure 32 on page 469, Figure 33 on page 468, Figure 34 on page 416, Figure 35 on page 472, Figure 35A on page 473, and Figure 36 on page 468.) (Refer to the FD excerpt below, and use the wind entry closest to the flight planned altitude.) Determine the time to be entered in block 10 of the flight plan.

Route of flight .... Figures 32, 33, 34, 35, 35A, & 36
Flight log & MAG VAR .... Figure 33
RNAV RWY 33 & Excerpt from AFD ...... Figs. 36A & 36

FT	3000	6000	9000	12000
DAL	2027	2239+13	2240+08	2248+05

A. 1 hour 35 minutes.

B. 1 hour 41 minutes.

C. 1 hour 46 minutes.

Answer (C) is correct. *(IFH Chap 10)*

DISCUSSION: To determine the estimated time en route to be entered in block 10, you must complete the flight planning log in Fig. 33. As you compare the flight log with the en route and arrival charts (Figs. 34, 35, and 35A), it will become apparent to you that some alterations of the flight log are necessary. On V573 (Fig. 34), there is a bend in the airway (COP) 10 NM southwest of MARKI INT., so an additional leg is required to accurately compute groundspeeds. Also, the check points in the STAR (Figs. 35 and 35A) are not labeled well in the flight log.

Having corrected the flight log as shown below, use the wind side of your flight computer to determine groundspeeds as shown. Remember that winds are given in true direction and must be converted to magnetic. Fig. 33 shows a variation of 4°E. Use the wind at 9,000 ft. (which is closest to the planned altitude of 8,000 ft.): 220° – 4°E var. = 216° at 40 kt.

	Distance	MC	Wind (Mag)	Ground-speed	Time
MARKI INT.	X	X	X	X	:12:00G
VOR COP	10	221°	216/40	140	:04:17
TXK VORTAC	45	210°	216/40	140	:19:17
CONNY INT	61	272°	216/40	154	:23:46
BUJ VORTAC	59	239°	216/40	142	:24:56
WEDER INT	24	215°	216/40	140	:10:15
Approach and Landing	X	X	X	X	:10:00G
					1:44:31

G = Given

Answer (A) is incorrect. An ETE of 1 hr. 35 min. does not take into account the flight time from the BUJ VORTAC to WEDER INT as explained in the STAR (Figs. 35 and 35A). Answer (B) is incorrect. An ETE of 1 hr. 41 min. requires a TAS of approximately 165 kt., not 180 kt.

TEXAS   **145**

DALLAS

| ADDISON | (ADS) | 9 N | UTC-6(-5DT) | 32°58'06"N 96°50'10"W | | **DALLAS-FT. WORTH** |

643   B   S4   FUEL 100LL JET A

H-2K, 4F, 5B, L-13C, A

RWY 15-33: H7201X100 (ASPH)   S-80, D-100, DT-160   MIRL   IAP

RWY 15: MALSR. VASI(V4R)---GA 3.0°TCH 51'. Thld dsplcd 980'. Ground.

RWY 33: REIL. Thld dsplcd 468'. Road.

AIRPORT REMARKS: Attended continuously. Numerous flocks of birds on and in vicinity of arpt. Use extreme care: numerous 200' AGL buildings within 1 mile East, and South of arpt, transmission towers and water tanks West of arpt. Rwy 33 REIL out of svc indefinitely. ACTIVATE MALSR Rwy 15---CTAF. Rwy limited to maximum gross weight 120,000 pounds. Control Zone effective 1200-0400Z‡ .

WEATHER DATA SOURCES: LAWRS

COMMUNICATIONS: CTAF 121.1   ATIS 126.8 (1200-0400Z‡)   UNICOM 122.95

FORT WORTH FSS (FTW) TF 1-800-WX-BRIEF. NOTAM FILE ADS.

Ⓡ REGIONAL APP CON 123.9   Ⓡ REGIONAL DEP CON 124.3

TOWER 121.1 (1200-0400Z‡)   GND CON 121.6   CLNC DEL 119.55

RADIO AIDS TO NAVIGATION: NOTAM FILE DAL.

LOVE (L) VORW/DME 114.3   LUE   Chan 90   32°50'51"N 96°51'42"W   002° 7.4 NM to fld. 490/08E.

BRONS NDB (LOM) 407   AD   33°02'40"N 96°52'13"W   153° 4.9 NM to fld.

ILS/DME 110.1 I-ADS Chan 38 Rwy 15. LOM BRONS NDB. Unmonitored when tower closed.

ILS 110.1 I-TBQ Rwy 33 LOC only. Unmonitored when twr clsd.

Figure 36. – Excerpt from Airport/Facility Directory.

FLIGHT LOG
HOT SPRINGS, MEMORIAL FIELD TO DALLAS, ADDISON, TX.

CHECK POINTS		ROUTE		WIND	SPEED-KTS		DIST	TIME		FUEL	
FROM	TO	ALTITUDE	COURSE	TEMP	TAS	GS	NM	LEG	TOT	LEG	TOT
HOT	MARKI	V573 CLIMB	221°					:12:00			
	TXK	V573 8000	210°		180						
TXK	BUJ3	BUJ3 8000	272°								
BUJ3	BUJ3	BUJ3 DESCENT	239°								
APPROACH & LANDING	DALLAS ADDISON							:10:00			

OTHER DATA:
NOTE: MAG. VAR. 4° E.

FLIGHT SUMMARY		
TIME	FUEL (LB)	
		EN ROUTE
		RESERVE
		MISSED APPR.
		TOTAL

Figure 33. – Flight Planning Log.

53. (Refer to Figure 32 on page 469 and Legend 26 on page 428.) What aircraft equipment code should be entered in block 3 of the flight plan?

A. A.

B. C.

C. I.

Answer (C) is correct. *(AIM Para 5-1-8)*
DISCUSSION: In block 3 of the flight plan, you enter the designation of the aircraft followed by a slash (/) and a letter for the equipment code. Fig. 32 indicates a transponder with Mode C and RNAV. Thus, Code I is required. (See Legend 26.)
Answer (A) is incorrect. A indicates DME and transponder with Mode C but no RNAV. Answer (B) is incorrect. C indicates RNAV and transponder but with no Mode C.

54. (Refer to Figure 32 below.) What CAS must be used to maintain the filed TAS at the flight planned altitude if the outside air temperature is +8°C?

   A. 154 KCAS.

   B. 157 KCAS.

   C. 163 KCAS.

Answer (B) is correct. *(PHAK Chap 15)*
   DISCUSSION: In the center of the slide rule side of your flight computer, on the right side, put the air temperature of +8°C over the altitude of 8,000 ft. (see block 7 of the flight plan). On the outer scale, find TAS of 180 (from block 4), which is over calibrated airspeed on the inner scale of 157 KCAS.
   Answer (A) is incorrect. Maintaining 154 KCAS would result in a TAS of 176 kt., not 180 kt. Answer (C) is incorrect. Maintaining 163 KCAS would result in a TAS of 187 kt., not 180 kt.

Figure 32. – Flight Plan and Aircraft Information.

55. (Refer to Figure 34 on page 416.) For planning purposes, what is the highest usable altitude for an IFR flight on V573 from the HOT VORTAC to the TXK VORTAC?

A. 16,000 feet MSL.

B. 14,500 feet MSL.

C. 13,999 feet MSL.

Answer (A) is correct. *(AIM Para 3-2-6)*
DISCUSSION: The VOR airway system consists of airways designated from 1,200 ft. AGL up to, but not including, 18,000 ft. MSL. Flying on V573 from HOT to TXK is a generally westerly course which requires an even-thousands altitude. Thus, 16,000 ft. MSL is the highest usable altitude.
Answer (B) is incorrect. This is a VFR, not IFR, cruising altitude from 180° to 359°. Answer (C) is incorrect. IFR altitudes are even or odd thousands of feet.

56. (Refer to Figure 34A below, and Figure 34 on page 416.) At which altitude and location on V573 would you expect the navigational signal of the HOT VOR/DME to be unreliable?

A. 3,000 feet at APINE intersection.

B. 2,600 feet at MARKI intersection.

C. 4,000 feet at ELMMO intersection.

Answer (A) is correct. *(ACL)*
DISCUSSION: The *A/FD* in Fig. 34A, under **Radio Aids to Navigation**, does not indicate that the HOT VOR/DME is unusable in any quadrants. APINE intersection is 26 NM from HOT, which means that the MEA, not MOCA, is the lowest altitude that assures acceptable navigational signals. The MEA at APINE is 3,500 ft.; therefore, 3,000 ft. is 500 ft. below the minimum required to receive acceptable navigational signals.
Answer (B) is incorrect. MARKI is 21 NM from HOT VOR/DME, and the MOCA is 2,500 ft. The MOCA assures acceptable navigation signals within 22 NM of the VOR; therefore, at an altitude of 2,600 ft., you would have acceptable navigation signals at MARKI intersection. Answer (C) is incorrect. The MEA at ELMMO is 3,500 ft. At 4,000 ft. over ELMMO, you will be above the MEA; this altitude assures acceptable navigation signals and meets obstacle clearance requirements.

ARKANSAS

HOT SPRINGS

MEMORIAL FLD   (HOT)   3 SW   UTC-6(-5DT)   34°28'41"N   93°05'46"W   MEMPHIS
540   B   S4   Fuel 100LL, JET A   ARFFIndex Ltd.   H-4G, L-14E
RWY 05-23: H6595X150   (ASPH-GRVD)   S-75, D-125. DT-210,   DDT-400,   HIRL   0.6%   NE   IAP
  RWY 05: MALSR. Tree.   **RWY 23:** REIL. Thld dsplcd 490'. Tree.
RWY 13-31: H4099X150 (ASPH)   S-28, D-36, DT-63 MIRL
  RWY 13: REIL. Road / Trees.   **RWY 31:** Pole.
AIRPORT REMARKS: Attended 1130-0400Z‡   CLOSED to unscheduled air carrier ops with more than 30 passenger
  seats except PPR, call   arpt manager 501-624-3306. Last 500' Rwy 05 CLOSED to takeoffs. Rwy 13-31 fair
  with extensive loose grvl-pavement debris. ACTIVATE HIRL Rwy 05-23 and MALSR Rwy 05---CTAF. Rwy 23 REIL
  out of svc indefinitely. Control Zone effective 1200-0400Z+.
COMMUNICATIONS: CTAF / UNICOM 123.0
  JONESBORO FSS (JBR) TF 1-800-WX-BRIEF. NOTAM FILE HOT.
  HOT SPRINGS RCO 122.1R 110.0T (LITTLE ROCK FSS)
  MEMPHIS CENTER APP/DEP CON: 118.85
RADIO AIDS TO NAVIGATION NOTAM FILE HOT.
  HOT SPRINGS (L) VOR/DME 110.0   HOT   Chan 37   34°28'43"N   93°05'26"W   at fld. 530/4E.
  HOSSY NDB (HW/LOM) 385   HO   34°25'21"N   93°11'22"W   050° 5.7 NM to fld.
  ILS/DME 111.5 I-HOT Chan 52 Rwy 05 LOM HOSSY NDB. Unmonitored.

Figure 34A. – Airport/Facility Directory (HOT).

---

57. (Refer to Figure 171 on page 471.) Under which condition should the missed approach procedure for the RNAV(GPS) RWY 33 approach be initiated?

A. When passage of the MAP waypoint is shown on the ambiguity indicator.

B. After the MDA is reached and 1.8 DME fix from the MAP waypoint.

C. Immediately upon reaching 4.1 DME from the FAF.

Answer (A) is correct. *(AIM Para 1-1-18)*
DISCUSSION: If a missed approach is necessary, the ambiguity indicator will show arrival and passage of the Missed Approach Waypoint (MAWP).
Answer (B) is incorrect. There is no requirement to continue past the Missed Approach Waypoint (MAWP) by 1.8 DME before initiating the missed approach. The ambiguity indicator will show arrival and passage of the MAWP. It is at that point the missed approach can be initiated. Answer (C) is incorrect. Although the missed approach point is 4.1 DME from the FAF (PORTR), it is the ambiguity indicator's display of arrival and passage of the missed approach waypoint that establishes the position where the missed approach should be initiated.

Figure 171.

58. (Refer to Figure 35 below, Figure 35A on page 473, and Figure 37 on page 473.) What is your position relative to the CONNY intersection on the BUJ.BUJ3 transition?

A. Left of the TXK R-272 and approaching the BUJ R-059°.

B. Left of the TXK R-266 and past the BUJ R-065.

C. Right of the TXK R-270 and approaching the BUJ R-245.

Answer (A) is correct. *(IFH Chap 10)*
DISCUSSION: Refer to Figs. 35 and 35A and note that this is actually the TXK.BUJ3 transition (to the BUJ.BUJ3 arrival). In Fig. 37, NAV 1 (an HSI) is tuned to 114.9 (BUJ VORTAC) and set to 239°. Since the bar is deflected to the northwest, you are southeast of the BUJ R-059, and thus approaching it (note the 270° heading). NAV 2 (an RMI) has the fat needle tuned to 116.3 (TXK VORTAC). The tail of the needle indicates R-270, which is south of R-272 and thus to the left.

Answer (B) is incorrect. The R-270 of TXK is right, not left, of the TXK R-266, and you are on, not past, the BUJ R-065.
Answer (C) is incorrect. You are on, not right of, the R-270 of TXK and approaching R-244 of LIT, not BUJ.

Figure 35. – En Route Chart Segment and Blue Ridge Three Arrival.

91094

SL-6039 (FAA)

BLUE RIDGE THREE ARRIVAL (BUJ.BUJ3)   DALLAS-FT. WORTH, TEXAS

ARRIVAL DESCRIPTION

FORT SMITH TRANSITION (FSM.BUJ3): From over FSM VORTAC via FSM R-213 and BUJ R-031 to BUJ VORTAC. Thence . . . .

LITTLE ROCK TRANSITION (LIT.BUJ3): From over LIT VORTAC via LIT R-244 and BUJ R-059 to BUJ VORTAC. Thence . . . .

TEXARKANA TRANSITION (TXK.BUJ3): From over TXK VORTAC via TXK R-272 and BUJ R-059 to BUJ VORTAC. Thence . . . .

TULSA TRANSITION (TUL.BUJ3): From over TUL VORTAC via TUL R-158 and BUJ R-031 to BUJ VORTAC. Thence . . . .

TURBOJETS LANDING DALLAS-FT WORTH INTL: (Landing South): From over BUJ VORTAC via BUJ R-230 to HAMAK INT. Expect vectors at BATON INT. (Landing North): From over BUJ VORTAC via BUJ R-230 to HAMAK INT, thence heading 170° for vector to final approach course.

NON-TURBOJETS LANDING DALLAS-FT WORTH INTL: (Landing South): From over BUJ VORTAC via BUJ R-230 to HAMAK INT. Expect vectors at BATON INT. (Landing North): From over BUJ VORTAC via BUJ R-215 to WEDER INT. Expect vectors to final approach course.

ALL AIRCRAFT LANDING DALLAS-LOVE FIELD, ADDISON, REDBIRD, NAS DALLAS, and PHIL L. HUDSON: (Landing South/North): From over BUJ VORTAC via BUJ R-215 to WEDER INT. Expect vectors to final approach course.

ALL AIRCRAFT LANDING MEACHAM, CARSWELL AFB, ALLIANCE, ARL-INGTON, DENTON and FT. WORTH SPINKS: (Landing South/North): From over BUJ VORTAC via BUJ R-260 to KORKS INT. Expect vectors to final approach course.

Figure 35A. – Blue Ridge Three Arrival Description.

Figure 37. – CDI and RMI - NAV 1 and NAV 2.

59. (Refer to Figure 36A on page 475.) Under which condition should the missed approach procedure for the VOR/DME RNAV RWY 33 approach be initiated?

A. Immediately upon reaching the 5.0 DME from the FAF.

B. When passage of the MAP way point is shown on the ambiguity indicator.

C. After the MDA is reached and 1.8 DME fix from the MAP way point.

Answer (B) is correct. *(FAR 91.175)*
DISCUSSION: The missed approach point (MAP) is the point prescribed in each instrument approach procedure at which a missed approach procedure shall be executed if the required visual reference has not been sighted. The MAP on the RNAV RWY 33 approach is arrival at the indicated MAP way point. Passage of the MAP way point is shown on the ambiguity indicator (TO-FROM flag).
Answer (A) is incorrect. The FAF is identified as 5.0 DME from the MAP, not vice versa. Answer (C) is incorrect. Assuming a 2.85° glide path, 1.8 DME from the MAP way point is where you would arrive at MDA.

60. (Refer to Figure 36A on page 475.) What is the MDA and visibility criteria respectively for the S-33 approach procedure?

A. 1,240 feet MSL; 1 SM.

B. 1,280 feet MSL; 1 and 1/4 SM.

C. 1,300 feet MSL; 1 SM.

Answer (A) is correct. *(ACL)*
DISCUSSION: The MDA and visibility criteria are found in the minimums section of the RNAV RWY 33 approach chart. The straight-in (S-33) MDA and visibility criteria for Category A and B aircraft are 1,240 ft. MSL and 1 SM, respectively (note that the question does not specify the aircraft category).
Answer (B) is incorrect. The minimum visibility is not shown to be 1 1/4 SM for any category of aircraft using the straight-in RNAV RWY 33 approach into ADS. Answer (C) is incorrect. These are the minimums for Category A and B aircraft only when the Dallas Love Field altimeter setting is used.

61. (Refer to Figure 36A on page 475.) What is the minimum number of waypoints required for the complete RNAV RWY 33 approach procedure including the IAF's and missed approach procedure?

A. One waypoint.

B. Two waypoints.

C. Three waypoints.

Answer (B) is correct. *(ACL)*
DISCUSSION: Two waypoints are given for the RNAV RWY 33 approach: ADDIS and the MAP.
Answer (A) is incorrect. The MAP is a waypoint (as shown by the box) even though it has no waypoint star. Answer (C) is incorrect. The FAF is not a waypoint; it is a DME fix off of the MAP waypoint.

62. (Refer to Figure 36A on page 475.) What is the MDA and visibility criteria respectively for the S 33 approach procedure?

A. 1,240 feet MSL; 1/2 SM.

B. 1,240 feet MSL; 1 SM.

C. 1,280 feet MSL; 1 and 1/4 SM.

Answer (B) is correct. *(ACL)*
DISCUSSION: The MDA and visibility criteria are found in the minimums section of the RNAV RWY 33 approach chart. The straight-in (S-33) MDA and visibility criteria for Category A and B aircraft are 1,240 ft. MSL and 1 SM, respectively (note that the question does not specify the aircraft category).
Answer (A) is incorrect. The minimum visibility is not shown to be 1/2 SM for any category of aircraft using the straight-in RNAV RWY 33 approach into ADS. Answer (C) is incorrect. The MDA for a circling approach, not a straight-in approach, is 1,280 ft. MSL, and the minimum visibility is not shown to be 1 and 1/4 SM for any category of aircraft using the straight-in RNAV RWY 33 approach into ADS.

Figure 36A. – RNAV RWY 33 (ADS).

63. (Refer to Figure 167 below, and Figure 168 on page 477.) At which point does the BYP.BYP6 arrival begin?

A. At the LIT VORTAC.

B. At GLOVE intersection.

C. At the BYP VORTAC.

Answer (C) is correct. *(ACL)*

DISCUSSION: The arrival, in contrast to the transition, begins over the BYP VORTAC as explained in the written description in Fig. 168.

Answer (A) is incorrect. The Little Rock transition, LIT.BYP6, begins over the LIT VORTAC. Answer (B) is incorrect. GLOVE INT. is an intersection along a feeder route within the LIT.BYP6 transition.

Figure 167.

(BYP.BYP6) 13178
BONHAM SIX ARRIVAL Arrival Routes
ST-6039 (FAA)
DALLAS-FORT WORTH INTL (DFW)
DALLAS-FORT WORTH, TEXAS

NOTE: Chart not to scale.

ARRIVAL DESCRIPTION

FORT SMITH TRANSITION (FSM.BYP6): From over FSM VORTAC on FSM R-215 to MAMEE INT, then on BYP R-035 to BYP VORTAC. Thence. . . .

LITTLE ROCK TRANSITION (LIT.BYP6): From over LIT VORTAC on LIT R-247 to MEEOW INT then on LIT R-247 and BYP R-064 to GLOVE INT, then on BYP R-064 to BYP VORTAC. Thence. . .

MC ALESTER TRANSITION (MLC.BYP6): From over MLC VORTAC on MLC R-188 and BYP R-010 to BYP VORTAC. Thence. . . .

PARIS TRANSITION (PRX.BYP6): From over PRX VOR/DME on PRX R-263 to MONTE INT then on BYP R-083 to BYP VORTAC. Thence. . . .

TEXARKANA TRANSITION (TXK.BYP6): From over TXK VORTAC on TXK R-286 to GLOVE INT then on BYP R-064 to BYP VORTAC. Thence. . . .

TULSA TRANSITION (TUL.BYP6): From over TUL VORTAC on TUL R-157 to MAMEE INT, then on BYP R-035 to BYP VORTAC. Thence. . . .

. . . . <u>ALL AIRCRAFT:</u> From over BYP VORTAC on BYP R-219, thence. . . .

<u>ALL AIRCRAFT LANDING SOUTH:</u> To LEMYN INT, expect vectors to final approach course.
<u>JETS LANDING NORTH:</u> FOR /E, /F, /G, and /R (RNP-2.0) EQUIPPED AIRCRAFT:
From over STONZ INT direct DIRKK, expect vector to final approach course prior to DIRKK, if not received by DIRKK fly present heading.
<u>ALL OTHERS:</u> To STONZ depart STONZ heading 175° for vector to final approach course.
<u>PROPS LANDING NORTH:</u> Depart LEMYN INT heading 190°, expect vectors to final approach course.

BONHAM SIX ARRIVAL Arrival Routes
(BYP.BYP6) 13178
DALLAS-FORT WORTH, TEXAS
DALLAS-FORT WORTH INTL (DFW)

Figure 168.

64. (Refer to Figure 174 below, and Figure 175 on page 479.) When DFW is landing to the north, at CURLE expect

A. to be instructed to maintain 200 knots.

B. to fly a course of 010°.

C. radar vectors.

Answer (C) is correct. *(IPH Chap 3)*
DISCUSSION: According to the arrival description in Fig. 175, "ALL AIRCRAFT LANDING NORTH; to CURLE INT, expect vectors to final approach course." Each aircraft landing north at CURLE intersection should expect vectors to final approach.
Answer (A) is incorrect. There are no notes indicating that an airspeed of 200 knots is to be maintained upon arrival at CURLE. Answer (B) is incorrect. A heading of 010° is for nonturbojets landing south.

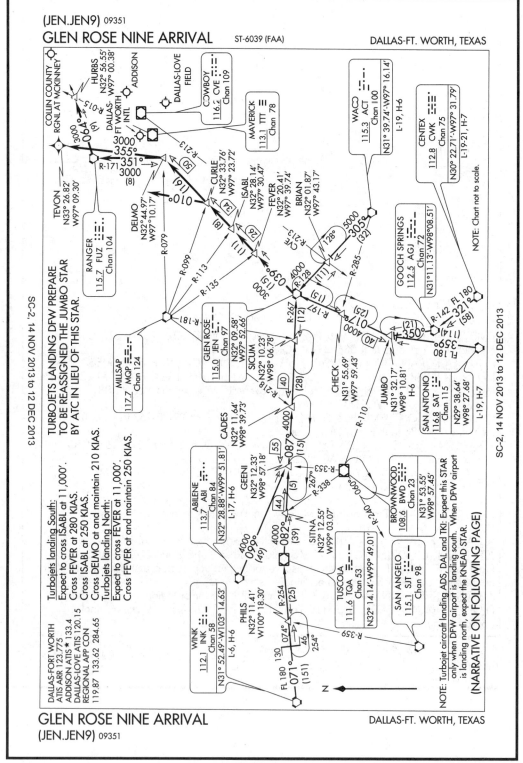

Figure 174.

(JEN.JEN9) 09351

GLEN ROSE NINE ARRIVAL ST-6039 (FAA) DALLAS-FT. WORTH, TEXAS

ARRIVAL DESCRIPTION

SC-2, 14 NOV 2013 to 12 DEC 2013

SC-2, 14 NOV 2013 to 12 DEC 2013

ABILENE TRANSITION (ABI.JEN9): From over ABI VORTAC via R-099 to GEENI INT, then via JEN R-267 to JEN VORTAC. Thence. . . .

CENTEX TRANSITION (CWK.JEN9): From over CWK VORTAC via CWK R-321 and AGJ R-142 to AGJ VORTAC, then via AGJ R-350 to JUMBO INT, then via JEN R-197 to JEN VORTAC. Thence . . . .

JUMBO TRANSITION (JUMBO.JEN9): From over JUMBO INT via JEN R-197 to JEN VORTAC. Thence . . . .

SAN ANTONIO TRANSITION (SAT.JEN9): From over SAT VORTAC via SAT R-359 to JUMBO INT, then via JEN R-197 to JEN VORTAC. Thence . . . .

WACO TRANSITION (ACT.JEN9): From over ACT VORTAC via ACT R-305 and JEN R-128 to JEN VORTAC. Thence. . . .

WINK TRANSITION (INK.JEN9): From over INK VORTAC via INK R-071 and TQA R-254 to TQA VOR/DME, then via TQA R-082 to GEENI INT, then via JEN R-267 to JEN VORTAC. Thence. . . .

. . . . ALL AIRCRAFT: From over JEN VORTAC via JEN R-039, thence . . . .

ALL AIRCRAFT LANDING NORTH: To CURLE INT, expect vectors to final approach course.

JETS LANDING SOUTH: To DELMO, depart DELMO heading 355°.
For /E, /F, /G and /R (RNP 2.0) EQUIPMENT SUFFIXED AIRCRAFT: From over DELMO WP direct TEVON WP, expect vector to final approach course prior to TEVON WP. If not received by TEVON fly present heading.
NON TURBOJETS LANDING SOUTH: To CURLE INT, depart CURLE heading 010° for vectors to final approach course.

AIRCRAFT LANDING DAL, ADS, TKI: To DELMO INT, depart DELMO via FUZ R-171 to FUZ VORTAC then FUZ R-064 to HURBS INT, expect vectors to final approach course.

GLEN ROSE NINE ARRIVAL DALLAS-FT. WORTH, TEXAS
(JEN.JEN9) 09351

Figure 175.

Questions 65 through 78 pertain to an IFR flight from Big Spring McMahon-Wrinkle Airport, Big Spring, Texas, to the Dallas-Ft. Worth International Airport, Ft. Worth, Texas.

The route of flight is given in block 8 on the flight plan portion of Fig. 38 on page 481. Information that pertains to your aircraft is given on the bottom portion of Fig. 38. The partially completed flight planning log is given in Fig. 39 on page 483.

The figures provided for this flight are listed below and are presented throughout the sequence of questions, except for Fig. 40, which is provided in color on page 417.

Fig.	Page	
38	481	Flight Plan and Aircraft Information
39	483	Flight Log and Excerpt from Airport/Facility Directory (21 XS)
40	417	En Route Chart Segment
41	484	ACTON Two Arrival
41A	485	ACTON Two Arrival Description
42	486	ILS-1 RWY 36L, Dallas-Fort Worth Intl.
42A	487	ILS RWY 36L
43	482	CDI and RMI – NAV 1 and NAV 2

65. (Refer to Figure 38 on page 481.) What number should be placed in block 12?

A. Total useable fuel on board.

B. Total fuel to destination, plus a 45 minute reserve.

C. Total fuel to destination, plus a 30 minute reserve.

Answer (A) is correct. *(AIM Para 5-1-8)*
DISCUSSION: Block 12 on the flight plan form is intended to record the total amount of usable fuel on board the aircraft in hours of endurance.
Answer (B) is incorrect. Block 12 records the total endurance of the aircraft, not the fuel required to the destination plus a 45 minute reserve. Answer (C) is incorrect. Block 12 records the total endurance of the aircraft, not the fuel required to the destination plus a 30 minute reserve.

66. (Refer to Figure 38 on page 481 and Legend 26 on page 428.) What aircraft equipment code should be entered in block 3 of the flight plan?

A. C.

B. I.

C. A.

Answer (B) is correct. *(AIM Para 5-1-8)*
DISCUSSION: In block 3 of the flight plan, you enter the designation of the aircraft followed by a slash (/) and a letter for the equipment code. Fig. 38 indicates there is a transponder with Mode C and RNAV. Thus, you need Code I. (See Legend 26.)
Answer (A) is incorrect. C indicates RNAV and transponder, but with no Mode C. Answer (C) is incorrect. A indicates DME and transponder with Mode C but no RNAV.

67. (Refer to Figure 38 on page 481.) What CAS must be used to maintain the filed TAS at the flight planned altitude if the outside air temperature is +05°C?

A. 129 KCAS.

B. 133 KCAS.

C. 139 KCAS.

Answer (A) is correct. *(PHAK Chap 15)*
DISCUSSION: In the center of the slide rule side of your flight computer, on the right side, put the air temperature of +5°C over the altitude of 11,000 ft. (from block 7 of the flight plan, Fig. 38). On the outer scale, find TAS of 156 (from block 4), which is over calibrated airspeed on the inner scale of 129 KCAS.
Answer (B) is incorrect. Maintaining 133 KCAS would result in a TAS of 161 kt., not 156 kt. Answer (C) is incorrect. Maintaining 139 KCAS would result in a TAS of 168 kt., not 156 kt.

68. (Refer to Figure 38 on page 481.) What fuel should be entered into block 12 of the flight plan?

A. Total fuel to destination.

B. Total fuel required to destination, plus the fuel to the alternate, plus 45 minutes.

C. Total usable fuel.

Answer (C) is correct. *(FAR 91.153, AIM Para 5-1-4)*
DISCUSSION: The total fuel measured in hours should be entered into block 12 of the flight plan.
Answer (A) is incorrect. 14 CFR Part 91 requires total fuel measured in hours to be entered into a flight plan, not just the amount of fuel required to reach the destination. Answer (B) is incorrect. 14 CFR Part 91 requires total fuel measured in hours to be entered into a flight plan, not just the amount of fuel required to reach the destination, then fly to the alternate, plus 45 minutes. That is the fuel requirement, not the requirement for flight plan information.

Figure 38. – Flight Plan and Aircraft Information.

69. (Refer to Figure 40 on page 417.) For planning purposes, what is the highest usable altitude for an IFR flight on V16 from the BGS VORTAC to ABI VORTAC?

A. 17,000 feet MSL.

B. 18,000 feet MSL.

C. 6,500 feet MSL.

Answer (A) is correct. *(AIM Para 3-2-6)*

DISCUSSION: The VOR airway system consists of airways designated from 1,200 ft. AGL up to, but not including, 18,000 ft. MSL.

Answer (B) is incorrect. Victor airways go up through 17,999 ft. but do not include 18,000 ft. Answer (C) is incorrect. The altitude of 6,500 ft. is the MRA at LORAN intersection.

70. (Refer to Figure 43 below, Figure 41 on page 484, and Figure 42A on page 487.) What is your position relative to CHAAR intersection? The aircraft is level at 3,000 feet MSL.

A. Right of the localizer course approaching CHAAR intersection and approaching the glide slope.

B. Left of the localizer course approaching CHAAR intersection and below the glide slope.

C. Right of the localizer course, past CHAAR intersection and above the glide slope.

Answer (A) is correct. *(IFH Chap 10)*
    DISCUSSION: NAV-1 (111.9) is on the I-BXN localizer indicating right of course because of the left deviation. Also, you are outside (approaching) CHAAR intersection since the DME readout is 7.5 DME (CHAAR is 7.2 DME). The glide slope is 3,000 ft. MSL at CHAAR, and thus you are beneath and approaching the glide slope. On NAV-2, the ADF frequency 233 does not appear on the approach chart. The VOR (114.3) is LOVE VOR, indicating R-230, and CHAAR is R-233, which confirms you are south of CHAAR position.
    Answer (B) is incorrect. The left localizer deviation means right, not left, of course. Answer (C) is incorrect. You are below, not above, the glide slope and have not passed CHAAR intersection.

Figure 43. – CDI and RMI - NAV 1 and NAV 2.

71. (Refer to Figure 38 on page 481, Figure 39 on page 483, Figure 40 on page 417, and Figure 41 on page 484.) (Refer to the FD excerpt below, and use the wind entry closest to the flight planned altitude.) Determine the time to be entered in block 10 of the flight plan.

Route of flight ....Figures 38, 39, and 40
Flight log & MAG VAR .... Figure 39
ACTON TWO ARRIVAL .... Figure 41

FT	3000	6000	9000	12000
ABI		2033+13	2141+13	2142+05

A. 1 hour 24 minutes.

B. 1 hour 26 minutes.

C. 1 hour 31 minutes.

Answer (C) is correct. *(IFH Chap 10)*
    DISCUSSION: To determine the estimated time en route to be entered in block 10, you must complete the flight planning log in Fig. 39. Using the wind side of your flight computer, determine groundspeeds as shown in the table below.
    Remember that winds are given in true direction and must be converted to magnetic. Fig. 39 shows a variation of 11°E. Use the wind at 12,000 ft. (which is closest to the planned altitude of 11,000 ft.): 210° – 11°E var. = 199° at 42 kt.

	Distance	MC	Wind (Mag)	Ground-speed	Time
BGS VORTAC	X	X	X	X	:06:00G
LORAN INT.	42	075°	199/42	176	:14:19
ABI VORTAC	40	076°	199/42	175	:13:43
COTTN INT.	63	087°	199/42	167	:22:38
AQN VORTAC	50	075°	199/42	176	:17:03
CREEK INT.	32	040°	199/42	194	:09:54
Approach and Landing	X	X	X	X	:08:00G
					1:31:37

G = Given

    Answer (A) is incorrect. An ETE of 1 hr. 24 min. requires a TAS of 175 kt., not 156 kt. Answer (B) is incorrect. An ETE of 1 hr. 26 min. requires a TAS of 170 kt., not 156 kt.

FLIGHT LOG

BIG SPRING McMAHON-WRINKLE TO DALLAS FT. WORTH (DFW)

CHECK POINTS		ROUTE	COURSE	WIND	SPEED-KTS		DIST	TIME		FUEL	
FROM	TO	ALTITUDE		TEMP	TAS	GS	NM	LEG	TOT	LEG	TOT
21XS	BGS	DIRECT CLIMB	DIRECT					:06:0			
	LORAN	V16 11,000	075°								
	ABI	V16 11,000	076°		156						
	COTTN	DIRECT 11,000	087°								
	AQN	AQN2	075°								
	CREEK	AQN2	040°								
APPROACH & LANDING		RADAR VEC-						:08:0			
	DFW AIRPORT	DESCENT									

OTHER DATA: NOTE:	MAG. VAR. 11° E. (STAR) ACTON TWO ARRIVAL (AQN2)

FLIGHT SUMMARY

TIME	FUEL (LB)	
		EN ROUTE
		RESERVE
		MISSED APPR.
		TOTAL

BIG SPRING McMAHON-WRINKLE   (21XS) 2SW UTC-6(-5DT).   **DALLAS-FT. WORTH**
    32°12'45"N101°31'17"W   H-21, 5A, L-13A, 15B
    2572 B S4FUEL 100LL, JET A   IAP
    RWY 17-35: H8803X100 (ASPH-CONC) S-44, D-62, DDT-101 MIRL
        RWY 17:SSALS.PVASI(ASPH)-GA3.0°TCH 41'.
    RWY 06-24:H4600X75(ASPH) MIRL
        RWY 24:PVASI(PSIL)-GA3.55°TCH31'. P-line.
    AIRPORT REMARKS: Attended 1400-2300Z . For fuel after hours call 915-263-3958. ACTIVATE MIRL Rwy 06-24
        and Rwy 17-35, SSALS Rwy 17 and PVASI Rwy 17 and 24-CTAF.
    COMMUNICATIONS:CTAF/UNICOM 122.8
        SAN ANGELOSFSS (SJT) TF 1-800-WX-BRIEF. NOTAM FILE SJT.
        RCO 122.4(SAN ANGELOFSS)
        FORT WORTH CENTER APP/DEP CON 133.7
    RADIO AIDS TO NAVIGATION: NOTAM FILE SJT.
        (L) VORTACW 144.3 BGS Chan 90 32°23'08"N 101°10.5NM to fld. 2670/11E.

EXCERPT FROM AIRPORT/FACILITY DIRECTORY (21 XS)

Figure 39. – Flight Log and Excerpt from Airport/Facility Directory (21 XS).

72. (Refer to Figure 42A on page 487.) Which navigational information and services would be available to the pilot when using the localizer frequency?

A. Localizer and glide slope, DME, TACAN with no voice capability.

B. Localizer information only, ATIS and DME are available.

C. Localizer and glide slope, DME, and no voice capability.

Answer (C) is correct. *(ACL)*
    DISCUSSION: ILS RWY 36L is an ILS (localizer and glide slope). On the NOS chart, a channel number indicates DME. The line under the I-BXN frequency 111.9 means no voice capability.
    Answer (A) is incorrect. There is no TACAN indicated in the IAP chart. TACAN is the military version of VOR/DME.
    Answer (B) is incorrect. It is an ILS approach with glide slope.

73. (Refer to Figure 41 below, and Figure 41A on page 485.) At which point does the AQN.AQN2 arrival begin?

A. ABI VORTAC.

B. ACTON VORTAC.

C. CREEK intersection.

Answer (B) is correct. *(ACL)*
   DISCUSSION: The arrival, in contrast to the transition, begins over the AQN VORTAC, as explained in the written description in Fig. 41A.
   Answer (A) is incorrect. The ABI VORTAC is the beginning of the Abilene transition. Answer (C) is incorrect. CREEK intersection is part, not the beginning, of the AQN.AQN2 arrival.

Figure 41. – ACTON Two Arrival.

74. (Refer to Figure 41A below, and Figure 41 on page 484.) Which frequency would you anticipate using to contact Regional Approach Control? (ACTON TWO ARRIVAL).

A. 119.05

B. 124.15

C. 125.8

Answer (C) is correct. *(ACL)*
DISCUSSION: The upper left-hand corner of the STAR chart (Fig. 41) shows the pertinent frequencies to be used. Since aircraft using this arrival are approaching from the west, the appropriate approach frequency is 125.8.
Answer (A) is incorrect. This frequency is for aircraft approaching from an easterly direction. Answer (B) is incorrect. This frequency is the DFW tower, not regional approach control, frequency for aircraft approaching from the west.

75. (Refer to Figure 41A below, and Figure 41 on page 484.) On which heading should you plan to depart CREEK intersection?

A. 010°.

B. 040°.

C. 350°.

Answer (C) is correct. *(ACL)*
DISCUSSION: Presumably, you should assume that you are flying a jet aircraft, since non-jet aircraft (such as the C-402 in this flight) do not fly to CREEK INT. (refer to Fig. 41A). The turbojet arrival indicates that you should maintain a heading of 350° after CREEK. Non-turbojet aircraft will proceed from AQN VORTAC via AQN R-040 to CREEK INT. and should expect radar vectors at BRYAR INT. (i.e., before CREEK INT.).
Answer (A) is incorrect. This heading is not an applicable heading in this STAR. Answer (B) is incorrect. This heading is the course from AQN to CREEK INT., not after CREEK INT.

ACTON TWO ARRIVAL (AQN.AQN2)   DALLAS-FORT WORTH, TEXAS

ARRIVAL DESCRIPTION

ABILENE TRANSITION (ABI.AQN2): From over ABI VORTAC via ABI R-087 and AQN R-255 to AQN VORTAC. Thence . . . .
EDNAS TRANSITION (EDNAS.AQN2): From over EDNAS INT via AQN R-199 to AQN VORTAC. Thence . . . .
WINK TRANSITION (INK.AQN2): From over INK VORTAC via INK R-071, TQA R-254, TQA R-073 and AQN R-255 to AQN VORTAC. Thence . . . .
TURBOJETS LANDING DALLAS-FT. WORTH INTL, MEACHAM, CARSWELL AFB, DENTON, ALLIANCE: (Landing South): From over AQN VORTAC via AQN R-040 to CREEK INT, thence heading 350° for vector to final approach course. (Landing North): From over AQN VORTAC via AQN R-040 to CREEK INT. Expect vectors at BRYAR INT.
NON-TURBOJETS LANDING DALLAS-FT. WORTH INTL, MEACHAM, CARSWELL AFB, DENTON, ALLIANCE: (Landing South): From over AQN VORTAC via AQN R-033 to RENDY INT. Expect vectors to final approach course. (Landing North): From over AQN VORTAC via AQN R-040 to CREEK INT. Expect vector at BRYAR INT.
TURBOJETS LANDING DALLAS-LOVE FIELD and ADDISON: (Landing South): From over AQN VORTAC via AQN R-040 to CREEK INT, thence heading 350° for vector to final approach course. (Landing North): From over AQN VORTAC via AQN R-079 to BRITY INT. Expect vector to final approach course.
NON-TURBOJETS LANDING DALLAS-LOVE FIELD and ADDISON: (Landing South/North): From over AQN VORTAC via AQN R-079 to BRITY INT. Expect vector to final approach course.
ALL AIRCRAFT LANDING FORT WORTH SPINKS, ARLINGTON, NAS DALLAS, REDBIRD, and PHIL L. HUDSON: (Landing South/North): From over AQN VORTAC via AQN R-079 to BRITY INT. Expect vectors to final approach course.

Figure 41A. – ACTON Two Arrival Description.

76. (Refer to Figure 42 below, Figure 41 on page 484, and Figure 42A on page 487.) Approaching DFW from Abilene, which frequencies should you expect to use for regional approach control, control tower, and ground control respectively?

    A. 119.05; 126.55; 121.65.

    B. 119.05; 124.15; 121.8.

    C. 125.8; 124.15; 121.8.

Answer (C) is correct. *(A/FD)*
    DISCUSSION: Refer to the **Communications** section of the *A/FD* in Fig. 42. Since the ACTON two arrival approaches from the west, approach control uses 125.8 or 132.1, tower uses 124.15, and ground uses 121.65 or 121.8.
    Answer (A) is incorrect. The frequency of 119.05 is for approach control from the east, not west, and 126.55 is for tower from the east, not west. Answer (B) is incorrect. The frequency of 119.05 is for approach control from the east, not west.

77. (Refer to Figure 42 below, and Figure 42A on page 487.) What is the difference in elevation (in feet MSL) between the airport elevation and the TDZE for RWY 36L?

    A. 15 feet.

    B. 18 feet.

    C. 22 feet.

Answer (A) is correct. *(ACL)*
    DISCUSSION: The airport elevation (603 ft.) is shown in the upper left corner of the airport diagram, and the TDZE (588 ft.) is shown to the left of the approach end of RWY 36L. The difference between the two is 15 ft. (603 – 588).
    Answer (B) is incorrect. The difference of 603 and 588 is 15 ft., not 18 ft. Answer (C) is incorrect. This is the difference between airport elevation and the TDZE for RWY 36R, not RWY 36L.

TEXAS

DALLAS-FORT WORTH INTL (DFW)   12 NW   UTC-6(-5DT)32°53'47"N 97°02'28"W   **DALLAS-FT. WORTH**
  603   B FUEL 100LL, JET A   OX 1, 3   LRA   ARFF Index E   **H-2K, 4F, 5B, L-13C, A**
  RWY 17L-35R: H11,388X150 (CONC-GRVD) S-120, D-200, DT-600, DDT-850 HIRL CL   **IAP**
    RWY 17L: ALSF2. TDZ.   RWY 35R: MALSR. TDZ.
  RWY 17R-35L: H11,388X200 (CONC-GRVD) S-120, D-200, DT-600, DDT-850 HIRL CL
    RWY 17R: MALSR. TDZ.   RWY 35L: TDZ. VASI(V6L).
  RWY 18R-36L: H11,388X150 (CONC-GRVD) S-120, D-200, DT-600, DDT-850 HIRL CL
    RWY 18R: ALSF2. TDZ   RWY 36L: MALSR. TDZ
  RWY 18L-36R: H11,387X200 (CONC-GRVD) S-120, D-200, DT-600, DDT-850 HIRL CL
    RWY 18L: MALSR. TDZ   RWY 36R: TDZ. VASI(V6L).
  RWY 13R-31L: H9300X150 (CONC-GRVD) S-120, D-220, DT-600, DDT-850 HIRL CL
    RWY 13R: MALSR. TDZ   RWY 31L: TDZ.
  RWY 13L-31R: H9000X2000 (CONC-GRVD) S-120, D-200, DT-600, DDT-850 HIRL CL 0.5% up NW
    RWY 13L: TDZ. VASI(VL6)--Upper GA 3.25° TCH 93'. Lower GA 3.0° TCH 47'.   RWY 31R: MALSR. TDZ
  RWY 18S-36S: H4000X100 (CONC)
AIRPORT REMARKS: Attended continuously. Rwy 18S-36S CLOSED indefinitely. Arpt under construction, men and
    equipment in movement areas. Partial outages of arpt lgt circuits will occur daily. Prior Permission Required from
    arpt ops for General Aviation acft to proceed to airline terminal gate except to General Aviation Facility. Rwy
    18S-36S located on taxiway G, 4000' long 100' wide restricted to prop acft 12,5000 lbs. & below and stol acft
    daylight VFR plus IFR departures. Prior permission required from the primary tenant airlines to operate within
    central terminal area. CAUTION: proper minimum clearance may not be maintained within the central terminal
    area. Landing fee. Helipad H1 on apt 104X104 (CONC) Heliport located at Twy G and Twy 24 intersection
    daylight VFR. Clearways 500X1000 each end Rwy 17L-35R, Rwy 17R-35L, Rwy 18L-36R and Rwy 18R-36L.
    Flight Notification Service (ADCUS) available.
WEATHER DATA SOURCES: LLWAS
COMMUNICATIONS: ATIS 117.0 134.9 (ARR) 135.5 (DEP)   **UNICOM** 122.95
    FORT WORTH FSS (FTW) LC 429-6434, TF 1-800-WX-BRIEF. NOTAM FILE DFW
  ®**REGIONAL APP CON** 119.05(E) 119.4(E) 125.8(W) 132.1(W)
    REGIONAL TOWER 126.55(E) 124.15(W)   **GND CON** 121.65 133.15(E) 121.8(W)   **CLNC DEL** 128.25 127.5
  ®**REGIONAL DEP CON** 118.55(E) 124.25 (WES) 127.75 (NORTH-SOUTH)
    TCA: See VFR Terminal Area chart.
RADIO AIDS TO NAVIGATION: NOTAM FILE DFW.
    (H) VORTACW 117.0   DFW   Chan 117   32°51'57"N 97°01'40"W   at fld. 560/08E.
       VOR Portion unusable 045°-050° all altitudes and distances, 350-100° beyond 30 NM below 2100'.
    ISSUE NDB (LOM) 233   PK   32°47'35"N 97°01'49"W   348° 6.2 NM to fld.
    JIFFY NDB (LOM) 219   FL   32°59'44"N 97°01'46"W   179° 6.0 NM to fld.
    ILS/DME 109.5 I-LWN Chan 32 Rwy 13R.
    ILS/DME 109.1 I-FLQ Chan 28 Rwy 17L. LOM JIFFY NDB.
    ILS 111.5 I-JHZ Rwy 17R. LOM JIFFY NDB.
    ILS 111.3 I-CIX Rwy 18L.
    ILS/DME 111.9 I-VYN Chan 56 Rwy 18R.
    ILS 110.9 I-RRA Rwy 31R.
    ILS/DME 109.1 I-PKQ Chan 28 Rwy 35R. LOM ISSUE NDB.
    ILS/DME 111.9 I-BXN Chan 56 Rwy 36L.

Figure 42. – ILS-1 RWY 36L, Dallas-Fort Worth Intl.

78. (Refer to Figure 42A below, and Legend 21 on page 267.) What rate of descent should you plan to use initially to establish the glidepath for the ILS RWY 36L approach? (Use 120 knots ground speed.)

- A. 425 feet per minute.
- B. 530 feet per minute.
- C. 637 feet per minute.

Answer (C) is correct. *(ACL)*

DISCUSSION: The profile view of the IAP chart (Fig. 42A) shows a glide slope angle of 3.00°. Legend 21 gives rates of descent based on various glide slope angles and ground speeds. Find the 3.0° on the left margin and move right to the 120-kt. groundspeed column to determine a rate of descent of 637 fpm.

Answer (A) is incorrect. This is the required rate of descent at 120-kt. groundspeed on a 2.0°, not 3.0°, glide slope. Answer (B) is incorrect. This is the required rate of descent at 120-kt. groundspeed on a 2.5°, not 3.0°, glide slope.

Figure 42A. – ILS RWY 36L.

11.7   4N1 to BDL

Questions 79 through 93 pertain to an IFR flight from Greenwood Lake Airport (4N1), West Milford, New Jersey, to the Bradley International Airport, Windsor Locks, Connecticut.

The route of flight is given in block 8 on the flight plan portion of Fig. 69 on page 489. Information that pertains to your aircraft is given on the bottom portion of Fig. 69. The partially completed flight planning log is given in Fig. 70 on page 490.

The figures provided for this flight are listed below and are presented throughout the sequence of questions, except for Fig. 71, which is provided in color on page 422.

Fig.	Page	
69	489	Flight Plan and Aircraft Information
70	490	Flight Planning Log
71	422	En Route Chart Segment
71A	490	CDI and OBS Indicators
72	495	JUDDS Two Arrival
73	493	ILS RWY 6 (BDL)
210	491	[title not provided by FAA]

79. (Refer to Figure 69 on page 489 and Legend 26 on page 428.) What aircraft equipment code should be entered in block 3 of the flight plan?

A. A.

B. B.

C. U.

Answer (A) is correct. *(AIM Para 5-1-8)*

DISCUSSION: In block 3 of the flight plan, you enter the designation of the aircraft followed by a slash (/) and a letter for the equipment code. Fig. 69 indicates that you have a transponder with Mode C and DME, which requires code A. (See Legend 26.)

Answer (B) is incorrect. Code B indicates DME and transponder but no Mode C. Answer (C) is incorrect. Code U indicates only a transponder with Mode C.

80. (Refer to Figure 69 on page 489, Figure 70 on page 490, Figure 71 on page 422, and Figure 72 on page 495.) Determine the time to be entered in block 10 of the flight plan. (Refer to the FD excerpt below, and use the wind entry closest to the flight planned altitude.)

Route of flight .... Figures 69, 70, & 71
Flight log and MAG VAR .... Figure 70
JUDDS TWO ARRIVAL
  and Excerpt from AFD .... Figure 72

FT	3000	6000	9000
BDL	3320	3425+05	3430+00

A. 1 hour 14 minutes.

B. 58 minutes.

C. 50 minutes.

Answer (B) is correct. *(IFH Chap 10)*

DISCUSSION: To determine the estimated time en route to be entered in block 10, you must complete the flight planning log in Fig. 70. Using the wind side of your flight computer, determine groundspeeds as shown in the table below. The arrow in Fig. 71 points to the departure airport.

Remember that winds are given in true direction and must be converted to magnetic. Fig. 70 shows a variation of 14°W. Use the wind at 6,000 ft. (which is closest to the planned altitude of 5,000 ft.): 340° + 14°W var. = 354° at 25 kt.

	Distance	MC	Wind (Mag)	Ground-speed	Time
SHAFF INT.	X	X	X	X	:08:00G
HELON INT.	24	029°	354/25	107	:13:27
IGN VORTAC	21	102°	354/25	134	:09:24
VOR COP	15	112°	354/25	138	:06:31
JUDDS INT.	17	100°	354/25	133	:07:40
BRISS INT.	6	057°	354/25	115	:03:07
Approach and Landing	X	X	X	X	:12:00G
					1:00:09

G = Given

Answer (A) is incorrect. An ETE of 1 hr. 14 min. requires a TAS of approximately 95 kt., not 128 kt. Answer (C) is incorrect. An ETE of 50 min. requires a TAS of 170 kt., not 128 kt.

81. (Refer to Figure 69 below.) What CAS should be used to maintain the filed TAS if the outside air temperature is +05°C?

A. 119 KCAS.

B. 124 KCAS.

C. 126 KCAS.

Answer (A) is correct. *(PHAK Chap 15)*
DISCUSSION: In the center of the slide rule side of your flight computer, on the right side, put the air temperature of +5°C over the altitude of 5,000 ft. (from block 7 of the flight plan, Fig. 69). On the outer scale, find TAS of 128 kt. (from block 4), which is over calibrated airspeed on the inner scale of 119 KCAS.

Answer (B) is incorrect. Maintaining 124 KCAS would result in a TAS of 134 kt., not 128 kt. Answer (C) is incorrect. Maintaining 126 KCAS would result in a TAS of 136 kt., not 128 kt.

Form Approved: OMB No. 2120-0034

U.S. DEPARTMENT OF TRANSPORTATION FEDERAL AVIATION ADMINISTRATION **FLIGHT PLAN**	(FAA USE ONLY)	☐ PILOT BRIEFING ☐ STOPOVER	☐ VNR	TIME STARTED	SPECIALIST INITIALS

1. TYPE		2. AIRCRAFT IDENTIFICATION	3. AIRCRAFT TYPE/ SPECIAL EQUIPMENT	4. TRUE AIRSPEED	5. DEPARTURE POINT	6. DEPARTURE TIME		7. CRUISING ALTITUDE
	VFR				GREENWOOD LAKE	PROPOSED (Z)	ACTUAL (Z)	
X	IFR	N2142S	C172/	128 KTS	4N1			5000
	DVFR							

8. ROUTE OF FLIGHT

DIRECT SHAFF INT., V213 HELON INT., V58 JUDDS INT., JUDDS2

9. DESTINATION (Name of airport and city) BRADLEY INTL. BDL	10. EST. TIME ENROUTE		11. REMARKS
	HOURS	MINUTES	INSTRUMENT TRAINING FLIGHT

12. FUEL ON BOARD		13. ALTERNATE AIRPORT(S)	14. PILOT'S NAME, ADDRESS & TELEPHONE NUMBER & AIRCRAFT HOME BASE	15. NUMBER ABOARD
HOURS	MINUTES		17. DESTINATION CONTACT/TELEPHONE (OPTIONAL)	2
		N/A		

16. COLOR OF AIRCRAFT BROWN/TAN/WHITE	CIVIL AIRCRAFT PILOTS. FAR Part 91 requires you file an IFR flight plan to operate under instrument flight rules in controlled airspace. Failure to file could result in a civil penalty not to exceed $1,000 for each violation (Section 901 of the Federal Aviation Act of 1958, as amended). Filing of a VFR flight plan is recommended as a good operating practice. See also Part 99 for requirements concerning DVFR flight plans.

FAA Form 7233-1 (8-82)   CLOSE VFR FLIGHT PLAN WITH _____ FSS ON ARRIVAL

AIRCRAFT INFORMATION

MAKE Cessna   MODEL 172

N 2142S   Vso 33

AIRCRAFT EQUIPMENT/STATUS**

**NOTE: X= OPERATIVE   INOP= INOPERATIVE   N/A= NOT APPLICABLE
TRANSPONDER: X (MODE C) X ILS: (LOCALIZER) X (GLIDE SLOPE) X
VOR NO. 1 X (NO. 2) X ADF: X RNAV: N/A
VERTICAL PATH COMPUTER: N/A DME: X
MARKER BEACON: X (AUDIO) INOP (VISUAL) X

Figure 69. – Flight Plan and Aircraft Information.

82. (Refer to Figure 70 below, and Figure 71 on page 422.) Which VORTAC navigational facility along the proposed route of flight could provide you with HIWAS information?

A. SPARTA VORTAC.

B. HUGUENOT VORTAC.

C. KINGSTON VORTAC.

Answer (C) is correct. *(ACL)*
DISCUSSION: The Kingston VORTAC (IGN) communication box contains a small square with a white H in the upper right-hand corner indicating availability of HIWAS.
Answer (A) is incorrect. The Sparta (SAX) VORTAC communication box has no small square with an H. Answer (B) is incorrect. The Huguenot VORTAC communication box has no small square with an H.

FLIGHT LOG

GREENWOOD LAKE (4N1) TO BRADLEY INTL. (BDL)

CHECK POINTS		ROUTE	COURSE	WIND	SPEED-KTS		DIST	TIME		FUEL	
FROM	TO	ALTITUDE		TEMP	TAS	GS	NM	LEG	TOT	LEG	TOT
4N1	SHAFF	DIRECT CLIMB	350°					:08:0			
	HELON	V213 5000	029°		128						
	IGN	V58 5000	102°								
		JUDDS2	112°								
	JUDDS	JUDDS2	100°								
	BRISS	JUDDS2	057°								
APPROACH & LANDING								:12:0			
	BDL INTL										

OTHER DATA:			FLIGHT SUMMARY		
NOTE: MAG. VAR. 14° W.		TIME	FUEL (LB)		
					EN ROUTE
					RESERVE
					MISSED APPR.
					TOTAL

Figure 70. – Flight Planning Log.

83. (Refer to Figure 71A below, and Figure 71 on page 422.) What is your position relative to the FLOSI intersection northbound on V213 airway?

A. West of V213 and approaching the FLOSI intersection.

B. East of V213 and approaching the FLOSI intersection.

C. West of V213 and past the FLOSI intersection.

Answer (A) is correct. *(IFH Chap 9)*
DISCUSSION: VOR-1 is tuned to IGN VORTAC (117.6) with an OBS setting of 265°. The FROM indication and right needle deflection indicate you are south of the IGN R-265 and thus approaching it. VOR-2 is tuned to SAX VORTAC (115.7) with an OBS setting of 029°. The FROM indication and right needle deflection indicate you are to the left or west of the SAX R-029.
Answer (B) is incorrect. A left, not right, needle deflection in VOR-2 would indicate right or east of the V213. Answer (C) is incorrect. A left, not right, needle deflection in VOR-1 would indicate that you have passed FLOSI intersection.

Figure 71A. – CDI and OBS Indicators.

84. (Refer to Figure 210 below.) Which sequence of marker beacon indicator lights, and their respective codes, will you receive on the ILS RWY 6 approach procedure to the MAP?

   A. White dots.

   B. Blue dashes, amber alternate dots and dashes.

   C. Blue and amber with alternating dots and dashes.

Answer (A) is correct. *(AIM Para 1-1-9)*

DISCUSSION: ILS RWY 6 shows no outer marker (OM) or middle marker (MM), leaving only the inner marker (IM) to contend with. The IM is identified by a series of white dots both aurally and visually at a rate of six dots per second.

Answer (B) is incorrect. Blue indicates an outer marker (OM), and amber indicates a middle marker (MM). Neither an OM or a MM are associated with ILS RWY 6 as depicted on the approach plate. Answer (C) is incorrect. Blue indicates an outer marker (OM), and amber indicates a middle marker (MM). Neither an OM or a MM are associated with ILS RWY 6 as depicted on the approach plate.

Figure 210.

85. (Refer to Figure 73 on page 493.) What is the minimum altitude at which you should intercept the glide slope on the ILS RWY 6 approach procedure?

    A. 3,000 feet MSL.

    B. 1,800 feet MSL.

    C. 1,690 feet MSL.

Answer (B) is correct. *(ACL)*
    DISCUSSION: In the profile section of the IAP chart, there is an <u>1800</u> with a lightning bolt pointing to the glide slope. This is the glide slope intercept altitude and final approach fix for precision approaches. Thus, here, one should not intercept below 1,800 ft. MSL.
    Answer (A) is incorrect. This is the minimum altitude in the holding pattern at PENNA INT. Answer (C) is incorrect. This is the altitude at which you will cross CHUPP LOM when descending on the glide slope.

86. (Refer to Figure 73 on page 493.) At which indication or occurrence should you initiate the published missed approach procedure for the ILS RWY 6 approach provided the runway environment is not in sight?

    A. When reaching 374 feet MSL indicated altitude.

    B. When 3 minutes (at 90 knots ground speed) have expired or reaching 374 feet MSL, whichever occurs first.

    C. Upon reaching 374 feet AGL.

Answer (A) is correct. *(ACL)*
    DISCUSSION: When flying the ILS RWY 6 approach, you should execute a missed approach when you have reached the decision height of 374 ft. MSL.
    Answer (B) is incorrect. The ILS is a precision approach and timing is only for the backup localizer approach. Answer (C) is incorrect. The decision height is 374 ft. MSL, not AGL.

87. (Refer to Figure 73 on page 493.) Which sequence of marker beacon indicator lights, and their respective codes, will you receive on the ILS RWY 6 approach procedure to the MAP?

    A. Blue - alternate dots and dashes; amber - dashes.

    B. Amber - alternate dots and dashes; blue - dashes.

    C. Blue - dashes; amber - alternate dots and dashes.

Answer (C) is correct. *(AIM Para 1-1-9)*
    DISCUSSION: The outer marker is identified with continuous dashes at the rate of two dashes per sec. and a blue marker beacon light. The middle marker is identified with alternate dots and dashes keyed at the rate of 95 dot/dash combinations per minute and an amber marker beacon light. Note that the inner marker, which is identified with continuous dots at the rate of six dots per sec. and a white marker beacon light, is crossed after (not before) the MAP.
    Answer (A) is incorrect. The outer marker has dashes, not dots and dashes, and the middle marker has dots and dashes, not just dashes. Answer (B) is incorrect. The outer marker is blue with dashes, and the middle marker is amber with dots and dashes, not vice versa.

88. (Refer to Figure 73 on page 493 and Legend 21 on page 267.) Using an average ground speed of 90 knots on the final approach segment, what rate of descent should be used initially to establish the glidepath for the ILS RWY 6 approach procedure?

    A. 395 feet per minute.

    B. 480 feet per minute.

    C. 555 feet per minute.

Answer (B) is correct. *(ACL)*
    DISCUSSION: The profile view of the IAP chart shows a glide slope angle of 3.00°. Legend 21 gives rates of descent based on various glide slope angles and groundspeeds. Find the 3.0° angle of descent on the left margin and move right to the 90-kt. groundspeed column to determine a rate of descent of 480 fpm.
    Answer (A) is incorrect. This is the required rate of descent at a groundspeed of 75 kt., not 90 kt. Answer (C) is incorrect. This is the required rate of descent at a groundspeed of 105 kt., not 90 kt.

89. (Refer to Figure 73 on page 493.) What is the touchdown zone elevation for RWY 6?

    A. 174 feet MSL.

    B. 200 feet AGL.

    C. 270 feet MSL.

Answer (A) is correct. *(ACL)*
    DISCUSSION: The IAP chart shows the TDZE in the airport diagram near the approach end of the landing runway. The TDZE is 174 ft. MSL.
    Answer (B) is incorrect. This is the HAT (height above touchdown) at the DH on the ILS. Answer (C) is incorrect. This is the height of an obstruction near the approach end of RWY 6.

Figure 73. – ILS RWY 6 (BDL).

90. (Refer to Figure 73 on page 493 and Legend 22 on page 211.) After passing the OM, Bradley Approach Control advises you that the MM on the ILS RWY 6 approach is inoperative. Under these circumstances, what adjustments, if any, are required to be made to the DH and visibility?

    A. DH 424/24.

    B. No adjustments are required.

    C. DH 374/24.

Answer (B) is correct. *(ACL)*
    DISCUSSION: Refer to Legend 22, Inoperative Components or Visual Aids Table. Since the MM is not listed in the table, no adjustments are required.
    Answer (A) is incorrect. No adjustments are required due to an inoperative MM. Answer (C) is incorrect. No adjustments are required due to an inoperative MM.

91. (Refer to Figure 73 on page 493 and Legend 19 on page 208.) Which runway and landing environment lighting is available for approach and landing on RWY 6 at Bradley International?

    A. HIRL, REIL, and VASI.

    B. HIRL and VASI.

    C. ALSF2 and HIRL.

Answer (C) is correct. *(ACL)*
    DISCUSSION: The airport diagram in Fig. 73 has a circle enclosing the letter "A," with a dot above it, near the approach end of RWY 6. Legend 19 indicates that this means ALSF-2 approach lighting. Information listed at the bottom left corner of the airport diagram (Fig. 73) indicates that RWY 6-24 has high-intensity runway lights (HIRL).
    Answer (A) is incorrect. REIL and VASI are not indicated for RWY 6. Answer (B) is incorrect. VASI is not indicated for RWY 6.

92. (Refer to Figure 72 on page 495.) At which location or condition does the IGN.JUDDS2 arrival begin?

    A. JUDDS intersection.

    B. IGN VORTAC.

    C. BRISS intersection.

Answer (B) is correct. *(ACL)*
    DISCUSSION: The IGN.JUDDS2 arrival on Fig. 72 indicates "from over Kingston VORTAC via R-112 ...." Thus, the JUDDS2 arrival begins over the Kingston (IGN) VORTAC.
    Answer (A) is incorrect. The JUDDS INT. is in the middle of the arrival route. Answer (C) is incorrect. The BRISS INT. is in the middle of the arrival route.

93. (Refer to Figure 72 on page 495.) How many precision approach procedures are published for Bradley International Airport?

    A. One.

    B. Three.

    C. Four.

Answer (B) is correct. *(A/FD)*
    DISCUSSION: To determine the number of precision approaches at Bradley International Airport, check the appropriate *Airport/Facility Directory*, which is reproduced in Fig. 72. At the end of the *A/FD*, note ILS/DMEs for RWY 6, RWY 33, and RWY 24.
    Answer (A) is incorrect. There are three, not one, ILSs. Answer (C) is incorrect. There are three, not four, ILSs.

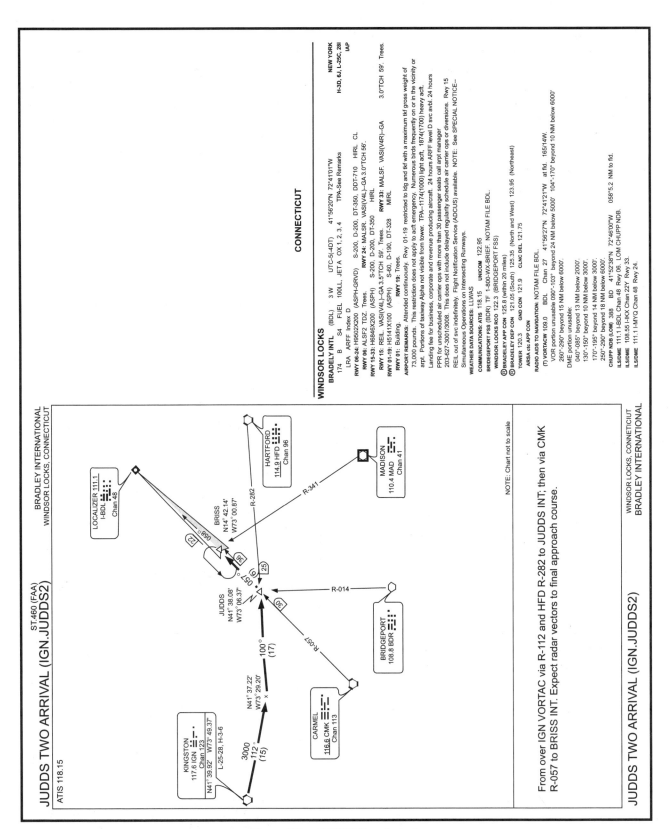

Figure 72. – JUDDS Two Arrival.

11.8 HLN to BIL

Questions 94 through 109 pertain to an IFR flight from Helena Regional Airport, Helena, Montana, to the Billings Logan International Airport, Billings, Montana.

The route of flight is given in block 8 on the flight plan portion of Fig. 74 on page 497. Information that pertains to your aircraft is given on the bottom portion of Fig. 74. The partially completed flight planning log is given in Fig. 75 on page 498.

The figures provided for this flight are listed below and are presented throughout the sequence of questions, except for Fig. 78, which is provided in color on page 423.

94. (Refer to Figure 74 on page 497 and Legend 26 on page 428.) What aircraft equipment code should be entered in block 3 of the flight plan?

A. T.

B. U.

C. A.

Answer (C) is correct. *(AIM Para 5-1-8)*

DISCUSSION: In block 3 of the flight plan, you enter the designation of the aircraft followed by a slash (/) and a letter for the equipment code. Fig. 74 indicates that you have a DME and transponder with Mode C, which requires code A. (See Legend 26.)

Answer (A) is incorrect. T indicates only a transponder with no Mode C. Answer (B) is incorrect. U indicates only a transponder with Mode C.

95. (Refer to Figure 74 on page 497, Figure 75 on page 498, Figure 76 on page 499, Figure 77 on page 500, and Figure 78 on page 423.) Determine the time to be entered in block 10 of the flight plan. (Refer to the FD excerpt below, and use the wind entry closest to the flight planned altitude.)

Route of flight..........................Figs. 74, 75, 76, 77, & 78
Flight log & MAG VAR..Fig. 75
VOR indications and
  Excerpts from AFD...Fig. 76

FT	6000	9000	12000	18000
BIL	2414	2422+11	2324+05	2126-11

A. 1 hour 15 minutes.

B. 1 hour 20 minutes.

C. 1 hour 25 minutes.

Answer (C) is correct. *(IFH Chap 10)*

DISCUSSION: To determine the estimated time en route to be entered in block 10, you must complete the flight planning log in Fig. 75. Using the wind side of your flight computer, determine groundspeeds as shown in the table below.

Remember that winds are given in true direction and must be converted to magnetic. Fig. 75 shows a variation of 18°E. Use the wind at 12,000 ft. (which is closest to the planned altitude of 11,000 ft.): 230° – 18°E var. = 212° at 24 kt.

	Distance	MC	Wind (Mag)	Ground- speed	Time
VESTS INT.	X	X	X	X	:15:00G
BZN VOR/DME	44	140°	212/24	151	:17:29
VOR COP	13	110°	212/24	163	:04:47
VORTAC					
LVM VORTAC	20	063°	212/24	180	:06:40
REEPO INT.	39	067°	212/24	179	:13:04
BIL VORTAC	38	069°	212/24	178	:12:49
Approach and					
Landing	X	X	X	X	:15:00G
					1:24:49

G = Given

Answer (A) is incorrect. An ETE of 1 hr. 15 min. requires a TAS of 195 kt., not 160 kt. Answer (B) is incorrect. An ETE of 1 hr. 20 min. requires a TAS of 175 kt., not 160 kt.

96. (Refer to Figure 74 below.) What CAS should be used to obtain the filed TAS at the flight planned altitude if the outside air temperature is +5°C?

A. 129 KCAS.

B. 133 KCAS.

C. 139 KCAS.

Answer (B) is correct. *(PHAK Chap 15)*
   DISCUSSION: In the center of the slide rule side of your flight computer, on the right side, put the air temperature of +5°C over the altitude of 11,000 ft. (from block 7 of the flight plan). On the outer scale, find TAS of 160 (from block 4), which is over calibrated airspeed on the inner scale of 133 KCAS.
   Answer (A) is incorrect. Obtaining 129 KCAS would result in a TAS of 156 kt., not 133 kt. Answer (C) is incorrect. Obtaining 139 KCAS would result in a TAS of 168 kt., not 133 kt.

Form Approved: OMB No. 2120-0034

U.S. DEPARTMENT OF TRANSPORTATION FEDERAL AVIATION ADMINISTRATION **FLIGHT PLAN**	(FAA USE ONLY)	☐ PILOT BRIEFING ☐ STOPOVER	☐ VNR	TIME STARTED	SPECIALIST INITIALS

1. TYPE		2. AIRCRAFT IDENTIFICATION	3. AIRCRAFT TYPE/ SPECIAL EQUIPMENT	4. TRUE AIRSPEED	5. DEPARTURE POINT	6. DEPARTURE TIME		7. CRUISING ALTITUDE
	VFR					PROPOSED (Z)	ACTUAL (Z)	
X	IFR	N242T	C310/	160 KTS	HLN			11000
	DVFR							

8. ROUTE OF FLIGHT
STAKK2, V365 BZN, V86

9. DESTINATION (Name of airport and city) LOGAN INTL. AIRPORT (BIL)	10. EST. TIME ENROUTE		11. REMARKS
	HOURS	MINUTES	

12. FUEL ON BOARD		13. ALTERNATE AIRPORT(S)	14. PILOTS NAME, ADDRESS & TELEPHONE NUMBER & AIRCRAFT HOME BASE	15. NUMBER ABOARD
HOURS	MINUTES			
		N/A	17. DESTINATION CONTACT/TELEPHONE (OPTIONAL)	2

16. COLOR OF AIRCRAFT RED/BLACK/WHITE	CIVIL AIRCRAFT PILOTS. FAR Part 91 requires you file an IFR flight plan to operate under instrument flight rules in controlled airspace. Failure to file could result in a civil penalty not to exceed $1,000 for each violation (Section 901 of the Federal Aviation Act of 1958, as amended). Filing of a VFR flight plan is recommended as a good operating practice. See also Part 99 for requirements concerning DVFR flight plans.

FAA Form 7233-1 (8-82)   CLOSE VFR FLIGHT PLAN WITH _____ FSS ON ARRIVAL

AIRCRAFT INFORMATION

MAKE Cessna   MODEL 310R

N 242T V_{so} 72

AIRCRAFT EQUIPMENT/STATUS**

**NOTE: X= OPERATIVE   INOP= INOPERATIVE   N/A= NOT APPLICABLE

TRANSPONDER: X (MODE C) X ILS: (LOCALIZER) X (GLIDE SLOPE) INOP

VOR NO.1 X (NO.2) X ADF: X RNAV: N/A

VERTICAL PATH COMPUTER: N/A DME: X

MARKER BEACON: X (AUDIO) X   (VISUAL) X

Figure 74. – Flight Plan and Aircraft Information.

FLIGHT LOG

HELENA REGIONAL AIRPORT TO BILLINGS LOGAN INTL.

CHECK POINTS		ROUTE	COURSE	WIND	SPEED-KTS		DIST	TIME		FUEL	
FROM	TO	ALTITUDE		TEMP	TAS	GS	NM	LEG	TOT	LEG	TOT
HLN	VESTS	STAKK2 CLIMB	103°					:15:0			
	BZN	V365 11000	140°		160						
	LVM	V86 11000	110° 063°								
	REEPO	V86 11000	067°								
	BIL	V86	069°								
APPROACH & LANDING											
	LOGAN INTL							:15:0			

OTHER DATA:
NOTE: MAG. VAR. 18° E.

FLIGHT SUMMARY		
TIME	FUEL (LB)	
		EN ROUTE
		RESERVE
		MISSED APPR.
		TOTAL

Figure 75. – Flight Planning Log.

97. (Refer to Figure 76 on page 499.) Which indication would be an acceptable accuracy check of both VOR receivers when the aircraft is located on the VOR receiver checkpoint at the Helena Regional Airport?

    A. A.

    B. B.

    C. C.

98. (Refer to Figure 76 on page 499 and Figure 77 on page 500.) Which en route low altitude navigation chart would cover the proposed routing at the BOZEMAN VORTAC?

    A. L-2.

    B. L-7.

    C. L-9.

Answer (C) is correct. *(ACL)*
    DISCUSSION: To determine the VOR receiver checkpoint at the Helena Regional Airport, consult the VOR receiver check table on Fig. 76. The checkpoint is on TWY (taxiway) E, midway between TWY C and RWY 27, and is on R-237 of Helena VORTAC. Thus, the RMI should show the tails of both needles on 237°, ±4°.
    Answer (A) is incorrect. The expected indication when using a VOT, not a ground VOR checkpoint would be R-180 ±4°. Answer (B) is incorrect. The tail, not the head, of the RMI needle indicates the radial.

Answer (C) is correct. *(ACL)*
    DISCUSSION: On Fig. 77, Bozeman VOR/DME is in the planview in the lower right corner. Below the frequency box, the notation L-9 is the number of the appropriate en route low-altitude navigation chart.
    Answer (A) is incorrect. Bozeman VOR/DME is found on L-9, not L-2. Answer (B) is incorrect. Bozeman VOR/DME is found on L-9, not L-7.

HELENA REGIONAL   (HLN)   2 NE   UTC-7(-6DT)   46°36'25"N 111°58'55"W   GREAT FALLS
  3873   B S4   FUEL 100LL JET A OX 1, 3   AOE ARFF Index B   H-IC, L-9B
  RWY 09-27: H9000X150 (ASPH-PFC)   S-100, D-160, DT-250   HIRL   IAP
    RWY 09: VASI(V4L)--GA 3.0°TCH 45'. Ground.   RWY 27: MALSR. VASI(V4L)--GA 3.0°TCH 55'. Rgt tfc.
  RWY 05-23: H94599X75 (ASPH-PFC)   S-21, D-30
    RWY 05: Road.   RWY 23: Fence. Rgt tfc.
  RWY 16-34: H2979X75 (ASPH)   S-21, D-30   MIRL
    RWY 34: Ground. Rgt tfc.
  AIRPORT REMARKS: Attended 1200-0800Z‡. East 2400' Taxiway C and first 900' Rwy 27 not visible from tower.
    Prior permission for unscheduled FAR 121 operation, Call 406-442-2821. AOE, 1 hour prior notice required.
    phone 449-1569 1500-0000Z‡, 0000-1500Z‡ 449-1024. Twys A;B; high speed C (between A and D)
    not available for air carrier use by acft with greater than 30 passenger seats. Rwy 16-34 and Rwy 05-23 (except
    between Rwy 09-27 and Twy D) not available for air carrier use by acft with greater than 30 passenger seats.
    When tower closed, ACTIVATE HORL Rwy 09-27 and MALSR Rwy 27----CTAF, when twr closed MIRL Rwy 16-34
    are off. Ldg fee for all acft over 12,500 lbs. NOTE: See SPECIAL NOTICE---Simultaneous Operations on
    Intersecting Runways.
  COMMUNICATIONS: CTAF 118.3   ATIS 120.4 (Mon-Fri 1300-0700Z‡, Sat-Sun 1300-0500Z‡)
    UNICOM 122.95
    GREAT FALLS FSS (GTF) TF 1-800-WX-BRIEF. NOTAM FILE HLN.
    RCO 122.2 122.1R 117.7T (GREAT FALLS FSS)
    APP/DEP CON 119.5 (Mon-Fri 1300-0700Z‡, Sat-Sun 1300-0500Z‡)
    SALT LAKE CENTER APP/DEP CON 133.4 (Mon-Fri 1700-1300Z‡, Sat-Sun 0500-1300Z‡)
    TOWER 118.3 (Mon-Fri 1300-0700Z‡, Sat-Sun 1300-0500Z‡)   GND CON 121.9
  RADIO AIDS TO NAVIGATION: NOTAM FILE HLN.
    (H) VORTAC 117.7   HLN Chan 124   46°36'25"N 111°57'10"W   254° 1.2 NM to fld.   3810/16E.
      VORTAC unusable:
        006°-090° beyond 25 NM below 11,000'   091°-120° beyond 20 NM below 16,000'
        121°-240° beyond 25 NM below 10,000'   355°-006° beyond 15 NM below 17,500'
        241°-320° beyond 25 NM below 10,000'
    CAPITOL NDB (HW) 317   CVP   46°36'24"N 111°56'11"W   254° 1.9 NM to fld.
      NDB unmonitored when tower closed.
    HAUSER NDB (MHW) 386   HAU   46°34'08"N 111°45'26"W   268° 9.6 NM to fld.
    ILS 110.1 I-HLN Rwy 27 ILS unmonitored when tower closed.

VOR RECEIVER CHECK

Facility Name (Arpt Name)	Freq/Ident	Type Check Pt. Gnd, AB/ALT	Azimuth from Fac. Mag	Dist. from Fac. N.M.	Check Point Description
Helena (Helena Regional)	117.7/HLN	G	237	0.7	On Twy E midway between Twy C and Rwy 27.
Kalispell (Glacier Park Intl)	108.4/FCA	A/4000	316	6.4	Over apch end Rwy 29.
Lewistown (Lewistown Muni)	112.2/LWT	A/5200	072	5.4	Over apch end Rwy 07.
Livingston	116.1/LVM	A/6500	234	5.5	Over northern most radio twr NE of the city.
Miles City (Frank Wiley Field)	112.1/MLS	G	036	4.2	On twy leading to Rwy 30.
Missoula (Missoula Intl)	112.8/MSO	G	340	0.6	On edge of ramp in front of Admin Building.

Figure 76. – VOR Indications and Excerpts from Airport/Facility Directory (HLN).

Figure 77. – STAKK TWO DEPARTURE.

99. (Refer to Figure 77 on page 500.) At which point does the basic instrument departure procedure terminate?

A. When Helena Departure Control establishes radar contact.

B. At STAKK intersection.

C. Over the BOZEMAN VOR.

Answer (B) is correct. *(ACL)*
   DISCUSSION: On the STAKK Two Departure in Fig. 77, the departure route description at the bottom indicates that, for takeoffs from RWY 9 and RWY 27, you should climb eastbound on HLN R-087 to cross STAKK INT. at or above 10,200 ft. "Thence via transition."
   Answer (A) is incorrect. Helena Departure Control will establish contact shortly after you get off the runway. Answer (C) is incorrect. The BOZEMAN VOR is the end of the BOZEMAN transition, not the basic DP.

100. (Refer to Figure 77 on page 500 and Legend 16 on page 292.) Using an average ground speed of 140 knots, what minimum rate of climb would meet the required minimum climb rate per NM as specified on the instrument departure procedure?

A. 350 feet per minute.

B. 475 feet per minute.

C. 700 feet per minute.

Answer (C) is correct. *(ACL)*
   DISCUSSION: On Fig. 77 on the DP, the note to the left indicates a minimum climb rate of 300 ft. per NM. To convert this to a climb rate (fpm), use Legend 16. Find the required climb rate of 300 ft. per NM on the left margin and move right to the 140-kt. groundspeed column to determine a rate of climb of 700 fpm.
   Answer (A) is incorrect. A 350-fpm climb rate at an average groundspeed of 140 kt. would result in a climb rate of less than 200 ft. per NM, not 300 ft. per NM. Answer (B) is incorrect. A 475-fpm climb rate at an average groundspeed of 140 kt. would result in a climb rate of approximately 200 ft. per NM, not 300 ft. per NM.

101. (Refer to Figure 78 on page 423.) When eastbound on V86 between Whitehall and Livingston, the minimum altitude that you should cross BZN is

A. 9,300 feet.

B. 10,400 feet.

C. 8,500 feet.

Answer (A) is correct. *(ACL)*
   DISCUSSION: On Fig. 78, the Bozeman (BZN) VOR/DME has a flag with an X, indicating a minimum crossing altitude (MCA). Near the center of the diagram, above the BZN VOR/DME communications box, is MCA V86-365 9300 SE. Thus, the minimum crossing altitude over the BZN VOR/DME for a flight southeast bound on V86 is 9,300 ft. MSL.
   Answer (B) is incorrect. This is the MEA on V86-365 between BZN and LVM, not the MCA at BZN VOR/DME. Answer (C) is incorrect. This is the MEA on V86 prior to BZN VOR/DME. The MEA is not the MCA when an MCA is specified.

102. (Refer to Figure 78 on page 423.) What is the maximum altitude that you may flight plan an IFR flight on V-86 EASTBOUND between BOZEMAN and BILLINGS VORTACs?

A. 14,500 feet MSL.

B. 17,000 feet MSL.

C. 18,000 feet MSL.

Answer (B) is correct. *(ACL)*
   DISCUSSION: Victor airways consist of altitudes from 1,200 ft. AGL up to, but not including, 18,000 ft. MSL. The jet route is from 18,000 ft. MSL through FL 450. Thus, the maximum altitude on an airway is 17,000 ft. MSL because IFR flight is conducted at cardinal altitudes: odd numbers for eastbound and even for westbound.
   Answer (A) is incorrect. The altitude of 14,500 ft. MSL (i.e., thousand-foot plus 500 ft.) is a VFR, not IFR, cruising altitude. Answer (C) is incorrect. Victor airways extend up to, but do not include, 18,000 ft. MSL. Jet routes begin at 18,000 ft. MSL (FL 180).

103. (Refer to Figure 78 on page 423.) What is the minimum crossing altitude over the BOZEMAN VORTAC for a flight southeast bound on V86?

A. 8,500 feet MSL.

B. 9,300 feet MSL.

C. 9,700 feet MSL.

Answer (B) is correct. *(ACL)*
   DISCUSSION: On Fig. 78, the Bozeman (BZN) VOR/DME (it is not a VORTAC) has a flag with an X, indicating a minimum crossing altitude (MCA). Near the center of the page, above the BZN VOR/DME communications box, is MCA V86-365 9300 SE. Thus, the minimum crossing altitude over the BZN VOR/DME for a flight southeast bound on V86 is 9,300 ft. MSL.
   Answer (A) is incorrect. This is the MEA on V86 prior to BZN VOR/DME. The MEA is not the MCA when an MCA is specified. Answer (C) is incorrect. This is the MEA on V365, not the MCA at BZN VOR/DME.

104. (Refer to Figure 79 below, and Figure 78 on page 423.) What is your position relative to the VOR COP southeast bound on V86 between the BOZEMAN and LIVINGSTON VORTACs? The No. 1 VOR is tuned to 116.1 and the No. 2 VOR is tuned to 112.2.

A. Past the LVM R-246 and west of the BZN R-110.

B. Approaching the LVM R-246 and west of the BZN R-110.

C. Past the LVM R-246 and east of the BZN R-110.

Answer (C) is correct. *(IFH Chap 9)*
 DISCUSSION: The tail of an RMI indicates the radial. You are on a 130° heading, so you are southeast bound. VOR-2 indicates R-105 of BZN (112.2). VOR-1 indicates on R-239 of LVM (116.1). Because you are on R-105 of BZN, you are to the east of BZN R-110. Because you are on R-239 of LVM, you have passed the LVM R-246.
 Answer (A) is incorrect. You are east, not west, of the BZN R-110. Answer (B) is incorrect. You are past, not approaching, the LVM R-246, and east, not west, of the BZN R-110.

Figure 79. – RMI Indicator.

105. (Refer to Figure 80 on page 503.) What is the TDZE for landing on RWY 27R?

A. 3,649 feet MSL.

B. 3,514 feet MSL.

C. 3,450 feet MSL.

Answer (B) is correct. *(ACL)*
 DISCUSSION: On the IAP chart, the TDZE is depicted in the airport diagram near the approach end of the landing runway (RWY 27R) as 3,514 ft. MSL.
 Answer (A) is incorrect. This is the airport elevation, not the TDZE. Answer (C) is incorrect. This is not a relevant altitude at an airport with a 3,649 ft. MSL elevation.

106. (Refer to Figure 74 on page 497 and Figure 80 on page 503.) Which aircraft approach category should be used for a circling approach for a landing on RWY 27?

A. A.

B. B.

C. C.

Answer (B) is correct. *(ACL)*
 DISCUSSION: Approach categories are based upon 1.3 V_{S0} and weight. Fig. 74 indicates V_{S0} of the Cessna 310 is 72. Using the general rule, 1.3 V_{S0} is 93.6, which is Category B (91 to 120 kt.).
 Answer (A) is incorrect. Category A is for approach speeds less than 91 kt. Answer (C) is incorrect. Category C is for approach speeds from 121 to 140 kt.

107. (Refer to Figure 80 on page 503.) How many initial approach fixes serve the VOR/DME RWY 27R (Billings Logan) approach procedure?

A. Three.

B. Four.

C. Five.

Answer (B) is correct. *(ACL)*
 DISCUSSION: Initial approach fixes are indicated by the designation "(IAF)" on instrument approach charts (Fig. 80). Note that there is an IAF at the 16 DME arc at R-157 INT and also at the R-040 INT. The Billings VORTAC is also indicated as an IAF, as is MUSTY INT.
 Answer (A) is incorrect. The VOR/DME RWY 27R approach has four, not three, IAFs. Answer (C) is incorrect. The VOR/DME RWY 27R approach has four, not five, IAFs.

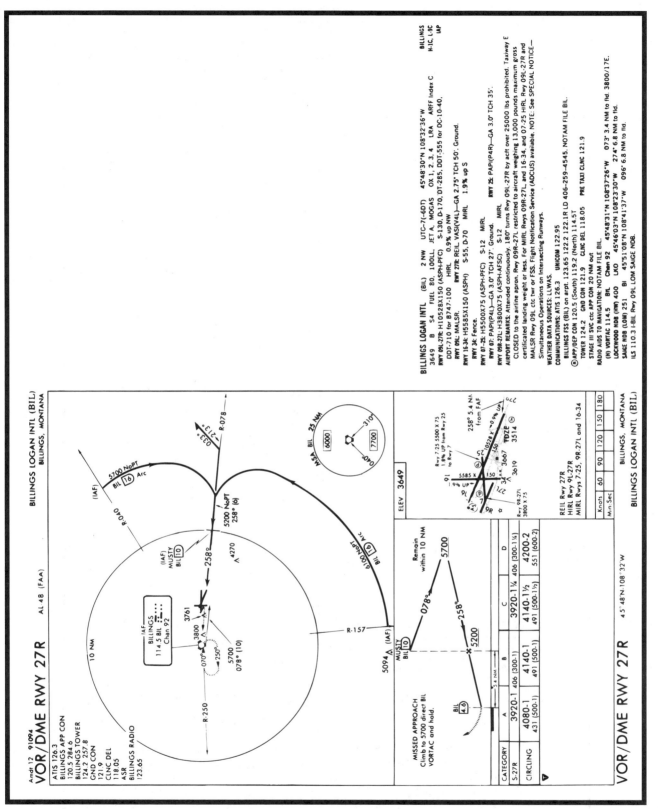

Figure 80. – VOR/DME RWY 27R and Airport/Facility Directory (BIL).

108. (Refer to Figure 211 below.) At which minimum altitude should you cross the STAKK intersection?

    A. 11,800 feet MSL.

    B. 10,800 feet MSL.

    C. 10,200 feet MSL.

Answer (C) is correct. *(ACL)*
    DISCUSSION: On the STAKK Two Departure (Fig. 211), the departure route description for either runway states, "Cross STAKK at or above 10,200'." Thus, the minimum altitude at which you should cross the STAKK INT. is 10,200 ft. MSL.
    Answer (A) is incorrect. This is not a pertinent altitude in this DP. Answer (B) is incorrect. This is not a pertinent altitude in this DP.

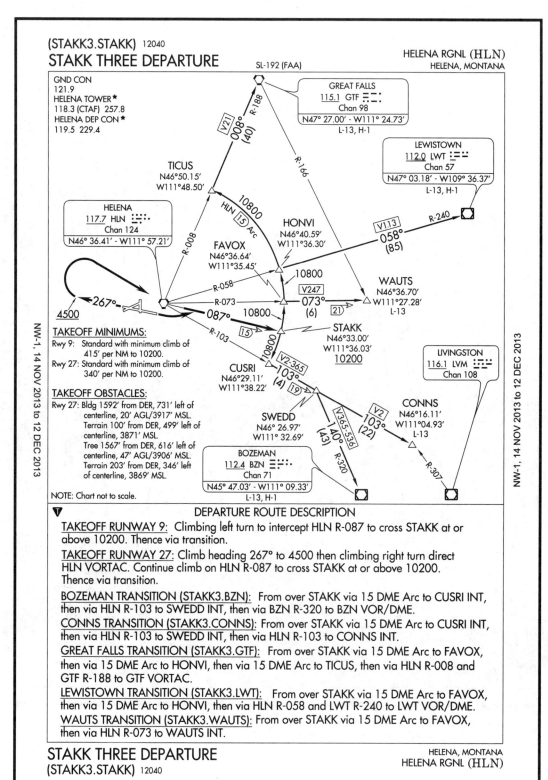

Figure 211.

109. (Refer to Figure 213 below.) How many initial approach fixes serve the VOR/DME RWY 28R (Billings Logan) approach procedure?

- A. Three.
- B. Four.
- C. Five.

Answer (A) is correct. *(IPH Chap 3)*
 DISCUSSION: Three initial approach fixes are associated with the VOR/DME RWY 28R approach depicted in Fig. 213. They are Pocov at 16 DME on the Billings 333 radial, Musty at 10 DME on the 082 radial, and Nelwn at 16 DME on the 160 radial. Each is labeled "IAF" on the overhead view of the approach plate.
 Answer (B) is incorrect. Three initial approach fixes are associated with the VOR/DME RWY 28R approach, not four. Answer (C) is incorrect. Three initial approach fixes are associated with the VOR/DME RWY 28R approach, not five.

Figure 213.

506

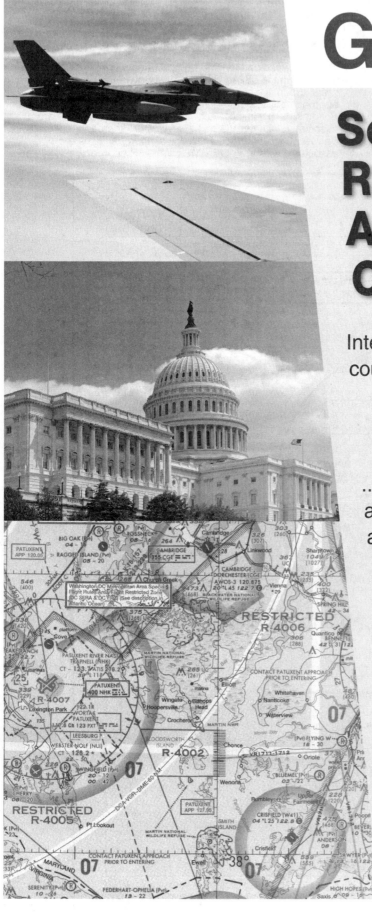

APPENDIX A
INSTRUMENT RATING PRACTICE TEST

The following 60 questions have been randomly selected from the airplane questions in our instrument rating test bank. You will be referred to figures (charts, tables, etc.) throughout this book. Be careful not to consult the answers or answer explanations when you look for and at the figures. Topical coverage in this practice test is similar to that of the FAA instrument rating-airplane knowledge test. Use the correct answer listing on page 512 to grade your practice test.

1. (Refer to Figure 50 on page 460.) What CAS must be used to maintain the filed TAS at the flight planned altitude? (Temperature 0°C.)

A — 136 KCAS.
B — 140 KCAS.
C — 147 KCAS.

2. (Refer to Figure 52 on page 463 and Legend 16 on page 292.) Using an average ground speed of 100 knots, what minimum rate of climb would meet the required minimum climb rate per NM as specified by the instrument departure procedure?

A — 425 feet per minute.
B — 580 feet per minute.
C — 642 feet per minute.

3. (Refer to Figure 51 on page 461, Figure 50 on page 460, Figure 52 on page 463, and Figure 53 on page 419.) Determine the time to be entered in block 10 of the flight plan. (Refer to the FD excerpt below, and use the wind entry closest to the flight planned altitude.)

Route of flight............................Figs. 50, 51, 52, & 53
Flight log and MAG VAR.................................... Fig. 51
HABUT ONE DEPARTURE
  and Excerpt from AFD.................................. Fig. 52

FT	3000	6000	9000
SBA	0610	2115+05	2525+00

A — 43 minutes.
B — 46 minutes.
C — 51 minutes.

4. Under which condition will pressure altitude be equal to true altitude?

A — When the atmospheric pressure is 29.92" Hg.
B — When standard atmospheric conditions exist.
C — When indicated altitude is equal to the pressure altitude.

5. If no MCA is specified, what is the lowest altitude for crossing a radio fix, beyond which a higher minimum applies?

A — The MEA at which the fix is approached.
B — The MRA at which the fix is approached.
C — The MOCA for the route segment beyond the fix.

6. (Refer to Figure 140 on page 220, and Figure 139 on page 221.) Which displacement from the localizer and glide slope at the 1.9 NM point is indicated?

A — 710 feet to the left of the localizer centerline and 140 feet below the glide slope.
B — 710 feet to the right of the localizer centerline and 140 feet above the glide slope.
C — 430 feet to the right of the localizer centerline and 28 feet above the glide slope.

7. (Refer to Figure 50 on page 460, and Legend 26 on page 428.) What aircraft equipment code should be entered in block 3 of the flight plan?

A — I.
B — T.
C — U.

8. (Refer to Figure 96 on page 100, and Figure 97 on page 99.) To which aircraft position does HSI presentation "D" correspond?

A — 1
B — 10
C — 2

9. (Refer to Figure 87 on page 424.) At STRUT intersection headed eastbound, ATC instructs you to hold west on the 10 DME fix west of LCH on V306, standard turns. What entry procedure is recommended?

A — Direct.
B — Teardrop.
C — Parallel.

10. (Refer to Figure 53 on page 419.) What is indicated by the inverse "H" symbol in the radio aids to navigation box for SAN MARCUS VORTAC?

A — VOR with TACAN compatible DME.
B — The availability of HIWAS.
C — The VOR has a high altitude SSV Class Designation.

11. (Refer to Figure 18 on page 377.) The 24-Hour Low Level Significant Weather Prog at 12Z indicates that southwestern Virginia will likely experience

A — ceilings less than 1,000 feet, visibility less than 3 miles.
B — clear sky and visibility greater than 6 miles.
C — ceilings 1,000 to 3,000 feet and visibility 3 to 5 miles.

12. (Refer to Figure 2 on page 374.) What approximate wind direction, speed, and temperature (relative to ISA) should a pilot expect when planning for a flight over ALB at FL 270?

A — 270° magnetic at 97 knots; ISA –4°C.
B — 260° true at 110 knots; ISA +5°C.
C — 275° true at 97 knots; ISA +4°C.

13. (Refer to Figure 124 on page 257.) What options are available concerning the teardrop course reversal for LOC RWY 35 approach to Duncan/Halliburton Field?

A — If a course reversal is required, only the teardrop can be executed.
B — The point where the turn is begun and the type and rate of turn are optional.
C — A normal procedure turn may be made if the 10 DME limit is not exceeded.

14. (Refer to Figure 126 on page 261.) What landing minimums apply for a 14 CFR Part 91 operator at Dothan, AL using a category C aircraft during a circling LOC 31 approach at 120 knots? (DME available.)

A — MDA 860 feet MSL and visibility 2 SM.
B — MDA 860 feet MSL and visibility 1 and 1/2 SM.
C — MDA 720 feet MSL and visibility 3/4 SM.

15. (Refer to Figure 129 on page 265.) What indication should you get when it is time to turn in bound while in the procedure turn at LABER?

A — 4 DME miles from LABER.
B — 10 DME miles from the MAP.
C — 12 DME miles from LIT VORTAC.

16. (Refer to Figure 55 on page 459.) Under which condition should a missed approach procedure be initiated if the runway environment (Paso Robles Municipal Airport) is not in sight?

A — After descending to 1,440 feet MSL.
B — After descent to 1,440 feet or reaching the 1 NM DME, whichever occurs first.
C — When you reach the established missed approach point and determine the visibility is less than 1 mile.

17. (Refer to Figure 12 on page 391.) What is the approximate wind direction and velocity at CVG at 34,000 feet (see arrow A)?

A — 040°/35 knots.
B — 097°/40 knots.
C — 230°/35 knots.

18. (Refer to Figure 144 on page 51.) Which illustration indicates a coordinated turn?

A — 3.
B — 1.
C — 2.

19. (Refer to Figure 108 on page 84.) Where should the bearing pointer be located relative to the wing-tip reference to maintain the 16 DME range in a left-hand arc with a left crosswind component?

A — Ahead of the left wing-tip reference for the VOR-2.
B — Ahead of the right wing-tip reference for the VOR-1.
C — Behind the left wing-tip reference for the VOR-2.

20. (Refer to Figure 54 on page 462, and Figure 52 on page 463.) What is the aircraft's position relative to the HABUT intersection? (The VOR-2 is tuned to 116.5.)

A — South of the localizer and past the GVO R-163.
B — North of the localizer and approaching the GVO R-163.
C — South of the localizer and approaching the GVO R-163.

21. (Refer to Figure 67 on page 405, and Figure 65 on page 421.) What is the significance of the symbol at GRICE intersection?

A — It signifies a localizer-only approach is available at Harry P. Williams Memorial.
B — The localizer has an additional navigation function.
C — GRICE intersection also serves as the FAF for the ILS approach procedure to Harry P. Williams Memorial.

22. (Refer to Figure 91 on page 426 and Legend 23 on page 412.) What is the function of the Great Falls RCO (Yellowstone vicinity)?

A — Long range communications outlet for Great Falls Center.
B — Remote communications outlet for Great Falls FSS.
C — Satellite remote controlled by Salt Lake Center with limited service.

23. Conditions that determine pitch attitude required to maintain level flight are

A — flightpath, wind velocity, and angle of attack.
B — airspeed, air density, wing design, and angle of attack.
C — relative wind, pressure altitude, and vertical lift component.

24. (Refer to Figure 138 on page 148.) What night operations, if any, are authorized between the approach end of the runway and the threshold lights?

A — No aircraft operations are permitted short of the threshold lights.

B — Only taxi operations are permitted in the area short of the threshold lights.

C — Taxi and takeoff operations are permitted, providing the takeoff operations are toward the visible green threshold lights.

25. (Refer to Figure 136 on page 155.) Which illustration would a pilot observe if the aircraft is "slightly high" (3.2°) on the glidepath?

A — 8.

B — 9.

C — 11.

26. (Refer to Figure 93 on page 173.) What is the maximum altitude that Class G airspace will exist? (Does not include airspace less than 1,500 feet AGL.)

A — 18,000 feet MSL.

B — 14,500 feet MSL.

C — 14,000 feet MSL.

27. What type clouds can be expected when an unstable air mass is forced to ascend a mountain slope?

A — Layered clouds with little vertical development.

B — Stratified clouds with considerable associated turbulence.

C — Clouds with extensive vertical development.

28. Which instrument is considered primary for power as the airspeed reaches the desired value during change of airspeed in a level turn?

A — Airspeed indicator.

B — Attitude indicator.

C — Altimeter.

29. Which procedure applies to instrument departure procedures?

A — Instrument departure clearances will not be issued unless requested by the pilot.

B — The pilot in command must accept an instrument departure procedure when issued by ATC.

C — If an instrument departure procedure is accepted, the pilot must possess a textual or graphic description.

30. Which DME indication should you receive when you are directly over a VORTAC site at approximately 6,000 feet AGL?

A — 0

B — 1

C — 1.3

31. (Refer to Figure 55 on page 459.) As a guide in making range corrections, how many degrees of relative bearing change should be used for each one-half-mile deviation from the desired arc?

A — 2° to 3°.

B — 5° maximum.

C — 10° to 20°.

32. What should be the indication on the magnetic compass as you roll into a standard rate turn to the right from a westerly heading in the Northern Hemisphere?

A — The compass will initially show a turn in the opposite direction, then turn to a northerly indication but lagging behind the actual heading of the aircraft.

B — The compass will remain on a westerly heading for a short time, then gradually catch up to the actual heading of the aircraft.

C — The compass will indicate the approximate correct magnetic heading if the roll into the turn is smooth.

33. You may cancel an IFR flight plan

A — at any time as long as you advise ATC.

B — only in an emergency.

C — if VMC outside Class A airspace.

34. What situation is most conducive to the formation of radiation fog?

A — Warm, moist air over low, flatland areas on clear, calm nights.

B — Moist, tropical air moving over cold, offshore water.

C — The movement of cold air over much warmer water.

35. Standing lenticular clouds, in mountainous areas, indicate

A — an inversion.

B — unstable air.

C — turbulence.

36. (Refer to Figure 95 on page 93.) On which radial is the aircraft as indicated by the No. 1 NAV?

A — R-175.

B — R-165.

C — R-345.

37. The rate of descent required to stay on the ILS glide slope

A — must be increased if the ground speed is decreased.

B — will remain constant if the indicated airspeed remains constant.

C — must be decreased if the ground speed is decreased.

38. Errors in both pitch and bank indication on an attitude indicator are usually at a maximum as the aircraft rolls out of a

A — 180° turn.
B — 270° turn.
C — 360° turn.

39. What instruments are considered supporting bank instruments during a straight, stabilized climb at a constant rate?

A — Attitude indicator and turn coordinator.
B — Heading indicator and attitude indicator.
C — Heading indicator and turn coordinator.

40. AIRMETs are issued on a scheduled basis every

A — 15 minutes after the hour only.
B — 15 minutes until the AIRMET is canceled.
C — six hours.

41. When making an instrument approach at the selected alternate airport, what landing minimums apply?

A — Standard alternate minimums (600-2 or 800-2).
B — The IFR alternate minimums listed for that airport.
C — The landing minimums published for the type of procedure selected.

42. (Refer to Figure 113 on page 235.) You receive this ATC clearance:

"...CLEARED TO THE XYZ VORTAC. HOLD NORTH ON THE THREE SIX ZERO RADIAL, LEFT TURNS..."

What is the recommended procedure to enter the holding pattern?

A — Parallel only.
B — Direct only.
C — Teardrop only.

43. When on a VFR-on-Top clearance, the cruising altitude is based on

A — true course.
B — magnetic course.
C — magnetic heading.

44. For IFR planning purposes, what are the compulsory reporting points when using VOR/DME or VORTAC fixes to define a direct route not on established airways?

A — Fixes selected to define the route.
B — There are no compulsory reporting points unless advised by ATC.
C — At the changeover points.

45. To preserve night vision, the most appropriate cockpit lighting is

A — Reducing the interior lighting intensity to a minimum level.
B — The use of regular white light, such as a flashlight, will not impair night adaptation.
C — Increase the interior intensity to slightly above the outside level.

46. Which precipitation type normally indicates freezing rain at higher altitudes?

A — Snow.
B — Hail.
C — Ice pellets.

47. The local altimeter setting should be used by all pilots in a particular area, primarily to provide for

A — the cancellation of altimeter error due to nonstandard temperatures aloft.
B — better vertical separation of aircraft.
C — more accurate terrain clearance in mountainous areas.

48. Which publication covers the procedures required for aircraft accident and incident reporting responsibilities for pilots?

A — FAR Part 61.
B — FAR Part 91.
C — NTSB Part 830.

49. What minimum weather conditions must be forecast for your ETA at an alternate airport, that has only a VOR approach with standard alternate minimums, for the airport to be listed as an alternate on the IFR flight plan?

A — 800-foot ceiling and 1 statute mile visibility.
B — 800-foot ceiling and 2 statute miles visibility.
C — 1,000-foot ceiling and visibility to allow descent from minimum en route altitude (MEA), approach, and landing under basic VFR.

50. Which procedure should you follow if you experience two-way communications failure while holding at a holding fix with an EFC time? (The holding fix is not the same as the approach fix.)

A — Depart the holding fix to arrive at the approach fix as close as possible to the EFC time.
B — Depart the holding fix at the EFC time.
C — Proceed immediately to the approach fix and hold until EFC.

51. In the event of two-way radio communications failure while operating on an IFR clearance in VFR conditions, the pilot should continue

A — by the route assigned in the last ATC clearance received.

B — the flight under VFR and land as soon as practical.

C — the flight by the most direct route to the fix specified in the last clearance.

52. Prior to which operation must an IFR flight plan be filed and an appropriate ATC clearance received?

A — Flying by reference to instruments in controlled airspace.

B — Entering controlled airspace when IMC exists.

C — Takeoff when IFR weather conditions exist.

53. When may you obtain a contact approach?

A — ATC may assign a contact approach if VFR conditions exist or you report the runway in sight and are clear of clouds.

B — ATC may assign a contact approach if you are below the clouds and the visibility is at least 1 mile.

C — ATC will assign a contact approach only upon request if the reported visibility is at least 1 mile.

54. Assume this clearance is received:

"CLEARED FOR ILS RUNWAY 07 LEFT APPROACH, SIDE-STEP TO RUNWAY 07 RIGHT."

When would the pilot be expected to commence the side-step maneuver?

A — As soon as possible after the runway environment is in sight.

B — Any time after becoming aligned with the final approach course of Runway 07 left, and after passing the final approach fix.

C — After reaching the circling minimums for Runway 07 right.

55. When is an IFR flight plan required?

A — When less than VFR conditions exist in either Class E or Class G airspace and in Class A airspace.

B — In all Class E airspace when conditions are below VFR, in Class A airspace, and in defense zone airspace.

C — In Class E airspace when IMC exists or in Class A airspace.

56. To carry passengers for hire in an airplane on cross-country flights of more than 50 NM from the departure airport, the pilot in command is required to hold at least

A — a Category II pilot authorization.

B — a First-Class Medical certificate.

C — a Commercial Pilot Certificate with an instrument rating.

57. What indication should a pilot receive when a VOR station is undergoing maintenance and may be considered unreliable?

A — No coded identification, but possible navigation indications.

B — Coded identification, but no navigation indications.

C — A voice recording on the VOR frequency announcing that the VOR is out of service for maintenance.

58. What wind condition prolongs the hazards of wake turbulence on a landing runway for the longest period of time?

A — Direct headwind.

B — Direct tailwind.

C — Light quartering tailwind.

59. Which force, in the Northern Hemisphere, acts at a right angle to the wind and deflects it to the right until parallel to the isobars?

A — Centrifugal.

B — Pressure gradient.

C — Coriolis.

60. The Hazardous Inflight Weather Advisory Service (HIWAS) is a continuous broadcast over selected VORs of

A — SIGMETs, CONVECTIVE SIGMETs, AIRMETs, Severe Weather Forecast Alerts (AWW), and Center Weather Advisories.

B — SIGMETs, CONVECTIVE SIGMETs, AIRMETs, Wind Shear Advisories, and Severe Weather Forecast Alerts (AWW).

C — Wind Shear Advisories, Radar Weather Reports, SIGMETs, CONVECTIVE SIGMETs, AIRMETs, and Center Weather Advisories (CWA).

PRACTICE TEST LIST OF ANSWERS

The listing below gives the correct answers for your instrument rating practice knowledge test and the page number in this book on which you will find each question with the complete Gleim answer explanation.

Q. #	Answer	Page	Q. #	Answer	Page	Q. #	Answer	Page	Q. #	Answer	Page
1.	B	462	16.	C	458	31.	C	458	46.	C	340
2.	C	462	17.	C	390	32.	C	27	47.	B	32
3.	C	461	18.	A	51	33.	C	161	48.	C	134
4.	B	36	19.	A	84	34.	A	334	49.	B	127
5.	A	397	20.	B	462	35.	C	336	50.	B	169
6.	B	220	21.	B	405	36.	C	92	51.	B	401
7.	A	460	22.	B	410	37.	C	225	52.	B	130
8.	C	98	23.	B	54	38.	A	40	53.	C	213
9.	A	406	24.	C	148	39.	A	57	54.	A	232
10.	B	464	25.	B	154	40.	C	366	55.	C	123
11.	A	376	26.	B	172	41.	C	256	56.	C	119
12.	C	374	27.	C	331	42.	C	235	57.	A	88
13.	A	256	28.	A	60	43.	B	400	58.	C	156
14.	B	260	29.	C	294	44.	A	166	59.	C	328
15.	A	264	30.	B	79	45.	A	317	60.	A	366

APPENDIX B
INTERPOLATION

The following is a tutorial based on information that has appeared in the FAA's *Pilot's Handbook of Aeronautical Knowledge*. Interpolation is required in questions found in the following three subunits:

Study Unit 9 - "Aviation Weather Services"
Subunit 9.7, "Wind and Temperature Aloft Forecast (FB)" (pages 359, 373)

Study Unit 11 - "IFR Flights"
Subunit 11.1, "GJT to DRO" (page 430)
Subunit 11.4, "SBA to PRB" (page 458)

A.   To interpolate means to compute intermediate values between a series of given values.

1.   In many instances when performance is critical, an accurate determination of the performance values is the only acceptable means to enhance safe flight.

2.   Guessing to determine these values should be avoided.

B.   Interpolation is simple to perform if the method is understood. The following are examples of how to interpolate, or accurately determine the intermediate values, between a series of given values.

C.   The numbers in column A range from 10 to 30, and the numbers in column B range from 50 to 100. Determine the intermediate numerical value in column B that would correspond with an intermediate value of 20 placed in column A.

A	B
10	50
20	X = Unknown
30	100

1.   It can be visualized that 20 is halfway between 10 and 30; therefore, the corresponding value of the unknown number in column B would be halfway between 50 and 100, or 75.

D.   Many interpolation problems are more difficult to visualize than the preceding example; therefore, a systematic method must be used to determine the required intermediate value. The following describes one method that can be used.

1.   The numbers in column A range from 10 to 30 with intermediate values of 15, 20, and 25. Determine the intermediate numerical value in column B that would correspond with 15 in column A.

A	B
10	50
15	
20	
25	
30	100

2.   First, in column A, determine the relationship of 15 to the range between 10 and 30 as follows:

$$\frac{15 - 10}{30 - 10} = \frac{5}{20} \text{ or } 1/4$$

a.   It should be noted that 15 is 1/4 of the range between 10 and 30.

3. Now determine 1/4 of the range of column B between 50 and 100 as follows:

$$100 - 50 = 50$$
$$1/4 \text{ of } 50 = 12.5$$

    a. The answer 12.5 represents the number of units, but to arrive at the correct value, 12.5 must be added to the lower number in column B as follows:

$$50 + 12.5 = 62.5$$

4. The interpolation has been completed and 62.5 is the actual value that is 1/4 of the range of column B.

E. Another method of interpolation is shown below:

1. Using the same numbers as in the previous example, a proportion problem based on the relationship of the number can be set up.

$$
\begin{array}{cc}
A & B \\
\left.5\left[\begin{array}{l}10 \\ 15\end{array}\right.\right. & X\left[\begin{array}{l}50 \\ ?\end{array}\right. \\
20\left[\begin{array}{l} \\ 20 \quad 50 \\ 25 \\ 30\end{array}\right. & \left[\begin{array}{l} \\ \\ 100\end{array}\right.
\end{array}
$$

Proportion: $\dfrac{5}{20} = \dfrac{X}{50}$

$$20X = 250$$
$$X = 12.5$$

    a. The answer, 12.5, must be added to 50 to arrive at the actual value of 62.5.

F. The following example illustrates the use of interpolation applied to a problem dealing with one aspect of airplane performance:

Temperature (°F)	Takeoff Distance (ft.)
70	1,173
80	1,356

1. If a distance of 1,173 feet is required for takeoff when the temperature is 70°F and 1,356 feet is required at 80°F, what distance is required when the temperature is 75°F? The solution to the problem can be determined as follows:

$$
10\left[\begin{array}{l} 5\left[\begin{array}{l}70° \\ 75°\end{array}\right. \\ 80° \end{array}\right. 183\left[\begin{array}{l} X\left[\begin{array}{l}1,173 \\ ?\end{array}\right. \\ 1,356\end{array}\right.
$$

$$\frac{5}{10} = \frac{X}{183}$$
$$10X = 915$$
$$X = 91.5$$

    a. The answer, 91.5, must be added to 1,173 to arrive at the actual value of 1,264.5 ft.

FAA LISTING OF
LEARNING STATEMENT CODES

Reprinted below and on the following pages are all of the FAA's learning statement codes for pilots. These are the codes that will appear on your Airman Computer Test Report. See the example on page 15. Your test report will list the learning statement code of each question answered incorrectly. The statements are designed to represent the knowledge test topic areas in clear verbal terms and encourage applicants to study the entire area of identified weakness instead of merely studying a specific question area. You should discuss your test results with your CFI.

When you receive your Airman Computer Test Report, you can trace the learning statement codes listed on it to these pages to find out which topics you had difficulty with. To determine the knowledge area in which a particular question was incorrectly answered, compare the learning statement code(s) on your Airman Computer Test Report to the listing that follows. The total number of test items missed may differ from the number of learning statement codes shown on your test report because you may have missed more than one question in a certain knowledge area.

Additionally, you should trace the learning statement codes on your Airman Computer Test Report to our cross-reference listing of questions beginning on page 521. Determine which Gleim subunits you need to review.

The FAA will periodically revise the existing learning codes and add new ones. As Gleim learns about any changes, we will update our materials.

PLT001	Calculate a course intercept
PLT002	Calculate aircraft performance - airspeed
PLT003	Calculate aircraft performance - center of gravity
PLT004	Calculate aircraft performance - climb / descent / maneuvering
PLT005	Calculate aircraft performance - density altitude
PLT006	Calculate aircraft performance - glide
PLT007	Calculate aircraft performance - IAS
PLT008	Calculate aircraft performance - landing
PLT009	Calculate aircraft performance - turbine temperatures (MGT, EGT, ITT, T4, etc) / torque / horsepower
PLT010	Calculate aircraft performance - STAB TRIM
PLT011	Calculate aircraft performance - takeoff
PLT012	Calculate aircraft performance - time/speed/distance/course/fuel/wind
PLT013	Calculate crosswind / headwind components
PLT014	Calculate distance / bearing to a station
PLT015	Calculate flight performance / planning - range
PLT016	Calculate fuel - dump time / weight / volume / quantity / consumption
PLT017	Calculate L/D ratio
PLT018	Calculate load factor / stall speed / velocity / angle of attack
PLT019	Calculate pressure altitude
PLT020	Calculate turbulent air penetration
PLT021	Calculate weight and balance
PLT022	Define Aeronautical Decision Making (ADM)
PLT023	Define altitude - absolute / true / indicated / density / pressure
PLT024	Define atmospheric adiabatic process
PLT025	Define Bernoulli's principle
PLT026	Define ceiling
PLT027	Define coning
PLT028	Define crewmember
PLT029	Define critical phase of flight
PLT030	Define false lift
PLT031	Define isobars / associated winds
PLT032	Define MACH speed regimes
PLT033	Define MEA / MOCA / MRA
PLT034	Define stopway / clearway
PLT035	Define Vne / Vno
PLT036	Interpret a MACH meter reading
PLT037	Interpret a Radar Weather Report / National Convective Weather Forecast
PLT038	Interpret aircraft Power Schedule Chart
PLT039	Interpret airport landing indicator
PLT040	Interpret airspace classes - charts / diagrams
PLT041	Interpret altimeter - readings / settings
PLT042	Interpret Constant Pressure charts / Isotachs Chart
PLT043	Interpret Analysis Heights / Temperature Chart
PLT044	Interpret ATC communications / instructions / terminology
PLT045	Interpret Descent Performance Chart
PLT046	Interpret drag ratio from charts
PLT047	Interpret/Program Flight Director/FMS/ Automation - modes / operation / indications / errors
PLT048	Interpret Hovering Ceiling Chart
PLT049	Interpret ILS - charts / RMI / CDI / indications
PLT050	Interpret information on a Brake Energy Limit Chart
PLT051	Interpret information on a Convective Outlook
PLT052	Interpret information on a Departure Procedure Chart
PLT053	Interpret information on a Flight Plan
PLT054	Interpret information on a Glider Performance Graph
PLT055	Interpret information on a High Altitude Chart
PLT056	Interpret information on a Horizontal Situation Indicator (HSI)
PLT057	Interpret information on a Hot Air Balloon Performance Graph
PLT058	Interpret information on a Low Altitude Chart
PLT059	Interpret information on a METAR / SPECI report
PLT060	Interpret information on a Performance Curve Chart
PLT061	Interpret information on a PIREP
PLT062	Interpret information on a Pseudo-Adiabatic Chart / K Index / Lifted Index
PLT063	*Removed by the FAA*
PLT064	Interpret information on a Sectional Chart
PLT065	Interpret information on a Service Ceiling Engine Inoperative Chart

PLT066	Interpret information on a Convective Outlook Chart
PLT067	Interpret information on a SIGMET
PLT068	Interpret information on a Significant Weather Prognostic Chart
PLT069	Interpret information on a Slush/Standing Water Takeoff Chart
PLT070	Interpret information on a Stability Chart
PLT071	Interpret information on a Surface Analysis Chart
PLT072	Interpret information on a Terminal Aerodrome Forecast (TAF)
PLT073	Interpret information on a Tower Enroute Control (TEC)
PLT074	Interpret information on a Velocity/Load Factor Chart
PLT075	Interpret information on a Weather Depiction Chart
PLT076	Interpret information on a Winds and Temperatures Aloft Forecast (FB)
PLT077	Interpret information on an Airport Diagram
PLT078	Interpret information in an Airport Facility Directory (AFD)
PLT079	Interpret information on an Airways Chart
PLT080	Interpret information on an Arrival Chart
PLT081	Interpret information on an Aviation Area Forecast (FA)
PLT082	Interpret information on an IFR Alternate Airport Minimums Chart
PLT083	Interpret information on an Instrument Approach Procedures (IAP)
PLT084	Interpret information on an Observed Winds Aloft Chart
PLT085	Interpret information on Takeoff Obstacle / Field / Climb Limit Charts
PLT086	Interpret readings on a Turn and Slip Indicator
PLT087	Interpret readings on an Aircraft Course and DME Indicator
PLT088	Interpret speed indicator readings
PLT089	Interpret Takeoff Speeds Chart
PLT090	Interpret VOR - charts / indications / CDI / NAV
PLT091	Interpret VOR / CDI - illustrations / indications / procedures
PLT092	Interpret weight and balance - diagram
PLT093	Recall administration of medical oxygen
PLT094	Recall aerodynamics - airfoil design / pressure distribution / effects of altitude
PLT095	Recall aerodynamics - longitudinal axis / lateral axis
PLT096	Recall aeromedical factors - effects of altitude
PLT097	Recall aeromedical factors - effects of carbon monoxide poisoning
PLT098	Recall aeromedical factors - fitness for flight
PLT099	Recall aeromedical factors - scanning procedures
PLT100	Recall aeronautical charts - IFR En Route Low Altitude
PLT101	Recall aeronautical charts - pilotage
PLT102	Recall aeronautical charts - terminal procedures
PLT103	Recall Aeronautical Decision Making (ADM) - hazardous attitudes
PLT104	Recall Aeronautical Decision Making (ADM) - human factors / CRM
PLT105	Recall airborne radar / thunderstorm detection equipment - use / limitations
PLT106	Recall aircraft air-cycle machine
PLT107	Recall aircraft alternator / generator system
PLT108	Recall aircraft anti-icing / deicing - methods / fluids
PLT109	Recall aircraft batteries - capacity / charging / types / storage / rating / precautions
PLT110	Recall aircraft brake system

PLT111	Recall aircraft circuitry - series / parallel
PLT112	Recall aircraft controls - proper use / techniques
PLT113	Recall aircraft design - categories / limitation factors
PLT114	Recall aircraft design - construction / function
PLT115	Recall aircraft engine - detonation/backfiring/ after firing, cause/characteristics
PLT116	Recall aircraft general knowledge / publications / AIM / navigational aids
PLT117	Recall aircraft heated windshields
PLT118	Recall aircraft instruments - gyroscopic
PLT119	Recall aircraft lighting - anti-collision / landing / navigation
PLT120	Recall aircraft limitations - turbulent air penetration
PLT121	Recall aircraft loading - computations
PLT122	Recall aircraft operations - checklist usage
PLT123	Recall aircraft performance - airspeed
PLT124	Recall aircraft performance - atmospheric effects
PLT125	Recall aircraft performance - climb / descent
PLT126	Recall aircraft performance - cold weather operations
PLT127	Recall aircraft performance - density altitude
PLT128	Recall aircraft performance - effects of icing
PLT129	Recall aircraft performance - effects of runway slope / slope landing
PLT130	Recall aircraft performance - fuel
PLT131	Recall aircraft performance - ground effect
PLT132	Recall aircraft performance - instrument markings / airspeed / definitions / indications
PLT133	Recall aircraft performance - normal climb / descent rates
PLT134	Recall aircraft performance - takeoff
PLT135	Recall aircraft pressurization - system / operation
PLT136	Recall aircraft systems - anti-icing / deicing
PLT137	Recall aircraft systems - environmental control
PLT138	Recall aircraft landing gear/tires - types / characteristics
PLT139	Recall aircraft warning systems - stall / fire / retractable gear / terrain awareness
PLT140	Recall airport operations - LAHSO
PLT141	Recall airport operations - markings / signs / lighting
PLT142	Recall airport operations - noise avoidance routes
PLT143	Recall airport operations - rescue / fire fighting vehicles and types of agents
PLT144	Recall airport operations - runway conditions
PLT145	Recall airport operations - runway lighting
PLT146	Recall airport operations - traffic pattern procedures / communication procedures
PLT147	Recall airport operations - visual glideslope indicators
PLT148	Recall airport operations lighting - MALS / ALSF / RCLS / TDZL
PLT149	Recall airport preflight / taxi operations - procedures
PLT150	Recall airport traffic patterns - entry procedures
PLT151	Recall airship - buoyancy
PLT152	Recall airship - flight characteristics / controllability
PLT153	Recall airship - flight operations
PLT154	Recall airship - ground weigh-off / static / trim condition
PLT155	Recall airship - maintaining pressure
PLT156	Recall airship - maximum headway / flight at equilibrium
PLT157	Recall airship - pressure height / dampers / position
PLT158	Recall airship - pressure height / manometers
PLT159	Recall airship - pressure height / super heat / valving gas

PLT160 Recall airship - stability / control / positive superheat
PLT161 Recall airspace classes - limits / requirements / restrictions / airspeeds / equipment
PLT162 Recall airspace requirements - operations
PLT163 Recall airspace requirements - visibility / cloud clearance
PLT164 Recall airspeed - effects during a turn
PLT165 Recall altimeter - effect of temperature changes
PLT166 Recall altimeter - settings / setting procedures
PLT167 Recall altimeters - characteristics / accuracy
PLT168 Recall angle of attack - characteristics / forces / principles
PLT169 Recall antitorque system - components / functions
PLT170 Recall approach / landing / taxiing techniques
PLT171 Recall ATC - reporting
PLT172 Recall ATC - system / services
PLT173 Recall atmospheric conditions - measurements / pressure / stability
PLT174 Recall autopilot / yaw damper - components / operating principles / characteristics / failure modes
PLT175 Recall autorotation
PLT176 Recall balance tab - purpose / operation
PLT177 Recall balloon - flight operations
PLT178 Recall balloon - flight operations / gas
PLT179 Recall balloon - ground weigh-off / static equilibrium / load
PLT180 Recall balloon gas/hot air - lift / false lift / characteristics
PLT181 Recall balloon - hot air / physics
PLT182 Recall balloon - inspecting the fabric
PLT183 Recall balloon flight operations - ascent / descent
PLT184 Recall balloon flight operations - launch / landing
PLT185 Recall basic instrument flying - fundamental skills
PLT186 Recall basic instrument flying - pitch instruments
PLT187 Recall basic instrument flying - turn coordinator / turn and slip indicator
PLT188 Recall cabin atmosphere control
PLT189 Recall carburetor - effects of carburetor heat / heat control
PLT190 Recall carburetor ice - factors affecting / causing
PLT191 Recall carburetors - types / components / operating principles / characteristics
PLT192 Recall clouds - types / formation / resulting weather
PLT193 Recall cockpit voice recorder (CVR) - operating principles / characteristics / testing
PLT194 Recall collision avoidance - scanning techniques
PLT195 Recall collision avoidance - TCAS
PLT196 Recall communications - ATIS broadcasts
PLT197 Recall Coriolis effect
PLT198 Recall course / heading - effects of wind
PLT199 Recall cyclic control pressure - characteristics
PLT200 Recall dead reckoning - calculations / charts
PLT201 Recall departure procedures - ODP / SID
PLT202 Recall DME - characteristics / accuracy / indications / Arc
PLT203 Recall earth's atmosphere - layers / characteristics / solar energy
PLT204 Recall effective communication - basic elements
PLT205 Recall effects of alcohol on the body
PLT206 Recall effects of temperature - density altitude / icing
PLT207 Recall electrical system - components / operating principles / characteristics / static bonding and shielding
PLT208 Recall emergency conditions / procedures
PLT209 *Removed by the FAA*

PLT210 Recall engine shutdown - normal / abnormal / emergency / precautions
PLT211 Recall evaluation testing characteristics
PLT212 Recall fire extinguishing systems - components / operating principles / characteristics
PLT213 Recall flight characteristics - longitudinal stability / instability
PLT214 Recall flight characteristics - structural / wing design
PLT215 Recall flight instruments - magnetic compass
PLT216 Recall flight instruments - total energy compensators
PLT217 Recall flight maneuvers - quick stop
PLT218 Recall flight operations - common student errors
PLT219 Recall flight operations - maneuvers
PLT220 Recall flight operations - night and high altitude operations
PLT221 Recall flight operations - takeoff / landing maneuvers
PLT222 Recall flight operations - takeoff procedures
PLT223 Recall flight operations multiengine - engine inoperative procedures
PLT224 Recall flight plan - IFR
PLT225 Recall flight plan - requirements
PLT226 Recall fog - types / formation / resulting weather
PLT227 Recall FOI techniques - integrated flight instruction
PLT228 Recall FOI techniques - lesson plans
PLT229 Recall FOI techniques - professionalism
PLT230 Recall FOI techniques - responsibilities
PLT231 Recall FOI techniques / human behavior - anxiety / fear / stress
PLT232 Recall FOI techniques / human behavior - dangerous tendencies
PLT233 Recall FOI techniques / human behavior - defense mechanisms
PLT234 Recall forces acting on aircraft - 3 axis intersect
PLT235 Recall forces acting on aircraft - aerodynamics
PLT236 Recall forces acting on aircraft - airfoil / center of pressure / mean camber line
PLT237 Recall forces acting on aircraft - airspeed / air density / lift / drag
PLT238 Recall forces acting on aircraft - aspect ratio
PLT239 Recall forces acting on aircraft - buoyancy / drag / gravity / thrust
PLT240 Recall forces acting on aircraft - CG / flight characteristics
PLT241 Recall forces acting on aircraft - drag / gravity / thrust / lift
PLT242 Recall forces acting on aircraft - lift / drag / thrust / weight / stall / limitations
PLT243 Recall forces acting on aircraft - propeller / torque
PLT244 Recall forces acting on aircraft - stability / controllability
PLT245 Recall forces acting on aircraft - stalls / spins
PLT246 Recall forces acting on aircraft - steady state climb / flight
PLT247 Recall forces acting on aircraft - thrust / drag / weight / lift
PLT248 Recall forces acting on aircraft - turns
PLT249 Recall fuel - air mixture
PLT250 Recall fuel - types / characteristics / contamination / fueling / defueling / precautions
PLT251 Recall fuel characteristics / contaminants / additives
PLT252 Recall fuel dump system - components / methods
PLT253 Recall fuel system - components / operating principles / characteristics / leaks
PLT254 Recall fuel tank - components / operating principles / characteristics

PLT255	Recall fueling procedures - safety / grounding / calculating volume
PLT256	Recall glider performance - effect of loading
PLT257	Recall glider performance - speed / distance / ballast / lift / drag
PLT258	Recall ground reference maneuvers - ground track diagram
PLT259	Recall ground resonance - conditions to occur
PLT260	Recall gyroplane - aerodynamics / rotor systems
PLT261	Recall hail - characteristics / hazards
PLT262	Recall helicopter hazards - dynamic rollover / Low G / LTE
PLT263	Recall hazardous weather - fog / icing / turbulence / visibility restriction
PLT264	Recall helicopter approach - settling with power
PLT265	Recall helicopter takeoff / landing - ground resonance action required
PLT266	Recall high lift devices - characteristics / functions
PLT267	Recall hot air balloon - weigh-off procedure
PLT268	Recall hovering - aircraft performance / tendencies
PLT269	Recall human behavior - defense mechanism
PLT270	Recall human behavior - social / self fulfillment / physical
PLT271	Recall human factors (ADM) - judgment
PLT272	Recall human factors - stress management
PLT273	Recall hydraulic systems - components / operating principles / characteristics
PLT274	Recall icing - formation / characteristics
PLT275	Recall ILS - indications / HSI
PLT276	Recall ILS - indications / OBS / CDI
PLT277	Recall ILS - marker beacon / indicator lights / codes
PLT278	Recall indicating systems - airspeed / angle of attack / attitude / heading / manifold pressure / synchro / EGT
PLT279	Recall Inertial/Doppler Navigation System principles / regulations / requirements / limitations
PLT280	Recall inflight illusions - causes / sources
PLT281	Recall information in an Airport Facility Directory
PLT282	Recall information in the certificate holder's manual
PLT283	Recall information on a Constant Pressure Analysis Chart
PLT284	Recall information on a Forecast Winds and Temperatures Aloft (FD)
PLT285	Recall information on a Height Velocity Diagram
PLT286	Recall information on a Significant Weather Prognostic Chart
PLT287	Recall information on a Surface Analysis Chart
PLT288	Recall information on a Terminal Aerodrome Forecast (TAF)
PLT289	Recall information on a Weather Depiction Chart
PLT290	Recall information on AIRMETS / SIGMETS
PLT291	Recall information on an Aviation Area Forecast (FA)
PLT292	Recall information on an Instrument Approach Procedures (IAP)
PLT293	Recall information on an Instrument Departure Procedure Chart
PLT294	Recall information on Inflight Aviation Weather Advisories
PLT295	Recall instructor techniques - obstacles / planning / activities / outcome
PLT296	Recall instrument procedures - holding / circling
PLT297	Recall instrument procedures - unusual attitude / unusual attitude recovery
PLT298	Recall instrument procedures - VFR on top
PLT300	Recall instrument/navigation system checks/inspections - limits / tuning / identifying / logging

PLT301	Recall inversion layer - characteristics
PLT302	Recall jet stream - types / characteristics
PLT303	Recall L/D ratio
PLT304	Recall launch / aero-tow procedures
PLT305	Recall leading edge devices - types / effect / purpose / operation
PLT306	Recall learning process - levels of learning / transfer of learning / incidental learning
PLT307	Recall learning process - memory / fact / recall
PLT308	Recall learning process - laws of learning elements
PLT309	Recall load factor - angle of bank
PLT310	Recall load factor - characteristics
PLT311	Recall load factor - effect of airspeed
PLT312	Recall load factor - maneuvering / stall speed
PLT313	Recall loading – limitations / terminology
PLT314	Recall longitudinal axis - aerodynamics / center of gravity / direction of motion
PLT315	Recall Machmeter - principles / functions
PLT316	Recall meteorology - severe weather watch (WW)
PLT317	Recall microburst - characteristics / hazards
PLT318	Recall minimum fuel advisory
PLT319	Recall navigation – celestial / navigation chart / characteristics
PLT320	Recall navigation - true north / magnetic north
PLT321	Recall navigation - types of landing systems
PLT322	Recall navigation - VOR / NAV system
PLT323	Recall NOTAMS - classes / information / distribution
PLT324	Recall oil system - types / components / functions / oil specifications
PLT325	Recall operations manual - transportation of prisoner
PLT326	Recall oxygen system - components / operating principles / characteristics
PLT327	Recall oxygen system - install / inspect / repair / service / precautions / leaks
PLT328	Recall performance planning - aircraft loading
PLT329	Recall physiological factors - cabin pressure
PLT330	Recall physiological factors - cause / effects of hypoxia
PLT331	Recall physiological factors - effects of scuba diving / smoking
PLT332	Recall physiological factors - hyperventilation
PLT333	Recall physiological factors - night vision
PLT334	Recall physiological factors - spatial disorientation
PLT335	Recall pilotage - calculations
PLT336	Recall pitch control - collective / cyclic
PLT337	Recall pitot-static system - components / operating principles / characteristics
PLT338	Recall pneumatic system - operation
PLT340	Recall positive exchange of flight controls
PLT341	Recall power setting - characteristics
PLT342	Recall powerplant - controlling engine temperature
PLT343	Recall powerplant - operating principles / operational characteristics / inspecting
PLT344	Recall precipitation - types / characteristics
PLT345	Recall pressure altitude
PLT346	Recall primary / secondary flight controls - types / purpose / functionality / operation
PLT347	Recall principles of flight - critical engine
PLT348	Recall principles of flight - turns
PLT349	Recall procedures for confined areas
PLT350	Recall propeller operations - constant / variable speed
PLT351	Recall propeller system - types / components / operating principles / characteristics
PLT352	Recall purpose / operation of a stabilizer
PLT353	*Removed by the FAA*
PLT354	Recall radio - GPS / RNAV / RAIM

PLT355	Recall radio - HSI
PLT356	Recall radio - ILS / compass locator
PLT357	Recall radio - ILS
PLT358	Recall radio - LOC / ILS
PLT359	*Removed by the FAA*
PLT360	*Removed by the FAA*
PLT361	*Removed by the FAA*
PLT362	*Removed by the FAA*
PLT363	Recall radio - VOR / VOT
PLT364	Recall radio system - license requirements / frequencies
PLT365	Recall reciprocating engine - components / operating principles / characteristics
PLT366	Recall regulations - accident / incident reporting and preserving wreckage
PLT367	Recall regulations - additional equipment/operating requirements large transport aircraft
PLT368	Recall regulations - admission to flight deck
PLT369	Recall regulations - aerobatic flight requirements
PLT370	Recall regulations - Air Traffic Control authorization / clearances
PLT371	Recall regulations - Aircraft Category / Class
PLT372	Recall regulations - aircraft inspection / records / expiration
PLT373	Recall regulations - aircraft operating limitations
PLT374	Recall regulations - aircraft owner / operator responsibilities
PLT375	Recall regulations - aircraft return to service
PLT376	Recall regulations - airspace special use / TFRS
PLT377	Recall regulations - airworthiness certificates / requirements / responsibilities
PLT378	Recall regulations - Airworthiness Directives
PLT379	Recall regulations - alternate airport requirements
PLT380	Recall regulations - alternate airport weather minima
PLT381	Recall regulations - altimeter settings
PLT382	Recall regulations - approach minima
PLT383	Recall regulations - basic flight rules
PLT384	Recall regulations - briefing of passengers
PLT385	Recall regulations - cargo in passenger compartment
PLT386	Recall regulations - certificate issuance / renewal
PLT387	Recall regulations - change of address
PLT388	Recall regulations - cockpit voice / flight data recorder(s)
PLT389	Recall regulations - commercial operation requirements / conditions / OpSpecs
PLT390	Recall regulations - communications en route
PLT391	Recall regulations - communications failure
PLT392	Recall regulations - compliance with local regulations
PLT393	Recall regulations - controlled / restricted airspace - requirements
PLT394	Recall regulations - declaration of an emergency
PLT395	Recall regulations - definitions
PLT396	Recall regulations - departure alternate airport
PLT397	Recall regulations - destination airport visibility
PLT398	Recall regulations - dispatch
PLT399	Recall regulations - display / inspection of licenses and certificates
PLT400	Recall regulations - documents to be carried on aircraft during flight
PLT401	Recall regulations - dropping / aerial application / towing restrictions
PLT402	Recall regulations - ELT requirements
PLT403	Recall regulations - emergency deviation from regulations
PLT404	Recall regulations - emergency equipment
PLT405	Recall regulations - equipment / instrument / certificate requirements
PLT406	Recall regulations - equipment failure
PLT407	Recall regulations - experience / training requirements
PLT408	Recall regulations - fire extinguisher requirements
PLT409	Recall regulations - flight / duty time
PLT410	Recall regulations - flight engineer qualifications / privileges / responsibilities
PLT411	Recall regulations - flight instructor limitations / qualifications
PLT412	Recall regulations - flight release
PLT413	Recall regulations - fuel requirements
PLT414	Recall regulations - general right-of-way rules
PLT415	Recall regulations - IFR flying
PLT416	Recall regulations - immediate notification
PLT417	Recall regulations - individual flotation devices
PLT418	Recall regulations - instructor demonstrations / authorizations
PLT419	Recall regulations - instructor requirements / responsibilities
PLT420	Recall regulations - instrument approach procedures
PLT421	Recall regulations - instrument flight rules
PLT422	Recall regulations - intermediate airport authorizations
PLT423	Recall regulations - knowledge and skill test checks
PLT424	Recall regulations - limits on autopilot usage
PLT425	Recall regulations - maintenance reports / records / entries
PLT426	Recall regulations - maintenance requirements
PLT427	Recall regulations - medical certificate requirements / validity
PLT428	Recall regulations - minimum equipment list
PLT429	Recall regulations - minimum flight / navigation instruments
PLT430	Recall regulations - minimum safe / flight altitude
PLT431	Recall regulations - operating near other aircraft
PLT432	Recall regulations - operational control functions
PLT433	Recall regulations - operational flight plan requirements
PLT434	Recall regulations - operational procedures for a controlled airport
PLT435	Recall regulations - operational procedures for an uncontrolled airport
PLT436	Recall regulations - operations manual
PLT437	Recall regulations - overwater operations
PLT438	Recall regulations - oxygen requirements
PLT439	Recall regulations - persons authorized to perform maintenance
PLT440	Recall regulations - Pilot / Crew duties and responsibilities
PLT441	Recall regulations - pilot briefing
PLT442	Recall regulations - pilot currency requirements
PLT443	Recall regulations - pilot qualifications / privileges / responsibilities / crew complement
PLT444	Recall regulations - pilot-in-command authority / responsibility
PLT445	Recall regulations - preflight requirements
PLT446	Recall regulations - preventative maintenance
PLT447	Recall regulations - privileges / limitations of medical certificates
PLT448	Recall regulations - privileges / limitations of pilot certificates
PLT449	Recall regulations - proficiency check requirements
PLT450	Recall regulations - qualifications / duty time
PLT451	Recall regulations - ratings issued / experience requirements / limitations
PLT452	Recall regulations - re-dispatch
PLT453	Recall regulations - records retention for domestic / flag air carriers
PLT454	Recall regulations - required aircraft / equipment inspections

PLT455   Recall regulations - requirements of a flight plan release

PLT456   Recall regulations - runway requirements

PLT457   Recall regulations - student pilot endorsements / other endorsements

PLT458   Recall regulations - submission / revision of Policy and Procedure Manuals

PLT459   Recall regulations - takeoff procedures / minimums

PLT460   Recall regulations - training programs

PLT461   Recall regulations - use of aircraft lights

PLT462   Recall regulations - use of microphone / megaphone / interphone / public address system

PLT463   Recall regulations - alcohol or drugs

PLT464   Recall regulations - use of safety belts / harnesses (crew member)

PLT465   Recall regulations - use of seats / safety belts / harnesses (passenger)

PLT466   Recall regulations - V speeds

PLT467   Recall regulations - visual flight rules and limitations

PLT468   Recall regulations - Visual Meteorological Conditions (VMC)

PLT469   Recall regulations - weather radar

PLT470   Recall rotor system - types / components / operating principles / characteristics

PLT471   Recall rotorcraft transmission - components / operating principles / characteristics

PLT472   Recall rotorcraft vibration - characteristics / sources

PLT473   Recall secondary flight controls - types / purpose / functionality

PLT474   Recall soaring - normal procedures

PLT475   Recall squall lines - formation / characteristics / resulting weather

PLT476   Recall stabilizer - purpose / operation

PLT477   Recall stalls - characteristics / factors / recovery / precautions

PLT478   Recall starter / ignition system - types / components / operating principles / characteristics

PLT479   Recall starter system - starting procedures

PLT480   Recall static/dynamic stability/instability - characteristics

PLT481   Recall student evaluation - learning process

PLT482   Recall student evaluation - written tests / oral quiz / critiques

PLT483   Recall supercharger - characteristics / operation

PLT484   Recall symbols - chart / navigation

PLT485   Recall taxiing / crosswind / techniques

PLT486   Recall taxiing / takeoff - techniques / procedures

PLT487   Recall teaching methods - demonstration / performance

PLT488   Recall teaching methods - group / guided discussion / lecture

PLT489   Recall teaching methods - known to unknown

PLT490   Recall teaching methods - motivation / student feelings of insecurity

PLT491   Recall teaching methods - organizing material / course of training

PLT492   Recall temperature - effects on weather formations

PLT493   Recall the dynamics of frost / ice / snow formation on an aircraft

PLT494   Recall thermals - types / characteristics / formation / locating / maneuvering / corrective actions

PLT495   Recall thunderstorms - types / characteristics / formation / hazards / precipitation static

PLT496   Recall towrope - strength / safety links / positioning

PLT497   Recall transponder - codes / operations / usage

PLT498   Recall Transportation Security Regulations

PLT499   Recall turbine engines - components / operational characteristics / associated instruments

PLT500   Recall turboprop engines - components / operational characteristics

PLT501   Recall turbulence - types / characteristics / reporting / corrective actions

PLT502   Recall universal signals - hand / light / visual

PLT503   Recall use of narcotics / drugs / intoxicating liquor

PLT504   Recall use of training aids - types / function / purpose

PLT505   Recall use of training aids - usefulness / simplicity / compatibility

PLT506   Recall V speeds - maneuvering / flap extended / gear extended / V_1, V_2, r, ne, mo, mc, mg, etc.

PLT507   Recall VOR - indications / VOR / VOT / CDI

PLT508   Recall VOR/altimeter/transponder checks - identification / tuning / identifying / logging

PLT509   Recall wake turbulence - characteristics / avoidance techniques

PLT510   Recall weather - causes / formation

PLT511   Recall weather associated with frontal activity / air masses

PLT512   Recall weather conditions - temperature / moisture / dewpoint

PLT513   Recall weather information - FAA Avcams

PLT514   Recall weather reporting systems - briefings / forecasts / reports / AWOS / ASOS

PLT515   Recall weather services - TIBS / TPC / WFO / HIWAS

PLT516   Recall winds - types / characteristics

PLT517   Recall winds associated with high / low-pressure systems

PLT518   Recall windshear - characteristics / hazards / power management

PLT519   Recall wing spoilers - purpose / operation

PLT520   Calculate density altitude

PLT521   Recall helicopter takeoff / landing – slope operations

PLT522   Recall helicopter – Pinnacle / Ridgeline operations

PLT523   Recall vortex generators – purpose / effects / aerodynamics

PLT524   Interpret / Program information on an avionics display

PLT525   Interpret table – oxygen / fuel / oil / accumulator / fire extinguisher

PLT526   Recall near midair collision report

PLT527   Recall BASIC VFR – weather minimums

CROSS-REFERENCES TO
THE FAA LEARNING STATEMENT CODES

Pages 521 through 530 contain a listing of all of the questions from our instrument rating knowledge test bank. The questions are in FAA Learning Statement Code (LSC) sequence. To the right of each LSC, we present our study unit/question number and our answer. For example, note that in one instance below, PLT002 is cross-referenced to 11-45, which represents our Study Unit 11, question 45; the correct answer is B.

Pages 515 through 520 contain a complete listing of all the FAA Learning Statement Codes associated with all of the instrument rating questions presented in this book. Use this list to identify the specific topic associated to each Learning Statement Code.

The first line of each of our answer explanations in Study Units 1 through 11 contains

1. The correct answer.
2. A reference for the answer explanation, e.g., *IPH Chap 1*. If this reference is not useful, use the following chart to identify the learning statement code to determine the specific reference appropriate for the question.

FAA Learning Code	Gleim SU/ Q. No.	Gleim Answer	FAA Learning Code	Gleim SU/ Q. No.	Gleim Answer	FAA Learning Code	Gleim SU/ Q. No.	Gleim Answer
PLT002	11–45	B	PLT012	11–27	B	PLT044	5–77	B
PLT002	11–54	B	PLT012	11–44	C	PLT044	5–78	B
PLT002	11–81	A	PLT012	11–52	C	PLT044	5–80	A
PLT002	11–96	B	PLT012	11–67	A	PLT044	5–88	B
PLT004	5–85	C	PLT012	11–71	C	PLT044	5–94	B
PLT004	11–16	C	PLT012	11–80	B	PLT044	5–96	C
PLT004	11–28	C	PLT012	11–95	C	PLT049	3–45	A
PLT004	11–47	C	PLT023	1–42	B	PLT049	3–47	B
PLT004	11–88	B	PLT026	9–10	C	PLT049	3–50	C
PLT004	11–100	C	PLT031	8–3	B	PLT049	3–66	B
PLT008	6–174	C	PLT033	10–1	A	PLT049	3–67	B
PLT008	11–19	B	PLT033	10–2	A	PLT049	3–68	C
PLT008	11–34	C	PLT033	10–3	A	PLT049	6–27	B
PLT008	11–40	A	PLT033	10–4	B	PLT049	6–28	C
PLT008	11–78	C	PLT033	10–5	A	PLT049	6–29	A
PLT012	1–17	C	PLT033	10–6	B	PLT049	6–30	B
PLT012	10–55	C	PLT033	10–8	C	PLT049	6–31	C
PLT012	10–56	B	PLT033	10–9	C	PLT049	6–32	A
PLT012	11–1	B	PLT033	10–10	A	PLT049	6–97	C
PLT012	11–2	A	PLT033	10–13	C	PLT051	9–55	B
PLT012	11–3	A	PLT036	1–16	A	PLT051	9–57	B
PLT012	11–8	A	PLT036	1–22	A	PLT051	9–58	A
PLT012	11–9	C	PLT041	1–29	C	PLT052	6–170	C
PLT012	11–12	B	PLT041	1–30	B	PLT052	6–172	A
PLT012	11–26	A	PLT041	1–32	B	PLT052	6–175	A

FAA Learning Code	Gleim SU/ Q. No.	Gleim Answer	FAA Learning Code	Gleim SU/ Q. No.	Gleim Answer	FAA Learning Code	Gleim SU/ Q. No.	Gleim Answer
PLT052	6–184	B	PLT058	11–5	A	PLT076	9–31	A
PLT052	6–185	C	PLT058	11–48	A	PLT077	5–129	B
PLT052	11–17	A	PLT058	11–49	B	PLT077	5–130	B
PLT052	11–99	B	PLT058	11–55	A	PLT077	5–131	B
PLT052	11–108	C	PLT058	11–69	A	PLT077	5–132	B
PLT053	11–10	C	PLT058	11–82	C	PLT077	5–133	B
PLT053	11–25	C	PLT058	11–102	B	PLT078	5–128	B
PLT053	11–43	A	PLT058	11–103	B	PLT078	6–165	B
PLT053	11–53	C	PLT059	9–9	C	PLT078	10–38	B
PLT053	11–66	B	PLT059	9–11	A	PLT078	10–39	A
PLT053	11–79	A	PLT059	9–12	A	PLT078	10–40	A
PLT053	11–94	C	PLT059	9–13	B	PLT079	10–50	C
PLT056	3–51	A	PLT061	9–14	C	PLT079	10–58	C
PLT056	3–54	C	PLT061	9–15	A	PLT079	11–101	A
PLT056	3–55	B	PLT063	1–61	C	PLT080	6–168	B
PLT056	3–56	C	PLT066	9–46	C	PLT080	6–177	B
PLT056	3–57	A	PLT066	9–47	A	PLT080	6–179	B
PLT056	3–58	C	PLT066	9–48	C	PLT080	6–181	B
PLT056	3–59	C	PLT066	9–49	A	PLT080	11–73	B
PLT056	3–63	C	PLT066	9–50	A	PLT080	11–92	B
PLT056	3–64	C	PLT067	9–8	B	PLT080	11–93	B
PLT056	3–65	A	PLT068	9–39	A	PLT083	6–19	A
PLT056	11–58	A	PLT068	9–40	A	PLT083	6–21	C
PLT058	10–34	C	PLT068	9–41	A	PLT083	6–92	A
PLT058	10–35	B	PLT068	9–42	B	PLT083	6–93	C
PLT058	10–36	C	PLT068	9–44	A	PLT083	6–96	C
PLT058	10–37	A	PLT068	9–61	C	PLT083	6–100	B
PLT058	10–41	C	PLT068	9–62	B	PLT083	6–101	A
PLT058	10–42	A	PLT068	9–63	B	PLT083	6–102	B
PLT058	10–44	C	PLT068	9–64	C	PLT083	6–103	C
PLT058	10–45	A	PLT068	9–65	C	PLT083	6–104	B
PLT058	10–46	C	PLT068	9–66	C	PLT083	6–108	A
PLT058	10–47	A	PLT068	9–67	B	PLT083	6–109	A
PLT058	10–48	B	PLT068	9–68	C	PLT083	6–114	B
PLT058	10–49	B	PLT068	9–69	C	PLT083	6–115	C
PLT058	10–51	C	PLT068	9–70	B	PLT083	6–118	B
PLT058	10–52	C	PLT071	9–56	C	PLT083	6–119	C
PLT058	10–53	A	PLT072	9–21	A	PLT083	6–120	A
PLT058	10–57	B	PLT075	9–16	C	PLT083	6–125	A
PLT058	10–59	B	PLT075	9–17	B	PLT083	6–126	A
PLT058	10–61	B	PLT076	9–29	C	PLT083	6–127	C
PLT058	11–4	B	PLT076	9–30	C	PLT083	6–129	C

FAA Learning Code	Gleim SU/ Q. No.	Gleim Answer	FAA Learning Code	Gleim SU/ Q. No.	Gleim Answer	FAA Learning Code	Gleim SU/ Q. No.	Gleim Answer
PLT083	6–131	C	PLT083	11–72	C	PLT091	11–14	B
PLT083	6–132	B	PLT083	11–77	A	PLT091	11–46	B
PLT083	6–134	B	PLT083	11–85	B	PLT091	11–70	A
PLT083	6–135	A	PLT083	11–86	A	PLT091	11–83	A
PLT083	6–136	B	PLT083	11–87	C	PLT091	11–104	C
PLT083	6–137	A	PLT083	11–89	A	PLT099	7–25	C
PLT083	6–138	A	PLT083	11–90	B	PLT100	5–113	A
PLT083	6–141	A	PLT083	11–91	C	PLT100	10–7	B
PLT083	6–142	C	PLT083	11–105	B	PLT100	10–43	B
PLT083	6–143	B	PLT083	11–106	B	PLT100	10–60	C
PLT083	6–144	B	PLT083	11–107	B	PLT100	10–62	B
PLT083	6–145	A	PLT084	9–71	A	PLT100	11–6	C
PLT083	6–146	C	PLT084	9–72	C	PLT100	11–98	C
PLT083	6–147	C	PLT084	9–73	C	PLT102	11–63	C
PLT083	6–148	C	PLT084	9–74	B	PLT102	11–64	C
PLT083	6–152	C	PLT085	11–21	C	PLT102	11–74	C
PLT083	6–153	B	PLT085	11–50	A	PLT102	11–75	C
PLT083	6–154	C	PLT086	2–4	A	PLT102	11–76	C
PLT083	6–155	A	PLT086	2–5	A	PLT104	1–77	C
PLT083	6–161	A	PLT086	2–6	B	PLT104	1–78	B
PLT083	6–162	C	PLT086	2–7	B	PLT104	1–79	A
PLT083	6–164	B	PLT086	2–8	C	PLT104	1–80	A
PLT083	6–166	B	PLT086	2–19	B	PLT105	8–65	A
PLT083	6–194	B	PLT088	1–15	A	PLT108	8–78	A
PLT083	6–196	C	PLT088	2–63	B	PLT116	3–82	C
PLT083	6–197	C	PLT088	2–68	B	PLT116	11–20	C
PLT083	6–199	B	PLT089	11–22	C	PLT118	1–47	C
PLT083	6–200	B	PLT089	11–24	C	PLT118	1–48	B
PLT083	6–202	C	PLT090	6–171	C	PLT118	1–50	C
PLT083	6–207	A	PLT090	11–7	B	PLT118	1–51	A
PLT083	11–18	A	PLT090	11–56	A	PLT118	1–52	C
PLT083	11–31	B	PLT091	3–6	B	PLT118	1–54	A
PLT083	11–32	A	PLT091	3–7	B	PLT118	1–55	C
PLT083	11–33	C	PLT091	3–8	A	PLT118	1–56	B
PLT083	11–35	C	PLT091	3–9	B	PLT118	1–57	B
PLT083	11–38	C	PLT091	3–10	C	PLT118	1–58	C
PLT083	11–39	A	PLT091	3–11	A	PLT118	1–60	C
PLT083	11–42	C	PLT091	3–12	C	PLT118	1–70	B
PLT083	11–59	B	PLT091	3–13	A	PLT120	8–58	C
PLT083	11–60	A	PLT091	3–15	A	PLT125	2–23	B
PLT083	11–61	B	PLT091	3–38	B	PLT125	2–29	C
PLT083	11–62	B	PLT091	3–53	C	PLT125	2–30	B

FAA Learning Code	Gleim SU/ Q. No.	Gleim Answer	FAA Learning Code	Gleim SU/ Q. No.	Gleim Answer	FAA Learning Code	Gleim SU/ Q. No.	Gleim Answer
PLT125	6–87	C	PLT141	5–14	B	PLT161	4–89	B
PLT125	6–90	B	PLT141	5–15	A	PLT161	4–90	A
PLT128	8–67	C	PLT141	5–16	B	PLT161	5–114	A
PLT128	8–90	A	PLT141	5–17	B	PLT161	5–115	B
PLT128	8–91	A	PLT141	5–18	A	PLT161	5–116	B
PLT128	8–92	C	PLT141	5–19	A	PLT161	5–118	B
PLT128	8–93	A	PLT141	5–20	C	PLT161	5–119	B
PLT128	8–98	B	PLT141	5–21	A	PLT161	5–120	B
PLT128	8–99	C	PLT141	5–22	B	PLT161	5–121	C
PLT128	8–100	A	PLT141	5–23	B	PLT161	5–122	B
PLT128	8–101	B	PLT141	5–24	B	PLT161	5–123	D
PLT128	8–102	C	PLT141	5–42	C	PLT161	5–124	C
PLT128	8–103	B	PLT141	5–55	B	PLT161	5–125	C
PLT128	8–104	B	PLT144	5–4	B	PLT161	5–126	C
PLT128	8–105	C	PLT145	5–1	C	PLT161	5–127	A
PLT128	8–106	C	PLT145	5–2	A	PLT161	10–24	C
PLT128	8–115	A	PLT146	6–71	C	PLT161	10–32	C
PLT132	1–62	A	PLT146	6–82	C	PLT162	5–117	A
PLT132	1–76	A	PLT146	6–83	A	PLT163	4–47	A
PLT133	5–84	C	PLT147	5–25	B	PLT163	4–48	B
PLT133	5–87	B	PLT147	5–26	B	PLT163	4–49	B
PLT133	5–99	C	PLT147	5–27	B	PLT163	4–50	C
PLT133	6–88	A	PLT147	5–28	C	PLT163	4–51	C
PLT133	6–89	C	PLT147	5–29	B	PLT163	4–52	B
PLT133	11–36	B	PLT147	5–30	C	PLT163	4–53	A
PLT133	11–37	B	PLT147	5–31	A	PLT163	4–54	C
PLT133	11–51	A	PLT147	5–32	A	PLT163	5–91	B
PLT136	8–94	A	PLT147	5–33	A	PLT165	1–44	B
PLT136	8–95	A	PLT147	5–34	C	PLT165	1–45	C
PLT136	8–96	B	PLT147	5–35	C	PLT166	1–27	C
PLT140	5–79	C	PLT147	5–36	A	PLT166	1–35	A
PLT141	4–1	A	PLT147	5–37	B	PLT166	1–37	C
PLT141	5–3	A	PLT147	5–38	B	PLT166	1–46	B
PLT141	5–5	B	PLT147	5–39	C	PLT166	2–49	A
PLT141	5–6	B	PLT147	5–40	A	PLT167	1–28	B
PLT141	5–7	B	PLT147	5–41	C	PLT167	1–33	B
PLT141	5–8	C	PLT161	4–40	B	PLT167	1–34	A
PLT141	5–9	B	PLT161	4–41	C	PLT168	2–9	B
PLT141	5–10	C	PLT161	4–42	A	PLT170	6–6	A
PLT141	5–11	C	PLT161	4–45	B	PLT170	6–45	A
PLT141	5–12	C	PLT161	4–73	C	PLT170	6–49	A
PLT141	5–13	B	PLT161	4–77	C	PLT170	6–53	B

FAA Learning Code	Gleim SU/ Q. No.	Gleim Answer	FAA Learning Code	Gleim SU/ Q. No.	Gleim Answer	FAA Learning Code	Gleim SU/ Q. No.	Gleim Answer
PLT170	6–57	C	PLT185	2–37	C	PLT201	6–169	C
PLT170	6–58	C	PLT185	2–41	C	PLT201	6–176	C
PLT170	6–94	B	PLT185	2–46	A	PLT202	3–1	A
PLT170	6–149	B	PLT185	2–50	C	PLT202	3–2	B
PLT170	6–159	A	PLT185	2–51	A	PLT202	3–3	B
PLT170	6–204	C	PLT185	2–52	B	PLT202	3–4	B
PLT171	5–71	B	PLT185	2–55	A	PLT202	3–14	B
PLT171	5–72	B	PLT185	2–57	C	PLT202	3–29	B
PLT171	5–86	B	PLT186	2–27	C	PLT202	4–83	A
PLT171	5–93	C	PLT186	2–36	B	PLT202	5–110	C
PLT171	5–98	B	PLT186	2–40	B	PLT202	6–163	C
PLT172	5–73	B	PLT186	2–42	C	PLT202	11–15	A
PLT172	5–74	B	PLT186	2–54	C	PLT202	11–29	A
PLT172	5–76	C	PLT187	1–63	B	PLT202	11–41	C
PLT172	5–97	C	PLT187	1–64	A	PLT203	8–7	C
PLT172	6–1	C	PLT187	1–65	B	PLT203	8–9	C
PLT172	6–63	C	PLT187	1–66	A	PLT203	8–11	C
PLT172	6–183	C	PLT187	1–67	A	PLT208	4–38	A
PLT172	9–4	A	PLT187	1–68	A	PLT215	1–1	C
PLT173	8–18	C	PLT187	1–69	C	PLT215	1–2	C
PLT173	8–19	C	PLT187	1–71	A	PLT215	1–3	C
PLT173	8–20	B	PLT187	1–72	A	PLT215	1–4	C
PLT173	8–21	A	PLT187	2–15	C	PLT215	1–5	A
PLT173	8–25	C	PLT187	2–16	C	PLT215	1–6	B
PLT173	8–27	B	PLT187	2–18	A	PLT215	1–7	C
PLT173	8–28	C	PLT187	2–22	A	PLT215	1–8	A
PLT173	8–29	A	PLT187	2–47	B	PLT215	1–9	B
PLT174	3–89	C	PLT187	2–48	B	PLT215	1–10	C
PLT174	3–90	B	PLT192	8–23	C	PLT215	1–11	B
PLT174	3–91	A	PLT192	8–47	C	PLT215	2–45	A
PLT185	2–11	B	PLT192	8–48	B	PLT220	10–14	A
PLT185	2–12	A	PLT192	8–51	B	PLT221	6–65	B
PLT185	2–13	C	PLT192	8–52	C	PLT222	5–81	C
PLT185	2–17	C	PLT192	8–53	B	PLT222	5–82	B
PLT185	2–24	A	PLT192	8–54	A	PLT224	3–71	C
PLT185	2–25	A	PLT194	5–48	C	PLT224	3–81	A
PLT185	2–26	B	PLT194	5–90	A	PLT224	5–60	A
PLT185	2–31	B	PLT194	7–27	A	PLT224	5–61	B
PLT185	2–32	C	PLT196	5–54	A	PLT224	5–63	C
PLT185	2–33	A	PLT196	5–57	B	PLT224	5–64	C
PLT185	2–34	C	PLT197	7–22	C	PLT224	5–65	A
PLT185	2–35	B	PLT197	8–4	B	PLT224	5–66	B

FAA Learning Code	Gleim SU/ Q. No.	Gleim Answer	FAA Learning Code	Gleim SU/ Q. No.	Gleim Answer	FAA Learning Code	Gleim SU/ Q. No.	Gleim Answer
PLT224	5–68	A	PLT275	3–52	C	PLT288	9–19	C
PLT224	5–69	C	PLT275	3–60	A	PLT288	9–20	C
PLT224	6–178	B	PLT275	3–61	B	PLT288	9–22	B
PLT225	5–59	B	PLT275	3–62	C	PLT288	9–23	C
PLT226	8–34	C	PLT275	11–84	A	PLT288	9–24	A
PLT226	8–35	A	PLT276	3–33	C	PLT288	9–25	B
PLT226	8–37	C	PLT277	6–25	A	PLT290	9–1	C
PLT226	8–38	C	PLT277	6–34	C	PLT290	9–3	A
PLT226	8–39	B	PLT277	6–35	B	PLT290	9–5	B
PLT226	8–40	A	PLT277	6–36	C	PLT290	9–6	C
PLT226	8–41	A	PLT277	6–48	C	PLT290	9–7	A
PLT226	8–42	A	PLT277	6–52	C	PLT290	9–51	C
PLT235	2–14	B	PLT277	6–99	B	PLT291	9–26	C
PLT237	2–2	A	PLT277	6–157	B	PLT291	9–27	C
PLT242	2–3	B	PLT278	1–59	A	PLT292	6–2	A
PLT248	2–1	C	PLT278	2–28	B	PLT292	6–3	C
PLT248	2–10	B	PLT278	2–38	C	PLT292	6–4	A
PLT263	2–69	B	PLT278	2–39	A	PLT292	6–12	B
PLT263	2–70	B	PLT278	2–44	C	PLT292	6–13	B
PLT263	8–49	B	PLT278	2–53	C	PLT292	6–14	B
PLT263	8–50	C	PLT278	2–56	A	PLT292	6–15	A
PLT263	8–97	C	PLT280	7–16	B	PLT292	6–16	A
PLT271	7–30	B	PLT280	7–17	A	PLT292	6–18	C
PLT274	8–66	C	PLT280	7–18	C	PLT292	6–47	C
PLT274	8–69	A	PLT280	7–19	A	PLT292	6–69	B
PLT274	8–70	A	PLT280	7–21	A	PLT292	6–70	C
PLT274	8–71	B	PLT280	7–23	A	PLT292	6–106	C
PLT274	8–79	A	PLT280	7–28	A	PLT292	6–107	B
PLT274	8–80	B	PLT280	7–29	A	PLT292	6–110	A
PLT274	8–82	C	PLT281	3–16	C	PLT292	6–111	C
PLT274	8–107	A	PLT281	11–30	B	PLT292	6–112	A
PLT274	8–108	A	PLT283	9–53	B	PLT292	6–113	A
PLT274	8–109	A	PLT283	9–54	C	PLT292	6–122	A
PLT274	8–110	B	PLT284	9–28	B	PLT292	6–124	B
PLT274	8–111	C	PLT284	9–33	A	PLT292	6–128	A
PLT 274	8–112	B	PLT284	9–34	C	PLT292	6–139	B
PLT 274	8–113	C	PLT284	9–35	B	PLT292	6–140	A
PLT274	8–114	B	PLT284	9–36	C	PLT292	6–156	B
PLT274	9–52	C	PLT284	9–37	B	PLT292	6–158	A
PLT275	3–46	C	PLT286	9–38	A	PLT292	11–109	A
PLT275	3–48	C	PLT286	9–43	C	PLT293	6–160	C
PLT275	3–49	A	PLT286	9–45	C	PLT293	6–180	B

FAA Learning Code	Gleim SU/ Q. No.	Gleim Answer	FAA Learning Code	Gleim SU/ Q. No.	Gleim Answer	FAA Learning Code	Gleim SU/ Q. No.	Gleim Answer
PLT294	9–18	B	PLT298	10–29	C	PLT322	3–85	C
PLT294	9–60	B	PLT298	10–30	A	PLT322	4–80	C
PLT296	6–20	C	PLT298	10–31	C	PLT322	5–89	A
PLT296	6–72	A	PLT298	10–54	C	PLT322	11–13	C
PLT296	6–73	B	PLT300	3–17	A	PLT323	5–52	C
PLT296	6–74	B	PLT300	3–18	B	PLT323	5–53	B
PLT296	6–75	B	PLT300	3–19	A	PLT323	5–58	A
PLT296	6–76	A	PLT300	3–20	B	PLT330	7–1	B
PLT296	6–77	B	PLT300	3–25	C	PLT 330	7–3	A
PLT296	6–78	C	PLT300	3–26	C	PLT330	7–4	C
PLT296	6–79	C	PLT300	3–30	C	PLT330	7–5	A
PLT296	6–80	C	PLT300	3–87	B	PLT330	7–6	A
PLT296	6–81	A	PLT300	3–88	C	PLT330	7–7	C
PLT296	6–84	B	PLT301	8–30	A	PLT330	7–8	C
PLT296	6–85	A	PLT301	8–31	A	PLT332	7–2	B
PLT296	6–86	C	PLT301	8–32	C	PLT333	7–24	A
PLT296	6–91	B	PLT301	8–33	A	PLT333	7–26	B
PLT296	6–117	C	PLT301	8–36	A	PLT334	7–9	C
PLT296	6–123	A	PLT301	8–122	A	PLT334	7–10	C
PLT296	6–130	C	PLT302	8–8	C	PLT334	7–11	C
PLT297	2–58	A	PLT302	8–10	B	PLT334	7–12	C
PLT297	2–59	B	PLT311	2–20	C	PLT334	7–13	C
PLT297	2–60	B	PLT311	2–21	B	PLT334	7–14	B
PLT297	2–61	C	PLT316	9–59	C	PLT334	7–15	A
PLT297	2–62	B	PLT317	8–124	C	PLT334	7–20	B
PLT297	2–64	A	PLT317	8–125	C	PLT336	2–43	C
PLT297	2–65	B	PLT317	8–126	B	PLT337	1–12	C
PLT297	2–66	C	PLT317	8–127	C	PLT337	1–13	B
PLT297	2–67	A	PLT317	8–128	A	PLT337	1–14	A
PLT298	10–15	C	PLT317	8–129	C	PLT337	1–18	C
PLT298	10–16	B	PLT317	8–130	C	PLT337	1–19	A
PLT298	10–17	B	PLT317	8–131	C	PLT337	1–20	C
PLT298	10–18	A	PLT318	5–103	C	PLT337	1–24	C
PLT298	10–19	A	PLT321	4–2	B	PLT337	1–25	C
PLT298	10–20	C	PLT321	6–39	A	PLT344	8–24	B
PLT298	10–21	A	PLT321	6–95	B	PLT344	8–68	C
PLT298	10–22	C	PLT322	3–31	C	PLT344	8–72	B
PLT298	10–23	B	PLT322	3–32	A	PLT344	8–73	A
PLT298	10–25	A	PLT322	3–35	C	PLT344	8–74	C
PLT298	10–26	B	PLT322	3–36	C	PLT345	1–23	B
PLT298	10–27	C	PLT322	3–83	A	PLT345	1–26	B
PLT298	10–28	B	PLT322	3–84	B	PLT345	1–31	B

FAA Learning Code	Gleim SU/ Q. No.	Gleim Answer	FAA Learning Code	Gleim SU/ Q. No.	Gleim Answer	FAA Learning Code	Gleim SU/ Q. No.	Gleim Answer
PLT345	1–36	B	PLT363	3–24	B	PLT407	4–11	B
PLT345	1–39	C	PLT366	4–97	C	PLT409	4–9	B
PLT345	1–40	B	PLT370	4–43	B	PLT411	4–7	B
PLT345	1–41	C	PLT370	5–92	B	PLT412	4–91	C
PLT345	1–43	A	PLT370	5–95	A	PLT412	4–92	A
PLT354	3–5	C	PLT379	3–86	C	PLT413	4–55	B
PLT354	3–69	A	PLT379	4–58	B	PLT413	4–56	B
PLT354	3–70	B	PLT379	4–59	C	PLT414	5–47	A
PLT354	3–72	B	PLT379	4–60	A	PLT415	4–25	A
PLT354	3–73	C	PLT379	4–61	B	PLT415	4–72	A
PLT354	3–74	A	PLT379	4–62	A	PLT415	4–74	C
PLT354	3–75	A	PLT379	4–63	C	PLT415	4–75	A
PLT354	3–76	A	PLT379	4–64	C	PLT415	4–76	B
PLT354	3–77	B	PLT379	4–65	A	PLT415	6–55	B
PLT354	3–78	A	PLT379	4–66	C	PLT415	6–182	C
PLT354	5–67	A	PLT379	4–67	B	PLT416	4–36	A
PLT354	6–186	B	PLT382	6–17	C	PLT420	3–79	A
PLT354	6–187	B	PLT382	6–38	A	PLT420	6–7	C
PLT354	6–188	A	PLT382	6–98	A	PLT420	6–22	A
PLT354	6–191	A	PLT382	6–192	A	PLT420	6–23	C
PLT354	6–193	A	PLT391	5–104	B	PLT420	6–50	B
PLT354	6–198	C	PLT391	5–105	B	PLT420	6–60	C
PLT354	6–201	B	PLT391	5–106	A	PLT420	6–61	C
PLT354	6–203	B	PLT391	5–107	A	PLT420	6–62	C
PLT354	6–206	A	PLT391	5–108	A	PLT420	6–64	A
PLT354	6–208	B	PLT391	5–109	A	PLT420	6–66	A
PLT356	6–40	B	PLT391	6–173	B	PLT420	6–67	B
PLT357	6–9	A	PLT391	10–33	B	PLT420	6–68	B
PLT357	6–26	A	PLT393	5–100	C	PLT420	6–105	A
PLT358	6–24	A	PLT395	4–3	C	PLT420	6–116	A
PLT358	6–33	B	PLT395	11–65	A	PLT420	6–133	A
PLT358	6–37	B	PLT403	4–37	A	PLT420	6–167	C
PLT358	6–41	B	PLT403	4–39	C	PLT420	6–195	B
PLT358	6–42	B	PLT405	4–4	B	PLT420	11–57	A
PLT358	6–44	B	PLT405	4–81	C	PLT421	4–32	A
PLT360	6–189	A	PLT405	4–82	A	PLT421	4–44	C
PLT360	6–190	B	PLT405	4–84	C	PLT421	4–46	C
PLT361	6–8	B	PLT405	4–93	B	PLT421	4–57	C
PLT361	6–10	B	PLT406	5–111	A	PLT424	8–77	B
PLT361	6–11	A	PLT406	5–112	C	PLT424	8–81	C
PLT363	3–21	C	PLT406	6–43	B	PLT429	11–11	C
PLT363	3–23	A	PLT407	4–8	A	PLT429	11–23	A

FAA Learning Code	Gleim SU/ Q. No.	Gleim Answer	FAA Learning Code	Gleim SU/ Q. No.	Gleim Answer	FAA Learning Code	Gleim SU/ Q. No.	Gleim Answer
PLT430	4–78	C	PLT451	4–6	B	PLT507	3–41	C
PLT430	4–79	B	PLT451	4–30	B	PLT507	3–42	B
PLT430	10–11	C	PLT454	4–94	C	PLT507	3–43	A
PLT430	10–12	C	PLT454	4–95	C	PLT507	3–44	B
PLT433	11–68	C	PLT454	4–96	C	PLT507	11–97	C
PLT434	5–101	C	PLT455	3–80	A	PLT508	3–22	B
PLT434	6–5	C	PLT455	5–51	B	PLT508	4–68	A
PLT435	5–70	C	PLT455	5–62	C	PLT508	4–69	A
PLT435	5–75	B	PLT455	6–121	C	PLT508	4–70	C
PLT435	5–102	B	PLT459	1–38	C	PLT508	4–71	B
PLT438	4–85	C	PLT459	4–33	C	PLT509	5–43	C
PLT438	4–86	C	PLT475	8–62	A	PLT509	5–44	C
PLT438	4–87	C	PLT484	6–150	C	PLT509	5–45	B
PLT438	4–88	C	PLT484	6–151	B	PLT509	5–46	C
PLT442	4–10	B	PLT484	6–205	C	PLT510	8–1	A
PLT442	4–12	A	PLT492	8–76	B	PLT510	8–2	C
PLT442	4–13	A	PLT492	9–32	C	PLT511	8–6	C
PLT442	4–14	A	PLT493	8–46	C	PLT511	8–12	A
PLT442	4–15	A	PLT493	8–75	C	PLT511	8–14	A
PLT442	4–16	A	PLT493	8–83	B	PLT511	8–15	C
PLT442	4–17	A	PLT493	8–84	A	PLT511	8–17	B
PLT442	4–18	A	PLT493	8–85	A	PLT511	8–22	C
PLT442	4–19	B	PLT493	8–86	C	PLT511	8–26	B
PLT442	4–20	A	PLT493	8–87	A	PLT512	8–43	B
PLT442	4–21	A	PLT493	8–88	A	PLT512	8–44	A
PLT442	4–22	B	PLT493	8–89	B	PLT512	8–45	A
PLT442	4–23	A	PLT495	8–55	C	PLT515	9–2	A
PLT442	4–24	B	PLT495	8–56	C	PLT516	8–5	B
PLT443	4–35	A	PLT495	8–57	B	PLT516	8–16	A
PLT444	4–31	C	PLT495	8–59	B	PLT518	2–71	B
PLT444	5–49	B	PLT495	8–60	A	PLT518	6–46	B
PLT444	5–50	C	PLT495	8–61	B	PLT518	6–51	B
PLT445	1–21	B	PLT495	8–63	C	PLT518	6–54	B
PLT445	1–49	A	PLT495	8–64	A	PLT518	6–56	C
PLT445	1–53	C	PLT497	5–83	B	PLT518	6–59	A
PLT445	4–34	C	PLT501	8–117	A	PLT518	8–13	A
PLT445	5–56	C	PLT507	3–27	A	PLT518	8–116	C
PLT448	4–26	C	PLT507	3–28	C	PLT518	8–118	C
PLT448	4–27	C	PLT507	3–34	B	PLT518	8–119	C
PLT448	4–28	C	PLT507	3–37	C	PLT518	8–120	C
PLT448	4–29	C	PLT507	3–39	B	PLT518	8–121	C
PLT451	4–5	B	PLT507	3–40	C	PLT518	8–123	A

FAA Learning Code	Gleim SU/ Q. No.	Gleim Answer
PLT524	1–73	A
PLT524	1–74	B
PLT524	1–75	C

ABBREVIATIONS AND ACRONYMS IN
INSTRUMENT PILOT FAA KNOWLEDGE TEST

A/FD	*Airport/Facility Directory*
AAH	*Advanced Avionics Handbook*
AC	Severe Weather Outlook Chart
AC	Advisory Circular
AC	convective outlook
AC Form	Airman Certification Form (i.e., AC Form 8080-2)
ACL	Aeronautical Chart Legend
ADIZ	Air Defense Identification Zone
AFH	*Airplane Flying Handbook*
AFNA	Aerodynamics for Naval Aviators
AGL	above ground level
AI	altitude indicator
AIM	*Aeronautical Information Manual*
AIRMET	Airman's Meteorological Information
ALS	approach light systems
ALT	altimeter
AME	aviation medical examiner
APV	approach with vertical guidance
ARTCC	Air Route Traffic Control Center
ASI	airspeed indicator
ASR	airport surveillance radar
ATC	Air Traffic Control
ATIS	Automatic Terminal Information Service
AvW	*Aviation Weather*
AWS	*Aviation Weather Services*
CAS	calibrated airspeed
CAT	clear air turbulence
CDI	course deviation indicator
CFII	Certificated Flight Instructor – Instrument
COP	changeover point
CTAF	common traffic advisory frequency
DA	decision altitude
DH	decision height
DME	distance measuring equipment
DP	departure procedure
DUATS	Direct User Access Terminal System
EFC	expected further clearance
ELT	emergency locator transmitter
ETA	estimated time of arrival
ETE	estimated time en route
FA	area forecast
FAA	Federal Aviation Administration
FAA-P-8740-50	On Landings, Part III
FAF	final approach fix
FAR	Federal Aviation Regulations
FBO	Fixed-Base Operator
FD	winds and temperatures aloft forecast
FDC NOTAM	Flight Data Center Notice to Airmen
FL	flight level
Fl Comp	flight computer
FSDO	Flight Standards District Office
FSS	Flight Service Station
GPH	gallons per hour
GS	glide slope or groundspeed
HAA	height above airport
HAT	height above touchdown
Hg	mercury
HI	heading indicator
HIRL	high-intensity runway lights
HSI	horizontal situation indicator
IAF	initial approach fix
IAP	instrument approach procedure
IAS	indicated airspeed
ICAO	International Civil Aviation Organization
IFH	*Instrument Flying Handbook*
IPH	*Instrument Procedures Handbook*
IFR	instrument flight rules
IGI	instrument ground instructor
ILS	instrument landing system
IM	inner marker
IMC	instrument meteorological conditions
INT	intersection
ISA	international standard atmosphere
KCAS	knots calibrated airspeed
LAA	Local Airport Advisory
LDA	localizer-type directional aid
LF	low frequency
LMM	middle compass locator
LNAV	Lateral navigation
LNAV + V	Lateral navigation with advisory vertical guidance
LNAV/VNAV	Lateral and vertical navigation
LOC	localizer
LOM	outer compass locator
LORAN	long range navigation
LP	Localizer performance
LPV	Localizer performance with vertical guidance
MAA	maximum authorized altitude
MAP	missed approach point
Mb	millibar
MB	magnetic bearing
MCA	minimum crossing altitude
MDA	minimum descent altitude
MEA	minimum en route altitude
METAR	aviation routine weather report
MH	magnetic heading
MHA	minimum holding altitude
MHP	Medical Handbook for Pilots
MIRL	medium-intensity runway lights
MLS	microwave landing system
MM	middle marker
MOA	Military Operations Area
MOCA	minimum obstruction clearance altitude
MP	manifold pressure
MRA	minimum reception altitude
MSA	minimum safe altitude
MSL	mean sea level
NAVAID	navigational aid
NoPT	no procedure turn
NOTAM	notice to airmen

NTSB	National Transportation Safety Board Regulations
OAT	outside air temperature
OBS	omnibearing selector
OM	outer marker
PAPI	precision approach path indicator
PAR	precision approach radar
PIC	pilot in command
P/C Glossary	Pilot/Controller Glossary *(AIM)*
PHAK	*Pilot's Handbook of Aeronautical Knowledge*
PIREP	Pilot Weather Report
PTS	Practical Test Standards
RAIL	runway alignment indicator lights
RB	relative bearing
REIL	runway end identifier lights
RIC	remote indicating compass
RMI	radio magnetic indicator
RNAV	area navigation
RPM	revolutions per minute (tachometer)
RVR	runway visual range
SDF	simplified directional facility
SIAP	standard instrument approach procedure
SIGMET	Significant Meteorological Information
STAR	standard terminal arrival route
SVFR	Special VFR
T&SI	turn-and-slip indicator
TACAN	Tactical Air Navigation
TAF	terminal aerodrome forecast
TAS	true airspeed
TC	turn coordinator
TDZ	touchdown zone
TDZE	touchdown zone elevation
UTC	Coordinated Universal Time
VASI	visual approach slope indicator
VDP	visual descent point
VFR	visual flight rules
VHF	very high frequency
VMC	visual meteorological conditions
VOR	VHF omnidirectional range
VORTAC	collocated VOR and TACAN
VOT	VOR test facility
VSI	vertical speed indicator
WAAS	Wide Area Augmentation System
Z	Zulu or UTC time

INDEX OF LEGENDS AND FIGURES

INDEX

AUTHORS' RECOMMENDATIONS

The Experimental Aircraft Association, Inc., is a very successful and effective nonprofit organization that represents and serves those of us interested in flying, in general, and in sport aviation, in particular. We personally invite you to enjoy becoming a member. Visit their website at www.eaa.org.

Types of EAA Memberships:

$40 - Individual (includes subscription to *EAA Sport Aviation* magazine)
$50 - Family (extends all benefits to member's spouse and children under 18, except for an additional EAA magazine subscription)
Free - Student (for those age 18 or under who have completed the EAA Young Eagles program)
$1,295 - Lifetime

Sign up online at www.eaa.org/en/eaa/eaa-membership/types-of-memberships, email membership@eaa.org, or call (800) JOIN-EAA.

The annual EAA Oshkosh AirVenture is an unbelievable aviation spectacular with over 10,000 airplanes at one airport and virtually everything aviation-oriented you can imagine! Plan to spend at least 1 day (not everything can be seen in a day) in Oshkosh (100 miles northwest of Milwaukee). Visit the AirVenture website at www.airventure.org.

Convention dates: 2016 -- July 25 through July 31
2017 -- July 24 through July 30

The annual Sun 'n Fun EAA Fly-In is also highly recommended. It is held at the Lakeland, FL (KLAL), airport (between Orlando and Tampa). Visit the Sun 'n Fun website at www.sun-n-fun.org.

Convention dates: 2016 -- April 5 through April 10
2017 -- April 4 through April 9

AIRCRAFT OWNERS AND PILOTS ASSOCIATION

AOPA is the largest, most influential aviation association in the world, with two thirds of all pilots in the United States as members. AOPA's most important contribution to the world's most accessible, safest, least expensive, friendliest, easiest-to-use general aviation environment is their lobbying on our behalf at the federal, state, and local levels. AOPA also provides legal services, advice, and other assistance to the aviation community.

We recommend that you become an AOPA member to get the most out of AOPA's resources. To join, call 1-800-USA-AOPA or visit the AOPA website at www.aopa.org.

LET'S GO FLYING!

The Aircraft Owners and Pilots Association (AOPA) hosts an informational web page on getting started in aviation. "Let's Go Flying!" contains information for those still dreaming about flying, those who are ready to begin, and those who are already making the journey.

The goal of this program is to encourage people to experience their dreams of flying through an introductory flight. Interested individuals can order a FREE copy of *Let's Go Flying: Your Invitation to Fly*, which explains how amazing it is to be a pilot. Other resources are available, such as a flight school finder, a guide on what to expect throughout training, an explanation of pilot certification options, a FREE monthly flight training newsletter, and much more. To learn more, visit www.aopa.org/letsgoflying.

INSTRUCTOR AUTHORIZATION FORM
INSTRUMENT RATING KNOWLEDGE TEST

Name: _____

    I certify that I have reviewed the above individual's preparation for the FAA Instrument Rating – Airplane knowledge test [covering the topics specified in 14 CFR 61.65(b)(1) through (10)] using the *Instrument Pilot FAA Knowledge Test* book, software, and/or online course by Irvin N. Gleim and find him/her competent to pass the knowledge test.

_____ _____ _____ _____ _____
Signed   Date   Name   CFI Number Expiration Date

GLEIM®
Aviation